ESSENTIAL
SHAREPOINT® 2013

ESSENTIAL SHAREPOINT® 2013

PRACTICAL GUIDANCE FOR MEANINGFUL BUSINESS RESULTS

Scott Jamison
Susan Hanley
Chris Bortlik

⋏⋏Addison-Wesley

Upper Saddle River, NJ • Boston • Indianapolis • San Francisco
New York • Toronto • Montreal • London • Munich • Paris • Madrid
Capetown • Sydney • Tokyo • Singapore • Mexico City

Many of the designations used by manufacturers and sellers to distinguish their products are claimed as trademarks. Where those designations appear in this book, and the publisher was aware of a trademark claim, the designations have been printed with initial capital letters or in all capitals.

The authors and publisher have taken care in the preparation of this book, but make no expressed or implied warranty of any kind and assume no responsibility for errors or omissions. No liability is assumed for incidental or consequential damages in connection with or arising out of the use of the information or programs contained herein.

The publisher offers excellent discounts on this book when ordered in quantity for bulk purchases or special sales, which may include electronic versions and/or custom covers and content particular to your business, training goals, marketing focus, and branding interests. For more information, please contact:

U.S. Corporate and Government Sales
(800) 382-3419
corpsales@pearsontechgroup.com

For sales outside the United States, please contact:

International Sales
international@pearson.com

Visit us on the Web: informit.com/aw

Library of Congress Cataloging-in-Publication Data.

Jamison, Scott.
  Essential SharePoint 2013 : practical guidance for meaningful business results / Scott Jamison,
  Susan Hanley, Chris Bortlik.—First edition.
      pages   cm
  Includes bibliographical references and index.
  ISBN 978-0-321-88411-4 (alk. paper)—ISBN 0-321-88411-6 (alk. paper)
  1. Microsoft SharePoint (Electronic resource) 2. Intranets (Computer networks) I. Hanley, Susan,
  1956– II. Bortlik, Chris. III. Title.
  TK5105.875.I6J353 2014
  004.6'82—dc23
                                                                                2013027429

ISBN-13: 978-0-321-88411-4
ISBN-10:   0-321-88411-6

Text printed in the United States on recycled paper at R. R. Donnelley in Crawfordsville, Indiana.
First printing, July 2013

To my lovely wife, Sung, who supported me tremendously during the writing of this book, and to my team at Jornata—the smartest and hardest-working bunch of folks I've ever worked with.

—Scott

For my family, whose support and dedication and willingness to eat takeout made it possible for me to write, and for the incredible SharePoint community, from whom I have learned so much and who inspire me to pay it forward.

—Sue

To my wife, Marisa, our four daughters, and our parents: thank you for all of your support and encouragement during the past 18 months. My contributions to this book would not have been possible without you and the sacrifices you have all made on my behalf. Love you all!

—Chris

CONTENTS

FOREWORD BY JEFF TEPER

We started the project that became SharePoint with an ambitious goal—bring together collaboration, content management, and portals into a single experience that connects people and teams inside and outside organizations. Amazingly, this same vision continues to drive us today—13 years later! We are fortunate that SharePoint has been one of the fastest-growing server products in Microsoft's history. Over 80% of the Fortune 500 depend on SharePoint every day to achieve business goals, and we're excited to deliver new releases of SharePoint to more customers every day through our Office 365 cloud service.

Much of the success of SharePoint has to be attributed to the early adopters who saw the vision way back in the 2001 release. Three of those early adopters were Scott Jamison, Susan Hanley, and Chris Bortlik. They helped shape the product, provided critical feedback, and have worked roughly 30,000 hours each on projects involving SharePoint technology. Combined, they contribute over 40 years of experience with the product and its precursor offerings. More expertise and insight is hard to imagine.

I'm proud to recommend this book—you'll find yourself reaching for it often; it will likely be one of the biggest factors in achieving your successful adoption of SharePoint.

—Jeff Teper
Microsoft Corporate Vice President, Office Servers & Services Program
Management
Redmond, Washington
May 2013

FOREWORD BY JARED SPATARO

This book will become a mainstay in your SharePoint library and should be one of the first books you read on SharePoint—no matter what your role. You will find yourself reaching for it whenever you need guidance on how to use and—more important—how to plan for the new SharePoint 2013 and Office 365 capabilities. I'm particularly pleased to see the breadth of coverage of the new functionality with the characteristic depth, expertise, and real-world recommendations that have made Scott, Sue, and Chris leaders in the SharePoint community. Anyone with an interest in SharePoint will benefit from the experience and best practices that they've developed over the years.

Enjoy the book, and enjoy the product. Tremendous work has gone into both.

—Jared Spataro
Microsoft Senior Director, SharePoint
Redmond, Washington
May 2013

ACKNOWLEDGMENTS

First, I'd like to thank Pearson for giving me yet another opportunity to write a book, with special thanks to Joan Murray and the rest of the Pearson team for shaping the book into something great.

This book could not have come to fruition without the expertise of Susan Hanley and Chris Bortlik. Their experience and perspective are invaluable to projects like this; every team should be lucky enough to have members like them. Sue and Chris provided useful insight, fantastic writing, and real-world expertise to make this a high-quality book. Their passion is unmatched in the SharePoint and Office 365 space.

As an authoring team, we'd like to thank our early reviewers, including Andy Kawa, Shelley Norton, and Ken Heft, who all provided insightful feedback and went above and beyond the call of duty. And thanks to Donal Conlon, who was instrumental in contributing useful insight and writing to the Web content chapter, and Dan Casey, who provided a fantastic user interface for the same.

Thank you to Corey Hanley, Michele Jones, and Donal Conlon for testing the Office 365 and on-premises security user experience; Tom Byrnes for permission to be quoted in Chapter 4; and the team of Marisa Bortlik, Brian Hanley, Corey Hanley, and Jamie Hanley for tacitly agreeing to serve as our "pretend" users so that we could test various permissions without creating fake names.

Special thanks to my wife, Sung, who, with a smile, always cheered me on, even in the wee hours.

And a final thank-you to the SharePoint community, who have read our previous books, encouraged us to write another one, and without whom none of this would be possible.

—*Scott Jamison*
Boston, MA
May 10, 2013

About the Authors

Scott Jamison is a world-renowned expert on collaborative, search, knowledge management, and ECM solutions and is an experienced leader with more than 20 years directing technology professionals to deliver a wide range of business solutions for customers. Scott is a strong strategic thinker, technologist, and operational manager. He is currently chief architect and CEO of Jornata (www.jornata.com), a premier SharePoint and Office 365 consulting firm.

Prior to joining Jornata, Scott was director of enterprise architecture at Microsoft and has held numerous leadership positions, including a senior management position leading a Microsoft-focused consulting team at Dell. Scott has worked with Microsoft teams at the local, regional, and international levels for years, often participating as an adviser to the Microsoft product teams.

Scott is a recognized thought leader and published author of several books and hundreds of magazine articles, and he has regular speaking engagements at events around the globe.

Scott received his M.A. in computer science from Boston University and did his postgraduate work at Bentley's McCallum Graduate School of Business. He is a Microsoft Certified Solution Master for SharePoint, a Microsoft SharePoint Server MVP, and a Microsoft Certified Architect for SharePoint.

Scott is on Twitter (@sjam) and hosts his blog at www.scottjamison .com. He lives in the Boston area with his wife, Sung.

Susan Hanley is an independent consultant specializing in the design, development, and implementation of successful knowledge management portal solutions based on the SharePoint platform, with a focus on information architecture, user adoption, governance, and business value metrics. She is an internationally recognized expert in knowledge management and has led hundreds of knowledge management, portal strategy, design, and implementation engagements based on the SharePoint platform and other platforms in the course of a 30-year consulting career.

Immediately prior to establishing Susan Hanley LLC, Sue led the Portals, Collaboration, and Content Management practice for Dell. Sue joined Plural (which was acquired by Dell in 2003) after more than 18 years at American Management Systems. In 1995, she became the first director of knowledge management for AMS, a position she held for five years. Prior to establishing the AMS Knowledge Centers, she was a project executive and business analyst on a variety of information systems deployment engagements.

Sue is a frequent writer and speaker on the topic of implementing successful intranet portal solutions, SharePoint governance and adoption, and measuring the value of knowledge management investments. She has made top-rated presentations at conferences all over the world. Sue is the coauthor of *Essential SharePoint 2007* (Addison-Wesley, 2007) and *Essential SharePoint 2010* (Addison-Wesley, 2011) and is a featured author of four books on knowledge management.

Sue has an M.B.A. in information systems management from the Smith School at the University of Maryland at College Park and a B.A. in psychology from the Johns Hopkins University. Sue writes the Essential SharePoint blog for Network World at www.networkworld.com/community/sharepoint. Her Twitter handle is @susanhanley.

Sue and her husband live in Bethesda, Maryland, and are the proud parents of three young adults.

Chris Bortlik works at Microsoft as an Office 365 technology specialist, working with enterprise customers and partners in the northeast region of the United States. Chris is a SharePoint "Insider" within Microsoft and works closely with the SharePoint product team. He holds the SharePoint 2010 MCITP and MCTS certifications and has been working with SharePoint since 2001.

Chris speaks frequently at Microsoft events (including the SharePoint Conference), SharePoint Saturday, and user group meetings. Chris was a contributing author of the *Essential SharePoint 2010* book (Addison-Wesley, 2011). He also publishes a blog on TechNet at http://blogs.technet.com/cbortlik. Outside of blogging, Chris is active on social networking sites, including Twitter, where you can follow him at @cbortlik.

Prior to joining Microsoft in 2008, Chris was a customer for 14 years, working in technical IT architect, development, and management roles—

primarily leading .NET- and SharePoint-related projects for large enterprise customers, including FM Global and John Hancock.

Chris holds a B.S. in computer science from Wentworth Institute of Technology and an M.B.A. from the Bentley University McCallum Graduate School of Business.

Chris lives in Woburn, Massachusetts, with his wife, Marisa, and their four daughters: Kayla, Jessica, Liliana, and Sophia.

Donal Conlon, vice president of delivery at Jornata, is a technology expert with 20 years in the IT industry, working primarily on Microsoft and IBM technologies. The majority of his career has been spent providing collaboration solutions on many platforms, with a focus on Microsoft SharePoint. Donal has held leadership positions at several companies in his career and currently works as a senior consultant at Jornata, delivering solutions on SharePoint and Office 365.

Donal holds an engineering degree from the University of Ireland, Galway.

CHAPTER 1

YOUR READING JOURNEY

SharePoint 2013 is the next version of Microsoft's popular content management and collaboration platform. With this version of the product, Microsoft has made the platform more Web-friendly, more mobile-friendly, and more social. They've also added a major deployment option: the cloud. A fast-moving, ever-changing platform like SharePoint deserves careful planning and guidance. Consider this book your guide.

What does it take to be successful with SharePoint? A quality SharePoint 2013 rollout relies not only on the structured design provided by an architect, but also on the collective content contributions of the user community. Through key activities like providing original content, ranking content that they like, collaboratively creating documents, and tagging content with their own taxonomy, users have the opportunity to improve an organization's ability to deliver and share knowledge and best practices. Successfully getting users to contribute content effectively should be one of your key goals.

Some features in SharePoint 2013 will be new to users of past versions of SharePoint. That said, many users will feel right at home with the platform because of its similarities to most Internet sites, which encourage users to actively participate rather than simply read static content. SharePoint 2013 recognizes the global nature of information and enterprises, making it easier to support multiple languages, on multiple browsers, and on multiple platforms, such as handheld devices. This book is designed to help you navigate this new world of SharePoint.

If you have read *Essential SharePoint 2007* and/or *Essential SharePoint 2010*, you will find a significant amount of new information in this book—not just about SharePoint's latest features, but also about key topics we've developed further by working with hundreds of clients who use SharePoint every day to solve real business problems. For example, since *Essential SharePoint 2010* was published, we've learned a great deal about effectively creating and deploying governance plans, operating and managing SharePoint from an IT perspective, and which SharePoint metrics really measure business value.

What Is This Book About?

Most books are designed to address the "how" behind SharePoint, from either an administrative perspective or a programming perspective. This book complements the typical SharePoint book with some of the "what" and "why" of SharePoint, provides insight into targeting business needs with collaboration technologies, and helps you understand how those needs might be addressed by using SharePoint.

This book addresses the multitude of decisions that must be made about topics within SharePoint in a way that speaks in simple language and bridges the gap between business and technical topics. Navigating the various client and server offerings from Microsoft can be confusing and daunting; this book will help you navigate these waters, providing direction and understanding. Specifically, this is a book about Microsoft's SharePoint offering, with a particular focus on four commonly requested topics: a business-focused overview, guidance for setting a proper strategy, governance and user deployment, and a business-focused discussion on how to apply SharePoint's key features. This book was written because collaboration, information management (knowledge and content), and Web accessibility are three of the most sought-after features in a corporate software solution[1]—and addressing those needs in a successful way is often no small feat. If you want to deploy SharePoint in your enterprise or upgrade from previous versions, or if you need a concise yet comprehensive introduction to collaboration solutions with SharePoint, you're starting in the right place. This book provides a great user-level guide to Microsoft's latest version of SharePoint, along with usage strategies and some insight into the technologies involved. This book is intended to be a tutorial as well as a handy reference.

Reader's Guide

While we hope that all readers will read the whole book from cover to cover, each chapter of this book can be read independently. The first

---

1. Note that throughout the book we use the word *solution* to refer to the business problem you are using SharePoint to solve. The solution includes the hardware and software platform, of course, but it also includes the people and business processes that are critical to a successful outcome. The solution itself might be an enterprise portal, a departmental collaboration site, a partner extranet, or any one of the many business activities you can enable with SharePoint.

section of the book is designed to help you think about planning your SharePoint project—the overall strategy for the solution you will build, the elements and features you will use, the organization of your information, your governance plan, your security model, and how you will launch the solution when development is complete. The second section describes how to optimize your solution, describing strategies for search, forms and work-flow, deploying your solution as a public-facing Web site, planning business intelligence capabilities, and building solutions that combine information from multiple sources, including other Office 2013 products. The final section includes a handy appendix that we provide as a freely downloadable Word document that you can incorporate into your own planning. The document, along with a collection of additional resources, is available at www.jornata.com/essentialsharepoint.

If you're familiar with Microsoft's marketing framework prior to SharePoint 2013, SharePoint was often described by breaking it down into six key feature areas. We'll discuss each of these key feature areas throughout the book.

- **Sites:** core capability to facilitate the creation and management of Web sites that contain, display, and aggregate content. Information about sites is described in many places in the book, but to get started, please review Chapter 3, "Introducing the SharePoint 2013 Platform."
- **Communities:** ability to interact with (and solicit feedback from) other users through social tools. Communities are discussed in Chapter 15, "Planning for Social Computing."
- **Content:** enterprise content management (documents, records, Web, rich media). Content management is a broad topic that is discussed in Chapter 6, "Planning Your Information Architecture," as well as Chapter 13, "Managing Enterprise Content."
- **Search:** ability to find information and people across SharePoint and other sources. Chapter 16, "Planning Enterprise Search," provides advice about planning the use of search in your SharePoint solution.
- **Insights:** business intelligence tools. Chapter 18, "Planning for Business Intelligence," talks about this topic.
- **Composites:** ability to create applications rapidly (mashups, composite applications, etc.). Developing composites is discussed in Chapter 17, "Planning Business Solutions."

Other key topics include

■ **Governance.** Chapter 4, "Planning for Business Governance," covers content governance, and Chapter 5, "Planning for Operational Governance," covers operational and application governance.
■ **Adoption and measurement.** Chapter 7, "Planning Your Adoption Strategy," and Chapter 8, "Developing a Value Measurement Strategy," cover important aspects of user adoption and measurement to ensure that you get the most out of your SharePoint investment.
■ **Cloud.** Chapter 11, "Taking SharePoint to the Cloud," covers important aspects of SharePoint Online as a deployment option.
■ **Architecture.** Chapter 9, "Understanding Architecture Fundamentals," provides an overview of the SharePoint technical architecture.

When you're finished reading this chapter, make sure you read Chapter 2, "Planning Your Solution Strategy," which provides a critical foundation for understanding your SharePoint-based solution objectives and is a foundation for the rest of the book. So put away Visual Studio and SharePoint Designer for a moment. Take a breath and a step back. Start thinking about why your organization needs SharePoint and how you know you'll be successful after your solution is deployed. Software is expensive to purchase and integrate. If you want to build a successful solution, you need a carefully defined plan. When you don't plan your SharePoint deployment, you could suffer from poor adoption, cluttered information, and low user satisfaction. Given all that, we recommend that you read through the first section of the book before you start your project to ensure that you don't miss any critical steps in your deployment.

What You Will Learn from This Book

To implement a content and collaborative system effectively, you'll likely need to consider a number of key questions:

■ Do I need an overall strategy? If so, how do I create one?
■ What should my governance plan look like?
■ How do users perform the top activities that they'll need to do?
■ What do I need to consider when I upgrade from previous versions of SharePoint?

- Where are documents stored currently? Where *should* documents live?
- How do users collaborate today?
- What kind of hardware do I need? Do I need hardware at all?
- How do I deploy the product properly?
- How does the Web fit into my collaboration needs? What about Office and smart client applications? What about mobile devices?
- Will I share information outside of my organization? Should I?

This book is designed to help you ask the right questions and get the right answers.

Who Should Read This Book

This book is not targeted to any one specific role. If you are a developer or solution architect, this book is the ideal companion to your SharePoint 2013 API guide and/or development books. It will help explain SharePoint best practices and help you understand your organization's business needs and how they might be addressed using this powerful solution platform. No developer should use SharePoint without first understanding the people and business considerations that are important to every SharePoint-based solution. Likewise, for IT pros and SharePoint administrators, the key to being successful with your SharePoint implementation is to first understand the big picture. If you are a project manager, consultant, or business analyst, you'll find that this book helps with the intangibles of a SharePoint rollout, for example, "What roles should exist to support SharePoint?" or "How can I best take advantage of the new features of SharePoint?"

A full list of enterprise roles is covered in Chapter 4, "Planning for Business Governance." If you're on the list, this book is for you.

How This Book Is Organized

This book is organized into three key parts.

Part I, "Planning," helps you determine what kinds of business needs are addressed by SharePoint and how you should think about SharePoint-based solutions within your organization. It's also a great introduction to the SharePoint feature set and architecture. Planning includes the following chapters:

- Chapter 2: Planning Your Solution Strategy
- Chapter 3: Introducing the SharePoint 2013 Platform
- Chapter 4: Planning for Business Governance
- Chapter 5: Planning for Operational Governance
- Chapter 6: Planning Your Information Architecture
- Chapter 7: Planning Your Adoption Strategy
- Chapter 8: Developing a Value Measurement Strategy
- Chapter 9: Understanding Architecture Fundamentals
- Chapter 10: Planning Your Upgrade
- Chapter 11: Taking SharePoint to the Cloud
- Chapter 12: Planning Security

Part II, "Optimizing," helps you implement SharePoint to its fullest potential by drilling into each of the key functional areas. Optimizing includes the following chapters:

- Chapter 13: Managing Enterprise Content
- Chapter 14: Managing Web Content
- Chapter 15: Planning for Social Computing
- Chapter 16: Planning Enterprise Search
- Chapter 17: Planning Business Solutions
- Chapter 18: Planning for Business Intelligence
- Chapter 19: Planning for Mobility
- Chapter 20: Integrating Office Applications

The third part is the appendix, which is designed to provide content that you can use as part of your governance and training plans as well as some of the trickier "how to" information for new capabilities in SharePoint 2013 that users and site owners should know.

What's New in SharePoint 2013?

At the beginning of most chapters is a section called "What's New in SharePoint 2013?" that summarizes the new features of SharePoint 2013 that align with the chapter topic.

Key Points

At each chapter's conclusion (except for this chapter) is a section called "Key Points," which summarizes the key facts, best practices, and other items that were covered in the chapter.

Thank You

Thank you for reading this book. Our goal was to write the most useful business-centric guide to SharePoint 2013 that will help you think strategically about planning and deploying SharePoint solutions for your organization. Enjoy!

PART I

PLANNING

CHAPTER 2

PLANNING YOUR SOLUTION STRATEGY

According to Microsoft market research, nearly 80% of Fortune 500 companies are using SharePoint.[1] Adding educational institutions, government agencies, small businesses, and nonprofits means that a significant number of people who go to work have access to SharePoint. But what does that really mean? Are all of these millions of SharePoint users getting value from the investments their organizations have made in SharePoint? It doesn't take too much Internet research to find that the answer to this question is . . . "Not always."

Our goal for this book is to help ensure that your organization can deliver value with your investment in SharePoint. One of the most powerful lessons learned from all of the previous releases of SharePoint is that truly successful SharePoint solutions have a significant user focus: from design to implementation to training to persistent communications. With SharePoint 2013, Microsoft has truly embraced this learning and has even overhauled the way it positions SharePoint. Instead of focusing on what SharePoint *is*, Microsoft is now focusing on what you can *do* with SharePoint. Understanding what you can do with SharePoint and what organizational problems you want to solve or scenarios you want to enable are critical inputs to business success. The most effective way to think strategically about SharePoint is to first make sure you have a good understanding of the business[2] problem you want to solve. Start with an understanding of what you want to accomplish, and then evaluate the features and capabilities of SharePoint that are available to help achieve the desired outcome.

---

1. http://technet.microsoft.com/en-us/magazine/gg981684.aspx
2. Note that within this book, we will use the terms *business* and *organization* somewhat interchangeably. We know that not all organizations are businesses (e.g., governmental agencies) and that SharePoint is just as appropriate in these environments—but unless we specifically make a point related to a type of organization, when we use the term *business*, we mean any type of organization.

While Microsoft would like to position SharePoint by talking about what you can do with it, we assume there are people reading this book who need to frame their strategy by better understanding what SharePoint is all about. We begin this chapter with a discussion of what SharePoint *is* and clarify its role as an application, a platform, and a framework. The remainder of the chapter provides a roadmap for framing your SharePoint solution strategy.

SharePoint: What Is It?

In the past, a great deal of the confusion around SharePoint has related to the difficulty in defining what it is. SharePoint has been compared to a Swiss Army knife—multiple tools in a single package. The Swiss Army knife typically includes a blade as well as other tools, such as a screwdriver, can opener, nail file, and corkscrew. Similarly, SharePoint has some built-in capabilities such as file libraries, calendars, task lists, Web publishing tools, and blogs that can be used to solve a variety of organizational problems.

Just as the Swiss Army knife is not the right tool for constructing a house or making a complex recipe, SharePoint is not the tool that you will use to solve *all* organizational problems. SharePoint 2013 is positioned as the "new way to work together."[3] This simple definition helps put an appropriate lens on the classes of organizational problems that are appropriate for SharePoint—and on a way to answer the "What is it?" question. As stated earlier, rather than focus on what SharePoint *is*, Microsoft wants to change the question entirely and focus on how you can use SharePoint to *get work done*.

What does that mean? It means that there are *classes* of organizational problems that are well suited to SharePoint's strengths, and those classes of problems are those that require collaborative work—both directly and indirectly. For example, SharePoint can be used to

- **Share information with your employees on your intranet:** because this is where you collaborate and communicate with your employees. Internally, the information that you share is about both people and content—and SharePoint enables both document-based and conversation-based internal collaboration.

---

3. http://sharepoint.microsoft.com/en-us/preview/sharepoint-benefits.aspx

- **Share information with trusted nonemployees on your extranet:** because this is where you collaborate with your current partners, suppliers, and even customers.
- **Share information with your organization's teams and communities:** because this is how day-to-day work gets done.
- **Share individual documents securely with people on an ad hoc basis:** because this is how to get some control over the myriad document-sharing methods that put your organization at risk.
- **Enable ad hoc and more permanent conversations:** because this is how people develop relationships and learn from one another.
- **Organize the information shared in each of these solution environments:** because this will make it easier to find information consistently.
- **Showcase key business data from operational systems:** because this will enable individual and collaborative decision making.
- **Manage the life cycle of the information in your organization:** because this will ensure that your content is compliant with the business rules and legal requirements of your organization or industry.
- **Discover enterprise information:** because this is how you can ensure that your users can get work done.
- **Share information about your organization on your public-facing Web site:** because this is the site where you collaborate and communicate with your external existing and prospective customers, partners, and suppliers. Of course, not all Web sites today are collaborative, but many of the most interesting and engaging sites have a collaborative component.

SharePoint includes features that make it particularly well suited to deliver information such as documents, videos, blogs, discussions, expertise, and even business data. But the overall goal for SharePoint solutions is to provide an environment in which this information can be used to solve organizational problems.

Not to leave the information technology (IT) community out of the conversation, SharePoint also includes capabilities for developers to use to *build* these applications and for IT professionals to use to *manage* the risk, cost, and time associated with the solutions that are enabled with SharePoint.

Is It an Application, a Platform, or a Framework?

In the world of information technology software, we often refer to the tools that we use as applications, platforms, or even frameworks:

- An *application* is computer software designed to help a user perform specific tasks.
- A computing *platform* includes a hardware architecture and a software framework that allow application software to run—for example, the operating system and programming languages.
- A software *framework* helps facilitate software development by providing generic capabilities that can be changed or configured to create a specific software application.

Are you confused yet? Well, so is the entire SharePoint community! For a long time, there has been a great deal of debate within the SharePoint community about whether SharePoint is an application or a platform or a framework. SharePoint has a little bit of functionality that could allow you to argue that it is all of these. In the past, SharePoint was positioned as a platform marketed to IT for businesses to build on to create the "center of gravity" for collaboration. Key elements of functionality were referred to as "workloads" that could be brought together to build solutions. The "workload" terminology never really caught on outside of Microsoft and the SharePoint consulting community—and has added to the confusion about "What is it?"

One of the reasons that the debate has raged for so long has to do with how easy it is to customize and configure SharePoint to do pretty much anything you want—that is, to use it as a framework. Unfortunately, by making things so easy to customize—by abstracting the details of the software code required to configure SharePoint enough so that business users can create complex custom solutions—Microsoft unintentionally introduced risk into many organizations because some of those user-created software solutions literally "brought the house down."

Another reason for the debate has had to do with a general dissatisfaction with the SharePoint "look and feel." There is probably no consultant or internal IT person responsible for SharePoint who has not heard a business sponsor say, "We'll use it, but make it not look like SharePoint." No business sponsors that we know of have ever told their IT folks or consultants, "We'll use Microsoft Word, but don't make it look like Word."

Applying a custom look and feel to Microsoft Word would be a colossal waste of corporate money—and it's just wrong for so many reasons. But pretty much everyone wants to brand SharePoint. When you can completely change the look and feel of a software product, it doesn't "feel" like an application, especially because when you go from one company to another, you might not be able to easily tell whether the Web site you are using is based on SharePoint or not—until you look under the covers.

With SharePoint 2013, Microsoft appears to want to stop the debating and define SharePoint clearly as an application—but not necessarily as an application with a single purpose. Unlike the Microsoft Word application, which has basically one functional purpose—to create documents—Microsoft considers SharePoint a multipurpose application—one that can be used to create other, highly "personal" applications, one that can be used as is to solve some specific collaboration scenarios, and one that can actually be used as a delivery vehicle to expose other applications (apps within the app, if you will). For some business scenarios, such as your public-facing Web site, it makes good business sense to not just configure how you want to organize and manage your content, but to also customize the look and feel of SharePoint to align with your corporate identity and the purpose and intention of your Internet site. SharePoint 2013 makes this much easier than with any prior version by providing capabilities so that any Web designer or developer can design a SharePoint site without having to become a SharePoint expert. Web designers can create beautiful state-of-the-art Web sites using the tools with which they are already familiar—and SharePoint will convert their HTML files to work with SharePoint automatically. For other business scenarios, such as your internal team collaboration sites, it may make more sense to leverage SharePoint much as you leverage Microsoft Word—as an application for which you spend far more time configuring how you will *use* it and less time on completely rebranding the look and feel. Minor cosmetic changes to include corporate colors and logos may be sufficient to support internal branding.

What's New in SharePoint 2013?

Planning a strategy for SharePoint 2013 starts, as it always has, with an understanding of the business problem(s) you are trying to solve. However, while the basic scenarios that SharePoint enables are still fundamentally similar, the features and capabilities of SharePoint 2013 are different enough that you will need to consider several key new areas when you are planning your strategy:

- Social collaboration
- Cloud computing
- Mobile
- Internet

SharePoint 2013 includes a rich new set of social collaboration capabilities enabling expertise discovery, conversations, and content evaluation that were previously supported only with additional third-party tools. Your users may hear about SharePoint 2013's new Twitter- and Facebook-style activity stream that supports familiar social capabilities like #hashtags, @mentions, following, and "likes." If you had previously considered internal social collaboration features to be of limited value in facilitating key moments of engagement within your organization, you should reevaluate these capabilities. Now would be the time to consider if these new social capabilities, which extend far beyond blogging and simple status updates, fit into your business strategy. For some organizations, these capabilities may be significant in driving an upgrade decision. Another new feature is the ability to introduce "gamification" attributes in SharePoint 2013 discussion lists. This new capability allows users to build "reputation points" toward up to five achievement levels by performing activities such as creating a post, replying to a post, achieving likes or a star rating of 4 or 5 for a post, or having a post marked as the "best reply." These features can be very effective in engaging users in some but not all scenarios, so it is important to think about the specific scenario you are enabling and the culture of the community in which the features will be leveraged.

Note   If social is in your future, you will want to pay particular attention to Chapter 7, "Planning Your Adoption Strategy," and Chapter 15, "Planning for Social Computing."

Microsoft has made an even bigger bet on cloud computing with SharePoint 2013, going so far as suggesting that some new capabilities may be available in the online versions of SharePoint prior to the more traditional on-premises versions. (For example, opening up a site collection for easy access by users outside your organization is a feature that is available only in SharePoint Online.) There may be very valid business and technical reasons why SharePoint in the cloud is not appropriate for your organization, but "cloudy with a chance of SharePoint" is a key theme of this release—and you shouldn't act as if the cloud doesn't exist—even if it doesn't apply to your current strategy.

Note   For more information about how using SharePoint in the cloud (SharePoint Online) might fit into your strategy, refer to Chapter 11, "Taking SharePoint to the Cloud," which covers the pros and cons and capabilities of using SharePoint in a cloud-based environment.

Another key area of enhancements in SharePoint 2013 is support for mobile computing. SharePoint 2013 provides new, optimized experiences for different mobile platforms. For smartphones, SharePoint 2013 offers a simplified view for navigating and accessing document libraries, lists, and Web Parts. SharePoint 2013 also includes the capability to define multiple device channels, which enables developers to render a single SharePoint site in multiple designs based on the user's device. While users were typically able to access SharePoint sites from mobile devices in previous versions, SharePoint 2013 automatically enhances that experience in some instances and allows developers and designers to explicitly define the user experience for different types of devices to create an even more functional experience for users. The most important strategic consideration for supporting a mobile experience for your SharePoint users, however, is evaluating the specific types of scenarios that your users will want to enable on their mobile devices on a regular basis.

As an example, while users may want to read and review a document occasionally on their smartphones, detailed document reviewing and editing will rarely be a critical scenario for mobile users. On the other hand, one could imagine that looking up a phone number or quickly finding someone with expertise in a specific topic might be a high-priority scenario. For the occasional-use scenario, it may not make sense to design a specific mobile capability. However, for the people-lookup scenario, it might make sense to build a highly focused and targeted mobile application designed to run on a smartphone.

Note   For additional information on thinking about mobile solutions and SharePoint 2013, be sure to read Chapter 19, "Planning for Mobility."

While many organizations developed rich and engaging public-facing Web sites using SharePoint 2010—for example, ConocoPhillips (www .conocophillips.com), Dell Financial Services (http://dfs.us.dell.com), and Ferrari (www.ferrari.com)—making the commitment to using SharePoint for externally facing Web sites previously required a very deep knowledge of SharePoint in addition to expertise in Web user interface (UI) development. SharePoint 2013 allows Web designers to leverage familiar Web site tools to design a SharePoint site. It also includes other capabilities that support public Web site development, including

- Features that support capabilities to promote and recommend content that is relevant to and popular with visitors based on their activity
- Significant improvements to search that enable sites to aggregate and present content in new and flexible ways
- Improved capabilities to reuse content in multiple publishing environments with the cross-site publishing feature
- The ability to organize navigation based on managed metadata terms rather than physical location

If you haven't previously considered managing both your internal and external Web sites with the same technology tools, SharePoint 2013 makes that decision much easier. It may be time to think about moving your externally facing Web site to SharePoint 2013 so that you can consolidate around a focused solution set.

Note For more information about using SharePoint 2013 for Internet-facing sites, read Chapter 14, "Managing Web Content."

SharePoint Strategy Roadmap

There are several key questions you need to address as you plan your SharePoint strategy. We discuss the first three steps of the SharePoint strategy roadmap in this chapter and focus on the remaining topics in subsequent chapters of the book. The key questions are illustrated in Figure 2-1.

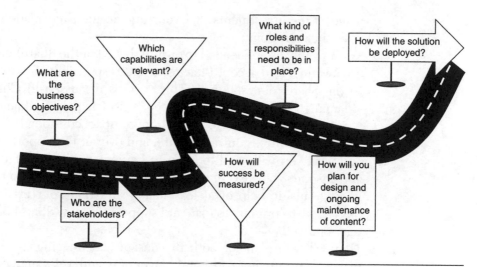

Figure 2-1 A SharePoint strategy roadmap

- What are the key business objectives or scenarios that you want to enable? How can SharePoint address these key business objectives? If the answers to these questions are unclear, the project should not proceed.
- Who are the primary stakeholders for these scenarios? These may include the CIO, the chief knowledge officer (CKO) or the person or team responsible for knowledge management, or business leaders in areas such as corporate communications, marketing, and human resources, among others. The stakeholders may be very different for different types of business problems.
- Which capabilities of SharePoint 2013 are relevant to the business problem?
- How will the organization measure the business success of the SharePoint initiative? In other words, which key business goals does the SharePoint solution address? Remember, technology solutions are not successful just because they are free of software defects. Successful solutions must be designed to have an impact on business objectives. The topic of planning how you will measure success is so important that we have given it a chapter of its own in this book. See Chapter 8, "Developing a Value Measurement Strategy," for an overview of a practical approach that you can use to measure the

value of the investments that your organization has made and will make in SharePoint.

- What processes are needed to ensure that all of the SharePoint users are aware of and accept their roles and responsibilities with regard to the SharePoint solution? This topic is discussed in Chapter 4, "Planning for Business Governance," and Chapter 5, "Planning for Operational Governance." It is important to consider the type of technical resources, infrastructure, and overall IT support you have and what you will need to learn to implement the new technology and migrate your existing environment. You may want to consider getting outside help or at least make sure that your existing staff has adequate training to plan and support the new SharePoint 2013 environment.

- How will you plan for both the design and ongoing maintenance of the content in SharePoint? Accurate and relevant content is the foundation of your SharePoint solution. Your strategy needs to include a plan to ensure that content remains relevant over time. This topic is also discussed in Chapter 4.

- How will you launch and deploy to ensure successful adoption? What types of communications and training do you need to provide for users? How will you ensure that your solution is adopted? Your rollout strategy needs to prepare both users and content for the new SharePoint solution. The strategy needs to include a communications plan to make sure that users are aware of and, ideally, eagerly anticipate the business value of the new SharePoint solution or solution capabilities. In addition, the strategy needs to include a plan for launching the new solution and training users. These topics are discussed in Chapter 7, "Planning Your Adoption Strategy."

What Is the Business Objective?

In the *Wizard of Oz*, Glinda the Good Witch says to Dorothy, "It's always best to start at the beginning." This advice is not just appropriate for starting out on the Yellow Brick Road; it also applies to SharePoint. The first step on the road to SharePoint success is making sure you have a good understanding of the business scenarios that you are trying to enable—and how important those scenarios are to the organization. In successful SharePoint implementations, business and IT stakeholders carefully frame the SharePoint project with clearly defined business goals and objectives that are used to guide the decisions that need to be made during the solution design and ongoing operations. More often than not, the key issues influencing the success of a SharePoint solution are organizational and political. Technical issues rarely derail a SharePoint project. As a result, it's particularly important to document why you are building the SharePoint solution in the first place and to ensure that all key stakeholders agree on the objectives.

Every organization has a strategic plan, though some may be more formal than others. It is often extremely helpful to start your SharePoint planning effort with that documented plan because it can help guide your understanding of the relative importance and business value of the scenarios you can (or should) enable with SharePoint. Earlier in this chapter, we discussed the types of business scenarios for which SharePoint is particularly well suited. The relative importance of these business scenarios is different for different types of organizations and organizations of different sizes. It's worth reviewing your organizational strategic plan because this document will provide the clues you need to understand how to position SharePoint strategically in your organization. Why is this important? Because your goal should be to tie the specific objectives for your SharePoint solution to one or more strategic objectives of the organization. Doing so enables you to ensure that your SharePoint project stays front and center in the organizational agenda and to minimize the risk of becoming number 11 on the organizational top-10 priority list. In other words, you want to avoid becoming the project that gets done "in our spare time," pretty much ensuring that the SharePoint project is not a career-making experience for the people working on it.

In addition to the business objectives and scenarios described earlier, there are other common business drivers that encourage organizations to consider SharePoint. Some or all of the following business objectives will probably resonate for your organization. If you can tie these specific objectives to your overall enterprise strategic objectives, you will be in even better shape to ensure that the right amount of attention and focus is directed to your SharePoint project. Sample business objectives include:

- Provide an organized "one-stop shop" for information by making it easier to find authoritative information.
- Provide easier and timelier access to the information employees need to get their work done.

- Improve the ability to share and exchange information across the organization by providing an electronic publishing method that is easy for users to leverage and assures "one version of the truth" for shared documents.
- Improve the ability to find and leverage expertise.
- Improve organizational learning by providing easier access to critical information and organizational memory.
- Improve the "time to talent," the speed with which new employees become productive.
- Reduce training costs for enterprise applications by providing a consistent user interface to all applications.
- Improve time to market for proposals and contracts by providing easier access to reusable assets.
- Improve decision making by providing an easy-to-use interface from which to review key business metrics.
- Improve project execution by providing an opportunity for work teams to collaborate and to electronically store project information in fully searchable, organized team sites.
- Maximize the reuse of best practices across the enterprise, enabling the organization to replicate successful business practices in all geographies.
- Provide more effective mechanisms to move work between business entities, such as self-service for customers or partners or enabling outsourcing by providing business partners with access to a collaboration environment or business data on an extranet.
- Improve customer service by providing direct access to the information customers need.

Note See Table 2-1 for examples of how SharePoint features can help address these business objectives.

Who Are the Stakeholders?

Who are your key stakeholders? As in most cases, the answer is that it depends on the specific business scenario you are enabling. Clearly, the executive for the sponsoring organization is an important key stakeholder. This individual will likely be your project sponsor. For intranet solutions, this is often the director of marketing or internal communications but can and should also include the executive in charge of knowledge management or quality or human resources. Including stakeholders from business groups outside communications will ensure that your intranet is not just about communications but will also effectively enable your collaboration strategy. For extranet portals, the stakeholders may also include key executives from an operational business unit. When you look to identify stakeholders, recognize that there are different types of stakeholders, all of whom should be included in the development of your solution strategy and ongoing governance model. Business executives should be included in the stakeholder community to provide overall direction and validate that the SharePoint deployment is critical to achieving business objectives. IT managers should be included to ensure that the solution meets IT standards for operations and development. Content providers should be included since great content is the key to valuable solutions of pretty much any type. Users should be included to ensure that the SharePoint solution rollout addresses more than just executive objectives and concerns.

Remember that while the executive sponsor may have the "grand vision" for the solution, the solution's users are critical to its ultimate success. Users need the solution to be easy to use in the context of their work and need to be able to see "What's in it for me?" For example, the key stakeholders for an intranet project to support a university should include administrators, faculty, and students. If the solution is externally facing, the "customer" community might be represented by examining the perspective of applicants or prospective students.

Keep in mind that if you choose to enable the social computing functionality available in SharePoint 2013, everyone in the organization, and even potential guest users in some scenarios, is both a producer and a consumer of information. Social features provide a rich and engaging opportunity to improve the ability to break down organizational silos and enable expertise location scenarios. However, enabling these capabilities requires a greater understanding of your organizational culture and user stakeholder community than if you are not leveraging these capabilities.

As you think about your key stakeholders, it's important to acknowledge the partnership that IT and the business will need to have in order to be successful with SharePoint. Because the success of SharePoint solutions is critically dependent on business user adoption, it is imperative that business stakeholders take an active role in solution design and governance planning and that IT staff fully understand how the solutions they build address business needs. A successful implementation often includes both process reengineering and culture change. A well-coordinated business and technical approach is essential to adoption.

In many organizations, the IT group is separated both physically and "emotionally" from the organization it is designed to serve. SharePoint projects provide an important opportunity for IT and business owners to collaborate.

One way to ensure that your SharePoint project will fail is to have IT build the solution without engaging a broad spectrum of potential users. In the past, technology projects were primarily driven by IT organizations. Many of these early solutions failed to gain user acceptance because they were essentially IT-only projects—driven by IT with limited user input. Today, more and more SharePoint projects are driven (and funded) by business users, though they are clearly dependent on IT. Many intranet projects are sponsored by the corporate department responsible for internal communications (though this may have the not-so-positive impact of the intranet being too communications-focused and less about enabling getting work done). One or more business units may fund and drive an external or customer portal or Web site initiative. As a result, it is critically important for IT to work with the sponsoring business unit as well as all key stakeholders to ensure that the inevitable trade-off decisions that will be made during solution design and development are made in favor of the business stakeholders as often as possible.

IT managers who fail to take advantage of this opportunity put their projects, and potentially their careers, at risk.

Take Action
Be inclusive rather than exclusive as you identify key stakeholders. It's important to gather as much business user support for your solution as possible.

Be sure to include users as key stakeholders. At the end of the day, these are the people who will help make your solution successful (or not).

In addition to traditional department or business executives, try to include employees who may not have the title but who are influential in your business. These people tend to have broad networks across the enterprise and can help drive your success because many people trust them.

Which Capabilities Are Relevant?

It is critically important to document business objectives at the start of your SharePoint initiative and to keep these objectives top of mind as you design and build your solution. Use the business objectives to guide your decisions about which features should go in each release of the solution and which features might not be relevant for your organization. Ask stakeholders to prioritize their business objectives so that you understand how to make trade-offs between alternative design approaches.

Stakeholders often have a very difficult time articulating requirements for SharePoint solutions, especially solutions that enable new ways of working together such as the capabilities enabled in the new SharePoint 2013/Yammer Newsfeed. This is because it is virtually impossible to envision how the solution will help solve business problems until users see the solution with "real" data or try the solution for a personal scenario. When users do express requirements, they may express them in very specific ways, which could require a significant amount of custom coding. However, if you understand the objectives or outcomes users are trying to achieve, you may be able to accomplish them using out-of-the-box or minimally customized functionality. To accomplish this, you will need SharePoint experts, both business analysts and developers, who know what you can and can't do easily. You may also need to create a small demo of some specific capabilities or features that you can show your stakeholders as part of the discussion about business scenarios. You really can't gather user requirements for SharePoint solutions the same way you do for a traditional software development project. Instead, solicit and try to understand business objectives. You can then, as a design team, *derive* requirements based on the business objectives and outcomes, and based on the feedback you get from providing a demo of the capabilities that are particularly important. It is critical to ensure that you understand the strategic objectives for the organization, the business objectives for SharePoint in general, and the specific business scenarios for the solutions you will enable with SharePoint.

Take Action

Identify three or four main features that will produce the most business impact and implement them exceptionally well.

Articulate, well in advance of launch, the long-term vision associated with your solution and how the first delivery sets the stage.

Set clear and reasonable expectations for business users—encourage them to focus on the business outcomes they want to achieve. In your requirements- (objectives-) gathering meetings, explain how you can accomplish the business outcomes using SharePoint's out-of-the-box capabilities so that you can get a feel for whether this will be acceptable to your users. Use statements such as "This is how we might accomplish what you are asking for in SharePoint 2013." Your goal is to rapidly deploy a first release of your solution so that your stakeholders can see the solution "in action" with their content. Develop and implement prototypes so that users can get a feel for SharePoint 2013, and alleviate any anxieties they may have about the new ways SharePoint enables work. You will probably find that it is only when users "meet SharePoint" with their own content that they can start to envision additional functionality that will add value to the business.

For each possible business objective, there are numerous SharePoint features you can implement to help enable that objective. Table 2-1 presents some of the features of SharePoint 2013 that you can leverage to explicitly accomplish your business objectives with indications where a feature is either new or significantly enhanced from SharePoint 2010. Use this table with great caution, however. Just because a feature can *help* achieve a business objective doesn't mean it *will*. People achieve business objectives, not software. While well-designed software solutions can *enable* people to achieve business objectives, simply implementing the features in this table will not guarantee that you will achieve the desired business outcomes.

Table 2-1 Mapping of General Business Objectives to SharePoint 2013 Features

Business Objective	Enabling Feature or Functionality
Provide an organized "one-stop shop" for information by making it easier to find authoritative information.	Search and search results refinement (for people and content) (ENHANCED) Integration with line-of-business systems Metadata Community discussion lists with "best reply" indicators (Where appropriate, the "best reply" helps users quickly filter information. However, the concept of a single "best reply" is not always appropriate in all contexts.) (NEW)
Provide easier and timelier access to the information employees need to get their work done.	Search (ENHANCED) Alerts Activity feeds with likes, follows, @mentions, and #hashtags (NEW) Blogs and wikis Mobile access (ENHANCED)
Improve the ability to share and exchange information across the organization by providing an electronic publishing method that is easy for users to leverage and assures "one version of the truth" for shared documents.	Document versioning Records retention (ENHANCED) Document sets Unique document IDs Default storage for documents attached to newsfeeds and discussions is a document library (rather than a list attachment) (NEW)
Improve the ability to find and leverage expertise.	People and expertise search (ENHANCED) Hashtag search (NEW) Follow people (NEW) Activity feeds with likes, follows, @mentions, and #hashtags (NEW) Community sites (NEW) Blogs and wikis

(continues)

Table 2-1 Mapping of General Business Objectives to SharePoint 2013 Features *(continued)*

Business Objective	Enabling Feature or Functionality
Improve organizational learning by providing easier access to critical information and organizational memory.	Search and search results refinement (ENHANCED) People and expertise search (ENHANCED) Follow people, documents, tags, and sites (NEW) Document repositories with metadata (both user and organizationally defined) Community sites (NEW) Blogs and wikis
Improve the "time to talent," the speed with which new employees become productive.	Search and search results refinement (ENHANCED) People and expertise search (ENHANCED) Follow people, documents, tags (NEW) Activity feeds with likes, follows, @mentions, and #hashtags (NEW) Community sites (NEW)
Reduce training costs for enterprise applications by providing a consistent user interface to all applications.	Search and search results refinement (ENHANCED) Integration with line-of-business systems Site templates Third-party solutions designed for integrating with SharePoint
Improve time to market for proposals and contracts by providing easier access to reusable assets.	Search and search results refinement (ENHANCED) People and expertise search (ENHANCED) Document repositories with metadata (both user- and organizationally defined)
Improve decision making by providing an easy-to-use interface from which to review key business metrics.	Dashboards with Excel Services Integration with line-of-business systems
Improve project execution by providing an opportunity for work teams to collaborate and to electronically store project information in fully searchable, organized team sites.	Team sites with enhanced project task tracking and monitoring features (ENHANCED) Document repositories with metadata (both user- and organizationally defined) Announcements and events (team calendar) Simple security model that users can administer

Business Objective	Enabling Feature or Functionality
Maximize the reuse of best practices across the enterprise, enabling the organization to replicate successful business practices in all geographies.	Site templates Search and search results refinement (ENHANCED) People and expertise search (ENHANCED) Follow people, documents, tags (NEW) Activity feeds with likes, follows, @mentions, and #hashtags (NEW) Document repositories with metadata (both user- and organizationally defined) Community sites (NEW) Blogs and wikis
Provide more effective mechanisms to move work between business entities, such as self-service for customers or partners or enabling outsourcing by providing business partners with access to a collaboration environment or business data on an extranet.	Extranets Ability to easily and securely share an individual document with an authorized external (or internal) user (NEW) Security model that business users can administer (ENHANCED)
Improve customer service by providing direct access to the information customers need.	Extranets Mobile access (ENHANCED) Public-facing Web sites managed with state-of-the-art Web content management features (ENHANCED) Search and search results refinement (ENHANCED) Integration with line-of-business systems Simple security model that users can administer

Key Points

Getting started with SharePoint 2013 means thinking about your strategy—not just your SharePoint strategy, but also your business strategy and the business outcomes that you want to enable with the SharePoint solutions you build. Remember:

- If you want to build a successful SharePoint 2013 solution, you need a carefully defined strategy focused on business outcomes and features that enable business outcomes.

- Identify and engage key stakeholders. Make sure they are involved as core members of your project team.
- Ensure that the SharePoint solutions you develop have a clear connection to business goals and objectives. Create a matrix to map your solution elements to your business strategy to ensure that you are focused on the right things.
- High-impact collaboration involves culture changes blended with the right technology. It is a small part technology and a large part business process change.
- Software does not achieve business objectives—people do. Just because a feature can help achieve a business objective doesn't mean it will.
- Not all content needs to be stored in SharePoint, but all business-critical data should be accessible through your portal.
- SharePoint 2013 provides a single application from which you can create modern, user-friendly solutions for many work scenarios, including intranet, extranet, collaboration, and Internet solutions. This allows you to engage not only employees, but also clients, partners, and prospects—the entire extended enterprise. A well-thought-out SharePoint strategy can make a significant contribution to enabling critical organizational results.

CHAPTER 3

Introducing the SharePoint 2013 Platform

In Chapter 2, "Planning Your Solution Strategy," we looked at essential factors in planning your overall enterprise portal, collaboration, and social strategy. An application, platform, and/or framework that supports this strategy will need to enable the tasks that users will do. This includes managing documents, sharing information, organizing content, communicating with others both synchronously and asynchronously, and using data to make business decisions. On top of this, the platform should also accommodate customizations that enable organizations to develop solutions that exactly meet the needs of their business.

All of these requirements are supported by Microsoft's collection of client and server products known as Office 2013 and SharePoint 2013, respectively. Together, SharePoint 2013 and Office 2013 form a comprehensive collaboration and knowledge management platform. Add in Exchange 2013 for e-mail and Lync 2013 for synchronous communication, and you've got a comprehensive collaboration and communication platform. Microsoft also provides this platform offering in the cloud in several flavors as a service called Office 365. This chapter provides an overview of this collection of technologies, a corresponding historical perspective, and what is new about SharePoint 2013. We'll also provide a walkthrough of how to build a simple but powerful solution by using SharePoint Online as a platform. Figures 3-1 and 3-2 highlight the core products and technologies in the overall Microsoft communications and collaboration platform. Note that SharePoint Workspace, a client application that provided offline access to content in the SharePoint 2010 time frame, has evolved into SkyDrive Pro, which focuses on synchronizing documents offline.

SharePoint *Foundation* 2013 is actually the *fifth* generation of Microsoft's foundation for the overall collaboration platform. SharePoint Foundation provides the core engine, toolset, and runtime that enable both users and IT

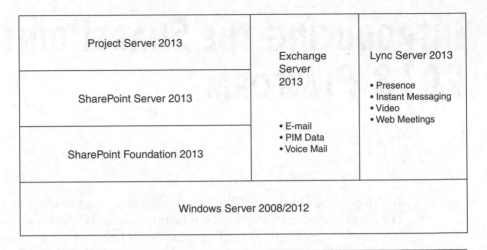

Project Server 2013	Exchange Server 2013	Lync Server 2013
SharePoint Server 2013		• Presence • Instant Messaging • Video • Web Meetings
SharePoint Foundation 2013	• E-mail • PIM Data • Voice Mail	
Windows Server 2008/2012		

Figure 3-1 The server products that make up Microsoft's Information Worker platform include capabilities to enable portals, collaboration, social computing, enterprise content management, e-mail, real-time communication, and other key features—deployed either on-premises or via the cloud

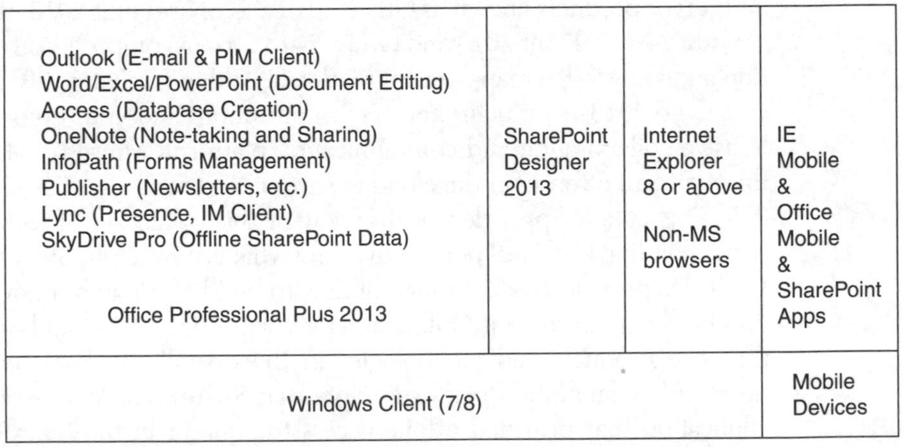

Outlook (E-mail & PIM Client) Word/Excel/PowerPoint (Document Editing) Access (Database Creation) OneNote (Note-taking and Sharing) InfoPath (Forms Management) Publisher (Newsletters, etc.) Lync (Presence, IM Client) SkyDrive Pro (Offline SharePoint Data) Office Professional Plus 2013	SharePoint Designer 2013	Internet Explorer 8 or above Non-MS browsers	IE Mobile & Office Mobile & SharePoint Apps
Windows Client (7/8)			Mobile Devices

Figure 3-2 The Microsoft client-side Information Worker components can be purchased separately (for example, Word, Excel), as an Office 2013 suite (Office Standard, Office Pro), or as a cloud-based service (Office 365)

professionals to create collaborative sites. Microsoft SharePoint *Server* 2013 is built on top of SharePoint Foundation and provides a large number of additional features, including aggregation, targeting, search, social computing, and content management functionality along with business intelligence and line-of-business (LOB) data integration. The next section describes how all of the pieces (including client tools like SkyDrive Pro and Lync, as well as related server-side products like Exchange) fit together in a typical environment. It also provides a little of the history behind the evolution of SharePoint products.

Microsoft's Collaboration Evolution

The world of Microsoft collaboration really started with Outlook 97 and Exchange 5.5 back in 1996, when public folders represented the extent of collaboration technology at Microsoft. At that time, Lotus Notes was the de facto enterprise collaboration product.

Exchange as a Collaboration Platform

When Microsoft Exchange 2000 Server was released, Microsoft positioned Exchange and its Web Store (the Exchange database plus some schema and Web-enablement features) as a collaboration server that would compete with, among other products, Lotus Notes. Exchange 2000 also provided a real-time communication piece that could provide instant messaging within an organization. The strategy seemed to make sense—use Exchange as the core asynchronous messaging, synchronous messaging, and collaboration platform. Build it and they will come.

Unfortunately, they never came. Using Exchange as the core collaboration platform never took off (mainly because applications had to be run directly on the server, a situation that didn't sit well with Exchange administrators). It became clear to Microsoft that messaging was a mission-critical application, and letting application developers build on top of Exchange was not going to be a popular option among Exchange administrators. (This is also now a trend in the SharePoint world since many SharePoint servers are now in the cloud and beyond the reach of administrators.) Microsoft repositioned Exchange as a pure messaging server. Microsoft also carved the real-time communication option out of Exchange 2000 and created a new product, called Live Communications Server (LCS) at the time and now called Lync, keeping Exchange firmly planted in the e-mail and personal information management (PIM) camp.

Office Server Extensions and SharePoint Team Services

Microsoft was addressing real-time collaboration with this new product LCS, but they still had a gap when it came to supporting groups that wanted to collaborate in a team environment. To meet this need, Microsoft leveraged existing technology originating with the FrontPage group and evolved it into SharePoint Team Services. On a technology basis, SharePoint has its roots in FrontPage Server Extensions, which became Office Server Extensions, then SharePoint Team Services, Windows SharePoint Services (WSS), and finally SharePoint Foundation. Based on FrontPage Server Extensions (a technology that enabled Web developers to save Web pages directly to the server over HTTP), Office 2000 included a server-side feature that provided list functionality called Office Server Extensions. This led to the next revision of the Web-based team collaboration concept in 2001—SharePoint Team Services (STS). STS was included with FrontPage 2002 and Office XP Developer.

Note   You may notice that certain file names in the SharePoint installation folders contain OWS or STS in them. These artifacts from previous versions of SharePoint stand for "Office Web Server" and "SharePoint Team Services," respectively. You may also wonder what VTI stands for (as in VTI_BIN) . . . it's "Vermeer Technologies, Inc.," which was acquired by Microsoft. Vermeer Technologies was the original developer of FrontPage.

SharePoint Portal Server 2001

The collaboration platform was moved out of Exchange 2000, but Microsoft was determined to use the Web Store database technology. At this point, Microsoft realized that there were three key collaboration/portal needs: real-time collaboration, ad hoc team collaboration, and an enterprise portal framework. SharePoint Portal Server (SPS) 2001 integrated a number of existing concepts into one product: search (which came from Index Server), workflow (which evolved from Exchange 5.5 workflow concepts), document management (which was based on the Web Store), and a customizable Web portal (which evolved from Digital Dashboard 3.0). The idea of a combined set of portal technologies was good; the implementation was, in hindsight, bad. SPS 2001 (code-named "Tahoe") wasn't based on the same technology as SharePoint Team Services (which provided the team collaboration solution). Worse yet, you couldn't even install them on the same machine. SPS 2003, mentioned next, fixed this, using a better architecture (mostly based on WSS 2.0) and better integration.

Windows SharePoint Services 2.0

The next revision of the Web-based team collaboration concept emerged as Windows SharePoint Services 2.0. Microsoft decided to include the platform with Windows Server 2003, rather than Office 2003. However, Office and WSS provided key integration points, which made each of them better when used with the other. The concepts from SharePoint Team Services were brought forward, with an emphasis on a scalable and consistent architecture.

SharePoint Portal Server 2003

SPS 2003 was based on WSS 2.0 and provided search, portal, and aggregation features. Microsoft took a big leap forward, basing SPS on WSS (instead of being a completely separate product). However, in the end it was still two teams, two architectures, and two different user experiences. Microsoft also realized that WSS belonged as a core part of the operating system—which had a huge impact in terms of development focus and installed base. Most customers bought SPS 2003 to implement a simple intranet and to search across WSS 2.0 team sites.

Windows SharePoint Services 3.0

Microsoft took key feedback from customers, which included the following core mandates:

- *Do* continue to provide core Web, management, and collaboration features in the WSS platform.
- *Do* add incremental improvements (like a recycle bin and workflow) that will enhance the experience and usability of the product.

■ *Don't* change the core architecture to the point where migration will be next to impossible.

Microsoft has done an impressive job evolving the SharePoint platform in a way that accomplishes those objectives.

Microsoft Office SharePoint Server 2007

Microsoft Office SharePoint Server (MOSS) 2007 was a true superset of WSS 3.0 and provided search, portal, and aggregation features, along with business data, Excel Services, and Web-based forms. And, in this release, the WSS and MOSS technologies were completely integrated, from the management to the UI to the user features to the programming APIs. In addition, MOSS 2007 represented the first integration of Web content management technology from another Microsoft product—Content Management Server—which enabled customers to use SharePoint as a true intranet/Internet site tool.

SharePoint Foundation 2010

With the 2010 release of SharePoint technologies, Microsoft evolved both the core platform as well as the development story through products like SharePoint Designer 2010 and Visual Studio 2010. SharePoint Foundation 2010 (4.0) proved to be the cleanest yet in terms of architecture and feature set.

Microsoft SharePoint Server 2010

Like MOSS 2007, Microsoft SharePoint Server 2010 was a superset of SharePoint Foundation and provided additional application features on top of the core SharePoint platform. In addition, Microsoft acquired the FAST search engine, which bolstered SharePoint's indexing and searching capabilities.

Current Versions of SharePoint Products and Technologies

The current-day world of Microsoft collaboration has made SharePoint the predominant content management product in the industry. SharePoint 2013 Foundation and Server not only provide comprehensive platform capabilities but also power the "Sites" capability of Microsoft's cloud-based Office 365 service.

SharePoint Foundation 2013

With the 2013 release of SharePoint, Microsoft has evolved both the core platform as well as the development story, mainly to accommodate Microsoft's own move into hosting SharePoint as a service in the cloud, rather than selling it as traditional software.

Microsoft SharePoint Server 2013

Like SharePoint 2010, Microsoft SharePoint Server 2013 is a superset of the corresponding SharePoint Foundation (2013) and provides additional application features on top of the core SharePoint platform. The next section describes the changes to Microsoft SharePoint Server 2013.

SharePoint Server 2013: The Details

There are three versions of SharePoint 2013 that can be deployed on-premises: SharePoint Foundation 2013, SharePoint Server 2013 with Standard CAL, and SharePoint Server 2013 with Enterprise CAL. Each version is a complete superset of the one it builds upon. In addition, there are many flavors of SharePoint Online—which is Microsoft's service that provides SharePoint via the cloud. We outline the differences in Table 3-3.

SharePoint Foundation 2013 is freely available as a downloadable component and can be installed on either Windows Server 2008 or Windows Server 2012. It provides core collaboration services with templates for team sites; it is based on ASP.NET and requires .NET Framework 4.5.

SharePoint Server 2013 comes in two distinct licensed versions from a CAL perspective: Standard and Enterprise. **SharePoint Server 2013 Standard** builds on SharePoint Foundation to provide portal, search, social computing, and enterprise content management (ECM) features. **SharePoint Server 2013 Enterprise** builds on SharePoint Server 2013 Standard to include services such as InfoPath Forms Services, Excel Services, and the Business Data Catalog.

Note Microsoft has eliminated the SharePoint FIS license, which stood for "For Internet Sites." This means that organizations that deploy SharePoint on-premises can simply purchase a regular SharePoint server license and do not need an additional license for external users who are not employees or contractors of the organization. This could save you significant licensing costs.

Microsoft SharePoint Server 2013 and Office 2013

Microsoft's goal is to provide consistent collaboration functionality in an architecturally sound manner. One of the core approaches to meeting this goal is the reuse of common services. The Windows operating system provides core Web server and workflow services (via .NET 4.5). The .NET Framework provides the Web Part Framework and Web concepts such as master pages. SQL Server provides database services. SharePoint Foundation provides core information services such as security, management, and a site provisioning engine. The rest of the SharePoint 2013 server components build on the core SharePoint Foundation platform to provide additional features. Figure 3-3 shows the component relationships that constitute the overall architecture. In the rest of this section, we will explore each component in more detail.

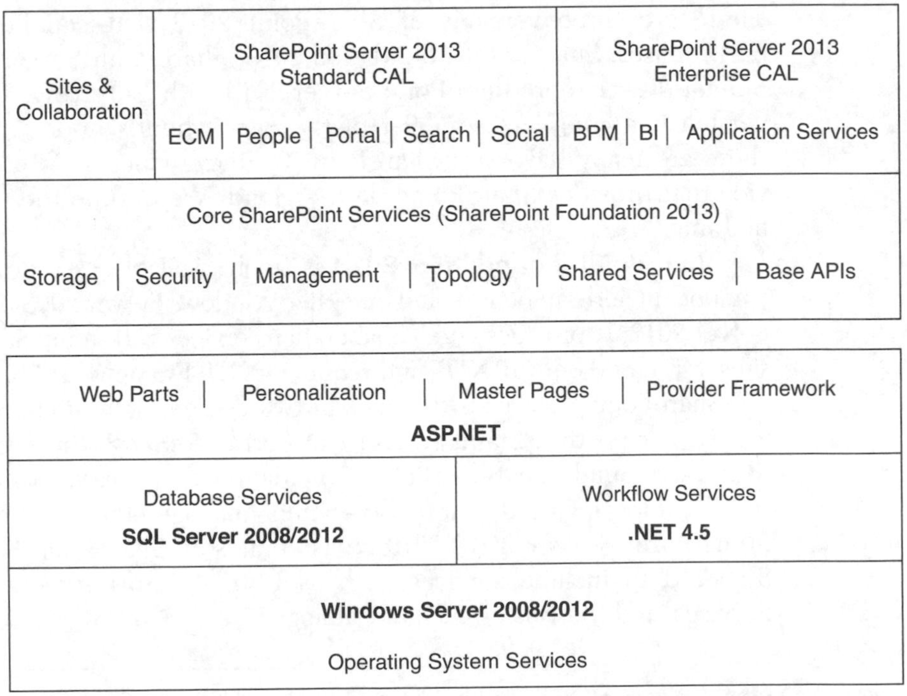

Sites & Collaboration	SharePoint Server 2013 Standard CAL		SharePoint Server 2013 Enterprise CAL	
	ECM | People | Portal | Search | Social		BPM | BI | Application Services	

Core SharePoint Services (SharePoint Foundation 2013)

Storage | Security | Management | Topology | Shared Services | Base APIs

Web Parts	Personalization	Master Pages	Provider Framework
ASP.NET			

Database Services **SQL Server 2008/2012**	Workflow Services **.NET 4.5**

Windows Server 2008/2012

Operating System Services

Figure 3-3 The SharePoint 2013 technologies provide a wide array of capabilities, built upon Windows Server and .NET and delivered in three tiers: SharePoint Foundation 2013, Microsoft SharePoint Server 2013 Standard CAL features, and Microsoft SharePoint Server 2013 Enterprise CAL features

Operating System Services: Windows Server

Windows Server provides base operating system services, such as the NTFS file system, the Internet Information Server (IIS) Web services, and application server features such as message queuing and component management services.

Note   The collaboration platform technologies discussed in this book run only on Windows Server 2008/2012 (64-bit) and are not supported on other operating systems such as Linux or Solaris. They are, however, accessible via a Web browser from clients on these systems.

Database Services: Microsoft SQL Server

Both SharePoint Foundation 2013 and SharePoint Server 2013 require a database server to store configuration information, metadata, and files. SharePoint 2013 requires either Microsoft SQL Server 2008 R2 SP1 (64-bit edition) or SQL Server 2012 (64-bit edition). For very small workgroup deployments, SharePoint will run using the SQL Server Express database included with SharePoint Foundation.

Note   SharePoint 2013 is not supported on non-Microsoft databases such as MySQL or Oracle.

Workflow Services: Windows Workflow Foundation

SharePoint 2013 supports workflow by building on the Windows Workflow Foundation 4 (part of Azure Workflow and .NET 4.5). There are essentially four ways to create workflows: use the out-of-the-box workflows (which ship via templates in Microsoft SharePoint Server 2013), create a workflow using SharePoint Designer 2013, use Visio 2013, or create a workflow in Visual Studio 2012 (for more complex workflows). SharePoint 2013 introduces a new Workflow Manager server role that is described further in Chapter 17, "Planning Business Solutions."

Web Page Services: ASP.NET

Core Web functionality in SharePoint 2013 is provided by the .NET Framework, specifically in the ASP.NET toolset. The Web Part Framework, included in ASP.NET, enables developers to create Web Parts that work in ASP.NET Web sites, SharePoint Foundation sites, and Microsoft SharePoint Server 2013 sites. (It is important to note, however, that ASP .NET Web Parts are not exactly the same as SharePoint 2013 Web Parts.) In addition, ASP.NET and SharePoint 2013 share some key features like master pages, which makes UI customization much easier.

Collaboration Services

SharePoint Foundation provides a core set of services for developing collaborative workspaces. We will focus on SharePoint Foundation as both a platform for the other SharePoint Server 2013 features as well as a rich collaborative technology in its own right.

Portal

Microsoft SharePoint Server 2013 provides a core set of services for developing sites that enable users to view aggregated lists of content, links, and other information. With SharePoint Server 2013, organizations can manage their intranets, extranets, and Internet sites with the same platform. Features like audience targeting enable content administrators to direct Web Parts and other content at dynamic groups of users. In SharePoint 2013, aggregation can be achieved both within a site collection via the Content Query Web Part, or across site collections by using a new Web Part called the Content Search Web Part, which uses the search index to power queries.

Enterprise Content Management

Microsoft SharePoint Server 2013 provides content management features that enable organizations to develop and manage HTML-rich Web sites. SharePoint Server 2013 provides approval, policy, rights management, retention, multilingual, and Web publishing features. Content is content is content—it doesn't matter whether you serve content up as HTML or a Word document anymore. ECM is discussed more in Chapter 13, "Managing Enterprise Content."

Search

SharePoint 2013 provides a number of key search features, including searching against disparate content sources, people search, and business data search. The FAST search engine, which was an additional component that required separate servers in SharePoint 2010, is now integrated into the core SharePoint 2013 search engine, making deployment topologies much simpler. For more information on search, see Chapter 16, "Planning Enterprise Search."

Social Computing (Community)

Microsoft SharePoint Server 2013 provides features that enable users to provide social feedback on content, including tagging, ratings, and comments. SharePoint Server 2013 also provides a number of people-centric features such as a profile store and My Sites. My Sites, which were introduced in SharePoint Portal Server 2003, provide sites for users to call their own. Through the social computing features in SharePoint Server 2013, businesses can create an experience akin to Facebook or LinkedIn for their users. Note that with the acquisition of Yammer, Microsoft has relegated the SharePoint 2013 social features to an inferior role. You should consider Yammer the premier social tool with respect to a SharePoint 2013 deployment. We discuss social computing in Chapter 15, "Planning for Social Computing."

Business Intelligence

Microsoft SharePoint Server 2013 brings business intelligence (BI) features to the mainstream, having dramatically improved the quality and user experience of this feature set. Excel Services, PerformancePoint Services, KPIs, dashboards, Report Center, and SQL Reporting Services all provide business intelligence via the SharePoint 2013 platform. We discuss the BI features in more detail in Chapter 18, "Planning for Business Intelligence."

Composite Applications

SharePoint sites become increasingly powerful when integrated with real business data. Being able to create rich applications quickly that combine information in SharePoint with information from other sources—such as a database, an LOB application, or the Web—is compelling. We cover how to quickly create dynamic applications ("mashups" and "composites") in Chapter 17, "Planning Business Solutions."

Table 3-1 shows the respective technologies that make up Microsoft's overall Information Worker platform. We focus on Microsoft SharePoint Server 2013 in this book, so when we use "SharePoint 2013," we typically mean the full server product.

Table 3-1 Microsoft's Communication and Collaboration Product Line

Technology	Description
SharePoint Foundation 2013	SharePoint Foundation is the core Web-based team workspace and site tool. SharePoint Foundation is licensed free with Windows Server 2008/2012 Server and available as a download from the Microsoft Windows Server site.
SharePoint Server 2013: Standard CAL	SharePoint Server 2013 builds on top of SharePoint Foundation to provide additional functionality along with aggregation, search, social, and content management features.
SharePoint Server 2013: Enterprise CAL	SharePoint Server 2013 Enterprise builds on SharePoint Server 2013 Standard to provide additional features such as InfoPath Web forms, the Business Connectivity Services (BCS), Visio, Access, Word Services, and business intelligence.
Lync 2013 (Client)	Lync is the core real-time messaging client.
Lync Server 2013	Lync 2013 is the server-side component that enables real-time communications features, such as instant messaging, presence, and real-time meetings.
Microsoft BizTalk Server 2010	BizTalk provides core integration functions and ships with an adapter for SharePoint. For example, BizTalk can automate your back-end business processes and pick up where SharePoint leaves off.
Exchange Server 2013	Designed to run on the 64-bit version of Microsoft Windows Server 2008 or 2012, Exchange Server 2013 is Microsoft's mail server product.
Office 2013	Office 2013 provides e-mail integration, offline content synchronization, Excel publishing, and other features that integrate with SharePoint 2013.
Office 365	This is Microsoft's cloud-based offering, which includes SharePoint, Exchange, and Lync hosted in Microsoft's cloud, along with Office Web Apps and cloud-based deployment of the Office client.

What's New in SharePoint 2013?

The prior version of SharePoint (SharePoint 2010) was a breakthrough version of Microsoft's core collaboration platform. Microsoft's plan for SharePoint 2013 was to build upon the far-reaching success of SharePoint 2007 and SharePoint 2010. Specifically, the architectural goals for SharePoint 2013 include

- Increased scalability
- Performance enhancements, including faster page load times
- Easier-to-manage security

- Richer social experiences
- Better offline document support
- Superior search capabilities
- Support for a large number of deployment scenarios, including the cloud
- Improved user experience for out-of-the-box features
- Easier upgrade for individual site collections
- Easier-to-manage solutions built for cloud-based deployment models

Once of the key objectives of the SharePoint 2013 team was to build upon the success of prior versions while preserving the items that made SharePoint 2010 a success. Thus, the SharePoint team kept the core architecture the same while adding a number of new features. Table 3-2 lists some of the new features in SharePoint 2013.

Comparing SharePoint Versions

SharePoint Foundation 2013 is a collection of services for Microsoft Windows Server 2008 that you can use to share information, collaborate with other users on documents, and create lists and Web Part pages. You can also use SharePoint Foundation as a development platform to create collaboration applications and information-sharing applications, as discussed in the next section.

Microsoft SharePoint Server 2013, a step up from SharePoint Foundation, is a scalable enterprise server that is built on SharePoint Foundation. You can use Microsoft SharePoint Server 2013 to aggregate SharePoint Foundation sites, other information, and applications in your organization. Because Microsoft SharePoint Server 2013 requires SharePoint Foundation, all features of SharePoint Foundation are available in Microsoft SharePoint Server 2013.

In addition to the core features of SharePoint Foundation (core site-based services and collaboration site templates), Microsoft SharePoint Server 2013 includes the following Standard and Enterprise features:

Microsoft SharePoint Server 2013 Standard:

- **Portal:** provides a way to create an intranet portal, an extranet portal, and an Internet-facing .com site on a single platform
- **News:** provides a way to create, maintain, and publish news articles for consumption by internal and external audiences

Table 3-2 SharePoint 2013: What's New?

Feature	Description
Collaboration	Collaboration with external users (for SharePoint Online)
	Enhanced OneNote integration with team sites
Social networking	Newsfeed enhancements
	Microblogging
	SkyDrive Pro for offline documents
	"Sites I follow" page
	Task timeline
	User profile enhancements
	Community Sites template
Document libraries	Drag and drop from desktop to browser
	Command usage via callout feature
	Offline synchronization via SkyDrive Pro
Mobile	Optimized mobile browser experiences
	Office on Demand
	Native Windows Phone and iPhone SharePoint apps
Branding and site customization	Create and edit lists as you edit a page
	Enhanced WYSIWYG page editing
	Enhanced themes ("Choose a Look")
	New Design Manager
	Site designs using any design product
Enterprise content management	Enhanced discovery and case management
	Site retention policies
	Video management
Search	People and expert search enhancements
	Navigation enhancements
	FAST engine integration—a single search engine
	Content Search Web Part
Business intelligence	Excel OData provider support
	Enhanced Business Intelligence Center

Feature	Description
Workflows	Redesigned workflow architecture (WWF4)
	Steps enable more complex logic
	Loops enable repeating of operations
	Visio 2013 Designer
	Enhanced e-mail editor
	New workflow actions
IT Pro changes	Deferred site collection upgrade
	Recycle Bin site collection restoration
	Shredded storage
	OAuth 2.0 and improved claims support (Note: Claims is now the default authentication model; Windows Classic is no longer supported for new Web applications and will be eliminated in future versions.)
Developer changes	New apps model
	Enhanced model for HTML, JavaScript, OData, REST, and OAuth
	Access Services uses Azure databases instead of lists
	New Napa Office 365 development tools
	BCS enhancements
	Machine translation service

- **User profiles:** provides an extensible profile for each employee and the ability for users to search and find expertise within the company
- **Social computing:** provides a way for users to socially tag, rate, and comment on content
- **Audiences:** provides a way to target content to groups of users based on rules
- **Search:** provides extensible search functionality across file shares, Web sites, Microsoft Exchange public folders, Lotus Notes, and Windows SharePoint Services sites (with the exception of the Content Search Web Part)
- **Records management:** provides document auditing, expiry, and other features that enable management of company records
- **Web content management:** provides functionality for business users to create and manage Web-based content (HTML) based on templates

Microsoft SharePoint Server 2013 Enterprise:

- **PerformancePoint Services:** provides business intelligence capabilities, a Report Center template and key performance indicator (KPI) lists, and Web Parts
- **Search:** adds the Content Search Web Part for aggregating information from across site collections by enabling queries of the search index
- **Business Connectivity Services (BCS):** provides a way to integrate line-of-business data into portal pages, team sites, document metadata, enterprise search, and employee profiles
- **InfoPath Forms Services:** provides the ability to publish, render, and consume InfoPath 2013 forms via a Web browser
- **Excel Services:** provides the ability to publish and render Excel 2013 workbooks on the server; enables calculations and graphics rendering via a Web interface
- **Access Services:** provides the ability to publish and render Access 2013 databases on the server; enables the Access application to store its data within a SQL Server or Azure database and run within SharePoint via a Web interface
- **Word Services:** provides the ability to publish and render Word 2013 documents on the server
- **Visio Services:** provides the ability to publish and render Visio 2013 diagrams on the server

Table 3-3 describes the core SharePoint 2013 product feature sets.

Note   For a complete feature comparison, you can view the official Microsoft comparison between an on-premises installation of SharePoint 2013 and SharePoint Online at http://technet.microsoft.com/en-us/library/jj819267.aspx.

So with all of these features, what does SharePoint 2013 provide from a collaboration and solutions perspective? For many companies still using file shares for document sharing and Access databases (and Excel, for that matter) for tracking applications, it provides a perfect next step. Let's take a look at these two trends: using SharePoint as a file share replacement and as an Access database/Excel workbook replacement.

Table 3-3 Comparison of SharePoint 2013 Feature Sets

Business Need	SharePoint Foundation 2013	SharePoint Server 2013 Standard CAL	SharePoint Server 2013 Enterprise CAL	SharePoint Online (E3/E4 plans)
Collaboration using user-created team sites	√	√	√	√
Browser-based user customization	√	√	√	√
Document management (check-in/checkout, versions, Content Types)	√	√	√	√
Blogs and wikis	√	√	√	√
Local search (sites and sub-sites)	√	√	√	√
Custom lists, surveys, templates	√	√	√	√
RSS feeds on any list	√	√	√	√
Offline (Sky-Drive Pro)	√	√	√	√
Integration with LOB data through Business Connectivity Services	√	√	√	√
Out-of-the-box workflow templates for approval and review		√	√	√

(continues)

Table 3.3 Comparison of SharePoint 2013 Feature Sets *(continued)*

Business Need	SharePoint Foundation 2013	SharePoint Server 2013 Standard CAL	SharePoint Server 2013 Enterprise CAL	SharePoint Online (E3/E4 plans)
Enterprise search (docs, sites, people)		√	√	√
Content Search Web Part			√	As of May 2013, not included. However, this is likely to change.
Records management (auditing, retention policy)		√	√	√
Centralized user profiles		√	√	√
Social tagging and feedback		√	√	√
Managed metadata services		√	√	√
Targeting content to rule-based groups (audiences)		√	√	√
Creating and maintaining news		√	√	√
Personal sites		√	√	√
Web content management		√	√	√
App catalog		√	√	√
Web-based InfoPath forms			√	√

Business Need	SharePoint Foundation 2013	SharePoint Server 2013 Standard CAL	SharePoint Server 2013 Enterprise CAL	SharePoint Online (E3/E4 plans)
KPI lists and Report Center		√		√
Excel Services			√	√
Access Services			√	√
Word Services			√	√
Visio Services			√	√
Licensing model	Windows Server + Windows Server CAL or Windows External Connector	Windows Server License + Windows CAL + Microsoft SharePoint Server 2013 Server License + Microsoft SharePoint Server 2013 Standard CAL (or Core CAL Suite)	Windows Server License + Windows CAL + Microsoft SharePoint Server 2013 Server License + Microsoft SharePoint Server 2013 Standard CAL (or Core CAL Suite) + Microsoft SharePoint Server 2013 Enterprise CAL (or Enterprise CAL Suite)	Office 365 Subscription or SharePoint Online Subscription

SharePoint: The File Share Killer?

SharePoint is commonly used as a file share and public folder replacement. Customers frequently ask whether SharePoint will replace file shares entirely. If you start encouraging users to put documents and other content into SharePoint, should you disconnect your file shares for good? The answer is a resounding *no*. File shares are not dead. But they are on life support.

SharePoint is designed for file collaboration, records management, and discovery. Windows file shares are good for file *storage*, housing a database, and for large amounts of read-only content. Determine if you have collaborative, findability, security, or e-discovery requirements. If so, your document storage needs are a good candidate for SharePoint. On the flip side, ask yourself whether the files in question have little collaborative value or are simply too large or costly to store in SharePoint. If either of these is true, a file share is probably a better place for those files, since the overhead of SharePoint might make it a poor choice.

In general, for business users collaborating on documents and for storing documents as records, SharePoint is probably a better fit. However, the following are many useful scenarios for file storage based on classic file shares:

- Product distribution, such as Office installation packages
- SMS distribution point (desktop patches and hot fixes)
- Backups
- Database storage, such as Access and SQL databases
- Very large audio/video and streaming media (over 2GB)
- Developer source control
- Executables and PowerShell scripts
- Archives and dumps

In short, users will need training to understand where to save their files. With most file-sharing scenarios, SharePoint libraries will be the Microsoft-recommended way of sharing files inside the corporation, and with collaborative SharePoint site extranet deployments, it's the way to share with partners. Most nontechnical users such as HR, sales, and marketing teams can say goodbye to using file shares for file sharing. To avoid replicating the limits of shared drives (for example, poor navigation and duplicate content), users will also need training to understand the use of metadata and folders to organize their content.

As you can see, there are a number of valid reasons for having *both* file shares and SharePoint document libraries in your organization. In fact, you may decide to keep *existing* collaborative content on your file shares as a read-only archive and simply use SharePoint 2013's search technology to enable users to search for existing documents (rather than migrating those documents to SharePoint).

So the file share question is answered . . . but what about Access databases and Excel workbooks? Are those dead?

SharePoint: The Access and Excel Killer?

Overheard at an organization near you:

Business user (to IT department): "We need an application to track donations to our upcoming fund-raising campaign."

IT department: "What are the requirements?"

Business user: "We need to track donors, contributions, project tasks, documents, and approvals, to search on items, and to provide reports to management."

IT department: "We can build it in four months."

Business user: (Gasp!)

IT department: "If you can secure additional funding, we can do it in two."

Business user: "Never mind. I'll create an Access database and throw it on a file share."

IT department: (Gasp!)

The problem with this fairly common scenario is that now there's yet another database out there that's probably not backed up properly, cannot support Web-based access, and is virtually unknown to and unsupported by IT. This is another reason why IT departments are putting SharePoint in place—to support requests by the business for collaboration and tracking applications.

Note   Q: What's the world's most widely used database application?
A: Microsoft Excel.

In addition to its great collaboration features, SharePoint 2013 can be very effective as a platform to create information-sharing and -tracking applications. Let's look at an example of the business need described by the business user—one that can be addressed in a matter of minutes, without code. Previously, this type of solution would take months for a development team to build, in addition to the time—perhaps months—it might take to deploy the infrastructure itself.

Let's say that one of the business units within your organization needs a simple way to track donations that are being solicited for a fund-raising campaign. There is a team of fund-raisers who need to track contributions, project managers who need to plan various fund-raising events, and managers who need to see the current status of the campaign's progress. Let's say that the team tracks donors in a spreadsheet that gets e-mailed around—a typical collaboration and tracking scenario. However, items such as actual contributions made by whom, event-planning documents, and other items are not tracked in an organized manner, since e-mail would be a difficult way to do this.

During discovery, some of the requirements that come to light are as follows:

- The need to track the following entities:
    - Donors (contacts)
    - Contributions (associated with donors)
    - Project tasks (for planning fund-raising events)
    - Team announcements (with RSS feeds)
    - Documents (including version tracking, multi-user editing, along with community tagging, ratings, and comments)
- A workflow-based approval process
- Highly scalable Web-based access
- Item-level security
- Keyword search
- Threshold reporting and visual indicators for management

While this type of application could be written as a custom Web application, it would likely take several weeks (or possibly even several months) of custom development. In addition, a Web server and database server would need to be deployed to accommodate the application. Let's see what a no-code method of creating the solution in SharePoint 2013, running in the cloud under Office 365, would look like. It's as simple as creating a new site, importing the existing spreadsheet, and configuring some new elements.

Walkthrough

The following steps illustrate how to build a collaborative application in SharePoint Server 2013. To get a peek at the application in its final form, check out Figure 3-10, which shows the completed collaborative application—created in less than an hour. You can follow along in your own SharePoint on-premises environment, or you can simply provision an Office 365 trial site at www.microsoft.com/office365.

Step 1: Create a new, blank site by first navigating to Sites (see Figure 3-4):

1. Click "new site."
2. Provide a name for the site—in this case **DonationTracking** (see Figure 3-5).
3. Click Create.

The result is a ready-to-use SharePoint site (see Figure 3-6).

Figure 3-4 The "Sites I'm following" page is a new feature in SharePoint 2013 that provides a list of sites that you've currently selected to follow. From here, you can click "new site" to create a site.

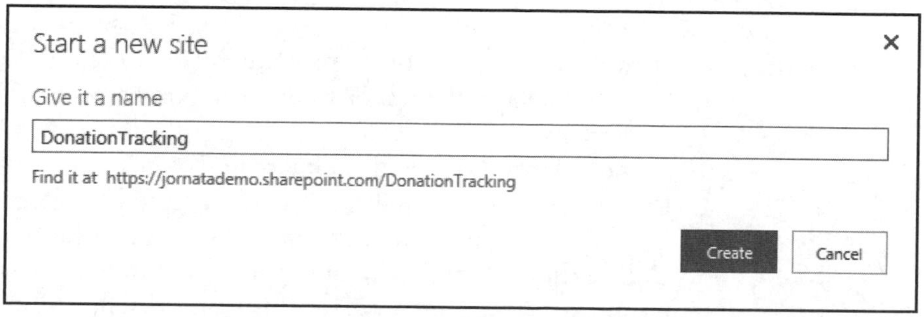

Figure 3-5 Simply provide a name for your new tracking site

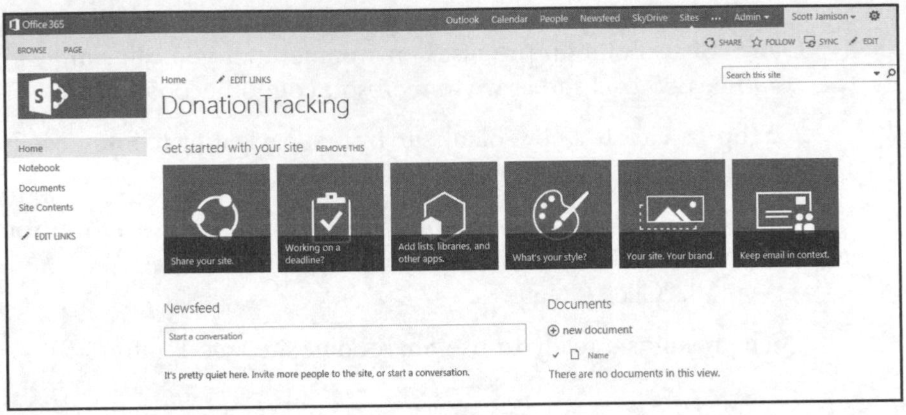

Figure 3-6 Once the site has been provisioned, you can add lists, Web Parts, and additional items to the site

Step 2: Create a new contacts list by adding a SharePoint 2013 app:

1. Click the gear in the upper-right corner and select "Add an app" (see Figure 3-7).
2. Click the Contacts app.
3. Name the list **Donors** and click Create.
4. The list will be created and show up in the list of Site Contents (see Figure 3-8).

Note If you keep getting prompted for a username and password when using your SharePoint site, or if you get an error trying to import a spreadsheet for a custom spreadsheet-based list, make sure that the site is added to your local intranet zone within your browser.

Step 3: Create a list to track donations made by donors in the contact list:
1. Click the gear in the upper-right corner and select "Add an app."
2. Select Custom List.
3. Name it **Donations** and click Create.
4. Under Site Contents, click the newly created Donations list.
5. Click the List tab in the Ribbon and select List Settings.
6. Under the Columns heading, click Title, change its name to **Donation** (you cannot delete this Column, since it provides the link to the item), and click OK.

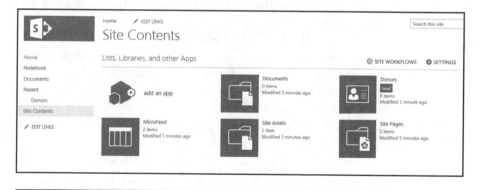

Figure 3-7 To create a new list within the SharePoint site, you now "Add an app" (which is different from prior versions of SharePoint)

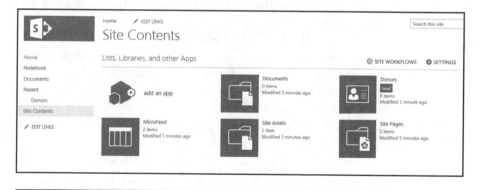

Figure 3-8 Your new list will show up under Site Contents, which displays Lists, Libraries, and other Apps

7. Under the Columns heading, click Create Column, and name the new Column **Donation Method**, making it a Choice field. Replace the default choices (Enter Choice #1, etc.) with Cash, Stock, and Clothing. Click OK.

8. Click Create Column and name the new Column **Donor**. This time, select the Lookup Column. Under Get Information From, select the Donors list, FullName Column. This will associate a

donation with a donor. Two features in SharePoint 2013 enable you to enforce unique values and to enforce relationship-linking behavior. We'll skip those for now. Click OK.

9. Click Create Column and name the new Column **Amount**, designating it as a Currency field. Click OK.

Step 4: Create a project task list:

1. Click the gear in the upper-right corner and select "Add an app."
2. Select Tasks, which enables you to track tasks and view Gantt charts.
3. Name the list **Event Planning Tasks** and click Create.

Step 5: Create an announcements list:

1. Click the gear in the upper-right corner and select "Add an app."
2. Select Announcements.
3. Name the list **Announcements** and click Create.

Step 6: Add the Web Parts for the lists just created to your site home page:

1. Navigate to the home page of your Donation Tracking site by clicking on the SharePoint icon in the upper-left corner of the page.
2. Click the Page tab and click Edit.
3. Next to "Getting started with your site" click Remove This to make some room for your Web Parts.
4. In the left Web Part zone, click Insert and then click App Part (see Figure 3-9).
5. One at a time, add your newly created list-based Web Parts, which will appear on the left under Parts, to the site. There's no need to add Documents since it's already on the page.
6. Click Save in the ribbon UI to return to user mode.

Step 7: To complete your application, arrange your Web Parts so that the site is organized well for a quality user experience. In addition, you'll want to add some sample data:

1. Click Edit under the Page tab in the ribbon.
2. Drag and drop your Web Parts to locations on the page that are to your liking. You will also want to create custom views and then set the Web Part to display those custom views.
3. Click Stop Editing in the ribbon UI to return to the site.
4. Start adding data to the site. See Figure 3-10 for an example of the new Donation Tracking collaborative site.

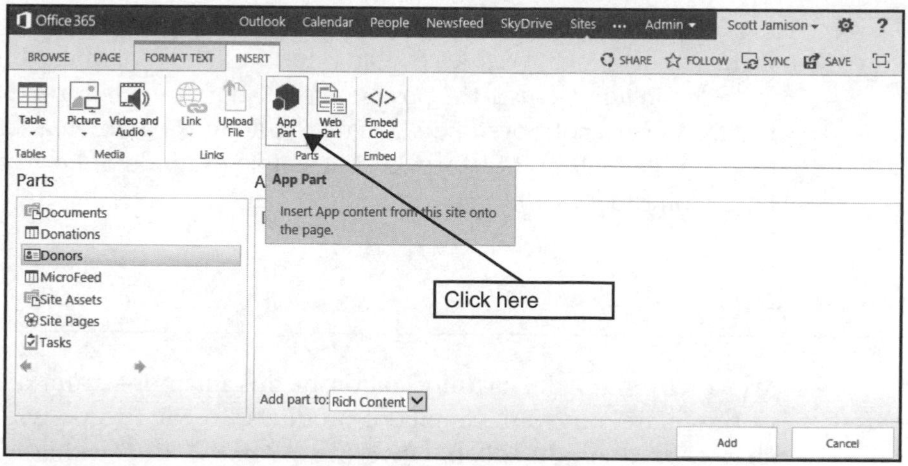

Figure 3-9 You can add the site's list-based Web Parts one at a time by selecting them from the site's Web Part gallery and clicking Add. (You can no longer add many Web Parts at once.)

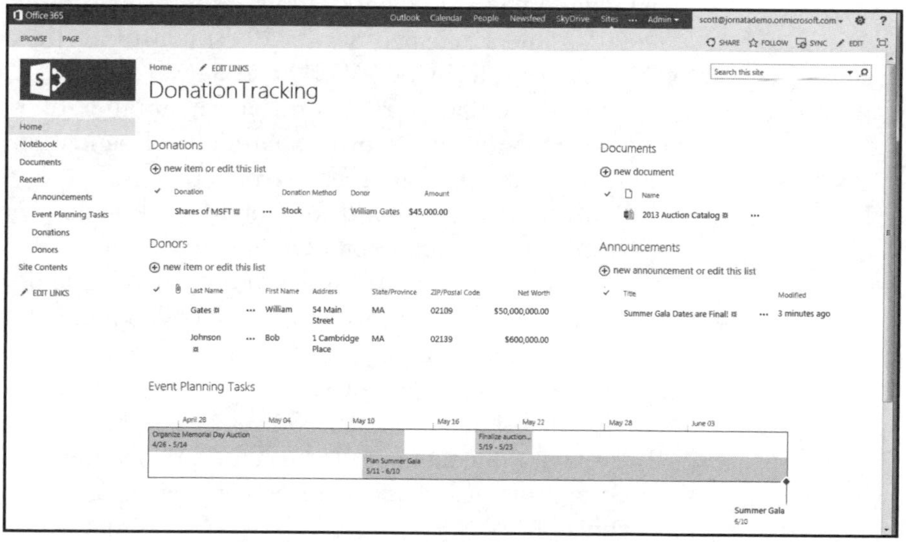

Figure 3-10 In less than an hour and with no code (and no servers if you use Office 365!), SharePoint 2013 enables a business user to create a collaborative application, complete with related custom list data, documents, search, project tasks, RSS-enabled announcements, and real-time usage reporting

Note that this solution enables the tracking of data, file storage with metadata, a secure, Web-accessible interface, and search capabilities—all in under an hour! This is the power of a collaboration platform that enables business users, not developers, to create solutions based on a set of ready-to-assemble tools and features. It is a simple example of how you can use SharePoint to *get things done*.

Key Points

We've covered a lot of information in this chapter—from an overview of the SharePoint 2013 family of products, to what to do with your file shares, to a sample collaborative SharePoint 2013 tracking application. We hope that you're starting to get a feel for the functionality of SharePoint and the types of business problems it can help address. In summary:

- Microsoft's family of communication and collaboration products (including Office client applications, Microsoft SharePoint 2013, Lync 2013, and Exchange Server 2013) constitute the foundation for Microsoft's Information Worker strategy.
- SharePoint Foundation 2013 provides a number of feature and developer enhancements over SharePoint Foundation 2010 but keeps the fundamental architecture intact.
- SharePoint 2013 is optimized for cloud-based deployment (specifically Office 365 and SharePoint Online).
- SharePoint Foundation 2013 is based on ASP.NET and .NET 4.5.
- SharePoint Foundation provides a set of collaborative functionality, including Web page support, collaboration, document management, and a team workspace platform.
- Microsoft SharePoint Server 2013 provides additional features built on SharePoint Foundation, including enterprise content management, social computing, search, business process management, and business intelligence.
- Both SharePoint Foundation 2013 and Microsoft SharePoint Server 2013 require the 64-bit versions of Windows Server (either 2008

R2 SP1 or 2012) and Microsoft SQL Server (either 2008 R2 SP1 or 2012) to run.

- Unlike previous versions, SharePoint 2013 requires claims-based authentication.
- SharePoint 2013 is a great place to build collaborative-style tracking applications with little to no code.

CHAPTER 4

PLANNING FOR BUSINESS GOVERNANCE

Danish philosopher Søren Kierkegaard said, "People understand me so poorly that they don't even understand my complaint about them not understanding me." If he lived in this century, Kierkegaard could have been talking about SharePoint governance—the most misunderstood and misrepresented concept in the SharePoint space! Though everyone seems to have a different definition for governance, we all seem to agree that it's one of the most important success factors for a SharePoint deployment. It's a bit like the story of the blind men and the elephant[1]—everyone has a different perspective.

With many controversial topics in the business world, it's helpful not to get hung up on definitions—especially if everyone agrees on the outcome. When it comes to "governance" (which we might as well call the "G" word since everyone seems to have his or her own unique perspective), the goal is something that most folks agree on—making sure that your solution is successful. What we all might disagree about is what is included in the "G" word and what you need to do to make it happen. We generally consider governance for SharePoint as the people, processes, and policies necessary to ensure that your SharePoint solution meets both short- and long-term business goals, including those that may be required for legal or regulatory purposes. Without clear business goals, a governance plan is really meaningless. Without a governance plan, it's virtually impossible to achieve your business goals.

For the discussion in this book, we will talk about SharePoint governance as having four dimensions, each of which requires a set of people

---

1. If you have never heard this story, a good explanation is available at http://en.wikipedia.org/wiki/Blind_men_and_an_elephant.

(roles), processes, and policies in order to achieve—and each of which helps reduce risk:

- Technology assurance
- Information assurance
- Guidance
- "Consumability"

Technology assurance—keeping the trains running on time. Whatever you want to call it, there is an element of the "G" word that is totally in the realm of the technology infrastructure team. Governance in this context means taking care of the "back end"—ensuring that backup and recovery plans are implemented (and tested), capacity planning for the solution (which includes understanding solution content, geographic distribution of the user base, and how the solution is used in a business context or contexts), ensuring performance, maintaining service-level agreements (SLAs), applying software patches and upgrades, and so on. Adding SharePoint to the mix of technology platforms in an organization may add a new element to technology assurance processes, but good IT departments are already doing this for other infrastructure applications— and the business users of SharePoint have a right to expect that the IT team will take care of the technology assurance required for SharePoint. If you are deploying SharePoint 2013 Online, Microsoft will take care of a lot of the technology assurance for you, and your IT shop can focus more on monitoring than on executing. When you are deploying SharePoint on-premises, there are certainly SharePoint-specific responsibilities that you need to worry about. If you are responsible for technology assurance in your organization, please read Chapter 5, "Planning for Operational Governance." If you are the business owner of a SharePoint solution, your role for technology assurance is to make sure that your service-level expectations for SharePoint are realistic and directly tied to business risk. As one of our colleagues used to be fond of saying, "You can have anything you want, as long as you have unlimited time and money."

Information assurance—ensuring that information in all its forms is adding value. Information assurance is the process of managing content—reviewing it, disposing of it, securing it, making note of when it is a record, and ensuring that records management processes are followed. We hope that you do not have to invent information assurance policies for SharePoint—your organization most likely already has an information assurance plan in place. If not, implementing SharePoint could serve as the catalyst for creating a formal records management/information assurance plan. The challenge you may face is that it's possible that your organization has an information assurance plan that is not actually followed or enforced. This all-too-common situation means that your organization has some significant exposure risk from an e-discovery perspective, but it also means that you may have some challenges getting users to comply with content management policies—especially those designed to remove or archive expired content—because you haven't enforced these policies in the past. The important thing to remember is that decisions about information assurance are not technology decisions; they are business decisions, and the IT team responsible for implementing SharePoint should be *following*, not *creating*, policies. Once the business requirements are identified, *business owners* should be accountable to ensure that the policies are communicated, applied, *and enforced* in the context of your SharePoint content. Information assurance is related to corporate compliance and risk mitigation—it is not optional. Security is a really big part of information assurance, and the security plan for your solution and your content is one of the most important areas of solution planning. Managing permissions is complicated—because business is messy—and this is a good area in which to invest in one of the several good third-party tools on the market to help manage and automate the application and review of permissions on your SharePoint site. For more information on this topic, refer to Chapter 12, "Planning Security." But remember, tools can only help you implement policies that you have already defined—so the first step is to define the policies.

Guidance—steering empowered users in the right direction to achieve business results. Making SharePoint governance "stick" is about education and support—ensuring that the people empowered with specific roles and responsibilities have the training and appropriate guidance to ensure that they can accomplish their business goals efficiently and effectively. Wherever possible, guidance should be built into site templates. For example, creating standard document library templates that already include enterprise metadata will make it painfully easy for site owners to understand how to leverage predefined metadata to help make their content more "findable." Proper guidance also includes the built-in critical role of the moderator that is part of the template for the SharePoint 2013 community site (see Chapter 15, "Planning for Social Computing"). And it means providing a training roadmap for new users that teaches them key SharePoint concepts just at the moment when they need to learn about them. There are often entire departments or teams dedicated to IT and information assurance, but rarely enough (or any) focus on providing users with another equally, if not more important, "G" word—guidance—about how to get the most value from the investments they have made in SharePoint.

"Consumability"—communicating your governance plan in a way that users can easily process and understand. Once you understand the basic governance elements, you can structure the conversations required to make good decisions about what you need to do for your specific solution. Documenting these decisions is important. But creating a massive governance document that no one reads or can process is almost as bad as not having a governance plan at all. Successful governance plans are "consumable" by the people who need to understand them. When your governance plan is consumable, it can also be enforced—and without some kind of continuous review, your well-documented governance plan is just a piece of paper. This doesn't mean that all of the elements of your governance plan need to be enforced in the same way. You will clearly need to monitor and enforce rules related to legal or regulatory compliance differently from guidance that results in better content "findability." But all elements of your governance plan need to be well understood by the people who have to follow them. And to do that, your governance plan must include a plan for making it consumable. We will spend some time talking about how to make your governance plan consumable in this chapter, but this is an emerging practice area and it is likely that you will want to keep up with our blogs and speaking engagements as we continue to learn more about successful approaches to ensuring the consumability of governance plans.

Chapter 5, "Planning for Operational Governance," focuses on the first governance dimension, technology assurance. The discussion in this chapter describes a series of steps to help you think about planning for SharePoint governance considering the last three dimensions: information assurance, guidance, and consumability. These three dimensions have the greatest impact on the business owner for SharePoint as a whole in your organization and the business owner of each individual SharePoint site.

Tom Byrnes, Enterprise SharePoint Architect at Biogen Idec, has a very simple definition for SharePoint governance that provides an excellent framework for the recommendations in this chapter and a guiding principle for the governance plans you create for your SharePoint solutions. According to Tom, governance means making sure that there are "no sharp edges." In other words, governance means ensuring that you are not creating a situation where your user, your organization, or your solution can get hurt either intentionally or accidentally.

> An effective governance plan means that your solution has "no sharp edges."
>
> —Thomas Byrnes, Enterprise SharePoint Architect, Biogen Idec

What's New in SharePoint 2013?

SharePoint 2013 adds a new dimension to the concept of governance, with new types of content (such as activity posts) and new user actions (such as liking, following, and mentioning) that will need additional governance focus. Here are some of the new governance concepts that you will want to think about:

■ **New types of content to govern—especially social content.** Each new version of SharePoint brings new types of content to govern for which we need to provide guidance, and SharePoint 2013 is no exception. The implication for governance planning is that there are new governance decisions to make. For example, if you are enabling the new, rich social conversation capabilities, you will need to discuss with your legal team whether there are any compliance issues associated with retaining conversations (i.e., legal discovery issues). There is no built-in process to automatically support "aging out" of the newsfeed, so you will need to consider how long to retain activity posts. You will also want to review what is legal to talk about in discussion posts (for example, certain types of personal information about yourself or others). Similarly, you will want to talk with your executives about what is *appropriate* to discuss. And you will need to communicate to your users that when they click the button to enable their personal sites for the first time, they are explicitly acknowledging that they are participating in a social conversation—that they can be followed and people can follow and mention them—without requiring explicit permission.

- **Easier to share.** SharePoint 2013 Online makes it easy to invite external users into a site or give them access to just one document on a site. You will need to think about whether you want to make this feature available (for the environment as a whole or on just some site collections) and if it will be available, what type of guidance to provide to users. For a more detailed discussion of the implications of some of the security decisions you will need to incorporate into your governance plan, refer to Chapter 12, "Planning Security."
- **New types of users.** Office 365/SharePoint Online customers can take advantage of a licensing model that allows organizations to give access to their SharePoint environment to "guest" or extranet users. Extranet user licenses are free, but extranet users have a "second-class" user experience that needs to be considered as part of your governance plan.

In addition, we've learned a lot about effectively creating and deploying governance plans since *Essential SharePoint 2010* was published; an increasing number of our clients have asked us to help them create effective governance plans. Even if you have read *Essential SharePoint 2007* and *Essential SharePoint 2010*, you will find a lot of new information about governance in this chapter. Some of the key lessons we've learned in the past three years include:

- Creating "consumable" governance plans is as important as (if not more so) creating a governance plan in the first place. Yes, you need to have a governance plan. But if it's not consumable, it's not worth the paper it's (ideally not) printed on.
- You can't talk about business and technical governance to the same audience—unless you want to put everyone to sleep (which is why we have added a separate chapter about operational governance to this edition of the book).
- If a particular action is required for legal or regulatory compliance purposes, the best approach in your SharePoint solution is to control it with technology—either with a third-party tool or with business rules that are applied with information management policies. It's critical to make a distinction between rules or policies that users have to follow for *compliance* purposes, and recommended *guidance*, which is more about the practices necessary to achieve desired business outcomes or, put another way, about risk mitigation

for business goals. Your users may not necessarily *have* to follow guidance, but if they don't, your organization may not achieve the desired business outcomes.

Not having an effective governance plan is just as detrimental to the success of SharePoint 2013 solutions as it was for previous versions. Since it is easy to build new sites and perhaps even easier to add new content in SharePoint 2013, it is easy for SharePoint solutions to quickly grow out of control. A carefully thought-out governance plan can ensure that you effectively manage your investment in SharePoint for organizational success.

Why Is Governance Planning Important?

A portal or collaboration solution is only as good as the value of its underlying content. A strong governance plan is essential to ensure that a solution delivers worthwhile content to its users in an effective way. Moreover, governance planning is especially important for SharePoint solutions because SharePoint is designed to empower users who are typically not IT or content management experts and may not be aware of best practices that will not only improve usability but save them a lot of time and energy when creating and deploying new sites.

A governance plan establishes the processes and roles required to

- Avoid solution, team site, and content "sprawl" (e.g., unmanaged sites and content that is not periodically reviewed for accuracy and relevance) by defining a content and site review process
- Ensure that content quality is maintained for the life of the solution by implementing content quality management policies
- Provide a consistently high-quality user experience by defining guidelines for site and content designers
- Establish clear decision-making authority and escalation procedures so policy violations are dealt with and conflicts are resolved on a timely basis
- Ensure that the solution strategy is aligned with business objectives so that it continuously delivers business value
- Ensure that content is retained in compliance with records retention guidelines

Adoption of a new SharePoint solution often involves a dramatic change in user behavior—specifically, greater integration of technology into day-to-day work and increased collaboration. This is especially significant if you are deploying the social features of SharePoint 2013. In more traditional IT solution deployments, the solution business logic changes relatively infrequently. In a SharePoint solution, both the back-end database and business logic change frequently and often significantly. Moreover, the business, market, and technology are guaranteed to change during the lifetime of the solution. This implies that business stakeholders must be continuously engaged since SharePoint's ability to meet user needs is critically dependent on areas such as data quality, content relevance and currency, and frequent updates, all of which are business user responsibilities.

When Should You Start Thinking about Governance?

The time to start thinking about governance is really when you are identifying the key business priorities for your solution. The key business outcomes for your solution define the context for the governance plan. This is really important because your business goals will help you define how much time and energy (and money) you need to invest in governance. For example, if improving content "findability" across the organization is not very important, or you have an alternative enterprise document management solution but having a single place for individual teams to collaborate is critical, you probably don't need to spend too much time on enforcing or planning strict document metadata rules in SharePoint. If, on the other hand, you expect SharePoint to help reduce "versionitis" (multiple versions of the same document in various repositories across the enterprise), your governance plan will need to include processes and policies and training to ensure that users follow the "one copy of a document" guiding principle and send links instead of attachments, and that you have a process to ensure that you are not unnecessarily creating more than one site for the same purpose.

While you need to start thinking about governance at the start of your SharePoint project, you may not have all the answers to the key governance questions at the beginning. Don't let that deter you—it's the governance *conversations* that are most important at the beginning because they get all the key stakeholders focused on the effort that will be required to ensure that your solution is optimized for success. No matter when you start thinking about governance and creating the first set of governance artifacts, do not think of governance as being "done" at any one point in time. Your governance plan needs to be something that you continuously revisit throughout the lifetime of your solution, so make time in your project plan to revisit the plan as you learn more about how users are using the solution and capture feedback from their experiences. As your SharePoint environment evolves, revisit your governance plan to adapt to changing needs. You may find that you need greater oversight to ensure conformance. You may find that you need less oversight to encourage more creative application of core features. You may find that the roles and responsibilities need to be updated to reflect changes in the solution or changes in how users are using SharePoint.

Communicating the substance of the governance plan is a core component of launch planning and the ongoing management of your SharePoint environment. For this reason, we have included "consumability" as a critical element of governance plans. But communication also has to include some type of enforcement and review. If you aren't committed to enforcing your governance plan, why bother? Remember: there are mandatory elements of your governance plan and "guidance" elements. The mandatory elements should be those related to regulatory, records management, or legal compliance as well as any element that is fundamentally vital to the success of your solution. If you are not prepared to enforce the mandatory elements of your governance plan, you should at least be aware of the organizational risks.

What Is in a Governance Plan?

An effective governance plan provides a *framework* for design standards, information architecture, service-level agreements, infrastructure maintenance, and your overall measurement plan. It is intended to summarize and tie together, not *replace*, the documents that describe these activities in detail. Referencing this related content rather than embedding it in the governance plan will keep the plan from becoming unnecessarily bloated and unmanageable.

In addition, the governance plan should reference all of your existing IT policies for topics such as the appropriate use of technology resources, confidentiality of content, and records retention. Since so much of the focus of SharePoint 2013 is on social computing, you will also need to reference or potentially update your social media policy. Again, your SharePoint governance plan doesn't need to *include* these policies, but it should reference them where appropriate.

The business governance plan is a business document; its primary audience is the business (content) owners of your SharePoint sites and the users who produce and consume the content on those sites. Since all users can effectively produce content in SharePoint via social tags and ratings, everyone in the organization needs to be generally familiar with the governance plan, at least at a high level.

Talking about the contents of your governance plan makes it seem like the governance plan should be a single document. If there is one key lesson we've learned about this topic in the past three years, it is that no one in your organization wants to read a big governance document—so don't create one! You will probably have better luck if you create a series of short governance documents, each targeted to people in a specific role related to your solution. But you might not even want to create documents at all and instead create a series of contextual Web pages that you can organize and display in multiple contexts—for example, in line with the tasks that users will execute or linked from your training environment. That's why we often refer to what you will create to "deliver" your governance plan as governance "artifacts," which may be Web pages, quick reference cards, videos, vignettes, tchotchkes, or, sometimes, actual documents.

The governance plan needs to include the following key elements, no matter what type of artifact you use to represent them:

- **Vision statement:** a clear statement of purpose reflecting the business outcomes for the solution.
- **Guiding principles:** statements that outline organizational preferences supporting the vision.
- **Roles and responsibilities:** descriptions[2] of the key roles required to support the solution and a summary of the responsibilities and, if appropriate, the skills and learning expectations for people serving in those roles.

---

2. In fact, your governance plan doesn't need the descriptions—it needs the people who fill the roles! If you have governance roles defined but no one filling the roles, you may be able to say you have a plan, but that's the point we are trying to make throughout this discussion: a plan without execution does not ensure success.

- **Policies:** documentation of the nonnegotiable aspects of your governance plan, policies that you will monitor and enforce. For example, this could include your expectations about how often content needs to be reviewed. You may have different policies (and levels of review) for content on the intranet versus content in team sites. Your policies should also include a review plan for the policies themselves as well as the entire governance plan.
- **Guidelines:** documentation of best practices and recommendations that will improve the user experience for your solution but that are not necessarily policies that you intend to enforce or mandate. Your recommended guidelines are designed to increase user comfort and make it easier for people to both comply with your policies and get value from the solution. Think of your guidelines as providing examples to manage expectations in addition to providing best practices. This is especially important for areas like the user profile and the new activity feed. For example, if you want users to complete an "About me" statement to improve the ability to find and leverage expertise, provide examples of what a helpful "About me" statement looks like.

In addition to these elements, your plan will likely also include procedures for common tasks such as requesting a new site, requesting a new shared Content Type or attribute, requesting a new site template, and so on. Publish these procedures so site owners and other users can easily find and follow the processes you define.

How Do You Create the Governance Plan?

Figure 4-1 shows a summary of suggested activities you will want to include in the process to create your governance plan. Though we show it as a sequence, you'll most likely work on several of these activities simultaneously—and revisit most of them as your solution and organization evolve.

Think about Governance during Design

As discussed earlier, governance planning should begin when you are first envisioning the solution (and any solution enhancements). You can and should start to raise the key governance questions during your initial stakeholder analysis and visioning sessions. You may not be able to answer

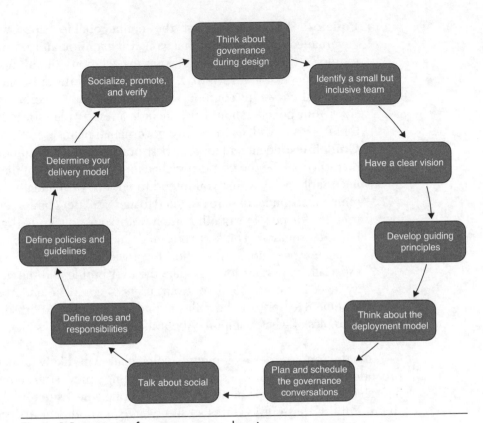

Figure 4-1 Activities for governance planning

every governance question before you have a solution design, but if you are going to need to establish new organizational roles or have to change job descriptions in order to ensure solution success, you will need to raise these issues as early as possible.

Identify a Small but Inclusive Team

If you are documenting your governance plan for the first time, you will probably find it most effective to put together a small team to review the key "framing" decisions for governance and then divide up the work to document the details and create the appropriate governance artifacts among the team members. The best reason to start with a small team is that you can actually make some initial decisions and have productive conversations about topics. Once your small team has made some initial recommendations, you can review and discuss your "straw man" proposal with your larger steering committee or governance board.

The team should clearly include representatives from IT, but you will also want to include people who can represent the interests of those responsible for training, human resources, communications, and knowledge management in the organization. For certain key decisions, you will need to bring in specialized resources—for example, you will probably want to review any fields you will expose in the user profile with your legal team, and you will clearly want to work with your records management team to identify policies required to ensure that your document repositories are compliant.

Have a Clear Vision

A vision statement describes, at a high level, what you want to achieve with SharePoint—essentially how the solution delivers value to the organization and to each individual employee. Use the vision statement your SharePoint project sponsors and stakeholders established for the solution as a foundation for your governance plan. Be sure that the vision is clear because the degree of formality and the depth to which you need to document the governance plan should align with the outcomes you want to achieve.

A clear vision statement provides critical guidance to the inevitable trade-off decisions you will need to make in thinking about your governance plan. For example, you may hear about the dangers of the SharePoint "wild wild west"—an uncontrolled environment with unstructured and "unfindable" content—and that this "chaos" is the primary reason you need to have a governance plan. If the solution you are developing is designed as a key element of your corporate knowledge management system, the "wild wild west" is indeed a scary and unacceptable environment. But what if your goal is to create an experimental environment where new SharePoint site owners can create "practice" sites to try out new skills or test alternative approaches for specific business problems? In this scenario, an overly restrictive governance plan doesn't make a lot of sense. You may determine that you can't afford an unlimited number of "practice" sites, so you may want a governance policy that says that all sites are deleted after a specific period of time, but in this scenario, the "wild wild west" is fine. But you know that only because there is a clear vision. The vision, thus, provides a framework for both the context and the investment in governance. Once you are clear about your vision, the next step is to gather your core project team together to think about the principles that will guide your governance plan.

Develop Guiding Principles

Guiding principles define organizational preferences supporting the vision. These critical statements reflect best practices that users and site designers must understand and internalize to ensure the success of your solution. It is very likely that your organization will share many of the same guiding principles that we've seen in successful SharePoint deployments.

Use the examples shown in Table 4-1 to help define a starter set of guiding principles for your solution. Think about how you might create some supplemental reference material to help users internalize these principles—or consider adding a "principle of the day" to the home page of your solution. If users have a good understanding of the guiding principles, you have a reasonable shot at getting them to follow your governance guidelines.

Table 4-1 Examples of Guiding Principles

Governance Guiding Principle	Implication	Remember . . .
General Principles		
Policies are tied to the scope and intention of the site. Governance policies will be more flexible for sites with more limited access than for sites that are shared with a broad audience.	The different audiences for sites allow you to adapt the governance model according to business needs. While some policies will be enforced across the entire organization, others may be determined by each site owner. This means that some content may not be as structured or searchable compared to other content that will be consistently "managed."	One size does not fit all. Yes, we've got rules, but we're smart enough to know when it's appropriate to deviate from a standard in order to achieve a business objective more effectively.

Governance Guiding Principle	Implication	Remember . . .
Even though SharePoint may be a new vehicle for collaboration, SharePoint content is governed by all general policies pertaining to the use of IT resources, including privacy, copyright, records retention, confidentiality, document security, etc.	Content ownership, security, management, and contribution privileges are distributed across the entire organization, including users who may not have had content contribution, security, or records management privileges in the past. All content contributors need to be aware of the organization's policies for business-appropriate use of IT resources.	Existing rules still apply: Would you want your mother/boss/customer/client to see this picture? Should your mother/boss/customer/client be able to see this content?
Security Principles		
Overall firm security policies about who can see what content still apply and govern SharePoint.	Users need to think about where content is published to ensure that confidential content is shared only on sites with limited access. This is especially critical for SharePoint 2013 if you are going to enable users to share content or sites externally. Think about what this means for your organization, and make sure you have a well-communicated principle that reminds your users about the benefits and risks of sharing content externally.	Publish to meet the "need to know" standards for your organization: no more, no less!
Role-based security will govern access control and permissions.	Users may have different permissions on different areas of SharePoint, which has an implication for both governance and training. While most users may not have content contribution privileges for tightly governed intranet pages, every user has Full Control privileges for his or her personal content.	You may not have the same permissions on every SharePoint page and site.

(continues)

Table 4-1 Examples of Guiding Principles *(continued)*

Governance Guiding Principle	Implication	Remember . . .
Site Design Principles		
Provide a consistent user experience—users should be able to consistently find key information on any collaboration site and search for the content they need.	All sites will also follow a consistent baseline design template to ensure consistency and usability across collaboration sites.	Hey—it's not about you, it's about the user!
Design to minimize training requirements for users—use the best (and simplest) feature for each business objective.	All users with site design privileges will be encouraged to participate in training to ensure that they use the most appropriate Web Parts and lists for each task.	Just because you can, doesn't mean you should. You don't really need to try every new feature!
Ensure that "findability" governs design decisions—optimize metadata and site configuration to provide the best value for the user audience, not just the content contributor.	In situations where design trade-offs must be considered (more metadata versus less, information above or below "the fold," duplicating links in multiple places), decisions should be made to make it easier for users rather than content contributors. "Findability" means designing sites so that important information is easily visible and navigational cues help users easily find key information. It also means using metadata to improve accuracy of search results. Both the "browse" and "search" experiences for users will guide design decisions in initial site development and modification over time.	Avoid building the "roach motel"—where content "checks in" but it never "checks out."
Site designers must understand the objectives of the recommended site design standards and make changes only when they can be justified with a valid business need.	Even though site designers may have permissions that allow them to make changes to site templates and other "controlled" site areas, they agree not to arbitrarily make changes to the basic site templates based on personal preference. Suggestions for changes to the standard site templates should be elevated to the governance board/ steering committee.	It's all about Spider-Man: "With great power comes great responsibility." Use your powers wisely.

Governance Guiding Principle	Implication	Remember . . .
All sites/pages must have a clearly identified content owner.	Users need to know whom to contact if information on a page or site is out-of-date or inaccurate.	Make it obvious who owns the content on all pages and sites.
Content Principles		
All content is posted in just one place. Users who need access to content should create links to the document to access the content from its "authoritative" location.	This means that the official version of a document is posted once by the content owner (which may be a department, not necessarily an individual). For the reader's convenience, users may create a link to the official copy of a document from anywhere in SharePoint but should not post a "convenience copy" unless required due to business needs. Users should not post copies of documents to their personal hard drives or SkyDrive Pro if they exist elsewhere in the solution.	Post only one copy of a document.
Edit in place—don't delete documents to create new versions.	Version control will be enabled in document libraries where prior versions need to be retained during document creation or editing. If prior versions need to be retained permanently for legal purposes, old versions of documents should be stored in an archive location or library. Documents will be edited in place rather than deleted and re-added so that document links created by other users will not break.	Someone may be linking to your documents. Update, don't delete!
Site sponsors/owners are accountable, but everyone owns the responsibility for content management.	All content posted to a site shared by more than a small team will be governed by a content management process that ensures content is accurate, relevant, and current. Site sponsors/owners are responsible and accountable for content quality and currency and for archiving old content on a timely basis, but site users are responsible for making site sponsors/owners aware of content that needs updating.	We're all responsible for content management.

(continues)

Table 4-1 Examples of Guiding Principles *(continued)*

Governance Guiding Principle	Implication	Remember . . .
Use links instead of e-mail attachments.	Users should send links to content whenever possible rather than use e-mail attachments.	No more e-mail attachments!
Copyrighted material will not be added to the portal without the proper licensing or approval.	Copyright violations can be very costly. This is probably one of the most frequently ignored principles on corporate intranets and one that your corporate librarian (if your organization still has one) is going to be particularly concerned about. It is very difficult to enforce this principle, but one way to help encourage users to "do the right thing" is to add a required metadata attribute to all image and site asset libraries that asks content publishers to acknowledge the source and ownership of each published image.	Don't publish what we don't own.

Think about the Deployment Model

SharePoint is typically implemented for four major categories of solutions: intranets, collaboration solutions, extranets, and Internet sites. Within each general category, you might also be using SharePoint for specific application solutions; for example, you might use your intranet to deliver business intelligence information or to approve purchasing requests with a business workflow. The degree of formality of your governance plan—as well as the extent to which you invest in enforcing your governance plan—will be tied not only to your overall vision, but also to the general category of solution you are deploying.

One way to think about how your deployment model impacts your governance is to consider two key deployment dimensions: risk and reach. In this context, risk means the degree of risk to the business if incorrect or invalid content is exposed. Reach indicates the breadth and depth of the audience to which your solution is exposed. For example, your Internet site has the widest reach and may also have the highest risk for your organization. If inappropriate content is exposed on your Internet site, it could be very damaging to your business. Figure 4-2 illustrates how you might think about plotting some of the typical solution categories along these two dimensions and how the formality of and investment in governance planning aligns with this framework. Remember that your particular deployments might not map exactly to the placement of each solution category in the model, so you will need to adapt this framework for your situation. The main point of thinking about your deployment model in this way is to help focus your investment in governance toward the solution areas that have the biggest impact and highest risk. When it comes to governance, one size does not fit all.

For team sites, you will probably want to establish general rules about what can be posted and how long the information needs to be retained. These rules might differ for temporary project sites versus persistent team sites to support an administrative or departmental team, but you will likely want some level of consistency at least by site type, especially if the content

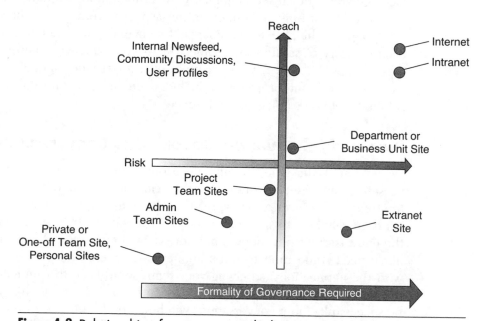

Figure 4-2 Relationship of governance to deployment scenarios

is exposed to the entire organization or, in the case of projects, where it is feasible that someone might be working on more than one project at a time. If each project team site is structured completely differently, team members will have to spend valuable knowledge cycles figuring out what is going on every time they go from project site to project site. But in addition, you may want to allow some flexibility for teams to think about their own governance plan. In the context of an individual team, that might mean creating a team compact or charter to define how they are going to use SharePoint to collaborate. Your governance plan might thus include some policies, if you want every team to work the same way, and some recommended guidelines, if you want to allow teams to choose a model that works best for them by giving some preferred examples so each team doesn't have to reinvent the wheel. As an example, one project team's governance plan could define a policy that all meeting minutes will go in the team notebook, and another might have a policy that says meeting minutes are stored in a document library called Meeting Minutes. Would it be better and more efficient if every team stored meeting minutes in the same place? Probably, but unless you are in an industry or on a project that has regulatory guidance that applies to meeting minutes, you may not want to invest a lot of time and energy in this aspect of your governance plan.

It can be helpful to summarize the overall governance model for each category of solution in a table so that you can review and compare expectations. Table 4-2 is an example of a governance model summary from a SharePoint project that included an intranet and collaboration solution that you can use as a reference.

Plan and Schedule the Governance Conversations

We've found that the framing decisions are easiest to discuss when presented as a set of questions that can be reviewed in a series of topic-focused conversations spread out over a couple of days or weeks. It's definitely best to spread out these conversations by topic and to limit the conversations per topic to no more than three to four hours. You will likely need some time to think about the answers and get comfortable with the implications, so giving your team some time to ruminate about the decisions and their implications will improve the odds that you will be successful. These conversations will help you fill out an overview table similar to Table 4-2, and they will also help you align expectations around

Table 4-2 Governance Model Summary for a Sample Deployment

Solution	Primary Audience	Content	Review Frequency and Responsibility	Governance Concepts
Home page (intranet)	Entire company	Company-wide news Targeted news	Daily review for news content by communications professionals in each business area	Tightly controlled Content managed by small number of designated communications professionals in each business area
Department/ functional area pages (intranet)	Entire company	Information about the services provided to the company by the functional area or department Links to more detailed information found in the department site	Annual review of each page and document by the functional area or department site owner	Tightly controlled Content managed by the functional area or department communications team following overall governance policies and design standards
Department site (collaboration)	Members of the business group or organizational unit	Documents, calendars, references, FAQs, contacts, links, and other content supporting the details of business services provided by the department	Annual review of each page and document by the functional area or department site owner	Content managed by individual document owner Site owner accountable for content quality Content review by business unit but must follow corporate guidelines

(continues)

Table 4-2 Governance Model Summary for a Sample Deployment *(continued)*

Solution	Primary Audience	Content	Review Frequency and Responsibility	Governance Concepts
Admin site (team collaboration)	Members of a persistent organizational group	Documents, out-of-office and event calendars, team roster, action items, links, and other content supporting the administration of the business team	Semiannual review of all content at the site level	Content managed by individual document owner Site owner accountable for content quality Looser governance standards Consistent template available to provide a best practice starting point for all admin teams
Community of practice site (team collaboration)	Cross-functional members of a topic- or event-based community	Documents, discussion board, member list, event calendar, action items, links	Semiannual review of all content at the site level	Content managed by individual document owner Site owner accountable for content quality Looser governance standards Consistent template available to provide a best practice starting point for all communities Some communities may have stricter governance policies based on reach and intent

Solution	Primary Audience	Content	Review Frequency and Responsibility	Governance Concepts
Project site (team collaboration)	Members of a project team	Documents, out-of-office and event calendars, team roster, action items, decisions, issues, links, and other content supporting the project	Semiannual review of all content at the site level	Content managed by individual document owner Site owner accountable for content quality Looser governance standards Consistent template available to provide a best practice starting point Additional governance policies and guidelines determined at the business unit level for projects within their domain

(continues)

Table 4-2 Governance Model Summary for a Sample Deployment *(continued)*

Solution	Primary Audience	Content	Review Frequency and Responsibility	Governance Concepts
Individual site (personal content/"My Site")	Individuals and their colleagues	Personal content and links—no corporate content	Semiannual review for each individual document	Content managed by individuals Individual site owner accountable for content quality Only general governance standards Site content quota helps ensure content management Blogs, profiles, and newsfeed content must follow corporate policies

just what it is going to take to ensure that you get the desired results from your SharePoint investment.

Each topic has a set of questions that you will need to answer to determine the substance of your governance plan. You will likely find that the conversations themselves provide an opportunity to clarify and manage expectations for all of your key stakeholders, and for the most part there is no single "best" answer to any question. The right answer is the one that works in your organization and for your solution. To make it easier for you to customize the list of governance questions—and to allow us to update the list based on our ongoing experiences—we have created the list of key governance questions as an online resource that you can download and adapt to meet your needs. The questions are all listed in this section, but you can find the latest list, along with all resources, at the following link: www.jornata.com/essentialsharepoint.

Vision and Overview

The questions in this first meeting are designed to help ensure that you have consensus about the expected solution outcomes. While some of the other governance questions will be difficult to answer until the solution is designed, the conversations about vision should be part of the early envisioning process.

- What are the desired business outcomes for the solution?
- How are these outcomes aligned with the key strategic objectives for the organization as a whole?
- What are the specific business objectives for the social features of SharePoint?
- What are the business-specific "moments of engagement" where social will drive value?
- Who is accountable for ensuring that the solution meets the expected outcomes?
- How will success be determined?
- Who are the key stakeholders for the solution?
  - Who is involved in content creation?
  - Who is involved in content consumption?
  - Who will be impacted?
- What types of overall corporate policies for information management, business, or technology management apply to the solution?
- Who is accountable for making sure that sites comply with governance policies and recommendations?
- Is there a penalty for noncompliance?
- What processes must be in place to ensure compliance?
- What are the expectations around user training (who takes which training)?
- What are the plans to incorporate policies and best practices into SharePoint training?
- Who will be responsible for maintaining the governance plan?
- Where will governance information "live"? How will it be communicated to users?

Enterprise Policies—Compliance

- Are there existing legal, IT, and information management policies that SharePoint solutions must follow?
    - Use of IT resources
    - Electronic communications
    - Social media policy
    - Protection of personally identifiable information (PII)
    - Records management
- How are these policies enforced in other systems?
- Are there standard policies that need to be included in each community site?
- Who is accountable for ensuring that policies are followed? How will accountability be evaluated?
- How do the corporate records and discovery policies address
    - Intranet pages
    - Intranet documents
    - Intranet news articles
    - Intranet images
    - Team site documents
    - Community or team site discussion lists
    - Other community or team site lists and images
    - Newsfeed
    - Individual user content in SkyDrive Pro
- Are there specific events in SharePoint that need to be logged for audit purposes? Are the right reporting tools in place to ensure that this can happen?

Enterprise Policies—Access

- Are there any overall access restrictions (specific Active Directory[3] or other groups permitted or not permitted to access the solution as a whole or individual types of sites)?
- Can users invite external people to access content? Are there restrictions on specific types of sites where external access is or is not permitted?

---

3. Active Directory is the Microsoft directory service used to manage access to a network and many applications, including SharePoint. Active Directory includes profile information about the employee such as name and e-mail address. Individual entries in Active Directory are combined into Active Directory Groups.

Enterprise Policies—Provisioning

- What is the provisioning process to get a new site collection?
- Who can request a new site collection?
- How is this decision reviewed?
- Are site owners required to take any training? If so, how will training be provided (online, in person, etc.) and monitored?
- What is the process to provision a team or community site within a site collection?
- How will sites be decommissioned?
- What is the plan for content archiving?

Enterprise Policies—Information Architecture

- Who is responsible for managing the overall information architecture for the solution?
- What type of information is most important for success?
- Are there specific information management policies that apply to different types of information?
- Who is responsible for ensuring that the information architecture supports effective information management?
- How will the effectiveness of the information architecture be evaluated over time?

Enterprise Processes

- What processes need to be in place to request new features or capabilities for the solution?
- Who will be accountable for reviewing and managing enhancement requests?

Overall Design—Branding and Functionality

- Are there required standards for branding?
- Is there an overall design style guide that all sites are required to follow?
- Who is responsible for branding decisions?
- Is SharePoint Designer permitted?
- Is the use of InfoPath permitted?
- Are any third-party tools/apps permitted? Restricted?

Enterprise Content

- Are there enterprise Content Types?
- What are the considerations for shared metadata?
- Is there any enterprise-wide mandatory core metadata?
- Are there any specific content requirements for users' personal content on SkyDrive Pro?
- Are there enterprise-wide supplemental terms (managed metadata in the term store)?
- How will metadata guidelines be communicated to site owners?
- Are there specific policies or guidance for different types of content (for example, news, links, discussions, data files, multimedia files, images)?
- Are there any overall requirements for dealing with inactive content? Does it get archived? (If so, how?) Does it get deleted? Who is accountable for managing inactive content?
- Is there a plan to archive content that might be required for e-discovery or during a regulatory audit?
- Are there specific types of content that cannot be stored in SharePoint?
- Is there a need to identify "work in progress" versus "final" content, or are there specific places that content of each type needs to be published?
- Who "owns" published documents? Contributor? Department? Does it depend on the site or site type?

Roles and Responsibilities

- Who is the business owner for the solution?
- Who is responsible for technical management of the environment, including hardware and software implementation, configuration, and maintenance? Who can install new Web Parts, features, or other code enhancements?
- Who will be responsible for ongoing evaluation to ensure that the solution continues to meet business and technical expectations?
- Who is allowed to set up new sites and who will be responsible for doing so? If this responsibility is controlled by the IT department, it is likely that IT will have to negotiate an SLA for site setup responsiveness with the business stakeholders. If this responsibility

is delegated, users will need training to ensure that they follow acceptable conventions for naming, storage, and so on.

- Who has access to each page/site? Who can grant access to each? Some organizations do not allow individual site owners to manage security on their sites. If this is something you decide to do, who will be responsible for managing security?
- Who is responsible for managing metadata? Who can set up or request new Content Types or Site Columns? How much central control do you want to have over the values in Site Columns?
- If the governance plan says that page and site owners are responsible for content management, are you prepared to decommission pages for which no one in the organization will step up to page ownership responsibilities? Who will be responsible for making these decisions?
- How do the existing organizational roles map to the roles required for the new solution?
  - Are there additional skills that people need to acquire?
  - Are there additional resources that need to be hired?
- Do the following roles already exist? (See the discussion later in this chapter for additional details about these specific SharePoint roles.)
  - Information architect
  - Center of excellence
  - Peer/business unit evangelists
- Is there a requirement for training to have a specific role overall or for an individual site?
- Who will be accountable for ensuring that lessons learned in various implementations across the organization are effectively shared with the rest of the organization?

Operational Decisions

- For each type of content or collection of sites:
  - What type of availability is required?
  - What are the expectations for disaster recovery and backup?
  - What are the expectations for response time?
  - What is the impact on storage, network infrastructure, and other elements of the IT backbone?
- What types of environments are needed to support the business outcomes (for example, development, QA, and production)?

- How will migration be supported from one environment to another?
- How will changes to the solution be managed?
- What types of processes are needed to ensure that the solution infrastructure is maintained and monitored?
- How will performance or infrastructure issues be escalated and resolved?

Site-Specific Governance Decisions

In addition to conversations at the enterprise level, you will also want to think about how your governance decisions may be different for each type of site or site collection.

- Who can request a new top-level site? What is the process?
- Who "owns" the persistent top-level navigation? What is the process for updating?
- Who decides where the new site goes in the navigation?
- Does the layout on each page/site need to be consistent?
- Are there specific templates that must be used? Can site owners use any available Web Part or app, or is there a specific list?
- Who can publish content?
- Can users outside the standard security permissions be invited into the site (external and internal)? Note: External users can be prevented from access globally, but users with Manage Permissions privileges control which internal users access the site.
- Are there specific policies or guidance for different types of content (for example, news, links, discussions, data files, multimedia files, images)?
- How critical is availability, backup, and response time to this site type?
- Who is accountable for ensuring that the content on the site follows governance policies and guidelines?
- How will you ensure that the purpose and relevance of the site have not changed?
- What happens to old or irrelevant content?
- How often does content have to be reviewed? By whom?
- Can content be deleted?
- What about an entire site?
- Who is accountable for determining and assigning permissions to access the site?
- Is there a requirement for training to have specific permissions?

Talk about Social

One of the governance conversations that you need to have for SharePoint 2013 relates to how you want to use the social features; we are emphasizing this because the social features are new and evolving, and unless you have already been using a social tool in your organization, you will want to put some additional focus on social content in your governance plan. Moreover, even before you talk about social in the context of governance, make sure you have considered the role social plays in your organization and what outcomes you are trying to achieve. You will probably need to bring in some expertise from legal and HR when you have your governance discussions about social computing. Even though some of your users may be familiar with the use of social tools in their personal lives, you need to think about conventions and norms for your organization.

Start by looking at your organization's existing social media policy because you may find that the "rules" for external conversations may be equally applicable internally. If your organization does not already have a social media policy, you can take a look at some of the publicly available policies from other organizations as a starting point to create one. For example, both Coca-Cola and Intel have made their internal social media policies public, and they include concepts and language that you may be able to reuse. There is a great Web site with links to many examples of social media policies that you can use as a reference: http://socialmedi-agovernance.com/policies.php. Here you will find links to both the Intel and Coca-Cola policies as well as many more from virtually every industry.

User Profile

- Do you want to have a customized statement of acknowledgment (in addition to what users see "out of the box") that reminds your users that when they create a profile, they are "opting in" to the social conversations in the organization and that they need to follow your internal social media policies?
- What are the fields planned for the user profile?
- Can users add their own picture? Any picture? Are there any privacy concerns associated with user pictures? Can users opt out of having their picture shared?
- What are the expectations for "About me"?
- What are the expectations for Ask Me About? How much of an expert does a user need to be in order to list a topic? Can users declare their own areas of expertise or does that need to be vetted by a third party?

- What are the expectations for Past Projects?
- What are the expectations for Skills? Can/should users enter non-work-related skills?
- Do you want users to update Schools?
- Can users enter Birthday if they choose? This is an optional default field in the profile, but some organizations consider this field personal information that should not be shared—even if someone wants to share it.
- Are both personal and business interested allowed in Interests?

Newsfeed and Discussions

The SharePoint 2013 Newsfeed (and Yammer) presents an entirely new type of content to govern. As mentioned earlier, there is no built-in process to automatically support "aging out" of the newsfeed, so you will need to consider how long to retain activity posts. Many organizations apply the same policies to their newsfeed content as they do to archiving e-mail, but this may or may not be appropriate for your organization. You will also want to review what is legal to talk about in discussion posts (for example, certain types of personal information about yourself or others). Similarly, you will want to talk with your executives about what is *appropriate* to discuss.

- Do you want to provide guidance about mentioning someone in the activity feed using an @mention or posting a photo of someone without asking permission?
- Is there an existing policy for social media that applies to the newsfeed or Yammer (or needs to be updated)?
- Are there specific topics or content that should not be included in activity posts? For example, in one legal implementation, attorneys were advised not to mention any specifics of open cases in newsfeed posts.
- How will newsfeed policies and guidance be enforced and communicated?

Define Roles and Responsibilities

Roles and responsibilities describe how each employee as an individual or in a particular role or group is responsible for ensuring success of the solution. Documenting roles and responsibilities is a critical aspect of the governance plan, which defines who has authority to mediate conflicting requirements and make overall branding and policy decisions. The conversations described earlier will help you focus on the types of roles that are necessary to ensure a successful SharePoint deployment. The discussion in this section defines each of these roles in more detail.

There are several key roles to consider. In smaller organizations, many roles may be fulfilled by a single individual. Tables 4-3 and 4-4 present lists of typical roles and responsibilities associated with SharePoint at the

Table 4-3 Enterprise Roles

Role	Key Responsibilities
Executive Sponsor	Serves as the executive-level "champion" for the solution. The primary responsibility of the executive sponsor is strategic, positioning the solution as a critical mechanism for achieving business value and helping to communicate the value of the solution to the management levels of the organization. The executive sponsor could come from different parts of the organization. In some very lucky organizations, the executive sponsor is the CEO. In others, it might be the person responsible for knowledge management or learning and professional development or even the chief operating officer. And, depending on how this role is positioned in your organization, you can be successful if the executive sponsor is also the CIO. We have found that the most successful SharePoint deployments are sponsored by an executive who is strategically aligned with the business outcomes for the solution.
Governance Board/ Steering Committee	Serves as a governance body with ultimate responsibility for meeting the goals of the solution. This board is typically composed of representatives of each of the major businesses represented in the solution, including corporate communications, knowledge management, HR, and IT.
Business Owner	Ensures that the solution objectives are achieved and that the needs of the business units are coordinated. Sets and evolves the solution strategy. Develops and maintains the SharePoint governance plan under the direction of the steering committee. The business owner does not have to be an IT expert, but his or her job function often includes responsibility for internal communications and/or knowledge management.
IT Owner	Implements technical direction and policy for SharePoint in the organization. Works in partnership with the business owner.
SharePoint Administrator	Oversees the technical administration functions for SharePoint. Runs audits on sites to determine usage, security, and quotas. Ensures that backup and recovery processes are implemented. Monitors performance issues within the environment and, along with the SharePoint architect, performs capacity management.

(continues)

Table 4-3 Enterprise Roles (*continued*)

Role	Key Responsibilities
SharePoint Architect	For on-premises deployments, responsible for SharePoint farm administration, including patch management, service packs, hot fixes, cumulative updates (CUs), and so on. Manages major deployments of new software or third-party tools. Develops and maintains overall branding and templates. Maintains documentation about custom configurations, design of custom Web Parts, and overall design decisions and feature deployments. Publishes and maintains an active catalog of custom Web Parts, third-party solutions, and custom development projects (with expected completion dates) in a site accessible by site owners and the power users community of practice.
SharePoint Infrastructure Support Team	For on-premises deployments, supports application servers, maintaining and updating security on all portal objects, providing ad hoc reporting, managing file size limits and quotas, and troubleshooting errors.
Application Development Team	Develops and maintains site templates and custom Web Parts. Configures and develops enterprise solutions as approved by the steering committee. Implements custom solutions for individual sites as approved by the steering committee. Oversees and provides technical development and ensures that standards are enforced during the development process.
Information Architect	Manages enterprise terms, Content Types, and metadata. Identifies candidates for promoted results within search (with support from site owners). Monitors search logs to identify candidates for new promoted results and synonyms. Designs and makes recommendations for adding new sites to the overall site architecture. Conducts regular usability tests to identify opportunities for improvement in navigation, page layout, and user experience. While some large organizations may already have an individual or group serving in this role, SharePoint 2013's enterprise content capabilities require an overall metadata management plan and an individual or team responsible for maintaining the "metadata dictionary" over the life of the solution.
SharePoint Coach	Provides coaching and design consulting to new users who have Full Control design privileges to ensure that best practices are followed and that the appropriate SharePoint features are applied in individual sites or site collections. In many organizations, a particular SharePoint feature becomes the de facto solution for any business problem—a "hammer in search of a nail." For example, you don't want to see users creating wiki sites when what they really need is a custom list. If you will be delegating site design capabilities to users who have limited solution design experience (which pretty much means every organization), having experienced site design coaches available to help users get started can ensure that you end up with a solution that actually gets used. One successful organization implemented "drop-in" office hours where new site owners could spend an hour or two with an experienced solution architect to ensure that they got appropriate guidance (in addition to formal training). Several others have established in-house consulting services to help new site owners get started. In many cases, the first hour or two of consulting is "free," and services beyond that require a charge code.

Role	Key Responsibilities
Power Users/ Evangelists	Supports the successful deployment of SharePoint in the organization by sharing best practices and lessons learned in a community of practice team sites. Members serve as SharePoint advocates and change agents in their local business units or departments. Several organizations create a special "brand" for their power user evangelists. At Best Buy, power users, who also function as coaches in their business units, are called "Ninjas." At Biogen Idec, power users are called "SharePoint PUMAs" (Power Users of Microsoft Applications).
Training Manager	Provides training for SharePoint users (all roles). Maintains a collection of SharePoint examples and sample solutions for site owners and site designers. Supports the successful deployment of SharePoint in the organization by sharing lessons learned in a SharePoint governance and best practices site. Serves as a SharePoint advocate and change agent within the organization.
Help Desk	Provides basic, first-tier support for users.

Table 4-4 Roles for Each Site or Site Collection

Role	Key Responsibilities
Site Sponsor	Provides executive sponsorship for the site. Ultimately accountable for content governance on the site. Defines business goals for the site. Very often, the site sponsor will not have any special access privileges on a SharePoint team site.
Site Designer	In an environment where site design is delegated to business users, creates and maintains the site (or site collection) design. Follows design best practices and guiding principles to ensure that even sites with limited access are optimized for user value. Defines and executes the security plan for the site. The site designer will likely be assigned to the Site Owner security group on a SharePoint site, which will afford this user with the Full Control privileges needed to configure the site, but having permissions to configure the site doesn't necessarily have to mean that the site designer is the business sponsor or owner of the site.

(continues)

Table 4-4 Roles for Each Site or Site Collection *(continued)*

Role	Key Responsibilities
Site Steward	Manages the site day to day by executing the functions required to ensure that the content on the site or page is accurate and relevant, including records retention codes. Monitors site security to ensure that the security model for the site matches the goals of the business and site sponsor and supports users of the site by serving as the primary identified contact point for the site. Depending on the level of training and expertise, the site steward may be assigned Full Control privileges.
Users	Uses the solution to access and share information. Users may have different access permissions in different areas of the solution, sometimes acting as a contributor (content producer) and other times acting as a visitor (content consumer).

enterprise level and then for each individual site or site collection. You will likely need to adapt both the responsibilities and even the terms you use to describe each role for your organization, but these lists will give you a good place to start.

One thing that you will notice is that it really "takes a village" to successfully support SharePoint in any organization—whether you have an on-premises or cloud deployment. And because of the different types of skills required to deploy and maintain both SharePoint and the solutions you build, it's virtually impossible to find a single person who can do it all or know it all. So, you will need a team—and the team may include specialized consultants that you bring in initially or from time to time in addition to your own staff and the extended SharePoint community. Many organizations find it helpful to organize their SharePoint resources in a center of excellence model, which may include full-time members of the IT staff supplemented with virtual members who work in various business groups around the company. Creating a center of excellence will help you create your SharePoint "brain trust," which collectively can help ensure that you distribute what will certainly be scarce expertise in the most effective way. But you will also need to keep in mind that the need for certain skills and roles will change over time—you may need more external application development and information architecture support in the beginning and less over time as your solution matures or as your internal team gains new skills. However, as the organizational needs change, you may find that you need some additional support in specific areas. This is where the extensive SharePoint community can provide significant value—as a source of both free and fee-based advice. Be sure that your SharePoint teams stay connected to the community via resources like Twitter, the public SharePoint community on Yammer "SPYam," hundreds of SharePoint blogs, the various LinkedIn and Microsoft forums, and the vast array of SharePoint Saturday and other conference events. You don't always have to "own" every SharePoint role, and when you have staff who are new to a role and need support, the SharePoint community provides a rich and vast collection of people and content available to supplement and guide.

Andrew Kawa, senior manager at Goodwin Proctor LLP, shares his view on the importance of having the power user/evangelist and coaching roles:

> We have several consultants that act in the SharePoint power user and coach capacities. It's interesting because these individuals have ended up playing a much bigger role in governance since they are the ones closest to the content in the SharePoint deployment. They are the ones that can say "no, don't create this site or don't add this content because this other group is already doing the same thing and you will be conflicting with or duplicating their content."

When site responsibilities are delegated to "business users," each team site or functional area site will also need specific roles and responsibilities defined to ensure success. These roles are business-oriented and do not necessarily have the same names as the *permission-based* groups that are automatically created for SharePoint sites.

Define Policies and Guidelines

Policies define rules for SharePoint use; guidelines describe best practices. From a governance perspective, policies are usually driven by statutory, regulatory, or organizational requirements. Users are expected to meet policies without deviation. If your organization is subject to regulatory oversight, be sure you can actually enforce your policies, as a failure to do so may target you as being noncompliant. Guidelines are usually established to encourage consistent practices. Users may adopt some elements of the guidelines that work for them, while not implementing others.

As applied to the topic of file names, a policy might state, "Do not include dates or version numbers in file names," while a guideline might state, "File names should be topical and descriptive." In another example, the policy might state, "All SharePoint sites will have a primary and secondary contact responsible for the site and its content," and the guideline might state, "The site contact is listed on the site home page and in the site directory."

Each organization will have its own set of policies and guidelines. General topics should include content oversight, site design, branding and user experience, site management, and security. To ensure that your content is relevant:

- Verify that your SharePoint polices and standards do not conflict with broader organizational polices.
- Publish policies and standards where users can easily find and follow them. Some policies may need to be published to "all readers," while others may need to be secured to protect the integrity of the application.
- Regularly review and revise policies and standards to keep them aligned to organizational needs.

Determine Your Delivery Model

One of the most important considerations for your governance plan is determining how you will "tell the governance story" to everyone who needs to know it. The challenge: not everyone needs to know the same things about governance, so your communications and delivery model are going to be messy.

We've already talked about the fact that you can't deliver the governance plan as one or more long documents, but that doesn't mean you don't need to document it. To create an optimal delivery model for your governance plan, you need to deliver just the right information to just the right people at just the right moment. This means that the ideal delivery model

- Automates policies wherever possible. For example, if records retention codes are mandatory and generally based on context, ensure that these codes are defaulted appropriately in each context. If your policy doesn't allow the use of SharePoint Designer, make sure that users do not have security privileges that would allow them to "accidentally" leverage a feature or tool you don't want them to use.

■ Includes communications and training to help users internalize the main elements of the governance plan, such as remembering to "update in place" and minimize the use of e-mail attachments.

■ Provides specific and targeted information to users based on their roles and tasks. Be sure to incorporate your policies as well as guidelines into all SharePoint training—so users only learn how to do things the "right" way. But, in addition, consider creating a series of brief "quick cards" or task guidance to help reinforce your best practices.

It's a good idea to create a central site for your governance policies and standards—a place where users can quickly look up both "how to" and "how should" information for the specific activities they need to execute in SharePoint. As with other compliance libraries, include a revision date and document owner metadata field to facilitate regular review to ensure that content is accurate and timely. System times/dates may not accurately reflect the revision schedule or subject expertise associated with the item(s).

Wherever possible, build your best practices into your site templates. Where you can't, make sure that it is painfully easy for users to learn both the required policies and beneficial guidelines to ensure that the entire organization gets the most value from your SharePoint investment.

Socialize, Promote, and Verify

The final activity in your governance planning roadmap is making sure that you socialize and monitor the governance plan. To help socialize the governance plan, in addition to your power user evangelists, it helps to find executive champions to reinforce the guiding principles and best practices. One organization decided to attack document "versionitis" by recruiting senior executives to commit to not responding to e-mail messages when they included a document attachment. We know your governance plan has executive sponsorship because an early step in the roadmap was to ensure that your solution has a defined vision and benefit. A great way to socialize the importance of good governance is to get your influential champions to do it for you. Integration with training is key—teach people "our way" or the "best practice way" to do things from the beginning and your best practices won't seem like something extra.

If you have a governance plan that you don't enforce or monitor, do you really have a governance plan? Probably not. Therefore, it's also important to think about how you are going to ensure that your policies and best practices are followed. Think about creating reports to show documents with limited or missing metadata or sites that are close to their "expiration date" and designate members of your center of excellence to work with site owners of sites that are not fully compliant. If ensuring that content is not ROTten (redundant, outdated, or trivial) is important, be prepared to delete pages or documents that do not follow the content management policies. Consider implementing a site audit plan that examines a small percentage of sites each quarter to try to get ahead of potential governance issues by looking for trends that can be addressed with training and communications. Actively promote stories about sites that demonstrate meaningful business value because they are following the governance plan to remind users that the governance plan is designed to ensure that your SharePoint solution meets business goals.

Key Points

The key take-aways to remember from this chapter are:

- Establish a governance plan to ensure quality and relevance of content and ensure that all users understand their roles and responsibilities.
- Remember that governance is really about both assurance and guidance—but it takes commitment to ensure that your governance plan is followed.
- Understand that your governance plan is successful if your solution has "no sharp edges."
- Keep your governance model simple. Solutions need a strong governance model, but they don't need complicated models with lots of bureaucracy. Make sure that all of your governance policies and guidelines can be tied to a specific business goal.
- Think about the fact that no one cares about governance—until you make it all about them! Be sure to create targeted governance content.

- Be sure to consider the new social features as part of your governance plan update for SharePoint 2013 even if you have a good governance plan for your SharePoint 2010 or 2007 solutions.
- Wherever you can, build best practices into your site templates. Make it as easy as possible for users to comply with governance policies and guidelines.
- Make sure that you have a governance board or steering committee with a strong advocate in the role of executive sponsor.
- Don't make the solution itself more complicated than it needs to be. Be careful about "overdesigning." Just because SharePoint has a cool feature doesn't mean that you need to deploy it—at least not right away.
- Ensure that all users with Design or Full Control privileges have internalized your design guiding principles and that content contributors understand guiding principles related to content.
- Think about how you will ensure compliance with your governance plan over time, particularly for highly visible sites. You may want to carefully monitor and review some sites and only spot-check others.
- Make sure that your governance plan is included in all of your SharePoint training. You will be most successful if your users never learn how to do a task in a way that doesn't follow your guidelines.
- Keep in mind that an effective governance plan doesn't have to constrain every move—it has to provide guidance to users to ensure that your solution remains effective and vibrant over time.

CHAPTER 5

PLANNING FOR OPERATIONAL GOVERNANCE

In Chapter 4, "Planning for Business Governance," we discussed the importance of governance planning for your business, which ensures that the most important part of your SharePoint environment—the content—stays in good shape over the life of your deployment.

This chapter, on the other hand, covers the governance of the underlying infrastructure—the actual SharePoint technical platform. This is especially important if you're managing your SharePoint farm(s) in-house, since you'll need to ensure uptime yourself. If you happen to be using Office 365 or SharePoint Online, Microsoft is doing most of the infrastructure governance for you, but you'll still need to manage some aspects of your environment.

There are two key parts to SharePoint infrastructure governance: operations and applications. Operational governance covers the maintenance of the servers, software, and backups of the data. Application governance covers the management of the customizations made to your SharePoint environment. Both are very important factors in ensuring that your SharePoint offering remains healthy over time.

An analogy we use frequently is that of governing cars and transportation through a "driving and roadway system." Business governance would focus on training drivers through driver's education and licensure, making sure they understand the "rules of the road" such as driving on the correct side of the road and stopping at intersections. Extending the analogy, operational governance would be ensuring that our infrastructure—such as roads and bridges—is maintained on a regular basis. And application governance would align with how we'd plan for getting new cars or adding lanes to existing roads (you can't just shut down a road for weeks on end—you've got to come up with a plan that accommodates future growth but does not inhibit existing usage). In all cases, the purpose of the governance plan that you come up with is to *manage risk*.

What's New in SharePoint 2013?

SharePoint 2013 adds a new dimension to both operational and application governance. First, with the cloud finally being a viable option with near-parity to what you can do on-premises, you'll need to consider the impact of both cloud and hybrid deployments on your governance approach. Next, with the new SharePoint 2013 apps model, the way you manage customizations and add-ons to your environment will change as well. Specifically, here are some of the new concepts that you will want to think about with respect to infrastructure governance:

- **Operational cloud considerations.** Choosing SharePoint 2013 in the cloud is now a viable option. This means that the role of a SharePoint administrator will likely shift from someone who manages the entire farm and underlying infrastructure to someone who manages the service applications and site collections in the farm. Or, you may be using a hybrid model (which is very likely if you're using Yammer for social features), where the SharePoint administrator manages both areas. Modeling your operational governance for these changes—and having the right staff members on the team—will be increasingly important.
- **Device options.** The ever-increasing list of devices supported by SharePoint could mean additional governance considerations for the various operating systems, browsers, and applications that you now must support. Gone are the days of dictating that the only supported combination is Windows 7 running Internet Explorer 8 and Office 2010. With additional Macs, iPads, iPhones, browser types, Office versions (both rich-client and Web-based), and accessibility modes, governing how and when to add or remove device support or upgrade to a CU will get more complex.
- **Apps model.** SharePoint 2013 has introduced a new app model for building and governing additional functionality that runs in the context of SharePoint. Understanding how to manage solutions in the new "apps" model is important, since full-trust and sandboxed

solutions are still viable options. Not only must you determine who may build and/or install solutions, you must also govern the way in which they may build and/or install them.

Planning for Operational Governance

The key to operational governance is simple: keep SharePoint up and running as a viable and dependable service for users. In general, this type of IT governance should be very familiar to IT pros, as it is similar to other applications in a server farm—Exchange, Lync, Windows, Active Directory (AD), or even SQL Server. That said, there are special considerations for SharePoint that are important and are discussed here.

Choose a Deployment Model (or It Will Choose You)

When planning your SharePoint deployment, you have a number of choices. Will you provide a central offering to your business? Will you use a single farm for everything? Will the cloud play a role? Who will administer the central farm(s), service applications, and site collections?

The key is to find the right balance for your organization (see Figure 5-1). Typically, a centrally managed offering, where software, services, and sites are hosted and managed centrally by a core IT group, is the most common type. However, some organizations allow various groups to manage their own farms locally or set up their own Office 365 subscriptions directly. Even if you do centrally manage SharePoint, you may find that if yours is a reasonably large

IT Governance

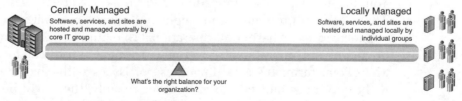

Figure 5-1 Your operational governance will need to balance the simpler management of a centralized deployment against the flexibility and scale of a distributed, locally managed one.

organization, you end up deploying several production farms, enabling you to provide different SLAs and configurations for various SharePoint offerings. For example, you might consider putting your intranet and document management system on one farm, your custom applications on a second farm, and your collaboration sites in the cloud.

It's important to note that if you don't plan for your deployment model to mature and evolve over time, you may find that you have multiple farms that spring up for dedicated business needs. This is where the deployment model chooses you, rather than the other way around. The last thing you probably need is for SharePoint to grow beyond your control—since you might be the one who has to pull it all back together later.

Correct Health Analyzer Issues

The SharePoint Health Analyzer, included in SharePoint 2013 as an integrated health analysis tool, is your friend. It will help you identify a lot of potential farm issues quickly. The Health Analyzer enables you to check for potential configuration, performance, and usage problems. The tool works by running predefined health rules against all of the servers in your SharePoint farm. A health rule (defined either by Microsoft or by you) runs a test and returns a status of whether the rule failed or not. When a rule fails, SharePoint Health Analyzer creates an alert on the "Review problems and solutions" page and writes the status to the Windows event log. Don't ignore these rules, since they could indicate early symptoms of a major problem later. In some cases, the rules provide a false positive, at which point you might need to disable or adjust a rule. This is OK, provided you know what you're doing!

Monitor Network Connectivity

You might read this subheading and think, "Network connectivity? That's not my problem." You might not consider monitoring network connectivity as a SharePoint operational role (and hence not an element of SharePoint operational governance), but it is critical to a healthy SharePoint farm. It's a leading cause of issues with SharePoint, since if the servers cannot talk to each other reliably, there will be a noticeable degradation in performance. In fact, that's the typical problem: it's not zero connectivity (which is obvious), but a slow environment that's not optimized. You should regularly check network performance and response times to and from SharePoint servers and SQL servers, AD servers, and users. You can test these items with standard monitoring tools such as Microsoft Systems Center Operations Manager (SCOM), or you can download a free script at www.jornata.com/essentialsharepoint. It's even more important—not less—to test connectivity when using Office 365, since the Internet connection coming into your organization (which is probably competing with YouTube, Facebook, and Lync calls) is the single point of failure for SharePoint performance.

Manage Capacity and Disk Space Effectively

Another major reason that SharePoint environments suddenly fail is lack of sufficient disk space. To ensure uptime, monitor disk space on a daily basis. This can be performed either by manual inspection or by enabling a monitoring tool such as SCOM. There are two primary locations that you should closely monitor: SQL database capacity and local file capacity. SQL database capacity is mostly impacted by growing data files and transaction files. Local file capacity observation is really only impacted by logging and search index partition files.

Manage Application Pools Effectively

Yet another reason that SharePoint environments suddenly fail is having a set of unstable application pools. Application pools run on the server and respond to requests for sites and other functionality. Two factors are pertinent to application pools: the application pool identity and the Web applications that the pool manages. Consider the account used from a security perspective, as this account must remain secure. You must also consider the Web applications associated from a process isolation perspective. Monitor the resources used by the application pool. If your application pool fails, so will all the Web applications that it manages. The primary cause of application pool failure is an expired application pool service account password. Make sure this service account is configured so that the password does not expire.

Manage Accounts and Passwords Effectively

If you are enabling password change management, carefully choose the accounts for which you do so. If the account is used in applications that do not understand or respect managed accounts, those applications will break after the password has been changed. In addition, ensure that service accounts used by SharePoint have passwords that do not automatically expire. Expiration of passwords is the number-two reason why SharePoint goes down.

Manage Databases Effectively

Because databases are at the core of the SharePoint farm, they need proper care. The SQL Server piece of the SharePoint puzzle often has inadequate governance—it's either completely ignored, with the assumption that there's nothing to do, or it's overmanaged, typically by overzealous database administrators. For the most part, SharePoint takes care of configuration items such as permissions and roles. And databases and tables shouldn't be messed with, since SharePoint will manage most other settings, too. However, there are a few items that should be checked on a regular basis: whitespace, fragmentation, and corruption. For details, you can consult the SharePoint TechNet article at http:// technet.microsoft.com/en-us/library/cc262731.aspx. In addition, content databases should still be kept below 200GB unless there is a valid reason to go above that number (a read-only archive database, for example, which can grow to 1TB or more).

Proactively Monitor the Health of Your SharePoint Environment

Finally, it's important to proactively monitor the health of your SharePoint environment. You'll mainly care about entries that appear in both the Windows application log and the SharePoint Unified Logging Service (ULS) logs. Being familiar with the diagnostics logs can save you valuable troubleshooting time. In addition, a tool like SCOM can monitor the event logs on all SharePoint servers in the farm, relying on preconfigured management packs that help you diagnose issues and recommend solutions. For some organizations that don't have dedicated SharePoint administrators but do have an on-premises environment, a program like Jornata's CoPilot for SharePoint infrastructure can help proactively address issues before they arise.

Note If you haven't done so already, download the ULS Viewer tool, available on CodePlex, to all your SharePoint servers to assist in troubleshooting Web and service applications.

Maintaining Operational Governance

The key to effective operational governance for SharePoint is to have a maintenance schedule for important tasks that should be done on a regular basis. Going back to our car-and-roadway analogy: Think about what would happen to roads and bridges if we didn't repair them regularly. And what about your car? Most cars need an oil change every three months or so. In fact, your owner's manual (you know, that thing in your glove compartment that you've never looked at) has a suggested maintenance schedule for your vehicle. We've come up with one for SharePoint, which can be performed manually by a SharePoint administrator or automated with PowerShell. Even if you automate it, an administrator should review the results on the regular schedule outlined here:

Daily

- Ping all servers in all environments (dev/test/prod):
  - Load balancers
  - Web Front Ends (WFEs)
  - Application servers
  - SQL servers
- Check backups to confirm that they completed the night before.
- Check available disk space on all servers.

Weekly

- Check Windows event logs for errors; investigate as needed.
- Check security logs.
- Perform an IIS reset on all SharePoint servers (WFEs and application servers).
- Review content databases for size (>50GB for site collections or >200GB for total database size).
- Check search crawl logs for errors; investigate as needed.
- Check User Profile Synchronization Service application synchronization status.
- Review SharePoint Health Analyzer errors; address as needed.
- Generate a report of newly created team sites.
- Review timer jobs for failures.
- Review services on the servers; ensure that all services have started properly.

- Check ULS logs for errors; investigate as needed.
- Ping SQL from the WFE (verify intrafarm communication).
- Check performance counters if issues have been reported during the week (memory, CPU, disk).
- Check if application pools are started.
- Generate a weekly report with
    - Usage data for the week (hits, unique users, total site collections, etc.)
    - Disk usage information, memory and CPU usage, uptime and availability, database sizes, top incidents and resolution
    - Summary of configuration changes to the environment

Monthly

- Review the environment for abandoned sites and orphaned content.
- Check SQL logs for problems.
- Do a SQL database consistency check.
- Verify backups by attempting a restore.
- Review and report on the SLA for the previous month.
- Do capacity planning based on current growth trends.
- Evaluate and apply hot fixes, service packs, update rollups, and security updates as needed.
- Perform a disaster recovery test.

Quarterly

- Review SharePoint Server documentation to ensure that it is still current based on changes introduced in CUs, service packs, server additions, and so on; update it if necessary.
- Review existing procedures, including backup, disaster recovery, maintenance, and so on, to ensure that they account for changes introduced in CUs, service packs, or other changes to the system.

Planning for Application Governance

So what do we mean by application governance? In short, it defines roles and responsibilities, along with policies and procedures, for building, deploying, and managing business solutions that will run on an organization's central SharePoint environment.

Application governance provides a roadmap and framework for how the organizational lines of business will qualify, build, and deploy a SharePoint solution. It also provides guidelines for how those applications should be constructed and validated before being handed off to the operations team for deployment. Finally, it covers how and when users can use SharePoint apps, whether available from an online store or provided directly by the organization. So if you're doing *any* kind of customization to your SharePoint environment, including custom master pages, Web Parts, SharePoint apps, SharePoint Designer changes, sandboxed solutions, third-party solutions, or anything else that changes the way SharePoint works, you'll need an application governance plan.

Account for the Three Categories of SharePoint Solutions

In general, there are three major classifications of SharePoint solutions: out-of-the-box customizations, declarative solutions, and custom-coded solutions. Your application governance plan should account for all three.

- **Out-of-the-box customizations:**
  - SharePoint provides a very flexible way to create simple solutions directly through the Web interface.
  - Each Line of Business (LOB) may develop its solutions freely.
- **Declarative solutions:**
  - These are typically solutions built by using SharePoint Designer.
  - Once authorization for SharePoint Designer is obtained, the LOB may develop its solution in a development environment. The solution is packaged and submitted for deployment.
- **Custom-coded solutions:**
  - These are built in C# via a .NET assembly deployed as a SharePoint solution package (.wsp) or SharePoint app.
  - These solutions need a design review.

Choose a Customization Policy (or It Will Choose You)

Much as when planning the operational governance side of your SharePoint deployment, you have a number of choices when it comes to application management (see Figure 5-2). Will you strictly manage any and all development, whereby customizations must adhere to strict rules? Or will you loosely manage development, letting application development teams build anything they want, including full-trust solutions and enabling the use of SharePoint Designer within sites?

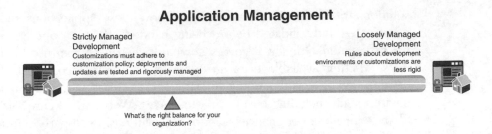

Application Management

Strictly Managed
Development
Customizations must adhere to
customization policy; deployments and
updates are tested and rigorously managed

Loosely Managed
Development
Rules about development
environments or customizations are
less rigid

What's the right balance for your
organization?

Figure 5-2 Your application governance policies will need to balance the ability to empower the business to build custom solutions with ensuring the stability of the farm

At the very least, your governance committee should consider the following questions before you deploy your SharePoint environment (or before your next upgrade):

- What customization policies do we adhere to as an organization? What is the "right balance" for us between flexible and open versus strict and cautious?
- Is a solution right for our central farm or should we suggest a stand-alone farm?
- When do we suggest that a business unit select a cloud-based SharePoint offering?
- Do we use life cycle management? For which applications?
- Do we have a checklist for which applications to let in?
- How do we know what SharePoint features/services we need to support business solutions?
- How do we evaluate third-party solutions, including SharePoint apps, for quality and/or appropriateness?
- Whom do we allow to create customizations? How are those users or developers or administrators trained, supervised, and supported?
- When do we deploy updates to the farm? Who does this?
- How do we regression-test custom solutions when a service pack or CU is released?

Your customization policy will determine which types of customizations will be allowed or disallowed, and how you will manage those customizations over time. In addition to answering the previous questions, your policy should include

- Service-level descriptions
- Processes for analyzing customizations
- Processes for piloting and testing customizations
- Guidelines for packaging and deploying customizations
- Guidelines for updating customizations
- Approved tools for development
- Roles and responsibilities for who will provide ongoing code support

Develop Governance Strategies for the New SharePoint Apps Model

The new SharePoint apps model, which provides a new way to deliver information or functionality to a SharePoint site, requires special governance considerations. Before you allow site owners to install apps in a SharePoint environment, you must plan how you'll support them.

Some key decision points regarding your overall apps policy include the following:

- Whether to allow site owners to be able to install and use SharePoint apps. If you decide to disable the use of apps, you'll need to prevent site owners from downloading them. Since the error that users get when trying to install an app is not intuitive, you'll need to communicate this policy to users and site owners. In addition, make this decision clear in your customization policy.
- Which specific SharePoint apps can site owners install and use. To restrict the list, you'll need to set up an app catalog to provide a set of apps for SharePoint that site owners can install and use, or use the app request feature to control the purchasing and licensing of apps for SharePoint. You can also restrict in which environments apps will run.
- Who can purchase SharePoint apps. You should create a request process that requires site owners to submit a request that your organization reviews to make sure that appropriate persons make purchases.
- Who can install SharePoint apps. Users must have the Manage Web Site and Create Sub-sites permissions to install an app for SharePoint. By default, these permissions are available only to users who have the Full Control permission level or who are in the Site Owners group.

- Which apps should be monitored. You can determine which specific apps should be monitored within a farm.
- How you'll control licensing, especially if you allow site owners to download and install SharePoint apps from the Internet. SharePoint 2013 does not enforce app licenses. The Office Store handles payments for the licenses, issues the correct licenses, and provides the process to verify license integrity. Note that licensing works only for apps that are distributed through the Office Store. Apps that you purchase from another source and apps that you develop internally must implement their own licensing mechanisms.

Maintaining Application Governance

For each type of solution, you'll want to have a checklist in place. Here's a suggested list of items for each type.

- **Out-of-the-box customizations:**
  - Encourage teams to create simple solutions directly through the Web interface.
  - Provide guidance to power users regarding the use of various tools such as Excel, Access, and Visio (since you might not support Excel Services, Access Services, or Visio Services).
  - Educate power users about the 5,000-item governor within lists; lists will support millions of items when partitioned and indexed properly, but views should always be used to limit the query for viewing purposes.
- **Declarative solutions:**
  - Decide which teams can make use of SharePoint Designer; enable the tool only for certified users.
  - Once authorization for SharePoint Designer is obtained, the LOB may develop its solution only in a development environment; the solution must be packaged and submitted for deployment using standard means.
- **Custom-coded solutions:**
  - Since these solutions are typically built in C# via a .NET assembly deployed as a SharePoint solution package (.wsp), they'll need extra scrutiny.
  - These solutions need a design review; see Table 5-1 for a suggested checklist.

Table 5-1 Suggested Checklist for Review of Custom-Coded Solutions for SharePoint

Phase	Checklist
Development	☐ All code checked into and maintained in source control
	☐ Code contains inline, method, and class-level comments
	☐ Installation and configuration docs complete
	☐ Configuration PowerShell scripts complete
	☐ Install and uninstall PowerShell scripts complete
	☐ SPDisposeCheck has been run and no issues have been identified
	☐ Solution review with central SharePoint team
	☐ Automated builds running nightly
	☐ Basic automated tests have been instrumented
	☐ Sign-off by QA manager to enter development stage
Test	☐ The requirements of all previous stages must be satisfied
	☐ Automated builds and tests running successfully in development environment
	☐ All major solution development has been completed
	☐ Solution dependencies documented
	☐ Solution compatibility issues documented
	☐ Code analysis shows proper code coverage of automated tests
	☐ Test plan for manual testing approved by central SharePoint team
	☐ FxCop (full-trust solution package) analysis has found no critical blocking issues
	☐ Functional, technical, and installation/configuration documentation completed
	☐ Satisfactory review and validation of solution by core SharePoint team
	☐ Sign-off by QA manager to enter test stage
Production	☐ The requirements of all previous stages have been satisfied
	☐ FxCop (full-trust solution package) analysis results submitted to SharePoint team—no errors found
	☐ Load and performance tests have met the requirements for performance and stability
	☐ Critical test phase functional tests successful—attained business sign-off
	☐ All known issues documented—attained business sign-off
	☐ Deployment plan approved
	☐ Sign-off by QA manager to enter production stage

Establish Development and Test Environments

If you plan to do any customizations outside of simple Web-based modifications to sites and lists, you'll need to establish at least one other environment in addition to your production farm.

For example, it's helpful to have a development integration environment for testing customizations; this environment should mirror production in terms of configuration. All new functionality, whether it be native to SharePoint, custom-developed, or third-party—should be first tested in the development environment.

It's also useful to have a staging environment, which should be updated with production content on a regular basis. Staging is typically done so that users can perform quality assurance testing with content that matches production content.

The number of non-production SharePoint environments really comes down to three factors: your tolerance for risk, how many and what kinds of changes you make to your environment, and your ability to adequately maintain the extra farms.

Key Points

The key points from this chapter are:

- Remember that managing risk is your key goal. Put policies and procedures in place to ensure uptime of the environment and deployability and stability of custom solutions.
- Establish an operational governance plan to ensure system uptime and to ensure that IT understands its roles and responsibilities with respect to SharePoint.
- Establish an application governance plan (also known as a customization policy) to ensure quality and relevance of custom applications built on top of SharePoint and to ensure that all users understand their roles and responsibilities.
- Remember that governance is really about both assurance and guidance—but it takes commitment to ensure that your governance plan is followed.

- Maintaining a central SharePoint farm is no small task; keep in mind that it's much more involved than other services like e-mail or instant messaging.
- The types of solutions you allow are critical—make sure you think through which solutions you want to allow, considering the trade-off between allowing lots of customization and keeping the server environment stable.
- Take the time to establish a methodology—it could closely align with your existing development life cycle, or it could be SharePoint-specific.
- Make sure that your governance plan is included in all of your SharePoint IT and developer training. You will be most successful if your IT team never learns how to do a task that doesn't follow your guidelines.
- Keep in mind that an effective governance plan doesn't have to constrain every move—it has to provide guidance to the team to ensure that your solution remains effective and vibrant over time.

CHAPTER 6

PLANNING YOUR INFORMATION ARCHITECTURE

One of the greatest strengths of SharePoint is the ease with which "regular" folks (i.e., non-IT people) can create incredibly sophisticated collaborative Web sites. Lots of them. With lots of content. As these Web sites start to acquire more content, it becomes very, very easy for small sites to grow into big messes—with usability and "findability" challenges, content management problems, and unhappy users and business sponsors. The information architecture (IA) for your SharePoint solution is the plan that helps you avoid the mess. It provides the structure and framework that help your users navigate and search to find what they need, complete the tasks they need to perform, and understand the context of information so that they can use it effectively.

Information architects create plans for Web sites much as architects create plans for new houses. They follow best practices and architecture design principles, but much of the work of the information architect is not an exact science. Just as an architect must accommodate your preference for a large family room in your new house and another client's preference for a small family room with a large kitchen, information architects need to understand their users' needs and preferences—and the kind of work that they do. Even more important, the information architect needs to understand whom the solution is *for*. In other words, it's not just about the people who live in the home and bring in all the furnishings; it's *also* about the visitors to the home, who may have different preferences and different needs.

Creating a good balance of experiences for both the owners and the visitors to a Web site is a particular challenge for information architects— and working hard to find the right balance for each site is what can make the difference between a SharePoint site that remains vibrant and adds value and one that gets stale and ignored.

The information architecture for the solutions you build with SharePoint includes the following:

- **Site architecture:** the navigational structure of the solution. The site architecture is important because it defines how users will "browse" through the solution—how they will move from room to room.

- **Page architecture:** the position of Web Parts and content on each page. The page architecture is important because consistency across similar pages helps users quickly find what they are looking for. In addition, placing the most important Web Parts in the most prominent and visible parts of the page ensures that users won't miss important information. To continue our analogy, the page architecture defines what furniture is inside each room and how it is placed for ease of use.

- **Metadata architecture:** the structure of the content within the solution. The metadata architecture is important because it attaches structure and meaning to all of the content in your solution. It defines the attributes that you will use to classify and organize your content in the same way a librarian uses classification terms like fiction or biography to organize (and find) content in a library. If all you knew about a book was its title, there would be only one way to organize books, and as your collection got bigger, it would be much harder to understand what you have and find similar books. The terms you use to classify your books represent the metadata about the books; the values and specific terms that you use depend on the type of your collection. For example, you would likely use different terms to describe your collection of scientific books from the ones you would use for your collection of science fiction books. This is one reason why you may find similar patterns for page and site architectures across different SharePoint solutions in different organizations, but you will rarely find identical metadata architectures, even in organizations in the same industry—because metadata terms are very closely related to the details of the domain of the collection and what the owner and consumers of the content need to know about it. In SharePoint terms, metadata architecture includes the content models that you will use (Content Types), the attributes for each content type (Columns), and the definition of which elements are shared on all sites and which are specific to just one site or list.

The metadata architecture is also important because it helps improve the search experience. The site architecture supports users who *browse*. The metadata architecture primarily supports users who *search*, but as you will see later, the metadata architecture also helps users browse for information in context because it allows you to add descriptive information about content that users can use to assess its value or filter and sort information in context.

If you get your information architecture right, your users will find that your solution is useful, valuable, accessible, and usable. If you get it wrong, you are likely to hear, "We put all our content in SharePoint and we *still* can't find anything!" You may also hear, "Every time I land on a different page, I have to reorient myself because every page is organized completely differently, even when it presents similar content." If you've heard either of these complaints as many times as we have, it is almost certain that the root cause of the problem is the information architecture—or lack thereof. Fixing a badly broken information architecture after the fact is a lot harder and more expensive than planning your IA up front. But don't assume that information architecture is a "once and done" process. It's unlikely that you'll get your IA right the first time. It is especially important to have skilled information architects who have permanent roles in your center of excellence for SharePoint support. You *want* your solution to grow and change as your business and information evolve. Similarly, you *want* your information architecture to be adaptable and align with evolving business needs. Investing in information architecture helps ensure that your organization will get the most value from its information assets. The investment is certainly greatest in the planning phase, but it's an investment worth nurturing as your solution matures to ensure that your content and valuable information assets remain current and "findable."

Information architectures should be driven by purpose. A well-designed IA increases the likelihood that users will find what they are looking for with minimal "clicks." An effective information architecture will assist users in understanding and interacting with the solution. Most important, the information architecture helps ensure that your organization can achieve the business value investment from SharePoint because a good information architecture ensures that users can both find and interact with the solution content.

Why Is Information Architecture Important?

SharePoint users expect intuitive navigation out of the box, but we often hear users complain, "It's not intuitive" when they talk about their organization's SharePoint solution. Most often, these users are not complaining about SharePoint as a platform; they are complaining about the way that their information architects have designed and implemented the sites they use. Investing in your information architecture helps

- **Improve user adoption.** Well-organized content gets found, which helps users see the value of the solution and participate in the collaboration process.
- **Improve user satisfaction and productivity.** When users can find what they are looking for, they are more productive.
- **Reduce IT costs.** A good information architecture helps eliminate redundant content, thus reducing both storage and retrieval costs. Planning your information architecture may also help you identify redundant solutions (for example, two solutions for storing the same type of content), which can reduce both maintenance and support costs.
- **Reduce information overload.** A good information architecture reduces information overload because it helps move the most relevant content to the top of search engine results, which means users can quickly get to the information they need.
- **Reduce compliance and bad information risk.** When users clearly understand how content is organized, they don't feel the need to store multiple "convenience" copies of the same document. Driving users to a single-source vetted document ensures that they will access accurate and timely content.

Your information architects need to understand how different audiences will navigate and search for information. The benefits of your SharePoint solution depend on how content is organized, labeled, and categorized. Your information architecture is thus critical to your solution's success.

Understanding the Role of the Information Architect

A good information architect is well versed in the concepts and principles of information organization. We'll provide a high-level overview of the most important concepts and some effective techniques in this chapter, but reading this chapter is not going to automatically turn you into an information architect. You will need to practice these skills in a variety of scenarios—and measure and evaluate the outcomes of various decisions—to be able to create solutions with effective organization, structure, and navigation. Additionally, a good information architect is also a business analyst—someone who can listen to, observe, and understand the needs of business users, both producers and consumers of information. An information architect cannot work alone; the information architect must work in partnership with the content or site owner and site users to iterate and validate the proposed structure and plan. Thus, information architecture is a team sport; the design process should be led by an experienced coach, but the coach needs a team—the users and sponsors of the solution.

Once the initial information architecture is created and tested, the ongoing role of the information architect depends on the type of solution being designed. Most organizations understand the need for a persistent information architect role for externally facing Web sites and large intranets. These highly visible sites impact a broad population of users, and the impact of a poor user experience can be costly in terms of lost revenue or compromised productivity on a large scale, so it's easier to understand the value of the permanent role of an information architect, even though it might not be full-time. It's a little harder to scale the same level of support for potentially hundreds or thousands of collaborative team sites.

We've found that in practice, it's very difficult for a typical team site owner who only occasionally has to make changes to the structure of a collaboration site or has a new type of content and needs to decide whether to add a list, library, folder, Content Type, or Site Column to instinctively know the most effective approach from an information perspective. This is one of the reasons we made the recommendation for the evangelist and coach roles and center of excellence model in Chapter 4, "Planning for Business Governance." While we definitely recommend training all site owners in basic information architecture principles, the practical reality is that information architecture is a skill that improves with practice, and you may find that your organization will get better outcomes by maintaining a central pool of information architects who can provide ongoing coaching and consultation to site owners who identify new information design challenges. If you can get your information architects to document the patterns they observe as they work with site owners over time, you can build best practices and models into your site templates or at least provide models that site owners can use if they encounter similar situations.

What's New in SharePoint 2013?

SharePoint 2010 introduced several features that significantly improved the ability to manage and maintain a consistent information architecture. The most important of these features was the ability to store taxonomy structures centrally and reuse them on any site or site collection. The Content Type hub and managed metadata were really breakthrough features for information architects. SharePoint 2013 retains these breakthrough features and provides some *evolutionary* rather than *revolutionary* features to help with your information architecture design—with one exception: information architecture for search. Some of the key new IA features for SharePoint 2013 include the following:

- **New top navigation bar that provides persistent navigational links to the information users need the most.** SharePoint 2013 has a new persistent navigation Suite Bar that shows links that are relevant to your access permissions. Figure 6-1 shows the new Suite Bar view for the administrator of an enterprise Office 365 deployment. The top navigation will show Admin only for the site administrator. Microsoft's information architects have predefined what they consider to be the most important categories of navigational links for users: Outlook, Calendar, People, Newsfeed,

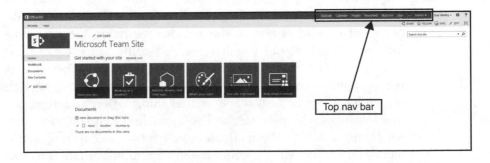

Figure 6-1 Top navigational architecture for an Office 365 environment

SkyDrive, and Sites. These links are collectively known as the Suite Bar, and they provide a "superstructure" for your site architecture. (Depending on your Office 365/SharePoint Online plan and your on-premises environment, you may see only Newsfeed, SkyDrive, and Sites.)

Microsoft has issued guidelines for how to replace Newsfeed in the Suite Bar with Yammer in SharePoint Online, but for the most part, you cannot change the Suite Bar links in SharePoint Online. You *can* change these persistent navigational links in your on-premises environment (it's not easy, but you can do it), but to ensure upgradability in the future, you should be intentional about changing the supersite architecture links provided natively in SharePoint. For the discussion in this chapter, we will assume that the Suite Bar is a predefined element of your navigational architecture and that you will use the Promoted Sites area of the Sites page to connect the "front door" to your major solutions in your environment (intranet and Internet home pages). Promoted Sites is a new centrally managed capability that allows you to promote links to different SharePoint sites to different users by leveraging SharePoint's Target Audiences feature. Promoted Sites provide another element of your supersite architecture. In addition, individuals can create links to the sites they care about by following these sites, which automatically places them on their personal Sites page.

- **New Sites page to provide a single place to connect different portal environments.** The Sites link on the Suite Bar takes you to the Sites "hub," which contains both shared and personalized navigational links that help users navigate within and between SharePoint environments, with a special focus on the sites that each individual user chooses to follow. The Administrator view of the Sites page is shown in Figure 6-2. The Promoted Sites shown at the top of the page are controlled by the portal administrator, and can be targeted using Target Audiences. The default Promoted Links are shown in Figure 6-2, but you may want to create a Promoted Link to the top-level site of your intranet portal (the intranet home page) and additional links to the home pages of departmental portals such as HR—sites to which everyone in the organization will likely need easy access. In previous versions of SharePoint, you would have had to make these cross-portal connections in your branding or in the "tabs" in each environment. In SharePoint 2013, you can use

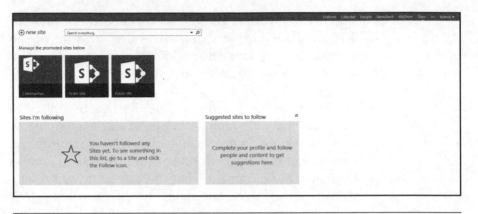

Figure 6-2 Administrator view of the Sites page

the Sites page to provide these connections and also use the same methods as in earlier versions within a specific portal.

- **New site templates to provide new "starter" site and page architectures.** As you will read more about later in this chapter, a key element of your information architecture is the organization of information on each site page. SharePoint 2013 sites have a new default user experience with changes to the default Quick Launch bar structure and site home page Web Part organization. These new page layout architectures reflect a much better understanding of how people actually work with SharePoint and, for some organizations and teams, might be usable out of the box with minimal configuration changes. Figure 6-3 shows the new home page of a publishing site (where you actually don't get a whole lot of help for your IA), and Figure 6-4 shows the new home page of a project site, which has a unique page layout and custom Web Parts designed to help direct the attention of project team members and managers to important dates and deadlines, which provides a little bit more help for the page layout element of your IA.

- **New ways to define site navigation.** The new managed navigation feature for publishing sites in SharePoint on-premises lets you define and maintain the navigation on a site by using term sets. Managed navigation supplements the existing SharePoint navigation that is based on site structure. Managed navigation is discussed in detail in Chapter 14, "Managing Web Content."

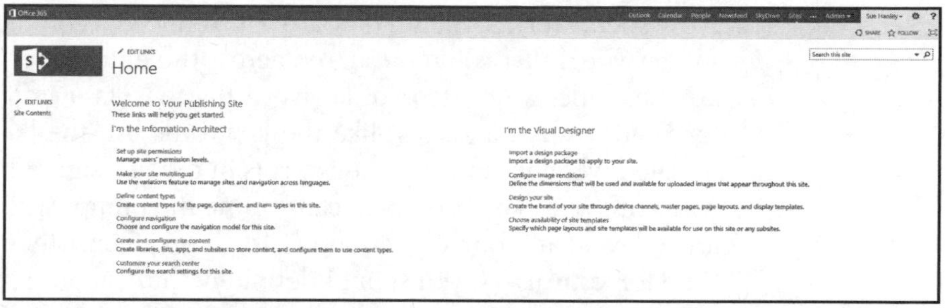

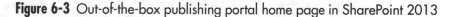

Figure 6-3 Out-of-the-box publishing portal home page in SharePoint 2013

- **New page layouts.** For example, the new category page layout is used to display structured content such as catalog data. You can use category pages when you want to aggregate content based on specific criteria. Category pages are also discussed in more detail in Chapter 14.

- **New ways to interact with managed metadata.** SharePoint 2013 includes a feature that many people in the SharePoint community were anxiously awaiting—the ability to edit managed metadata in a "datasheet" view, which is now called the Quick Edit view. This allows you to update any type of metadata "in bulk" in a view that looks and acts like a spreadsheet. In SharePoint 2010, you needed to open the properties of each document to change the values for any managed metadata attributes. (If you are new to SharePoint, managed metadata is described in the "Understanding Metadata Architecture" section of this chapter.)

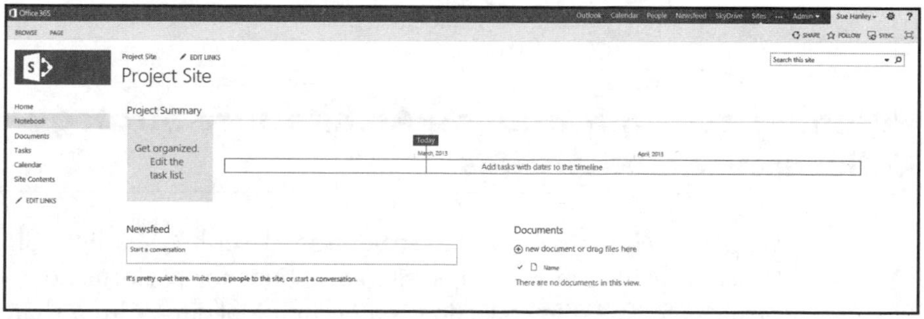

Figure 6-4 Home page of a project site in SharePoint 2013

- **New social terms.** SharePoint 2010 introduced a common term set for keywords that could be shared across the enterprise. SharePoint 2013 includes a new type of keyword that has its own home in the term store—hashtags. Just like the keywords list, the hashtag list is updated when users create new terms in the newsfeed. However, as with enterprise keywords, you can "prime the pump" with terms that are relevant to your organization. To ensure consistency and save time for your users, you should definitely think about predefining a list of enterprise keywords as well as hashtags; both types of metadata leverage "type-ahead" features, so if a term has already been defined, it can easily be reused. For example, if yours is an engineering company, you may want to predefine keywords and hashtags for each major discipline, such as civil or mechanical. If you are going to ask users to enter values in the Schools field of the user profile, you might want to consider predefining keywords for the most common schools attended by your employees, which will ensure consistent spelling and acronyms and make it much quicker and easier for people to complete their profiles. Hashtags are stored in a separate term store and must be one word, so if you wanted a hashtag for business development, you could enter "BusinessDevelopment." Enterprise keywords can have multiple words and include spaces.
- **New requirement to configure search as an application.** Overall, the new search engine in SharePoint 2013 provides a far superior experience for users—even if you do no configuration at all. However, unlike SharePoint 2010 search, which automatically configured facets for you based on the managed metadata Site Columns in your information architecture, SharePoint 2013 search requires a more intentional approach to defining search refiners since no custom properties are automatically promoted to become search facets.

Planning Your Information Architecture Strategy—Site Collections and Sub-sites

Within each of the portal structures described earlier, SharePoint is typically divided into multiple site collections for performance, storage, and management. A site collection is a grouping of sites with a shared top-level site. Each site in the collection shares administrative settings, such as permissions, and can also share navigation. There are site collections that you will get by default. For example, each SharePoint 2013 user has a private site collection in which to manage his or her personal content called My Site[1]; this augments the My Site of previous versions with an offline synchronization feature—a new Sky Drive Pro document library within the My Site. In addition, if you choose to implement the new Community Portal in SharePoint 2013 or a Search Center, these are instantiated as unique site collections.

If you plan to create both collaborative team sites and a "publishing-based" intranet, you could simply implement two unique site collections, each configured with different portal templates. But one of the first decisions you will need to make from an information architecture perspective is whether or not you actually need a unique site collection for *each* team site or within your intranet, for each departmental area, as an example.

As shown in Figure 6-2, the Sites page provides a convenient way to visually "connect" your publishing and collaboration portals if you want to provide your users with an easy way to navigate back and forth between the two environments. But, if you choose to implement multiple site collections *within* your collaboration portal, you may also want to figure out how to connect some or all of those sites to one another. If navigation and administrative settings are scoped to a single site collection, you may wonder why you would *ever* want to create more than one site collection in your collaboration portal. Isn't that going to create a more complicated management structure and user experience? The simple answer is yes, but there are other reasons why you may not want to use just one site collection for all of your content—and this is why the information architect cannot make a recommendation about an overall IA strategy entirely without help from the solution technical architect. In addition to understanding how users will experience your solution, you also need to understand how much content will be managed and how actively content will be updated, because there can be significant performance implications associated with managing all of your content in a single site collection. You may need to isolate security permissions, for example, if you have a highly sensitive collection of content; or you may want to restrict a particular custom feature to a specific site collection. Table 6-1 lists some of the pros and cons of implementing your solution as multiple site collections versus a single site collection with sub-sites.

---

1. You'll notice that we use the term *My Site* in the book—as does Microsoft in its online documentation. Although the feature set lives on, we anticipate that Microsoft will move away from the My Site branding in favor of the individual capabilities such as Newsfeed, SkyDrive Pro, and Sites.

Table 6-1 Criteria for Evaluating One versus Multiple Site Collections

	Multiple Site Collections	Single Site Collection with Multiple Sub-sites
Pros	Unique set of users and permissions. Unique and separated content databases are possible, which allows you to create individual "sites" of up to 200GB each. Creates a much more "scalable" infrastructure. Unique workflows, Site Columns, and Content Types. Responsibilities for site administration can be delegated, though users to whom site collection administration or site design privileges have been delegated should have training in information architecture skills. Shared Content Types if you use a Content Type hub (described later in this chapter). Unique quotas (without a third-party tool, you can set a quota only at the site collection level, not for an individual site). Shared farm services such as search and user profiles. Ability to upgrade, back up, and restore each site collection independently. Recommended for extremely active sites that generate a lot of database activity so the performance of other sites is not affected.	Shared navigation and content across all sites. Site collection galleries and libraries provide a way to create a single, branded user experience for all the sites in the collection. Shared permissions across all sites. Single content database to back up. Can use "lookup lists" on any site in the site collection. Site Columns that use lookup lists work only in the same site collection. Lookup lists cannot be replicated across site collections, even if you are using a Content Type hub.
Cons	No out-of-the-box solution to roll up data from site collection to site collection. However, in publishing portals, you can use the cross-site publishing and managed navigation features of SharePoint 2013 to surface content from one content authoring site collection into one or more publishing site collections where users will "consume" information. Navigation is more complicated since there is no automatic hierarchy or inheritance between site collections in collaboration sites except as described for publishing portals (and only if you use these relatively complicated features). In collaboration sites, unless you use custom controls or code, you will be doing a lot of manual updates to keep every site collection in sync.	Using a single content database could create an issue if your content grows to more than the recommended limit of 200GB. You can move a sub-site to a new site collection, but when you do, you will have a new URL for the new site that you will need to provide to all users. Managing permissions and security groups can be confusing if you have a lot of sub-sites with unique permissions. If you have to restore a content database, the entire solution will be unavailable.

Planning Your Information Architecture Strategy— Gathering the Right Information

Building your information architecture includes four key foundational elements:

- Knowledge of the domain to be modeled
- Content organization
- Firsthand understanding of site owner and user needs and capabilities
- Knowledge of the features available to model the IA in SharePoint

The first key element of a well-designed information architecture is knowledge of the domain to be modeled. Information architects must work with content owners to establish an effective and useful taxonomy, which describes the structure and classification of your content. Carefully and thoughtfully designing the optimal model for site organization and the structure and values for metadata is a very detailed process. As painful as the process might be, content owners must actively participate in detailed data and site design reviews because they have the best knowledge of the domain. (It often helps to have a lot of chocolate available when you are working on your detailed metadata and site design!)

The second key element is content organization—this involves a combination of data modeling and library science skills. Content needs to be organized so that users who are not content experts can find it. In other words, the content taxonomy should not assume that all users have an in-depth knowledge of the content, the domain, or the authoritative terms that describe them. In addition to the authoritative terms content editors apply when they assign metadata to sites and documents, users can add "social" metadata in the form of tags and notes (also called "folksonomy"), which provides additional information to help users find what they need. Together with your content organization, authoritative metadata and social metadata can greatly enhance "findability"—the key goal of your information architecture. Of note, while search recognizes and leverages authoritative metadata and "social" tags, it does not (at least not at the time of the writing of this book) use likes and ratings (which are a form of metadata) to promote results. In other words, the likes or high ratings that a SharePoint item has will not help boost its "findability" in search results (though they can help users evaluate and compare content).

The third key element is a firsthand understanding of the users. In general, when there are trade-offs to be made in information architecture, design for the consumer of the content, not the person who contributes the content. For example, our experience has been that most people who are contributing content will have about 10 to 15 seconds of patience available for entering metadata. This means that you can probably include no more than about five contributor-entered fields in your design for most content types. The exception (and the trade-off) is for content that you will publish for a specific discipline or audience, where the *job* of the contributors is to communicate everything they can about the content they are publishing so that people can find it later. Entering more metadata (more than the recommended five or so fields) is generally not an issue for people contributing, as an example, human resources content on your intranet. In that type of scenario, the additional time spent entering metadata makes it significantly easier for people to filter or search for content and ultimately saves time for the human resources team responsible for the content—they get fewer phone calls asking for content that can be easily found via search.

The fourth key element is understanding how you can model the IA in SharePoint, which means that the information architect needs to understand how site collections, sites, page layouts, Content Types, Site Columns, and Web Parts all work together in SharePoint to model your information architecture. It also helps to understand how to represent the architecture to a stakeholder so that you can get feedback to ensure that the IA is going to work.

In Chapter 2, "Planning Your Solution Strategy," we talked about the process you should go through with your key stakeholders to understand both their objectives for the solution and how they use and create information. The questions about information creation and use form the basis of the information-gathering activities that inform your information architecture. As a reminder, you will need the following general types of information to develop your information architecture:

- Who are the key users/stakeholders? Do they include only people inside the organization, or do they also include your clients or customers, partners, and vendors? Look at who uses content and why they need it. Why is the content relevant to users? What is their desired outcome?
- Do your users include the entire organization or just selected departments or roles?
- Do geographical boundaries matter for your content access or storage?

- How do your stakeholders use and access the information they need today?
- Who creates content? What types of content do they create?
- Who reviews and edits content and who might need to approve publication?
- What types of content need to be identified as records?
- How is information organized today? Take a look at your existing file shares, intranet, and collaboration sites. Do a comprehensive inventory and decide what can be deleted or archived.
- What information will be migrated to SharePoint? Is there any information that might be indexed "in place" or migrated to archival storage?
- How is content managed throughout the life cycle?
- How much content will be managed of each type?

Manually defining and documenting information architectures requires significant effort and cost, but some manual effort is usually required. A good information architect starts by examining existing structures—typically found in folder hierarchies, existing intranets, industry sources, or organizational charts—and uses these existing structures as a starting point to review proposed architectures with domain experts. The process will most certainly be iterative—starting at the top and working down as well as working up from the bottom. As an alternative or complement to a completely manual process, automated classification tools can suggest an information architecture by analyzing the content from a collection of documents. Some of the automatic classification engines include algorithms that help the engines train themselves from example data. At best, automated classification systems can get you started with building your information architecture. For the most part, building effective information architectures requires at least some human analysis and manual effort. In this chapter, we provide a general overview of three different levels (site, page, and metadata) of information architecture or taxonomy. Each of these levels probably deserves a book of its own, so simply reading this chapter will not make you an expert information architect.[2] Getting your information architecture right is not a one-time process—a

---

2. In fact, there is actually a great book that focuses entirely on building practical information architectures for SharePoint: *Practical SharePoint 2010 Information Architecture* by Ruven Gotz. In addition, there are excellent courses you can take that focus on building and managing information architectures for SharePoint 2013. Earley & Associates offers detailed IA training specifically for SharePoint. More information can be found at www.earley.com.

good IA needs to evolve as your organization changes. Investing in expert support for your initial information architecture is well worthwhile. Look for an expert who will help transfer knowledge about IA best practices to your organization. You may not need someone to hang around for life, but you should consider engaging an expert, ideally someone with a background or degree in library science or information management, to help you get started and help your organization develop the skills needed to maintain and evolve your IA.

To improve adoption, we encourage usability testing of your site, page, and metadata architecture by representatives of key user areas and roles. Retest as your architecture evolves to ensure that you will continue to have highly satisfied users when you deploy or alter your solution.

Creating an Effective Site Architecture

In a portal or content management system, an effective site architecture helps users to navigate to content without having to search. Your site architecture allows users to see documents and other components of the solution in context, which helps them assess whether a document or component is relevant to what they are trying to accomplish. Our experience indicates that users use a combination of hierarchical navigation and search when both are available. It is impossible to predict who will be a "browser" and who will be a "searcher" in advance. The challenge is that while creating an optimal site architecture for navigation and content organization is vitally important, you probably won't get it right until you get real users using the solution with real data. As you learn more about how users interact with your solution by observing their behavior, reviewing usage statistics, and gathering feedback after deployment, you can evolve your site architecture to make your solution even more effective.

As you conduct interviews and workshops to develop an understanding of user objectives for the solution and how they use information to guide their work, think about how that information fits within the overall conceptual organization of the company. Think about how content can be separated into major groups based on key business processes, major projects, key business roles, or organizational functions. Within each major classification, you may need to break each concept into subunits, depending on the type of content, who will "own" the content, and how you believe people will use the content.

Creating a new SharePoint solution is a great opportunity to learn about your organization. You will almost certainly discover that people in different parts of the organization or in different geographies have very different information needs. You want to be as comprehensive as possible when you do your analysis—be sure to include users who represent different roles, departments, and geographies. One key lesson we have learned: don't ask your prospective users what they want on the new Web site. Instead, try to find out what kind of information they need to do their jobs—and the sources from which they gather this information. Focus on the work instead of the Web site. Focus on the outcomes and objectives, not the specific steps your users might define as requirements. User requirements are often expressed in the context of the user's mental model and prior experience. If you focus on outcomes instead of requirements, you are often able to leverage more out-of-the-box functionality, which can save considerable time and money. If you can, observe people doing their jobs. It's always amazing how much you can learn from watching what people do, which is sometimes very different from what they say they do. If you are replacing a current site, you can also gather key content concepts from an audit of the existing site. If you have only limited access to "real" users, you can create personas to stand in for different user segments. Personas represent archetypes of the key groups of users for your site. Creating and using personas can help guide decisions about the functionality and the design of your site. For example, a common persona helpful for the site architecture of an intranet is that of a new employee. Approaching your site architecture design from the perspective of each persona will help ensure that your design recognizes that different users have different needs and also that users may have different needs at different times based on what they are trying to do or the work that they have to get done.

Site Architecture Design Techniques

Information architects use many different techniques to design and validate proposed site architectures. In this section, we talk about two: card sorting and tree testing.

Card Sorting

One helpful technique you can use to create and iterate insights for your site architecture design is card sorting. The idea behind card sorting is to use the prospective list of content topics you have gathered during your stakeholder interviews, brainstorming, and content audit to engage users to help organize the information in a way that is useful and relevant to the people who will use the solution. The challenge with information organization design is that until you have validated the proposed approach with real users, anything that you do is purely theoretical. Card sorting is a technique that helps validate that your theory can actually work in practice. A word of caution: card sorting should be used only as an *input* to your site architecture, not the only approach to defining it. The main goal of card sorting is to look for patterns—to identify groupings of information that you didn't expect and to validate some that you did expect. It sometimes tells you more about what you got wrong than about how to get the site architecture right, but it's a great design technique to have in your IA toolbox. As you iterate through the site architecture process, you will want to take out duplicate items, combine similar items, and look for opportunities to create primary and secondary groups or subgroupings where appropriate.

In theory, card sorting is very simple. To start, you write on an index card each of the content topics that you have gathered during your stakeholder analysis, from existing documents and manuals, from the existing site, from planned solutions and processes, and from future content. Get prospective users (the ideal number seems to be around 20 to 30 but you can certainly use more) to group the cards into related piles and give the piles a name. Collate all the results and use them as input to your site architecture design. Donna Spencer has written an entire book on the topic—called *Card Sorting* (published in 2009)—and she has also written an excellent blog post that includes a spreadsheet you can download to record and analyze the results of a manual card sort. The blog post can be found at http://boxesandarrows.com/card-sorting-a-definitive-guide/. Manual card sorts can provide incredible insight because you can learn a lot about how users think about information by listening to their dialog as they work through the decisions they make during the card-sorting process. But tracking the results of multiple participants in a manual card sort takes a lot of effort. For this reason, many information architects also use online card-sorting programs (such as OptimalSort from Optimal Workshop) to supplement the insights from manual card sorts.

Tree Testing

Tree testing is a variation of card sorting that is focused more on tasks than on topics. While you can potentially use card sorting before you have an IA in mind, with tree testing you need to have your proposed site architecture defined—and then you can use this technique to validate which parts of your navigational "tree" are more aligned with user expectations and which ones may need rework. With card sorting, you give your users topics and ask them to categorize the information in meaningful groups. With tree testing, you give the users a task and then, using your proposed site architecture, ask them to tell you where in the navigational structure they would expect to find the information to accomplish that task. Tree testing is a form of usability testing that you can use to test your proposed architecture even before the site is developed.

Tree testing can also be done manually, using a series of index cards large enough to include all of the elements of a particular "branch" in your site. Tree testing can also be conducted online using software such as Tree-jack from Optimal Workshop.

Note   Neither tree testing nor card sorting helps you with other factors that help users navigate your site and find content such as the visual design and layout of the Web Parts on each page. This is why the page architecture design, described later in this chapter, is also critical for your overall IA.

Site Architecture Best Practices

One mistake made by novice information architects is organizing their site architecture based on the organizational structure of their company or department. The company organization chart should *not* be the starting point for your site architecture. That doesn't mean you should ignore how your company is organized; it just means that you should use the organization chart to *inform* your site architecture, not to *guide* it. That said, there are some organizational units that are also functional units—for example, human resources and legal. It is perfectly fine to represent HR and legal in your intranet site architecture because while these may, in fact, be represented on the organization chart as "departments," each is also a function within a typical organization that all of your users will understand. The mistake designers often make is putting a business function like corporate communications "under" HR in the site architecture because the corporate communications department happens to report to the head of HR in their company (or when they put HR and legal under finance because these two business units report to the chief financial officer). This structure might make sense temporarily, but if there is a reorganization and communications moves to another business group, the site architecture will no longer make sense. In addition, new employees who are not familiar with the company's organizational structure will be far less likely to understand the site navigation if functions are aligned by organizational "ownership" rather than key functional area.

A well-designed site architecture can contribute to organizational goals and objectives. It should allow people to quickly find the information they need to do their jobs, effectively improving operational efficiency. It should also help people place the context of their work in the overall context of the organization, enabling them to gain an understanding of what is available in the solution as a whole, even if they primarily focus on their own particular space. It is important to provide meaningful labels to the elements of your site architecture. It is even more important to test your chosen labels with representative users to make sure that your nomenclature makes sense. (You can use the tree testing described previously to validate that your nomenclature resonates with your users.) Labels should be succinct—not more than three words each. Terms should be straightforward and consistent and should convey the desired tone for your solution. Try not to make up words for your navigation—use terms that users will understand (like "Human Resources" rather than "People Team"). There is no single "right" way to organize the content in your site. However, there are some approaches that are frequently used in well-regarded solutions:

- **About:** Many Internet sites and internally facing intranet sites group general information about the organization in a section called "About Us" or "About [Company Name]" or "Our Firm." You can put information such as the mission and vision, directions, company history, and organization charts in this section. Because this is such a familiar concept, users will generally know what to expect in this category. (But be careful, because this can easily become the catchall for new content that doesn't seem to fit anywhere else.) The SharePoint 2013 community site has a predefined About page built into the template. This is a site-specific About page that allows the community moderator or owner to describe the community objectives as well as "rules of the road" for participating. This particular page template also includes a Web Part called "About this community" that displays the date that the community was established, a property of the community site that can be set by the moderator or site owner but defaults to the date that the site was created. Figure 6-5 shows the default About page for a community site. A navigational link to the About page is included in the left-hand site navigation (Quick Launch) by default. All of the site templates in SharePoint 2013 have some elements of the site architecture predefined. For the most part, these are suggestions based on feedback from real users and usability testing, but that doesn't mean that you can't change them for your environment if you find that they are either distracting or confusing for your users. As stated earlier, you can't validate that your site architecture is "correct" without testing it—before, during, and after deployment.

- **Functional groupings based on "what we do," "who we serve" (both customer groups and industries), and what employees need to do their jobs.** Different organizations will have different terms for these groupings, for example, Customers, Clients, Life and Career, My Role.
- **Activity groupings based on primary activities.** This structure may work for a departmental-level in addition to an enterprise-level solution. For example, the following types of activities might form a basis of your site architecture:
  - **Project work:** activities that are designed to produce a specific result during a finite period of time
  - **Support work:** ongoing services that maintain an existing process (such as application maintenance and support)

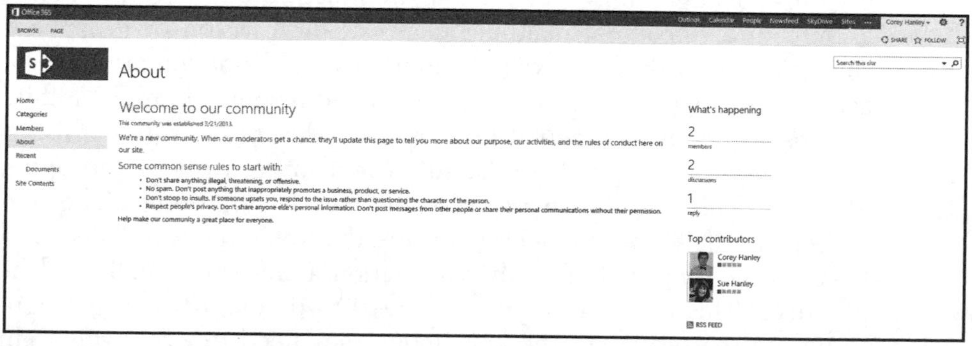

Figure 6-5 Community Site About page

- **Enabling work:** initiatives such as career planning, a project management office, or portfolio tracking that help your organization deliver project or support activities
- **Customer work:** activities related to engaging with partners, suppliers, and customers
- **Team work:** activities related to administering a team such as managing vacation and travel schedules and conducting regular team meetings
- **Leadership work:** information and activities for management personnel only, such as performance management, budgeting, and sharing other confidential information

- **"Duplicate" groupings if content "belongs" in more than one collection.** One of the biggest benefits of organizing information online is that the same content can be grouped logically in more than one location even if it "lives" physically in only one place. For example, you may organize your sites based on industry groups, but there may be a subgroup that could be classified in more than one industry. For example, imagine an information architecture for an executive search firm. The site that supports the CIO practice could appear under the CxO group and the Information Technology group, which would help users navigate to the practice page no matter where they are looking for it. However, be careful about overusing this capability and creating lots of "weak" categories to organize your content because this will confuse your users, who will wonder why the same topic appears in so many places.

In some organizations, the solution design team will define the major organizational groupings for the site architecture but leave the detailed architecture to content-planning teams at the division or group level. This practice works effectively if experienced information architects are available to support the divisional teams and if some common architecture principles are defined at the enterprise level to ensure consistency in user experience across the solution and to ensure that the optimal SharePoint features are leveraged in the architecture design. The key to success in a delegated model is to ensure that you empower all users who have Design permissions with information architecture skills and best practices. This means that you will need to define a training program to ensure that users get the knowledge they need to effectively define their information architecture. In addition to training, you should also consider providing expert coaching to new information architects until they feel proficient.

Before you implement your site architecture, it is important to review it with several stakeholders and, ideally, use one of the techniques described earlier to gather data to validate that you are on the right track. While you may be tempted to immediately implement your proposed architecture in SharePoint, this is not a good idea. You should go through at least one round of "paper" site architecture documentation and testing. There are several techniques that information architects use to document a site architecture visually. Many information architects like to use mind maps and a mind-mapping tool such as MindManager (www.mindjet .com) to document a proposed site architecture. Others use Microsoft Office Visio or PowerPoint. The goal of your site architecture diagram is to show the relationship of the high-level elements of your proposed site navigational structure in a picture that allows you to review your proposal with your key stakeholders. The documentation technique you use isn't nearly as important as the conversation that you need to have, so choose a diagramming technique that best facilitates your conversation. Figure 6-6 shows a very simple site architecture diagram created with Microsoft Office Visio. This example shows some diagramming techniques that you might use to help facilitate your architecture conversation. The first level of sites below the "home" page represents the top-level tabs for this site architecture design. Each of the pages below the home page could be a sub-site or just a page, depending on how you want to manage the content.

Your site architecture diagram should include the following:

- Hierarchical diagram showing each level ("node") and how the nodes are connected. Try to limit your nodes to no more than three levels deep. This is not a hard-and-fast rule, just a guideline. Don't use this rule to eliminate useful "landing" pages for major sections in your site. Category or landing pages help provide context when users land on sub-pages or sub-sites from search results.
- Labels for each sub-site or page and, if possible, a general description of the content on the page.
- Plan for navigation (using tabs and/or other navigational links).

As you consider whether a particular topic, process, or function needs a separate "node" (page or site) in the site architecture, it is also helpful to consider several factors in overall site administration:

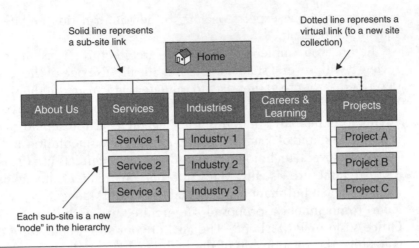

Figure 6-6 Example site architecture

- **Content ownership.** If a particular business group is the primary owner of all of the content to be published on the page or site, creating a separate site ("node") for that business group probably makes sense.
- **Security.** If a significant collection of content is highly sensitive or targeted to a specific user group, creating a separate node in the architecture allows you to more easily control the security settings for that content.
- **Database administration.** If you think that you might want to back up, restore, or otherwise manage content in a single group, having a unique portal node for that content will make these processes easier to manage.
- **Navigation.** Try to minimize the levels of nesting in your information architecture. It's a good practice to keep the number of levels in the hierarchy to no more than three so that users do not have to continuously "click through" if they are browsing for content. If you don't need to create a node in the architecture for any of the other reasons previously outlined or your content group does not need a "landing" page, don't create it.

Effective site architecture design is not a simple or quick process, even for small organizations or simple sites. If you invest the time to learn about your users' information needs, the result will be a site that is easy to learn and use and provides much greater value. Once your site architecture is established, you will need to have a process to maintain it and to review suggestions for changes as part of your governance process, as discussed in Chapter 4, "Planning for Business Governance."

Implementing Your Site Architecture

Once you have designed how your sites will be organized in your architecture, you have several options for how to display the architecture for your users. As outlined in Table 6-1, if you implement your solution in a single site collection, SharePoint can "automatically" surface your site architecture because you can show each sub-site in the top links or "tabs" area of your site. Collaboration sites have simple navigational options that allow you to automatically show one level "below" the root site as your top links and share parent navigation on all child sites. Publishing portals (or collaboration sites with publishing features enabled) allow you to automatically create a multilevel hierarchy for your solution. Figure 6-7 shows the site architecture diagram for a team site. Figure 6-8 shows the navigational settings required to automatically surface a link to Sub-site 1.1. The screen shot shown in Figure 6-8 was made from a collaboration site where publishing features have been enabled. Selecting Structural Navigation and "Show sub-sites" displays a navigational link to the "grandchild" site called Sub-site 1.1 when the user clicks the drop-down button next to the child site called Sub-site 1 on the parent site called Team Site.

Figure 6-9 shows the more limited top links navigational options available in a collaboration site where publishing features have not been enabled. In this instance, you can automatically surface a child site of the parent site, but you do not have the option of automatically surfacing a grandchild site (a sub-site of Sub-site 1).

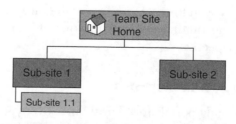

Figure 6-7 Example multilevel site architecture diagram

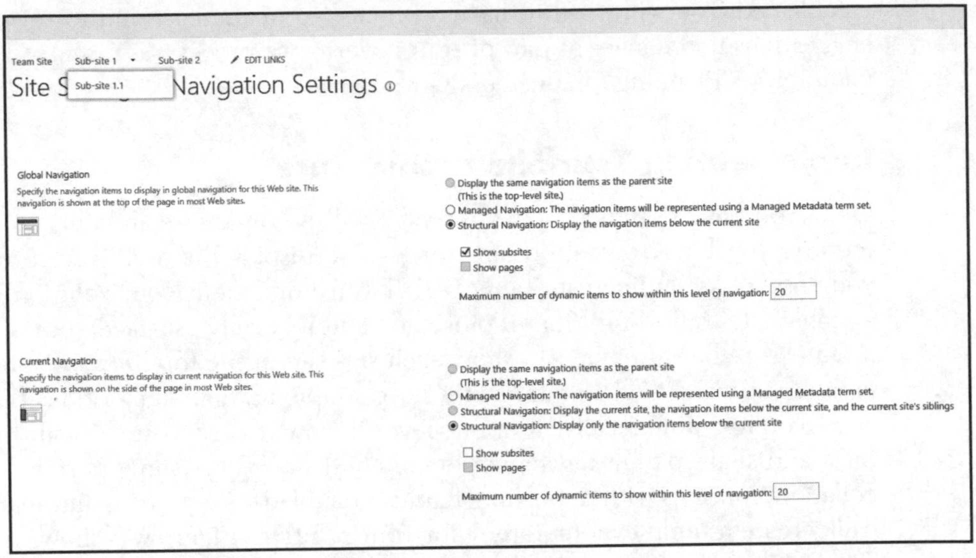

Figure 6-8 Navigation settings for sites with publishing features

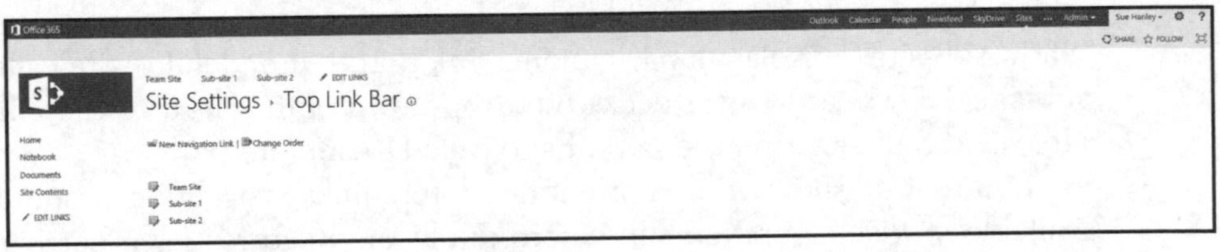

Figure 6-9 Top link settings for a collaboration site

In either of the two scenarios (publishing or collaboration), you can manually add links to sites that fall outside the physical sub-site hierarchy. This allows you to create a site architecture that reflects how users need to find information no matter how your sites are implemented from a structural perspective.

Managed Navigation

In publishing portals for SharePoint 2013, you can use managed metadata to define and maintain site navigation. This feature is described in more detail in Chapter 14, "Managing Web Content." Using managed navigation doesn't really change any of the best practices for site architecture design, but it does allow you to create a more dynamic site architecture with "friendly URLs" for pages. It also allows you to break up your content into multiple authoring site collections and use the central term store to manage a navigational framework that you can reuse in one or more publishing site collections.

> **Note** Refer to Chapter 14, "Managing Web Content," for more information on how to leverage these new features to manage your site navigation.

Page Architecture

The overall site architecture for your solution is typically reflected in the top links area of your site. Think of the top links area as where you will most often provide navigation to functional topics that reflect how your solution is structured. However, each of these functional sites has a home page that needs to be laid out in a way that helps your users find what they need in the most expeditious way. As described in the previous section, these logical "home pages" don't actually have to be implemented as separate sites. But to simplify the discussion, we'll assume that to be the case, because whether they are separate sites or just pages in a site, you still have to answer the following question: When a user lands on the home page of the site represented in the site architecture, what does that page look like? The answer to that question is found in your page architecture or page layout design.

Consistent page layouts contribute to an effective user experience. Following consistent layout patterns, such as always showing links on the right side of the page and a contact person at the bottom, makes it easier for users who navigate from page to page to find what they need on your site because while the content differs, the orientation of the page follows a pattern. This doesn't mean that every page has to look exactly the same—especially if an element of the pattern doesn't apply to your content. However, if every page that has essentially the same purpose is completely different, users will have to spend valuable time orienting themselves as they go from page to page or site to site, and that wasted time can significantly impact productivity.

There are several best practices when it comes to page layout design, and these practices apply whether you are using a publishing or a collaboration template for your solution. In both cases, SharePoint includes a starter layout for all pages. Depending on how you customize your site, either with custom branding or by taking advantage of the many options available out of the box via the "Change the look" settings option, your page layout may not include all of the same layout configuration areas because some of the different layout themes include a left-hand navigational area (Quick Launch) and others do not. In most cases, however, you will have the Quick Launch (left-side navigation) and body of the page to design (because we are assuming that the top links or tabs are going to reflect your navigational site architecture).

In a typical Web site design (publishing portal), you will have at least two different page layout templates—one for the home page of the site and one for pages below the home page—but most often you will have several additional structural page layout templates that content owners could choose to use based on the "story" they are trying to communicate on their page. SharePoint provides several publishing page layouts out of the box, including some of the ones shown in Figure 6-10. And, of course, you can design your own to meet your specific needs. Be careful how many you design because this becomes a supportability and upgrade challenge. Try to be flexible in the design so that users will have the options to lay out their page, but consider your ability to support a large number of alternative page layouts. There is no magic number to recommend; the goal is to find the minimal number of page layouts that provides a balance between consistency of user experience and flexibility to present information in the most "consumable" way. With a publishing portal, you will almost always create custom page layouts that provide structured content areas and sometimes areas where page owners can add their own Web Parts. Publishing portals are designed to be configured using page layout templates that you will customize to best meet your business needs, though you may need to do only minimal configuration. If you look at the default home page for a publishing portal as shown in Figure 6-3, you can see that you are expected to look at your publishing portal design from the perspective of both an information architect and a visual designer. With collaboration sites, however, anyone with Full Control privileges (typically site owners) has the ability to configure the layout of a page.

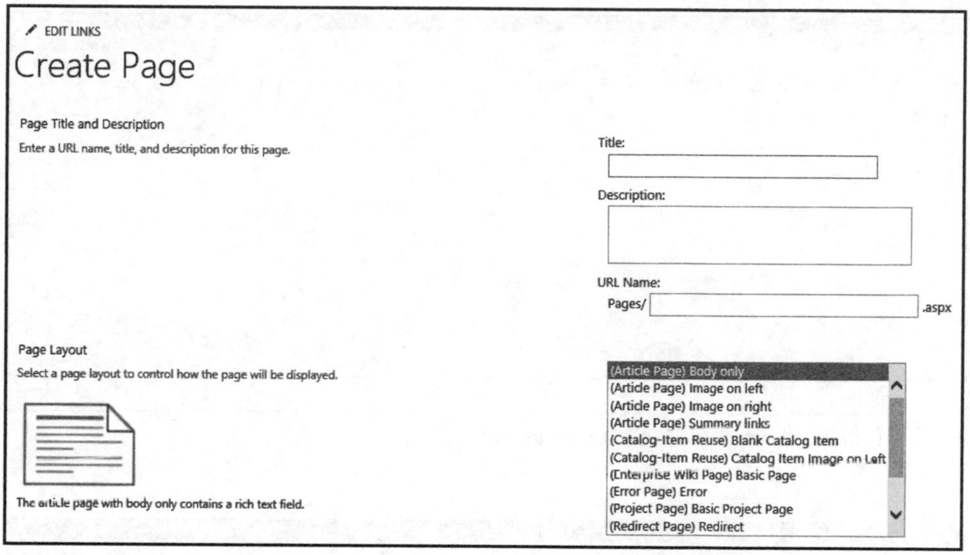

Figure 6-10 Default publishing page layouts (partial list)

Every collaboration site template in SharePoint 2013 also comes with several "starter" page layouts, including a home page. Figure 6-11 shows the home page for a team site in edit mode. This view shows the areas of the page layout that you can edit in a default team site. Notice that you can select alternative text layouts in the ribbon. The default text layout shows two columns with a header, but as you can see in Figure 6-12, you can change the layout of the home page, a wiki page by default, to create the specific experience you want to provide for your users. In the default template "theme," the Quick Launch links on the left of the page remain permanently in the layout even if you change the structure of the rest of the page. This means that you will design the Quick Launch navigation only once for each team site, no matter how many pages you have within it. If you create a child sub-site of your team site, it can share the top navigation from the parent as described earlier, but the Quick Launch is always local to the individual site. The default Quick Launch shows several predetermined links (Home, Notebook, Documents, Site Contents), but you can edit the list. Different types of team site templates have different initial links in the Quick Launch area.

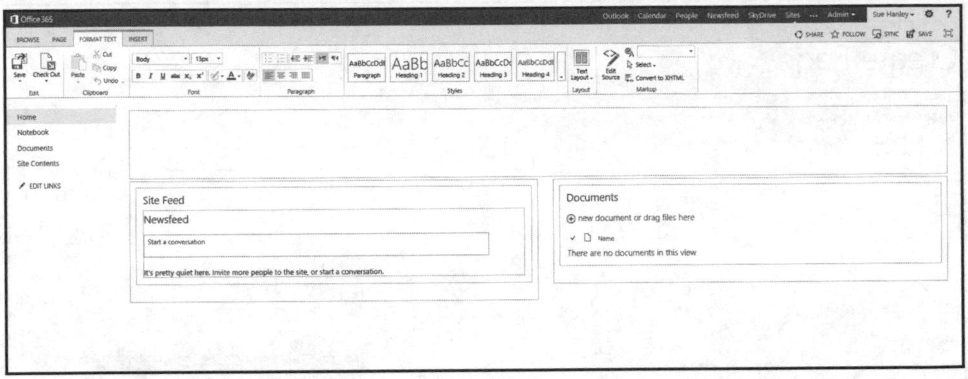

Figure 6-11 Default page layout for a team site

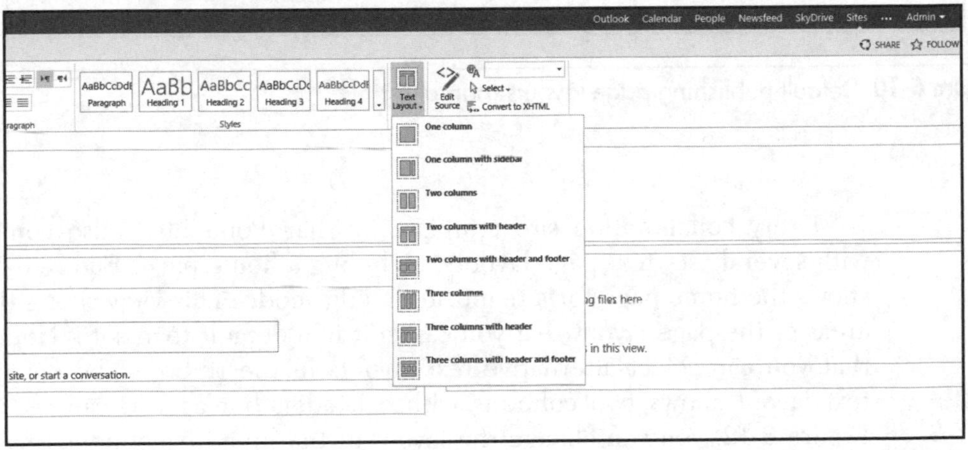

Figure 6-12 Default text layouts for a team site

Designing a page layout for a site thus includes thinking about what goes in the Quick Launch, the layout of the page (the number of columns, whether you have a header, and so on), and the Web Parts (or content areas in the case of a publishing page) that you will display on the page.

Even if you start with a template provided in SharePoint 2013, you still need to think about how users will use each site. Consider the following basic design principles when configuring your page layout architecture:

- **Consistency:** Provides standard design templates for all pages on the portal, and take steps in your governance processes to ensure that these design standards are followed. For intranets and Web sites, this ensures that users can navigate around the solution without getting surprised by changing design standards. But even in a collaboration environment where you are distributing Full Control permissions to different team site owners, consistency helps. If each team site has a completely different layout, people who work on more than one team will have to spend time learning the structure of every different site for all the teams or projects they work on. Consistency provides a very real benefit for your organization because you will not have to pay people to spend their time trying to figure out what the site or page owner is trying to say as they navigate through the solution or start work on a new team or project.

- **Speed:** Make sure that users can get information as fast as possible. This goes along with consistency but should inspire you to think about a few additional design principles. For example, does the information or placeholder you are adding improve the ability for users to quickly find what they are looking for, or does it get in the way? Think about using the new Promoted Links feature of SharePoint 2013 to direct users to important content on your site.

- **Scrolling:** Does the page layout require that users scroll up or down or left to right to find important information? Design your page to fit your organization's standard screen size, and then make sure that users do not have to scroll to find the most important information or Web Parts on the page. Scrolling may be acceptable in your design standards, but scrolling should never be tolerated for critical information. Think about designing your page the way that news editors design a newspaper—the most important information should be "above the fold." As a best practice, avoid designing sites that require left-to-right scrolling for sites viewed using your organization's standard display size; up-and-down scrolling is generally OK.

- **Important content at the top, above the fold:** Put your most important content toward the top left of the page. This is where readers will "land" visually when they get to your page. If the most important information is in this location, you have a better chance of capturing your user's attention than if the information is buried somewhere else on the page. One mistake we see pretty often is that site designers put large images or content that never changes (for example, "welcome" messages) in prime real estate on the site. You want to avoid this at all costs—put content that changes frequently in the places where users will be most likely to see it. Move content that never changes or changes infrequently to a page that you might reference in the Quick Launch or "below the fold" on your page. The Community Site template in SharePoint 2013 includes an About page that is in the default Quick Launch for this type of site. You can add an About page to any type of site, and if the About page is in a consistent place in the Quick Launch on every team site, your users will learn where to find helpful reference information about the team or the site. A separate About page is generally a better approach than a lot of wasted space with "welcome" messages that never change.

- **Identified content owner(s).** Every top-level site and major content page should have an owner clearly identified and visible on the page. Some organizations list both a sponsor, the executive or manager sponsoring the page and ultimately accountable for quality, and an owner or content manager/steward who is accountable for day-to-day management of the site or page and to whom content questions should be directed.

- **One link per page:** One of the key decisions that you will need to make in the layout of a team site is whether to provide links to content in the Quick Launch, in a Web Part, or neither. This decision is what we call the page layout dilemma, and the options are discussed in the sidebar. As a general rule, however, you want to have one visible link to a content area on each page. For example, if you show your Announcements or Links list in Web Parts on your page, don't *also* have a link to each list in your Quick Launch. This is by no means a hard-and-fast rule, but the idea is to minimize link confusion for your users. Also, make sure that the label for your link clearly tells your users what they will find when they click it. A link labeled "Miscellaneous" is not likely to be helpful to anyone.

- **Images:** Use images to help create visual interest on your site and also to provide visual cues for key site content. You can easily create clickable images by inserting an image in a content editor Web Part and adding a hyperlink to the target content, or use the out-of-the-box Promoted Links feature to create friendly, visual navigation to important content. However, be sure to size your images to work effectively in your screen real estate, and use an appropriate resolution for the Web to minimize screen "paint time," especially for users who will access your site at slower speeds. When you select images for your site, be sure they are relevant, and be sure that you have the right to publish them on your site. One of the things that you will quickly notice about SharePoint 2013 site templates is that you can easily add a background image to your sites. Be very, very careful about using this feature because in many cases, background images obscure text content and make it much harder to read. This is what we call a "bright shiny object" feature—it's tempting to try because it's new and shiny. Keep in mind: just because you *can*, doesn't mean you *should*. Our best advice: don't use background images on your sites, even if you are tempted to do so.

- **Images that move:** Avoid moving or rotating images, especially when the user has no control over the movement. You have probably seen a lot of Web sites with image rotators or image carousels, especially for news. They've become the de facto standard on many, many Web sites, and as a result, your users will probably want one on at least the intranet home page (if not also on their team sites). Use them if you must, but be aware that many of your users will find automatic rotation very annoying, so be sure to do some usability testing to get user feedback. You can have a news carousel without automatic movement—or one that changes the image each time the user lands on the page. You don't *have* to automatically rotate the images—even if your business sponsor is enamored with that feature. If you must automatically rotate, be sure the frequency of rotation is not so fast that users don't have time to process the image or text that you are rotating. Make absolutely sure that users can stop the rotation by clicking on an image. Finally, make sure that the number of items in the rotation is visible so that users know where they are in the rotation and how many items there are in total.

The Page Layout Dilemma: Web Parts versus Quick Launch Links

One of the many decisions that information architects wrestle with is determining what content gets to be promoted as a Web Part and what content is surfaced in the Quick Launch bar. The general guideline is that you want to make the most important content easy to find on the page, which means that you don't want users to have to work too hard to find it. Since Web Parts surface individual content item details and links in the Quick Launch surface only a type or class of content, you should use Web Parts for important content where your users need to see the details of the content or content item and the content is time-sensitive, and the Quick Launch bar for more reference-type information. This is why you will see many sites with an Announcements Web Part—because each individual announcement is important, and if the details aren't surfaced in a Web Part, site visitors would never know that there is something new to see.

As a general rule, documents are more likely to fall into the reference information category, so you probably don't need to have a Web Part to surface document content. However, you might consider having a link to your document library in the Quick Launch and have a Web Part that shows New Documents (a view showing the most recently updated five to ten documents). Since Web Parts provide a window into the content of lists and libraries, use them to surface information that you don't want users to have to click to see, such as the most recent content for a list or library.

Page architecture designs (also called wireframes) are often configured on paper before a prototype is created in SharePoint. There are several wireframe tools that you can use to help lay out the content on your site, including Visio or even PowerPoint. However, we love a very inexpensive mockup tool called Balsamiq (www.balsamiq.com). James Sturges has shared a set of SharePoint 2010 wireframes configured with Balsamiq that you can download from his blog at http://sharepoint.jsturges.com/2011/11/sp2010-wireframe-template/. In addition, the folks at Flucidity have created a downloadable set of Balsamiq templates for SharePoint 2013 sites at http://flucidity.com/2013/02/sharepoint-2013-balsamiq-mock-up-template/. There are also quite a few community-contributed mockups for Balsamiq that you can find at https://mockupstogo.mybalsamiq.com/projects. There are several SharePoint elements in the community-generated content, though most are for SharePoint 2007. Figure 6-13 shows a very simple page wireframe for a community site created using Balsamiq. What we really like about Balsamiq is that the layouts clearly are not meant to be "real"; they are meant to help facilitate a design conversation with your users and sponsors.

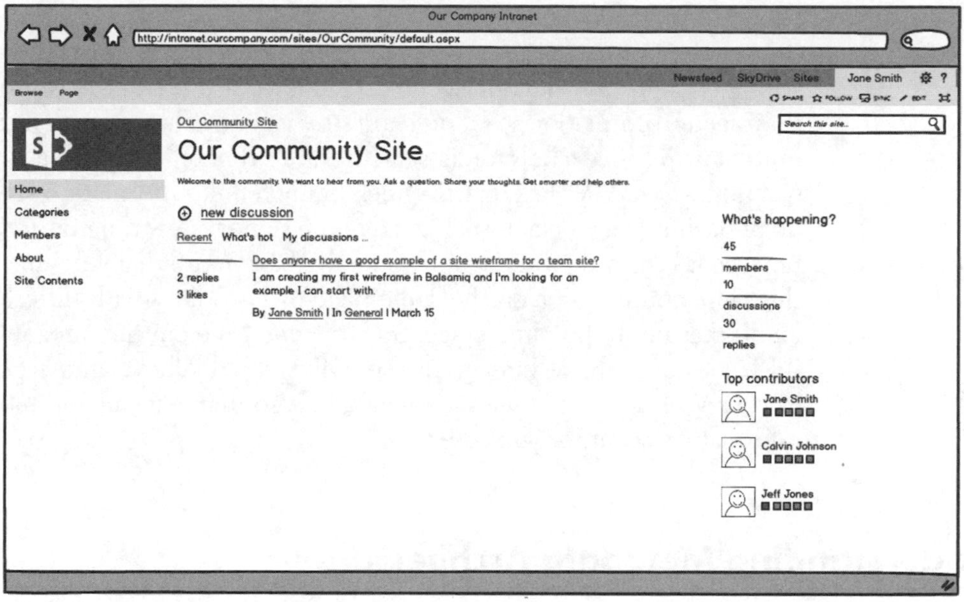

Figure 6-13 Sample page architecture created with Balsamiq

In general, plan to develop an initial page layout proposal when you are designing your site, but consider offering stakeholders additional opportunities to reevaluate page layout design as you configure each layout. Use the recommended usability testing approaches described earlier to validate the effectiveness of both your site and page architectures. You will get a chance to improve even your best ideas for page layout when users can see the solution with "real" data.

Page Architecture and the Three-Click-Rule Myth

Do not get hung up by thinking that all content has to be "findable" with no more than three clicks because the "three-click rule" is just a myth. The truth of the matter is that users are very willing to click to find information as long as they are confident that with each click they are headed in the right direction. That doesn't mean that you shouldn't try to surface the most important or most frequently used content toward the top of each page. That is always a good practice. The three-click rule is a myth because in practice, we have seen that the number of clicks doesn't matter as long as you are providing a strong enough "information scent" to guide your users to the content they need. Information scent on team sites can be achieved with clear, mutually exclusive labels for lists and libraries that tell users what they will find when they click on the Quick Launch link. Information scent on publishing pages can be achieved in the same way. Strong information scent is also achieved when you don't have more than one link to the same content area on the same page or have links with different labels that go to the same place. Spend some time crafting meaningful labels and take advantage of the ability to add "hover messages" in your Web Part and Quick Launch labels so that you can add more information scent for your users.

Understanding Metadata Architecture

Metadata (literally, data about data) defines the structure of the content within your SharePoint solution—the attributes that you will use to classify and organize your content the way a librarian organizes content in a library. Why do you need to think about metadata? Metadata makes it easier for users to find content; in other words, "findability" is the key rationale for metadata, just as it is for the other elements of your information architecture. Metadata can also provide context for content, helping users to quickly identify whether a document or other asset will be helpful—without having to examine the content of the document in detail. Now you understand metadata, right? Probably not so much. So, let's try to make the point about why metadata is important by using an analogy that you can use with your users as well.

Explaining Metadata

Think about your online music collection. Every song in the collection is a unique item, just like documents in a document library. And, whether you know it or not, you are already taking advantage of metadata to organize them. Every song is by a specific artist or artists. Unless the song is a single, it comes from a specific album (though it's possible that some of you reading this book have never actually *seen* a real record album). And each song was written by one or more composers. Each of those attributes—artist, album, and composer—represents different metadata associated with each song. The *values* of these attributes, along with the name of the song, are what you need to be able to find an individual song in your library—because without these attributes, the song is just a bunch of bits and bytes on your computer. Artist, Album, Composer, and Name are among the many attributes used to describe songs in an online collection. Each of these particular attribute values is something that you as a user typically don't have to enter because in the world of online music, they are already associated with the songs that you purchase online. Essentially, they are part of the metadata that you get "for free," along with other attributes such as Genre. The collection of attributes that you (and others) use to understand or make sense of your online music collection represents the metadata for the item Song. With just a little information about each song in my collection (see Figure 6-14), I can find

- How many songs in my collection were cowritten by Elton John and Bernie Taupin
- All the songs on the album *Here and There*
- All songs sung by Elton John

Now let's think about how this concept applies to the documents that we store in SharePoint. In the world of documents, just as with songs, there is some metadata that we get "for free" when we create or upload a document in SharePoint. The most obvious is the file name, which your document acquired when you saved it to your hard drive or your file share. If I am the author of a document, I get to decide its file name when I save it the first time, no matter where I save it. When the contributor or "uploader" adds a previously saved document to SharePoint, the file name is still a primary reference for the document in SharePoint—but it is not the only metadata attribute available to identify the document. In a single document library, the only metadata value that must be unique is the file

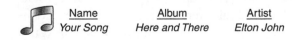

	Name	Album	Artist	Composers
	Your Song	*Here and There*	*Elton John*	*Elton John* *Bernie Taupin*

Figure 6-14 Sample song metadata

name.[3] In other words, every document in a document library must have a unique name. In SharePoint lists, every item also has a unique identifier, but this unique identifier is stored "behind the scenes," so you *can* have a list where each item has the same name (or Title) unless you add a rule to require the name/Title to be unique. Some of the other "free" metadata attributes for documents are Created (the date the file was first uploaded to SharePoint or created inside SharePoint), Modified (the date that the file was last modified), Created By (the user ID of the person who first created or uploaded the document), Modified By (the user ID of the person who last changed the document or any of its attributes), Version, and File Size. But notice that the "free" attributes of your music collection are actually very descriptive, and if you wanted to group your songs by album or sort them by artist, you could pretty easily do that without ever having to add any metadata of your own (but note that *someone* has added the metadata for your music; it just wasn't you). In the case of documents, the "free" metadata isn't very descriptive. And, because every document creator or "uploader" has complete and total control over how his or her documents are named, you can see that even with file-naming standards you might not get very valuable metadata to help you find a document if all you can use is the metadata you get "for free." Figure 6-15 shows a list of all the "free" metadata that SharePoint 2013 provides out of the box for all documents and that you can expose in document library views. The Type shows an icon if SharePoint recognizes the file type such as Word, Excel, and PowerPoint but also any of the standard image formats and .pdf files. Name is the file name. All of the other attributes are determined by SharePoint, and with the exception of the file Name and Title, users do not enter or maintain these values. As you can see, these attributes are not particularly descriptive even if they might be useful in some scenarios.

"But wait," you say. "I know how we can help organize and find our documents! That's what folders are for!" Folders, also known as the dreaded "F" word, are, in fact, the way we have traditionally organized our online documents in file shares. It's the metaphor that we all know and are used to. Here's the problem: Have you ever actually tried to find a document in a hierarchy of folders that someone else has set up? Was it easy? Probably not. What if your library is designed to hold sales reports and your organization is divided into six sales regions and you sell four different products? Are you going to name your documents Sales Report-[Product Name]-[Month]-[Year]-[Region]?

---

3. Technically, file names have to be unique only within *folders* in a document library.

Column Name

Type (icon linked to document)

Name (linked to document with edit menu)

Modified

Modified By

App Created By

App Modified By

Check In Comment

Checked Out To

Content Type

Copy Source

Created

Created By

Edit (link to edit item)

File Size

Folder Child Count

ID

Item Child Count

Name (for use in forms)

Name (linked to document)

Title

Version

Figure 6-15 Default document metadata available in list views

Are you going to create a folder for each product and then a sub-folder for each region and then a sub-folder for each year and then a sub-folder for each month and expect contributors to click-click-click their way through all of your folders to store a document? Are you then going to expect users to click-click-click their way through all of your folders to *find* a document? What happens if I am looking for the August 2013 sales reports and they haven't been added to the folder yet? I just clicked my way through multiple levels only to find out that the folder is empty! As you can probably imagine, while your folder structure technically adds some descriptive metadata about your document, that metadata isn't that *useful* because it doesn't really help users quickly find what they need the way the song metadata does. And the folder metaphor gets really complicated when a document needs to go in more than one place. For example, how would you file a sales report that covers more than one region? Would you store it in two folders, thereby creating a duplication issue? What if the report gets amended? Will you remember to update the file in both locations? As you might be able to tell, your folder idea may not be as useful as you thought.

Metadata provides a far superior organizational framework for document classification than folders because it allows you to "slice and dice" your information depending on what you need to know at the time. Metadata also doesn't "bury" content behind multiple clicks, and, more important, if you use metadata to organize your content, you have to store each item only one time, but you can associate it with more than one attribute value. You can then use your metadata attributes to create different views grouped by any single-choice value, which allows you to create the illusion of folders in views that provide the ability to visualize document lists in multiple ways without the problems associated with folders. This is the same concept as using the same song in multiple playlists in your music collection. You don't have to buy the song twice to use it in your "road trip" and "exercise" playlists. For the type of content called Song in a music collection, you have seen that there are some standard attributes (aka metadata) that provide meaningful descriptive information to help us organize, navigate, and find music in our collection. For the type of content called Document, there are no universal descriptive attributes that will apply in all organizations or sometimes even in all departments of the same organization. So, for each type of content in your SharePoint solution, you need to create your own collection of helpful descriptive metadata so that users can answer the same types of meaningful questions that you can about your music collection and authoritatively find all of the content they need to make a decision or take an action. In the folder example, you could have used just a few simple descriptive metadata attributes to organize your sales reports—Product Name, Sales Region, and Month/Year—and you would be able to easily fulfill the following types of information requests:

- Show me all the sales reports for any product in April 2012.
- Show me all the sales reports for Product A in June of 2013.
- Show me all the sales reports for Product C in Regions 1 and 2 for July 2011.

Moreover, you wouldn't have to do any clicking at all to find out that no sales reports have been posted for August 2013. A quick sort of the files would show that nothing has been added with a Month/Year value of August 2013.

One thing that is important to note about creating custom descriptive metadata for documents in your SharePoint collection is that you need to keep it simple. While you could certainly add an unlimited number of attributes that would help describe your documents the way all the song information describes your songs, since you have to both define *and* add the metadata for documents and essentially *all* of your metadata is "custom," you want to define custom metadata only for attributes that you need frequently enough to take an action or make a business decision to make the tagging and defining process worthwhile. In other words, the constraining factor for defining your metadata architecture is reusable business value. You don't need to create a metadata attribute for every possible way you could want to sort or group your documents; you just want attributes for the most common and business-critical ways.

So let's go back for a moment to the "F" word (folder). You are now probably wondering if folders are bad in the context of SharePoint. The answer is mostly no, folders are not "bad." In fact, starting with SharePoint 2010, folders can have metadata, and when you put a document in a folder that has its own metadata, the document "inherits" the metadata from the folder, so you can define the values of metadata one time for each folder and then automatically "tag" your documents with those values. In other words, you can use a combination of folders *and* metadata to create a familiar construct for filing or storing documents but still create a "findable" asset collection by using views to display content that show documents without folders. Folders are also helpful if you want to add security within your document libraries because you can secure a folder, and then all of the documents in it will share the parent folder permissions. This does not eliminate the issue that a document can live in only one physical folder, but, as you can see in the sales example, that is a problem only for reports that span multiple regions. If no reports ever span multiple regions, you could technically mimic your folder hierarchy within SharePoint and, in views that don't show folders, find the information listed above. The problem with that approach is that it's massively confusing if human beings are doing the uploading—because each contributor still has to navigate or find the one and only one folder where his or her documents need to be stored. If you are getting your sales reports from a reporting *system*, on the other hand, using the folders for uploading and "no folders" views for consuming information would be perfectly fine.

If Metadata Is Good, Are Folders Always Bad?

One of the most challenging jobs for any information architect is convincing users of the benefit of organizing their documents with metadata rather than folders. Folders, the traditional organizational framework for documents in file shares (and file cabinets), have several problems:

- It takes lots of clicks to get to the content you are looking for.
- Folders are inflexible—you either put the same content in two different folders if it applies to more than one folder, which immediately creates version control challenges, or you have to live with the structure you created and make sure all users understand how to correctly put documents "where they are supposed to go."
- Using folders to organize content assumes that you and your colleagues all have the same mental model for content organization.
- Folders don't let you easily sort, filter, and create ad hoc views of your content—folders assume you know today how you might want to see your content tomorrow.

Metadata is a better organizing principle for several reasons:

- It's easy to see what content is available in a library or list.
- Users can look at, sort, or filter content by any dimension that is useful today ... and use a different dimension tomorrow.
- Metadata improves the ability to serendipitously discover what is available in a content repository—it surfaces rather than buries content.
- With metadata, you have the option to use "group by" in views if you need to collect content of a similar type to create an organizing experience similar to folders, but still have the flexibility to group your content along multiple dimensions.
- Metadata improves search engine results. SharePoint search uses the content metadata in the algorithm that returns results. In essence, metadata provides bonus points that can boost the content's position or rank on a results page.

Information architects and good SharePoint designers have spent many years trying to break users of the "folder habit." However, starting with SharePoint 2010 and continuing in SharePoint 2013, folders have an opportunity for a comeback because they are the vehicle through which location-based metadata is assigned. In SharePoint 2013, you can assign default metadata values to a folder using the "Column default value settings" feature in Library Settings, and then all the documents that you create in or upload to that folder will automatically "inherit" the metadata value associated with the folder. Since folders can actually provide a valuable "service," they may have a place in your information architecture—especially if you create views that show your items without folders. Folders have other benefits as well, including the fact that you can assign security to folders and thus use the same document library for documents that have different access privileges so that users with the highest level of privileges can see all content and users with lower privileges can see only the content that their permissions allow. But while you *can* use folders for security, you do not want to use folders for both security and metadata grouping in the same library because you will create a very confusing model for content contributors.

Does this mean that we are now recommending that you use folders to organize your content by default? Not necessarily. However, you have additional *options* you can consider for your information architecture depending on the type of repository you have and whether or not you want to take advantage of document routing and location-based metadata features that are described in Chapter 13, "Managing Enterprise Content." Chapter 13 also talks about a special type of folder called a document set that effectively allows you to create a template and act on a group of documents at one time. Document sets can have default metadata just like regular folders, but they can also provide a way to manage a deliverable that contains multiple documents in a unified way.

Basic Metadata Concepts for SharePoint

For the most part, people think of metadata as attributes that are assigned to documents, but you can use metadata attributes to classify and organize any type of list content. The basic design principles are the same, no matter what type of content you are organizing. However, we will primarily talk about document metadata in this section.

There are two primary constructs in SharePoint that you will use to design your metadata architecture: Content Types and Columns.

- **A Content Type** is a collection of settings that define a particular type of information, such as document, list item, or folder. Content Types allow you to manage the settings for a particular type of information in a central, reusable way. One type of setting associated with a Content Type is its Columns or attributes. For example, the Columns of a Content Type called Sales Report might include Name, Product, Region, and Month/Year. A Content Type can be defined at the top level of your site collection (the root) and be reused in any document library and/or any site below the root, or in a sub-site and be used on any library on that site or in sites "below" that site. You can also define Content Types in a single site collection (called a hub) and share them across multiple site collections. All SharePoint assets are associated with a Content Type, so even if you don't *think* you are using them, you are! The attributes shown in Figure 6-15 are the ones that are included in the base Document Content Type in SharePoint, but you can also add attributes of your own. SharePoint includes a long list of base Content Types for all different types of content. (To see the list, navigate to Site Settings and click on Site Content Types under Web Designer Galleries.) As a best practice, you should not modify these core Content Types. Instead, create a custom Content Type that is derived from the most appropriate core Content Type and add your custom metadata to your custom variation.[4] Content Types can be associated to a specific list or library, which essentially allows you to restrict the type of content you can add to that list or library to just the Content Types that you have specified. Users see the list of associated Content Types for your document libraries in one of three ways: when they click the New button to create a document, when they upload a document with required metadata attributes, or when they edit an existing document's metadata properties. Note that when a user uploads a document to a library that has more than one Content Type associated with it, the document is associated with the first Content Type in the list by default.
- **Columns** are the properties or attributes of a particular type of content. Columns have a unique type such as "single line of text" or "date" or "number." Columns can be defined at the "root" of a site collection

---

4. Microsoft strongly recommends that you do not modify any of the core Content Types. However, if you must do so, please refer to the "Guidance for Editing Pre-defined Content Types and Site Columns" white paper from Microsoft at http://go.microsoft.com/fwlink/p/?LinkId=260922.

so that they can be used across the entire site collection. They can also be defined at the root of a sub-site and then be used in the sub-site and its children. Columns can also be shared across your entire environment when they are used in Content Types that are shared via a Content Type hub. Columns at the root of a site collection or site are called Site Columns, but the context of "site" depends on whether you are at the root site of the collection or a sub-site. Columns can also be defined in an individual list or library. In this case, they are usable only within that list or library, and they are typically referred to as "local" or List Columns. Column labels are scoped to the location where they "live," but behind the scenes each Column has a unique identifier called a GUID. Though you might have a local Column called Document Type in each of two different libraries, the values for Document Type are not shared across the two libraries and you have really created two different Columns with two different GUIDs behind the scenes. To avoid Column name confusion, especially if you want to share values across more than one list, library, or site, you should try to create most Columns at the highest possible level in your collection—at the root of the site collection where the values are scoped to a single site collection or in a Content Type hub where you want to share values and labels more broadly. (But please keep reading, because there are even more variations for sharing Columns and Column values.)

You will need to plan how you will use these features across your entire solution as well as in individual sites, lists, and libraries. Metadata planning requires careful thought and a significant interest in details. However, a wonderful feature of SharePoint is that your metadata architecture can evolve and grow as your business and knowledge about user needs change. Your metadata architecture should be thoughtfully planned, but you do not have to agonize over every decision that you make. Put a stake in the ground, try it out, and continue to monitor your solution over time.

Content Types

It is often difficult to find related information when you are searching through a large repository. For example, let's assume that you need to create a project plan for a new project and you know that there have been other projects similar to yours in the past. In a portal with many project team sites, it can be challenging to find all of the project plans. Content Types in SharePoint help simplify this task. If you define Project Plan as a Content Type, you can then find all project plans in your portal easily with a single search. Content Types also let you associate specific Columns with different types of content. For example, you can associate an Effective Date with a Policy but not with other types of documents. If you share and manage the Policy Content Type across your entire farm, you can ensure that all policy documents, created in any site collection, will have Effective Date as an attribute. You can also share a Column in *all* Content Types, such as a Records Retention Code.

A Content Type contains these elements:

- **Metadata (Site Columns).** Every Content Type has an associated set of Columns or attributes. A specific Column might be required in one Content Type and not required in another. You cannot define default values for Columns based on the Content Type in which they are used, just which Columns are associated with the Content Type. The values for a particular metadata Column are defined for the Column, not the Content Type. If the values for a particular Column are unique to a Content Type, consider defining a separate, unique Column that is associated with a particular Content Type.

- **Properties.** When a user edits a Microsoft Office document in SharePoint 2013, a Document Information Panel is displayed at the top of the document. The Document Information Panel provides a convenient way to update the document's properties. You can configure a custom Document Information Panel using InfoPath 2013, which would allow you to, for example, create a custom document creation experience for different types of users.

- **Template.** Document (or Column) templates can be used to create files with predefined styles and boilerplate content. You can assign one unique document template to each Content Type. For example, you can associate a predefined Excel spreadsheet for a Content Type called Expense Report. You can have only one template for each Content Type, but you can add multiple Content Types to a single library to make different templates available in one location. For example, in the Expense Report library you could have a Content Type for Expense Report: Travel and a different one for Expense Report: Entertainment, each with its own template to capture different metadata, support different layouts, or trigger separate workflows if needed.

- **Workflows.** Some Content Types have a consistent process that can be assigned for approval. For example, all status reports may have to be routed to the project manager before they can be published on the portal. A workflow can be associated with a particular Content Type. Workflows can be triggered automatically based on a specific event or manually with a user's action.
- **Information management policies.** Your organization may have rules about how particular Content Types should be managed. This is particularly useful for records management. You can associate policies with a Content Type to manage characteristics such as retention period.

You can also associate workflows, properties, templates, and policies directly in a list or library. However, when you associate these items locally, they are not reusable, even within a specific site.

Content Types are organized in a hierarchy that allows one Content Type to inherit characteristics from another Content Type in a parent-child relationship. For example, while a memo is an "instance" of a document, if your organization wants users to leverage a standard template when creating a memo, you will want to create a new Memo Content Type as a child of the parent Document Content Type. The Memo Content Type can inherit all of the properties of the Document Content Type but can leverage a different template.

As a general rule, define Content Types at the highest possible level in your solution so that they are reusable and manageable across the entire solution:

- If you want a Content Type to be available to a specific site (and its sub-sites), define it in the site Content Type gallery.
- If you want a Content Type to be available to all sites in a site collection, define it in the site *collection* Content Type gallery.
- If you want to create a Content Type to be used across multiple site collections (at the enterprise level), define a site collection to be a Content Type hub. The Content Types created in the hub can then be associated with each site collection using the Managed Metadata Service. Once an enterprise Content Type is published, it can't be changed within the local site collection.

As you might imagine, if you are going to define metadata at the enterprise level, you are potentially introducing the need for a new governance role—an enterprise information architect or metadata planning group. Someone (or some group) in the organization should be responsible for planning and managing enterprise-level Content Types and other shared metadata. This does not have to be a full-time job (though it may be in large organizations), but the role will clearly need to be defined in someone's job description.

As much art as science is required to determine what Content Types you need in your solution. Consider the following when you are planning Content Types for the enterprise, site collection, or individual site:

- Does this type of content have unique requirements based on the Content Type elements listed previously?
- Should this Content Type be available across the entire enterprise or in one site collection or one site? For example, if your organization has implemented a records management policy, you may want to add a Records Retention Code to one or all enterprise Document Content Types and make it a required field. This will ensure that users will assign a Records Retention Code to all content assets.
- Would a user want to search for this type of content uniquely? For example, if you think that your users might want to be able to search for all project plans in your portal, no matter who publishes the document, you will want to create a unique Content Type called Project Plan. However, if IT project plans have a different template or workflow from Accounting project plans, you will want to create a parent Content Type called Project Plan and two children Content Types, perhaps called IT Project Plan and Accounting Project Plan.
- Many users find that having too many unique Content Types creates more confusion than value. A smaller number of Content Types is probably better, especially for document repositories.

The Content Types that you define will be very specific to your organization; however, here are a few examples of the types of documents for which you might want to create unique Content Types:

- Article
- Brochure
- Case study
- Job description
- Lesson learned
- Policy

- Project plan
- Sales report
- Trip report

Figure 6-16 shows a simple example of how Content Types can inherit metadata (Column) values from their parent.

Columns

Columns are basically the lowest level of your SharePoint metadata architecture. The "container" in SharePoint where metadata attributes are defined is called a column, but a SharePoint Column is an attribute or property of a list or library. Columns allow you to define descriptive attributes for documents

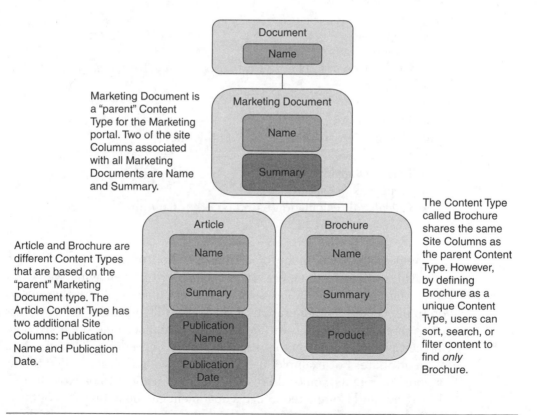

Marketing Document is a "parent" Content Type for the Marketing portal. Two of the site Columns associated with all Marketing Documents are Name and Summary.

Article and Brochure are different Content Types that are based on the "parent" Marketing Document type. The Article Content Type has two additional Site Columns: Publication Name and Publication Date.

The Content Type called Brochure shares the same Site Columns as the parent Content Type. However, by defining Brochure as a unique Content Type, users can sort, search, or filter content to find *only* Brochure.

Figure 6-16 Content Types and Columns: working together to organize content and improve reuse

or lists. In a document library, the file name is one of the default Columns, but as we discussed earlier, the name alone is usually not descriptive enough to help organize content in a document library. If you want to be able to get insights from your content or even group and organize your documents in meaningful ways, you will need to create custom Columns that are relevant to the type of content you are trying to organize. Going back to the music library example, if your songs were stored in SharePoint, Song would be the Content Type, and Artist, Composer, Genre, and Release Date are examples of the Columns that you could use to describe each individual song. People often use the term *metadata* to mean the Columns in your list or library even though technically Content Types are metadata, too.

Columns can be defined at the site collection or site level and can be inherited by child sites or defined locally in a library or list. Columns have a name and a type, such as

- Single line of text
- Multiple lines of text
- Choice (menu to choose from: drop-down, check box, radio button)
- Number
- Currency
- Date and time
- Lookup (information already on this site)
- Yes/No (check box)
- Person or group
- Hyperlink or picture
- Calculated (calculation based on other Columns)
- Managed metadata

There are other Column types that are used primarily in publishing sites, which you can learn more about in Chapter 14, "Managing Web Content." Managed metadata is a special type of choice Column that allows you to define and use a hierarchical set of centrally managed terms across your entire SharePoint infrastructure or just within a single site collection. Choice Columns allow you to present users with a predefined list of values for an attribute. For example, if you want to have a Column called Status for your documents, you could restrict the list of choices to be Not Started, In Progress, and Completed. Since a document can be in only one of those states, you would further restrict the choice Column to be a drop-down or single-choice Column. "Regular" choice Columns can have only a flat list of values. Managed metadata, on the other hand, allows you to store attributes in a hierarchy that can be up to seven layers deep. Refer to the "Managed Metadata" section later in this chapter for additional information about this special type of Column.

Even if you are not using managed metadata to share values for Columns, you should still consider creating all Columns as Site Columns at the top site in a site collection. Managing Columns centrally allows you to automatically propagate new values to any library or list that uses that Site Column. For example, if you maintain a list of offices centrally in a "global" (site-collection-level) Site Column called Office and you open a new office, you have to update the list of offices in only one place if Office is a Site Column at the top level of your site collection. You can also use lookup Columns with reference lists supplying value choices. Unlike managed metadata, lookup Columns are scoped to an individual site collection, and if you need to use a lookup Column across your entire site collection, you must create the list and the Column that "looks up to it" at the top or root site. Of course, you may also want to manage Office as a managed metadata term if it makes sense to share these values across multiple site collections or if you want to maintain an office hierarchy by country or state. Deciding the best structure for your metadata requires knowledge of the domain and business purpose, but it is also possible to evolve your metadata architecture over time.

Effectively planning your Content Types and Columns can make or break the effectiveness of your SharePoint solution. It's very frustrating to look at solutions in organizations that have been "experimenting" with SharePoint by essentially throwing the platform at users without providing any support for metadata architecture design. What typically happens is that users tend to use the same structures they are used to—folders—as the only method for organizing content rather than exploring the multiple ways of collecting and organizing content that are enabled by assigning just a few Columns and Content Types. While SharePoint supports the concept of folders in document libraries, folders can be a restrictive way of organizing content because a piece of content can "live" in only one folder. By contrast, the same document can be classified into multiple "groups" using Columns. For example, Columns allow you to create views that group the documents in your document library by author (to associate a document that was written by Sue and Scott and then find all of the documents written or cowritten by Sue) or all of the documents for the West region or all of the documents written by Sue for the West region. Folders do have a new role to play in your information architecture, but they are not necessarily the best organizing principle for your content (see the earlier sidebar on folders for a discussion about when you should consider using folders in your document libraries).

In addition to planning whether or not you will use folders to organize your content, another very common IA dilemma is whether to use multiple Content Types in a document library to identify the types of documents in the library or whether to use a single content type with a Column called something like Document Type to differentiate the different types of documents. There is no right answer to the "Content Type versus Document Type" or "Content Type versus Column" decision, but Table 6-2 summarizes some of the pros and cons of each method for organizing the types of documents in a document library.

Table 6-3 provides a list of metadata Column best practices to help guide you in the choices you need to make regarding metadata Column labels and values.

Table 6-2 Choosing between Multiple Content Types and a Single Content Type in a Library

	Multiple Content Types	One Content Type with a Document Type Column
Pros	You can have different Columns for different types of content—and still keep all the content in the same document library.	Users do not have to choose the Content Type when they upload—and you can make Document Type a required Column.
	You can have a different template for each type of document in the library.	You can use a "group by" view to organize documents.
	You can share the same structure across multiple document libraries and multiple site collections by sharing reusable Content Types in a hub.	Much simpler concept for users to understand.
	You can apply different workflows and retention policies based on each unique Content Type.	Easy to modify in bulk in a Quick Edit (formerly Datasheet) view.
	Provides scalable long-term flexibility.	
Cons	Users often miss the option to select the Content Type when they upload a document to a document library. Unless the default Content Type is very obviously not relevant, users often forget to "switch" the default to the more appropriate choice.	You can't use a template to create a new document other than the default one for the document library.
	You can't use a "group by" view to group documents by Content Type.	No ability to automatically assign different workflows to different documents based on Content Type.
	You can't change the value of Content Type in the Quick Edit (formerly called the Datasheet) view, so it is hard to update in bulk.	Not as flexible over the long term.

Table 6-3 Metadata Column Best Practices

Best Practice	Recommendation
Identify universal metadata applied to all content assets.	Many organizations require a records retention code for all document (and some other content) assets. This is the most consistently applied "universal" metadata attribute we see in practice. Some organizations also find it helpful to require an owner and a revision date attribute for all documents. This helps identify the person responsible for the content (who may or may not be the author) and determine content freshness.
Limit the number of required Columns.	One of the most important Column-related decisions you will make is determining which Columns should be required. The following are recommended guidelines for determining which and how many Columns should be required: • If the site is primarily used to publish information (a small number of content contributors with a large number of readers), make all content classification decisions based on whether or not the user will use the value to find or filter results. In this scenario, don't worry too much about whether or not you have too many required Columns. Remember, if users can find content more easily with better content classification, content owners or managers will have fewer phone calls requesting information that distract them from their daily work. Since it's their job to provide information, they usually won't mind if they have to spend additional time entering required fields for documents. • If the site is a collaboration site where the objective is to get users to change their behavior from storing reusable assets on their local or shared drive and putting them in a team site or publishing page on the portal, assume that most users will have about 15 seconds of patience available when they are saving or uploading content. That means that you'll probably be able to have at most five required Columns. • When applicable, include thoughtful default values so that users have to enter a Column value only if their content is different from the expected norm. This is an example of a scenario where you may want to consider creating a folder structure for your content. For example, if you have a large repository of project deliverables and each document needs to have an associated project name, you can create a folder for each project and assign a default value for Project Name that is unique for each folder. This will make it easier for users to comply with a requirement to post their deliverables in the repository because they will not have to add Project Name as an attribute. This may seem contradictory given that as a general rule, we don't like to encourage the use of folders in document libraries. However, as you can see, there are some scenarios where the use of folders for metadata "inheritance" will give you a "best of both worlds" capability to find and share content.

(continues)

Table 6-3 Metadata Column Best Practices *(continued)*

Best Practice	Recommendation
Follow the basic principles of good data design.	Make sure that • Each metadata property is unique and that each property is really necessary to describe the content. • List values represent a single category of knowledge. For example, a Column defining Color might include values such as Red, Blue, and Green, but not an entry such as Plaid. Instead, define a second category for Pattern to present values such as Stripes, Polka Dots, and Plaid. • The list of values for an attribute is complete, so that users are not forced to pick an inaccurate field. • Choice values in a drop-down list are mutually exclusive. • Required Columns are listed first for data entry if they do not have a default value. • Default values are entered judiciously. Many users accept default values without reading them. This unconscious choice can skew filtering and search results. • The use of "fill-in" fields in list choices is avoided where possible.
Use descriptive, meaningful labels.	Try to use terms that your users will recognize. Do not make up a label value—use the "regular" term if that's what people know.
Use singular nouns for Column names.	For example, use Document Type, not Document Types.
Use a logical order in value lists.	For the most part, list values should be in alphabetical order to help users quickly scan items. If you need to sequence or sort lists using another sort order, you can insert a number in front of a text term, for example, 1-Design, 2-Development, 3-Train, 4-Deploy. Note that you can create a custom display order for managed metadata, so this guideline applies only to Site and list Column values that are not derived from managed metadata term sets.
Avoid using "None," "N/A," or "Other" as metadata values if possible.	If you must use these options, add them to the end of your metadata list, even if the value is out of alphabetical order. If you need to include "Other," consider using a fill-in option to allow users to capture a different value. Beware that this may degrade the effectiveness of a choice list if users add alternate values such as an acronym for an existing value option. List/library owners should be trained to monitor lists with this option periodically to ensure that data is cataloged effectively.
Consider using a Summary attribute in document libraries (and encourage users to fill it in).	Adding a brief description/summary (abstract) to documents helps users quickly scan a list of documents to see if they are relevant.

Enterprise Keywords: the "Folksonomy" Column

Document libraries in SharePoint 2010 and 2013 include the ability to enable a special type of enterprise managed metadata Column called enterprise keywords. Unlike other managed metadata, enterprise keywords are stored in a single, flat list in a system term set called Keywords. In other words, there is no hierarchy of enterprise keywords. This Column can be added as part of a Content Type, or it can be enabled in a setting called Enterprise Metadata and Keywords Settings for a document library. If you enable enterprise keywords, users who have content contribution privileges can associate one or more keywords of their own choice to a document. These attributes are best thought of as "sort of controlled" because as with other types of managed metadata, enterprise keyword values are displayed with a "type-ahead" feature so that when a user starts typing, keywords entered previously by other users are displayed. However, users don't *have* to select a previously entered term, and they don't have to spell any new terms they enter correctly. In fact, you cannot restrict the values—these are truly user-generated attributes. Newly entered terms become part of the overall list of enterprise keywords that become available for everyone in the organization to reuse. (The administrator for the portal can update or delete enterprise keywords.) If enterprise keywords are enabled, they essentially allow content contributors to create their own attribute tags for a document.

In SharePoint 2013, there are thus three ways an attribute can be assigned to a document:

- When a content contributor or editor selects or adds a value in a Column defined by the content designer. This is a form of authoritative metadata; it is assigned by the content contributor in a structured field.
- When a content consumer assigns a social tag to a document. A social tag can be any value entered by the user using the Tags and Notes property in the document library ribbon. As the user starts typing a value, SharePoint provides a list of previously used social terms (from the same term set used by enterprise keywords), and the user can select from this list. Since any user can add social metadata, these tags (or keywords) are not considered authoritative.

- When a content editor adds an enterprise keyword. Enterprise keywords are authoritative tags because they are added by users with content-editing privileges, but the source of their values includes both the managed terms for the site as well as the social data values used by other content contributors and visitors. You can think of enterprise keywords as social tags assigned by a content editor.

Like any other Column, enterprise keywords help users find content in a library. However, unlike other Columns, the values of enterprise keywords are more flexible and less structured, which provides a very dynamic way to quickly react to evolving terms, opportunities, and emerging business needs.

More than one enterprise keyword can be assigned to the same document. By default, enterprise keywords act like a check box attribute. However, there are some conventions that must be used to assign enterprise keywords:

- Separate values with semicolons.
- Do not use commas to separate values. Commas in a list of enterprise keywords will automatically be replaced with semicolons; so, for example, if you enter "X, Y, and Z" as your keyword, SharePoint will replace your entry with three separate values (and the third will be called "and Z").
- Use "&" or spaces to separate words that should be combined as a single keyword.

Managed Metadata

As mentioned earlier, managed metadata is a special type of Column that allows you to create a hierarchy of options as choices. In addition, when you select managed metadata as a Column type, you can manage the value list centrally even if you are not using centrally managed Content Types. Note that managed metadata is not available in SharePoint Foundation 2013. It is available only with the enterprise versions of SharePoint, whether on-premises or online. In SharePoint 2010, information architects had to make trade-offs when they wanted to use managed metadata for a Column because you were not able to edit managed metadata in a Datasheet view (which is called the Quick Edit view in SharePoint 2013). In SharePoint 2013, managed metadata can be edited in the Quick Edit (or Datasheet) view, which allows you to make changes to any type of metadata in bulk using features available in spreadsheets like dragging a value across adjacent rows.

With managed metadata, you can create a "local" label for a shared list of values. For example, one part of your organization may refer to your external partners as Business Partners. Another part of the organization may call them Third-Party Organizations. A third part may call them Vendors. Even in an ideal world, each part of the company may have valid reasons for referring to these external parties by different names, even though the actual values—the names of the external companies—are the same. In SharePoint 2007, you would have had to try to get everyone to agree to the same label and values and used either manual processes, custom code, or third-party products to ensure that everything stayed synchronized across multiple sites and site collections. With managed metadata, you can create a shared list of values once, use the *values* to group similar content in search results, but allow each department to refer to the "external people who might be business partners, vendors, or third-party organizations" by whichever Column label makes sense in their context.

There are a few important terms that are used to describe managed metadata:

- A *term* is the word or phrase that is associated with an item. Terms are the values that you select when you assign managed metadata to an item.
- A *term set* is a collection of related terms. Term sets belong to a *term set group*. When you define a Column as being of the type Managed Metadata, you associate the Column with a particular term set and restrict its values to the values in the term set.
- A *local term set* is created in the context of an individual site collection. Its values are visible only to users who have access to the site collection.
- A *global term set* is created outside the context of a site collection. What makes managed metadata special is that you can maintain the values for the terms separately from the Column itself. And you can delegate responsibility for managing the term set to someone who wouldn't otherwise have Full Control privileges in the libraries where the term set is used. So, for example, the overall term store administrator could create a term set called Offices and designate a person in the facilities department to manage and maintain that group.

Managed metadata is "consumed" in a Managed Metadata Service. You must have at least one Managed Metadata Service to share Content Types and term sets across more than one site collection.

The Term Store Management Tool is used to create and manage terms and term sets. You can use this tool to

- Create a new term set or delete one that is no longer needed.
- Add, change, or remove terms.
- Create a hierarchy for terms and identify which terms in the hierarchy can be used to assign tags to content and which terms are just used for grouping terms. (You typically will want to use only the lowest level in the term hierarchy for tagging.)
- Define alternate terms (synonyms) so that if users use different terms for the same thing or you are introducing a new term to replace an old one, "taggers" will be able to use their familiar term to find a tag but the new authoritative term will actually be assigned to the document. Note that the synonyms that you define for terms in a term set are not automatically available as search synonyms. Search synonyms must be configured independently, as described in Chapter 16, "Planning Enterprise Search."
- Import terms from an existing list. Unless you have only a few terms to add to your term set, you will probably want to use the import capability to add your terms. You act on each term independently in the Term Store Management Tool, so while it is convenient to use for updates to existing terms, you will not want to use it to add a large collection of terms.
- Predefine enterprise keywords. If you already know that there are some common terms that your users will want to associate with documents, you can add some enterprise keywords in advance to create consistent spelling and formatting. For example, if your organization is an engineering firm, consider adding enterprise keywords for each of the major engineering disciplines used in your work.

There are some helpful worksheets on the Microsoft Web site that you can use to document and plan potential term sets for your solution. You can download the Term Set Planning Worksheet at http://technet.microsoft .com/en-us/library/ee519604.aspx. Table 6-4 shows how this worksheet could be used to organize a small set of sports-related products. (The list of

Table 6-4 Planning a Term Set

Sports Product Term Set	Level 2	Level 3	Level 4	Description	Available for Tagging	Synonym of
Golf					No	
Golf	Bags				Yes	
Golf	Balls					
Golf	Books					
Golf	Clothing & Shoes					
Golf	Clothing & Shoes	Shirts			No	
Golf	Clothing & Shoes	Shirts	Short-sleeved shirt	Short-sleeved shirt without a collar	Yes	T-shirt
Golf	Clothing & Shoes	Shirts	Long-sleeved shirt		Yes	
Golf	Clothing & Shoes	Shirts	Polo shirt	Short-sleeved shirt with a collar	Yes	
Golf	Clothing & Shoes	Pants			No	
Golf	Clothing & Shoes	Pants	Short pants	Appropriate for warm weather	Yes	Shorts Capris
Golf	Clothing & Shoes	Pants	Long pants	Appropriate for colder days on the course	Yes	
Exercise & Fitness					No	
Exercise & Fitness	Boxing				Yes	
Exercise & Fitness	Yoga				Yes	

product names was borrowed from eBay.) As part of the planning exercise for a term set, you will want to look for existing places where potential term set values are stored (such as product lists, regional office lists, or department lists) and organize the values into a meaningful hierarchy. This process should include a data cleanup exercise where you will remove duplicates and rationalize terms (select one term to be the primary value and then identify synonyms for alternative values). Standardizing terms may require negotiating. When it is clear that differences are minor (such as different abbreviations or spellings for the same value), our best advice is to use the "get over it" approach—pick a primary term, make the others synonyms, and move on with your life.

Figure 6-17 shows the first step in creating a new term set. This tool can be accessed from either central administration or from within Site Settings if you have the appropriate permissions. The Term Set Name and

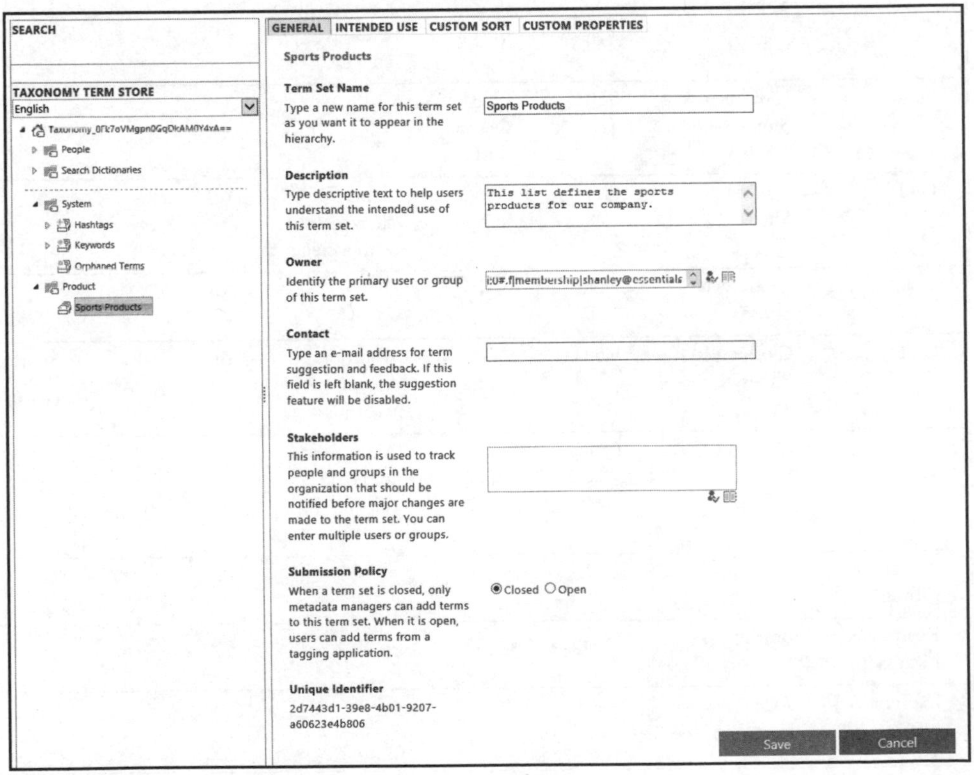

Figure 6-17 Create a term set

Description are identified, along with an Owner, a Contact, Stakeholders who should be notified before major changes are made to the term set, and whether or not new terms can be added to the term set.

Figure 6-18 shows the new Intended Use tab. This allows you to specify whether a term set is intended to be used for tagging, as in this example, or for managed navigation (see Chapter 14, "Managing Web Content").

If you plan to manually add terms, or if you need to assign synonyms for terms after you have imported a term set, you will use the term properties editing screen shown in Figure 6-19. For parent terms in the hierarchy, you will see an additional tab called Custom Sort that will allow you to specify a custom sort order to child terms. Using a custom sort order ensures that terms appear in consistent order, even if the default label for a term is changed.

Figure 6-20 shows how the product term set appears to users when it has been associated with a Column called Product in a document library. In this example, you can see an instance where the user is attempting to assign a Product value of "T-shirt" to the document. Notice that since

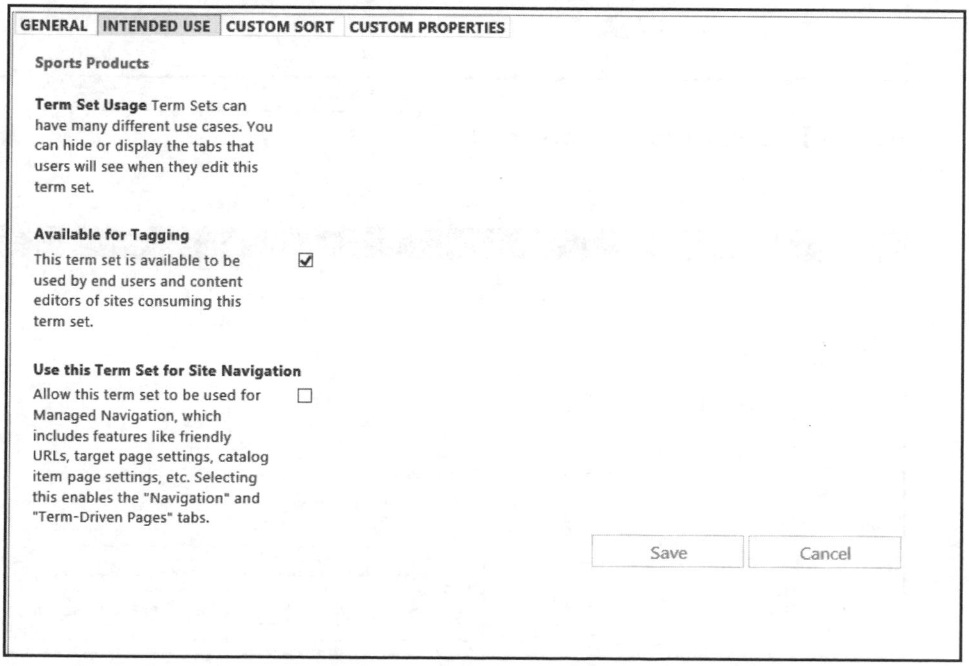

| GENERAL | INTENDED USE | CUSTOM SORT | CUSTOM PROPERTIES |

Sports Products

Term Set Usage Term Sets can have many different use cases. You can hide or display the tabs that users will see when they edit this term set.

Available for Tagging
This term set is available to be used by end users and content editors of sites consuming this term set. ☑

Use this Term Set for Site Navigation
Allow this term set to be used for Managed Navigation, which includes features like friendly URLs, target page settings, catalog item page settings, etc. Selecting this enables the "Navigation" and "Term-Driven Pages" tabs. ☐

Save   Cancel

Figure 6-18 Define the intended use for the term set

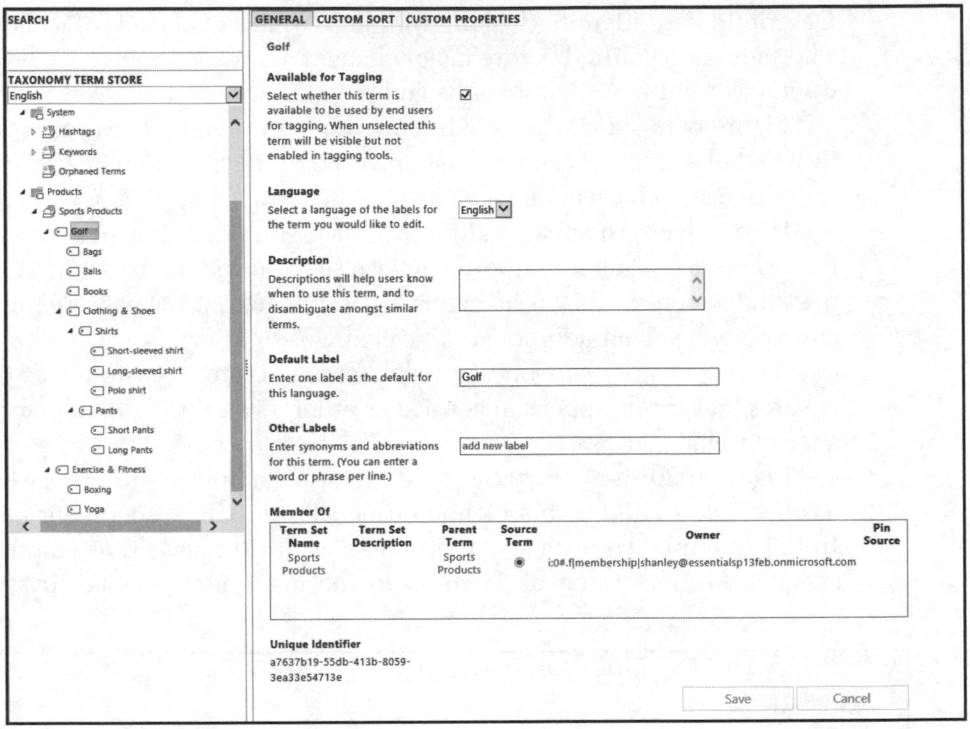

Figure 6-19 Define terms in the term set

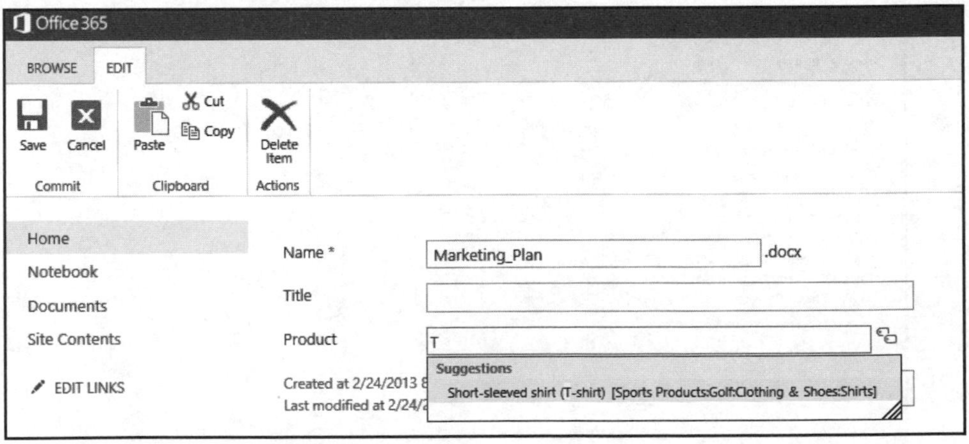

Figure 6-20 Synonyms help users use familiar terms to assign metadata

"T-shirt" has been declared a synonym for "Short-sleeved shirt," this term is "available" as a tag. The actual tag value that gets assigned to the document is "Short-sleeved shirt," not "T-shirt," because "Short-sleeved shirt" is the primary term.

One of the best features of managed metadata terms is that when you manage term values in a term set and you change the value of a term for any reason, the value will be updated automatically in all the locations where you have used that term. For example, let's say that you accidentally typed Puter instead of Putter when attempting to add metadata to a collection of golf-related documents. By the time you realize that the term has been misspelled, several hundred documents have been added and assigned the incorrect term. When you change the spelling of Puter to Putter in the term set, all of the documents with the incorrect spelling will be automatically corrected, *even if you don't open them.* This feature will be particularly useful in organizations like pharmaceutical firms where a drug starts out as a compound and may get several interim names before it gets an official brand name prior to public launch. When the drug is approved, a single change to the term store is all that it takes to assign all content tagged Compound ABC to Blockbuster Drug. The term Compound ABC can also be added as a *search* synonym for Blockbuster Drug so that a single search for either term will return all relevant documents, even if the document metadata or content has not been updated with the new managed term. This feature alone should encourage you to carefully plan your use of managed metadata and who will be allowed to make changes to it.

It may not be necessary to run out and hire a consultant to support this process (though it's not a bad idea for your first deployment). If your organization has a corporate library staffed with someone with a library science degree, you already have a great resource with the relevant knowledge and experience to guide the planning and implementation of your managed terms hierarchy.

Metadata and Search

In SharePoint 2010, search recognized managed metadata in search results and automatically created search refiners based on those attributes. If you wanted to see additional attributes (nonmanaged metadata) as search refiners, you had to configure them manually. With SharePoint 2013, none of your content attributes are automatically "promoted" as search refiners and so you must be much more intentional about determining which attributes of your content should be "promoted" as refiners in search results. This means that you really need to commit to spend time planning and configuring the user experience for search and should incorporate this effort into your project plan. We discuss how to create search refiners in Chapter 16, "Planning Enterprise Search." Use the following suggestions to help determine which properties should be added as search refiners:

- SharePoint automatically creates refiners for Result Type, Author, and Modified Date. You will need to determine which additional attributes will be helpful as refiners.
- If you have attributes that you are using in all content types, such as Business Unit or Geography, it makes sense to create refiners for these attributes.
- If you have an attribute that you use in a lot of document libraries, like Topic, this value will also be a good candidate for a search refiner. Many if not all of your managed metadata properties will be good candidates for search refiners.
- You do not actually have to have metadata to create a search refiner; you can also use the entity extraction feature of SharePoint search to extract terms from content and then create refiners from these terms. Using this capability requires a detailed understanding of the content and user scenarios, but the capability is extremely helpful when you want to try to extract a structure from a large number of unstructured documents.

Maintaining Your Information Architecture

Ideally, when you first deploy your new SharePoint solution, the information architecture is well structured and content is appropriately cataloged because designers and application sponsors have taken a lot of time to ensure that the initial implementation is successful. Over time, new content enters the system, along with new sites, and if you aren't careful, the well-structured information architecture devolves into chaos. When the information architecture becomes less relevant, so do the applications that depend on it. When that happens, users become frustrated and management wonders why they continue to make investments in the solution.

Even though features such as managed metadata give you more opportunities to control your information architecture, it is still important to pay attention to your IA to ensure that it evolves with your business and user needs. There are many reasons that an information architecture can degrade over time. The key to overcoming the challenges associated with maintaining your information architecture is to recognize up front that maintaining your information architecture requires a continual investment. Building a successful information architecture is not a "build it once and walk away" process. There are several business process recommendations that can help you manage and maintain your information architecture. Table 6-5 provides a list of some of the reasons an information architecture can degrade over time and proposes several mitigating strategies to overcome these problems.

Table 6-5 Recommended Actions to Maintain Your Information Architecture

Problems	Solutions
Site owners may incorrectly assign Column values to content, or when users can't find a "bucket" in which to place their new content, they may put it in a "Miscellaneous" topic, which makes searches and queries far more difficult.	Assign content managers (or content stewards) to ensure that new content is assigned appropriate metadata values. Content managers can be domain experts who allocate a portion of their time to review new contributions to the site or library.
	Content managers can also be librarians, specialists who help design meaningful taxonomies, tag content as it appears, and maintain the information architecture over time.
	Leverage automated classification software if the volume of content is too large for librarians to study and classify manually.
When the system allows users to add Column values of their own, they may create a redundant value or concept.	Establish governance policies for managing the information architecture's structure and adding new documents to document libraries, adding new Site Columns, and adding new Column values. Use managed metadata to control list values.
	Governance policies should define who does which tasks, procedures for performing tasks, and feedback mechanisms for suggesting changes and improvements.
New terms may get added that are merely synonyms for existing terms, creating unnecessary redundancy.	You can also define synonyms for managed terms as shown in the Other Labels attribute in Figure 6-19.

(continues)

Table 6-5 Recommended Actions to Maintain Your Information Architecture *(continued)*

Problems	Solutions
The organization can change direction so that the information architecture becomes less relevant to the business.	Revise the information architecture on a regular basis. At a minimum, conduct an information architecture review once a year (or more frequently if content is being added continuously or major organizational or business changes have occurred). Note that this is less likely to happen if you organize your sites functionally as recommended in the site architecture section, but either way, conducting periodic usability tests is a great way to make sure that your information architecture is still relevant.
Old or irrelevant content may remain in the solution because content owners are not actively engaged in a content recertification process.	Maintain the content itself by archiving old documents and monitoring content usage so that content that is not current or is no longer relevant does not appear in search results. Consider mandating at least an annual content recertification process as part of your content management governance strategy.

Key Points

Keep the following key points in mind as you plan your information architecture:

- Effectively planning and deploying an information architecture for your solution should be an iterative process. Assume that you will not get it right the first time out of the gate, and plan to engage users in a series of deployment reviews to evolve the architecture based on user needs and organizational changes over time.
- Conduct usability tests before you deploy your solution to make sure that your information architecture makes sense to users, and conduct usability tests at least annually as your solution matures.
- Leverage Content Types and Columns to manage metadata, using inheritance to propagate changes throughout the solution.
- Take advantage of the enterprise metadata management features, especially the ability to share Content Types across site collections and the ability to create managed metadata terms.

- Allocate time to plan search and configure search refiners when you are creating your solution design.
- Emphasize the user experience over the content contributor experience in most information architecture trade-off decisions.
- Ensure that maintaining your information architecture is a continuous investment—don't assume that you can design your architecture and walk away. The information architecture and portal content need continuous nurturing in order to remain relevant and valuable.
- Consider adding a new role to your solution team for an enterprise information architect (or enterprise "taxonomist") to ensure that someone is accountable for ensuring that your information architecture is maintained.

CHAPTER 7

PLANNING YOUR ADOPTION STRATEGY

The most important step for planning your adoption strategy is making sure you have a solution worth adopting! It doesn't make much sense to focus on planning adoption until you are absolutely certain that your proposed solution addresses a critical business need. While this may seem like an unusual way to begin a chapter on adoption, consider this: people don't get promoted because their solution is "adopted." People get promoted because their solution delivers business *value*—because they produce meaningful and measureable business results. As you think about adoption and what it means for your organization, do not be fooled into thinking that a metric such as "800 (or 8,000) contributions from 200 different users in 6 months" means your solution is successful. While this kind of measure might *seem* to indicate that the solution is "adopted," interest and activity alone do not necessarily mean that organizational performance has improved. For this reason, we will sum up the entire message of this chapter in a single thought: the real secret of user adoption for your Share Point 2013 solution is making sure that the solution solves a meaningful organizational problem—and that it does so in a significantly better way than the alternative solutions that may be available. While there may be a small portion of your users who are excited by new technology just because it is new, most users care about solving their practical, every-day business problems. If your solution solves these problems in a more effective way than any other alternative, you will achieve adoption and, more important, put your solution on a path to deliver business results. If your solution does not solve a key business problem, all the adoption planning in the world isn't going to make a difference.

This chapter could have been very short, especially since we've just given you the secret to adoption success—create solutions that solve real business problems. However, we know that even with a fantastic, easy-to-use SharePoint solution that addresses a critical business problem, user adoption may still be a challenge. Why? Because almost any time you ask people to *change*, even if it's ultimately going to make their lives much easier, you will get some resistance. Almost all change requires some "activation energy" to overcome initial resistance. You may have heard something like this during stakeholder interviews: "We don't *like* the current system, but we're *used* to it and it works for us." Kenneth Murphy, writer and former HR senior vice president at Altria Group, once said this about change: "Change is good—you go first." While the most important foundation for adoption planning is having a solution worth adopting, the next most important element in user adoption planning is thinking about how you will address the issue of change. As described in Chapter 2, "Planning Your Solution Strategy," involving your users in the design process helps to ensure that they will be engaged about the changes that they may need to make in order to achieve their business objectives. But involving your users in the design process may not be enough to ensure adoption. We will spend most of our time in this chapter sharing some practical ideas to help ensure that your solution will be adopted and your users will want to "go first" and change. Keep in mind that any of the approaches suggested in this chapter should be evaluated in the context of your own organizational goals and the goals of the specific solution you are building. Adoption is "personal." While we provide techniques that have worked in some organizations, just because they worked in one culture doesn't mean they will work for your culture—or for your specific situation. Make sure to evaluate every suggestion in the context of your solution and your organization. Don't be afraid to try something new, but make sure it's relevant to your situation. User adoption is far more challenging for internal solutions, so this chapter focuses almost exclusively on adoption of internally facing SharePoint solutions. If you are using SharePoint for an Internet-facing solution, the most important adoption criteria will be ease of use and overall design, topics that are addressed in Chapter 14, "Managing Web Content."

What's New in SharePoint 2013?

In general, features in SharePoint 2013 will not themselves help you get your solution adopted—it's what you *do* with the features to create great solutions that will make it easier to gain adoption. That said, SharePoint 2013 provides some new capabilities to make it easier for users to use SharePoint to get work done, which can be important elements of your solution and, therefore, your adoption plan. Some of the top features that will help deliver outcomes that add value to the user experience include the following:

- **Modern graphical user interface.** The out-of-the-box user interface for SharePoint has been streamlined to make it easier to present information in engaging ways. The Promoted Links app shown in Figure 7-1 makes it very easy to create engaging visual cues to help users navigate to content. Each link can have its own background image (which can be a photograph), title (such as "Link to Financial Reports for our business group"), and description that appears when you move your mouse over the "tile" (see Figure 7-2). The images in Figures 7-1 and 7-2 show examples of what the tiles view of a Promoted Links list looks like on a SharePoint page. You can use this type of app to help direct users to content on your site (such as documents or tasks) or off the site (such as a link to a frequently needed application system or Web site). Does "pimping" your site help encourage adoption? Not on its own, but a visually engaging site captures attention that will help direct users to the information

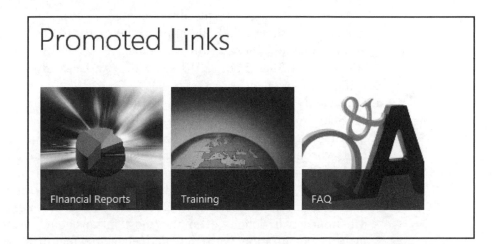

Figure 7-1 Example of how Promoted Links tiles look on a SharePoint 2013 site

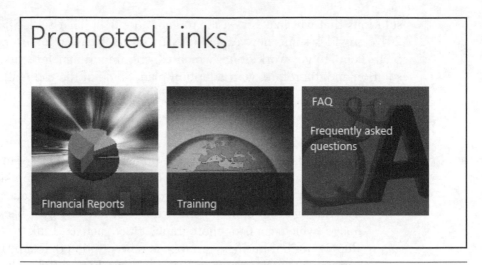

Figure 7-2 View that users see when they mouse over a link tile

that they need the most (assuming that you use this feature for just that purpose, of course).

- **Familiar social features.** SharePoint 2013 uses the same terminology and functionality that many users will be familiar with from Twitter and Facebook. For example, users can indicate agreement in the newsfeed and discussion lists with "likes"; evaluate document or discussion content with star ratings; follow sites, people, documents, or terms; direct content to others using @mentions and #hashtags; and add apps to their sites to easily integrate new capabilities. These features will make it easier for users to take advantage of SharePoint 2013 since they will already be familiar with the experience.

- **One vastly improved search engine for all.** Previous versions of SharePoint had different search engines. This presented information-finding challenges that created different experiences for users who leveraged versions of SharePoint in different organizations or even different contexts in the same organization. With SharePoint 2013, there is one search engine for all versions—the former FAST engine acquired by Microsoft in 2008. The SharePoint 2013 search experience will delight even the most intransigent curmudgeon in your organization with rich and engaging features, including document previews in the context of search results (including the ability to step through PowerPoint presentations), the ability to find a document in context with one click to the document library, and faceted navigation.

Note For more information about SharePoint 2013 search, refer to Chapter 16, "Planning Enterprise Search."

- **Simple sharing.** SharePoint 2013 makes it far easier to share documents both inside and outside the organization without the risk of users going "off the reservation" with tools like Dropbox to share confidential documents.
- **Project task tracking in one place.** Many organizations want to use SharePoint to manage project activities. SharePoint 2013 makes it much easier to get users to participate in project collaboration with features such as the visual project task timeline and the ability to automatically roll up all of your tasks from any project site to a consolidated personal task list that can be synchronized with Outlook. Figure 7-3 shows an example of the project summary timeline from a standard SharePoint 2013 team site with the project apps enabled.
- **Simple offline synchronization with SkyDrive Pro.** Your users are probably already very familiar with Microsoft's public file-sharing solution in SkyDrive. SharePoint 2013 brings a very similar

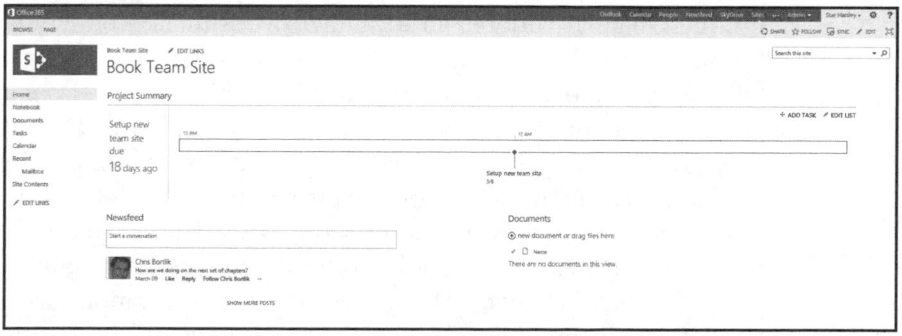

Figure 7-3 Project task list Web Part on a SharePoint 2013 team site

but more IT-friendly (i.e., manageable and secure) solution to the enterprise with SkyDrive Pro, making it easy for users to share content and take it offline.

■ **Enhanced discussion lists with recognition and reward capabilities.** The new Community Site template and the community features that can be enabled on any team site allow you to easily and visually recognize and reward contributions by community members. Even if you choose not to enable the "gamification" features in the community template, the new discussion list is much more engaging and includes "like" and "mention" capabilities to enrich the discussion experience. For your users who have viewed or contributed to an online forum, this will be a very similar experience that will encourage participation.

Why Is Adoption of New Solutions So Hard?

In 2004, Harvard marketing professor John Gourville published interesting research in the *Harvard Business Review* about the adoption of new products.[1] In the article, Gourville traced the commonly used phrase about building a "better mousetrap" to a quote from Ralph Waldo Emerson: "If a man can write a better book, preach a better sermon, or make a better mousetrap, than his neighbor, though he build his house in the woods, the world will make a beaten path to his door." Gourville concluded that this quote was compelling but wrong, noting that there are many examples of products that have offered an advantage over similar products in the market but haven't actually replaced them in popularity. In the article, Gourville talks about some of the reasons why it is so difficult to get people to adopt new products or technologies—even if they are better than those which they are replacing. The reasons all boil down to one important point: *we tend to overvalue the status quo*. New solutions, by definition, ask people to change the way they currently work. To get users to adopt something new, the new solution must either offer the user some benefit or help avoid a "cost." The challenge is that even if the new solution has a direct net benefit, it will almost always involve some degree of *loss*. In other words, if

---

1. John T. Gourville, "Why Consumers Don't Buy: The Psychology of New Product Adoption," Harvard Business School Note #504-056 (Boston: Harvard Business School Publishing, 2004).

I accept the new technology, I may have to give up something I am already comfortable with—such as an existing way of working; the new technology might also involve a new cost that must be incurred. Unfortunately, these losses represent significant psychological switching costs, which may not match the objective net benefit of the solution we have just developed. Gourville states, "More precisely, the adoption of an innovation almost always involves *giving up* things we currently have and *getting* other things we do not have."[2] This means that no matter how great your solution is, your users will have to change in order to use it. But, more important, since people inherently overvalue that which they already have or know over that which they don't have or don't know, getting people to make the transition to new technologies can be very difficult.

Gourville talks about the gap between the value perceived by the developer of a new solution and the value acknowledged by the consumer. Typically, developers or innovators overvalue what they are offering. Remember, if you are building the solution, you are already invested in the benefits. Once you are invested, it's often hard to look at the solution from the perspective of someone who is not as invested. On the other hand, consumers or users typically value the new solution in contrast to their status quo, which has a perceived "endowment" bias because it is what they already own or know. The gap between these two perceptions results in a compounding of biases that Gourville calls the "9X Problem." Simply put, the problem says that a new product has to offer at least a nine to ten times improvement over the incumbent solution in order for it to be easily or rapidly adopted. Since it is rare that you will be creating a solution that offers this much of an improvement, you need to find strategies to clearly demonstrate value, minimize resistance, and maybe even incent users to make the initial change and incorporate these strategies in your adoption plan.

The remainder of this chapter will explore several practical approaches that should be considered for your adoption plan:

- Design a solution that delights your users.
- Plan your deployment to optimize adoption success.
- Plan effective training to increase user comfort with the new solution.
- Carefully consider incentives and rewards.
- Design and implement persistent communications to engage users on an ongoing basis.

---

2. Ibid., 5.

Design a Solution That Delights

Designing a solution that meets business needs is clearly your most important goal. But there are solutions that just "answer the mail" and solutions that are truly designed to engage users in a meaningful way. Delighting your users will be less important for solutions that people are required to use—for example, to process an expense report or update a general ledger entry. But when you are implementing the types of collaboration and intranet solutions that people typically create with SharePoint, you have an additional challenge to think about—your users typically don't *have* to use the solution in order to get their work done. Unless you ban e-mail attachments, users can always send an attachment instead of the preferred approach of sending a link to the document in SharePoint. Users don't *have* to post questions to a newsfeed or a discussion list—they can also call someone, send an e-mail to a distribution list, or ask their manager for an answer. So, for these types of solutions—and this is especially important if you want to leverage the social features of SharePoint 2013—it's critical to make sure that you do more than just answer the mail; you also want to make your users *enjoy* the new way of working.

There are some great examples of organizations that have designed features into their SharePoint solutions that help decrease the activation energy required to try a new way of working. Microsoft has provided some great ones out of the box that you can leverage without much effort:

- Provide opportunities for users to give feedback.
- Provide contextual help and tips.
- Target content where it makes sense.
- Feature people and faces.
- Provide guidance and use cases for new capabilities—but in the context of how people already do their jobs.
- Create one list or library view for contributors and a different view for consumers of information.
- Pay attention to search.
- Create delightful content.
- Be mindful of feature abuse: just because you can, doesn't mean you should.
- "Prime the pump" by predefining keywords and terms that users are likely to use in their profiles.
- Eliminate "sharp edges" by carefully managing user permissions.

Provide Opportunities for Users to Give Feedback

Vancity is Canada's largest credit union. Their intranet has multiple "points of engagement" for users. One of the most unique is the search "Find-o-meter," which is a graphic that appears on the right-hand side of search results that asks users to rate the quality of the results that they got with their query. There are only three choices, ranging from "Awesome, it's like you read my mind," to "Okay, but Google still kicks our butt," to "Yikes, not even close. Waaaaaay off!" For all kinds of reasons, the reference to Google is probably not a good idea to copy, partly because there is virtually no way Google's page rank and optimization algorithms are going to kick the butt of the new SharePoint's search results in your organization. In addition, the team is sending a not-so-subtle message that even if the results are viewed as "Okay," Google's results would be better. This is not only untrue but also sends a very, very bad message about search results confidence to system users. But the concept is still great, and even more important, the "Find-o-meter" has a large open text box that asks users to help the team improve if the results are less than awesome by describing what they were looking for and what happened. Users can then optionally tick a box that asks if they want to get a response from a member of the intranet team.

At a large global pharmaceutical, the policy for all SharePoint sites is that a clearly identified site steward (day-to-day content manager) and site owner (business sponsor) must be listed on the home page of every site with links to their contact information. This helps drive home the important guiding principle that "we're all responsible for collaboration success." All team site visitors are encouraged to use the contact links to advise the site steward of any issues with the site or its content.

Note The site steward and site owner are two of the potential roles that are discussed in more detail in Chapter 4, "Planning for Business Governance."

Provide Contextual Help and Tips

One of the best ways to delight your users is to provide "just-in-time" help—in other words, to provide help in the context of the task rather than on a separate training site. There are some third-party tools that can do this, and you can also create your own context-sensitive help in page, list, and library templates. SharePoint 2013 includes a great example of context-sensitive help in the default search results page when no answers are returned. This page includes a hyperlink to tips for searching that are worth noting and including in your training programs. For example, the tips include explaining the conventions for making queries more (or less) specific by using logical operators such as AND, OR, and NOT and using wildcard characters (*). It is very possible that your users are not aware that Boolean operators and wildcards have been available in SharePoint search since SharePoint 2010, and they probably haven't used these capabilities in Google either—though they work in both contexts. For a direct link to these search tips, go to www .jornata.com/essentialsharepoint and be sure to check out the detailed tips for searching in the appendix of this book. You may also want to consider adding some "permanent" search tips to your search results page. Adding a few quick references to expanding searches with OR and narrowing searches with AND and using wildcards when you are not sure about spelling or extensions can be very helpful. You can also automatically provide additional context for search by creating custom search result "verticals" or scopes that help users restrict their search results to only a certain type or location for content.

Target Content Where It Makes Sense

Though not new to SharePoint 2013, the ability to target content to specific audiences is an underutilized SharePoint feature. When you are using SharePoint as the platform for your intranet, consider leveraging this feature to ensure that your home page in particular is more relevant to your users. If the home page provides more relevant information, users will be incented to open the intranet on a regular basis, not just to get the latest expense report form but to learn more about what is going in the organization. Many organizations allow users to choose the news channels that they would like on their home page; others "prescribe" the corporate news channel and let users choose additional channels; and others make assumptions based on role, geography, and/or business unit to explicitly target news, links, and other content. In most cases, users can elect to see additional information that was not explicitly targeted, but by ensuring that the most relevant information is front and center, users are more likely to want to engage.

Feature People and Faces

Humans are hard-wired to react to human faces and human stories. Leverage opportunities to associate pictures of people in news articles and feature stories about people, and strongly encourage your users to associate a picture with their user profiles. One of the simplest and easiest ways to engage and delight people is to give a human face (literally) to technology. The user profile picture brings a human face to virtually every interaction users have in SharePoint 2013—not just in their profile but also in many other places such as newsfeed postings and discussion lists. The use or choice of pictures in user profiles is often a hotly debated topic in governance discussions. As we discussed in Chapter 4, "Planning for Business Governance," you can and should provide guidance about user-provided pictures, and certainly allow users to opt out if they don't want their picture included. From an adoption perspective, forcing users to use their employee ID picture is almost never positively received, but this is definitely a topic for your governance plan.

Provide Guidance and Use Cases for New Capabilities—but in the Context of How People Already Do Their Jobs

A great way to delight users is to design a solution that is fully compatible with existing behavior—but makes it easier, faster, cheaper, or even just more fun to do that behavior. If you don't have to ask your users to make too many drastic changes to leverage the new solution, it will be easier to get them to adopt it. However, it also helps to provide guidance and examples to help people understand any differences and to manage expectations. This will be particularly helpful to encourage the adoption of the new social features of SharePoint 2013.

Create Different Views for Contributors and Consumers of Information

The messaging about the use of the "F" word (folders) in SharePoint has changed since the introduction of SharePoint 2010. As we discussed in Chapter 6, "Planning Your Information Architecture," folders should not be considered a dirty word when they can be used to automatically populate metadata into documents (to improve "findability"). However, if your solution is one where most users are viewers and only a few are contributors, you should strive to make default views without folders and create special "contribution" or "publishing" views for the people who will contribute content into folders. Even if you are using a team site where most people have both roles, having different views for consuming and contributing will make it much easier for users to make the shift from their trusty file shares to SharePoint to create a much more useful and delightful content experience.

Pay Attention to Search

Improving the ability to find information may be the one single shared goal of every SharePoint deployment. Finding information means making sure that search works, and even with the very delightful SharePoint 2013 search capabilities, you will still need to pay attention to search in order to delight your users on an ongoing basis. This means making sure that you have someone whose role includes monitoring search results to identify candidates for promoted results (formerly called best bets) and synonyms. Don't even think that you don't know what people are searching for. This isn't the Internet—this is your organization! You *know* what you do! If you are upgrading, you've got usage data you should have been looking at anyway, so if you haven't, now would be the time. If you are implementing SharePoint for the first time, consider some of these suggestions for how you can nurture the search experience to delight and engage your users:

- Does your company make products? Well, then have a promoted result for your products by name. Include a link to the product manager's user profile, the home page for that product on the intranet or Internet site, and other top content or sites relevant to that product. Do the same for other concepts (such as business units, frequently used forms or reports, key benefits, or even industry terms) that are relevant to your organization.
- Look at what people are searching for by examining the Top Queries by Day and Month report. This report shows the most popular search queries. Use this report to understand what types of information visitors are seeking.
- Find out what searches are not yielding great results by examining the Abandoned Queries by Day and Month report. This report shows popular search queries that received low click-through. Use this report to identify search queries that might create user dissatisfaction and to improve the discoverability of content. Then, consider using query rules to improve the query's results.
- Identify opportunities to configure search verticals, search results sources, and search refiners to improve the user search experience. Refer to Chapter 16, "Planning Enterprise Search," for additional suggestions about configuring search.

- Pay particular attention to the terms that yield no results by looking at the No Results Queries by Day and Month report. This report shows popular search queries that returned no results. Use this report to identify opportunities to create new content or new search synonyms (for example, this report helps identify common misspellings that can cause user frustration).

Create Delightful Content

Content is really king—and queen and duke and prince. If you do not have great content (ideally, content that is not available anyplace else), you cannot possibly expect users to "adopt," much less use, your system. Writing great content to be consumed on the Web is not the same as writing great content for print. For example, when you write for the Web, you want to write much more concisely than you would for print, using short bullet points whenever possible. When you want to add more detail by using a link to another location, avoid the much abused "click here" by rewriting links to be more meaningful. People read differently when they are consuming Web site content, so creating content that is easy to scan creates delightful user experiences that can significantly improve adoption. There are lots of great guidelines for writing for the Web and creating content for SharePoint. We have compiled several in a document you can download at www.jornata/com/essentialsharepoint. Your organization may also have a corporate style and branding guide that will help ensure that your communications reflect your business effectively.

Be Mindful of Feature Abuse: Just Because You Can, Doesn't Mean You Should

SharePoint 2013 has lots of new and improved features, but that doesn't necessarily mean that every feature is right for your solution or your organization right out of the gate or even at all. It is important to understand how people work and the culture of your organization and the specifics of the problems you are trying to address. It is not always a good idea to promote a feature to see if it will "stick" without doing the work to make sure that the feature has a context or that you have the content and support that you will need to be successful. For example, the "gamification" aspects of the new community site and community feature set may not be appropriate in your organizational culture or for your specific community. If these features are not appropriate, turn them off—you can always enable them later on as your needs change. Delight your users by paying close attention to how they work and what they need, not the bright-shiny-object features that your users may not be ready for now, or maybe ever.

"Prime the Pump" by Predefining Keywords and Terms That Users Are Likely to Use in Their Profiles

If you haven't yet launched your SharePoint solution, you still have time to catch something that will help make your solution feel more polished and engage your users. If you can, try to "prime" your enterprise keywords (this requires Administrator privileges to your farm) with the terms and spellings that you would like people to use. For example, if you want users' skills to be entered using a capital letter (for example, Accounting, Organizational Development, JavaScript, SharePoint), enter as many enterprise terms as you can before the first users start creating their own. This helps ensure consistency of structure and spelling so that you can avoid the issue of having the first user to list JavaScript as a skill enter "JaavScript" and then, using the type-ahead feature in keywords, having every other user select this incorrect spelling in their skills list. While capitalization issues tend to be minor, other issues of inconsistency can make search less functional, so if you can predefine (and enter) common terms, you will delight your users by saving them time (because they will be able to take advantage of type-ahead) and not making them think too hard about the right "level" at which to make an entry. In addition, when you are launching social features like Communities and Newsfeed, it helps to engage early adopters to ensure that no community starts empty and the organizational newsfeed has some activity when the majority of your users are introduced to the solution.

Eliminate "Sharp Edges" by Carefully Managing User Permissions

While this may be a tip that is more appropriate for a discussion of governance, one sure way to delight your users is to make sure that they don't have permissions that allow them to accidentally break something. One of the interesting challenges with SharePoint implementations is that when we use this wonderful software to empower users to create and modify their own solutions, we often end up with users with just enough knowledge and just enough permission to make mistakes. This is especially important with SharePoint 2013 team sites because the default permission set for users in the Members group is "higher" than in SharePoint 2010 and earlier editions. By default, members have Edit privileges in SharePoint 2013 team sites, not Contribute. This new permissions set—Edit—allows users to edit pages, lists, and libraries. And, to be extra-"helpful," Microsoft has exposed the Edit page button in the upper-right corner of each page. The risk (which comes from experience, not theory) is that users who have not been fully trained will see the Edit button and think that it means edit an *item*; however, once the page is in Edit mode, a small update to the text on the page changes the text on the page for all users, and a click of the "x" next to a discussion list entry doesn't just delete the entry, it closes the Web Part—for not just one user, but for everyone!

To increase the opportunity to delight, eliminate as many opportunities for users to get hurt from a "sharp edge" as possible. If your user community is not SharePoint savvy, consider making the default member permissions set Contribute, not Edit. If you want to ensure that site access security is tightly controlled, consider not allowing users to have access to features that allow them to manage permissions. Or, better yet, have a graduated permissions option that extends permissions as users have completed predefined training, and implement a service-level agreement that manages "rescue" expectations when a user with privileges accidentally gets stuck on a sharp edge.

Plan Your Deployment to Optimize Adoption Success

There are all kinds of factors that will influence the adoption of your SharePoint solution—and different factors will impact different types of solutions. For example, you may have a different deployment strategy for your new intranet as a whole than you will for the social features or for your new team site templates.

Deployment Strategies for Intranets

Adoption strategies for intranets typically focus on communications—and we will address both launch and "persistent" communications strategies later in this chapter. But there are several other deployment considerations that have an impact on adoption success:

- **Launching the new while you still have the old.** It's important to think about the timing of your intranet launch and how you will transition from your old intranet. Organizations often launch with a new home page only and then point users back to the old solution for all content below the home page. While this may create a disjointed user experience if you are also updating your site branding, if you have a content navigational strategy that works, this approach can be viable. Just remember that you will need to have a plan for how you will transition your old content and pages, and your content producers will need to understand where and how to publish content during the transition.

- **Replacing existing functionality and content.** While it may be necessary to create a transitional deployment plan due to budget and organizational considerations, many organizations prefer to build out the entire infrastructure in the new environment and then migrate all existing content at once. In the most optimistic of situations (which rarely matches reality), all the existing content is current and relevant and simply needs to be moved to the new platform. If you already have a working SharePoint 2010 intranet, your transition to SharePoint 2013 can be very simple from a user adoption perspective. If you are changing your site templates, there may be some work (both with third-party tools and manual) to transition content, but if your changes are not drastic, the work will not likely be too difficult because behind the scenes, not much has changed from a content perspective. So, you can effectively migrate your entire intranet as is. The question is, Should you? The answer is not "one size fits all," but as a general rule, when you are upgrading to a new platform that will cause any disruption or extra work for your content consumers or publishers, it's worth providing some new capability to make the transition effort worthwhile. The good news is that out of the box, SharePoint 2013 provides an incredibly powerful new capability that often makes the transition effort worth it on its own—the new search experience.

- **Deploying new functionality and features.** If your new intranet involves a complete redesign, then in addition to thinking about how you want to transition the old site and its content, you will also have to consider if and how you are going to leverage the new capabilities of SharePoint 2013. For example, are you going to launch with a "big wow" and just make all the new features available (such as Newsfeed and Communities) on Day 1, or are you going to slowly release capabilities over time, not a "big wow" but a "long wow"? Consider this: except for the intranet design and implementation team, in most organizations the majority of people just don't get all that excited about changes to the intranet. Sadly enough, that is often true for even the business owners of the intranet. And, as we talked about earlier, change is not always welcome, even when it is good. Change management is a continuous process. So, when you launch your new intranet, you may want to consider limiting the amount of change you foist on your users all at once and think about planning a series of incremental releases, each designed to provide features that will inspire users to use the intranet. You don't always have to jump on the next new feature that comes along, but when a new feature "fits," it will be much easier to get users to change. While this may involve extending the implementation of your intranet over a longer period of time, the best intranets are never "done," so the approach may actually contribute to a sense that the intranet team is much more responsive to the needs of the business.

Deployment Strategies for Social Features

There is no question that the new social computing (or social collaboration) features of SharePoint 2013 will require extensive change management and adoption planning in organizations. Some experts believe that social collaboration will eventually replace e-mail as the primary means of collaboration within the enterprise. Even if e-mail is here to stay, there is no question that social collaboration represents the next generation of enterprise collaboration technology. Despite the prevalence of social collaboration in the consumer space, especially for the "Facebook generation," it is still a relatively new capability inside companies, and both organizational leaders and employees are still trying to understand how it can drive business value. Until "social" is pervasive within the organization, there will be a need to plan and guide its adoption—and if your organization is planning to deploy the social features of SharePoint 2013, you will need to think about a specific adoption plan. These features are discussed extensively in Chapter 15, "Planning for Social Computing."

- **Choosing between enterprise and controlled deployments.**
  One of the first decisions you'll want to make is whether to launch
  your social features to the entire organization or to a smaller group
  of users, potentially rolling out to one or more communities or
  departments at a time. Social solutions tend to work best with larger
  populations, if only because it is difficult to engage a large population
  with any "traditional" method of collaboration. An advantage of an
  enterprise deployment is that you can engage the entire organization
  at one time. That advantage can also be a disadvantage—especially
  if you do not have some meaningful use cases to showcase at launch
  time. A more controlled deployment allows you to build use cases
  and lessons learned with a smaller population and thus limit your
  risk if you need to tweak any aspect of the solution or your launch
  or adoption plans. But a controlled deployment generally loses the
  "large-group advantage." The good news is that these strategies are
  not really mutually exclusive; you may be able to start with a controlled deployment, and once a few communities are successfully
  "on-boarded," you can then move to an enterprise launch.
- **Starting top down versus bottom up.** A top-down approach
  involves reaching out to executives in the organization to become
  active users and then promoting their involvement to encourage
  others to follow their example. This strategy worked very effectively
  for IBM, where CEO Sam Palmisano actively reinforced the use of
  internal collaboration tools by using them himself and encouraging
  others to do so as well. In most organizations, getting executives to
  "model the behavior" is a great way to encourage change—but the
  executives need to be committed to ongoing use of the tools for
  the initial launch success to be sustained. A bottom-up approach
  involves introducing the tools first to the staff and letting them
  create a groundswell of adoption at the grassroots level that will help
  evangelize the benefits of the technology. While these strategies are
  also not mutually exclusive, you may have to choose one primary
  approach because it is rare that the SharePoint team will have
  sufficient time and budget to simultaneously pursue every single
  approach to the same degree at one time.
- **Engaging early adopters and evangelists.** No matter which
  other adoption strategies you choose, identifying a core group of
  early adopters and evangelists is a good idea. There will never be
  a large enough SharePoint team to individually support all of your

users. As a result, the central SharePoint team in any organization needs to build up an extended team of experts or "power users" across the organization. When it comes to the adoption of social tools, your early adopters should include some of your subject matter experts or just anyone who is willing to "go first" who can be engaged to start conversations in a discussion list or newsfeed. In one client organization, we launched our new discussion list with a "content blast" workshop where we scripted some conversations to get things going. This was part of a concerted "fake it till you make it" approach that was actually very effective. Each participant came prepared to be an "asker" and to have a document ready to upload to serve as an answer to a set of predefined frequently asked questions. At another organization, the first step to launching the social tools was to engage the top subject matter experts to create profiles. At a conference where the solution was officially launched, virtually every member of the community first asked, "Are John and Jim on yet?" Both directly and indirectly, the community members were telling us that if the key thought leaders were going to use SharePoint to collaborate, they would use it, too.

Deployment Strategies for Collaboration Solutions (Team Sites)

If you spend some time carefully planning your approach for deploying your collaborative team sites, you can save a lot of time for individual teams. Collaborative activities tend to have patterns, and if you can identify what patterns apply in your organization, you will improve not just adoption but also the quality of search results.

- **Starting with templates.** One of the most important adoption strategies you can use for team sites is to create templates for the typical types of teams in your organization. Don't expect the generic templates included with SharePoint 2013 to work for your organization as is. Your templates can have both default content and default permissions—and you should think about making it easier for your users by including both. For example, if your organization, like many others, has standard records retention codes that need to be added to all SharePoint documents, be sure to replace the out-of-the-box Document Content Type in your default team site document libraries with your customized Document Content Type that includes the Records Retention Code Column. By default, the new Community Site template does not include a document library other than Site Assets. If your communities typically share documents, create a custom version of the Community Site template that includes a document library and also changes the permissions on the Site Assets library so that all users have Read access but only moderators and/or site owners have Contribute permissions. If your project management office has prepared templates and guidelines that all project teams must use, make sure that your project team site template includes a permanent link to the site where the most recent version of these templates will be stored.

■ **Encouraging good collaboration practices.** Most successful projects start with some type of project charter—either formal or informal. As a best practice, it's great if you can get your project teams to include how they will collaborate using SharePoint as part of the way they will work together to deliver the charter objectives. On some teams, these behaviors are implicit, but when users are new to SharePoint or online collaboration in general, it is a good idea to make these shared behaviors more explicit—in the form of a written team agreement or "compact." There are some teams where the behaviors are explicitly defined but not written down, so not everyone follows them. The recommended approach is to document a set of shared expectations for how each team will use SharePoint to work together more effectively so that they can achieve both their project and organizational collaboration objectives.

Suggested Elements for a Team "Compact"

■ We will use a consistent, approved team site template. Common organization of standard project content will make it easier for users to interact with site content.

■ We will send links to documents in our team site instead of e-mailing document attachments to one another.

■ We will use authoritative versions of shared content and create links to content on other sites instead of creating duplicate content.

- We will make sure that all of the work for the project, even documents that are not finished, is stored in the team site.
- We will all make sure to use the Status attribute when we share documents, indicating whether a document is a Draft, Ready for Review, or Final.
- We will use ratings to indicate whether a document is potentially reusable or a candidate for a best practice example. (In other words, this is the framework we will use to apply document ratings—this is what ratings mean for our team.)
- When we are assigned a task to review a document for a colleague, we will review the document *and* update the assigned task.
- We will tag content as it is added, even if the attributes aren't required!
- We will let the team leader/project manager know if the metadata scheme needs to be adjusted.
- We will use the discussion list or site newsfeed instead of e-mail to post questions and solicit feedback from each another.
- We will be accountable for checking the team site regularly—either by setting up alerts or by using any other approach that fits within our personal work process.

- **Establishing a coaching team in the center of excellence.** We talk about the concept of a center of excellence in Chapter 4, "Planning for Business Governance." The general concept is that the center of excellence is a team (which can be virtual) dedicated to helping your organization successfully develop, promote, and adopt SharePoint to achieve business value. One especially helpful role in the center of excellence is that of the coach. In organizations where this role has been successfully deployed, each new site owner is assigned a coach from the center of excellence team. The role of the coach is to help ensure that users who are new to SharePoint have access to someone who can help disseminate best practices and guide new SharePoint users in the best way to use SharePoint successfully for their team or project. At some organizations, coaches stick with their "customers" for the life of the solution, providing expert resources who can be called upon as needed for guidance and support. At others, the coach is assigned to the "customer" for the initial launch only. Coaches don't have to come from IT or even the central SharePoint organization. In fact, the best coaches will come from inside each business unit. It takes time to develop new coaches, and in some cases you may want initially to outsource coaching to a consulting partner with the idea that your potential internal coaches can shadow your external coaches until they are ready to become coaches themselves.

Both the coach and the "customer" receive the benefit from their collaboration. Coaches learn about business processes and needs when the customer presents a new problem or challenge, and customers learn how to leverage others' solutions to meet their own needs. You can quickly build a cadre of internal consultant coaches by providing opportunities for your coaches to be exposed to different problems from other site owners or teams. The coach role may or may not be a full-time job. We have seen this approach work very well in organizations where the cadre of coaches comes from volunteers among the power users community. A moderated online user community that publishes vetted, successful solutions can provide an essential resource for both coaches and customers.

■ **Providing initial and ongoing support.** Just as it is important to provide opportunities for your users to provide feedback on your intranet, it is equally important to provide opportunities for ongoing support for your teams using SharePoint. A key suggested strategy is to provide regular "office hours" similar to the way university professors hold office hours for their students. One organization staffed a "hotline" every Friday afternoon with members of the virtual center of excellence so site owners and users knew that if they called during that time, they would get the "hotline" to the top SharePoint experts in the company. Another scheduled monthly office hours in the lobby of the headquarters building with members of the SharePoint development and support team available at "kiosk" workstations where site owners could bring their challenging SharePoint problems. No matter which approach you choose, the important outcome is ensuring that you are making expertise and support easily available to users who are committed to using SharePoint in your organization.

Plan Effective Training

When it comes to training, one size does *not* fit all. Training needs to be targeted to your users in the context of your specific solution—not generic

SharePoint training. Training does not ever work best when you bombard users with every possible feature and function of SharePoint all at one time. You don't want your colleagues to feel like they are drinking from a fire hose. The best training programs are designed to give users just the right amount of information at just the point when they need it. While it is virtually impossible to make all training "just in time," your goal should be to tailor your training programs to make your users comfortable enough to get their work done using SharePoint and then provide opportunities for them to learn more when they have a need or are interested in expanding their knowledge.

Educational experts know that not everyone learns in precisely the same way. This is especially true for busy adults. You will get the best outcomes from your training initiatives if you can offer training in multiple ways: classroom, online, "just-in-time" via computer-based training (CBT), short online videos, quick reference cards, and so on. If time and money were unlimited, you could consider creating an individual training program for each person in the organization—but of course that will never be the case. Instead, it makes sense to think of developing training for users based on their role—both what they do in their job and their role for the SharePoint site (for example, reader, contributor, or site owner).

It is critically important to align training with your governance plan— don't train users in how they *could* do something; train users in how you do it in *your* organization. A client, Mike, once told his SharePoint consultant, "Don't give me an answer that says you can do that task seven different ways—just tell me the *best* way to do it for my team." If your organization has file-naming conventions, teach the naming conventions as you are teaching users how to upload a document. If you have optional Columns for all documents (for example, a field called Summary where users can briefly describe the document), showcase the benefit of adding content in that Column in all training for content contributors.

Three Practical Tips for Training Content

- **Teach your users how to create an effective search query.** If you do, you will have a friend for life! It's actually pretty easy to get users to pay attention to search training because any new search skill can be applied not just in SharePoint but on the Internet as well in either Bing or Google search. This is especially important if your organization skipped SharePoint 2010 and you are upgrading to SharePoint 2013 from SharePoint 2007. Be sure to show users how to narrow search results by using AND between words and to expand search results by using OR or the wildcard character (*). Boolean operators were not available in SharePoint 2007 search, and it is possible that your users have never used them before. Refer to the appendix for more search query tips.

- **Encourage users to separate words in file names with underscores (or hyphens) but not spaces.** Have you ever noticed the ugly "%20" between words in SharePoint URLs? SharePoint itself isn't responsible for inserting the "%20" characters in your URLs. This is what happens when your references are "URL encoded." A single character space in a name translates to %20 (three characters). Since your URL cannot be longer than 255 characters and the %20s are not very readable, it's a good idea to eliminate as many spaces as possible—without compromising usability. As with most user experience items, you need to balance readability with usability. As a best practice, train
  - Site owners/solution builders when creating site assets that have more than one word in the name (sites, lists, libraries, and views) to "smush" words together in "CamelCase" with no spaces but using capital letters to distinguish the words, for example: CamelCase.
  - Content contributors to use an underscore (_) instead of a space between words when file names have more than one word. Capitalize each word of the file name, for example, My_File_Name.docx. The underscore is the best option because almost all search engines understand the underscore as a word separator, which means each word will be part of the search index. Using an underscore eliminates %20s in the URL and still allows each word of the file name to be indexed for search. Users can also use a hyphen (-) between words in a file name, but hyphens are used as break points to wrap text on separate lines. URLs that contain hyphens often cause problems in e-mail because when you click on them from your e-mail program, the characters on the second line are not included in the URL, which makes the link appear to be broken.
- **Explain the Title property and how it works.** Teach contributors to review the value in the Title property for all documents (and be sure that your default document library views

show the Title Column). Title is an important value in SharePoint. Out of the box, the document title is ranked close to the top for search relevance. More important, the title of a document is what is featured in search results, not the file name, so you really want a meaningful title. The problem with Title is that it is a value promoted from the Office properties of a document, and if you start your documents with a template or from a document created by someone else, you could end up with really, really inaccurate titles, which seriously compromises the ability to find your documents easily later on. To improve "findability," teach users about the importance of the Title property, or optionally create custom Content Types where you make Title required.

Your training strategy should encompass all aspects of your new solution—not only the SharePoint 2013 technology but also business processes impacted by SharePoint 2013. Users who are very familiar with your current SharePoint version will be especially interested in learning about things that have changed in SharePoint 2013, so a critical component of your training plan will need to include specific "upgraded features" training for those users.

This section discusses the following elements of your training plan:

- **Audience:** who should be trained and what training content is appropriate for each audience
- **Timing:** when training should be offered
- **Approach:** examples of successful training approaches that you can consider for your organization

Audience

Develop a training program for SharePoint 2013 that carefully addresses the specific needs of each constituent community based on their role in the organization and their role in the context of the solution. If you implement personal sites, all users will have Contribute (or Edit) permissions for at least that area of the portal. This means that every user in the organization should know *something* about best practices for organizing information. However, not all users will have the same level of interest, so your training plan will need to be adjusted accordingly. While you may *think* that all users want to learn everything that they can about SharePoint, in practice, this doesn't always turn out to be the case. Think about how you can structure your training plan so that you offer multiple levels of training for users with varying degrees of both interest and time. One successful approach that several organizations have adopted is to create a "SharePoint Basics" offering that introduces all users to the solution, shows them effective search techniques, and explains the basics of your content organization and site navigation schemes. This introductory topic shouldn't require much more than about an hour to deliver. The Basics offering can then be supplemented with additional training content based on user interest and role.

One approach that can be very helpful for training is to provide users with a "sandbox" environment in which to practice. Either before or immediately after training, provide users with a test environment that is a mirror image of the production site. Allowing users to experiment in a safe place can prepare them for a production launch and can also help the development team identify bugs and other issues if this approach is used prior to a major upgrade or launch.

Timing

Training for SharePoint is ideally scheduled immediately prior to the launch of your new solution and on an ongoing basis as users need new and expanded skills. Some users, particularly users who are responsible for loading the initial content, will need to be trained (either formally or informally) prior to the start of content conversion. The majority of users, particularly those with Read access, should be trained just before or at the time of your solution launch.

One of the biggest training challenges, of course, is figuring out just what users need and when they need it. There is no single best answer to this challenge because each solution is different. It's really hard to figure out what is "just enough" when it comes to training for SharePoint. It depends on the user's role, how frequently they will use the skill, and a host of other factors, including their learning style. If your user community includes a significant number of engineers or scientists, it is likely that no matter how much or how little you teach them about SharePoint, they will try to figure out what else it can do! As you plan training, the important thing to remember is that you want to engage the natural curiosity of your user community *before* they propagate a "wrong" or ineffective approach by exploring on their own. We've seen too many cases where eager users "discover" a feature and share it with their colleagues even if there is actually a much simpler or more effective feature. You will need to negotiate a careful balance between overwhelming the user with too much content and making sure that each user has enough knowledge to get the job done. If you have nontechnical users who will be given Full Control or Design privileges on a SharePoint site, it is important to empower them with site design best practices training, not just how to use SharePoint features. These new "site designers" should be familiar with the guiding principles documented in your governance plan (see Chapter 4, "Planning for Business Governance") and information architecture fundamentals (see Chapter 6, "Planning Your Information Architecture"). One thing to remember: do not expect to train "casual" users to become information architects. You will want your site owners to understand the fundamentals of information architecture, but you should plan on staffing your center of excellence with "professional" information architects.

While you will definitely need to develop a training plan that is specific to your organization's needs, you will not always need to develop training material. There are many commercial SharePoint training offerings (including vast collections of free and low-cost short training videos) as well as documentation and online training that are available at Microsoft.com. Many training companies seem to find it most effective to teach SharePoint classes as multiday events. Unfortunately, not all training participants will be able to participate or find this type of training effective. For the most part, we have seen only limited success with this type of training if large communities need to be trained. Furthermore, many users find it difficult to schedule that much time away from their job duties.

Identifying a more effective delivery approach is challenging. Should you consider multiday training options for *all* of your SharePoint users, even if the class is called SharePoint Basics? Absolutely not. Should you consider it for *some* users? Definitely yes. For the majority of your users, you will need to consider frequent "mini-training" events that allow users to consume training "just in time," as they need it.

Here are some suggested approaches for just-in-time SharePoint training:

- **SharePoint Basics.** This is online or in-person brief introductory training to be offered in conjunction with the launch of your new solution and then at additional intervals for new employees or people who want a refresher. Be sure to supplement this with task-based videos and/or checklist refreshers as well.

- **Online, topic-based computer-based training.** There is already a wealth of video training offerings for SharePoint 2013, as well as additional "on-demand" training from Microsoft Office online. Short, topic-focused training videos or online training can be delivered to users just as they need the knowledge in the course of doing their work. The ideal training modules require no more than ten minutes to "consume" and can be accessed by users as they are trying to accomplish specific tasks. While you can certainly develop these modules on your own, it's worth checking out the existing offerings, even if they reflect a generic SharePoint solution. In some cases, you can work with the solution provider to customize the materials for your specific implementation.

- **User documentation, delivered online or in print form.** Some users will not be comfortable without written documentation. Many successful organizations create generic documentation for key tasks such as uploading and assigning metadata to documents or changing security permissions that they make available to teams to use as is or customized for their sites. Others create formal documentation only for tasks or processes that are customized in their deployment. Still others "create" documentation for their environment by linking to existing Microsoft documentation on the various SharePoint features. As you think about the approach that will be most successful in your organization, keep in mind that to be useful, your documentation needs to be consumable. This means that you should think about small documents rather than 20-page "books" that no one will ever read. In addition, remember that to be valuable, documentation should be delivered in context. This means that while you may want to create a document library or site for user documentation, you should *link* to each relevant chunk of documentation from the site where the user will need it—create links in the context of where users will do their work. For example, on a page where a user will submit a form, provide a link to the document describing how to submit the form.

- **Recurring training events such as regular meetings or "lunch and learn" sessions.** One very successful organization implemented a regular "Get Sharp on SharePoint" weekly training event. Each week, they planned and delivered a 30-minute online meeting focused on a unique SharePoint topic such as search, creating your personal SharePoint site, assigning metadata, and so on. The first 15 minutes of the meeting were typically devoted to a presentation, and the second 15 minutes provided an opportunity for participants to ask questions and share experiences (either on the topic of the day or not). Each meeting was recorded so that users could replay the video at any time. The combination of real-time, online topic-based training plus recorded playback was extremely effective in both introducing and reinforcing key topics. Because the topics were publicized as part of the communications plan, users could plan their participation based on their interest and workload.

- **"Office hours" consulting sessions.** Several companies offer recurring drop-in help centers where users can bring their SharePoint design or usage concerns to their internal SharePoint experts. This effectively provides one-on-one private training to supplement other just-in-time training offerings.

While not always considered part of training, another important resource for just-in-time training is your power users community and SharePoint center of excellence team. A powerful way to deliver training just at the moment when a user needs it is to offer a "live" person for quick questions. Creating an "Ask the Experts" discussion forum, establishing a best practices wiki with a searchable repository of tips and tricks, publishing a list of SharePoint subject matter experts in your own organization, and adding links to SharePoint training in your default site templates can also help support your training program. In addition, the popularity of SharePoint has led to many SharePoint user groups around the world, in just about every city and region. These user groups typically meet at least monthly and can be a great way to both learn and benefit from the best ideas of other organizations.

Approach

Training should be tailored to how each constituent community will use SharePoint to do their jobs. To maximize the effectiveness of your training plan, you may want to consider training a few employees from each department or business unit or office in a "train the trainer" scenario and ask them to train their peers. You may also want to identify some initial candidates to become power users of SharePoint 2013 and consider providing additional, in-depth training for these individuals, who can then be engaged to train or coach others. Ideally, the power users should be distributed across the organization so that they can provide first-level support and ongoing training to members of their local department, business unit, or office.

Each organization has unique business roles that may require specialized SharePoint training. Don't kid yourself—certain types of users will absolutely require custom approaches to training. For example, in a law firm, you should not plan to deliver the same training to both partners and paralegals. In a hospital, clinicians and administrators will probably have different training needs and learning styles.

In general, there are three types of user roles for a SharePoint solution: Visitors (readers), Members (contributors or editors), and Owners (designers). These roles are generally described using SharePoint terminology for the permissions that users have on a given page or site.

- **Visitors** have Read permission for the specific page or site—at least for the "authoritative" content. One of the unique training challenges for SharePoint is that you may have certain types of content (for example, social tags or ratings) that any user can add to a page or site, even if they have only Read permission for the primary content. These users will need both training in when and how they should add social content and, even more important, training in the organizational governance policies for this type of information.
- **Members** generally have both Read and Contribute permission in the Community Site template and a new permission set called Edit in team sites. These users will need the same training as visitors but must also understand how to add content and how to assign metadata to contributed content and the governance policies for content contribution. In the default Team Site template in SharePoint 2013, members have a new permission level called Edit. Note that Edit permissions are a higher level than Contribute and allow users to create and delete lists, add or remove Columns in a list, and add or remove public views of a list. Many organizations will want to revert to the default Contribute permission to control who has access to edit the lists and libraries on a site.
- **Owners** typically have Full Control permission, which means that they have the ability to modify the structure, lists, libraries, and content metadata for the site in addition to being able to add content, and they can also manage user permissions. These users need a comprehensive set of "how to" training for SharePoint as well

as a complete understanding of all of your governance principles and policies, especially those related to security. In addition, any user with Full Control or Design privileges needs to understand some basic information architecture and Web site usability best practices.

As you roll out SharePoint solutions inside your organization, you are making an implied assumption that your users have basic "information literacy" skills. This may not always be the case in all organizations. Because SharePoint includes so many social computing features, your training plan may need to address the needs of users who have not yet mastered each of these basic skills. Refer to the sidebar for a list of some of the basic information literacy skills you will want to ensure are part of the core competencies of your solution users.

Information Literacy Competencies for Successful Collaboration and Portal Solutions

Some of the basic information literacy skills that are important for your solution users to have include

- **Locating:** the ability to understand and use IT-based tools required to conduct research on the Internet, including basic search competencies (narrowing or expanding search scopes, understanding metadata concepts)
- **Evaluating:** the ability to distinguish between authoritative and nonauthoritative information sources (for example, social tags versus other types of metadata) and current versus old information, as well as the ability to critically evaluate the strengths and weaknesses, benefits, and costs of information technologies
- **Communicating:** the ability to format and publish ideas electronically, both in document format as well as on blogs and wiki pages
- **Organizing:** the ability to classify and organize information in ways that benefit both personal and shared retrieval (understanding the fundamental concepts of "findability" and views to surface critical or frequently used content)
- **Learning:** the ability to adapt to and make use of continuously evolving innovations in information technology, including the ability to determine how to apply emerging technologies inside the business

Carefully Consider Incentives and Rewards

At some point in any discussion of user adoption, the topic of incentives and rewards will come up. Should you create a plan to specifically incent or reward users for using SharePoint? Well, of course, it depends. Over the long term, the solution you are developing needs to provide value to your users or no amount of incentives will encourage them to use it. However, that doesn't mean that you might not want to create some initial incentives to encourage users to engage with your solution, and in certain circumstances you may even want to create some ongoing incentives to recognize and reward certain behaviors.

Try It, You'll Like It

Most mothers will at some point utter the same words their own mothers used to try to coax their children to try a new food: "Try it, you'll like it." Sometimes, getting a user to try a new way of collaborating or a new way of searching only takes a little encouragement. A small incentive— even the promise of "You'll like it"—may be enough to get your users to give your solution a try. If your solution is easy to use and meets or, better yet, exceeds your users' expectations, the little incentive or push can be very effective, even if it involves a small reward. If you need a little incentive to jump-start usage, just make sure that it aligns with your culture and with the goals of the system.

Make the Launch Fun

Consider a fun activity, such as a SharePoint scavenger hunt, to get users excited about the new solution. For example, one organization created a portal treasure hunt that provided participants with a list of ten questions whose answers could be found by either searching or browsing for content within the solution environment. One question asked users to find the author of a specific document published to the portal. This answer was found by searching or browsing for the document and then examining its metadata properties to identify the author. Another asked users to find out what would be offered for lunch in the cafeteria on a date two weeks into the future. This answer was found by navigating to or searching for the cafeteria menu, which was published monthly, and looking in the document for the lunch item on that date. A third question asked users to identify whom to call for questions related to medical benefits. This answer could be found in several ways, including searching for the term *medical benefits*, which turned up a frequently asked question with the answer, or by navigating to the HR page and looking at the Key Contacts list for the medical benefits expert, whose name and contact information were prominently featured. Users who turned in correct answers for all ten questions were entered into a drawing for a dinner for two at a local restaurant. The activity not only promoted the new SharePoint environment, but it also walked new users through some valuable information-seeking activities for which the solution could provide quick and accurate results.

Function Follows Food

In many organizations, if you want to get people's attention, promise them food. Don't underestimate the value of "lunch and learn" or "cookies and conversation" or an event like "Share-toberfest: inebriate while you collaborate," an event offered at Del Monte Foods at the launch of its new intranet to showcase the capabilities of its new solution (which happened to be in October).

Consider Game Dynamics

Organizations where the employees are engaged will outperform those whose employees aren't on many dimensions.[3] Employee engagement can thus be a real competitive advantage, and a workplace trend that seems to have come of age at the time SharePoint 2013 was launched is "gamification." At its core, gamification is about finding the fun things in the work that we do to create more engagement—with our organization, with our work, with the tools we use to do our work, and with each other. According to Wikipedia, "gamification is the use of game-thinking and game mechanics in non-game contexts in order to engage users and solve problems."[4]

---

3. www.gallup.com/consulting/121535/employee-engagement-overview-brochure.aspx
4. http://en.wikipedia.org/wiki/Gamification

Why is gamification important to user adoption and SharePoint? Because gamification is built into the Community Site template and community features in SharePoint 2013, and if you plan to use these features, you will need to think about how they apply to the business contexts in which you intend to use them. And you may want to think about other ways to use gamification to encourage specific user behaviors.

There are typically three elements to most "gamified" systems: points, badges, and leaderboards, often referred to as PBL. SharePoint 2013's community features include all three elements—users get *points* for both asking and replying to discussion posts, the moderator of a community site can determine up to five levels of *badges* out of the box based on accumulated point totals or "gift" a badge to specific users based on expertise or seniority, and the "top contributors" Web Part provides a *leaderboard* display of who has the most points in the community. These features are included in the community features—but you don't have to enable them if you don't want to. If you choose to enable them, make sure that they are appropriate for your user community. These features are helpful if they make collaborating more engaging for your users. They can be harmful if they make users feel patronized.

Giving users feedback to encourage or incent desired behaviors is not a bad idea. Let's say that you want to encourage users to write articles for your home page. Providing information showing how many times their articles have been read, featuring their contributed stories in the "featured stories" area on the home page, and featuring "most commented" or "most read" articles gives authors positive feedback about their contributions and creates an incentive to write more articles. The same approach might apply if you want to encourage users to write blog articles. Gamification applied right can help drive behavior change. Gamification applied incorrectly can be demotivating.

Consider doing some research on gamification and game thinking before incorporating it into your adoption strategy. As with any new business practice or technical feature, you need to first have a strong understanding of user needs and the work that your users do to determine whether and which game approaches will be effective in your organization. There is a lot of emerging content on this topic, but a good place to start is with a book called *For the Win: How Game Thinking Can Revolutionize Your Business* by Kevin Werbach and Dan Hunter, two college professors and lawyers who created the world's first college course on gamification at the Wharton School of the University of Pennsylvania. In the book, Werbach and Hunter talk about how game thinking and addressing problems by thinking like a game designer can create engaging experiences for employees that can help drive business value—which is, of course, why we care about user adoption in the first place.

Design and Implement Persistent Communications

Don't assume that your new SharePoint solution is going to launch itself—a communications plan is absolutely essential for successful solutions. One mistake many organizations make is that they leave communications planning to the end of their project plans and forget to engage the internal marketing and communications teams early enough in the project so that they can have an impact. The other big mistake that organizations make is assuming that communications planning is over once the solution is launched. A good communications strategy must be persistent; until your solution is embedded into the fabric of your organization, you should use every opportunity to promote awareness of both the features and the benefits of the solution. Everyone in your organization is listening to the same radio station: WIIFM (What's In It For Me?). Your persistent communications plan needs to ensure that you are constantly promoting the value of your solution to ensure that the business benefits that are so critical to your organizational success can be realized.

The communications strategy should promote both awareness and the value of the new SharePoint solution. Your communications plan will likely include some awareness activities that begin during design, but the majority of activities will begin just before you are ready to launch the solution and continue persistently. Communications activities must also be an active part of sustaining user acceptance throughout the entire life of the solution, and thus your plan needs to include not just communications when the solution launches, but also ongoing activities that keep the portal and collaboration tools "top of mind" throughout their lifetime. As you begin to think about your communications planning, be sure to

- Leverage existing expertise and experts to help develop your communications plan. Work with your internal communications or marketing teams to develop both communications messages and materials. Consider what activities and messages have worked in the past, and think creatively about new ways of engaging users and solution contributors.

- Leverage existing newsletters and "town hall" or business unit meetings to deliver key messages about the solution, collaboration tools, and other productivity initiatives. You can also demonstrate the solution "live."
- Draft a memorandum for the CEO or similar high-level executive to send when you are ready to launch. Active sponsorship by key business executives can go a long way toward getting users over their initial reluctance to try the new solution.
- Tailor messages in communications plans to each target audience. For example, messages may be different for field personnel and home office personnel because the value of the solution and collaboration tools and the business reasons for using them may be different based on the various roles and locations in the organization. The same user will leverage the solution for different reasons at different times, and the communications plan should address these different scenarios. An attorney in a law firm will play the role of "employee" when she uses the company portal to update the beneficiary of her 401K plan. However, the attorney will approach the same portal as a business stakeholder when she uses the portal to find last month's billing for her current clients. Make sure that both the communications medium and the message are targeted to your audience and the roles they play in the organization. In the attorney example, this might mean designing a communications message for all employees that reminds users that the company portal can be used for basic HR self-service. In addition, this could also mean designing a completely separate message targeted to just attorneys that describes how Attorney Smith used the portal while on the phone with a client who was requesting additional work to quickly identify that this client was 60 days past due and that this timely information resulted in an immediate collection of the past due amount. Work with key individuals within each business group to ensure that messages and medium work for their locations and roles.
- Encourage influential executives to talk about the solution, and better yet, use the solution for information distribution instead of sending e-mail. One successful organization found an executive who refused to respond to internal e-mail messages that included attachments that should have been added as links to documents in the portal. When he got an e-mail with an attachment, he politely replied to the sender that he would read the e-mail when the

attachment was referenced as a link to a document in the portal. This helped rapidly enforce "no more e-mail attachments" as a guiding principle to eliminate "versionitis" (multiple versions of the same document floating around the organization).

- Eliminate paper-based or e-mail distribution for regular reports or targeted communications if they can be found on the portal. For example, you may want to consider eliminating paper-based newsletters if you can use the portal to create targeted news items, or simply post the existing newsletter to the portal and allow users to print it only if they want a paper copy. (This will not only help drive users to your solution, but it will also help support your organization's "green" initiatives!)

- Promote enthusiasm and eagerness by including high-value content and functionality in the first release. One important activity is to ensure that you have correctly identified a "killer application" and critical content for the first release of SharePoint 2013. This will be a key component of your plan if you are migrating from earlier versions because users will want to understand the benefit (to them) of the upgrade. Be sure that you are implementing at least one type of content or application that users really want and have not been able to get before—this is the "wow" factor that helps encourage user adoption. If you are not already using FAST for search, your killer app for SharePoint 2013 won't take much work because the new search functionality is likely to delight even your most reluctant users. In addition to search, however, your portal might include a dashboard that integrates information from different applications and provides a comprehensive view of a customer or an account. Your portal might also include a collection of links to all of the resources a new employee needs to quickly get up to speed in your organization. Identify valuable content or applications that users can get only on the portal to encourage users to try it. Design specific communications to promote the use of this content.

- Manage user expectations about what SharePoint is and isn't, emphasizing that it is a platform that is designed to evolve over time. Communications vehicles should emphasize and reiterate this point and should focus on the objectives of this first release and ask users to provide feedback regarding metadata (Did we get it right?), satisfaction (Are users happy with the user experience, and can they find what they are looking for?), and training (Do we need more?).

Make sure you have a contact on each page so users know who is responsible for content.

- Create a launch video. For some great ideas and examples, check out Ellen Van Aken's collection of intranet launch videos at www. scoop .it/t/intranet-launch-videos-and-teasers.
- Remember that communication is an ongoing activity—you need to think about messaging beyond the initial launch and after the solution is operational. It will be difficult for your users to learn and appreciate all of the features of SharePoint in a single newsletter or training class. An ongoing communications effort provides additional opportunities to promote the features and functionality of SharePoint as well as your specific implementation.

A good communications plan identifies the method, the message, and the audience for each element. A good plan also includes activities for multiple phases of solution development, including messages that you may communicate during design, pilot, launch, and post-release. Use the structure in Table 7-1 as a starting point for developing your own communications plan.

Table 7-1 Sample Communications Plan Worksheet with One Example Item

Item	Description	Audience	Key Messages	Expected Outcomes	Timing	Responsibility
Article in corporate newsletter	Brief article (with no major commitments regarding timing) that talks about the plans for the new solution	Entire organization	Acknowledgement of stakeholders who participated in the initial interviews Key benefits of solution Status of project Initial deployment plan—where we are with pilots, etc. Expecta tions for new processes For more information call …	Awareness raised about the solution Expectations managed regarding enterprise rollout and impact on individual users	During design	Corporate comms team with input from solution design team

Key Points

As you prepare your user adoption, training, and communications plans, consider the following take-aways from this chapter:

- User adoption is not the end game. Adoption defined as the number of users who access your solution does not provide an indicator of performance improvement or business benefit. The real secret of user adoption for your SharePoint 2013 solution is making sure that the solution solves a meaningful organizational problem and that it does so in a significantly better way than the alternative solutions that may be available.
- Successful adoption planning recognizes that adoption is about managing change—which is an ongoing process, not a one-time event.
- Be sure you understand the business objectives that can be solved with each SharePoint feature you deploy, and if you can't tie a feature to a business outcome, defer or don't deploy the feature.
- Think about the story of the Three Bears as you create your training plan. Too little training and you run the risk of ineffective SharePoint sites. Too much training and people will feel like they are drinking from a fire hose. Your goal: use the suggestions in this chapter to try to get your training just right.
- Train just enough and just in time. Consider offering training topics to supplement basic SharePoint training so that users can focus on areas of interest at the time when they need to learn more about a topic. SharePoint 2013 has even more features and functionality than SharePoint 2010. This will definitely be overwhelming to many users. To ensure that people retain and can process what they learn, think about how both training and communications can be offered in "consumable chunks."
- Provide training in more than just how to use the various SharePoint features. Make sure that training covers best practices that define which features to use in a variety of business scenarios.
- Supplement training in "why" and "how" with a set of reusable examples of common configurations such as sites to manage a team, sites to manage a project, or sites to provide or publish information.
- Explain the concept of metadata and show examples of document libraries "before" (with folders) and "after" (with metadata) so that users can understand how using metadata instead of folders

improves content "findability." Do not use generic examples—make sure all examples include real data from your organization.

- In general, don't try to train all users in all features at one time. Consider introducing more advanced SharePoint functionality over time (for example, the ability to target content via audiences and managing security) so as not to overwhelm users with too much information. Consider targeted groups, however, for more advanced functionality.
- Think about communications as a persistent, not a one-time, process.
- Focus on value to the user in your adoption, communications, and training messages, emphasizing "what's in it for me" and the business benefit of participation in the solution.

CHAPTER 8

DEVELOPING A VALUE MEASUREMENT STRATEGY

Measurement is critical to being able to determine the level of success of your solution. As a foundation, you should focus on both the objectives for measurement and the various perspectives for your metrics. Many organizations see measurement and calculating a return on investment (ROI) as a mechanism to justify a project. However, measurement should be more than that. It should provide a process to ensure that you get the most value out of each project and initiative. This is especially true of SharePoint projects, where an effective measurement process will provide the necessary feedback about where you are going along the road to successfully leveraging your investment. At every stage in the journey, measurement (the process) and metrics (the indicators) provide a valuable means for focusing attention on business outcomes—not just ROI alone, but specific, meaningful business results described in a way that clearly demonstrates value. Having a measurement program in place helps managers assess, encourage, and reward relevant behaviors. You also can't influence what you don't measure.

In this chapter, we approach measurement from exactly this perspective—no matter what type of solution you are building with SharePoint, you need to understand and quantify the problem you are trying to solve so that you can determine whether the investment you will make in solving that problem is worth making. Furthermore, you have to measure your progress toward achieving that outcome objective so that you can focus your "solution energy" in the right place. Our objective is to provide a practical approach for measuring the value of investments in SharePoint solutions.

Here's the main point: the only truly sustainable measure of value for a SharePoint solution is business impact. No matter what type of solution you are building using SharePoint 2013 as a foundation application—a public-facing Internet site, a decision support system, an intranet site, or a team or community collaboration solution—the only way to measure its value is to determine whether the estimated business benefits for the solution are greater than the estimated cost. It seems so simple, doesn't it? Well, in theory, it is. Unfortunately, the fact is that it can be very difficult to understand the true cost for some of these types of solutions, and it can seem impossible to estimate the benefits, especially for intranet, social, and collaboration solutions where the benefits are not always direct.

Too often, organizations view adoption as the key measure of SharePoint success. Unless a solution is adopted, it cannot possibly deliver value. However, adoption alone is not a sufficient measure of success. While it is true that many failed or failing deployments can point to poor user adoption as a key indicator, the more important trait to consider is whether the solution has a clear connection to business goals. A good SharePoint solution includes a plan for demonstrating business value—a practical measurement plan that recognizes the key solution stakeholders and tells the success story in a way that clearly demonstrates business impact. The goal of this chapter is to help you identify and document these success stories.

What about the Cloud? Cloudy with a Chance of SharePoint

SharePoint 2013 presents an additional dimension in calculating both the costs and benefits of SharePoint solutions because you will need to consider the option of leveraging SharePoint in the cloud. In Chapter 11, "Taking SharePoint to the Cloud," we talk about the benefits, risks, and considerations of on-premises versus cloud-based SharePoint solutions. However, many of the cloud-versus-on-premises trade-offs are about a dimension of measurement that will be more critical to technical decision makers than business decision makers and for the overall SharePoint investment, not specific business solutions. As long as your compliance and risk officers are comfortable with cloud-based solutions, the fact that SharePoint runs in the cloud versus on-premises will not have much relevance to the business impact assessment for an individual SharePoint solution. There can be many advantages to thinking strategically about the value of SharePoint in the cloud, not the least of which is Microsoft's long-term commitment to a "cloud first" strategy and the fact that you will likely find it much easier to take advantage of new features and capabilities. However, you will likely be making your cloud-versus-on-premises decision for Office as whole, including not only SharePoint, but also Exchange, Lync, and the Office client itself. As a result, we cover the topic of assessing whether it is beneficial to look at SharePoint in the cloud for your organization only in Chapter 11. If you would like to explore a financial model that might help with the cloud-versus-on-premises solution, MIT professor Andrew McAfee has done some work with Google to create a model that is appropriate for small to medium-size businesses. It can be found at https://docs.google.com/spreadsheet/ccc?key=0AjFVAaH_U6vidG9EdFNrN3FyYTFhMWJERG03MERuX2c#gid=32.

What's New in SharePoint 2013?

The fact that you need to measure is not new—but with SharePoint 2013, there are some new features that provide important measurable benefits that can be incorporated into your measurement plan. This section is by no means exhaustive, but it will help identify where you may find opportunities to focus your measurement plan for moving or upgrading to SharePoint 2013.

- **Improvements to "social" that provide increased opportunities to benefit from people-to-people connections.** Whether you are upgrading to SharePoint 2013 or starting with SharePoint for the first time, it's likely that you are at least thinking about the social collaboration features. As we discuss throughout this book, Microsoft has made a significant investment in improving the social features of SharePoint in this latest release, and this investment will continue to mature in future upgrades. The ability to make more "people connections" and provide rich social interactions makes it much easier to find experts and keep track of topics of interest. Some of the places to look for the benefits of richer people connections include the number of new product or service innovations, reduction in the number of redundant or duplicative tools or approaches, and lower cost of doing business. SharePoint 2013, along with

Yammer, enables a new suite of social interactions that previously required additional costly third-party add-on products to achieve, so there are also opportunities to reduce costs.

- **Improvements to search that save time and improve productivity.** Search functionality has also improved significantly in SharePoint 2013. In addition to the many search improvements "behind the scenes," users will immediately notice and be able to take advantage of rich results previews as well as many improvements to search relevance that can result in faster decisions, less wasted time getting answers, and overall improvements in information-finding activities. New analytics functionality in search can display recommendations based on usage patterns. By including recommendations on a page, you can guide users to other content that may be relevant for them, saving time and ensuring that important and valuable content is more easily found.

- **Improvements to mobile access that enable better access to critical information "on the go" with a lower investment effort.** SharePoint 2013 provides new viewing experiences across different mobile platforms, providing capabilities to work anytime, in any place, and on any device in far easier ways than in previous versions. If mobile access scenarios are critical to your business, you will likely find measurable business impact with these new features because SharePoint 2013 makes it far more cost-effective to build solutions for mobile access.

- **Improvements to the ability to brand SharePoint solutions that allow you to leverage a wider community of resources at potentially lower cost.** From a technical perspective, SharePoint 2013 has some beneficial improvements for support, especially when it comes to designing user experiences and branding SharePoint sites. New features for publishing sites minimize the specialized SharePoint knowledge that was previously required to successfully brand a SharePoint site. With SharePoint 2013, designers can create a site design as they typically would using their preferred design tool (e.g., Dreamweaver or whatever else is popular these days) without having to learn to use SharePoint Designer or Visual Studio 2013 to brand a SharePoint site.

As with any new technology, there will be a learning curve cost associated with upgrading or migrating to SharePoint 2013. If you currently use an earlier version of SharePoint, the upgrade decision is probably more "when" rather than "if"—but you should make the timing decision based on your business needs and whether or not you actually have critical business impact scenarios that will be enabled by SharePoint 2013 and whether the cost of enabling those scenarios over the long term is greater than the short-term migration and upgrade costs. There is no magic wand to make this decision easy, and the answer will be very different for each organization. In addition to the learning curve, be aware that as with the introduction of enterprise Content Types and managed metadata in SharePoint 2010, some of the features of SharePoint 2013 cannot be effectively and successfully deployed without an investment in people resources. One key cost area to evaluate is the ongoing investment in moderators for community sites. If you are going to enable the "gamification" features in communities, moderation is not optional—someone will need to monitor how reputation points are earned and valued and ensure that communities and the conversations they enable are adding value to the business.

Why Measure?

Measurement is critical to being able to determine the level of success of your solution. As a foundation, you should focus on both the objectives for measurement and the various perspectives for your metrics.

Performance measures support decision making and communication throughout an organization to understand the progress, efficiency, value, and strategic alignment of SharePoint solutions. Performance measures for SharePoint solutions have several objectives throughout different parts of the solution life cycle—before you get started, during the solution development, and after the initial deployment—as outlined in Table 8-1.

Having a measurement program is important, not just to understand the business case for your investment, but also to understand the trade-offs or impact of selecting investment A over investment B and to help guide your deployment after your solution is operational. It's not just about "Show me the money"; it's also about "How can we achieve an even greater impact?"

The perspectives of the customer, department, organization, and individual in an organization are critical to its success. The implication of this for SharePoint metrics is important—when you think about metrics and the measurement process, it is important to identify who is likely to use the performance measurement information. Potential users include strategic decision makers, project decision makers, funding and approval stakeholders, government agencies involved in approval or regulation, users, and customers. There is no one "right" set of metrics for SharePoint solutions. Metrics should be stated in terms that are familiar to the stakeholder. For this reason, you may find that there are several different metrics that need to be captured for your solution. Most solutions will require a combination of measurement types and classes to effectively communicate with the key stakeholders.

Table 8-1 Objectives for SharePoint Performance Measures Throughout the Life Cycle

Before	During	After
Help make a business case for implementation—to quantify the "before" and estimate the "after" situation.	Provide a target or goal for each phase of a deployment. Help make investment trade-offs—to decide which of several proposed projects has the greatest organizational impact. Help guide and tune the implementation process by providing feedback to users or sponsors to encourage desired behaviors or modifications to the solution.	Describe, retrospectively, the value of the initial investment decision and the lessons learned. Help develop benchmarks for future comparisons and for others to use. Focus learning from the effort and developing lessons learned.

Measurement Process Overview

The measurement process (see Figure 8-1) is presented as a series of questions that will help guide you through the decisions required to define, choose, and use the most appropriate metrics for your SharePoint solution.

The first two questions are actually outside the scope of the measurement process, but because they provide a critical foundation for the approach, the process is not really complete without them. The remainder of this chapter discusses each question and provides examples of how they might be answered in your organization.

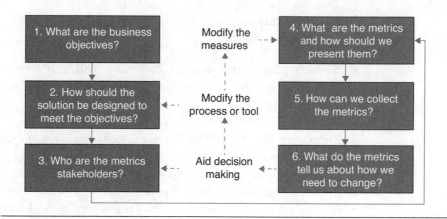

Figure 8-1 Measurement process

Question 1: What Are the Business Objectives?

Designing any good technology solution requires a comprehensive understanding of the business problem you are trying to solve. This is especially true if you are implementing the social computing features of SharePoint because one of the reasons many "social" solutions fail to gain traction is that they are disconnected from the key business challenges in the organization. There is only one reason for implementing SharePoint or any other collaboration or portal platform: you have a business problem to solve.

If you aren't addressing an important or valuable business problem with your SharePoint solution, you need to go back to the beginning to find that problem, as well as a business sponsor who is committed to solving it. Be sure you are tying your SharePoint solution to a key organizational initiative or goal. If not, you are working on a "sideshow" project—one whose funding is going to be at risk no matter what your measurement program concludes. (This could also become a career-limiting move if you are the one responsible for the solution.)

Another reason to have a clear connection to business goals is to help make decisions about which potential SharePoint project(s) to implement. With limited time, budget, and resources, most organizations find that there are more possible projects for the SharePoint team than can possibly be accomplished. In this scenario, it's important to have a framework for differentiating among opportunities that are competing for scarce resources.

Many organizations share a common list of objectives for SharePoint solutions. For example:

- Reducing the volume of organizational e-mail and e-mail attachments to save time and reduce the confusion resulting from multiple document versions
- Reducing communications costs
- Improving the ability to connect with partners, customers, and suppliers by making it easier to publish content on the Internet
- Increasing speed of access to existing knowledge assets
- Improving the ability to find experts and expertise
- Improving decision-making time (search helps find things quickly, which can, in turn, streamline decision making and even business processes)
- Improving response time for nonroutine issues that don't follow standard processes by providing tools to enable navigation across boundaries—connecting people to people to accelerate exception resolution
- Decreasing travel costs
- Increasing customer, employee, and partner satisfaction
- Reducing time to market and improving the ability to create innovative products or services

While it's easy to say, "Yes, I want that too," it's important that you understand what these objectives mean for your business and how you specifically plan to measure your solution results. It's really difficult (if not impossible) to plan your measurement strategy around these broad goals. Of course, we all want to achieve these strategic objectives in general, but to produce meaningful and measureable results, it's far more helpful to identify a specific, tactical approach that works in your organization. Getting more tactical means getting SMARTer about your solution goals.

Get SMART

SMART is a mnemonic for thinking about setting meaningful and realistic objectives for any type of performance evaluation. The acronym describes the key characteristics of meaningful performance indicators:

- **S**pecific (concrete and well defined)
- **M**easurable (quantifiable, comparable)

- **A**chievable (feasible, actionable)
- **R**ealistic (consider resources)
- **T**ime-bound (deadline driven)

Thus, a good objective for measuring performance is expressed in a SMART way. For example, a good collaboration solution can speed the time to create critical deliverables. For a consulting organization, a SMART objective for a SharePoint proposal library solution might be to reduce the average amount of time it takes to produce complex proposals by 10% in Year X. (This is actually relatively easy to do if your organization assigns a unique project number to major proposal efforts.) When you start with a SMART business objective, you immediately have two critical elements of your measurement plan: a baseline measure to capture and the outcome that defines success.

The good news is that most important business problems in your organization will already have at least one baseline measure—but this is not always the case. Before you even think about getting started, try to quantify both the problem and the target—and get management buy-in regarding the change in outcome that means success. In other words, understand how success is spelled in *your* organization.

In addition, take a look around the organization to find examples of solutions that are already delivering value—solutions that users really like and that management holds up as examples of successes. If you can understand why those projects or solutions are considered successful, you can look for analogous problems or opportunities to find what might work in your own backyard.

Question 2: How Should the Solution Be Designed to Meet the Objectives?

There is not much point in trying to develop a measurement plan for a solution that doesn't solve a critical business problem, so you really have to answer Question 1 before you can move on to Question 2. However, if you have a critical business problem to solve, it's also critical to make sure that you are following good practices to design a solution to solve that problem. It's not enough to just understand the business objective; it's also essential to design a solution worth measuring! Fortunately, most of the content in this book is focused on sharing good practices for designing SharePoint 2013 solutions.

In the context of SharePoint, creating a great design means thinking about the answers to even more important questions, including these:

- What is the most appropriate site architecture and technical infrastructure for your solution?
- Which features of SharePoint will enable you to achieve your objectives?
- What types of customizations make sense for your solution?
- How will you support any planned customizations over the long term, and what impact will these customizations have on the ability to upgrade?
- What is the plan for security?
- What is the governance model for your solution?
- Do you have a clear set of roles and responsibilities for deploying the solution?
- What types of training and communications are planned?

Question 3: Who Are the Metrics Stakeholders?

Part of understanding the business objective is identifying your key stakeholders. From the perspective of metrics, you need to identify who will use the measures, how your solution addresses the business problems they care about, and which solution metrics most effectively demonstrate an impact on those problems. Sue's late Uncle Phil used to always say, "Everyone has their own set of nerves." Think about her Uncle Phil when you think about your stakeholders—each one has a different set of objectives, business goals, and responsibilities. Your metrics story needs to speak directly to their needs.

In most cases, your solution stakeholders and your metrics stakeholders are the same people. However, not all stakeholders need the same type of information, and you may have a metrics stakeholder who has only a peripheral relationship to the solution itself—such as a high-level business executive. A helpful approach is to create a list of solution stakeholders and use brainstorming to identify additional stakeholders who care about specific metrics. Use that list to create a table to identify the type of information each stakeholder needs to know about your solution.

The type of information stakeholders will care about depends on the types of decisions that they need to make. Identify the key decisions and questions for each of your key stakeholders:

- How is their business unit or team evaluated?
- What keeps them up at night?
- What are the metrics that they use or review already to evaluate the success of business initiatives?
- What information do they need to derive from your metrics in order to make better decisions or understand their business operations?

A word of caution: sometimes, stakeholders get carried away with the level of detail and measures they *think* they need to measure the success of the solution. As you work with your stakeholders to determine what they need to know, **focus on the outcomes, and then work backward to figure out how you will measure those outcomes**. For example, in a consulting firm, there was a core business objective related to understanding employee expertise so that the firm could both staff projects with the best possible resources and quickly respond to client questions. One of their initiatives included maintaining expertise information about their employees. While they could create reports to show the percentage of employees who had entered at least one expertise topic at the "expert" level (and to be sure, several executives really wanted to know that number), that metric was pretty useless in terms of telling executives the value of the data itself or the processes they had created to maintain it. In this example, high "adoption" told virtually nothing about the value of the information or the processes they had enabled to keep it up-to-date. The firm realized that the only true and useful measure of the value of the expertise identification information was how it was used. To capture the value of the information, they conducted an annual survey and offered prizes for people who could tell the best story about how the expertise information delivered value to their business unit or project or client. The firm asked the storyteller to quantify the value—typically in terms of time saved or revenue generated—and then applied a consistent, fully loaded average salary cost to estimate the monetary value of the story.

Question 4: What Are the Metrics and How Should We Present Them?

Once you identify your key stakeholders and understand what they need to know, you need to focus on identifying the *types* of metrics, how you will *collect* the metrics, and how you will *communicate* the metrics. Together, these three elements will form the measurement approach.

SharePoint and Traditional ROI Analysis

ROI is one way of looking at the potential value of a capital investment. The purpose of an ROI metric is to measure the per-period (typically annual) rate of return on money invested in order to make a financial decision. Quite simply, the ROI is the difference between the value of the benefits and the investment cost over a defined period of time.

Traditional ROI analysis is tricky for SharePoint solutions. The approach that you take to communicate about metrics will likely depend on where you are in the life cycle of your project. If you are at the beginning and you are focused on demonstrating why SharePoint 2013 is the right application to use to build your solution, and you are not already using SharePoint for other business solutions, you may have some unique criteria for your ROI analysis. For example, if you are building a solution to support just one small area of the business, but everyone in the organization will need to use it, you will want to understand how much of the cost burden for SharePoint should be factored into the first SharePoint solution. While the initial cost analysis might be perceived as supporting just one solution (and might seem expensive), that same cost infrastructure will eventually be shared by all of your SharePoint solutions—and shouldn't be unfairly associated with just the first one. However, if that initial solution is your company's public Web site or intranet, you may want to consider the infrastructure cost as primarily being associated with the initial enterprise project. The point is that a traditional ROI analysis where you need to consider ongoing operational and infrastructure costs is easier and most appropriate for investing in SharePoint as an application platform but may be less relevant for analyzing alternative SharePoint investments or measuring the impact of an ongoing SharePoint solution. However, each solution, as well as the platform as a whole, has a total-cost-of-ownership element, which includes calculating the time and effort and resources that will be needed to fix the solution when it breaks. These costs, plus the cost of fielding user support calls, should also be included in your overall analysis of costs.

Once the SharePoint infrastructure is in place, the incremental cost of each new investment is relatively trivial, so if you choose a traditional ROI measure for your solution, you will need to determine whether and how to account for infrastructure costs. The best advice here is to choose an approach and be consistent. It can be very challenging to estimate how much data storage one solution will need as opposed to another and very difficult to determine a consistent method for estimating storage in advance. So, if you decide to leave storage infrastructure or the ongoing operational cost of maintaining the SharePoint environment out of the measurement equation, leave it out for all of your prospective or existing solutions. From a practical perspective, it's impossible to imagine an ROI calculation that is 100% precise—and that really shouldn't be your goal. Your measurement goal is to ensure that you have a consistent approach to ensure that value is being delivered with each solution or incremental investment.

"ROI-Lite" in Practice

One organization we know employs an "ROI-lite" measurement approach to prioritize and evaluate potential SharePoint projects—but the ROI that they calculate does include cost measures for routine projects. Many of these projects involve using SharePoint to automate an existing process or workflow. They have a small team of internal resources to help with the creation of SharePoint solutions. To determine which projects to work on, they calculate a baseline metric for executing the process before SharePoint—sometimes by measuring process throughput and other times by observing the time it takes to do a task. They then estimate the process or throughput times expected in the "after" situation and multiply this number by the number of times the process is executed in a year and then by an average fully loaded hourly cost for an employee. The initial calculation helps prioritize which projects to work on. Then, to ensure that the solutions are delivering the expected value, they go back to each project after about 90 days and measure actual results. These new metrics help provide insight into potential repeatable solutions for other business areas. While metrics based on averages may not provide a precise measure of ROI, the repeated use of a consistent calculation can be used to assess priorities and disseminate best practices—both of which are important elements of an overall measurement program.

ROI is really only part of the measurement story for SharePoint—and it won't be the right metric for all of your stakeholders. While employees using a collaboration solution might appreciate the benefit the organization gets from the platform, it's not the measurement that they really care about. The metric that drives their day-to-day behavior is not the overall benefit for the company; it's a more personal metric that answers the question "What's in it for me?"

User Adoption and Measurement

The most important characteristic to consider when choosing or defining a performance measure is whether the metric tells something about the outcome you are trying to achieve. Just because you have 75% of your organization completing a robust user profile in SharePoint 2013 does not necessarily mean that SharePoint 2013 is successful. Adoption is not the end of the road. Business results are the only true measure of SharePoint success.

Choose the metrics you want to capture in terms of the use cases that are of highest interest to your stakeholders and their business objectives. It's also important to pick a small number of metrics that are both relevant to the business and have a more direct relationship to business outcomes—and can be collected at a relatively low cost. For example, a possible metric for a best practices library is the number of times the library has been accessed. A large number of accesses or "hits" for the library or an individual document suggests that people are reading documents, but this does not definitively indicate whether the content was useful to anyone or whether it improved operational efficiency or quality. To get a better measure of value, you could enable the ratings function in SharePoint 2013 along with very clear directions regarding the context of the ratings (in this context, a good rating metric would be to ask users to rate the degree to which they were able to reuse the document). Adding ratings makes the hits or downloads metric much more valuable than either would be on its own because it combines a quantitative measure of usage with a qualitative measure of value. Adding a user survey to seek out specific cases where the information helped and how it was used would add even more meaning to your metric—because you would now have specific examples that your stakeholders can relate to (and share with others).

Types of Measurement

The specific measurement approaches you choose for your SharePoint initiative can be *quantitative* or *qualitative*. In general, a measurement program should include both types:

- **Quantitative measurement** approaches use numbers and typically provide "hard" data to evaluate performance between points (such as last month to this month) or to spot trends. For example, you can collect quantitative data on site usage or the number of hours spent on a particular task. Even if the absolute value of hard data such as the number of site accesses in a given month doesn't tell you much about the *value* of the solution, a significant drop or increase in that metric can give you important clues about the content or the solution itself. Some quantitative measurements can be obtained automatically from native SharePoint 2013 usage data, and others require third-party tools. One of the major investment areas for SharePoint 2013 is in the area of usage measurement. Examples of some of the quantitative system measurement data you can obtain from SharePoint 2013 are described later in this chapter.
- **Qualitative measurement** approaches, often referred to as "soft" data, include stories, anecdotes, and future scenarios. When it is difficult to capture meaningful quantitative metrics (for example, at the beginning of a project), qualitative metrics can have a significant benefit. The best measurement programs incorporate both quantitative and qualitative measurements. The qualitative metrics—especially those with a quantitative "punch line"—add richness to your quantitative metrics.

Quantitative Metrics

Too often, SharePoint solution owners spend too much time capturing metrics that have very little impact on the true value of the SharePoint solution. Every metric you capture, whether it's a *system metric* that is automatically provided or a *business metric* that might require some additional effort to record, needs to fit into the story you are trying to tell.

System metrics (often called "usage analytics") are captured directly from SharePoint 2013 or a third-party tool. System metrics alone do not directly measure business value, but they can be especially useful in providing clues to where users are getting value and to help quickly spot content problems or gaps and areas for improvement. System metrics don't typically cost very much to collect, but because they are more loosely coupled with the outcome you are trying to measure, you will almost always need to make a decision about how much and which "nonsystem" metrics you need to add to your system metrics to create a meaningful measurement approach.

Figure 8-2 lists some of the most helpful usage metrics that are available out of the box with SharePoint 2013 and the business value objective for each of these metrics. Not all metrics and targets should be the same. For example, usage metrics depend on the type of content. A news site, especially if it is the home page, is likely to be visited every day. A policy site would not need to be visited daily to deliver the same value. In SharePoint 2013, all analytics processing is part of the search service. Usage analytics are significantly improved with SharePoint 2013 and, when combined with search analytics, provide new and useful information that can add value to the SharePoint experience.

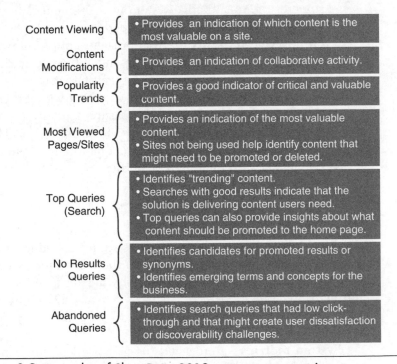

Figure 8-2 Examples of SharePoint 2013 system usage metrics

In SharePoint 2013, usage analytics capture user actions such as clicks and viewed items. These usage events are added to the search index. Each time a user views an item, SharePoint creates a usage event. SharePoint 2013 logs every click in SharePoint sites and provides a count of hits for every document. This information is used to provide "item-to-item" recommendations (people who viewed this also viewed this), to show "view counts" in search results, to provide a count of the top items in a list or a site, and to influence relevancy in search results. There are three types of usage events that are configured by default, and if needed, you can configure up to 12 additional custom events. The default usage events are

- **Views:** the number of times an item, page, or document has been viewed
- **Recommendations displayed:** the number of times an item, page, or document was shown in a recommendation
- **Recommendations clicked:** the number of times an item, page, or document was clicked when it was shown in the context of a recommendation

In practice, these events help more than just "count" system usage; they are used dynamically by SharePoint to influence search results and create a more helpful user experience.

Business or outcome metrics are used to tell the story of how the solution impacts the organizational business processes. It is very likely that your organization is already tracking a significant number of business metrics related to the core business activities you perform. These may include metrics such as the number of new customers acquired over a given period, metrics related to order processing, or metrics related to financial accounting such as average accounts receivable. In the ideal world, you should look to your SharePoint deployment to have an impact on these key business metrics—because if your solution is solving a core business problem, you clearly want to make sure you can directly impact the "main event." But it's almost impossible to measure SharePoint's unique impact on these metrics. If your story can be shown alongside positive movement in key corporate metrics, or if your solution is really directly related to one or more of these metrics, you need to track and showcase them in your metrics reports or dashboards. You may not always be able to directly impact the "main event," but you really want the problem you are addressing to be at least part of or connected to the bigger picture. Here are a few examples of business metrics that might help you get started:

- **Number of hours per week to process data or execute a business process:** Let's say that your business objective is to reduce the amount of time it takes to execute a specific task. For example, you've designed a data capture and workflow solution in SharePoint 2013 to improve the processing flow. The first thing you need to do is get a baseline measure for the current process—the "as is." There are a number of techniques that you can use, ranging from asking the people who are doing the job today to timing them either informally or with a time and motion study. If your process is less concrete, such as finding experts to work on an assignment or answer a question, you will have to be creative about identifying your baseline metric. As discussed later in this chapter, you may need to try to quantify the current problem through the capture and use of stories, anecdotes, interviews, surveys, and other qualitative measures. As long as you apply consistent assumptions in your baseline and post-project metrics, you should be in a good position to demonstrate a positive impact.

- **Number of [proposals, contracts, etc.] produced per month/quarter/year:** If the objective for your solution is to improve the ability to create new proposals, contracts, or other documents that rely on reusable content, one useful outcome metric is the number of these artifacts that you produce in a given time period. For proposals, you might want to track both the number produced and the number of *successful* proposals.

- **Number of "[Your Organization] All" e-mails:** Reading e-mail messages that aren't really targeted to you takes time—time that could be spent focused on other critical tasks. In addition, untargeted e-mails have a cost to the organization in terms of mailbox storage. Transferring even a small portion of the "All" e-mails to targeted SharePoint news or announcements can have a direct positive impact on productivity and e-mail cost.[1] Calculating a

---

1. If you are looking for a great way to estimate the cost of the "info-glut" related to e-mail, take a look at *The Hamster Revolution* by Mike Song, Vicki Halsey, and Tim Burress (Berrett-Koehler Publishers, Inc., 2007). They estimate that if you send and receive as few as 60 e-mails per workday and spend an average of two minutes per e-mail, you are spending a total of 60 days per year just on e-mail! If you multiply that by the number of people in the organization, you can see that you wouldn't have to eliminate too many messages in order to make a significant impact on productivity. (If you combine the impact of using SharePoint 2013 to publish information and some of the other great suggestions in this book, you could make an even bigger impact.)

baseline number for "[Your Organization] All" e-mails is a good productivity-related metric.

- **Number of e-mail attachments:** E-mail attachments have a significant cost in terms of both productivity (users may never know if they are looking at the most recent version of a document) and storage.
- **Average application training costs:** One benefit that many organizations find from investing in SharePoint portal solutions is the ability to significantly reduce the amount of money they spend on application training. The reason is that many users of enterprise applications use only a small fraction of the functionality, and by creating Web Parts for the most common functions, you may be able to eliminate application training for these users.
- **Cost savings to retire an existing application:** Many organizations are slowly retiring existing third-party or custom applications and are rebuilding the solutions with SharePoint. For a baseline metric, look to the annual hardware and software maintenance costs for your legacy solutions.

If you want to translate the time it takes to execute a current business process to dollars, you'll need to know the average fully loaded hourly cost of the employee who performs the task currently. You can probably get this number from your human resources or finance department.

Qualitative Metrics

Qualitative metrics provide context and meaning for quantitative metrics. When it is difficult to capture meaningful quantitative metrics (such as the value to the individual for being a member of a community), qualitative metrics (such as a story from a member about how the community helped solve a critical problem) can have as much or more impact on stakeholders. Qualitative metrics can augment quantitative metrics with additional context and meaning.

The best qualitative metrics are what we like to call "serious anecdotes." A serious anecdote is a story with a meaningful (dollar value) punch line—a story that describes a measurable business result. The serious anecdotes in the sidebars describe examples from several industries. Even though these anecdotes describe specific instances, they may be relevant to your situation. If you can collect and quantify multiple similar serious anecdotes as part of your measurement program (approaches for *collecting* these stories are described later in the chapter), the *combination* of the serious outcomes of your qualitative stories demonstrates a real and significant metric to associate with your solution investment.

Example Of a Serious Anecdote: Consulting

I joined the organization on March 16 without previous experience. After one week of training, I joined a project team.

After one day of training on the project, I was assigned a task to learn a particular technology that was new to everyone on the team. I was given a bunch of books and told that I had three days to learn how to create a project using this technology.

In my first week of training, I remembered learning about the company's expertise database. I sent an e-mail to four people I found in the database asking for their help. One of them sent me a document containing exactly what I wanted.

Instead of three days, my task was completed in one-half a day.

Example of a Serious Anecdote: Pharmaceutical

A scientist with expertise in thrombotic and joint diseases in Frankfurt began a project to isolate and culture macrophages and needed some help.

Meanwhile, two scientists in the United States had deep experience with protocols for this area.

The Frankfurt scientist consulted the intranet to find expertise within the company and contacted the two U.S. scientists.

Both scientists in the United States quickly responded with assistance. One helped with culturing protocols and the other helped with information about magnetic cell sorting.

By reaching out to the other scientists via online search, the Frankfurt scientist was able to leverage existing internal expertise and, in the process, reduced his research effort by four weeks.

Example of a Serious Anecdote: Construction

ICA is a construction company in Mexico with operations in the Americas and Europe. They created an enterprise content management system using SharePoint. It provides a way to organize and search terabytes of documents and create knowledge communities.[2]

From the case study: "Because ICA stores and organizes project documentation in one place, it can better track customer change orders throughout project life cycles, which can **add up to tens of thousands of dollars' worth of work**."

Prior to the implementation of the SharePoint solution, it was difficult to charge customers for changes because they were not well documented. According to the Web infrastructure manager, "Now, we can track and document every task completed so that we can bill for it."

Even if you have a rich collection of quantitative metrics, you will want to have some qualitative metrics to provide context and meaning for your measurement program. The collection of anecdotes or stories is probably the most common type of qualitative measurement approach. But what if you haven't yet implemented your solution and you don't yet have any stories to capture? In this case, there is a special type of story that is particularly helpful. These types of stories describe a future vision for the organization or business unit or describe a "day in the life" of one or more types of employees and are often referred to as "future scenarios." A future scenario might start like this: "Imagine the future . . . " The following example is an excerpt of a future scenario for a "next-generation" intranet at a management consulting firm.

Future Scenario Example

Imagine the future . . . On December 15, 2016, just after his morning coffee, Rick Jones, a consultant working with a financial institution, is asked by the client for advice on creating a social media strategy.

---

2. www.microsoft.com/casestudies/Microsoft-Sharepoint-Server-2010/ICA/Construction-Firm-Speeds-Project-Completion-with-Centralized-Content-Management/4000010862

Rick has limited social media experience, and the client wants a proposal with a fairly detailed plan before the holidays so the budget money can be allocated prior to the end of the year.

Over his next cup of coffee, Rick accesses the intranet and searches the topic "social media strategy." A graphic view of a knowledge map helps him navigate the abundance of information.

Rick finds the firm's social media strategy methodology, several sample proposals for similar clients that have five-star ratings by the Social Computing Community of Practice, 25 applicable qualification statements, a list of the members of the Social Computing Community of Practice, and links to their personal profile pages.

Rick clicks on a three-minute embedded video that features social media expert Liz Picone talking about the key challenges for "social business" engagements.

Rick sees that the qualifications in the business area of the financial institution he's working with are limited, so he executes a search outside the intranet, using research services to which the company subscribes and Web sites "certified" by the corporate library.

After lunch, Rick sees that several of the social media experts are online, and he calls a few to ask their advice on how to address a particularly unique aspect of the potential engagement.

Rick downloads one of the proposals recommended by an expert for a head start. As he begins adding details that are unique to his client's needs, the search agent built into the intranet pops up with three additional proposals that are also similar to Rick's and an article in a Gartner research database that rates his company as a premier provider of social media consulting services.

On December 18, the proposal is completed and mailed to the client.

When the proposal is completed, Rick clicks the option "save to intranet" so that his newly completed proposal is immediately available to others across the firm.

Rick is prompted for some simple metadata so that his proposal can be indexed and cataloged appropriately.

In three weeks, the system prompts Rick for a status update on the proposal: Did we win? What was the feedback from the client? Rick updates the proposal database simply by replying to the automatically generated e-mail message.

This example "future scenario" concluded with a summary of the vision for knowledge management at the company. Did it work? Draw your own conclusion. In the meeting where this vision was presented, one of the executives in the room raised his hand and said, "I can't *wait* to work for that company!"

SharePoint 2013 provides yet another particularly interesting way to capture qualitative metrics with the ratings and likes features. Consider using ratings for a very simple purpose: to ask users to indicate whether a page or document is helpful. In other words, the messaging for your ratings program is both simple and clear—all you are asking users is "Was this asset helpful?" or "Were you able to get value from this asset?" This simple approach gives you a way to quantify your qualitative metrics in a meaningful way, and it also gives you a way to capture more meaningful stories by reaching out to those people who liked or rated a document or page. People will typically tell you more in a conversation than they will write down, so if you use a "journalist approach" to find the lead and then interview the storyteller, you will probably get much better results.

Telling the Measurement Story

Communicating the measurement story is as important as picking the measures in the first place. Telling the measurement story for your SharePoint solution is no different from telling any other type of business story—you need to understand your audience, what they need to know, and their preferred platform for evaluating metrics. And, even more important than for other business stories, you need to consider carefully where you are in the life cycle of your investment—because the story you tell and the measures you use will be different at each phase.

Determine a Baseline

If you've selected a key business problem to automate using SharePoint 2013, it's likely that you already have some baseline measures in place. Note that one major mistake people often make when documenting their measures of success with SharePoint is that they try to demonstrate business impact without knowing where they started. This approach is doomed to failure. **You need to have a good baseline or you will have**

no ability to measure the impact of your SharePoint solution. The first places to look for outcome measures are the metrics that you are already capturing for the business problem that you are trying to solve. If those metrics do not already exist, you will want to establish a good baseline measure before you get started. You can't tell how far you've come if you don't know where you started!

With that in mind, you will most likely want to capture both quantitative measures and qualitative metrics for your baseline "before." After you have deployed your solution, and sometimes along the way as you are implementing it, you will want to use the same approach to capture your "after" story.

Package and Present

The approach you use to package and present your metrics should be aligned with your solution objectives, your overall strategic goals, the expectations of your key stakeholders, and techniques that are already being used in your organization. You may need to present your metrics in multiple ways depending on the audience. Two options that are particularly helpful include preparing a balanced scorecard and a metrics "dashboard" summary.

There are dozens of other approaches that you could consider for presenting your metrics. In one organization, the portal team prepared a dashboard in a report card format each year to show the impact of the intranet and collaboration solution on the business. The criteria were similar to what was used in their balanced scorecard, but the presentation style helped highlight where they were especially successful and where their approach or communications or user adoption needed improvement.

The **balanced scorecard** is a strategic planning and management system that was made popular by Drs. Robert Kaplan and David Norton as a measurement framework that added key nonfinancial performance metrics to traditional financial metrics so that executives would get a more balanced view of organizational performance. An approach based on a balanced scorecard is especially useful in creating a framework for looking at SharePoint solution investments—even if not all of the elements of an organizational balanced scorecard are applicable. One organization used a very successful balanced scorecard approach to craft a metrics model for a new expertise location system. The team knew that the solution required both changes in user behavior (to create their profiles and to use the system to find expertise) and the implementation of new technology. The goal for the initial metrics plan was to create a meaningful way of showing executives specific measurement targets for the pilot deployment along with the ability to objectively track the metrics results. The most important thing they did in advance was to gain consensus from the executive sponsors that if the target goals for the pilot were achieved, the executives would consider the pilot a success and recommend funding a full deployment. The team wanted to emphasize that there were several different types of measures that together presented the most balanced way to evaluate the pilot success, so they adapted the balanced scorecard model to show information that was especially meaningful to their stakeholders.

Figure 8-3 shows three specific categories of measures you can use to create a balanced scorecard for SharePoint projects.

For each category in your scorecard, you will likely have multiple metrics. For each metric, you will want to track three key attributes:

- **Target:** the goal for the metric during the period covered by your SMART objective. Review target metrics with management in advance so that the key stakeholders and decision makers can define how they will measure success.
- **Actual:** the results measured at the end of the evaluation period.
- **Differences:** percentage that the target differs from the actual.

Table 8-2 shows examples of metrics that you can consider adapting for your balanced scorecard or dashboard report.

Figure 8-3 Balanced scorecard categories

Table 8-2 Balanced Scorecard Metrics

Scorecard Category	Critical Success Factors	Sample Metrics	Source
Business Value			
Demonstrate clear value with respect to the business strategy	Tangible, quantifiable examples of reductions in process cycle time	No. of anecdotes $ value of anecdotes Cycle time improvement (in hours)	"Serious anecdotes" collected via surveys and follow-up Estimates and/or direct measurement of cycle time
Health			
Gain frequent and sustained adoption of solution	High volume of needs that can't be met through existing channels Positive impact on existing workload or work processes	No. of searches per week No. of average users per week No. of unique users per week No. of "hits" on key pages/sites "Usefulness rating" from user surveys Percentage of users who say, "Don't take it away" at the end of the pilot	System metrics User surveys
Capabilities			
Provide reliable, easy-to-use technology that can be incorporated into work processes	Solution user friendliness and intuitiveness Solution reliability Integration of the solution with work processes and existing tools	"Usefulness rating" from user surveys No. of searches per week No. of average users per week No. of unique users per week No. of "hits" on key pages/sites No. of Help Desk calls/week	System metrics User surveys Direct measurement

Scorecard Category	Critical Success Factors	Sample Metrics	Source
Ensure that users understand objectives and how to leverage the solution	User training Effective help resources Persistent, clear communications Active, sustained management support Incorporation of collaboration into performance objectives and evaluations	Percentage of users trained Percentage of pilot milestones achieved No. of communications events/activities	User surveys Direct measurement

Table 8-3 shows a template that you can use to create a balanced scorecard for your SharePoint initiative. If relevant, consider using some of the sample metrics shown in Table 8-2 in your scorecard.

If a balanced scorecard doesn't quite work to present your metrics, SharePoint 2013 provides some excellent dashboard and charting tools that can be used to present quantitative metrics and qualitative survey results in meaningful ways. A good metrics dashboard tells a story visually without overwhelming the user. Not all data requires visualization to make the point. Don't go overboard picking the coolest-looking visualization approach just because you can. Be careful when choosing colors; to a colorblind person, red-green indicators can be very difficult to discern unless combined with other indicators that are not dependent on color. Try to stick with simple and familiar approaches (pie and bar charts will almost always win out over speedometer-type gauges), but the best approach depends on the type of data you are presenting.

While some of your usage data might be interesting in real time, most of your measurements will not need to be presented in real time to tell an effective story. Choose a time period for both collecting and presenting metrics that achieves a balance between the cost of collecting and presenting the metrics and the value that they provide.

Table 8-3 Balanced Scorecard Template

Category	Metric	Value	Outcome
Business value			
Health			
Capabilities			

Question 5: How Can We Collect the Metrics?

As you identify the metrics that you want to capture, you will need to define a measurement process to collect them. Be careful not to overdo capturing and producing metrics for your key stakeholders. You are looking for the appropriate balance; you want to capture and report on just the right metrics—not too few and not too many. You want to make sure that you are not spending more time counting than you are "doing."

Some of the available system metrics in SharePoint 2013 were provided in Figure 8-3. Wherever possible, use automated approaches to capture system metrics. Qualitative metrics are harder to collect. The following approaches have been successful in several organizations.

Usability Testing

The goal of usability testing is to identify any usability problems, collect quantitative data on participants' performance (e.g., time on task, error rates), as well as determine user satisfaction with the solution.[3] For successful solutions, usability testing is an ongoing process, which means that you can and should be using this process to capture value metrics for your solution! At a minimum, consider some type of usability testing every six months as an element of your measurement program.

Usability testing does not have to be an expensive proposition. Usability expert Jakob Nielsen says that elaborate usability tests are not always necessary. Excellent results can come from testing no more than five users and running as many small tests as you can afford.[4]

---

3. Marissa Peacock, "The What, Why and How of Usability Testing," April 13, 2010. www.cmswire.com/cms/web-engagement/the-what-why-and-how-of-usability-testing-007152.php
4. Jakob Nielsen's Alertbox, "Why You Only Need to Test with 5 Users," March 19, 2000. www.useit.com/alertbox/20000319.html

One organization incorporated measures of usability in a post-pilot survey for a new collaboration solution in addition to a more formal usability study and used both as part of its balanced scorecard. Table 8-4 shows the questions in the usability survey and the "metrics" that were derived from the survey results.

User Feedback

A great way to collect qualitative metrics on an ongoing basis is to make sure that all your sites and pages include a feedback button or link and/or a link to a site or page owner that provides the ability for users to provide feedback. If feedback is distributed to individual site owners, you will need to provide a mechanism to ensure that qualitative feedback is shared with the team responsible for solution metrics, which could be the site owner but might also be the business owner of SharePoint as a whole. Keeping track of what users take the time to note about your solution is a great way to monitor value on an ongoing basis.

Ongoing User Surveys

Periodically survey users to identify users with good value stories—and then interview the users to capture both the story and their estimate of value. Ask questions such as

- What have you found on [the solution] that you have been able to reuse?
- How much effort did that save?

Table 8-4 Usability Testing Metrics

Usability Test Question	Metric
If presented with the choice, do you want to keep the solution? (Choices: "Don't take it away" and "Take it away")	"Don't take it away"
How does the usability of this solution compare to other solutions you use on a regular basis? (Choices: 5-point scale—Much harder to use, Harder to use, About the same, Easier to use, and Much easier to use)	"User-friendliness rating"
How easy and intuitive is the solution for each of the following [specific tasks]? (Choices: 5-point scale—Very difficult, Difficult, Moderate, Easy, Very easy)	"Intuitiveness rating"

One technique that might help collect good "serious anecdotes" from periodic surveys is to give respondents an option to follow up the survey with an interview. Here is a question that you might add to your user survey: "If you prefer, we can contact you directly to gather this information. We would take no more than a couple of minutes to record your experience. Would you rather have us contact you?"

Keep all stories in a document library or list with good metadata so that you have the results available to report or demonstrate as needed. Keep a list of user quotes to use in presentations and reports.

Question 6: What Do the Metrics Tell Us about How We Need to Change?

In an article in *Washingtonian* magazine in August 2012, Chris Tracy, president and chief operating officer of the Chef Geoff's restaurant group started by his brother, Geoff Tracy, was quoted as saying, "Numbers are just tools. The idea is to get better. To constantly improve."[5] This is as important for managing restaurant groups as it is for running any type of organization. The goal for your measurement program is to use the information to make good decisions—about the solution as well as the business. Figure 8-1 shows not just the six key measurement process questions, but also a feedback loop as a reminder that your measurement program provides critical input to how your SharePoint solution can be adapted over time to continue to provide value. The complex and dynamic nature of pretty much all organizations means that the SharePoint solutions we build are going to have to be flexible enough to change in order to continue to provide value. The only way to understand what changes you need to make is to execute your measurement plan.

Use your measurement framework to assess how users are taking advantage of the solution and let it act as an early-warning system to identify both new metrics and new capabilities that can help achieve your business objectives. When a metric shows an unexpected result, try to find out whether it was a one-time event or an indicator of a trend. Ask yourself if the result you are seeing tells you that you may be measuring the wrong thing. At the very least, metrics will help you get ideas for how to improve your solution. Collect and prioritize these new ideas and

---

5. Todd Kliman, "Everywhere at Once," *Washingtonian*, August 2012, p. 172

go back to your original plans and assumptions to see if they need to be changed. Then, build consensus on what needs to be changed, how to make the change, and when and how to introduce the change to your users.

Key Points

Metrics alone won't make your SharePoint solution successful. To be helpful, the metrics need

- A person whose job it is to monitor them
- A person or team who is accountable for making changes based on metrics analysis

In other words, it's as important to have a plan for acting on metrics as it is to collect them in the first place! Identify who will be responsible for producing and reviewing metrics reports. This will likely include people from both your SharePoint administration team and business owners. Your measurement plan puts a sharp focus on the things that you are measuring. This gives everyone a clear indication of what is important to the organization. And if it's important, someone needs to have responsibility for paying attention!

Evaluate whether the best approach to capture and monitor metrics is via a third-party tool or custom code. Custom reports using existing data may provide the least expensive option for capturing the desired metrics, but using a third-party tool will provide the most flexible long-term solution. Most of the third-party tools that are designed to work with SharePoint have capabilities to leverage out-of-the-box metrics and collect and capture additional custom metrics. They typically provide a repository for collecting metrics so that trending analysis can be accomplished for key metrics.

Once you decide the specific approaches you will use for your SharePoint measurement program:

- Develop a plan to capture qualitative metrics.
- Develop a library or list to capture and categorize qualitative metrics.
- Develop an approach to produce regular metrics analysis (e.g., a balanced scorecard showing both qualitative and quantitative metrics as well as actions taken as a result of metrics analysis).

CHAPTER 9

UNDERSTANDING ARCHITECTURE FUNDAMENTALS

No matter your role, you'll want to understand the fundamental structure and core terminology of SharePoint 2013, since it will influence many choices you make, such as internal business ownership and total infrastructure costs. After reading this chapter, you'll understand the difference between sites and site collections, what shared services are and how they've changed, and why you may need as many as 20 servers or as few as *zero*.

If you're using SharePoint Online (either stand-alone or as part of the Office 365 suite), Microsoft is running the core infrastructure in the cloud. That said, you'll still need to understand how site collections, sites, and service applications will impact your overall solution, along with how you might consider connecting your on-premises environment to a cloud-based one.

In this chapter, we'll cover the following topics to help you think about your SharePoint service from a high-level design perspective:

- New features of SharePoint 2013
- An overview of key SharePoint functions
- Sites, site collections, templates, and services
- Managing SharePoint administration
- Deployment options

What's New In SharePoint 2013?

In general, SharePoint 2013 retains the fundamental architecture of SharePoint 2010. Topology concepts such as flexible server roles (including Web Front Ends, application servers, and database servers) are still in play. In addition, the logical hierarchy of SharePoint, which includes Web applications, site collections, sites, and lists, is untouched.

New items include the following:

- The consolidation of SharePoint search and FAST search into a single search offering
- The removal of workflow and Office Web Apps as internal SharePoint offerings (and into stand-alone services)
- The introduction of the cloud as a tier-one architecture option

A Functional Overview

Let's first review the key components of Microsoft SharePoint 2013 and associated dependencies, including the operating system, database services, SharePoint Foundation, SharePoint applications, and SharePoint application services. It is important to understand which functionality is provided by which component, and how these components relate to each other.

Operating System

Microsoft SharePoint Server 2013 is built on top of SharePoint Foundation, which, in turn, is built on top of the technologies and services provided by Microsoft Windows Server 2008 or 2012. The core platform services use the Microsoft .NET 4.x Framework. This combination of Windows and .NET provides SharePoint with the following technologies:

- Internet Information Services 7/8 (for hosting Web applications)
- ASP.NET master pages, content pages (Web Part pages), Web Parts, personalization, membership, navigation
- Azure Workflow

Database Services

Microsoft SQL Server (either SQL 2008 SP1 R2 or SQL 2012) is the relational database used for storing all content, data, and configuration information used by SharePoint 2013, including documents and other BLOBs uploaded by users. All content (including large documents) is stored in the database, and not as files in the file system. SharePoint does provide an option for storing BLOBs outside of the database; this option is called Remote BLOB Storage (RBS). Several third-party vendors, and Microsoft itself, provide options for storing documents outside of the SQL Server database via RBS.

Since SQL Server is required for SharePoint, other relational databases, such as Oracle or MySQL, do not work and are not supported. If a separate database is not specified during installation, a specialized version of SQL Server 2008 Express is installed locally. The SharePoint-specific version of SQL Server 2008 Express has a database limit of 4GB and cannot be managed directly by SQL Enterprise Manager. For this reason, most organizations install SharePoint 2013 in a farm configuration and specify a separate SQL Server machine for the database server.

SharePoint Foundation 2013

SharePoint Foundation builds on the operating system and database services to add additional features, such as team sites and collaboration features. Specifically, SharePoint Foundation provides the following platform capabilities:

- **Storage.** The primary storage mechanism for SharePoint is through content databases, which are literally SQL databases managed by SharePoint to accommodate the pages, data, and documents stored in the various sites.
- **Management.** Configuration of settings, along with management functions, is provided via administration pages with deep configuration options.
- **Deployment.** The deployment topology, including Web farms, physical servers, and defined roles, is provided by SharePoint Foundation.
- **Site model.** The overall logical design consists of Web applications, site collections, and sites.
- **Extensibility.** The ability to extend SharePoint with additional features such as Web Parts and templates, along with the overall apps model, is also provided by SharePoint Foundation.

SharePoint Foundation provides more than just these core technology services. Microsoft decided to make SharePoint Foundation a useful application out of the box, and thus SharePoint Foundation provides the following application capabilities:

- **Document collaboration.** The core SharePoint platform provides document storage, check-in/checkout, version control, and other fundamental features for storing and managing documents. (Full capabilities require the SharePoint Standard CAL.)
- **Wikis and blogs.** Templates like wiki templates and blog templates are provided for social collaboration features.
- **RSS support.** The ability to consume and publish content as RSS (Really Simple Syndication) enables easier integration with content sources outside of SharePoint.
- **Project task management.** Lightweight project management functionality is provided for simple task management. This should not be confused with Microsoft Project Server 2013, which is built on top of, and requires, the Microsoft SharePoint Server 2013 Enterprise CAL.
- **Contacts.** The ability to manage contact information for external persons is provided as a list item template.
- **Calendars.** The ability to manage appointments and events is available as a list item template.
- **E-mail integration.** Core integration with an SMTP server is an important feature that provides alerts and other mail-based notification.
- **Integration with Office client applications.** Saving to and from the Office applications, such as Word and PowerPoint, is provided by SharePoint Foundation.

Application Features

Architecturally, Microsoft SharePoint Server (Standard and Enterprise) 2013 consists of a common set of application features that support a number of areas:

- **Portals and publishing.** SharePoint Server provides publishing templates that enable the storage and formatting of HTML content for both private and public Web sites.
- **Search.** Capabilities for finding and surfacing content via the Search Center, cross-site search, and the Content Search Web Part is provided by a new unified search engine.
- **Content management.** The ability to provide enterprise-scale authoring, advanced document management, and records management is something that the SharePoint Server standard CAL provides.

- **Business process.** Most processes involve capturing data via forms and integrating with other systems. SharePoint's forms server and line-of-business (LOB) integration feature (BCS) provide these services respectively.
- **Business intelligence.** SharePoint 2013 dramatically improves BI features such as status indicators, PerformancePoint functionality, and Excel Services.
- **Composite Applications.** The ability to create fast, dynamic applications, including mashups and agile applications, is provided by SharePoint Server.

Each of these is built upon the platform services and core application components of SharePoint Foundation, plus the application services components of Microsoft SharePoint Server 2013.

Service Applications

Service applications provide the features that are shared by multiple applications in Microsoft SharePoint Server 2013. What does that mean? Let's use an example—user profiles. You may want to use the user profile feature, which provides an out-of-the-box employee directory, including basic information (e.g., name, phone number), along with some custom properties and a photograph. You may also want to create several different sites within your organization, all of which use very different URLs and have different users—for example, an Internet presence, an employee intranet site, and a collaboration portal for self-service team site use. You wouldn't want to create and manage three separate profile databases. In this case, the user profile service can be shared across the various portals—hence it is a *shared service*. Specifically, the following features are provided by shared service applications in Microsoft SharePoint Server 2013:

- The User Profile Service Application enables you to store and synchronize user profiles and is the foundation for My Sites, audiences, and social features.
- The Search Service Application provides indexing and querying capabilities via a new engine based on underlying FAST technology.
- The Managed Metadata Service Application enables you to manage a central list of terms for tagging purposes.
- The Excel Services Service Application provides the ability to render Excel content and charts via a browser.

- The Word Services Service Application provides the ability to render Word documents via a browser.
- The Access Services Service Application provides the ability to create Access-based applications through SharePoint.
- The PowerPoint Services Service Application provides the ability to render PowerPoint documents via a browser.
- The Visio Services Service Application provides the ability to render Visio documents via a browser.
- The PerformancePoint Services Service Application enables a number of business intelligence scenarios including charts, graphs, and drill-down reporting.
- The Business Connectivity Services Service Application provides the ability to connect to databases and LOB systems outside of SharePoint.

So what exactly do service applications support? They are the middle-tier feature that supports SharePoint site collections by providing either processing functionality or data support (or both).

SharePoint 2013 does not change the service application architecture that was introduced in SharePoint 2010. For example, proxy groups are still used to define a collection of service applications that can be shared across a set of Web applications.

Sites, Site Collections, Site Templates, and Service Applications

There are fundamental concepts in SharePoint that comprise every portal, team site, Internet page, and extranet site:

- **Farm.** A farm is simply a collection of physical or virtual servers acting as one logical SharePoint environment. The SharePoint configuration database tracks all servers in the farm and treats the farm as one logical entity.
- **Web application.** Within a farm, you can split SharePoint into multiple Web applications. Each Web application is defined with a set of URLs, a logical partition in SharePoint, related settings, and a mapping to one or more Web sites in Internet Information Server (IIS). While not a technically perfect definition, you can

think of a Web application as a URL such as http://my.intranet .com or http://sharepoint.intranet.com.

- **Tenant.** Within a Web application, SharePoint can host many different organizations on a single farm. SharePoint can optionally provide a logical grouping just above the site collection level. This provides a tenant with the ability to configure settings for multiple site collections independent of other tenants. This is mainly used by Office 365 for hosting multiple cloud-based SharePoint deployments on a single farm.

- **Site collection.** Within a Web application (or tenant), you can create one or more site collections. A site collection consists of a top-level site, its sub-sites, and numerous configuration settings. It is a logical unit for administration—there are settings that can be configured only at the site collection level. Each Web application can host many site collections. A site collection is the primary dividing line for SharePoint logical groupings.

- **Sites.** A site collection can contain one or more sites. A site consists of a data repository, visual elements, administration, and almost every other core element of the functionality and experience for the user. Visually, a site is represented as one or more Web pages, lists, and Web Parts. In short, a site is a container for housing lists and libraries—along with certain configuration settings.

- **Lists and libraries.** Within a site, lists and libraries are data repositories that can hold columns of data and/or documents. They are analogous to a database table or Excel worksheet. Lists typically store rows and columns of information (such as contacts, issues, or other related data). Libraries typically store BLOBs of data, such as documents, images, or videos. Visually, lists and libraries are represented by Web Parts, views, and input forms.

- **Items.** The contents that lists and libraries contain are called items. Examples of items include documents, list contents such as contacts or appointments, and Web pages.

Sites and Site Collections

To explore the concepts of SharePoint, let's start with a simple example composed of a single Web server and its logical elements (see Figure 9-1).

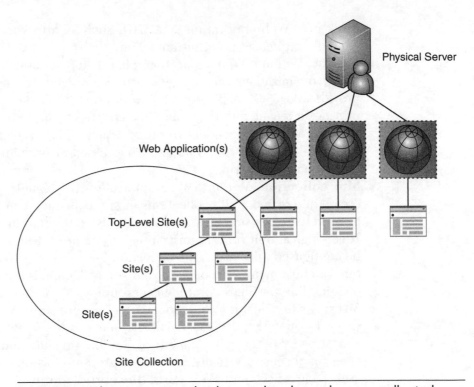

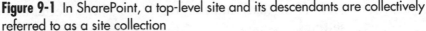

Figure 9-1 In SharePoint, a top-level site and its descendants are collectively referred to as a site collection

At the highest level, you have a physical server running IIS. Within IIS, you have a Web application, which maps to a URL (such as http:// myportal), a port (such as 80), and an IP address (such as 192.168.1.4). Once a Web application is extended with SharePoint functionality, one or more top-level sites can be created. Each top-level site can contain one or more child sites. The collection of sites that includes a top-level site and all of its descendants down to the leaf site(s), along with the collective configuration settings, is called a *site collection*. This is important, since much of SharePoint administration (quotas, backup and restore, Content Types, and many others) is based on the site collection concept.

After you determine what kind of Web page elements and storage your solution requires, the next step is to plan how your sites will be implemented across site collections. A site collection is a hierarchical set of sites that can be managed together. Sites within a site collection have common features, such as shared permissions, galleries for templates,

Content Types, and Web Parts, and they often share a common navigation. All sites in a site collection are (and must be) stored together in the same SQL-based content database. An intranet portal is often implemented as a site collection with the top-level Web site's default page as the home page of the portal.

In general, we recommend that you put each of the following types of sites in separate site collections right from the start. This will help you manage site collections and content databases better in the long run.

- Intranet portals
- Extranet sites
- Team collaboration sites
- My Sites (by default, each personal site is its own site collection)
- Internet sites (staging)
- Internet sites (production)
- Lines of businesses within a conglomerate
- Document Center sites
- Records Center sites

So, for example, if you were to deploy a company intranet, a corporate Internet-facing site, and a records management repository, you'd want to create three site collections right at the start. This enables you to manage the site collections individually, provide separate content databases, and more easily accommodate growth over time.

The downside of multiple site collections is that there are some features that do not work *across* site collections. This is important, since a large deployment of SharePoint will dictate multiple site collections. The following features do not work across site collections:

- **Content Types.** Content Types provide the facility to define the manner in which common documents, forms, and other content are normalized in your organization.
- **Content Query Web Part.** This Web Part aggregates information from across sites but does not work across site collections.
- **Workflow.** When you deploy workflow, it is accessible only within the site collection in which it is deployed.
- **Information management and retention policies.** Records management policies are set at the site collection level, forcing organizations to deploy the same policy multiple times for large enterprises.

- **Search.** Certain features of search are configured at the site collection level.
- **Quotas.** You should absolutely define quotas so that users are used to limited storage from Day 1. Quotas are also configured at the site collection level, which means that you will need to configure quotas separately at each top-level site.

Let's say you decided to create two site collections to accommodate project sites: one site collection for IT and one site collection for finance. Due to the site collection limitation just described, if you wanted consistent document metadata properties on a particular document type, you'd have to deploy the Content Type twice—once for each site collection. You could also employ the Content Type hub feature, but that's somewhat of a work-around for the fact that Content Types don't span site collections. In addition, if you wanted to aggregate content from both site collections, the Content Query Web Part wouldn't work; you'd need to use the Content Search Web Part instead.

Site Templates

Since a site is simply a container with some administration, some lists to back it up, and a default page for viewing its contents, how do we get a different (or consistent) look and behavior for each site in SharePoint? We use templates. Templates arc simply a definition of which lists, Web Part pages, and Web Parts are to be packaged together to define a starting point for your site. Since everything is a SharePoint Foundation 2013 site in SharePoint, the template defines the look and behavior of the page(s). Table 9-1 lists the out-of-the-box templates in SharePoint 2013. In addition to the out-of-the-box templates, you can make custom templates available to users. Templates are your building blocks, allowing you to quickly create complex solutions that include custom branding and functionality.

A template defines what the site will look like, the lists that constitute the site initially, how publishing will work on the site, and a number of other settings. It enables a site to be created by using a predefined definition. You can think of a site as a cookie (that you eat) and a template as the cookie cutter. This typically means that unless you've updated the underlying site definition (which is not recommended), your site is disassociated with the template the moment the site is provisioned. The implication is that if you need to make any changes to your template later, existing sites will not update automatically.

Table 9-1 Out-of-the-Box Templates in SharePoint Foundation 2013 and Microsoft SharePoint Server 2013

Category	Name	Best Suited for . . .	SharePoint Server Only?	New for 2013?
Collaboration	Team Site	Team collaboration.		
	Blog	Posting information in chronological order; others can comment.		
	Project Site	Managing and collaborating on a project.		√
	Community Site	A place where community members discuss topics of common interest. Members can browse and discover relevant content by exploring categories, sorting discussions by popularity, or viewing only posts that have a best reply. Members gain reputation points by participating in the community, such as starting discussions and replying to them, liking posts, and specifying best replies.		√
Enterprise	Document Center	Centrally managing documents (active, broadly published items).	√	
	Records Center	Centrally managing records (corporate "sealed" items).	√	

(continues)

Table 9-1 Out-of-the-Box Templates in SharePoint Foundation 2013 and Microsoft SharePoint Server 2013 *(continued)*

Category	Name	Best Suited for . . .	SharePoint Server Only?	New for 2013?
	Business Intelligence Center	Managing reports and BI information.	√	√
	Enterprise Search Center	Delivering an enterprise-wide search experience. Includes a welcome page with a search box that connects users to four search results page experiences: one for general searches, one for people searches, one for conversation searches, and one for video searches.	√	
	Basic Search Center	A basic search experience. Includes a welcome page with a search box that connects users to a search results page, and an advanced search page.	√	
	Visio Process Repository	Viewing, sharing, and storing Visio process diagrams. It includes a versioned document library and templates for basic flowcharts, cross-functional flowcharts, and BPMN diagrams.	√	

Category	Name	Best Suited for . . .	SharePoint Server Only?	New for 2013?
Publishing	Publishing Site	A blank site for quickly publishing HTML Web pages.	√	
	Publishing Site with Workflow	A site for publishing Web pages on a schedule by using approval workflows.	√	
	Enterprise Wiki	Publishing knowledge that you capture and want to share across the enterprise. It provides an easy content-editing experience in a single location for coauthoring content, discussions, and project management.	√	
Duet Enterprise	SAP Workflow Site	Aggregating business tasks for use with SAP.	√	√

Service Applications

In MOSS 2007, services were grouped together within a Shared Services Provider (SSP). In SharePoint 2010, this was no longer the case; the configuration of services was made more flexible by enabling single services to be configured independently. SharePoint 2013 does not change the service application architecture.

Figure 9-2 shows how service applications work in SharePoint 2013.

Note SharePoint 2013 does not support shared services over a WAN. This factor can impact design and deployment in large organizations.

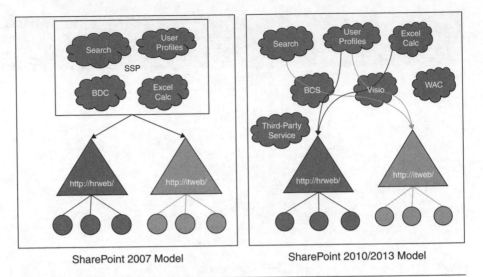

SharePoint 2007 Model   SharePoint 2010/2013 Model

Figure 9-2 You can create multiple service instances if your environment needs them—for example, if you need to keep searches between your business units separate

Understanding SharePoint Administration

Administration in SharePoint is managed through a set of Web pages that allow both IT pros and business users to configure settings and add new content. In general, administration is broken out by role and grouped by type of task.

There are four tiers to SharePoint administration:

- Central administration (which is where all global SharePoint settings are configured)
- Tenant administration (which can be used in any deployment but is most commonly used with SharePoint Online)
- Site collection administration (with unique settings for each site collection)
- Site-level administration (with unique settings for each site)

Central Administration

With central administration, there is one central administration site per farm. It enables settings like topology, security, and application services. Figure 9-3 shows an overview of the Central Administration site.

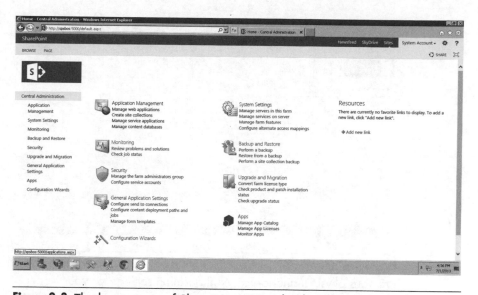

Figure 9-3 The home page of SharePoint Central Administration provides access to core tasks you'll need to perform to manage your farm

- Who? On-premises IT administrators
- Where? Farm-level
- How many? One per farm
- What? Used for actions like adding a new physical server to the farm or configuring Web application settings

The main page is organized into eight sections, each of which contains links to pages that help you manage your server or server farm, such as changing the server farm topology, specifying which services are running on each server, and changing settings that affect multiple servers or applications. For example, the System Settings section enables you to manage servers in the farm (see Figure 9-4).

Finally, the Application Management page contains links to pages that help you configure settings for Web applications and site collections that are on the farm (see Figure 9-5).

Within the Application Management area is also the section called Service Applications where shared services are now configured (see Figure 9-6). This section includes administration of user profiles, My Sites, search, usage reporting, audiences, Excel Services, Business Connectivity Services, and the other service applications.

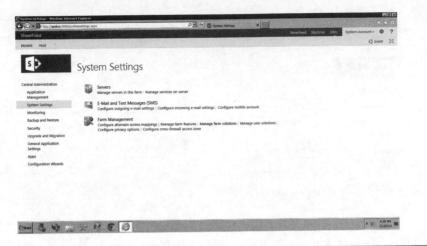

Figure 9-4 The System Settings section of SharePoint Central Administration provides physical and logical configuration settings for your farm

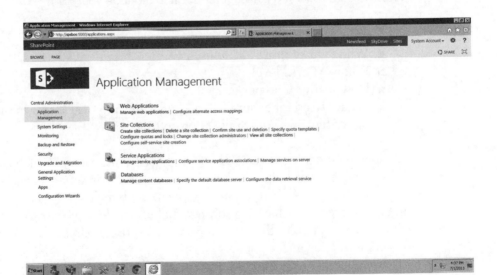

Figure 9-5 The Application Management section of SharePoint Central Administration provides ways to configure your core application components, such as Web application settings and site collection settings

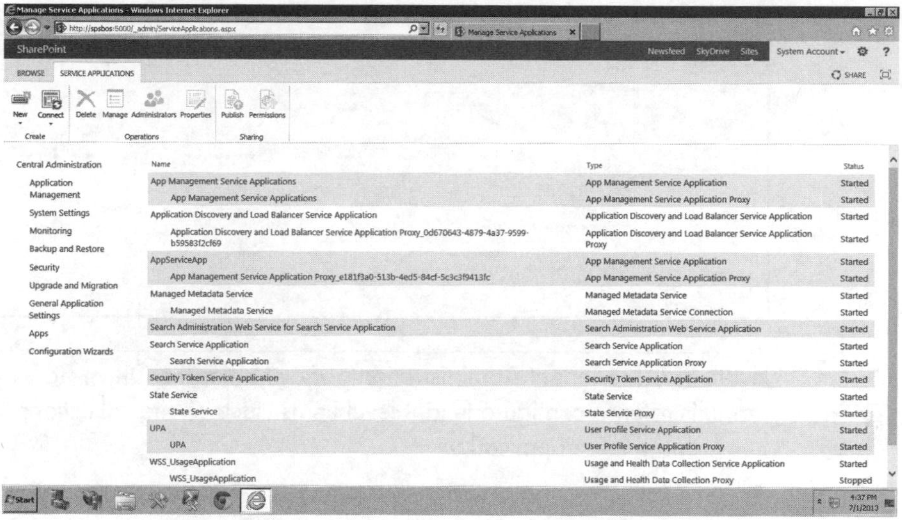

Figure 9-6 SharePoint Central Administration also gets you to a place where you can administer service applications

Tenant Administration

Tenant administration provides administration for a specific set of site collections that belong to a tenant subscription (see Figure 9-7).

- Who? IT or business IT liaison (typically used with SharePoint Online)
- Where: One per SharePoint Online/Office 365 subscription
- How many? One per SharePoint Online tenant
- What? Used for actions like creating site collections or managing service application settings in a SharePoint Online environment

Site Collection Administration

Site collection settings provide administration for a specific site collection.

- Who? Business user or IT (site collection owner)
- Where: Every site collection
- How many: One administration page per site collection
- What? Used to configure site-collection-level configuration settings

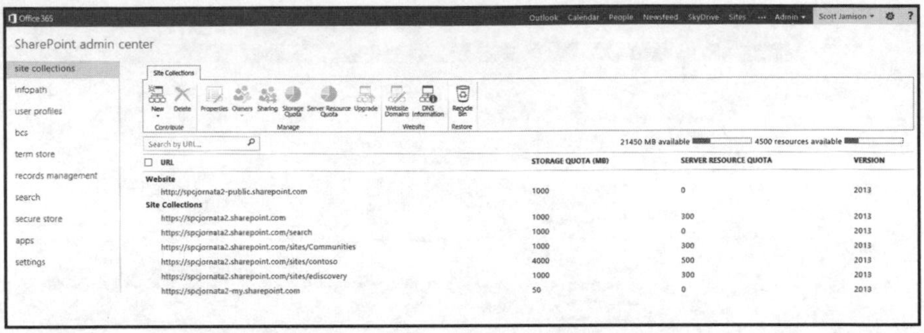

Figure 9-7 The Tenant Administration page enables the Office 365 subscription administrator to configure tenant-level items, such as site collections, overall settings, and service applications

The primary use of the Site Settings page(s) is to provide a UI where business users can manage site collection settings and the top-level sites in the site collection. By clicking the gear icon in the upper-right corner of the screen and selecting Site Settings at the top-level site, the site collection administrator can configure settings at the site collection level.

Site-Level Administration

Site settings provide administration for a specific site (see Figure 9-8).

- Who? Business user or IT (site owner)
- Where: Every site
- How many: One administration page per site, with an extra column for site collection settings for top-level sites
- What? Used for things like site configuration, creating a new list, adding users to the site, storage, site hierarchy

The primary use of the Site Settings page(s) is to provide a UI where business users can manage an individual site. This includes the site-specific permissions, the look and feel of the site, a view of out-of-the-box usage reports, and miscellaneous site settings. We recommend that business users who will be administering a site get adequate training on the Site Settings pages.

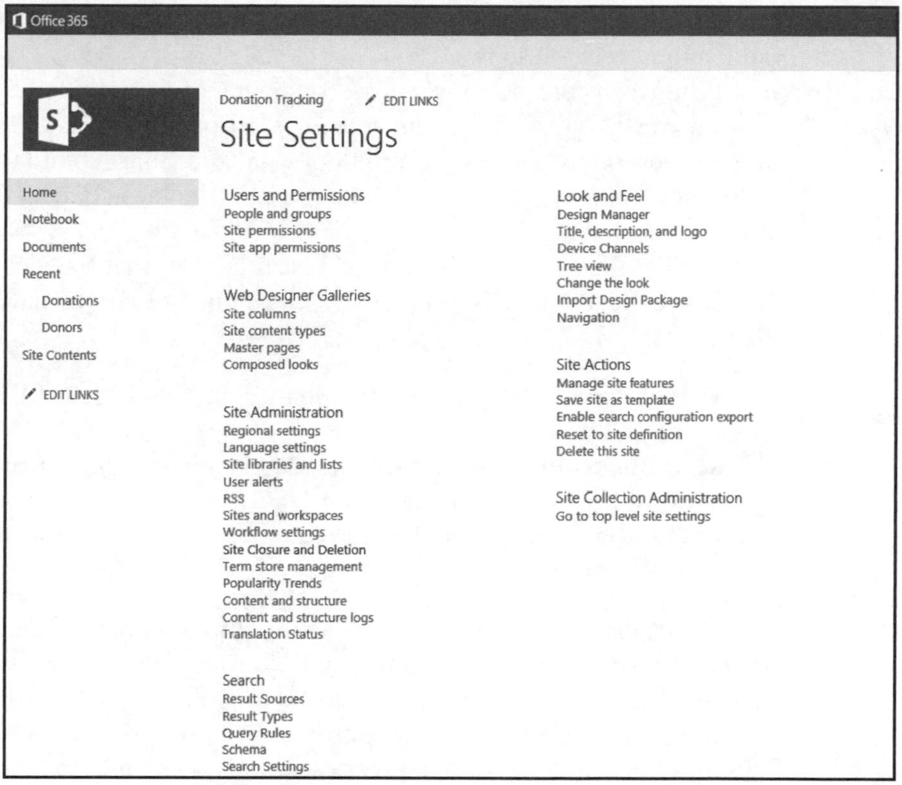

Office 365

S> Donation Tracking   ✎ EDIT LINKS
Site Settings

Home
Notebook
Documents
Recent
    Donations
    Donors
Site Contents

✎ EDIT LINKS

Users and Permissions
People and groups
Site permissions
Site app permissions

Web Designer Galleries
Site columns
Site content types
Master pages
Composed looks

Site Administration
Regional settings
Language settings
Site libraries and lists
User alerts
RSS
Sites and workspaces
Workflow settings
Site Closure and Deletion
Term store management
Popularity Trends
Content and structure
Content and structure logs
Translation Status

Search
Result Sources
Result Types
Query Rules
Schema
Search Settings

Look and Feel
Design Manager
Title, description, and logo
Device Channels
Tree view
Change the look
Import Design Package
Navigation

Site Actions
Manage site features
Save site as template
Enable search configuration export
Reset to site definition
Delete this site

Site Collection Administration
Go to top level site settings

Figure 9-8 The administration page on a site lets a user (typically the site owner) configure site-specific items, such as site-level permissions, the lists and libraries stored within the site, and the look and feel used by the site

As you have seen, the various SharePoint configuration and administration settings require multiple administrators. You should carefully plan and designate which users should be administering which pieces of the SharePoint administration puzzle.

Deployment Options

In addition to administration options, another major consideration for your SharePoint rollout is your physical deployment. Even if you're deploying in the cloud, this will mean "How many servers do I need to deploy?" This section helps you think through the answer to this question by helping you understand your options.

When considering on-premises deployment options for SharePoint, you are really considering your *topology*. In other words, you are determining how many servers you will deploy in your SharePoint farm and the roles they will play. In SharePoint Server 2013, how you deploy SharePoint is very flexible.

In SharePoint Server 2013, servers can have virtually any combination of services enabled. For simplicity, let's define servers as having one of three roles:

- **Web Front End (WFE):** the SharePoint bits with just Web rendering enabled
- **Application server:** may include search indexing, Excel calculations, Project Server, and other features
- **Database server:** no SharePoint-specific software is installed (only SQL Server)

Depending on need, you may have multiple servers performing each role or a single server performing multiple roles. This results in any number of physical configuration options when rolling out SharePoint. Your environment will have special requirements around server roles, authentication, DMZ, and application services, among other needs.

The following sections describe some configurations to consider. They are by no means the only ways to build your environment, but they do represent common deployment scenarios.

Zero-Server Deployment

How could you possibly deploy SharePoint without any servers at all? Quite simply, you choose a cloud deployment. By using SharePoint Online, either by itself or through Office 365, you can configure and deploy a production SharePoint offering as a pure service, rather than hosting any of your own servers.[1] A cloud deployment limits certain customization

---

1. While small deployments of Office 365 and SharePoint Online require no on-premises servers, most larger deployments will use Active Directory Federation Services (ADFS) to provide single sign-on for user authentication. This requires an organization to deploy an on-premises ADFS server that can communicate with the Internet.

options, such as full control over your farm, but does provide a fast and lower-maintenance option for using SharePoint 2013.

Single-Server Deployment

If you elect to host the servers yourself, you may start with a single server. A single server hosts all three roles (WFE, application server, and database) on a single machine. From a logical perspective, all SharePoint objects are located on this server (content sites, shared services, central administration, and databases). This is good for very small deployments, since it is fast and easy. The major downsides include scalability issues (since there is no room to grow except for expanding things like memory and processor) and availability issues (if the server goes down, SharePoint is down).

There are two ways to deploy on a single server: let SharePoint include the database for you (which will limit your total storage space) or first install SQL Server separately.

Note Choose your deployment topology carefully. There is no direct upgrade from a stand-alone installation to a farm installation.

Two-Server Deployment

In a two-server scenario, one of the servers hosts the WFE and the application server, and the second server hosts the SQL Server database. This provides a way to manage the database separately but adds complexity without adding scalability or availability. This step adds a second tier to the deployment. In most organizations, this is the smallest deployment that is recommended for anything other than a demonstration environment or very small group.

Three-Server Deployment

By adding an additional server to the two-server deployment that acts as an additional WFE/application server, we gain scalability (by being able to service more requests) and availability (by load-balancing requests, so that if one server goes down, the system stays up and running on the other machine). The single point of failure is now the SQL machine.

Four-Server Deployment

By adding a machine to the database role and upgrading the SQL Server machine to a full cluster, we can achieve availability on both tiers of the environment. This is the smallest highly available environment, meaning that there are no single points of failure. Note that clustering is not a simple upgrade but rather a reinstall where you must move databases.

Five-Server Deployment

The next step that you should consider is to start breaking out the application services for additional performance. For example, the indexing process is very CPU-intensive and should often be put onto its own server. In a five-server deployment, the fifth server would host just an application server, primarily serving as an indexing machine. This creates a three-tier environment, with a new application server tier being added.

N-Server Deployment

The beauty of the scale-out process is that we can continue adding servers at each of the tiers, depending on the needs of the business. Do we need to serve more Web pages per second? Add more WFEs. Do we need to dedicate processor time to calculating Excel sheets? Add more application servers, specifically dedicated to Excel Services. You get the idea. Let's say you decide that ten production machines make sense. You may then want to deploy a separate Internet farm in the DMZ and an intranet farm behind the firewall. In addition, you may want staging and testing machines so that you can adequately test new features and Web Parts. This may bring your server count to 20 servers or more. In the next section we'll provide three specific examples: departmental, corporate intranet, and Internet-facing deployments.

Deployment Examples

The most common examples of SharePoint deployment are for departmental use, a corporate intranet, and/or an Internet-facing deployment, either as a secured extranet or a public Web site.

Departmental

A departmental solution—typically for collaboration, but it may include a team portal—will often consist of a single SharePoint server and a database server (see Figure 9-9). However, savvy departments should deploy a second SharePoint server for availability.

Corporate Intranet

A corporate intranet—serving anywhere from hundreds to up to tens of thousands of employees—will start to incorporate dedicated application servers (see Figure 9-10). All servers are deployed within the company firewall.

Internet (Web Content Management)

A corporate Internet presence gets a bit more complicated, since you'll not only want to have enough Web servers to serve a large number of external users, but you'll also want an internal cluster for

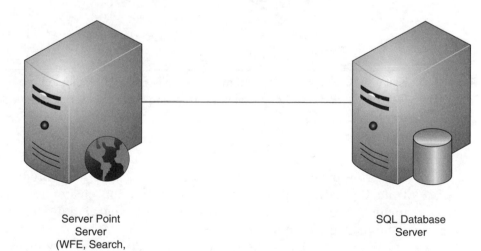

Server Point
Server
(WFE, Search,
Application)

SQL Database
Server

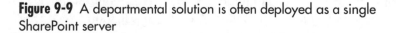

Figure 9-9 A departmental solution is often deployed as a single SharePoint server

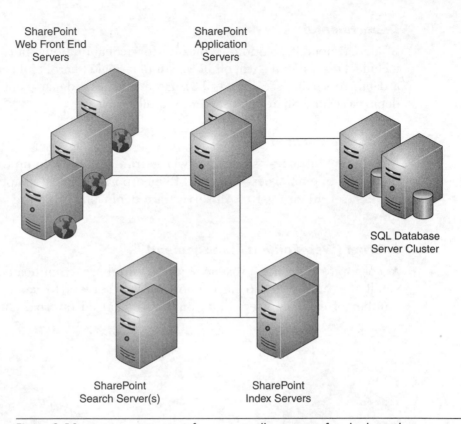

SharePoint Web Front End Servers

SharePoint Application Servers

SQL Database Server Cluster

SharePoint Search Server(s)

SharePoint Index Servers

Figure 9-10 Corporate intranet farms typically consist of multiple Web Front Ends, dedicated application servers, and dedicated search and index servers

authoring purposes. SharePoint will then deploy all content changes from the authoring cluster to your production cluster in a one-way manner. Figure 9-11 shows an example of a SharePoint deployment in a publishing environment.

When considering the question "How do I know how many servers I will need?" the short answer for deployment is this: carefully consider your usage plan (collaboration, portal, Web content management, and so on), uptime needs, number of users, application processing demands, geographic dispersion, and budget when determining your deployment architecture.

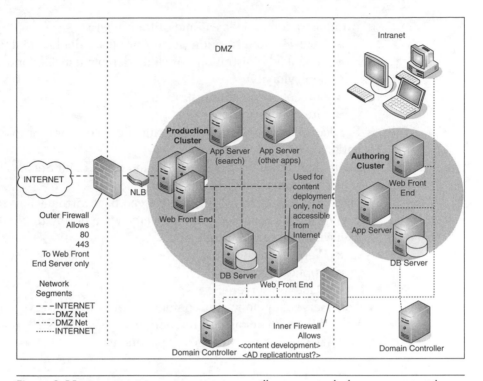

Figure 9-11 For your Internet presence, you'll want to include servers outside your corporate firewall (for Internet user access) as well as servers inside the firewall (for employee access)

Key Points

- In SharePoint 2013, virtually everything is a site, including central administration itself.
- A site is a container for lists, libraries, and settings.
- Pages are items that are stored in libraries.
- A site collection is a hierarchical collection of one or more sites that are managed together. All sites in a site collection must be stored together in the same content database. Some features do not work across site collections, so it's important to plan how you use them.
- A Web application is something that SharePoint manages and maps to between one and five IIS Web sites.

- Administration happens at one of four levels:
  - Central administration (for on-premises deployments)
  - Tenant administration (for cloud deployments and multi-tenant deployments)
  - Site collection administration
  - Site administration
- Service applications provide functionality to one or more Web applications.
- Both SharePoint Foundation 2013 and SharePoint Server 2013 support shared services.
- In SharePoint Server 2013, servers can have virtually any combination of services enabled; for simplicity, we typically think of servers as having one of three roles:
  - Web Front End (WFE)
  - Application server
  - Database server
- Your server topology can contain as few as zero servers if you're using Microsoft's cloud-hosted option, or as many as 20 (or more!) if you have a large on-premises deployment.

CHAPTER 10

PLANNING YOUR UPGRADE

The key challenges in moving to SharePoint 2013 from previous versions are twofold. First, you must decide what to do with your existing content (and the organization of that content) that is currently in SharePoint 2007 and/or SharePoint 2010. Second, you must decide whether to move to an on-premises SharePoint farm or to a cloud-hosted instance of Office 365.

In this chapter, we help you decide how best to prepare to move your current SharePoint environment(s) to SharePoint 2013. Then we cover the two primary options for upgrading to SharePoint Server 2013: database-attach and content migration. In either case, you'll want to build a new SharePoint 2013 farm and then move your data to it.

Before we even get into upgrade and migration, the key question is "Should you upgrade to SharePoint 2013?" As we've mentioned in earlier chapters, SharePoint has been widely accepted and deployed across many organizations of all sizes and vertical markets. The success of SharePoint has primarily been centered on the ease of use and administration around building collaboration and communication forums for employees, partners, and clients. With SharePoint 2013, Microsoft looks to extend the success of its SharePoint technologies by introducing new features like enhanced social computing—mainly via Yammer. Additionally, improved search and advanced browser and device support make the argument for upgrading to the newest version very compelling. We assume that since you've got a copy of this book in your hands, you're ready to move to SharePoint 2013.

What do you do if you already have an intranet or extranet or virtual team space using an earlier version of SharePoint and you want to move to SharePoint 2013? Should you upgrade some of your existing environments or all of them? Or should you build an entirely new infrastructure and move all of your data, which could help you to take better advantage of some of the new functionality offered—and perhaps reorganize and consolidate some of your content? In this chapter, we take a look at these questions and help you plan your upgrade.

Before we begin, however, it is important to emphasize that natively, SharePoint 2013 only supports migrating directly from SharePoint 2010. For those users who are still using SharePoint 2003 or SharePoint 2007 and are considering a jump to SharePoint 2013, there are two options: (1) upgrade to SharePoint 2010 as an interim step by using the content database-attach method, and follow the guidelines offered in this chapter; or (2) use third-party tools (AvePoint, Axceler, Metalogix, or Quest, for example) to migrate your old content directly into a new SharePoint 2013 environment. In any case, the planning advice offered in this chapter is critical to a seamless and smooth transition.

What's New in SharePoint 2013?

SharePoint 2013 presents a number of changes from previous versions of SharePoint with respect to upgrade. The following upgrade features are of particular note:

- In-place upgrade is no longer supported
- Site collection upgrades can be deferred
- The default authentication mode has changed to claims
- Master page customizations have changed
- Search is now a single, consolidated offering
- SharePoint 2013 can host sites in both SharePoint 2010 and SharePoint 2013 modes, enabling a "true" SharePoint 2010 mode
- Database-attach upgrade, which is the preferred solution for content databases, is now available for some service application databases

Let's review each of these features in a bit more detail.

In-Place Upgrade Is No Longer Supported

The hard truth about in-place upgrade in SharePoint 2010 is that it rarely ever worked. In light of that, Microsoft has made the decision to drop support for in-place upgrades of an existing environment. And since there is no more gradual upgrade—a feature introduced in SharePoint 2007—the database-attach upgrade method is the only upgrade option left for directly upgrading your databases via the product itself to a new environment that is based on SharePoint 2013.

Site Collection Upgrades Can Be Deferred

In SharePoint 2013, when a farm administrator upgrades a content database, he or she can elect to either upgrade the user interface on every site collection or to defer the user interface upgrade. If user interface upgrades are deferred, the site collection owners are able to upgrade their sites to the new SharePoint 2013 user interface on their own timeline. Commands for upgrading a site collection are available on the Site Settings page in the site collection administration section. In addition, there are also Windows PowerShell cmdlets to upgrade site collections to the new user interface if the farm administrator wishes to selectively upgrade the UI in bulk.

The Default Authentication Mode Has Changed to Claims

In SharePoint 2010, you could configure your Web application to support either Windows authentication or claims authentication. In SharePoint 2013, the default mode for new Web applications is claims. In addition, future versions of SharePoint will support only claims mode. Thus, you'll need to consider any sites or custom applications that might be impacted by moving to claims. If you do switch from Windows Classic mode to claims, you may have to rewrite custom applications.

Master Page Customizations Have Changed

If you've done any major branding customization in previous versions of SharePoint, you could be in a situation where you need to make some changes to your branding when moving to SharePoint 2013. SharePoint 2013 introduces a new way of creating and managing master pages, so even the smallest amount of branding or styling demands at least a basic understanding of how the new master page model works. We recommend creating an inventory of the server-side customizations in your environment (branding features, Web Parts, master pages, page layouts, CSS files, etc.). That way, you'll have a list of items that you can verify still work, or a list of items you'll need to update.

Search Is Now a Single, Consolidated Offering

In SharePoint 2013, a number of changes have been made to search to accommodate the consolidation of the two previous search engines

(SharePoint and FAST) into a single search platform. This will change the way you approach your upgrade, since you'll need to determine whether to reconfigure search or let SharePoint upgrade your settings directly. In many cases, you might consider a search-first migration, where you build a new SharePoint 2013 server farm, enable search, and crawl your SharePoint 2010 environment from there. This allows you to create a new environment and immediately get benefit from your new farm; you can then migrate your content databases over time to the new farm.

SharePoint 2013 Can Host Sites in Both 2010 and 2013 Modes

The SharePoint 2010 visual upgrade feature enabled site owners and administrators to see how their sites would look and behave in the new user interface. In reality, the feature didn't provide a "true" preview because the site had already been upgraded to the new functionality!

In SharePoint 2013, the farm can host sites in both SharePoint 2010 and SharePoint 2013 modes simultaneously, mainly since the farm code contains both SharePoint 2010 and SharePoint 2013 versions of features, site templates, site definitions, Web Parts, the "14" and "15" SharePoint paths, and two parallel IIS support directories under /Layouts. This means that existing SharePoint 2010 solutions can often be deployed to SharePoint 2013 and continue to run within a SharePoint 2010–mode site without changes.

In SharePoint 2013, the upgrade of the software and database has been separated from the upgrade of the site. This means that a site can remain running in SharePoint 2010 mode until a site owner or administrator explicitly upgrades it to the new user interface. Site collection owners can also request an evaluation site, which is a *separate, temporary copy* of the site, to review the new interface and functionality. This enables site administrators to review the new site, make updates in their original site, and then upgrade their site to the new version.

Database-Attach Is Now Available for Some Service Application Databases

To make the upgrade easier for a new SharePoint 2013 farm, the most common service application databases are available for database-attach. The method for upgrade is the same: create a new SharePoint 2013 farm, copy the existing content databases and/or service application databases to the new farm, and execute a database-attach.

For SharePoint 2013, you can use the database-attach upgrade method to upgrade the following service application databases:

- Managed metadata
- User profile
- Search administration
- PerformancePoint
- Business data connectivity
- Secure store

Planning for Upgrade or Migration

With SharePoint 2013 you can upgrade the database schema of existing SharePoint 2010 environments automatically for all of your content databases and site collections. Current SharePoint applications will be fully functional with the new dual-mode capability, so all existing capabilities will still be enabled, and all existing custom and third-party Web Parts will continue to execute. Sounds simple, right? Well, it's probably not. Although SharePoint 2013 does provide a better migration experience, don't expect your upgrade to be that simple. Things will likely break.

The reality is that upgrading to the new version of SharePoint, if done right, could be very hard. This statement is not meant to scare or deter, but rather to inspire and motivate. Really. The most critical task in the upgrade process is planning. One possible scenario is to upgrade the software and leave the content and associated taxonomy alone; another choice might be that you choose not to upgrade but rather completely redesign and rebuild from scratch—including which content goes and which content stays. Technology can update the available functionality and introduce new database tables, but it cannot fix poorly designed taxonomies or appease overwhelmed users. SharePoint 2013 upgrade planning involves the evaluation of new technical features, validation of the usefulness of those features in your environment, and integration of those features into your existing SharePoint framework. It will take time to do these steps properly, but it will pay off in the long run.

Upgrades are a good time for introspection and analysis. How has your current environment evolved over time since your initial deployment? Has your organization shifted strategically? Are you capturing and leveraging your organizational content effectively? There is a lot to evaluate. Take a look at your organization's use of SharePoint and consider the following questions. For questions to which you answer yes, think about how functionality, processes, and support will change in SharePoint 2013. For questions to which you answer no, will you introduce this functionality with SharePoint 2013 or continue to avoid it? Your answers will influence the means of your upgrade. And as we show later, your answers also impact the timing of your upgrade.

- Do you have business processes that are driven by (or enabled within) SharePoint?
- Are you currently taking advantage of SharePoint-based work-flows?
- Do you have a culture of e-mailing document attachments as a means of workflow, review, and collaboration? Do you want to change this?
- Do users require offline or remote access?
- Are your content contributors responsible for tagging your documents? Are they diligent in this effort?
- Are your navigation, search, and document-tagging taxonomies in good shape? Do your users agree?
- Do you have a well-defined list of compelling reasons that is driving your decision to upgrade to SharePoint 2013? Or is it simply to "do the newest thing"?
- Are users ready for the move to Office 2013 and the new features of SharePoint 2013? How will you train and support them?
- Did you heavily customize your SharePoint 2007/2010 environment? Are you invested in third-party or custom solutions?
- Do you have additional infrastructure (over and above your current farm infrastructure) available to you that complies with the SharePoint 2013 technical requirements (this includes 64-bit technology, increased RAM requirements, new operating systems, and so on) for a new farm?
- After your upgrade, will you present the new SharePoint 2013 interface, or will you wait to alter your user interface in a subsequent phase?
- Are you using Internet Explorer 8 or above? Or a browser that supports HTML5?

As this list shows, there is a lot to think about when moving a well-established environment to the next version of the associated technology. Many of these issues are connected directly with business users and processes. We look at some of them in more detail in the next sections.

Governance Considerations

As we have mentioned, one of the biggest challenges with a SharePoint 2013 upgrade is executing a well-thought-out plan. You'll need a plan not just for the technical component of applying new software, but more important, for two other elements: (1) the details of what you will (or won't) do with the software product after it is enabled, and (2) communication with your user community. That's where governance comes in. As mentioned in Chapter 4, "Planning for Business Governance," governance implies having a documented strategy for managing content (among other things). If you have a governance strategy in place for a current SharePoint 2010 environment, modifying or adapting it to SharePoint 2013 is evolutionary. If you don't have a governance policy today, consider developing one prior to the upgrade. This will establish clear rules on the use of native or customized SharePoint functionality. With this control and guidance in place, you will feel more comfortable with having some of the additional features of SharePoint 2013, such as the social computing components, more widely used and in a consistent manner. A governance plan is not a requirement for the upgrade but is critical to the ultimate success of post-upgrade usage.

SharePoint-Driven Business Processes

SharePoint 2013 is a great tool that you can use to build more efficient business processes. With SharePoint 2010, many of these business processes (organizational workflow, e-mail-driven discussion threads, and lightweight project management, for example) became more widely used.

SharePoint 2013 not only builds on previous business process capabilities, but it also integrates business processes deeper into the SharePoint environment by supporting additional features through the use of enhanced forms, workflow, Excel, Visio, and Access-based business applications and by incorporating LOB data into your portal with greater simplicity, resulting in an enhanced user experience. In addition, with the introduction of stronger social computing capabilities through tools like

Yammer, SharePoint users can be consumers, producers, and influencers of content more than ever before.

When planning for SharePoint 2013, it is important to identify and resolve barriers to business process adoption. Consider the following questions and associated recommendations:

- Is your organization ready for the upgrade? User adoption and education are critical to introducing and leveraging change. Make sure everyone understands when the upgrade is happening and why.
- Does your current SharePoint content organization support an upgrade to this new technology, or does it limit it? If users currently complain about the "findability" of content or the overall organization of intranet sites, an upgrade is a good time to make the necessary changes to increase ease of use. You might even consider a "search-first" upgrade, whereby you build a new SharePoint 2013 farm, enable search functionality that provides indexing of existing SharePoint 2010 content, and then slowly migrate your content to SharePoint 2013 over time. Just remember that if your content metadata is of poor quality (such as a bevy of incorrect titles), simply upgrading to a new version won't correct your findability woes.
- Are there technology limitations that would prevent adoption? Are you still using Office 2003 or 2007? If yes, you will need to consider moving to Office 2013 (or at least Office 2010) before upgrading to SharePoint 2013.
- Is sufficient user training available? Especially in an organization that is still getting used to the ribbon user interface and browser-based document access, user training (for both content owners and administrators alike) is critical in advance of an interface change.
- Are the users and site collection administrators comfortable with the change? Communicate the changes and associated features of SharePoint 2013 well in advance of an upgrade so users can process and embrace these changes, and so site collection administrators can start planning their move to SharePoint 2013 for the site collections they own.
- Is there adequate IT support? Ensure that IT staff is properly trained and prepared for supporting the new features in SharePoint 2013; this includes direct (SharePoint administrators) and indirect

(infrastructure personnel) resources. You might want to consider a SharePoint center of excellence to assist users and site owners through the upgrade.

Electronic Forms and Document Workflow

Does your organization still use paper-based forms? Or are you using an electronic forms–based tool like InfoPath? Or can you take advantage of new flexibility with designing and customizing HTML5 forms in SharePoint? Have you invested in data collection capabilities in SharePoint 2010, and how can these be enhanced?

How is workflow managed in your current SharePoint environment? Are rules in place to control the movement of data before it gets to SharePoint? One of the challenges of enabling the workflow capabilities in SharePoint 2010 (and this is still true with SharePoint 2013) was the discipline needed to enforce the rules around how the stages of the workflow are executed. Because the workflow is system-based, it needs to be well defined. Typically, organizations use e-mail as the primary vehicle for workflow-based approval and validation. A number of e-mails are exchanged, decisions are made, and the workflow plan is ultimately executed, but the record of the decision is not typically stored with the document.

Planning for enabling electronic forms and/or automated workflow involves investigating the current forms and workflow processes within your organization and then defining how SharePoint will manage them. Define your users (and/or roles) and document the decision points and time constraints of the various stages. This will help validate the usefulness of SharePoint's forms and workflow tools and help define if and where they should be implemented.

Another thing to consider is that SharePoint 2013 changes the native workflow capabilities by moving them to Windows Workflow Foundation 4, which was substantially redesigned from earlier versions. Why does this matter? If you've invested in workflow with SharePoint 2010, whether through custom application development or third-party product or both, you should investigate how these processes might be simplified or enhanced by using new native functionality.

It is also important to note that new features like Web-based forms and document workflow should be part of a broader functional upgrade and should be used only to meet specific business requirements. There is a danger in using new features of SharePoint 2013 for the sole purpose of building a stronger *perception* associated with ROI without clear ties to the business needs. If that happens, users are more discouraged than excited.

Although your existing in-flight workflows should complete without issue, your upgrade can be impacted based on your ability and willingness to alter existing data collection and workflow processes in SharePoint 2010 prior to upgrade. This may include simple edits to data entry forms or more advanced initiatives like migrating away from a third-party workflow or business process tools.

Preparing for Social Computing and Yammer

Even with the introduction of various new technologies, the most likely place that organizational information exists, aside from inside people's heads, is in their e-mail mailboxes. And we're not talking about notes to your spouse—we're talking about important corporate knowledge like domain expertise, business intelligence, and key decisions. Most of this is information that can't be accessed by other users and may walk out the door when an employee leaves, leaving the company without some important organizational knowledge.

How much corporate knowledge is lost in your organization's e-mail? Does your company have a formal process in place to capture, catalog, and store information gathered through e-mail communication with peers, clients, and partners? One of the challenges in solving this problem with SharePoint 2010 was that while it was very good at storing structured content (such as documents), the social features were introduced but still lacking.

That said, SharePoint 2010 did offer new alternatives to help with the storage and retrieval of unstructured knowledge. As an example, users could follow topics and view a newsfeed, but most serious social features required a third-party tool such as NewsGator's Social Sites. The challenge, however, was that these types of social tools were used sparingly, mainly because organizations were concerned about giving "too much freedom" to users. This has changed as the world itself has changed. Now, with Internet applications like LinkedIn, Facebook, and Twitter, organizations see the value in capturing real-time, unstructured information.

Is your organization ready to embrace changes in the way people communicate using tools like wikis and blogs? Are you willing to give employees the freedom to publish content in small, unformatted bits (think of Twitter)? Does your current SharePoint taxonomy support the inclusion of this new type of information? The promise of capturing "lost" corporate knowledge, currently buried in various employee e-mails, is very exciting. It does, however, come with some cost and cultural change. This is an important point. Often (and this is especially true with SharePoint 2013), functional upgrades require one part technology, two parts business process adjustment, and a good measure of culture change. Users must clearly understand the benefits of altered approaches to their activities. This is a requirement for general user adoption.

Will you look to take advantage of social computing capabilities in SharePoint 2013? If yes, do you have a formal plan for managing and monitoring these features? More important, does the content organization and/or security model you are using in SharePoint 2010 prevent or limit any part of your vision? In addition, with the advent of Site Mailboxes in SharePoint 2013, which communications should still reside in e-mail and which should go into a social dialog? That decision will depend on your culture. No matter what you decide, you should have a decision before you actually upgrade. Otherwise, you're taking the old "ready, fire, aim" approach, perhaps without even realizing it.

There are a couple of challenges here for existing SharePoint 2010-based organizations. First, if you have dabbled in social computing capabilities (with native functionality or third-party add-ons), you need to consider whether these will be left alone or redone with native SharePoint 2013. The impact on your upgrade is that these steps will happen after the physical upgrade and may or may not be addressed before the new launch. Second, if you have not formalized a social computing strategy but would like to do so as part of your SharePoint 2013 deployment, you will want to begin the education and design pieces before the upgrade so that users are well prepared when this functionality is made available to them. Finally, you'll need to consider whether you should use SharePoint 2013's native social features, or if you should instead use Yammer. You should consider using Yammer for newsfeed capabilities, as it will likely replace SharePoint's social features over time.

Working with SharePoint Content Offline

How often are your SharePoint users, publishers, or readers disconnected from your corporate environment? Are your remote users forced to check out or download a collection of documents before getting on a plane? What if they're planning to use an iPad instead of their laptop? Are you concerned that document versions fall out of sync because of your remote users? SharePoint 2013, with the integration of SkyDrive Pro, offers substantially improved offline access to document library content. Users can retrieve, alter, and synchronize much of the data in SharePoint easily and automatically.

While this may sound like a wonderful thing, there are configuration issues. There are also levels of functionality that go from simple (copy files for offline access) to advanced (How does putting corporate data into the cloud impact security policies?). Are you currently using an offline solution? Would you like to introduce this capability with your upgrade? How many users will be impacted, and how will your organization be rewarded with the use of offline capabilities? And since not all features work on tablets and other devices, you could potentially be forced into purchasing a third-party tool.

A primary goal of offline-enabled tools is to provide users with a strong sense that they are still part of the larger organizational community, even when disconnected or out of the office. Ways to achieve this are to provide Web-based meetings, Web cams, and instant messaging. In SharePoint terms, enabling users to always access the current version of a given document helps maintain synchronization across the user community. The cascading implication of remote devices is the desire to access SharePoint over any Internet connection without going through a virtual private network (VPN). Are you prepared to not only upgrade to SharePoint 2013, but also provide iPad tools, enable direct-to-Web access, and turn on SkyDrive Pro?

Getting Your Timing Right: When Should You Upgrade?

Determining when to upgrade is not a simple task. The best reason to select a particular time is to take advantage of capabilities that have been introduced in the latest version, such as browser compatibility, mobile device support, or better offline capabilities—tying those features into business goals that are of importance to the organization. That said, do you need any of the new SharePoint 2013 features in your current deployment? If you do, and they clearly tie to business goals and align with your corporate cadence, an upgrade in the short term makes sense. If you do not need SharePoint 2013 features now but think you will over time, include them in your post-upgrade strategy—but spend some time planning this before you push through an upgrade process. If you are not likely to need those features for some time, you might want to consider deferring your upgrade until you have greater momentum within your current deployment. In short, resist upgrading just to get a shiny new toy or because Microsoft said you should.

Recall the list of questions about your current SharePoint environment that we asked at the beginning of this chapter. Let's look at how the answers to those questions might impact your readiness for an upgrade to SharePoint 2013. Table 10-1 highlights the questions and recommended actions and timing.

Fixing Your SharePoint Structure

A big part of SharePoint is an easy-to-use information architecture. Simply doing an upgrade won't automatically fix problems like hard-to-use navigation and searches that don't find anything. You'll need to step back and ask a few more questions.

Does your current SharePoint navigation taxonomy (the structure and hierarchy of your site) make sense to users? What content do employees use on the portal? (If you don't know, look at the usage reports and use surveys to find out.) What content is missing or misplaced? Has your business changed since your last SharePoint rollout, or might it change in the future so that the current portal structure does not map to that vision? These are tough questions, but the answers will ultimately have a significant influence on your upgrade path. SharePoint 2013 has incredible new features, but they alone cannot make your portal "better."

Implementing good technology to manage bad content will not help your users work better, smarter, or faster. We just can't say it enough.

Is an upgrade to SharePoint 2013 the right time to reorganize your portal content and better align it with what users want or the business demands? Or is your page and content organization stable and successful with less of a need for radical change? Can new functionality be included in these specific sections or added as additional pages without a major disruption to page organization? Believe it or not, your best tool in this piece of the planning will be a whiteboard. Draw your current portal structure. Use sticky notes to represent pages and/or sites (this way, you can move things around as you brainstorm). Think about where new functionality might be introduced. Change your marker color (or sticky

Table 10-1 Recommendations on Timing Your Upgrade Based on Current Environment Attributes

	Answered "Yes"	Answered "No"
Do you have business processes that are driven by (or enabled within) SharePoint? Are you currently taking advantage of SharePoint-based workflow?	We recommend pausing before you upgrade to determine if existing workflows will be left as is, or if an evolution to the new Workflow Manager–style workflows is warranted. If you keep the existing workflow architecture, users will be using the SharePoint 2010 workflows for backward compatibility, which might require training. In addition, ask yourself if there's an opportunity to improve any of those processes before you upgrade, since just upgrading the tool won't make the processes any better.	Upgrade will likely be easier since training won't be needed to educate users about why they might still need to use SharePoint 2010 workflows even after upgrade. It could be a good time to identify two or three ways you could use the improved workflow features in SharePoint 2013 to automate a business process.
Do you have a culture of e-mailing document attachments as a means of workflow, review, and collaboration?	We recommend using upgrade as an opportunity to educate users on the merits of uploading a document to a site and sending a link, rather than e-mailing attachments (single source of the truth, for one). Identify ways to streamline document creation and revision directly in SharePoint.	Congratulations! Since your team isn't e-mailing attachments, we'll assume you've conquered a fundamental working habit. At this point you can educate business users about how new SharePoint 2013 features might enhance current document sharing and review.
Do users require offline or remote access?	If you're currently using SharePoint Workspace, you'll need to train users on its disappearance. Investigate SkyDrive Pro or a third-party tool and how it might be leveraged for offline access for SharePoint 2013.	Determine whether offline access may be needed in future phases. Is this a good time to introduce SkyDrive Pro or a mobile tool?

	Answered "Yes"	Answered "No"
Are your content contributors responsible for tagging your documents? Are they diligent in this effort?	Congratulations! If content contributors are tagging documents well, your data hygiene is good and your search results even better.	Before you upgrade, investigate why current tagging processes aren't being helped by existing features such as the term store or location-based metadata. Use the upgrade as an opportunity to introduce these features into the culture if you didn't do so in SharePoint 2010.
Are your navigation, search, and document-tagging taxonomies in good shape? Do your users agree?	Congratulations! Since you got it right in a prior SharePoint build, simply ensure that you have planned for proper search configuration post-upgrade. Don't assume that it will just work, as the engine introduces anomalies such as Office Web Apps not working for non-2013 content.	We recommend that you take a step back and determine if changes should be made in content organization as part of the upgrade process. A technology upgrade alone won't help; focus instead on the information architecture and combine this with the overall effort.
Do you have a well-defined list of compelling reasons that is driving your decision to upgrade to SharePoint 2013?	Good news. Just ensure that IT and the business agree on the priority and timing. Don't assume that your list matches everyone else's. Make sure you get buy-in, which will increase the odds of success.	Take a step back and develop a strategy for implementation of new features. Ensure that they align with business goals. If you're upgrading due to a mandate, find out the underlying reason. If you're upgrading simply to stay in support from Microsoft, that's actually OK . . . just add that to the list as a reason.
Are users ready for the move to Office 2013 and the new features of SharePoint 2013? How will you train and support them?	Ensure that any training is offered in advance of upgrade deployment. Communicate the changes early; users don't like change. Or surprises.	Understand how the SharePoint experience will be impacted by the version of Office in use. Develop a comprehensive training and adoption plan prior to upgrade.

(continues)

Table 10-1 Recommendations on Timing Your Upgrade Based on Current Environment Attributes *(continued)*

	Answered "Yes"	Answered "No"
Did you heavily customize your SharePoint 2007/2010 environment? Are you invested in third-party or custom solutions?	Analysis recommended. Ensure that all custom components will work and be supported in SharePoint 2013. Determine whether custom code could be replaced by out-of-the-box functionality. Consider how deferred migration of site collections might benefit your migration planning. Do lots of testing.	Verify that no additional customization will be required post-upgrade to support missing features.
Do you have additional infrastructure available to you that complies with the SharePoint 2013 technical requirements (this includes 64-bit technology, increased RAM requirements, operating systems, and so on) for a new farm?	You're in good shape. Simply ensure that you have room for other environments (development, staging, and so on) and that you have a good story around availability and uptime.	Perform the necessary analysis to prepare your environment and support staff on the requirements associated with an additional SharePoint farm. Procure additional hardware (or virtual machines) in advance since your upgrade will necessitate having two environments simultaneously, at least during the upgrade period.
After your upgrade, will you present the new SharePoint 2013 interface, or will you wait to alter your user interface in a subsequent phase?	Ensure that site collection administrators understand how to evaluate and upgrade their collections during a testing phase and that your users are well trained on how to manage content in the new SharePoint 2013 interface.	Consider keeping the SharePoint 2010 interface in use until most sites are sufficiently tested and users are comfortable with the new 2013 interface. Train site collection administrators on the proper timing for upgrading their site collections.
Are you using Internet Explorer 8 or above? Or a browser that supports HTML5?	You're in good shape. Have a pilot team in place prior to upgrade to ensure a quality user experience.	Consider upgrading all power users to IE8 before conducting the SharePoint 2013 upgrade. To ensure that other users on Safari or Chrome or mobile devices have a quality experience, test thoroughly and engage in user acceptance testing in a staging environment.

note color) and start to make changes. In the end, which color dominates? This will help you decide how you should proceed. note color) and start to make changes. In the end, which color dominates? This will help you decide how you should proceed.

Note Chapter 6, "Planning Your Information Architecture," walks you through defining your SharePoint taxonomy and metadata in more detail. Use the tips in that chapter even if you've done an IA design before—you'll be surprised at how much better you can make your SharePoint environment with some simple design changes.

Addressing New Features in SharePoint 2013

As you plan your SharePoint 2013 rollout, what are its two or three features that are organizational "killer applications" (that is, they draw your users to higher levels of adoption)?

Will social computing functionality in Yammer draw people to participate more? Will more flexible browser and device options for content management give users a greater sense of empowerment? Will enhanced search help users find the "right" content faster? How do these new features fit into your existing portal taxonomy and complement your organizational strategy?

The challenge is to sift through the long list of features of SharePoint 2013 and identify those that will be used and are useful to your organization. This list will help your planning and will excite users about the new system. Think about how these capabilities change what information is being stored in SharePoint and, more important, how users (readers, contributors, administrators) will be affected. With that list, decide how implementation may be impacted by changes to the existing site taxonomy, security model, or governance plan.

User Comfort, Skill Level, and Training

This is the big question: How ready are your users for SharePoint (and Office) 2013? What will the impact be on productivity and overall SharePoint adoption if you choose to change things radically? How will you prepare employees for SharePoint 2013 and potential changes in how business processes and content creation are managed? How can you do all of this within a timeline that works for the business units and IT? This is the piece most SharePoint implementers forget.

Even if Microsoft did have a "magic button" to seamlessly upgrade your current SharePoint environment to 2013—as they do in the cloud with SharePoint Online—and all the features you really need are enabled (and everything worked), would users be thrilled or terrified? The biggest disadvantage of having an existing SharePoint environment is that an upgrade means change—and change is scary. You'll need to manage that fear by not overwhelming users, providing them with proper instructions, and giving them a clear roadmap for how to use the new features (and associated benefits). A SharePoint upgrade cannot happen in a vacuum. Users need to be informed and prepared. Manage risk by managing change. Deviate from your existing framework only if there are recognizable benefits to the user community in doing so.

SharePoint 2010 Customizations

Finally, how much have you altered your existing SharePoint environment? Have you created custom Web Parts or site definitions? Have you unghosted pages (that is, have you detached them from the standard template so that the pages are now stored in the database)? Have you stayed with native functionality or created a highly customized environment? These items could have a major impact on the usefulness (and success) of Microsoft's built-in upgrade process. If you have created a SharePoint environment with little to no customization, an automated upgrade may be more likely to succeed. If you have customized SharePoint, you will need to identify those customization points and validate that each will successfully upgrade. Are you using third-party Web Parts? Have you created your own custom Web Parts? Will they work? Have you altered the underlying JavaScript or XML or ASPX pages? Take an inventory of changes you have made to SharePoint since you installed the software and use this list as a gauge for how hard an automated upgrade will be. Consider the list at http://technet .microsoft.com/en-us/library/ff382641.aspx, which is a good checklist of things to review and correct before attempting an upgrade.

In addition, don't forget to assess whether any custom tools or add-ons you are using are (1) still needed with SharePoint 2013 (that is, do native components now provide the custom functionality and displace the old add-on?) and (2) operational in a SharePoint 2013 environment (that is, does the vendor support the new platform, or does the custom code still work?). You will need to determine this for all nonnative components that you currently manage.

Understanding Upgrade and Migration Options

Now that we've scared you into never upgrading again . . . Just kidding. Now that we've identified key issues to consider before you move to SharePoint 2013, let's cover the ways in which you'll get there. Natively, Microsoft supports a *single* overarching strategy to move from 2010 to 2013: build a new SharePoint 2013 environment and use database-attach. A potential second, which is not directly supported by the product, is to build a new SharePoint 2013 environment and migrate content as needed with a third-party tool. Table 10-2 highlights some of the details associated with each choice.

In-Place Upgrade

The in-place upgrade that was available in SharePoint 2010 and prior versions is no longer an option in SharePoint 2013.

Database-Attach Upgrade

A database-attach upgrade requires that you build a brand-new SharePoint 2013 farm for the new environment. Once SharePoint 2013 is installed in the new farm, you then attach the SharePoint 2010 content database to the 2013 farm. At that point, the content upgrade will run automatically for that content database. The old SharePoint 2010 farm remains available and untouched by the upgrade, which allows you to keep the old farm up and running. This is a good method for large and complex deployments and is the most common upgrade approach. Another advantage is that you can test the process in a virtual test environment. If your upgrade fails during initial testing, you can troubleshoot and resolve these issues before going live.

Selective External Migration

Selectively migrating content by moving content with third-party or custom tools (as opposed to letting SharePoint upgrade the databases directly) is a potential option if you want to completely redesign your SharePoint 2013 environment from the ground up or if you are migrating content from a variety of sources. Like the database-attach migration, you build a new SharePoint 2013 server farm. But rather than letting SharePoint upgrade your content databases automatically, you create a

Table 10-3 Guidance about Selecting the Appropriate Upgrade Strategy

Business Case	Recommended Upgrade	Comments
Simple SharePoint 2010 environment Few customizations Simple taxonomy that is consistent with future business needs	Database-attach.	A database-attach will provide the quickest path to an operational SharePoint environment.
Many organizational, team, and project sites in use with varied ownership and varied desire for upgrade timing	Separate content into site collections with dedicated content databases; perform a content database-attach and instruct site collection owners to upgrade their sites at their own pace.	Site collection owners can recognize benefits from using SharePoint 2013 if they choose but are not forced to upgrade until they are ready.
Very mature SharePoint 2010 environment with significant amount of outdated content Site taxonomy is dated and docs not reflect current business vision Lots of customizations that need to be eliminated	Rebuild and selectively migrate. or Build a new farm, perform a database-attach, and then selectively migrate content within the new farm.	Moving to SharePoint 2013 can be a good time to evaluate your current portal design and do any necessary course corrections. The advantage of starting from scratch (and selectively migrating content) is that it allows you to leverage the new capabilities and structure as they were intended (without having to retrofit changes).
Upgrading from SharePoint 2007 to SharePoint 2013 directly	Use an interim farm to database-attach from 2007 to 2010 and then from 2010 to 2013. or Build a new SharePoint 2013 farm and use a migration tool.	Moving from SharePoint 2007 to SharePoint 2013 cannot be achieved directly via database-attach.

- **Customized JavaScript (for example, OWS.JS) as well as jscript.** You will need to test these to ensure that they still function properly.
- **Profile database.** You will need to reimport your profiles, which takes roughly an hour for every 200 profiles. Make sure you budget this time.

- **Audiences.** You will need to recreate audiences in the new environment.
- **Hard-coded URL references.** If you change the underlying site topology, the URLs associated with sites and/or documents may change, causing references to break. Try to identify these early in your analysis.
- **Custom search scopes, content sources, and best bets.** You will need to recrawl your content and reestablish many of the search settings you created in SharePoint 2010. Depending on the size of your corpus, a recrawl could take a long time.
- **Custom security applied to portal, sites, sub-sites, and document libraries.** You will likely need to revisit the permissions.

The following are some things you absolutely must do before your upgrade:

- Create a full backup of your databases.
- Ensure that you meet all infrastructure requirements associated with SharePoint 2013.
- Inventory all custom Web Parts and custom coding in your SharePoint 2010 environment.
- Install all prerequisites.
- Create custom elements (site definitions and so on) for things you've customized.
- Establish new DNS names for the new environment, which may take time to propagate across your network.
- Conduct a survey of users of the current SharePoint offering. Use this as a baseline for what is and isn't working. Identify areas for improvement.
- Create a communication plan to let users know when SharePoint will be down, when things will be ready, and what to expect.

After your upgrade, you should

- Review the sites: Did SharePoint migrate the sites correctly? Are they using the right template? Is the new look and feel acceptable?
- Validate that the security model is correct.
- Test search and ensure that any custom scopes or managed properties are enabled.

- Look for errors in the SharePoint log or event logs. The format of the upgrade, upgrade error, and site upgrade log files are now in ULS format.
- Ensure that all services are running properly.
- Conduct a survey of users of the new SharePoint offering. Compare this to your baseline to see how your assumptions panned out. Use metrics, both quantitative and anecdotal, to continually improve your SharePoint environment.

Additional Considerations

In this chapter, we've outlined several questions to consider in advance of your decision to upgrade your SharePoint 2010 environment to a new SharePoint 2013 environment. The goal is to give you food for thought and, we hope, convince you that a move to SharePoint 2013 requires careful planning and consideration. The decision to upgrade or migrate will be different for each organization. It will depend on the items we discussed here, your users, and your ability to effectively deliver on the value proposition of SharePoint 2013 technologies. So what's your plan? Here is an outline of some final steps to help you get ready:

1. Educate yourself on SharePoint 2013 features. Read, get a demo, and find training materials that will help you appreciate the new functionality in SharePoint 2013 and how it maps to your business.
2. Educate yourself on how SharePoint 2013 will work in your environment. Will the features you need really be available in the configuration you have?
3. Decide on the proper version of SharePoint 2013. Will you use SharePoint Foundation 2013 only? Or SharePoint Server 2013 Standard? Or do you need extended business intelligence capabilities, Excel Services, or Business Connectivity Services offered by SharePoint Server 2010 Enterprise?
4. Is this an opportunity to move your infrastructure into the cloud, either partially or fully, via Office 365?
5. Identify the new features that you would like to implement (workflow, offline, and so on) and think about how they will integrate with the existing information architecture.
6. Document all the customizations made in your current environment. These include templates, Web Parts, and styles. This will serve as your checklist for functional validation as you go to step 7.

7. Create a test SharePoint 2013 environment with a copy of your existing SharePoint environment. Test a database-attach upgrade. Whether or not you have already made your decision, it is best to validate the upgrade process and identify any potential problem areas.

8. Next, verify that you can get all items that you documented in step 6 to work successfully. Does the environment meet your needs? Will the potential downtime of the migration process be acceptable to users?

9. Conduct focus group testing with representative users. Show them an upgraded site. Demonstrate some of the new features. Talk to them about the positives and negatives of the existing environment. Identify your "killer applications."

10. Do a whiteboard session with SharePoint governance stakeholders. Lay out your current taxonomy. Talk about some of the feedback from the focus groups and from user surveys you've conducted. Identify how the features identified in step 5 will be integrated. Devise a proposed new portal taxonomy if necessary.

11. Take a step back and reflect. After going through the process, how do you feel? Is this an opportunity to build something new (and better) and introduce significant business value? How will you get there? How long will it take? Do you need help from a professional?

12. Finally, visit the Microsoft TechNet site for detailed upgrade information at http://technet.microsoft.com/en-us/library/cc303429.aspx.

Key Points

- Plan your upgrade. Plan which Web applications, content databases, and site collections will go first. Plan how you will communicate to site collection owners and to users. Plan how you will deal with customizations.

- Test your upgrade in another environment before you upgrade production. Even the simplest upgrade process could fail, leaving your environment unstable or unavailable.

- Consider the cloud. Is this the point at which SharePoint Online or Office 365 could be a viable option?

- Use your upgrade as an opportunity to improve business processes or collaboration practices. For example, you may decide to introduce a new feature (such as social computing or business intelligence capabilities) into your rollout so that users see immediate benefit. This will enable you to more easily justify any downtime users might experience.

- You don't have to upgrade everything at once. You may decide, for example, that you can leave your existing team sites alone (for now) and stand up another server farm for blogs and wikis. Then you can slowly migrate existing team sites to SharePoint 2013. You can also use SharePoint 2013's option to upgrade the databases only, upgrading the user experience at another time. Finally, you can use a search-first cross-farm shared services approach to have two farms running at once. This phased approach is very important to consider.
- Consider your needs: Are you best suited for SharePoint Foundation 2013, SharePoint 2013 Standard, or SharePoint 2013 Enterprise?
- Most important, involve the user community. Survey them before and after. Provide communication early and often. Offer training.

CHAPTER 11

TAKING SHAREPOINT TO THE CLOUD

On March 4, 2010, Microsoft CEO Steve Ballmer made the public statement that Microsoft was "all in" with the cloud and that Microsoft was betting the future of its company on cloud computing.[1] In October 2012, Ballmer redefined Microsoft as a "devices and services" company in his annual shareholder letter.[2] It is clear that cloud computing is viewed as strategic by Microsoft.

In this chapter, we will

- Define what cloud computing is
- Review the past, present, and future for SharePoint in the cloud
- Discuss some of the key questions and considerations about developing a successful strategy for using SharePoint in the cloud
- Compare the differences between SharePoint Server 2013 and SharePoint Online
- Review the implications that the cloud has for SharePoint governance, adoption, migration, and overall planning

Microsoft has been in the cloud computing business for roughly 20 years. Services such as Hotmail, Bing, the Microsoft Network (MSN), SkyDrive, and Xbox Live are among the largest consumer services available. In recent months, Microsoft has acquired online service companies, including Skype and Yammer. Microsoft has also launched the Azure online service to enable organizations to run their servers, databases, and applications in a Microsoft-managed data center.

Microsoft has offered a managed version of Exchange and SharePoint Online since the launch of Business Productivity Online Services (BPOS)

---

1. Steve Ballmer, "Cloud Computing." www.microsoft.com/en-us/news/exec/steve/2010/03-04cloud.aspx
2. Steve Ballmer, Microsoft shareholder letter. www.microsoft.com/investor/reports/ar12/share holder-letter/index.html

in 2009. BPOS was based on SharePoint 2007, which was not truly designed to be run as a cloud service offering. Because of these limitations, SharePoint Online in BPOS did not offer much more than the basic functionality that Windows SharePoint Services (WSS) provided.

With the 2010 wave of products (Exchange, SharePoint, Lync, Office), BPOS was rebranded as Office 365. SharePoint Online then supported many of the core features of the standard version of SharePoint Server but still lacked some of the higher-end SharePoint Server enterprise features, including FAST search and business intelligence.

SharePoint 2013 now offers near-perfect feature parity between what Microsoft delivers as a service via SharePoint Online and what it ships as part of SharePoint Server. The SharePoint engineering team designed this release to be delivered as a service while still offering customers and partners choices about whether to deploy everything online, on-premises, hosted by a third party, or a hybrid combination.

What's New in SharePoint 2013?

SharePoint 2013 is designed to be a cloud service. There are now some capabilities that exist only in the online version of SharePoint, such as external sharing of content and new developer tools known as Napa. We will discuss these new capabilities later in this chapter.

SharePoint (2013) Online supports many of the same capabilities already described elsewhere in this book, including the new social computing features, SkyDrive Pro, eDiscovery, and enterprise search capabilities. There are also new online services that are built on top of SharePoint Online. Project Online provides the ability to perform enterprise project, task, portfolio, and resource management via Office 365. Duet Online adds the ability to more deeply integrate SharePoint Online with SAP.

SharePoint Online now has tighter integration with Exchange Online. Key examples of this include the new capabilities for eDiscovery and Site Mailboxes, which are described in Chapter 13, "Managing Enterprise Content." The task view within your SharePoint Online personal site provides an aggregated view of all of your tasks across various SharePoint Online sites as well as tasks assigned to you in Exchange Online and Project Online.

SharePoint Online search now supports hybrid scenarios where there may be some content on-premises and some online. In this model, SharePoint Online indexes content stored within Office 365. SharePoint on-premises indexes the content stored on-premises, including file servers and other content stores. The major change is that both SharePoint Online and on-premises can now display results from a remote SharePoint farm. For example, SharePoint Online can display results from the on-premises search index using the new result sources and query rules capabilities that are described in more detail in Chapter 16, "Planning Enterprise Search."

SharePoint Online is also integrated with other Microsoft cloud services such as Windows Azure and SQL Azure. When developing applications for SharePoint Online, one option is to have the application automatically hosted to run inside of Windows Azure. Access Services (when used via SharePoint Online) now automatically creates databases within SQL Azure and stores data within that service—as opposed to storing data within SharePoint Online. These are two examples of how Microsoft is seeking to provide new ways for scaling and building applications targeted at the multi-tenant SharePoint Online offering—applications and services now extend beyond Office 365.

Cloud Computing Concepts

Cloud computing has become an industry catchphrase with many different definitions and interpretations. Before we discuss SharePoint Online and Office 365, we will explain some of the different cloud computing concepts and options.

Private Clouds

The first option is a private cloud. In a private cloud, your organization owns and manages the physical servers and networking and is responsible for items that include the operating system, patching, databases, backup, disaster recovery, and high availability. You have full control over SharePoint and all of its related components. Many organizations today leverage this model and have a mix of physical and virtualized servers using technologies such as VMware and Microsoft's Hyper-V and are taking advantage of private cloud benefits, including self-service provisioning and scalability.

Infrastructure as a Service

Infrastructure as a service (IAAS) has become much more prominent in recent years. Companies such as Amazon offer organizations large amounts of computing power and elasticity to handle things like seasonal spikes in business. In this model, the service provider manages the physical services and resources, including the server and its hardware resources such as memory, storage, and networking. Your organization owns the virtual machine that runs within the service provider's data center, and you are responsible for the operating system and applications (such as SharePoint, SQL Server) that run within the virtual machine as well as the patching and management of these virtual servers and products. Microsoft is beginning to offer its own IAAS offering as part of the Windows Azure service offering.

Platform as a Service

Platform as a service (PAAS) is still a relatively new service offering. In this case, the service provider manages all of the infrastructure (physical and virtual), and you focus on your applications and data management. Your organization does not need to deal with sizing or patching the underlying servers. An example of this is Microsoft's Azure Media Services where Microsoft manages the servers and storage for your online media files (such as streaming videos).

Software as a Service

Software as a service (SAAS) has been around for a while. SAAS offers consumers and organizations the ability to subscribe to a product that is delivered via the public cloud. The service may be free of charge, advertiser funded, or charged per user on a regular monthly or annual basis. The service provider manages all aspects of the service, including providing regular updates to the application and ensuring that it is highly available and backed up. Many consumers are using services such as Hotmail, Xbox Live, or Skype. Enterprises may be using services such as Salesforce.com or Yammer. Microsoft has been moving into the enterprise SAAS business over the past few years, including Office 365, which is where SharePoint Online runs.

Key Differences

Figure 11-1 summarizes the key differences among on-premises (private cloud), IAAS, PAAS, and SAAS from a Microsoft cloud services perspective. One of the main things to consider is the level of control and customization your organization needs. Typically, the more control you

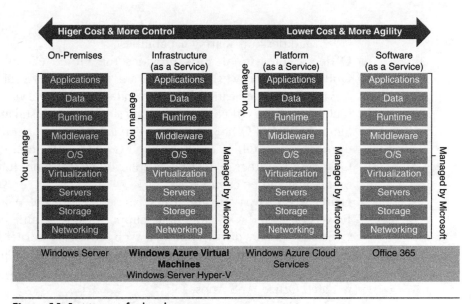

Figure 11-1 Microsoft cloud services comparison

keep, the higher your long-term costs will be since you will be responsible for management, patching, storage, backup, disaster recovery, and other operations. However, the further you move toward the SAAS model, the less you control, which typically means less long-term cost since the service provider can realize economies of scale by providing a standardized service to multiple customers.

Office 365 Overview

Office 365 is one of Microsoft's SAAS offerings. The following services are key components of Office 365 with the wave of products released online in early 2013:

- **Exchange Online** is for e-mail, calendaring, and personal task management. Microsoft also offers Exchange Online Archiving and Exchange Online Protection as services for storing archived messages and handling e-mail spam and virus and malware protection.
- **SharePoint Online** is very similar to what is available in SharePoint Server 2013 on-premises. This chapter will highlight key differences between the online and on-premises versions.

- **Lync Online** provides presence status, instant messaging, audio, video, and desktop-sharing capabilities.
- **Office Professional Plus** provides the Office clients (such as Outlook, Word, PowerPoint, Excel, and OneNote) as a subscription service. Office applications can be installed on demand via streaming technology from Office 365, including side-by-side installations with older versions of Office. Office as a service is licensed per user. Each user can install Office on up to five PC or Mac devices. Please see Chapter 20, "Integrating Office Applications," for more information on the new Office clients.
- **Office Web Apps** provide browser-based versions of Word, Excel, PowerPoint, and OneNote that support viewing and editing of Office documents directly within a Web browser; Internet Explorer, Firefox, Safari, and Chrome are supported. Please see Chapter 20, "Integrating Office Applications," for more information on the updated Office Web Apps.
- **Project Online** is a new offering with the 2013 SharePoint Online service update. Project Server is now available as an online service for enterprise project, resource, and portfolio management. Project Online integrates with SharePoint Online by providing a rolled-up view of all tasks assigned to an individual across Exchange, SharePoint, and Project sites. The Project desktop client is also available on a per-user subscription basis and is installed and managed in a manner similar to the Office clients.
- **Visio Online** is an update to Visio Services (first introduced in 2010) and includes the new ability to subscribe to a user-based service for managing the deployment of the Visio client software.
- **Duet Online** is a new joint offering from Microsoft and SAP that offers the ability to integrate SharePoint Online with an SAP implementation.
- **Information Rights Management (IRM)** is now available as a service offering from Microsoft and can be integrated with Exchange and SharePoint Online. It enables the ability to apply policies to messages and documents stored within Office 365 to manage who can view or edit items and for how long. You can also set policies to prevent messages and files from being sent or viewed by people outside of your organization.

Office 365 Licensing Considerations

Microsoft offers a variety of Office 365 pricing plans for individual components; discounts are offered when multiple services (such as Exchange Online and SharePoint Online) are purchased as part of a suite. Various options are available based on the size of the organization, and there is the option to have different license types for different user roles. For example, kiosk workers who need only browser-based access to e-mail and Office documents can be covered under a less expensive plan than others who need to fully use SharePoint and Office. More details on the various Office 365 license offerings can be found at www.office365.com.

One of the main licensing items to consider is whether or not your organization is able to run in the standard multi-tenant environment or if it needs to be in its own dedicated environment. In a multi-tenant environment, multiple organizations share the same hardware, but their content and data are kept separate. For example, multiple organizations may be managed within the same SharePoint farm, but each organization resides within its own "tenant" (essentially a separate Web application within the SharePoint farm), and all of its content is stored within its own private site collections and content databases. In a dedicated environment, a single organization is in a single SharePoint farm. One of the main trade-offs between dedicated and multi-tenant is cost. Typically a dedicated environment costs more since Microsoft needs to allocate and manage specific hardware for a single customer.

Note The SharePoint Online standard (multi-tenant) and dedicated versions offer different capabilities, benefits, and feature roadmaps. The primary focus of this chapter is on the standard offering.

Office 365 Identity Management

There are multiple ways to set up user access to Office 365. Smaller organizations will likely use the Office 365 user management system to manually create user accounts and set passwords within Office 365. Organizations that already have Active Directory in place on-premises will often want to set up single sign-on (SSO) and identity federation with Office 365. In this scenario, the organization will typically synchronize its user accounts (but not the user passwords) with the Windows Azure Active Directory service with which Office 365 integrates. When users log in to Office 365, they use their normal Active Directory user accounts and domain passwords. The benefit of this is that users do not have to remember different usernames and passwords between online and on-premises systems. From the perspective of your organization, this enables you to manage a single set of user accounts and apply your corporate policies to them, such as password complexity and expiration. This common user identity configuration is also important for supporting hybrid scenarios, which will be discussed later in this chapter.

Note More information on the options and setup for SSO and directory synchronization can be found at http://technet.microsoft.com/en-us/library/hh967619.aspx.

SharePoint Online also offers the option of inviting people outside of your organization to collaborate. The SharePoint Online tenant administrator for your organization can determine whether to allow external sharing within your tenant and, if external sharing is enabled, whether to require external users who accept sharing invitations to sign in as authenticated users or if they can access resources anonymously (no login required). Your organization can also specify different external sharing policies for different site collections within SharePoint Online. For example, your organization may have a site collection set up for collaboration only within your organization. In this case, external sharing should be disabled for that site collection. Your organization may have a separate site collection for external collaboration for areas such as working with customers, partners, or boards of directors. Additional considerations for security in this scenario are discussed in Chapter 12, "Planning Security."

Office 365 Administration

Most organizations use Office 365 in a multi-tenant environment. A tenant is the boundary that separates your organization's content and data from what belongs to other organizations. Office 365 offers a consolidated management console for tenant administrators to manage their Office 365 environment. From this environment you can

- View a dashboard (see Figure 11-2) to see the overall health of the Office 365 service and whether there are any issues or planned maintenance activities for the individual service components, including SharePoint Online. You can also view and open new service requests and see what users have been assigned Exchange mail licenses but have not logged in to use the service.

- View the "setup" resource area to help your organization determine the right approach for setting up your user accounts in Office 365. This area is also used to facilitate migrating to Exchange Online or running in a hybrid environment where some users are kept on-premises while others are online.
- Access the "users and groups" area where you can manually create Office 365 online user accounts or learn how to set up Active Directory synchronization, single sign-on, and federation. This is also the area where you assign and manage individual user licenses based on the services and plans you have purchased.
- View the "domains" area to associate your organization's domain (such as myorganization.com) with the Office 365 service.
- Update service settings where you will see direct links to manage the various components of Office 365, for example, Exchange Online archiving, auditing, or data loss prevention policies.

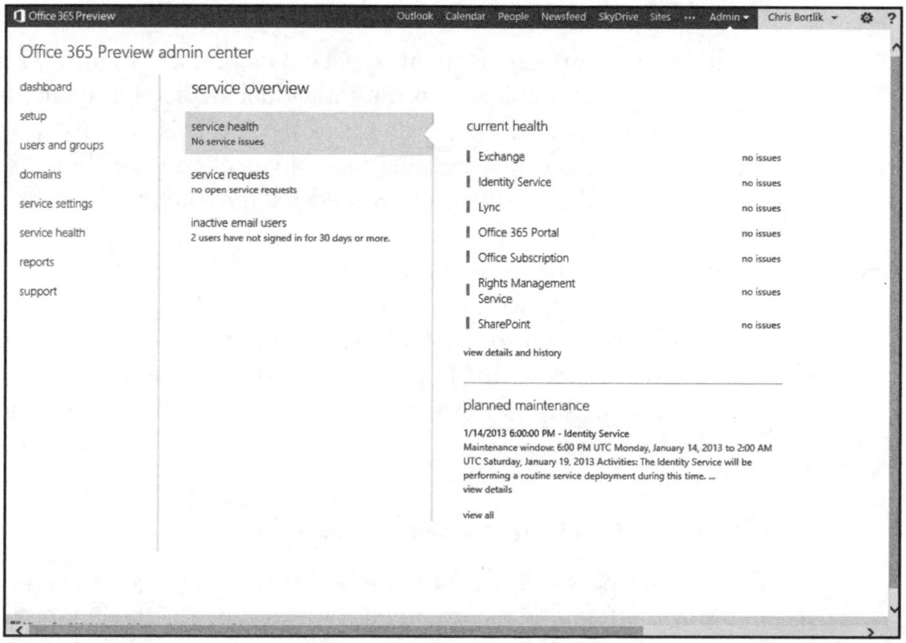

Figure 11-2 Office 365 tenant administrator dashboard

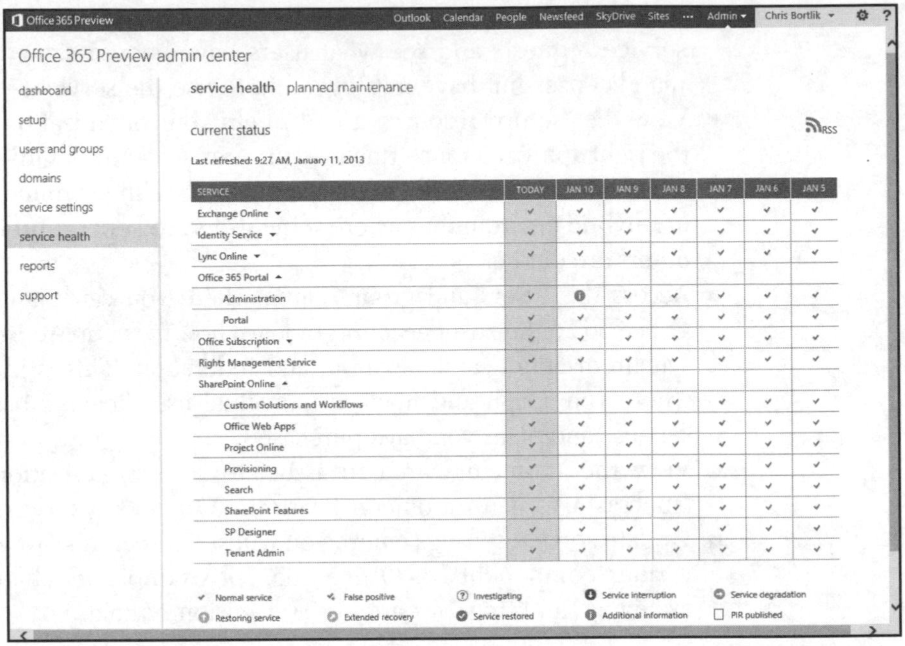

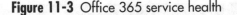

Figure 11-3 Office 365 service health

- View information about service health (see Figure 11-3) to have additional visibility into the individual service components and their availability over the previous seven days. This area also provides additional details on upcoming maintenance. You are able to subscribe to service alerts using an RSS feed reader (such as Outlook or Internet Explorer) as well.
- View reports to see how your tenant is being used.
- View a "support" area that offers links to frequently asked questions, forums, and resource tools. Depending on your contract and support agreements with Microsoft, your organization may have different forms of support available, including telephone support for tenant administrators.

Office 365 User Experience

From a user perspective, Office 365 seeks to bring together various products in a single integrated environment. One example is the common navigation bar at the top of the page in Office 365 (see Figure 11-4).

Figure 11-4 Office 365 navigation bar

This navigation bar enables you to navigate to the following:

- **Outlook** takes you to your Exchange Online mailbox via the Web-based version of Outlook—Outlook Web Application (OWA). If you are using Lync Online, your presence status (free, busy, in a meeting, etc.) is also visible within the browser.
- **Calendar** shows a Web-based view of your personal calendar stored within Exchange Online.
- **People** displays your contacts from Exchange Online and provides the ability to show integrated contact information from social networks that you may belong to such as Facebook or LinkedIn.
- **Newsfeed** is your SharePoint Online activity stream for the people, sites, documents, and tags that you are interested in. Please refer to Chapter 15, "Planning for Social Computing," for additional information on the SharePoint 2013 Newsfeed capabilities.
- **SkyDrive** is your personal storage within SharePoint Online. Each user with a SkyDrive in SharePoint Online is allocated 7GB of personal storage. (Though the tab says SkyDrive, this is actually SkyDrive Pro. SkyDrive is your personal documents area. SkyDrive Pro is where you can synchronize SharePoint documents with your computer to work with them offline. You will likely need to explain this to your users as part of your training plan.) Please refer to Chapter 20, "Integrating Office Applications," for additional information on the SkyDrive Pro capabilities.
- **Sites** provides a list of the sites you are following within SharePoint Online and provides the ability for your organization to promote certain sites to be visible at the top of the page for each user. Please refer to Chapter 15, "Planning for Social Computing," for additional information on the SharePoint 2013 Sites capabilities.
- **Office Store** (listed on the ". . ." more options menu) is a link to the Microsoft public store where you can preview or purchase applications for Microsoft Office applications and SharePoint. Please refer to Chapter 17, "Planning Business Solutions," for additional information on the new Office and SharePoint application model and store.

- **Office.com** (listed on the "..." more options menu) is a link to the Microsoft Office site where you can search for information, access online help resources, and download Office document templates.
- **Admin** is where Office 365 tenant administrators are able to access the Exchange Online, SharePoint Online, and Lync Online administrative features.

Note that these features and links are dependent upon the Office 365 services to which your organization has subscribed and the specific license that has been assigned to each user. For example, users with a kiosk license will not have access to SkyDrive Pro for personal storage and will not have a SkyDrive link available at the top of each page.

SharePoint Online Functionality

In most cases, SharePoint Online is run as a multi-tenant service, which means that multiple organizations exist within the same physical SharePoint farm. SharePoint Online provides the ability to administer your tenant within Office 365.

Note When managing SharePoint Online, you do not have access to the physical server, nor can you access SharePoint's central administration area to manage farm-wide services and features. This means that, among other things, you cannot install new farm-level solutions in SharePoint Online.

The SharePoint Online tenant administration screens allow you to centrally manage many shared settings across your various SharePoint site collections, including the following:

- **Site Collections** (see Figure 11-5) enables a SharePoint Online administrator to create new site collections and manage existing site collections. Key considerations include specifying who will be the administrators for the site collection and whether or not you will add a third-party "support partner" to help administer and manage SharePoint Online on behalf of your organization. This screen is also where you can specify unique external sharing

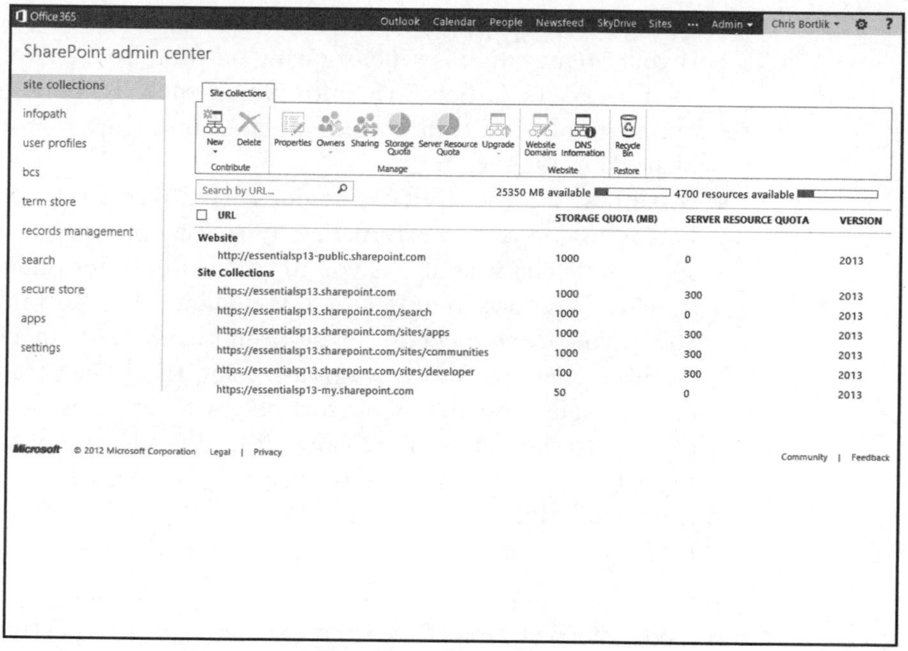

Figure 11-5 SharePoint Online site collections administration

policies on a per-site-collection basis. From this screen you can also allocate how much of your organization's pooled SharePoint Online storage quota is allowed for each site collection and how many resources can be allocated to each site collection to run custom applications.

- **InfoPath** enables a SharePoint Online administrator to specify if browser-based InfoPath Forms Services can be used by authorized users, based on their license and permissions.

Note Please see Chapter 17, "Planning Business Solutions," for additional information on InfoPath Forms Services.

- **User Profiles** supports maintenance of properties that are available for each user and management of their personal content (formerly referred to as My Site), including individual components such as Newsfeed and SkyDrive Pro. User profiles are discussed in depth in Chapter 15, "Planning for Social Computing." If your organization is synchronizing on-premises Active Directory information to Office 365, information such as the user's name, phone number, and title are populated in the user profile within SharePoint Online.

- **Business Connectivity Services (BCS)** enables SharePoint Online to connect to external systems. Two primary scenarios are supported. The first allows you to connect to other online services such as Windows Azure or CRM Online. The second scenario allows you to connect to an on-premises system. In both cases, BCS connects to the data service using the oData standard and an externally available Web service. BCS provides the option to connect to the data source using either the identity of the current logged-in user or a system user account that has been specified by the SharePoint Online administrator and stored within the secure store.

Note More information on BCS can be found in Chapter 17, "Planning Business Solutions."

- **Term Store** supports sharing enterprise keywords across SharePoint Online site collections. Note that out of the box, the term store can be used only within a single SharePoint Online tenant and cannot be integrated with an on-premises term store. A variety of different third-party tools and programmatic options are available if you have a requirement to have a single term store in use for hybrid scenarios between SharePoint Online and on-premises.

Note For more information on the term store, please see Chapter 13, "Managing Enterprise Content."

- **Records Management** provides the ability for SharePoint Online administrators to specify "send to" connections for content to be routed either manually or via defined retention policies. For example, a corporate Records Center could be established within SharePoint Online and certain document types could be automatically copied or moved to that location based on a defined policy.

Sales proposals, for instance, could be moved three years after they were last modified.

Note Please see Chapter 13, "Managing Enterprise Content," for more information on records management capabilities within SharePoint.

- **Search** presents SharePoint Online search management settings such as defining the location of the primary Search Center and configuring result sources for searching content from a remote SharePoint server on-premises or another search provider (such as Bing or Google) using the OpenSearch federation standard.

Note For additional information about search, see Chapter 16, "Planning Enterprise Search."

- **Secure Store** enables SharePoint Online administrators to centrally define the username and password used to authenticate and connect to other systems using Business Connectivity Services.
- **Apps** provides the ability to manage SharePoint Online policies for acquiring third-party applications from the public SharePoint marketplace as well as establishing an organizational application catalog for centrally publishing and managing applications that can be used across the SharePoint Online environment. You can also monitor application usage and track license allocations from this area.
- **Settings** (see Figure 11-6) is a key page for managing your overall SharePoint Online environment. From here you can specify whether or not authorized users should be able to invite external people to collaborate in SharePoint and whether or not they need to log in to gain access. You are able to specify if new site collections can be created using the older SharePoint 2010 user experience or if they must use the new SharePoint 2013 style. This is an important item to consider as you plan for your training, adoption, and migration to SharePoint 2013. You can also enable or disable the integration of the IRM service with SharePoint Online for applying policies to Office documents stored within SharePoint. Site self-provisioning policies are defined here, and you can specify whether to use the default SharePoint site provisioning form or a custom form.

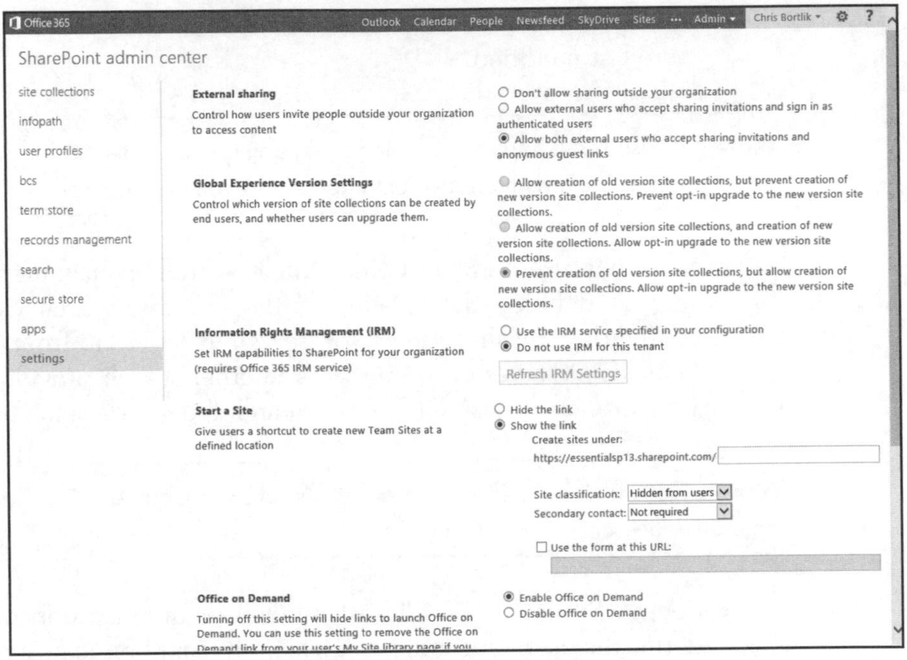

Figure 11-6 SharePoint Online tenant settings

You can also define whether information classification policies must be assigned to the site and if an additional site owner must be specified before the site can be created. Office on Demand (described further in Chapter 20, "Integrating Office Applications") can be enabled or disabled here if you want to allow people to temporarily install an Office application (such as Word) on devices they are using (such as at a library, kiosk, or family member's house) when they need the full Office client features to make document edits. Finally, you can specify whether or not you want preview features to be enabled within your SharePoint Online tenant or if only fully released and supported capabilities should be provided.

Comparing SharePoint Online with SharePoint Server 2013

At the time of the writing of this book, there continue to be differences between capabilities that are available in SharePoint Online and what is available within SharePoint Server 2013 on-premises. With the third major service update to SharePoint Online in early 2013, Microsoft has shortened the list of capabilities that can be used only within SharePoint Server and has started to add capabilities that now will be available only within SharePoint Online.

The SharePoint Online service descriptions are regularly updated to provide information on what capabilities and features are available across the various licensing plans and how they compare to what is available via SharePoint Server. Refer to http://technet.microsoft.com/en-us/library/jj819267.aspx for the latest information. It is strongly encouraged that organizations evaluating SharePoint Online carefully review these service descriptions to confirm that they meet their needs.

Capabilities Missing from SharePoint Online

One of the main differences between SharePoint Server and SharePoint Online is the degree of administrative control provided to the SharePoint administrator. As we described earlier, SharePoint Online does not provide access to central administration. Instead, your organization is provided access to a SharePoint Online tenant administration area for performing the available tasks. One of the primary impacts of this is that there are some farm-level settings that you are not allowed to modify. These include the maximum size of a file that can be uploaded to SharePoint Online (currently limited to 250MB per file), the types of files that can be uploaded, and the quota allocation to personal sites and SkyDrive Pro, which is currently set at 7GB per user. This is one of the main trade-offs that organizations need to assess when evaluating SharePoint Online. For some organizations, not being able to turn all of the knobs and dials within SharePoint is acceptable in exchange for potentially lower administrative costs and having a standardized offering that is managed by Microsoft. For others, these limitations present a decision point where they need to assess if they can modify their requirements to accept the capabilities offered by the service.

Applications are another significant area to review and assess when considering SharePoint Online. The new SharePoint apps model and marketplace discussed earlier provide new ways to develop and purchase applications for SharePoint. Applications can also be developed within SharePoint using the Client Side Object Model (CSOM). Sandbox solutions are still available, although Microsoft has deprecated sandbox solutions with this release to encourage the new application model to be considered for SharePoint-hosted applications. One major difference between SharePoint

Online and SharePoint Server is that full-trust farm-level solutions cannot be deployed to SharePoint Online. This includes both applications that your organization may build and those you may purchase from third parties. The main reason for this is that your organization does not have access to the physical server in SharePoint Online and therefore does not have permission to deploy and manage full-trust applications. Microsoft also needs to maintain its SLAs for all customers in multi-tenant scenarios where more than one organization is running within the same SharePoint farm.

Business intelligence capabilities have been improved in SharePoint Online but still have some restrictions. Excel Services can be leveraged, including support for PowerPivot and Power View. However, there are limitations on Excel file size and how external data sources can be accessed from SharePoint Online. PerformancePoint Services is not currently supported within SharePoint Online. One alternative that some organizations consider is leveraging other cloud services, such as Windows and SQL Azure, to provide the more advanced business intelligence and reporting capabilities that are required and then have that information surfaced within SharePoint Online. Additional information about SharePoint business intelligence capabilities can be found in Chapter 18, "Planning for Business Intelligence."

Search has been improved in SharePoint Online and now provides many of the enterprise search capabilities that were previously part of FAST search for SharePoint. However, there are limitations on what content sources can be indexed and made available via SharePoint Online. While SharePoint Online has added the ability to connect to a remote SharePoint server in a hybrid scenario, it does not currently enable you to directly crawl and index content sources outside of SharePoint Online, such as on-premises file shares or other content stores. If this is something that your organization requires, you will need to implement an on-premises SharePoint server to index that content and then have the SharePoint Online search service connect to that as an external content source. Note that when implementing hybrid search in this manner the results are not interwoven for relevancy. This means that the results of online and on-premises cannot be shown within a single search results block. There are third-party applications available, such as those provided by BA Insight, that provide additional capabilities for working with SharePoint search in hybrid environments. Another limitation of SharePoint Online's search capabilities is the range of file formats that can be full-text indexed. SharePoint Online does not allow organizations to install and configure additional file format handlers beyond what is standard with SharePoint 2013 (refer to http://technet.microsoft.com/en-us/library/jj219530 for the complete list). This means that file types not on this list will only be searchable based on the metadata attributes associated with the files such as their title, author, and any other attributes that you associate with the files within SharePoint.

Note For additional details and a full comparison of SharePoint search differences between SharePoint Online and SharePoint Server, please see Chapter 16, "Planning Enterprise Search."

Usage reporting and auditing are currently not as robust in SharePoint Online as they are in on-premises. One example is that SharePoint Online does not allow organizations to audit who has viewed an item, but it does support auditing the create, edit, and delete actions. Usage reporting and administrative reporting are also areas where third-party tools such as Axceler, AvePoint, Metalogix, Quest (now part of Dell), and Webtrends may provide enhancements.

Capabilities Available Only in SharePoint Online

There are a number of capabilities that exist only within SharePoint Online. As Microsoft announced at the SharePoint Conference in November 2012, going forward, the online service will be updated on a much more frequent release cycle than SharePoint Server. At a minimum, Microsoft plans to update SharePoint Online on a quarterly basis. This suggests that additional SharePoint Online–only features will be added before the next version of SharePoint Server is released.

External sharing (see Figure 11-7) is one area that is unique to SharePoint Online. As discussed earlier in this chapter, external sharing enables sites, lists, and/or individual items (such as documents) to be selectively shared with people who do not have an account within your Office 365 tenant. If enabled, users can send an anonymous guest link to specific items or invite people to log in to the site by using any e-mail address.

If a login is required, the recipient of the e-mail (see Figure 11-8) will need to first associate his or her e-mail address with a Microsoft account (such as hotmail.com, outlook.com, or live.com) or an existing Office 365 account (see Figure 11-9).

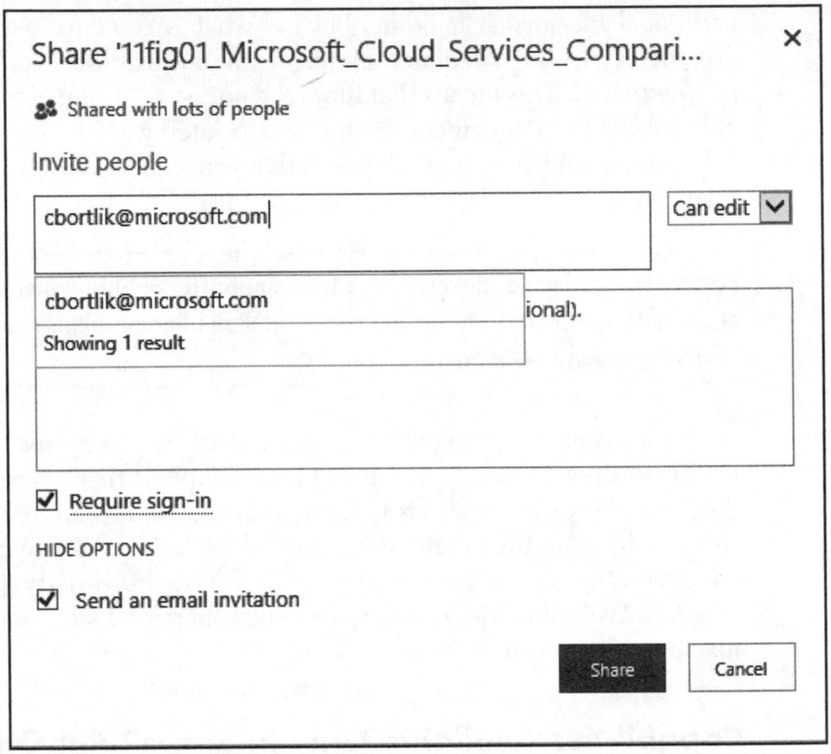

Figure 11-7 Inviting an external user to edit a file in SharePoint Online

External sharing can be used in a variety of scenarios such as working with customers, partners, boards of directors, and others outside of your organization. However, you should carefully consider if and where to enable external sharing and confirm that proper governance and audit controls are in place to ensure that sensitive information is not being shared inappropriately with people outside of your organization—similar to policies that may be in place today for e-mail, FTP sites, and extranets. You should also ensure that access requests and permissions are regularly reviewed (see Figure 11-10) to ensure that access is revoked when it is no longer required.

SharePoint Online includes a public Web site that may be useful for some organizations. The Web site (see Figure 11-11) comes prebuilt with a basic Publishing Site template and supports many of the core Web content management capabilities described in Chapter 14, "Managing Web

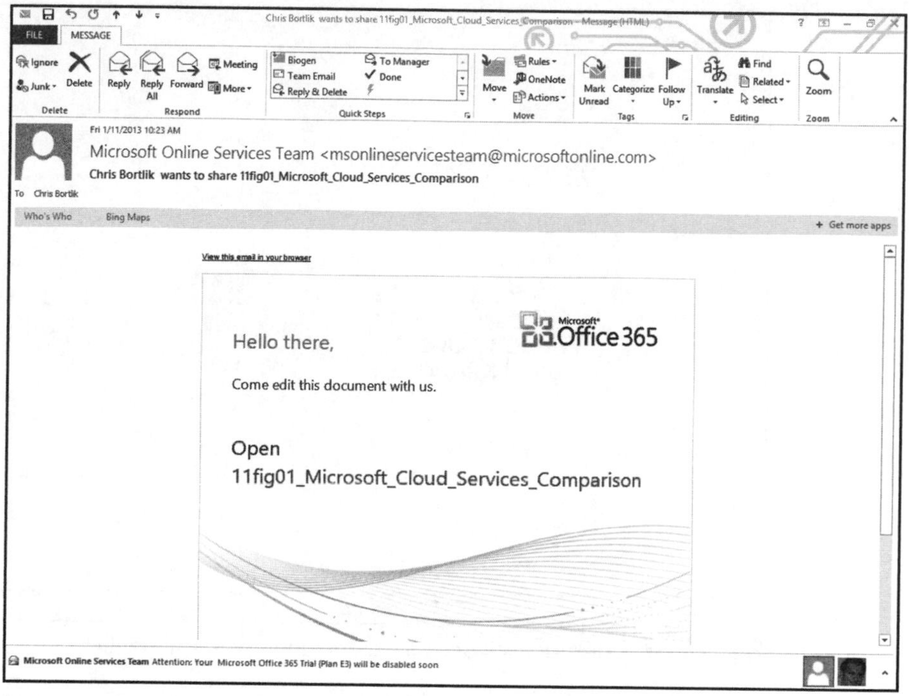

Figure 11-8 External user invitation e-mail

Content." Note that this site does not support the full set of capabilities often required by large organizations to manage their public Web sites, such as the new Content by Search Web Part. In those scenarios, organizations may find that running their public-facing Web site based on SharePoint on-premises, or hosted by an IAAS provider such as Windows Azure or Amazon, to be a better alternative.

SharePoint Online provides a Developer Site template that can be used to build applications for SharePoint and Office using the new apps model described earlier. SharePoint Online also supports an application called Napa (see Figure 11-12), which provides the ability to build and run SharePoint-hosted applications directly in a Web browser. These applications can be built quickly without additional developer tools. If a full development environment is needed for advanced applications, Napa solutions can be exported to Visual Studio 2012, where they can be further developed and debugged with a richer toolset.

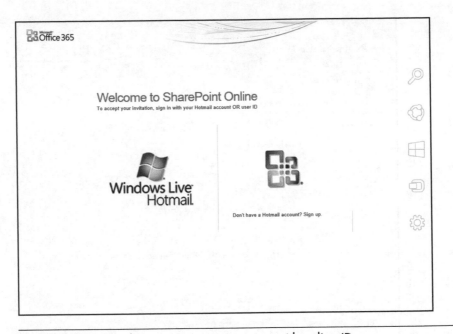

Figure 11-9 External user account association with online ID

Figure 11-10 Reviewing access requests within SharePoint Online

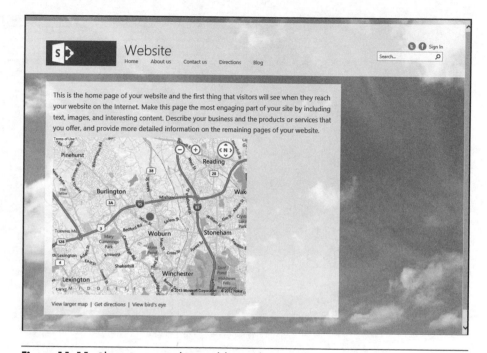

Figure 11-11 SharePoint Online public Web site

Office 365 has a variety of features for integration between Office clients and SharePoint Online. Office on Demand, the ability to temporarily stream and use the Office clients on another device, is available only from the SharePoint Online personal site. The ability for Office to remember the documents that you recently viewed and where you left off when reading or editing a document works only if your Office clients are connected to Microsoft online services—either SkyDrive (as a consumer) or Office 365 (as an organization). More details on these topics are discussed in Chapter 20, "Integrating Office Applications."

Yammer, an online-only social networking solution that Microsoft acquired in July 2012, is available in two licensing models. The free version of Yammer provides organizations with user social and document-sharing capabilities. The paid enterprise version of Yammer allows organizations to integrate Yammer with other systems, including SharePoint, and to perform advanced administrative functions, including integration with on-premises Active Directory environments to help ensure that user access to Yammer is terminated when an individual no longer works for an organization.

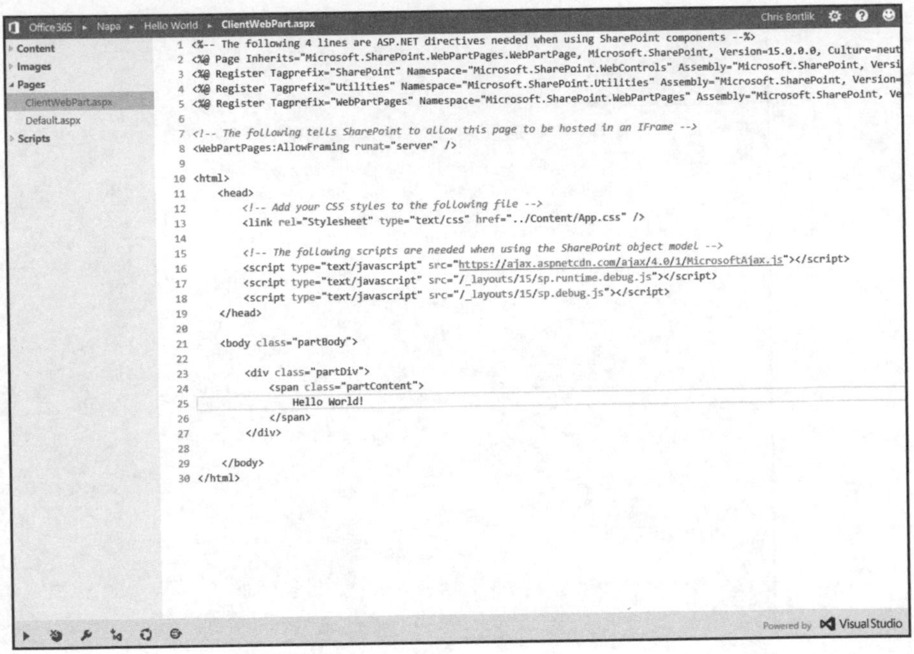

Figure 11-12 SharePoint Online Napa development tools

At the SharePoint Conference in November 2012,[3] Microsoft announced licensing changes that now provide SharePoint Online users with a license to also use Yammer enterprise capabilities. Microsoft also demonstrated how in the future Yammer and SharePoint will become integrated for social computing and file sharing. Given Microsoft's focus on Office 365 and the fact that Yammer is delivered only as an online service, it is expected that integration between Yammer and SharePoint Online will be accelerated and delivered prior to additional integration with SharePoint Server.

Planning for SharePoint Online

How do you know if SharePoint Online is right for your organization? There are a number of different considerations and trade-offs that you need to consider. For organizations that are new to SharePoint or those

---

3. Jared Spataro, Senior Director, Microsoft Office Division, "Putting Social to Work," November 12, 2012. http://blogs.technet.com/b/microsoft_blog/archive/2012/11/12/putting-social-to-work.aspx

that have limited resources to manage their SharePoint infrastructure (including backups, disaster recovery, patching, and upgrades), going to SharePoint Online may be an easy decision. For organizations that have made a large investment in SharePoint on-premises, or have developed or purchased many custom solutions that are not yet compatible with SharePoint Online, the decision may be more challenging.

With SharePoint 2013, many organizations are considering starting with SharePoint Online in a few key use case scenarios:

- **SkyDrive Pro** for providing 7GB of personal file storage per user. This may help to replace unsupported consumer file-sharing services (such as Box, Dropbox, SkyDrive consumer, or Google Drive) that people are using outside of established IT security policies. Hosted in SharePoint Online, SkyDrive Pro is also available from any corporate, personal, or mobile device, which is a frequent requirement to support flexible work styles.
- **Social** via either SharePoint 2013 Newsfeed or Yammer, which is now included with the price of SharePoint Online. Providing these services via the public cloud allows you to support mobile scenarios and enable external collaboration.
- **Mobile** by leveraging the SharePoint and Office Mobile and Web Applications to access files and social information via SharePoint Online. This includes providing access to phone and tablet devices and supporting bring-your-own-device (BYOD) scenarios.
- **External sharing and collaboration** by using SharePoint team sites and the ability to invite external users to view or edit a document, library, or site. Examples are board of director sites or collaborating with customers and partners.
- **Basic team sites** for utility SharePoint environments with minimal customization, such as basic document management and collaboration requirements.
- **Project management** using the new SharePoint 2013 task management capabilities or Project Online.

Getting Started with SharePoint Online

If you do decide to move to SharePoint Online, your planning process will be similar to what has been covered elsewhere in this book. Topics such as governance, measurement, and adoption remain just as important online as they do on-premises. You will need to review your existing policies, training plans, and support procedures to see what needs to be revised to factor in your move to SharePoint Online.

Migrating to SharePoint Online

When planning your migration to SharePoint Online, you will first need to determine what needs to be migrated—if anything. Will you be migrating all existing content to SharePoint Online or just some content? Will you operate in a hybrid mode where some content will be kept on-premises and other content will be moved to SharePoint Online?

Information classification is an important consideration. Some organizations may have a policy that all content classified as "high business impact" (HBI), such as Social Security numbers, credit card numbers, or patient information, cannot be stored in the cloud. There may be business or geopolitical regulations in place that require content to be stored in a particular country. These requirements must be considered and documented before beginning to move content to SharePoint Online.

Once you have determined what needs to be migrated, you next need to determine how that migration will occur. Unfortunately, Microsoft does not allow you to connect your existing SharePoint content databases to move them to SharePoint Online. Microsoft also does not currently provide tools to support the content migration process. There are a few options to consider:

- Migrate nothing and start with SharePoint Online for new content and sites going forward.
- Request that users manually migrate their own content, recognizing that dates and the user ID for the Created By and Modified By users are not preserved with a manual migration.
- Develop and test your own migration utilities by leveraging remote PowerShell scripts or the new Client Side Object Model.
- Purchase a third-party migration tool, such as those provided by vendors like AvePoint, Axceler, Metalogix, and Quest (Dell), to support the migration process.

In addition to planning for content migration, you need to review any application and integration requirements that you may have in place.

Have you developed or purchased any third-party applications that are actively being used in your existing SharePoint environment? If so, do you still need the application or does the supplier have a version that is compatible with SharePoint Online?

Understanding SharePoint Online Governance and Operational Implications

A number of areas within your SharePoint governance and operational plans will need to be reviewed and updated for SharePoint Online:

- Can your operational procedures be simplified since you may no longer need to be concerned with patching, backups, and restores?
- Is your organization building applications for SharePoint? If so, you will need to think about whether to build those applications with the new SharePoint apps model. You will also need to review your SharePoint application development life cycle model to consider where applications will be developed and tested and how they will be deployed and managed with SharePoint Online.
- Will people have access to SharePoint Online from computers that are not managed by your organization? If so, have you considered your policies and requirements for encrypting data on those devices if users will be able to synchronize files offline with SkyDrive Pro?
- Is any training needed for SharePoint Online tenant administrators? If you are using SharePoint on-premises today, will the online administrators be the same people?
- Will you enable external sharing to be leveraged within SharePoint Online? If yes, will it be for all site collections or just specific ones?
- Do you need to connect SharePoint Online with other data sources and systems either on-premises or via other cloud services, such as an online customer relationship management (CRM) system? Are these systems already externally accessible?
- Will you need to have a hybrid search environment set up to span searching across online and on-premises content sources?

> **Note** Microsoft has published documentation and reference architectures to help customers plan for and implement a hybrid between SharePoint Online and SharePoint 2013 on-premises. These resources can be found on TechNet at http://technet.microsoft.com/en-us/library/jj838715.aspx.

Other Online Options

While most of this chapter has focused on Microsoft's SharePoint Online offering via Office 365, it should be noted that there are many other hosted SharePoint offerings available for organizations that do not want to manage SharePoint on-premises.

Companies such as Fpweb, Rackspace, NaviSite, and Amazon offer the ability for organizations to have their SharePoint environment hosted elsewhere. Microsoft is also offering IAAS offerings via its Azure cloud service for organizations that require more control and ability to customize than are available via SharePoint Online, such as for advanced Web content management and business intelligence requirements.

When considering these options, you need to decide how much control and management your organization wants to have over the environment. There are pros and cons of each of the cloud options described earlier—especially when comparing IAAS and SAAS.

Many of the hosting providers also offer services to assist with the migration and management of your SharePoint environment. It is important to review these options and have clear contract terms regarding SLAs and roles and responsibilities between your organization and the service provider.

Key Points

Consider the following points as you determine your cloud strategy for SharePoint:

- Microsoft has stated that they are "all in" with the cloud and will be moving toward making the latest SharePoint capabilities available first through SharePoint Online as part of Office 365.
- Going forward, Microsoft has begun to publicly state that it intends to develop for SharePoint Online as the primary delivery model.

This does not mean that Microsoft is abandoning SharePoint Server, which can be run by organizations on-premises or hosted by third-party providers. What this strategy means is that new functionality will be made available first in SharePoint Online, likely in a series of regular service updates.

- During the SharePoint Conference in November 2012, Jeff Teper, corporate vice president and head of the SharePoint engineering team at Microsoft, stated that SharePoint Online would be receiving updates at least once per quarter.
- In July 2012, the Microsoft SharePoint team acquired Yammer, which is an online-only social computing platform. Yammer and SharePoint will be integrated more as the two services evolve.
- There are a variety of different options available for moving SharePoint to the cloud. Microsoft and a variety of third-party service providers offer different hosting models that you should carefully consider. Whether you look at running SharePoint on-premises using an IAAS provider, or moving to a full SAAS option such as Office 365, there are many different pros and cons to carefully consider.
- Document your requirements and evaluation criteria. Determine if the cloud is right for your organization. Microsoft and its partners have tools and resources to help determine if there is alignment. One example is the Office 365 alignment index calculator tool that can be found at https://onramp.office365.com.
- Consider your software currency requirements. For some organizations, the fact that Office 365, including SharePoint Online, is updated regularly is a benefit. You need to think about your organizational culture and training requirements. You also need to make sure that you can maintain the necessary operating system, Web browser, and Office version levels to stay current with usage of the service.
- If you do decide to go with Office 365, think about your identity management requirements. Will you require synchronization with an existing Active Directory environment, or will you use cloud identities that are unique to Office 365?
- Determine if you will license just SharePoint Online or other components of the Office 365 suite such as Exchange, Lync, Office, or Project Online as well. You may also want to consider segmenting your user population to have different license types for different people,

such as kiosk workers who may not require the same capabilities as a power user.

- Consider your security requirements and make sure that the standard multi-tenant offering meets your needs. If not, you may want to explore the dedicated option, keep SharePoint hosted on-premises, or consider a third-party provider. Microsoft provides an online "trust center" that explains the processes, controls, and certifications that are in place for Office 365 which can be found at http://trustoffice365.com/.

- If you do decide to move to the cloud, consider starting with a pilot team or department before moving your full organization. Use this pilot to confirm and validate that your requirements are being met and to update your communications, training, migration, and adoption plans for further rollout within your organization.

CHAPTER 12

PLANNING SECURITY

Planning security for your solution is about balancing and optimizing the various security elements for all of the people who will use the solution, including content contributors, content users, and administrators who manage and maintain security groups. It also involves defining a model that works for the current business requirements but is also defined well enough to grow and be altered as requirements and content change. Planning security is also about deciding how you will "put the 'share' in SharePoint." Especially for SharePoint 2013, where there are new and simplified options for sharing content, planning security involves deciding what content will be closed off all the time, but also what content will be closed off some of the time or to some users.

There is no single best way to design security and manage security groups. Each business scenario is different. Because the risks associated with getting your security model wrong are pretty big—three main issues come to mind: (1) not allowing required access, (2) allowing inappropriate access, and (3) not understanding where permissions have been broken or applied to individuals instead of groups so that granting permissions in one place does not result in the access you expect—we often find ourselves suggesting that planning security should come with the same kind of warning you see on television shows with crazy stunts: "Don't try this at home." In other words, if this is the first time you are implementing security for SharePoint, try to get support from someone who has in-depth knowledge of SharePoint security best practices.

In this chapter, we share as many of these best practices as we can, but it's really important to remember that almost every planning decision has to be carefully considered from multiple perspectives to arrive at the best solution for the situation. If you delegate design privileges for sites or site collections within your solution, you need to remember that it's not enough to train "site designers" in information architecture best practices; they must also understand how SharePoint security works and best practices for both creating and maintaining a security model or plan. In one organization, users are not given new sites or site collections until they prepare and document a security plan for their sites that can be reviewed with a senior-level solution architect. This approach is one that might be worth emulating because it ensures that a "solution analyst" working with an experienced information architect or security specialist collectively defines the security model for the site or solution. In another organization, site administrators are required to attend internal training to ensure that they understand both SharePoint site administration and specifically security best practices before they can assume full control of a SharePoint site.

One of the challenges that continues to be true for SharePoint 2013 is that it is not easy to figure out who has what privileges across your entire SharePoint environment. It is also not easy to replicate security permissions— for example, to hire a new employee into the role of a former employee and easily assign the same access privileges. In a small environment with only a couple of site collections, these actions will not be too time-consuming. However, these relatively typical transactions will be really, really difficult in large, complex environments. For this reason, most large organizations use one of the excellent third-party security management tools (such as those from AvePoint, Axceler, or Dell) to help manage and govern their SharePoint environments. Whether you are just beginning or are well into your SharePoint journey, it is worth considering this type of investment.

The discussion of security planning in this chapter is focused on the perspective of the business owner of the solution or site. Some of the implementation tasks may require support from your technical solution administrator, but ultimately, planning security is a business responsibility. This may seem like an overwhelming task for nontechnical resources who perceive security management as something IT has always owned. It's not. While IT may own the *implementation* of security requirements, security *decisions* are the responsibility of the business. Very much like a shared folder, security management in SharePoint is about determining who should and should not have access to various types of content. However, unlike your file share resources where security is generally only managed by IT and external users generally cannot access them, business users can have a lot more access to implementing security permissions in SharePoint, and external users can also "get in" pretty easily (at least in Office 365/SharePoint Online),[1] depending on how you manage your implementation. The new capability of SharePoint

---

1. There are some security differences between SharePoint 2013 on-premises and Office 365/SharePoint 2013 Online. In this chapter, when we refer to SharePoint 2013, we mean both online and on-premises. When a capability is available only in Office 365/SharePoint Online, we will explicitly call that out. We use the term SharePoint Online to refer to SharePoint 2013 Online or an Office 365 plan that includes SharePoint Online.

2013 to more easily share content with anyone, even external users, creates a risk area that must be clearly understood—and governed, as we discussed in Chapter 4, "Planning for Business Governance." Thus, business users have a critical need to understand how security in SharePoint works.

What's New In SharePoint 2013?

In general, security relationships in SharePoint 2013 work very much the same as they did in SharePoint 2010. Permissions are inherited from the root site unless you intentionally "break" them. Security can be managed down to the individual document or "item" level, though this is still not a recommended practice as we explain later in this chapter. However, SharePoint 2013 makes breaking permissions (and sharing content) easier, and because it is now so easy to do, it's also very easy to make mistakes and accidentally share content that you don't want to share. For this reason, you will want to be very, very intentional about what you allow users to do, especially when it comes to sharing content outside the organization.

Even if you are very familiar with how security works in previous versions of SharePoint, you will want to make sure you understand some of the new security capabilities in SharePoint 2013:

- **Simplified sharing of documents with both internal and external users.** From a business user perspective, the most significant change with SharePoint 2013 is that it is now very easy for individuals to give access to sites, lists, or documents to both internal and external users—but only in Office 365/SharePoint Online. Office 365/SharePoint Online environments and site collections can optionally be enabled for external sharing, but this capability is not available in SharePoint 2013 on-premises.
- In previous versions of SharePoint, you could not "manage permissions" on an item unless your permission set included the Manage Permissions feature. This was typically available only to Full Control users. However, in SharePoint 2013 Online, any user of your site has access to the new Share option. (Figure 12-1 shows the Share option for a document, and Figure 12-2 shows the Share option for a site.) The Share option allows that user to create a request to share the site, list, or document with someone who does not otherwise have access.

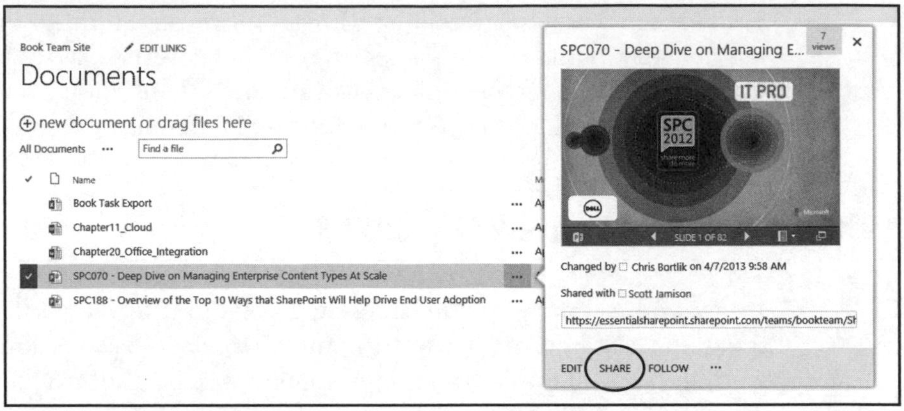

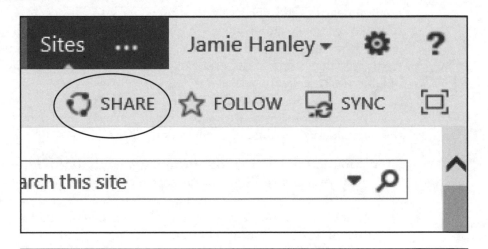

Figure 12-1 Share option for a document in SharePoint 2013

Figure 12-2 Share option for a site in SharePoint 2013

- Users who do not have the ability to manage permissions do not actually get to share anything without approval, even though they have access to the Share option. All requests to share are sent to the site owner, who then can approve or deny them. Unfortunately, it won't be obvious to your users that they aren't really sharing, so you will need to explain this during training. (When a visitor or member of a SharePoint site initiates a sharing request, a pop-up displays that lets them know that the request has been sent to the site owner. However, the pop-up does not display for very long, so it might be missed by busy users.)

■ The ability to share documents and sites is different in the online and on-premises versions of SharePoint 2013. Table 12-1 summarizes the user experiences for sharing documents and sites in both types of SharePoint 2013 environments.

Note In SharePoint 2013 on-premises, there is a confusing user experience with the ability to "share" documents for visitors and members unless you have set up outgoing e-mail on your farm and enabled access requests for your site. While the Share option is not available in the document ribbon for visitors and members, it is visible from the list item dialog as shown in Figure 12-13. Clicking the Share option in this scenario without access requests and e-mail enabled returns an error message: "Sorry, something went wrong. Only a limited set of people are allowed to share this content." This is actually by design, though the error message is a little confusing. Nothing really went wrong; the user just doesn't have permission to share a document if the site doesn't have "Allow access requests" turned on. This capability is enabled in Site Settings β Site permissions, and when enabled, it allows visitors and members to initiate an internal document-sharing request that goes to the site owner. In SharePoint Online, visitors and members can initiate a sharing request for a document in both the ribbon and in the item dialog, but all of the requests go to the site owner for approval.

Table 12-1 User Experience for Sharing Documents and Sites in SharePoint 2013 On-Premises and Online

Scenario	SharePoint 2013 On-Premises	Office 365/SharePoint 2013 Online
Visitors (Read Permission)		
Share a site	No option available.	Yes, visitors can initiate an **internal** sharing request that goes to the site owner for approval.
		When a visitor tries to initiate a sharing request for an **external** user, an error message is displayed that says, "Sorry, you are not allowed to share this with external users."

(continues)

Table 12-1 User Experience for Sharing Documents and Sites in SharePoint 2013 On-Premises and Online *(continued)*

Scenario	SharePoint 2013 On-Premises	Office 365/SharePoint 2013 Online
Share a document	No option available to share a document **internally** from the ribbon, but the Share option is available in the document item dialog (see Figure 12-13). **See important note on the previous page.**	Yes, visitors can initiate an **internal** sharing request that goes to the site owner for approval. When a visitor tries to initiate a sharing request for an **external** user, an error message is displayed that says, "Sorry, you are not allowed to share this with external users."
Members (Contribute or Edit Permission)		
Share a site	No option available.	Yes, members can initiate an **internal** sharing request that goes to the site owner for approval. When a member tries to initiate a sharing request for an **external** user, an error message is displayed that says, "Sorry, you are not allowed to share this with external users."
Share a document	No option available to share a document **internally** from the ribbon, but the Share option is available in the document item dialog (see Figure 12-13). **See important note on the previous page.**	Yes, members can initiate an **internal** sharing request that goes to the site owner for approval. When a member tries to initiate a sharing request for an **external** user, an error message is displayed that says, "Sorry, you are not allowed to share this with external users."

- **New default access groups.** There are two special new Domain Groups in SharePoint 2013. The **Everyone** group is the new name for "All authenticated users." It is available in SharePoint on-premises as well as SharePoint Online. It maps to "all authenticated users in the tenancy, including external users" in SharePoint Online. The **Everyone except external users** group is available only in SharePoint Online. This group includes all of your authenticated users plus anyone invited with a "guest" user account. In SkyDrive Pro, the default access for the Shared with Everyone folder in SharePoint 2013 on-premises is Everyone. In SharePoint Online, the default access for the Shared with Everyone folder is Everyone except external users.

- **Ability to share externally with or without authentication required.** In SharePoint Online, you have the option of sharing content with external users. When you share a document with external users, you can require that they authenticate with a free Microsoft account or without any authentication. (The ability to do this is controlled globally and at the site collection level by the administrator.) When you share an individual document, you can also specify whether access is read-only or whether the external user can edit the document. If you do not require authentication and you allow a guest user to edit a document, the Modified By user shows up as Guest Contributor. If you require authentication, which means your external user will have to sign in with an existing Microsoft account, you will see the username associated with the Microsoft account in the Modified By field. As a best practice, it is always a good idea to require authentication if you are allowing an external user to edit a document.

- **Easily exchange information with users requesting access to sites.** As in previous versions, site owners can use the "Site permissions" setting in Site Settings to enable access requests for a specific SharePoint site. The setting allows you to enter the e-mail address of the user who will receive access requests. When unauthorized users try to access a site for which access requests have been enabled, they get a dialog box where they can respond to the new "Let us know why you need access to this site" prompt. The completed access request is then visible to the site owner in a new area of Site Settings called "Access requests and invitations." By opening the individual access request menu, the site owner can decide whether to approve or decline access to the site. If access is declined, the requester sees a "Sorry, your request has been declined" message the next time he or she tries to access the site along with a dialog box in which to provide supplementary information to ask the site owner to reconsider.

- **New Community Site template with special security features.** The new Community Site template (see Chapter 15, "Planning for Social Computing") provides an engaging concept for encouraging topic-focused discussions but also introduces some unique security concepts that site owners may find confusing. It is especially important to use the out-of-the-box security groups created with new community sites and to set up each new community site with unique permissions. Special security considerations for community sites are discussed later in this chapter.

■ **New authentication options.** SharePoint 2013 offers claims-based authentication using the Open Authorization 2.0 (OAuth) model. OAuth is an industry-standard security protocol that allows SharePoint to give applications access to SharePoint resources such as sites and lists without the app having to obtain, store, or submit the users' credentials. This allows apps and services to act on behalf of users for limited access to SharePoint resources. For example, an application may be allowed to read or write to a calendar or newsfeed on SharePoint. The new SharePoint apps model functions very similarly to what consumers may be used to on Facebook and how Facebook applications, such as Farmville, are authorized to post messages on behalf of users after they have authorized it to do so.

Planning How Users Will Access SharePoint

The first security decisions you will make about your SharePoint implementation relate to user access. You will need to decide if you will allow people to access SharePoint from outside of your corporate network and, if so, from which devices. You will also want to determine if people outside of your organization will need access.

Historically, many organizations started by using SharePoint on-premises and set up the SharePoint servers on their internal network behind a firewall that prevented people from accessing SharePoint externally. In this scenario, people could access SharePoint only when they were in the office using a computer issued by the organization and connected to the organization's internal network.

As people have become more mobile, many organizations have set up external access to their internal SharePoint server environments using a VPN or methods such as Microsoft's Direct Access technologies. These enable individuals to connect remotely to the corporate network from a company-supported computer.

As SharePoint use has expanded to secure extranets, or even public-facing Web sites, organizations have been setting up SharePoint environments outside of their corporate networks to enable people outside of their organizations to access SharePoint without having to open up their networks too widely.

Setting up SharePoint externally to your organization offers the ability for people to access your SharePoint environment from their mobile devices (such as a phone or tablet device) and to use their own personal computer equipment from any location, something that has become more prevalent with the BYOD trend that many organizations have been supporting.

SharePoint Online (as part of Office 365) offers additional capabilities to securely support access to your SharePoint environment from any environment, from any device, and adds some new capabilities that are not available via SharePoint 2013 on-premises, including the new external sharing capabilities that are described in this chapter.

Planning How You Will Share

One of the reasons most organizations implement SharePoint is that they want to be able to improve and facilitate the way they manage and share content. "Versionitis," the insidious disease that results in documents being replicated all over the organization's file shares in different states or versions, has a potential cure with SharePoint. So clearly, we *want* to share with SharePoint—sometimes. From a knowledge management perspective, the organizational goal is generally to allow Read access to internal content by default, unless there is a regulatory or business reason to secure it. As you are planning SharePoint security, you may want to challenge some of the existing security models for your file shares and see if the files are secured because they need to be or because they always have been historically even though no one can remember why. Use the implementation of or upgrade to SharePoint 2013 to revisit security on your file shares and existing SharePoint sites and to make sure that you are protecting content that needs to be protected but allowing content that could benefit the organization, by preventing "versionitis" and promoting reuse, to be discovered. That said, you will still need to think about how to allow sharing of content and make sure that your site owners understand their responsibilities when it comes to content security.

> **You Can't Prevent Internal Sharing by Site Owners—You Can Only Educate Site Owners about the Implications**
> While your administrator can prevent users from sharing content with external users with a setting at the environment or site collection level (in SharePoint Online), you cannot prevent site owners from sharing content internally. You need to make sure your training and governance plans ensure that site owners understand the responsibility with which they have been entrusted. This is not different from previous versions of SharePoint, but because the ability to share content is more "exposed" in SharePoint 2013, the risk of making security mistakes is increased.

Planning How You Will Share Internally

With earlier versions of SharePoint, only site owners (users with Full Control[2] permissions) had the ability to manage security on the site or on any content within a site. In SharePoint 2013 Online, all users have access to the Share option (refer to Figures 12-1 and 12-2) to request that a site or document be shared with an internal user, but only the site owner can approve these requests. In SharePoint 2013 on-premises, the user experience for sharing is different. These differences are summarized in Table 12-1.

Sharing Documents Internally

Users with the ability to share can click the Share option for each of the documents they want to share and enter the name or e-mail address of any internal user with whom they wish to share the item. Figure 12-3 shows an example of the view that users other than the site owner see when they click the Share option for a document from the document "callout" box in a document library. To see the "callout" box, click the ellipsis (...) to the right of the document name (refer to Figure 12-1). As shown in Figure 12-3, the document is already shared with Scott Jamison. To invite additional internal users to see a document, all you need to do is start typing the name or e-mail address and the users that match the typed characters will be displayed so you can select the appropriate name. If you are not the site owner, the invitation to the guest user doesn't actually go to the user. Instead, when someone

---

2. Any user with the Manage Permissions permission level can manage permissions on content. By default, however, Manage Permissions is included only in the Full Control and Manage Hierarchy permission sets.

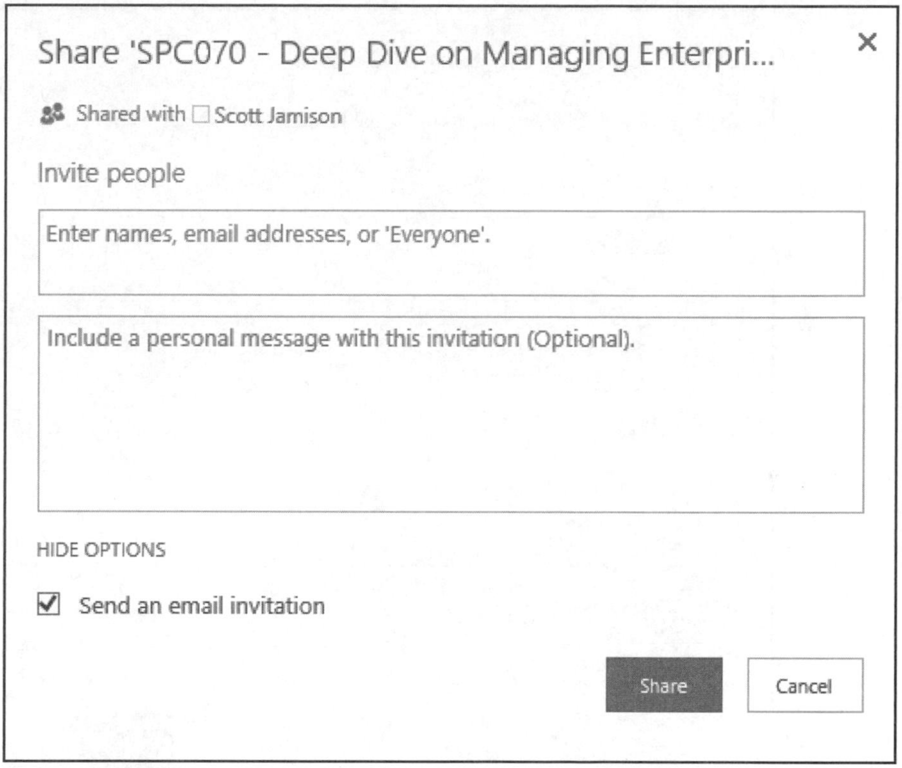

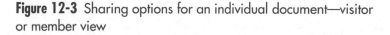

Share 'SPC070 - Deep Dive on Managing Enterpri...   ✕

👥 Shared with ☐ Scott Jamison

Invite people

Enter names, email addresses, or 'Everyone'.

Include a personal message with this invitation (Optional).

HIDE OPTIONS

☑ Send an email invitation

Share   Cancel

Figure 12-3 Sharing options for an individual document—visitor or member view

other than the site owner initiates the Share action, a request is sent to the site owner, who then has the ability to approve, decline, or engage in a dialog with the requester to discuss why the request has been made and then decide the permissions the new user will get (Read, Contribute, etc.).

When a site owner initiates the Share action, the view shows the permission selection option directly, since the site owner does not need to request approval to share content. The site owner view for sharing a document is shown in Figure 12-4.

Sharing Sites Internally

Sharing a site works very much the same way as sharing a document. The best way to share a site is by clicking the Share option in the upper right-hand corner of the site (see Figure 12-2), but site owners can also

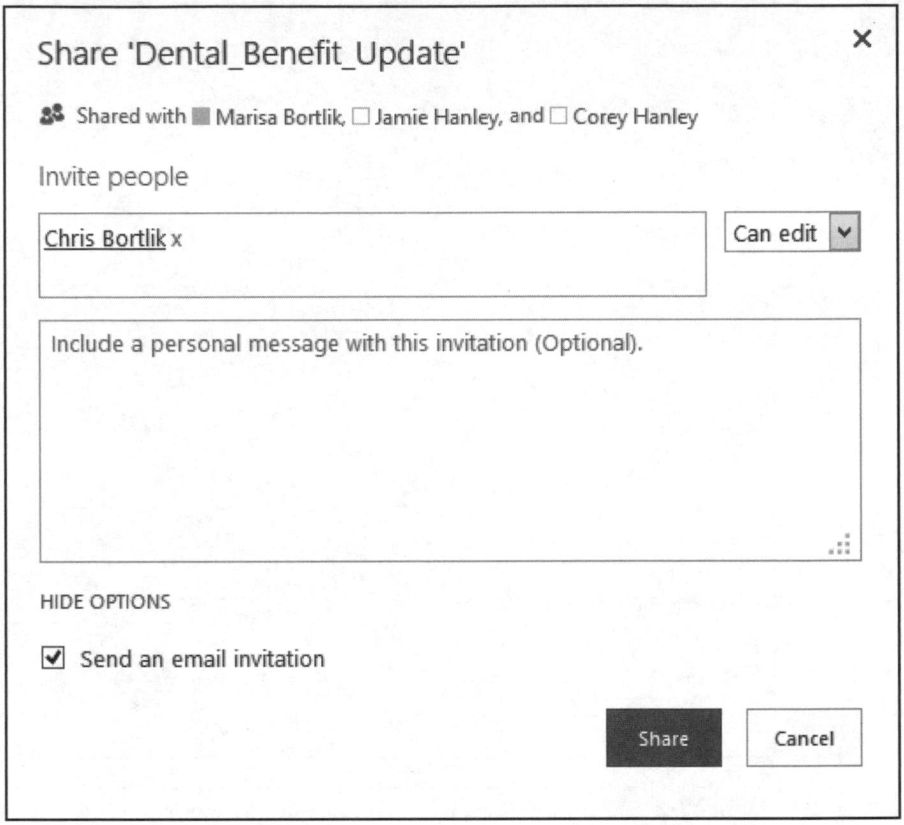

Share 'Dental_Benefit_Update'   ✕

👥 Shared with ■ Marisa Bortlik, ☐ Jamie Hanley, and ☐ Corey Hanley

Invite people

| Chris Bortlik x | Can edit ▾ |

Include a personal message with this invitation (Optional).

HIDE OPTIONS

☑ Send an email invitation

[Share]   [Cancel]

Figure 12-4 Sharing options for an individual document—site owner view

grant permissions from Site Settings → Users and Permissions → Site permissions. When users other than the site owner in SharePoint Online want to share a site (remember, the Share option for sites is not visible to users with Visitor and Member permissions in SharePoint 2013 on-premises), they see the share request screen shown in Figure 12-5. The share request is submitted to the site owner, who can determine the level of access to grant the new user. When site owners share a site, they see a view that allows them to specify the type of permissions the new internal user should have, as shown in Figure 12-6.

You don't have the ability to restrict sharing internally within your SharePoint environment, so planning how you will share internally is largely a training and governance exercise. Think about it this way: Sharing is generally a good thing when you need to share. Being able to easily invite a specific person from outside your team to edit a single document without

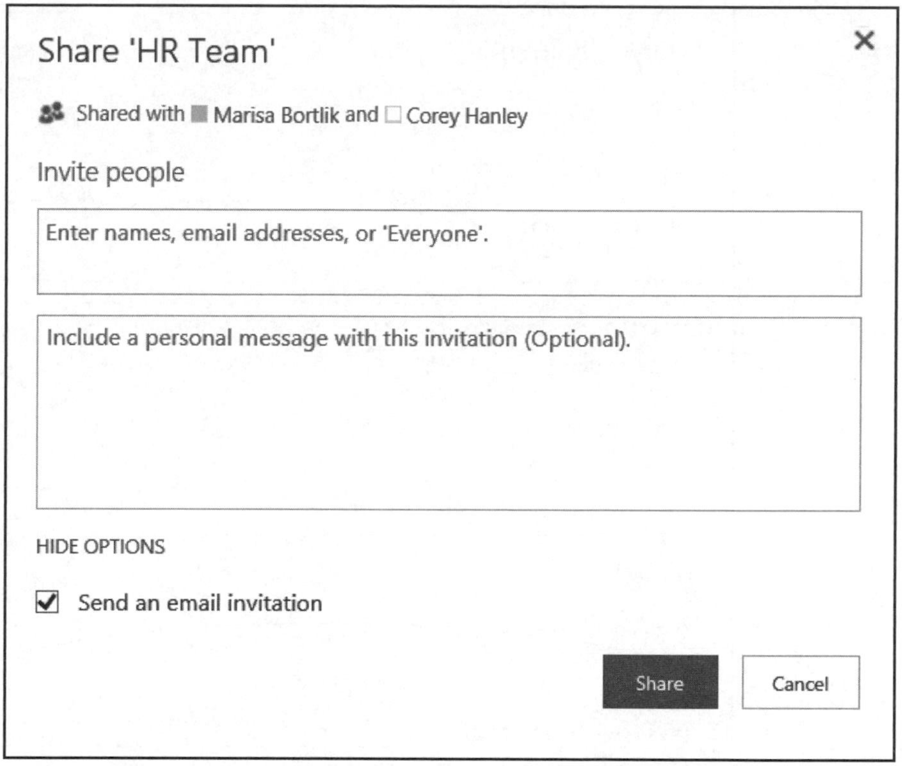

Share 'HR Team'   ✕

👥 Shared with ■ Marisa Bortlik and ☐ Corey Hanley

Invite people

    Enter names, email addresses, or 'Everyone'.

    Include a personal message with this invitation (Optional).

HIDE OPTIONS

☑ Send an email invitation

                              Share   Cancel

Figure 12-5 Share request options for a site—visitor and member view in SharePoint Online

editing your other documents is a really helpful feature. However, you should consider the following:

- Introducing unique permissions on individual documents introduces a security risk and adds complexity to your environment. If you invite someone to collaborate on a document, you may want to remove those permissions when the editing process is complete.
- Think about the implications of allowing anyone to invite others to edit content. You will introduce some risk in situations where a busy site owner might inadvertently approve access requests that shouldn't be approved. Another risk is that someone will share the entire site when they mean to share only one document.

Our best advice is to make sure your site owners understand that "with great power comes great responsibility." Simplified content sharing will definitely enhance many collaboration scenarios—but this new

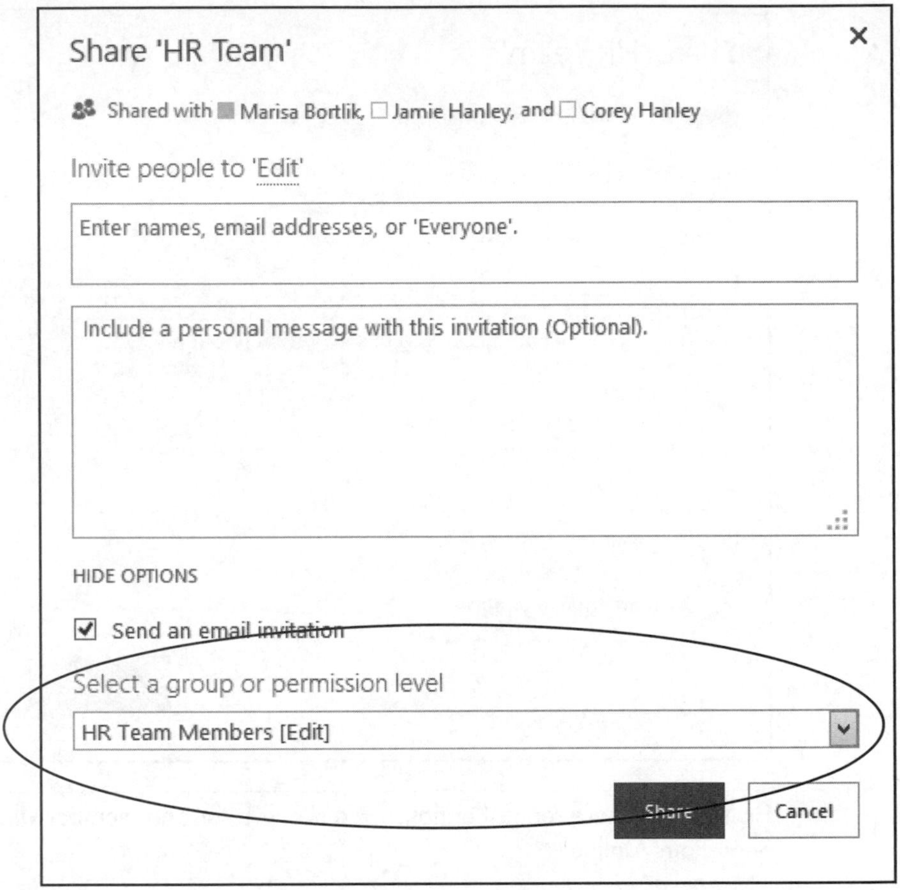

Figure 12-6 Share request options for a site—site owner view

capability is not without risk, and you should take the time to consider the implications when you grant site owner privileges.

Planning How You Will Share Externally

If your teams do work that involves collaborating with external partners, SharePoint Online provides the capability to easily invite external users to access sites or documents. There are three scenarios that you can enable:

■ You can share an entire site by inviting external users to sign in to your site using any e-mail address, and then Office 365 will require the person receiving the invitation to associate with an existing

Microsoft account (for example, a Hotmail or Outlook address) or a Microsoft Office 365 user ID.

- You can share individual documents by inviting external users to sign in to your site using a Microsoft account or a Microsoft Office 365 user ID.
- You can send users a guest link that they can use to view or edit individual documents on your site anonymously.

Setting up your SharePoint Online site to allow external sharing depends on the version of SharePoint Online that your organization uses. Since inviting external users into your site introduces a security risk, you should carefully consider the implications of external sharing and make sure that the site owners and administrators who can authorize these permissions have sufficient training and time to properly administer external users. External sharing is turned on by default no matter which version of SharePoint Online your organization is using. You should consider turning it off globally before anyone starts using sites or until you know exactly how you want to use and support this feature. No matter which version of SharePoint Online you are using, only users with Full Control privileges are allowed to share sites or items with external users initially. Once these users are "in the system," their user IDs are available in the People Picker for any site user to select. However, sharing requests for external users are always routed to the site owner for approval before access is granted.

- If your organization is using Office 365 Small Business Premium, the Office 365 administrator is the only person who can enable or disable the external sharing feature for all sites. When this feature is deactivated, any external user previously invited to sites can no longer access the sites. To enable or disable external sharing, go to Admin → Service Settings → Sites and Document Sharing. You can also use this same location to remove individual external users.
- If your organization is using one of the Office 365 enterprise plans, you can configure external sharing at two levels within the SharePoint administration center. First, you can turn external sharing on or off globally for the entire environment. Additionally, you can turn external sharing on or off for each individual site collection. You can also specify whether or not you want to allow sharing with only authenticated users or with both authenticated and anonymous users through guest links. Remember, if you plan to allow external users to edit documents, you should consider

restricting access to only authenticated users. Note that if your site has been upgraded from SharePoint 2010, you will not be able to manage external sharing through the SharePoint admin center for sites still using the SharePoint 2010 experience. For these sites, you will need to explicitly activate the site collection feature called "External user invitations."

It is important to think about external sharing as part of your overall security planning for SharePoint Online. You may want to create a special permissions group to which external users are assigned when they receive invitations to be sure that you do not "overshare." You may also want to create separate site collections that are used only for collaboration with external users so that you can allow external users to access specific content without opening up the entire environment. Remember that in all cases, your goal is to balance the ease of getting work done with trusted external partners with minimizing the governance "sharp edges" discussed in Chapter 4, "Planning for Business Governance."

Sharing Sites Externally

If you share an entire site with an external user, that person can log in and function as a full member of the site but with some limited privileges.[3] Your external user will be able to see the names of other site users in the People Picker. You will want to think seriously about whether this is a good idea if you have a site that you share with multiple external partners and you don't want each partner to know the names of the other partners. You will also introduce some risk because once your external user has access to the site, some of your existing site users may be able to grant permissions to the external user that are different from the ones you originally assigned.

If you invite external users to your top-level team site, they will be able to view content on the top-level team site and all sub-sites. If you have sensitive content, it's a better idea to create a unique sub-site (with unique permissions) where you will put content for external users and then share only the sub-site externally. (This same concept applies when you are sharing content with internal users if the content is highly sensitive.) Remember that there

---

3. Guest users in SharePoint Online/Office 365 will see no links on the Suite Bar, nor will they see the ability to access an "About me" page for themselves or someone else. They will not be able to follow items or access the public newsfeed. However, if the site has a site feed, external users will be able to participate but will not see other users' photos, and there will be no entry points for following people, topics, or documents.

is no single best practice for sharing site content with external users. It is important to think about the business purpose of your site and the level of trust you have with your external collaborators and choose an approach that minimizes risk while maximizing the ability to get work done.

Sharing Individual Documents Externally

If you are going to share documents externally in your SharePoint Online site,[4] you can either use anonymous guest links or links that require authentication. If you allow anonymous guest links, anyone who gets an invitation can also share that same link with others. You should never use anonymous guest links to share documents that are sensitive, and as a best practice, you should never provide an anonymous link to allow *editing* of a document. Remember, even though any site user can use the Share option to share a document with an external user in SharePoint Online, only site owners (users with Full Control privileges) can authorize the access request.

You must be a site owner or have Full Control permissions to share a document with external users the first time. Once individual external users have been granted access to any internal content, however, their user IDs are available in the People Picker, so that any user can use the Share option to initiate an access request even though the request will be routed to the site owner for approval. In addition, the external sharing feature must be turned on in either the Office 365 Service Settings or the SharePoint Online administration center, depending on which Office 365 plan your organization uses. For enterprise plans, external sharing must also be turned on for your site collection.

Planning How You Will Secure SharePoint Sites

Securing SharePoint sites consists of granting *permissions* to *people* who should belong to *groups* and then assigning those permissions to *securable objects*. Simple, right? We review each of these key security elements,

---

4. Note that unless you have implemented some form of rights management on SharePoint content, your internal users will still be able to download a document and then share it externally via e-mail. You can have a governance policy (see Chapter 4, "Planning for Business Governance") that tells users this is not permitted, but without some form of rights management software, you will not be able to *prevent* this from happening. Sharing individual documents with guest users from within your SharePoint Online site provides more control over external access, but it is not completely without risk as stated earlier. As a general rule, sharing is always best if you are working with trusted partners.

which are shown in Figure 12-7, in the discussion that follows. Securing or providing access to content in SharePoint comes from the combination of these three security elements, as shown in Figure 12-8.

Just as with previous versions of SharePoint, only users with the permission called Manage Permissions can grant security permissions. By default, only the Full Control and Manage Hierarchy permissions sets include the Manage Permissions item, and typically only the site owner will have this ability.

Securable Objects

Securable objects consist of all of the SharePoint elements to which permissions can be applied. These include a site collection, a sub-site or site within a site collection, a list or library, a folder, or an individual item in a list or library. By default, permissions are assigned at the site level, and lower-level objects inherit permissions from their parent site. For example, security permissions for the top-level site are inherited by all sub-sites unless you explicitly "break" the inheritance. Permissions for each object in a site are inherited from the

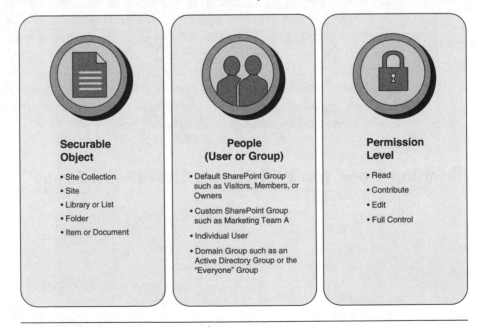

Securable Object

- Site Collection
- Site
- Library or List
- Folder
- Item or Document

People (User or Group)

- Default SharePoint Group such as Visitors, Members, or Owners
- Custom SharePoint Group such as Marketing Team A
- Individual User
- Domain Group such as an Active Directory Group or the "Everyone" Group

Permission Level

- Read
- Contribute
- Edit
- Full Control

Figure 12-7 SharePoint security elements

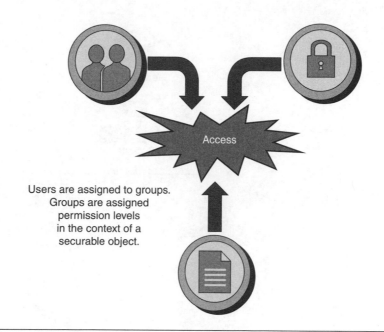

Users are assigned to groups. Groups are assigned permission levels in the context of a securable object.

Figure 12-8 Access in SharePoint happens when people are assigned permission levels for a securable object

parent site, and permissions for documents or list items are inherited from the library or folder, as shown in Figure 12-9.

As a general best practice, you always want to apply security at the highest level possible in your solution because it's easier to manage and maintain security in fewer places. The menu option used in SharePoint to apply unique permissions depends on the type of object.

To restrict, assign, or examine permissions for a site, select the gear icon in the upper-right corner (see Figure 12-10) and then select Site settings → Site permissions in the Users and Permissions group on the Site Settings page. Alternatively, to allow users to have access to a site, you can also click the Share option in the upper-right corner (see Figure 12-11), but be sure to select the appropriate security group for each user. As a reminder, if you do not see all of these options, you most likely do not have permissions that allow you to manage security on your site (or you are not the site owner).

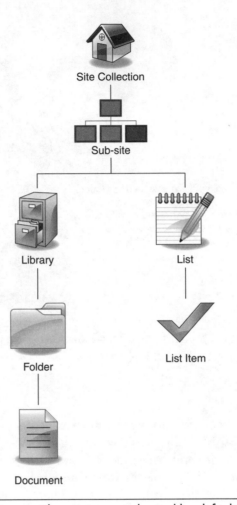

Site Collection

Sub-site

Library

List

Folder

List Item

Document

Figure 12-9 Permissions in SharePoint are inherited by default

- To restrict, assign, or examine permissions for a library, select the Library tab in the ribbon and then select Library Settings and the Shared With button, as shown in Figure 12-12.
- List permissions work exactly the same way. Be very careful if you want to assign permissions to just a list or library and not an entire site. The Share option in the upper-right corner of the page assigns permissions to the entire site, not the list or library. The only way to manage permissions for a list or library is to access the list or library settings from the ribbon.

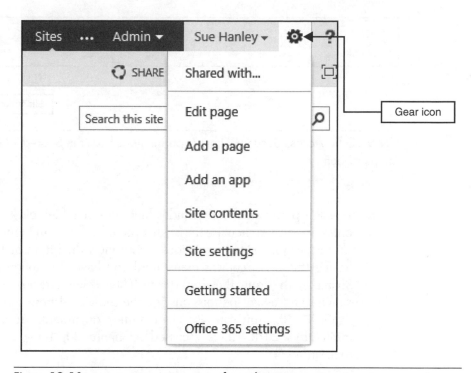

Figure 12-10 Access site permissions from the "Site settings" option on a site

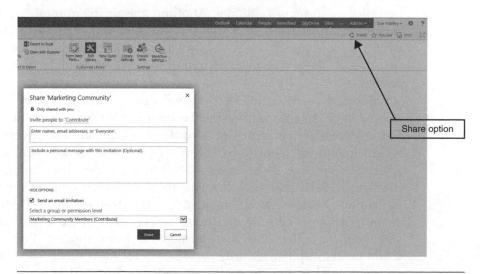

Figure 12-11 Assign site permissions from the Share option for a site

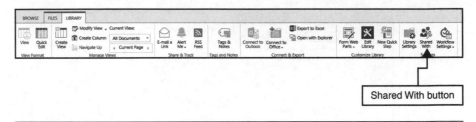

Figure 12-12 Access document library permissions from the Shared With button on the ribbon

- To assign permissions for an individual item or folder, click the ". . ." context menu and then use the Share option (as shown in Figure 12-13). You can also manage permissions for an individual item or folder by clicking the ". . ." context menu until you have the option to select "Shared with" from the drop-down. Then select Advanced to both examine and assign permissions for the individual item as shown in Figure 12-13. (You can also share Office documents from directly within Office 2013. This is discussed in Chapter 20, "Integrating Office Applications.")

It's easiest to understand how security permissions have been applied if permissions are the same for all elements of the site. This is clearly not always possible or practical, but it should be a guiding principle for your security model. Another reason for minimizing security exceptions in SharePoint is that the interface does not easily show you where permissions have been "broken" unless you examine each item or use the Check Permissions option for each individual user in every context.

Because there is no way to scroll down a list or library view and immediately determine if a specific item (or list or site) is secured differently from its peers, it can be difficult to quickly identify or change where item-level security has been applied. Site owners can, however, select Site Settings → Site permissions to see a view like the one shown in Figure 12-15 and click the link to show which content on the site has unique permissions. This capability is extremely helpful, but it still requires a lot of clicking and must be repeated in each context where you want to understand how permissions were applied. Furthermore, if you need to update security permissions for individually secured items, you will need to update each item independently. If you are the Help

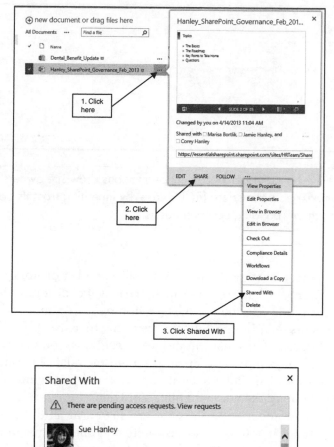

Figure 12-13 Site owners can access permissions in multiple ways, including navigating from the document context menu to access the Advanced options (individual document permissions) screen shown in Figure 12-14

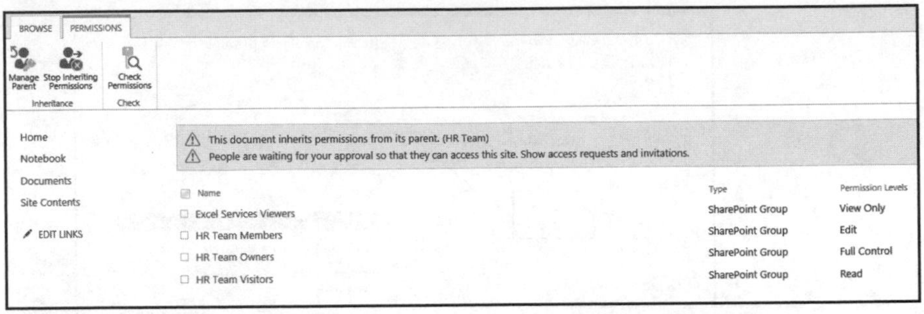

Figure 12-14 Individual document permissions show site owners how a document gets permissions (in this case, by inheriting from its parent) and if there are any pending access requests

Desk person trying to help a user navigate a list or library, you will need to remember that your permissions may be different from the user's permissions inside the same list or library, so you may see more or fewer documents than the person you are trying to assist. If you have a security model that contains many item-level exceptions, you may want to consider documenting the exceptions in the item metadata or using a third-party solution for SharePoint security analysis and management such as those available from Axceler, AvePoint, and Dell.

Because security permissions are shared in all documents in a document library, if you have permission to edit one document in a library, you have permission to edit all documents in that library unless security has been "broken" (managed) for an individual document in the library. By editing, we mean the ability to alter or delete those documents. If you store documents in folders, security in the folder is inherited into each document in the folder. This is one reason that you may want to use folders in a document library—to apply shared editing permissions to separate groups of documents and minimize the use of item-level permissions. This is one example of how security has an impact on your user experience and content topology. Introducing folders or document sets to manage collective security may solve authorization issues but may introduce an inconsistency in how content is managed (for example, other libraries may group documents by metadata). Consider this when balancing security management and usability.

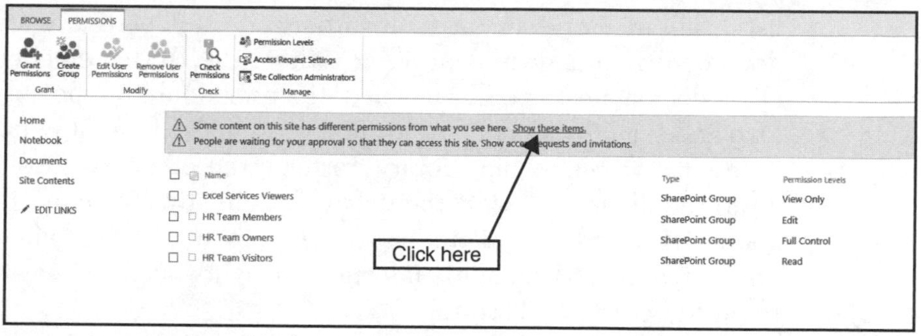

Figure 12-15 If libraries or documents within a site have been assigned permissions directly, SharePoint alerts the user

Security Trimming

Any object that you secure in SharePoint is secure in both "browse" and "search" scenarios. If a document, list, or site has unique permissions, users who do not have access to the object will not see it in lists or search results. This is called *security trimming*. If an unauthorized user attempts to access this content directly via a URL link, that user will be denied access and prompted for alternate credentials. Security trimming also impacts search results. If two different users execute the same exact search, they may see different results based on their permissions. Security does not affect the relevancy of results; it only affects the number of items that are returned.

Security Exceptions

Information Rights Management (IRM), which is part of most SharePoint Online enterprise plans and can be added to and integrated with SharePoint 2013 Server Standard and Enterprise on-premises, offers another way to secure items stored in SharePoint. Microsoft IRM allows users to create a persistent set of access controls that live with the content itself as well as in the location where the item is stored if your administrator has enabled IRM for your environment. IRM services can be used, for example, to protect an individual item from being downloaded or printed. When enabled, IRM security takes precedence in a list or library. For example, if an authorized user opens a rights-managed document from a document library where the IRM protection does not allow documents to be downloaded, the user would not be able to download and send that document to another user, even if that person also has access to the SharePoint library. Instead, the other user would have to go to the library and view the document directly. For more information about IRM and SharePoint 2013, refer to http://office.microsoft.com/en-us/sharepoint-help/apply-information-rights-management-to-a-list-or-library-HA102891460.aspx.

There are several objects in SharePoint that *cannot* be secured. These include views, audiences, Web Parts, and list Columns. Be sure to consider the following implications about which objects can be secured and how security is inherited:

- Because you cannot secure an individual view of a document library, you cannot use unique views to get around the fact that you cannot secure an individual Column in a list. For example, you may want to have a Column in a list that shows financial numbers that you don't want all users to see. You cannot secure the financial *Columns* using Manage Permissions or secure a *view* that doesn't display the financial Columns. In this scenario, you should consider using an alternate means of sharing the sensitive data. For example, one approach might be to use Excel to store the information and secure the Column in Excel. You can then use Excel Services to display the information in a SharePoint Web Part. (See Chapter 18, "Planning for Business Intelligence," for a description of how to leverage Excel Services.) Another approach would be to show the protected data in a separate list and use an event handler to keep the two lists synchronized.

- You cannot secure a Web Part, but you can use an audience to *target* a Web Part so that it shows up only for users who "belong" to that audience. (Note that the content displayed in a Web Part is always secure, but security cannot be applied to the Web Part itself.) Targeting a Web Part using an audience does not secure the content displayed in the Web Part—you must secure the object displayed in the Web Part by managing permissions on the content. This is an important distinction. Audiences are used to personalize presentation and effectively manage screen real estate with relevant content. Use audience targeting to feature or showcase information, not to protect it.

People (User or Group)

In the context of SharePoint, "people" are individual users who need access to a SharePoint site and can be defined individually or as members of a group. A group is a named collection of people (users) in SharePoint.

While individual people can be granted permissions inside of SharePoint, it is generally more desirable to first add a person to a group and then grant permissions to the group. That way, new users can be added in one place, to either a SharePoint or Active Directory Group, and they will automatically get all the permissions associated with that group. This methodology is also helpful in two other ways: (1) it is easier to replicate security permissions for new users, and (2) it reduces the amount of legacy security that accumulates over time (for example, someone has left the company but his or her name is still associated with a collection of sites across the environment).

In SharePoint, there are two types of groups that you will work with:

- A **Domain Group** is created outside SharePoint in Active Directory. A Domain Group (also called an Active Directory or AD Group) is defined for the entire enterprise and can be used in any site collection in SharePoint or to manage access for other applications used by your organization. Domain Groups are generally created by a security administrator in your IT organization, but some organizations allow business teams to request the creation of a new Domain Group that they can manage themselves. Domain Groups are most often created to represent persistent roles or geographic groups of people inside your organization. If you can, take advantage of existing, automatically maintained Domain Groups to assign permissions for your site. For example, if there is already a Domain Group for managers and you have content or sites that are for managers only, you should use this existing group to secure your site. When new managers are added or if someone is no longer a manager, you will not need to worry about (or be responsible for) adding or deleting the person's name from the group. If your organization allows you to create Domain Groups that are not automatically populated, you may have to manage "comings and goings," but you will still need to do so in only one place. It is not always possible or practical to have an Active Directory Group for individual sites in SharePoint. This is especially true if you are creating highly granular, low-membership groups. You should not clutter AD with SharePoint-specific groups. You should also avoid creating AD Groups that cannot be repurposed (that is, used in multiple security applications inside and outside of SharePoint). In these instances, you are better served by leveraging SharePoint security groups.

■ A **SharePoint Group** can be defined by a site collection administrator or a user with Manage Permissions privileges and can be used to secure objects within a *single site collection only*. Groups created in SharePoint for one site collection can be used only within that individual site collection and must be separately created and maintained if needed in another site collection. All SharePoint Groups are created at the site collection level and are available to any subsite or other securable object in the site collection.

SharePoint Groups can include Active Directory Groups and/or individual users. However, SharePoint Groups cannot include other SharePoint Groups. There are two types of SharePoint Groups: Default Groups and Custom Groups. There is a raging debate in the SharePoint community about whether Active Directory or SharePoint Groups are "better" for managing security. As with pretty much all things related to SharePoint, the right answer is "It depends." There are pros and cons of each type of security group as described in the discussion that follows.

Default SharePoint Groups

SharePoint provides several *default* SharePoint Groups for team sites; additional default SharePoint Groups are provided in publishing sites or when publishing features are enabled. Each SharePoint Group is associated with a default permission level. (Refer to the next section of this chapter for a detailed review of permissions and permission levels.). The out-of-the-box security groups in SharePoint are essentially a combination of "role" and "permissions."

In addition, the SharePoint model is inclusive, not exclusive. That is, you cannot define activities that users or groups are *not* allowed to perform. For example, the Visitors group has the Read permission level by default, so people often associate the Visitors group with Read permissions, even though this doesn't have to be the case. For example, when you want Visitors to be able to respond to a survey, they will need Contribute permissions.

As a general rule, you always want to give a person or group the least amount of permissions to effectively achieve the required business functionality . . . and no more (the "principle of least privilege"). This may create additional administrative overhead, but it is a core tenet of ensuring the stability and security of a SharePoint environment.

Default team site SharePoint Groups and associated permission levels are described in Table 12-2. Additional default security groups and associated permission levels are created if you use templates other than the Team Site template or if you activate publishing features for a site; these groups are described in Table 12-3.

Table 12-2 Team Site Default SharePoint Groups and Associated Permission Levels

Group Name	Default Permission Level
[Site Name] Owners	**Assigned *Full Control* permission level for the site.** Generally, there should be a small number of users in this group. Make sure that anyone you assign to the Owners group has had sufficient SharePoint training for all of the features available to owners.
Designers	**Assigned *Design* permission level for the site.** You might use this group to give users permission to design the structure of the site without giving them permission to assign security or create sub-sites. In practice, we don't find this default group used very often.
	For SharePoint Online, applies only to the public Web site and any site based on the Publishing Site template.
[Site Name] Moderators (community sites)	**Assigned the new *Moderate* permission level.** Moderators have similar permissions to the new Edit level in the context of community sites and sites where community features have been enabled. In addition to all of the permissions assigned to the Edit permission set, the Moderate permission level also includes the "Override list behaviors" permission (which allows users to discard or check in a document that is checked out to another user) and permissions that allow moderators to access the special community features for moderators. (Refer to Chapter 15, "Planning for Social Computing," for a more comprehensive discussion of the permissions for moderators in community sites.)
[Site Name] Members (team sites)	**Assigned *Edit* permission level for the site.** The Edit permission level is new for SharePoint 2013 and includes the ability to "Manage Lists." This allows users to create and delete lists, add or remove Columns in a list, and add or remove public views of a list. See the sidebar for additional discussion of the implications of this permission level.

(continues)

Table 12-2 Team Site Default SharePoint Groups and Associated Permission Levels *(continued)*

Group Name	Default Permission Level
[Site Name] Members (community sites)	**Assigned *Contribute* permission level for the site.** Users can add, edit, or delete content on existing lists and libraries.
[Site Name] Visitors	**Assigned *Read* permission level for the site.** Generally, the largest number of users will be in this group.
Viewers	**Assigned *View* permission level for the site.** These users can see content but cannot edit or download it (for intranet sites only in SharePoint Online).

Table 12-3 Publishing Site Default SharePoint Groups and Associated Permission Levels

Group Name	Default Permission Level
Restricted Readers	**Assigned *Restricted Read* permission level for the site.** This group is rarely used and is most often leveraged when users should have very limited visibility into presentation page content only without the ability to view prior versions of content. For SharePoint Online, applies only to the public Web site and any site based on the Publishing Site template.
Style Resource Readers	**Assigned *Limited Access* permissions that allow the member to have Read access to the Master Page Gallery and Restricted Read to the Style Library.** This group is used for design team members who may want to see associated styling elements.
Quick Deploy Users	**Assigned *Contribute* permissions that allow the user to contribute to the Quick Deploy Items library plus Limited Access to the rest of the site.** For SharePoint Online, applies only to the public Web site and any site based on the Publishing Site template.
Approvers	**Assigned *Approve* permission level for the site.** This group is used for content publishing purposes. Members have the authority to see, validate, publish, or reject/propose content changes prior to public consumption. For SharePoint Online, applies only to the public Web site and any site based on the Publishing Site template.

Group Name	Default Permission Level
Public Site Designers	**Assigned *Design* permission level for the public Web site in SharePoint Online sites.** Used to assign permissions for people who need to be able to view, add, update, delete, approve, and customize the public Web site.
Hierarchy Managers	**Assigned *Manage Hierarchy* permission level for the site.** The permissions for this group allow users to manage but not create security groups. For SharePoint Online, applies only to the public Web site and any site based on the Publishing Site template.

Caution: New Edit Permission for SharePoint 2013 Team Sites

In response to requests from some SharePoint users, Microsoft added a new Edit permission level in SharePoint 2013 to the default Members group settings. In addition to standard Contribute rights (add, edit, delete on current lists/libraries), the Edit permission level includes the ability to "Manage Lists." This allows users to create and delete lists, add or remove Columns in a list, and add or remove public views of a list.

This is likely to catch many SharePoint administrators off guard because members in SharePoint 2013 team sites have "more powers" than they did in previous versions.

In our experience, Manage Lists permissions should not be given to users who have not had sufficient training to use the power that comes with this permission. If members can create or delete metadata Columns, lists, and libraries ad hoc, it is difficult to create and maintain meaningful site structure or prevent content fragmentation. (Note that if users with Edit permissions create a list or library, they do not get Full Control permissions for that list or library. They still have only Edit permissions, which do not include the ability to manage permissions or override list behaviors, which is granted with Full Control privileges.)

Unless both your business needs and training plans are aligned to support assigning the ability to manage lists to team site members, you may want to consider adjusting the Team Site templates in your organization to allow members to have only the Contribute permission set by default, as it was in previous versions.

If you want to allow more users than the site owner to manage lists, consider creating a new security group called Editors and assign Edit permissions to this group.

If you enable publishing features for your site but decide that you do not need any of these security groups, you can leave these groups unpopulated or delete the default groups that you are not using. It is usually better to leave only those security groups that you are actually using on your site to create a "cleaner" and less confusing experience for site owners. However, you should be thoughtful about which groups you delete because your site and business needs may evolve over time.

Special SharePoint Groups

In addition, SharePoint includes several special users and groups for administering SharePoint sites:

- **Site collection administrators** have an "all-access pass" to every element of content and all site permissions in all sites in the collection. In addition, they are recorded as the contact for the site collection and can audit site content, enable site collection features, and monitor site and search usage. A SharePoint site can have a primary and secondary site collection administrator, and if you are the site collection administrator, you can add additional admins. You cannot hide content from a site collection administrator, so if you have content that can be visible only to members of the executive committee in your organization, you will need to designate a member of the executive committee as the site collection administrator. You need to designate individual people, not a group, as site collection administrators, with the ideal number being more than one, but no more than a handful of users. It is recommended that site collection administrators (or any administrator) be named users and not service accounts. Using service accounts eliminates auditing capabilities as you can't track changes to specific resources.

■ **Farm administrators** control which users can manage settings for the server farm in on-premises deployments. By default, farm administrators do not have access to site content, though they can take ownership of a site if they want to view content. This group is used only in central administration; you won't see this group in any individual site collection.

■ **Administrators** have the same privileges as farm administrators, but they can also install new products and applications, deploy Web Parts to the entire farm, create new Web applications, and start services (such as a search crawl) on-premises. This group does not have access to site content by default and is not visible in an individual site collection.

There are additional standard special security groups for SharePoint Online:

■ **Company administrators** include any user who is a global administrator for Office 365. By default, the Office 365 Company Administrators group is added to the SharePoint Owners group and the list of site collection administrators and thus has Full Control privileges. Be cautious about changing the group membership for company administrators or removing any of these special high-level groups. As an example, if you remove a company administrator from the SharePoint Owners group, you could remove permissions from the Global Admin group and eliminate the ability of this group to configure access for SharePoint Groups.

■ **SharePoint Online administrators** is a group included with SharePoint Online for Enterprises. Users in this group can configure user profile and InfoPath Forms Services, set up search and Business Connectivity Services, create a term store, or define a records management system. Users with these privileges can also monitor quotas; set up the ability to invite external users to access the SharePoint Online site; create, update, or delete site collections; and assign primary and secondary site collection owners to any site collection.

■ **Tenant_Users** include every user who is added to Office 365. These users are automatically added to the Members group on the

SharePoint team site and are thus given Edit permissions by default. You should consider changing this if you do not want to provide this level of permissions for every single user. You can instead add the Tenant_Users group to the SharePoint Visitors group, which is a safer option. That means that all users will get Read permissions by default, which is probably more in line with the expected behavior in most scenarios.

Custom SharePoint Groups

There may be situations where you have groups of people who need different access permissions to various objects in your site and it may not be possible or practical to create an Active Directory Group for them. While you can add multiple Active Directory Groups to a SharePoint Group, you cannot "nest" SharePoint Groups. If the same group of people need different permissions in different sites (for example, Contribute in one and Read in another) and you can't use an Active Directory Group, you will want to create a custom SharePoint Group.

You may also want to create a custom group because the terms *visitors*, *members*, and *owners* just don't make sense in your organization and you want to use terms that will resonate better with users. As a best practice, when you create a custom SharePoint Group, choose a name for the group to reflect the people in the group and their collective role in the organization, not their security permissions. This is hard to explain without an example, so please continue reading to the section of this chapter where the step-by-step planning process is described to see an example of a situation where you might want to create custom SharePoint Groups.

Special Considerations for Community Sites

As a best practice, you should always set up your community sites with unique permissions—and use the default security groups that the template creates for you. (For more information about the Community Site template, refer to Chapter 15, "Planning for Social Computing.") Microsoft has built in some special permissions for community sites and, unfortunately, changed the meaning of the term *member* in the context of sites built using the Community Site template. Actually, the term *member* in the context of a community site is probably closer to the generally accepted English definition of this term. As discussed earlier, the use of the term *member* in the context of all other types of SharePoint team sites is confusing because it is used to refer to a permission group, not the group of people who are actually members of the team. In the context of a community site, there are actually two completely different types of "members":

- **Members of the SharePoint security group called [Site Name] Members.** Just like other team sites in SharePoint, when you create a new community site with unique permissions, SharePoint 2013 automatically creates the default security groups [Site Name] Owners, [Site Name] Members, [Site Name] Visitors, and the new [Site Name] Moderators. These default groups have Full Control, Contribute, Read, and Moderator permissions, respectively. This is actually different from "regular" team sites, where [Site Name] Members have Edit permissions by default. You definitely do not want most community site users to have Edit permissions, so the default permissions are very helpful in this context.

- **Members of the community site (who will be listed in the members view in the default template).** In the community site, a member also means someone who has explicitly joined the community using the join option on the community site. Until users explicitly join a community, they are not listed in the members view on the site. Even if users are in the Members security group, until they have either explicitly joined the community *or* made a contribution to the discussion group, they are not listed in the members view. It is fortunate that the only people who really have to understand these distinctions are the people who create community sites and your Help Desk, who will get the calls when something goes wrong. The best advice to solution planners is to be aware of this distinction and document it very carefully for your Help Desk.

Permission Levels

Individual permissions (such as view items, open items, edit items, and delete items) are grouped together into permission "levels," such as

Contribute, which allow users to perform specific actions. Permission levels are created and managed at the root site level only but inherit down for use at any sub-site. You can also create custom permission levels, but when you do this, you may make managing a site more difficult and you will also make it more difficult to audit your site's security. That doesn't mean that you shouldn't create custom permission levels, but it does mean that you should carefully document all the permission levels that you create for your site. In some organizations, we have seen users set up a custom permission level that offers content contribution but not deletion rights. This allows users to create and edit content but not delete it. (Note that the Recycle Bin minimizes the need for this type of customization, but there are scenarios where site owners really want this level of control.) Since you create permission levels at the root of the site collection, you can configure this custom permission level once and it will be available for all sites in the collection.

Individual permissions are assigned to one or more permission levels, which are in turn assigned to individual users or SharePoint Groups. Remember that the preferred approach is that permission levels should always be assigned to SharePoint Groups, not individuals.

The out-of-the-box or default permission levels for team sites include the following:

- **Full Control** provides administrator access to the site. This permission level contains all permissions and cannot be customized or deleted. As a general rule, you will allow users to have Full Control privileges only when they have demonstrated an understanding of how SharePoint works, SharePoint best practices, and, most important, your organization's governance model. This user can give anyone else permissions, including Full Control.
- **Design** allows the user to create lists and document libraries, edit pages, and apply themes, borders, and style sheets in the site.
- **Edit**, a new permission level for SharePoint 2013, allows the user to create and delete lists, add or delete Columns in lists, and add or delete public views of lists in addition to all of the privileges afforded users with Contribute permissions.
- **Contribute** allows the user to add, edit, and delete items in existing lists and document libraries.
- **Read** allows read-only access to the site. Users and groups with this permission level can view items and pages, open items, and download documents.

- **Limited Access** is a special permission level that is automatically assigned to users who have access to some areas of the site but not all areas. For example, users with Contribute access to a document library on a sub-site will appear in the permissions list of the home page as having Limited Access permissions. This does not allow them to view anything on the home page unless they belong to a group that has home page access. Limited Access is automatically assigned by SharePoint when a user or group is provided unique access to a specific securable object. This permission level cannot be customized or deleted.

The out-of-the-box or default permission levels for publishing sites include the following:

- **Manage Hierarchy** allows users to create sites and edit pages, list items, and documents. This permission level does not include permission to approve items, apply themes and borders or style sheets, or create groups. However, this permission level is otherwise very similar to Full Control.
- **Approve** allows users to edit and approve pages, list items, and documents.
- **View** allows users to view pages, list items, and documents. Document types with server-side file handlers can be viewed in the browser but not downloaded.
- **Restricted Read** is designed to give users access to a specific list, document library, item, or document without giving them access to the entire site. Previous document versions and user rights information are not available to people and groups with this permission level.

It is possible to create custom permission levels based on business needs. As a best practice, you should not change the out-of-the-box permission levels. Always create a copy of an existing permission level to create a new one. This can be done by going to Site Settings → Site permissions → Permission Levels and then clicking to the permission level that is closest to the new one you want to create. Scroll to the bottom of the page and click the Copy Permission Level option. Custom permission levels, like securable objects that require unique security, add complexity to the maintenance of your security model. Some individual permissions have dependencies, but in general, SharePoint will not allow you to delete an individual permission from a permission level if other individual permissions depend on it. With 33 individual permissions, you can see that creating custom permission levels can get very complicated. If you do create custom permission levels, be sure to carefully document and describe what you have done and why you have created the custom levels. Examples of possible custom permission levels that we have seen in practice include the following:

- **Restricted Contributor:** for users who can upload and edit documents but cannot delete documents. This custom permission level can help ensure that users cannot accidentally delete documents but still have the capability to upload and edit them. To create a custom Restricted Contributor permission level, create a copy of the Contribute permission level and then remove (uncheck) the Delete Items and Delete Versions permissions. Users without delete permissions will not be able to edit the document name (file name) after uploading the document. If the name needs to be changed, a user with Edit, Contribute, Design, or Full Control permissions will have to make any necessary changes to the document name. Users with custom Restricted Contributor permissions (add, change, but not delete) can edit other metadata properties.

- **Manage Permissions:** for users who need to manage permissions for the site or library but not necessarily have Full Control access. By default, a user must have Full Control permissions to manage security for a site. However, you may want to delegate the responsibility for managing security to a user who should not have Full Control access to the site. In this case, create a custom permission level that starts with the Contribute (or Edit) set but *adds* the Manage Permissions user permission. This custom permission level will allow users to upload, edit, and delete documents and manage user access without having Full Control privileges. You'll want to be careful about creating this type of access because in addition to allowing a group with this custom permission set to add and remove users from groups, it also allows them to create new groups and change permissions on existing objects. As with Full Control, only highly trusted and trained users should have the ability to manage permissions on your site.

Use the following best practices for creating and managing permission levels:

- If a custom permission level is needed for a SharePoint site collection, *always start with an existing permission level* and then either add to or delete from that set of permissions to create the custom permission level.

- Try to create short, meaningful names for each custom permission level, and be sure to add a description that summarizes what type of access is associated with the permission level. In some cases, it is helpful to prepend your organization's name to customizations to have them stand out as unique and personalized.

- As a general rule, *do not change the "default" permission levels.* Remember the saying "You touch it, you own it." SharePoint does not offer any indicator that shows alterations to native security levels. If a similar permission level is needed and you are tempted to modify one of the default permission levels, follow this process instead:

  - Start with a copy of that permission level and make a custom permission level.
  - After copying the default permission level, make additions or deletions to individual permissions.

Defining and Documenting Your SharePoint Security Plan

A well-thought-out security model is crucial for the successful assignment of security in any SharePoint site collection. This section describes a process you can use to work through the steps required to properly secure your site (or site collection). We recommend that you complete and document your security model before actually creating groups or assigning permission levels in a site collection.

Note As a best practice, you should save your security plan and any other administrative documents for your site in a secure document library visible only to the Site Owners group or individuals with Full Control or Design privileges.

The following steps describe the progressive design and documentation of a security schema for a corporate site with sub-sites for marketing, finance, and human resources:

Step 1. List and describe where unique security is required. Table 12-4 shows an example of the first level of a security model for

Table 12-4 Sample Security Table

Securable Object	Description	Unique or Inherited Permissions
Home	Top-level site in the hierarchy. Everyone in the company can see the home page, but only the people in the marketing department can edit most content on the page.	Unique
Home/Discussion Board	Discussion board on the home page to which anyone can contribute.	Unique
Home/Sub-site for Team A	Sub-site for just the finance team.	Unique
Home/Sub-site for Team B	Sub-site for the marketing team where only a few people will edit.	Unique
Home/Sub-site B/ Document Library 2	Private library where the marketing department will work on documents before everyone else in the company can see them.	Unique
Home/Sub-site for Team C	Sub-site for human resources where all users can read but only members of HR can edit.	Unique

an intranet site collection—where you describe each securable object and document whether it needs unique or inherited permissions.

Step 2. List and describe who needs access. Table 12-5 identifies who needs what type of access to each securable object in the site collection.

Step 3. List and describe the permission levels. Table 12-6 describes the permission levels needed for the site collection.

Step 4. Define and create the SharePoint security groups you need.

Step 5. Apply security permissions.

These steps are described in detail in the following sections.

Table 12-5 Sample Security Table with Access Defined

Securable Object (Level in the Site Hierarchy)	Description	Unique or Inherited Permissions?	People or Roles That Need Access	What Do These Users Need to Do?
Home	Top-level site in the hierarchy. Everyone in the company can see the home page, but only the people in the marketing department can edit most content on the page.	Unique	Entire company Members of the marketing team Fred and Sally	Read Contribute content Design or manage the entire site collection
Home/ Discussion Board	Discussion board on the home page to which anyone can contribute.	Unique	Entire company	Contribute content
Home/ Sub-site for Team A	Sub-site for just the finance team.	Unique	Members of the finance team John (site owner for this site)	Contribute content Design or manage this site
Home/ Sub-site for Team B	Sub-site for the marketing team where only a few people will edit.	Unique	Members of the marketing team Bob, Jane, Seth Sarah (site owner for this site)	Read Contribute content Design or manage this site

(continues)

Table 12-5 Sample Security Table with Access Defined *(continued)*

Securable Object (Level in the Site Hierarchy)	Description	Unique or Inherited Permissions?	People or Roles That Need Access	What Do These Users Need to Do?
Home/ Sub-site B/ Document Library 2	Private library where the marketing department will work on documents before everyone else in the company can see them.	Unique	Members of the marketing team	Contribute content
Home/Sub-site C	Sub-site for human resources where all users can read but only members of HR can edit.	Unique	Entire company Members of the HR team	Read Contribute content

Step 1: List and Describe Where Unique Security Is Required

To simplify the ongoing management of security of each site collection, it is important to partner with your business sponsor(s) to determine which parts of a site collection have common security requirements and which parts have unique requirements. As discussed in Chapter 4, "Planning for Business Governance," you need to carefully consider the implications of "oversecuring" content. If every site is locked down for Read access, it will be hard to achieve your knowledge management objectives. Remember that SharePoint security is inclusive—you need to fully understand the requirements associated with protecting highly secured content and know what should never happen (for example, security breaches).

Table 12-6 Permission Levels for This Site

What Are the Permission Levels for This Site?	Describe Each Permission Level
Full Control	Administrator rights—all permissions.
Design	Create lists and document libraries, edit pages, and apply themes, borders, and style sheets in the site.
Contribute	Add, edit, and delete items in existing lists and document libraries.
Read	Read-only access to the site—view items and pages, open items, and documents.
Manage Permissions	**Custom:** Create and change permission levels on the site and assign permission to users and groups.
Restricted Contributor	**Custom:** View, add, and edit items or documents in lists, document libraries, and discussion comments; cannot delete items.

As you think about creating the permission structure for each site collection, you need to carefully balance the ease of maintaining and administering the security model with the need to control specific permissions for individual securable objects. As a general rule, try to manage security *at the site level*. If there are particular items that contain sensitive information that must be even more secure than the site as a whole, you can apply security to individual securable objects. But remember, applying detailed security permissions at the object level can be a very time-consuming task. SharePoint includes the capability to identify how permissions have been assigned in your site collection, but "unpacking" permissions is a group-by-group, site-by-site, object-by-object process, so the more complex your model, the more complex it will be to examine and maintain security. When you examine permissions at the site level, SharePoint 2013 identifies if unique permissions have been applied somewhere in the site and provides a link to show you which lists and libraries have unique permissions (see Figure 12-15). However, you will not be able to tell just by looking at a document library or site whether unique security has been applied—you will have to examine the settings for the object or group to see how it has been secured. This is why it is easier to maintain security at the site level: you have only one place to look when you need to understand how security has been applied.

Consider each part of a site when determining the security assignments for the top-level site, the sub-sites, and document libraries and lists. Document the overall site security model and note the parts that require unique security levels. One way to initially document the security that will need to be applied is to start with the site architecture diagram and add a visual indicator to define where unique security is needed. As discussed in Chapter 6, "Planning Your Information Architecture," there are several tools you can use to create a site architecture diagram, including MindManager, Visio, PowerPoint, or Word (if the diagram is not very complex). Figure 12-16 shows a simple site architecture diagram that includes an indicator (the word *unique*) to show where unique security permissions will be applied (no indicator assumes inherited permissions).

Notice that "Discussion Board" on the home page is displayed in **bold**. This is a visual cue indicating that the discussion board will have different security from the rest of the home page—all employees have Read access to most of the content on the home page, but they can contribute to the discussion board. The same would be required for surveys. You could also create a "node" in your diagram for each object in the site and use dotted lines or different colors to indicate where unique security is required. Planning security is an iterative process, and you may find that you need a more text-

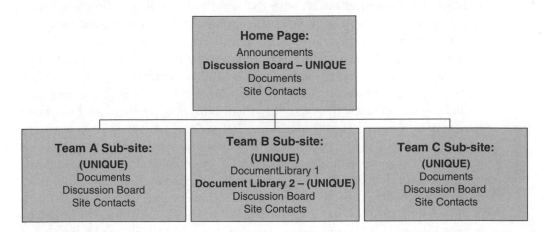

Figure 12-16 Site architecture diagram with security indicator

based approach to evolve your model. As an alternative to a site architecture diagram, you can create a table like Table 12-4 to facilitate conversation with the business sponsor(s) about the permissions types that are needed for the site. As we go through steps 2 and 3, we'll expand the columns in the table. At the end of the steps, we will have documented our security model for this site collection. A similar approach can be used to prepare the security model for an extranet (that is, an externally accessible site for content presentation or collaboration with partners or customers), but more care would be required to define shared and exclusive partner/client areas.

Note that this example assumes a home page where a small number of individuals can contribute content but a large number can read content. The home page is a site where the primary purpose is communications. On the home page, there is a discussion board to which all users can contribute even though they have only Read permissions for the rest of the content on the home page.

When planning security, keep in mind the following:

- The security of each object is inherited from its parent unless inheritance is explicitly broken. For example, by default, every object (for example, list or library) on a site has the same security as the site itself. If users have Contribute access to the site, they have Contribute access to every object on the site. Similarly, if users have Contribute access to a document library, they have Contribute access to every document in the library unless unique permissions have been applied to a document.
- Permissions from the parent can be reapplied if previously broken. However, any special permission levels that were previously created at the object level will be removed when permissions from the parent are reapplied.

Given these characteristics, think about the following regarding security as the site is designed:

- Try to design the site to allow assignment of permissions at the site level.
- If security at the object level is required, consider security for an entire object (an entire list or library, for example) before securing individual items. This may mean creating a second document library (or a folder within a library) if you need unique permissions for a particular group of documents.

- Always consider navigation. If you assign unique security to a nested sub-site, you must ensure that the user has a navigation path to it. That is, if users have access to a sub-site but do not have any access to the parent site, they will have no way to get to the sub-site. This is why it is good practice to examine your security model from the top down (that is, home page to lowest-level sub-site), then in reverse (lowest-level site back to home page).

Step 2: List and Describe Who Needs Access

The next step is to carefully consider who needs access to a site collection or part of a site collection. The easiest way to document this is to add columns to the table created in step 1 to identify who needs what type of access to each securable object in the site collection. This is shown in Table 12-5.

This step may require several iterations as the plan is reviewed with key stakeholders for the site and as the site design evolves. It should account for expected functional growth and anticipated security changes.

Step 3: List and Describe the Permission Levels

Next, evaluate the out-of-the-box permission levels to ensure that they meet your needs. As described earlier, permission levels are the collection of individual permissions that describe what users can and cannot do with the securable objects on a site. You can use a table structure like that shown in Table 12-6 to describe the permission levels needed for your site. For example, if we were to need custom permission levels, we would list those in addition to the out-of-the-box permission levels we plan to use.

Step 4: Define and Create the SharePoint Security Groups You Need

Out-of-the-box groups like Members or Visitors may not provide sufficient granularity for your permissions requirements. You can address this by creating custom SharePoint Groups for the following scenarios (among others):

- A group of users in a site collection needs different permission levels in different areas of the site (e.g., Read in one area, Contributor in another).

- You need to clearly identify a group of users by role (e.g., Senior Leadership Committee).
- It is not possible or practical to create an Active Directory Group for these users.

When you create a custom SharePoint Group, it is best to choose a business-oriented name for the group—such as Marketing Team—rather than a permission-oriented name like Reader or Contributor. Create your custom SharePoint Groups at the top level of the site with no permissions. Then, grant the group appropriate permission levels for the specific securable objects where unique access is needed within the site collection.

For simple sites and most team sites, you can begin by using the default SharePoint Groups (which are [Site Name] Owners, [Site Name] Members, and [Site Name] Visitors) and assign permissions at the site level. In our example, by examining the security requirements, we decide that we want to create a custom SharePoint Group called Marketing Team because we want a clearly named group of *people* that we can maintain as a group but assign different *permission levels* to this group depending on the securable object within the site. As a best practice, after creating the [Site Name] Owners group, use that group as the owner of related groups. This will allow any member in the Owners group to manage the subgroups. In addition, using consistent group name prefixes will help you easily identify related groups as they will display together in the SharePoint Group directory. Using generic group names (e.g., Administrative Assistants) is helpful if the group includes all administrative assistants in the business but not if it includes only the marketing or HR administrative assistants.

Whether or not you use custom or default security groups, you will generally follow a model similar to the inverted triangle shown in Figure 12-17. In general, you should assign users only the permissions they need to do their jobs.

Most of your users will belong to a group with Read permissions. Fewer users will belong to groups with Edit or Contribute permissions. Do not add every user as a member of the [Site Name] Owners SharePoint Group. Instead, limit Full Control rights to a small set of well-trained users who will be responsible for all aspects of site maintenance. Because users with Full Control permissions can change permissions for themselves and others or even delete the site, it is easy to lose control of the site if too many people have this level of access.

Do not confuse business ownership of a site with the default security group called [Site Name] Owners. In most cases, the business executive

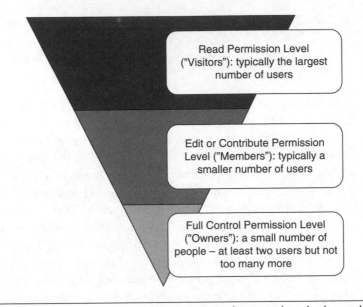

Read Permission Level ("Visitors"): typically the largest number of users

Edit or Contribute Permission Level ("Members"): typically a smaller number of users

Full Control Permission Level ("Owners"): a small number of people – at least two users but not too many more

Figure 12-17 Assign users only the permissions they need to do their jobs

who is the "owner" or sponsor of the site does not have (or need) Full Control privileges for the site.

Step 5: Apply Security Permissions

Security is assigned *from the perspective of the securable object*. Therefore, in the last step of the process, permissions and objects that need security are combined with any existing Domain Groups and default or custom SharePoint Groups.

In this step, extend the security table to include the securable objects requiring unique security (from step 1), the security group name (Owners, Members, Visitors from step 4), the permission level (from step 3), and the people who need access (from step 2) in a table similar to the complete security table example shown in Table 12-7.

In this example, two custom SharePoint Groups are created for marketing and HR because these groups of people have different levels of access in different areas of the site collection. For all other securable objects, the default groups created by SharePoint are used. In addition, we explicitly removed permissions for any security group that was initially inherited from the parent (top-level) site but should not have permissions for the uniquely secured object.

Maintaining Your Security Model

It may seem overly ambitious to expect you to keep your initial security plan document up-to-date, but if there is any documentation worth maintaining as you evolve your site design, this is the one to try to maintain. In fact, it may not be a single document but a collection of documents (if you choose to decentralize security management). If you always follow the best practice of assigning users to groups rather than assigning permissions to individuals, maintaining the document won't be too difficult because you will need to make an update only if you add a new group or add unique permissions to a securable object. Is it realistic to assume that you can keep the security model document current in a dynamic environment? Probably not. So you will definitely want to take advantage of the ways SharePoint allows you to "unpack" your security model directly in your site. Here's what you can do pretty easily:

- Check the permissions on a site.
- Check the permissions that have been assigned to an individual or group across the entire site collection.
- On an individual object, display the permission levels and how those permissions were applied. Figures 12-12, 12-13, 12-14, and 12-15 show the various ways to review access permissions and requests for access for an individual document, list item, or site.

Here's what you can't do easily with the native interface: audit who has made security changes to various securable objects. To easily audit how security permissions have been assigned and changed over time, you will want to consider deploying a third-party tool.

Managing and checking security permissions can be very time-consuming, with or without a third-party tool. As a best practice, it is a good idea to create a test user account and use it for security validation. If you are someone with security application privileges, you automatically have access to the associated content when you change permissions. To verify that the security changes you make work as expected, add the test user as a member of the appropriate security group. Log in as that test

Table 12-7 Sample Complete Security Model

Securable Object	Description	Unique or Inherited Permissions	Security Group	Permission Level	Who Is in This Group?
Home	Top-level site in the hierarchy.	Unique	Home Visitors	Read	Everyone or Everyone except external users.
	Everyone in the company can see the home page, but only the people in the marketing department can edit most content on the page.		Home Members	Contribute	No one—so this default group can be deleted.
			Marketing Team	Contribute	People who work in marketing. Users are added and maintained by the site owner in SharePoint.
			Home Owners	Full Control	Fred (IT resource). Sally (SharePoint super user).
Home/ Discussion Board	Discussion board on the home page to which anyone can contribute.	Unique	Discussion Board Visitors	Read	Not explicitly used—Read access inherited from parent.
			Discussion Board Members	Contribute	AD Group for the entire company.
			Discussion Board Owners	Full Control	Not explicitly used—inherited from parent.

Home/Sub-site for Team A		SharePoint Group	Permission	Description
Sub-site for just the finance team.	Unique	Team A Site Visitors	Read	No visitors for this site—need to remove permissions for the parent Visitors group when this site is created.
		Team A Site Members	Contribute	Individual members of the finance team added to this default SharePoint Group for this sub-site. There is no need to create a custom SharePoint Group for the finance team because they have unique privileges only on this one site.
		Team A Site Owners	Full Control	John (team leader or project manager).
		Home Site Owners	Full Control	Inherited from the parent level; includes Fred and Sally. It's usually a good idea to share this group across all sub-sites and ask the sub-site owner not to remove permissions for this group on an individual sub-site.

(continues)

Table 12-7 Sample Complete Security Model *(continued)*

Securable Object	Description	Unique or Inherited Permissions	Security Group	Permission Level	Who Is in This Group?
Home/Sub-site for Team B	Sub-site for the marketing team where only a few people will edit most of the content.	Unique	Marketing Team	Read	People who work in marketing. Set up and managed at the top of the site collection. Note that the parent SharePoint Groups will be removed from access for this sub-site because it is an exclusive, private site for the marketing team.
			Team B Site Members	Contribute	Bob, Jane, Seth (implementers, content creators).
			Team B Site Owners	Full Control	Sarah (site owner for this site).
			Home Site Owners	Full Control	Inherited from the parent level; includes Fred and Sally.

Location	Description	Inheritance	Group	Permission	Members/Notes
Home/Sub-site B/Document Library 2	Private library where the entire marketing department will work on creating documents before everyone else in the company can see them.	Unique	Marketing Team	Contribute	People who work in marketing.
			Team B Site Owners	Full Control	Sarah (site owner for this site)—inherited from sub-site.
			Home Site Owners	Full Control	Inherited from the parent level; includes Fred and Sally.
Home/Sub-site C	Sub-site for human resources where all users can read but only members of HR can edit.	Unique	Entire Company	Read	AD Group for the entire company.
			HR Team	Contribute	Members of the HR team.
			Home Site Owners	Full Control	Inherited from the parent level; includes Fred and Sally.

user and validate that the content is accessible. Then, remove the user from the group and test again to ensure that the content is no longer accessible.

The concept that the "highest" set of privileges will always apply is an important one to remember. This means if a user is a member of two groups, Group A and Group B, where Group A has Read permission for a site and Group B has Edit permission, the user will have Edit access.

Checking Permissions for a Site

To check how permissions have been assigned on an individual site, you must have Full Control privileges. To check permissions for a site, navigate to the root of the site and click the gear icon at the upper right and select "Shared with ..." as shown in Figure 12-18. This will show you a list of names of people and groups with which the site has been shared. From this Shared With box, which is shown in Figure 12-13, you can click the Advanced option to see the details displayed in Figure 12-14. This will tell you if there are uniquely secured items in the site. If not, you know what you see at the site permissions is inherited to all objects in the site. If there are uniquely secured items, you will be able to see which items have unique permissions. To find out what these unique permissions

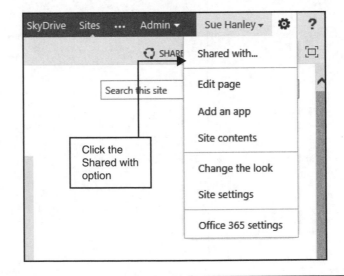

Figure 12-18 Use Shared With to display how permissions have been assigned in an individual site

are, you will need to navigate to the item and check the permissions as described below.

Checking Permissions Assigned to an Individual or Group

To examine how permissions have been assigned to an individual or group across a site collection, you must have Full Control privileges. The easiest way to do this is to go to the root of the site collection and select Site Settings → Site permissions and click the Check Permissions button in the ribbon (refer to Figure 12-15). This will display the Check Permissions dialog box shown in Figure 12-19. Start typing the name of the individual or group, and you will see a drop-down list of names matching what you have typed. Click the Check Now button to see a view of the permissions for that user or group in the site collection. You will see a list that enumerates the permissions for the individual or group. The list shows the URL of each securable object and the permission level that has been assigned to each group.

Alternatively, to check permissions for a group you can also go to the root of the site collection and select Site Settings → Users and Permissions, and then People and Groups. Highlight the group in the Quick Launch and select Settings → View Group Permissions as shown in Figure 12-20.

Displaying Permission Levels for an Object

To examine permission levels for an individual object, you need to navigate to the object. From the individual object where you want to display permissions, navigate to the settings for that object.

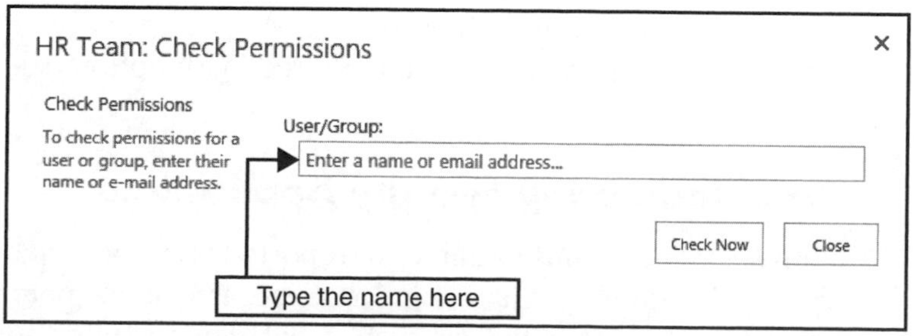

Figure 12-19 Use Check Permissions to display how permissions have been assigned to an individual or group in a site collection

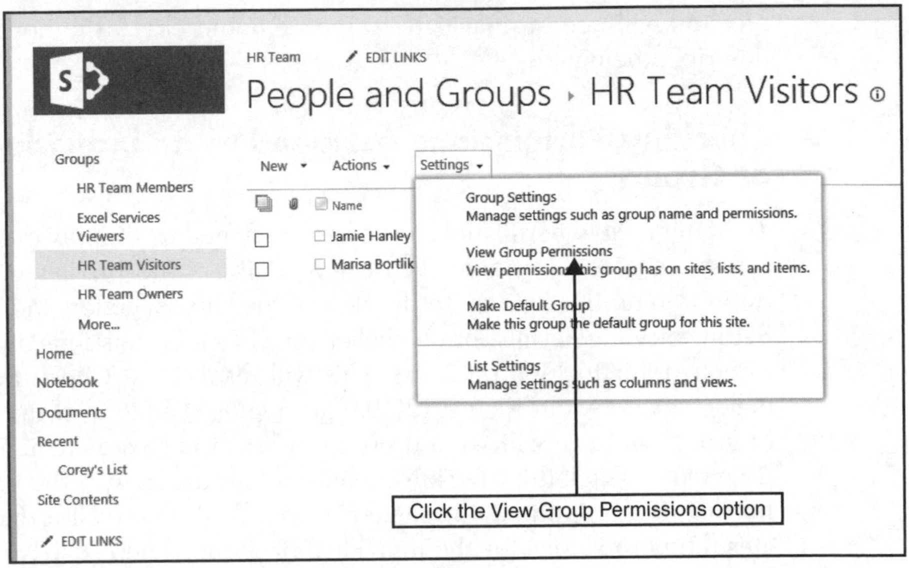

Figure 12-20 Use View Group Permissions to display how permissions have been assigned to a group in a site collection

For a site, this is found under Site Settings → Users and Permissions. Click "Site permissions" to access the Check Permissions option in the ribbon. Note that People and Groups will show individuals and site groups that are available to the entire site collection, not just the current site.

- For a document library or list, click the Shared With option in the ribbon and then use the Advanced option for additional detail (see Figures 12-12 and 12-13). You can also access the library or list settings and then the "Permissions for this library or list" option under Permissions and Management.
- For a document, click the Shared With option (see Figure 12-13).

Troubleshooting Security Applications

This section contains examples of reported issues and questions with security applications in SharePoint and the associated potential resolutions/answers. This list is not exhaustive but demonstrates additional learning elements associated with SharePoint security management.

- **"SharePoint is denying me access to a site."** First, it is very important to note that SharePoint handles *authorization* but not *authentication*. You can't get to a SharePoint site without first being authenticated (that is, associated with valid credentials). Once a user is authenticated, SharePoint applies security to determine whether that user is authorized to see all, some, or none of the content. If users do not have access rights to a site or object for which they have a link, a page is presented so an access request can be sent to the site owner (Figure 12-21). Note that the only way users can see the message shown in Figure 12-21 is if they have been given a link to content from another user or from a page or site or object to which they have access. Search will never return objects to which a user doesn't have access—but people can easily place hyperlinks to secured content in documents or on site pages without knowing that the content to which they are linking may not be available to all users.

- **"Certain users can no longer access their team site, and security has not been changed."** There is a scenario worth mentioning here. If a site contributor places an image on the site and the image is located (and secured) in a different location, that security is applied at the time of page rendering. So in this example, a user may

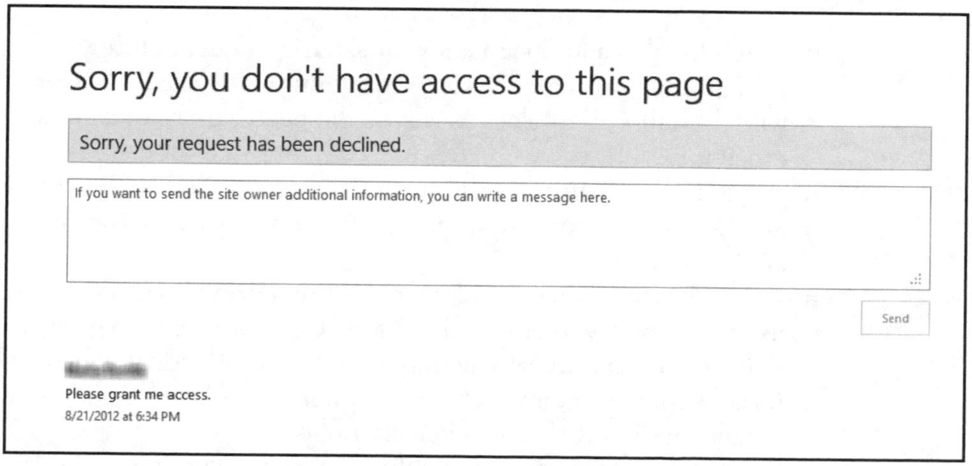

Sorry, you don't have access to this page

> Sorry, your request has been declined.

> If you want to send the site owner additional information, you can write a message here.

Send

Please grant me access.
8/21/2012 at 6:34 PM

Figure 12-21 Users who are denied access can engage in a dialog with the site owner to request access

be prompted with the security dialog box because that user does not have access to the image. This is why security must be well mapped in early stages where, in this case, an openly available image library has the necessary Read access.

- **"I'm the site owner and I no longer have access to my site."** Users with Full Control privileges (typically, users in the Site Owners group) have permission to manage all permissions—including their own. Even after being trained, a site owner might accidentally remove his or her own permissions from a site, usually while adding or removing other users from the Site Owners group. When this happens, the site collection administrator can add the user back to the Site Owners group.

- **"How do I know if I have contribution rights to a library?"** If you see the "+ New document or drag files here" instructions when you are viewing a library, you have contribution rights to that library.

Key Points

Consider the following recommended actions when you think about security:

- Carefully plan and document your security model before you begin configuring your site. This involves defining the security associated with the full-site topology as well as the necessary roles and security exceptions.
- Try to apply security at the highest level, preferably the site. Pay attention to the concept of permission inheritance as you plan and apply security.
- As much as possible, avoid giving access permissions to individual users. Always try to ensure that users will be assigned to groups and that permissions are assigned to groups, not individual people. This makes support and maintenance simpler and reduces the amount of clutter that is left behind when staff depart.
- Be sure to document and justify all custom permission levels you create for your site.

- Use the "principle of least privilege" to assign permissions to users. As a general rule, give users only the permissions that they need to perform their roles. Your business sponsor may be the effective "owner" of your site, but that doesn't mean that you should give your business sponsor Owner (Full Control) privileges for the site. Think about a variation of the phrase that is often associated with the Hippocratic Oath for assigning security permissions—"First, don't assign permissions that allow a user to do harm to the site"—as you place users into security groups.

- In Office 365/SharePoint Online environments, pay attention to whether or not something should be shared with Everyone or Everyone except external users. There may be scenarios where you want to explicitly restrict access to guest user accounts. While you can, as suggested, create a separate site collection where you allow external access and have some internal-only sites where this will never be an issue, you have the option of providing even more explicit restrictions even if the site collection content would otherwise be available to be shared with external (guest) users.

- Think about whether the new default Edit permissions set for members is appropriate for your users. You may want to consider changing the default back to Contribute.

- If you are not using the Community Site template, be sure to use the out-of-the-box security groups and give users access via the Share option to make sure that you don't give members the wrong permissions.

- If you are using SharePoint Online and will allow access for external users, it is always a good idea to require authentication if you are allowing an external user to edit content.

- If you are using SharePoint 2013 on-premises and want visitors and members to be able to initiate sharing requests for documents, be sure to enable access requests for your site and make sure e-mail is enabled for your farm.

- If you need to create custom permission levels, start by making a copy of an existing permission level and then add or remove individual permissions. Don't go overboard with creating custom permission levels or you will make yourself crazy trying to understand and maintain your security model.

- Be sure to create a process or plan to monitor security as your solution evolves.

- Don't give service accounts or generic user accounts security privileges. An effective security audit includes the ability to associate any task with a specific individual.

- Factor security into any navigation strategy. In traveling from site A to site B, a user must have at least Read permission to all nodes in that path or the navigation fails.

- If you can, try to keep the security model document up-to-date. In addition, use the processes described in the "Maintaining Your Security Model" section to audit permissions and access for critical sites on a regular basis. At a minimum, try to document where and why you have applied individual item-level permissions in a list or library—you don't necessarily have to document how you have secured each item, just the "method to your madness"! The third-party tools mentioned earlier can help identify where you have broken permissions, but your security model helps you understand why this might have occurred.

PART II

OPTIMIZING

MANAGING ENTERPRISE CONTENT

Enterprise content management (ECM) is a widely recognized IT industry term for software technology that enables organizations to create, capture, present, access, view, print, store, secure, manage, publish, personalize, distribute, search, retain, and destroy digital content related to organizational processes. Whew—that's a mouthful. So what does this mean? In short, it means storing document content electronically and then making sure it is managed appropriately. Whether it's the simple creation of content, sharing the content with others, or a full document life cycle that represents your organization's processes (see Figure 13-1 for an example life cycle), understanding how SharePoint can help is critical to the successful management of content.

With the 2010 release, SharePoint finally could be considered a document management system, rather than just a document collaboration environment. Prior to SharePoint's emergence in this manner, many organizations used SharePoint for document sharing, only to purchase a more expensive system (such as EMC Documentum or IBM FileNet) to provide actual document management features for a central collection of artifacts. While this model eases some of the traditional bottlenecks associated with a central team managing all content, it poses several new challenges. First, consistency is hard to enforce. Different users will likely apply different metadata or inconsistent security around content (this includes pages as well as documents and other types of content). In addition, with many owners come varied processes for managing how content gets published and ultimately removed. Finally, with this inconsistency around process and control comes a potential conflict with corporate compliance mandates.

SharePoint 2013 changes the way documents and other data are managed by easing the burden associated with effective content management of corporate data. Because ECM is now embedded in the main SharePoint feature set—even in SharePoint Online—users can take advantage of traditional ECM processes like document management

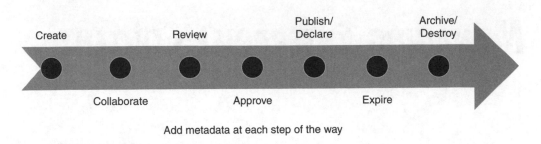

Add metadata at each step of the way

Figure 13-1 For individuals, simply creating a document is sufficient; however, when sharing with teams or organizing content for the enterprise, a more complete definition of the document life cycle is needed—you should take a step back and determine yours

and records management, all within a familiar user interface. This allows users to participate in the management of documents and records without changing the way they work—at least to some degree—within their SharePoint environment. Because SharePoint supports a wide variety of document and records management strategies that can be used in combination to accommodate various levels of document processing, integrity, and disposition, it is important to plan carefully to achieve your business goals.

Getting Started with ECM

Before we dive into some of the functionality associated with ECM, let's look at key terms we'll use throughout this chapter:

- **Enterprise content management (ECM).** ECM refers to activities related to document management (DM), forms management, Web content management (WCM), and records management (RM).
- **Document management (DM).** Document management refers to the active use of "living" documents, along with a set of capabilities, such as check-in, checkout, and version control, designed to put structure around those documents. These are documents authored by individuals and teams that exist in a state in which they may be changed or moved at any time.
- **Digital Asset Management (DAM).** Digital asset management typically refers to the storage and organization of media content,

such as videos, images, and audio files. While we don't specifically cover digital asset management in this chapter, the principles of ECM that we do cover can apply to this type of content.

- **Records management (RM).** Records management refers to documents and other content (Web pages, physical assets, etc.) that exist in an official, stable state. These are documents that the organization has effectively authored and should not be changed. A document may move from a normal state and later become a record. Records are often archived, tracked, and audited. The most common scenario for records management is legal/regulatory compliance—ensuring that a document is retained/unchanged/purged according to a predictable, known schedule.

- **E-discovery.** Electronic discovery is the process of identifying and delivering electronic information that can be used as evidence. SharePoint Server 2013 introduces a new feature called the eDiscovery Center, which is a new type of site collection that is used as a portal for managing e-discovery cases. From this central location you can discover content in the same SharePoint farm or other SharePoint farms, content in Exchange Server 2013, and content on file shares.

- **Legal holds.** During an e-discovery process, you can apply a legal hold to SharePoint and Exchange content that you discover. The hold ensures that a copy of the content is preserved while still allowing users to work with (and even change) the content. When you have identified the specific items that you will have to deliver, SharePoint provides a way to export them in an industry-standard format.

With these terms defined, let's dig into the main pieces of ECM within SharePoint 2013. For this discussion, we'll focus our ECM topics on three main components: document management, records management, and e-discovery. Web content management (WCM) has its own chapter (Chapter 14, "Managing Web Content").

What's New in SharePoint 2013?

Let's take a high-level view of what's new in SharePoint 2013. In general, the document and records management features haven't changed drastically. The following sections describe the new or enhanced features in SharePoint 2013 that will impact how you manage and organize content.

Site Retention Policy

New in SharePoint 2013 is the ability to manage the open/close status of a site, complete with retention policies (see Figure 13-2). When a site is closed, it is trimmed from places that aggregate open sites to site members such as Outlook, OWA, and Project Server. In addition, a site can automatically be deleted after it is closed. Before you apply a policy to a specific site, you'll need to create site policies that define specific rules for exactly how a site is closed and deleted, when the deletion should occur, and whether a site should be marked as read-only upon closure. If you have any kind of retention policy for compliance reasons, or you simply wish to clean up sites after they're no longer in use, this feature can be very useful. From an overall content management perspective, site retention can work

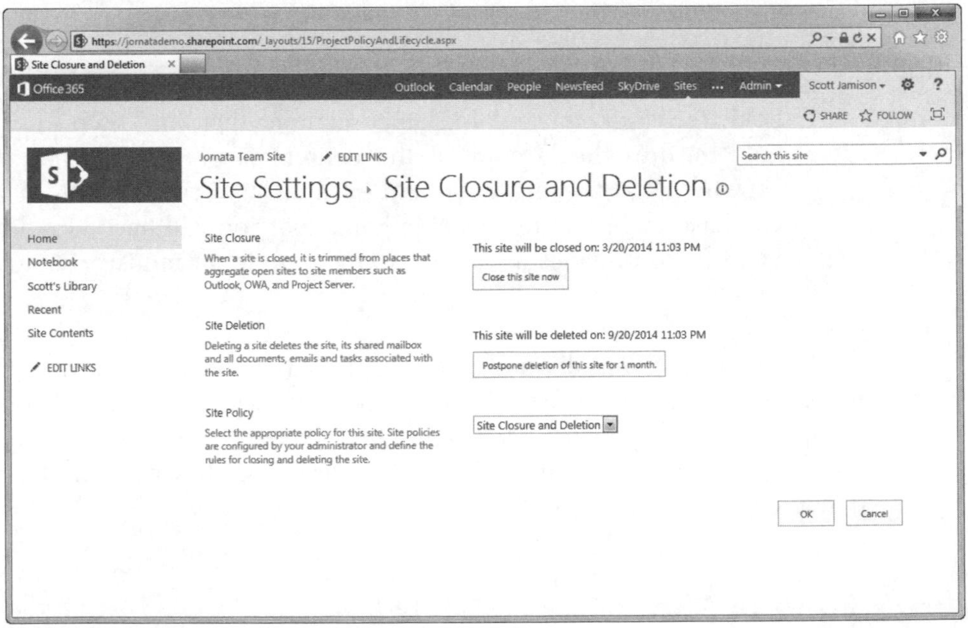

Figure 13-2 Site retention policies enable you to set when a site gets closed, whether sites are deleted automatically, and whether closed sites should be read-only

hand in hand with item retention to complete an overall content retention policy within your organization. Even if you haven't considered it before, we recommend taking the time to determine whether cleaning up content—regardless of the legal requirement to do so—could be of benefit.

Site Mailbox

Site Mailboxes enable you to manage e-mail and documents together by connecting a SharePoint site to an Exchange mailbox especially created for the site. Users can then view the project or team-related e-mail from SharePoint and view site documents in Outlook. You can add a site mailbox to any site by adding the Site Mailbox app and then clicking into the app to complete the configuration (see Figure 13-3). Once you configure the site mailbox, a link to the mailbox will show up in the Site Contents page, just as for lists and libraries. When users click the Mailbox link, they are redirected to a page that displays an Outlook Web Access–based view of the mailbox content, complete with a breadcrumb back to the SharePoint site.

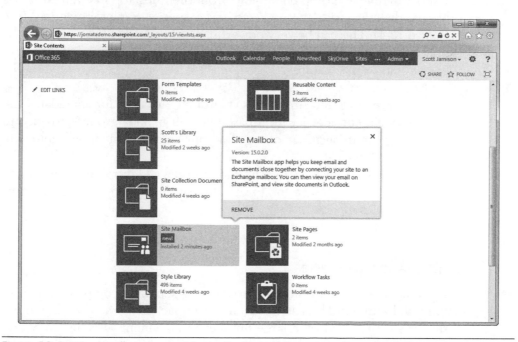

Figure 13-3 Site Mailboxes provide an Exchange-based mailbox to jointly manage documents and e-mail

Note that the Site Mailbox capability is included with Office 365 but not SharePoint Online by itself. In addition, for the Site Mailbox functionality to work on-premises, you'll need both SharePoint 2013 and Exchange 2013 installed.

We recommend considering this feature if you

- Need to have a consistent retention policy between project-related e-mail and SharePoint document content
- Manage teams and projects for which overall content needs to be managed together
- Want to provide the ability for team members to view and contribute documents stored in SharePoint document libraries directly from Outlook 2013

Document Drag and Drop

Users can drag and drop documents from their desktop into a SharePoint library directly—without the need for a special Explorer window (see Figure 13-4). This can be very powerful, since the ease of use provided by drag and drop will encourage SharePoint document library use. There are two caveats to this feature:

1. Since drag and drop doesn't prompt the user for metadata, you should consider location-based default metadata values to encourage the implicit use of tags for your content, which will help with searching later.
2. Internet Explorer 9 doesn't support drag and drop, so you'll need to use IE10, Chrome, or Firefox to use this feature—these browsers are all supported.

Shredded Storage

Document versions are no longer stored as separate, complete copies of the full document. This can have a major impact on storage needs and can save costs if you rely on a large number of document versions. In Share-Point 2010 (when combined with Office 2010), Microsoft introduced the concept of transmitting only the changes made to Office documents when

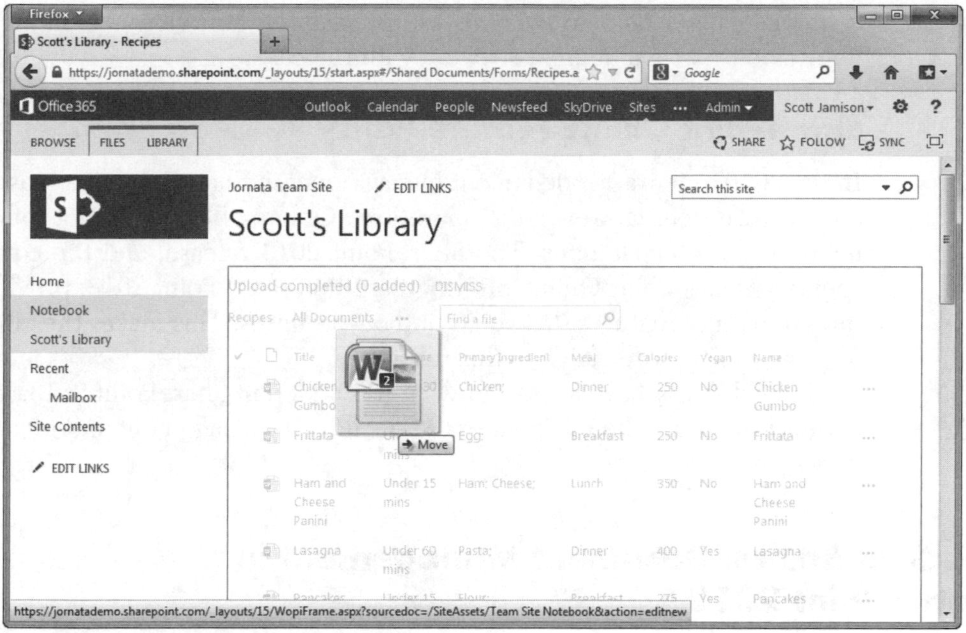

Figure 13-4 SharePoint 2013 supports browser-based drag and drop in almost any browser, providing a much improved user experience for document contributors

updating them in SharePoint; SharePoint 2013 takes this a step further and saves differences to the databases as well, saving both network bandwidth and database storage space.

eDiscovery Center

SharePoint Server 2013 introduces a new feature called the eDiscovery Center, which is a new type of site collection that is used as a portal for managing e-discovery cases. From this central location, you can discover content in the same SharePoint farm or other SharePoint farms, content in Exchange Server 2013, and content on file shares.

When an organization receives a request for e-discovery, perhaps from legal or as an outside request, you create an eDiscovery *case* in the eDiscovery Center. An eDiscovery case is a collaboration site that you can use to organize information (located via search) related to that particular e-discovery request. From within an eDiscovery case, you can search for content, apply a hold to content, export content, and view the status of holds and exports that are associated with the case.

SharePoint Online Feature Parity

In the 2010 time frame, document management in SharePoint was reasonably feature-rich. However, the SharePoint Online offering did not reflect many of those capabilities. The SharePoint 2013 release, and the corresponding SharePoint Online offering based on SharePoint 2013, provides the same set of features that you'd find on-premises. This makes the cloud offering much more viable in this release.

Now that you have an idea of what was added in SharePoint 2013, let's review how to get the most out of the document management and records management features.

Back to Basics: Document Management in SharePoint 2013

Technically, document management has been a core piece of SharePoint since its inception, with features such as document libraries and custom Columns (metadata). Some might argue that versions of SharePoint prior to 2010 offered "document collaboration" or perhaps document management "lite." The new document management features that have been added in SharePoint 2010 and 2013 bring SharePoint's document management capabilities up to par with—or at least close to—industry expectations. This section discusses each of the key document management features as well as how and when you'd use them, and then provides a step-by-step walkthrough of a typical configuration for document and records management within SharePoint. In this section, we intentionally focus on some key features that might have existed prior to SharePoint 2013—such as location-based default metadata values—since many of these valuable features are still underused in most organizations, and because the features that have been introduced in SharePoint 2013, while useful, are marginally evolutionary and not revolutionary.

Document Libraries

A document library is simply a SharePoint list that is designed to accommodate documents. In SharePoint, *libraries* are designed to hold large items such as documents, images, videos, and reports, whereas *lists* typically hold structured data. In most cases, a document library is the best place to store and manage document content, with features such as versions, check-in/checkout, and tagging.

Note Document libraries are also used to hold Web pages. For example, every team site in SharePoint 2013 has a library called Site Pages. This library holds the pages that display the user interface to the user, including Home.aspx, which is the start page for the site.

Versioning Settings

Version management is a core component of any document management system. It involves tracking the change history associated with a particular item. SharePoint 2013 offers several options: don't track prior versions, track major versions only, or track major and minor version numbers.

- **No versioning** indicates that only the most recent version of the document will be retained.
- A **major version** is a published version (1.0, 2.0) that indicates that the document is published and available to all readers. Previous versions are stored in the version history.
- A **minor version** (1.1, 1.2) indicates that the document is in progress. It will eventually be published but has not yet been. Minor versions can be made visible to contributors only or to all readers. Previous versions are stored in the version history.
- SharePoint also retains document metadata/Column information within the version history.

Version options are set *directly within* the document library and *apply to the library as a whole*.

The document library Versioning Settings page allows you to specify if items should require content approval prior to publication, configure version setting details, set draft item security, and indicate checkout requirement options for a document library (see Figure 13-5).

Content Approval

You can think of content approval (see Figure 13-5) as a one-stage approval process. When this setting is enabled, all major-versioned documents need

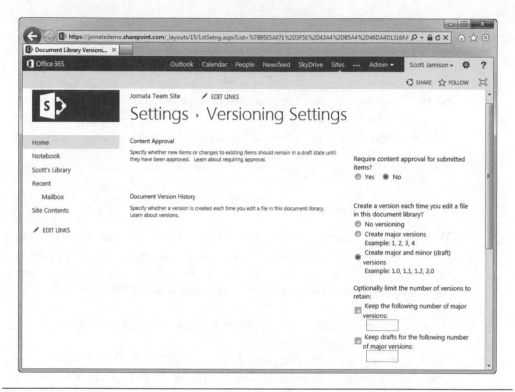

Figure 13-5 The Document Library Versioning Settings provide content approval, version history, draft item security, and checkout requirement options for a document library

approval from an Approver user role. New and changed items remain in a pending state until approved or rejected by someone who has permission to approve them.

- If the item or file is approved, it is assigned an Approved status in the list or library, and it is displayed to anyone with permission to view the list or library.
- If the item or file is rejected, it remains in a pending state and is visible only to the people with permission to view drafts. Minor versions (drafts) don't require approval.

Content approval settings apply to what is returned in search results as well.

Document Version History

Depending on the options selected in this section, SharePoint tracks revisions to both the document content and its metadata properties. Libraries can track both major and minor versions, and you can limit the number of versions that people can store (see Figure 13-6).

Tracking both major and minor versions provides a more detailed way to track the version history of an item. Major versions are more likely to represent a milestone, such as when a file is ready to be viewed by a wide audience. Minor versions are typically used as a routine increment, such as a version that a user saves or checks in while he or she is still writing the content. When you want to view the version history of a file, major and minor versions make it easy to identify the stages of the file's development. Note that users can add a version comment for minor versions only if they check out and check the document back in; this means that if you want to require comments on every version (including minor versions), you need to require checkout.

When you save and close a file, the version is tracked as a minor version by default. If you check out the file before working on it, you can designate the type of version you are checking in. You must publish a major version of the file for it to become visible to all readers. You do not need to publish a file as a separate step if you designate it as a major version when you check it in.

Versions are numbered when they are created. When major and minor versions are tracked, the major versions are whole numbers, and the minor

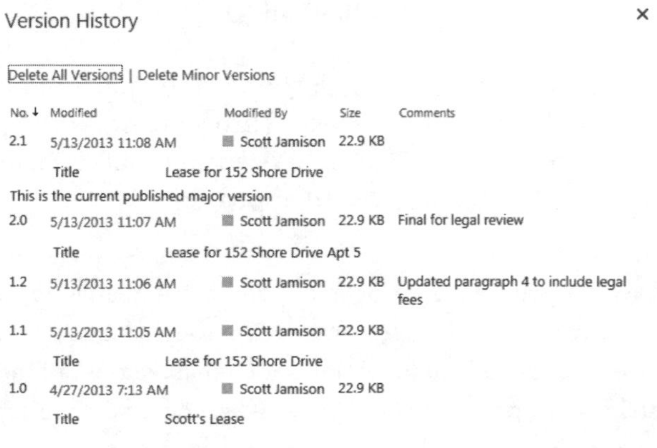

Version History   ×

Delete All Versions | Delete Minor Versions

No. ↓	Modified	Modified By	Size	Comments
2.1	5/13/2013 11:08 AM	Scott Jamison	22.9 KB	
	Title	Lease for 152 Shore Drive		
This is the current published major version				
2.0	5/13/2013 11:07 AM	Scott Jamison	22.9 KB	Final for legal review
	Title	Lease for 152 Shore Drive Apt 5		
1.2	5/13/2013 11:06 AM	Scott Jamison	22.9 KB	Updated paragraph 4 to include legal fees
1.1	5/13/2013 11:05 AM	Scott Jamison	22.9 KB	
	Title	Lease for 152 Shore Drive		
1.0	4/27/2013 7:13 AM	Scott Jamison	22.9 KB	
	Title	Scott's Lease		

Figure 13-6 Versioning enables you to save the various changes to an item over the course of its editing history

versions are decimals. For example, 0.1 is the first minor version of a file, 1.2 is the second minor version of a file that was published once, and 2.0 is the second major version of a published file.

Let's walk through an example to illustrate how the version numbering might work. Assume that a user creates a new file in a document library; the document is labeled 0.1. When the user publishes the document, it is labeled as version 1.0. After being checked out, edited, and checked in an additional time, version 1.1 is visible to team members but not seen by the organization. (Note that the specific visibility of draft items depends on the Draft Item Security setting, described in the next section.) The rest of the organization continues to see only version 1.0. It's the same with a second draft, tagged as version 1.2. Finally, when the document is published, version 2.0 is created, and it supplants version 1.0 from a visibility perspective so that everyone sees version 2.0.

Again, let's recap:

- Version 0.1 (created at check-in; visible to author and/or approval team only)
- Version 1.0 (created when published; visible to all after approval takes place)
- Version 1.1 (created at check-in; visible to author and/or approval team only)
- Version 1.2 (created at check-in; visible to author and/or approval team only)
- Version 2.0 (visible to all)

The power of the major/minor version functionality is the ability to manage the document revision process within the portal (versus on a local drive) while at the same time ensuring that a document is not made available until it is complete and approved.

Note If you delete a document and subsequently restore the document, all stored versions will be restored in the source document library.

If you choose to limit the number of versions that SharePoint stores, the oldest versions are permanently deleted when the limit is reached and not sent to the Recycle Bin.

A major change in SharePoint 2013 with respect to version history is that a full copy of every version is no longer stored in the database. In prior versions of SharePoint, regardless of the versioning control method that you chose, a complete copy of each version of the document would be stored in SQL Server. This made some organizations stop and think about whether to enable versioning due to the sheer cost of storage. With a new feature in SharePoint 2013 called "shredded storage," only the differences between the document versions are stored. This could make you reconsider your stance on enabling versioning since the overall storage savings could be significant.

Draft Item Security

The Draft Item Security setting allows you to control which groups of people can read drafts. As discussed in the last section, drafts are the minor versions of a file and are created in one of two ways: either when a minor version of a file is created or updated in a library that tracks major and minor versions, or when a list item or file is created or updated but not yet approved in a list or library in which content approval is required.

You can specify which groups of people can view drafts—either by enabling all users with Read access to view them, or by restricting viewing only to users who can edit items. This allows you to restrict readers to access only the major versions of documents or the documents that are approved.

- **If content approval is required**, you can specify whether files that are pending approval can be viewed by people with permission to read, people with permission to edit, or only the author and people with permission to approve items.
- **If both major and minor versions are being tracked**, the author must publish a major version before the file can be submitted for approval. When content approval is required, people who have permission to read content but do not have permission to see draft items will see the last approved major version of the file.

If you plan to use minor versions and content approval, we recommend configuring Draft Item Security so that only editors and/or approvers see draft items. This ensures that general site users don't see unapproved versions of documents.

Require Checkout

You can also configure the document library to require checkout before items can be edited (see Figure 13-7). Requiring checkout prevents multiple people from making changes at the same time. When this setting is enabled, new files are initially set as checked out. The person who creates or adds the file must check it in before other people can see it. Checkout is also required to update metadata properties on the file.

When checkout is required, a file is checked out automatically when someone opens it for editing. When a file is checked out, no one can edit it except the person who checked it out. Changes that someone makes to a file while it is checked out are not visible to others until the file is checked

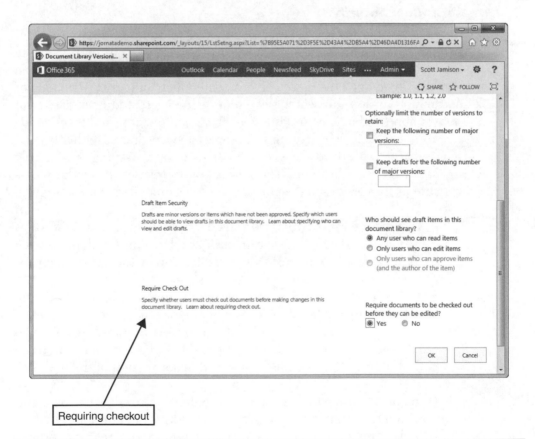

Requiring checkout

Figure 13-7 The Require Check Out setting enables you to require that users check out items before they can be edited

back in. This is true regardless of whether the person is working on the file locally or on the server.

Note In general, if users are planning to edit documents in place, they are typically better off not requiring checkout and instead using the simultaneous editing feature of SharePoint and Office. In this scenario, you should instruct site designers and users to use check-in/checkout only if they're going to take documents offline and edit them, or if you require very strict controls. Just note that no conflict resolution process will be available; multiple users will simply edit the same document at the same time. In Word and PowerPoint, they'll see each other's changes as they save the document. In Excel, changes are saved as soon as the user tabs out of a cell.

When users check in a file, they are prompted to enter comments about the changes that were made. If a library tracks versions, the comments become part of the version history. If both major versions and minor versions are tracked, users are prompted to choose which type of version they are checking in (major or minor).

Item-Level Security

SharePoint enables library owners to configure permissions at the item level; this means a single document library can hold a collection of similar (by content) documents that have different security definition(s). Item-level security can also be applied at the folder level (all documents in a folder share the security settings of the folder) or at the document level (unique permissions for the item).

Users looking at the list may see different documents based on their security privileges. In addition, security can be applied not just for viewing but for editing as well. In this case, specific users can edit only certain documents in the list. Again, one document library is managing a collection of similar content but the visibility or accessibility is being managed at the item level.

Consolidated libraries with item-level security can be far more efficient to present, navigate, and manage, but it is important to carefully consider the design and application of item-level security. By definition, permissions are broken from the parent, so if users or groups are added, modified, or deleted at the parent level, they will not automatically be updated in the folder or document. Furthermore, neither folders nor documents show an item-level security indicator. This can make document management challenging. Consider adding a metadata field to indicate if item security is applied. This can be a simple yes/no or a text field to capture who has access.

The recommendation here is to use item-level security as sparingly possible, mainly due to the burden that it can put on site administrators. When you enable item-level security, you break the security inheritance model. Therefore, if you change the security on either the library itself or the site as a whole, your documents will not inherit the new permissions and you will have to find each document that is uniquely provisioned and adjust the permissions manually. This can be a huge problem if you have a large number of items with item-level security in a library.

Managed Metadata

Managed metadata services play a large role in effectively tagging content. SharePoint 2013's Managed Metadata Service (or *term store*) provides a simple means of centrally managing a keyword taxonomy and providing an easy-to-use interface for updating and leveraging the keyword hierarchy. In addition to a central store of terms, this service provides many useful items: "type-ahead" on keyword selection (which works as an auto-complete function), easy management of the keyword associations, synonym management, and security trimming that allows for the decentralization of metadata ownership.

With managed metadata, SharePoint 2013 allows you to create centrally managed taxonomies and use them across lists and document libraries. In addition, users are able to navigate by using the metadata items. As an example, you might want to tag company documents with a custom property that identifies the client to which the document is aligned, which would then contain a well-managed list of client names. This ensures that metadata values are consistent, making searches more accurate. To add a Column in this manner, you can create a new Column in SharePoint called Offering and select Managed Metadata as the Column's type. This enables you to point the new Column at a managed term set in the term store. When users enter information into this property, they are able to select from a hierarchical view of preset value choices (see Figure 13-8).

You can also use the Managed Metadata type to provide hierarchical navigation for users. For example, users can view a navigation tree

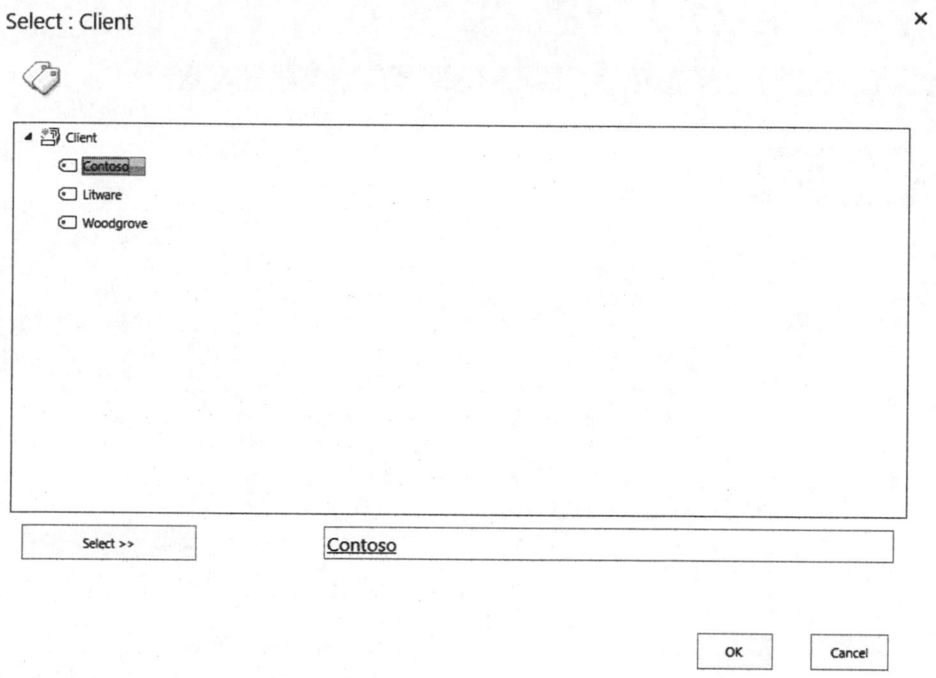

Select : Client   ✕

Client
  ⬡ Contoso
  ⬡ Litware
  ⬡ Woodgrove

Select >>	Contoso

OK   Cancel

Figure 13-8 The Managed Metadata Column type enables users to select from a set of predefined, centrally managed terms

(Figure 13-9). If a user selects the company Contoso under Client, SharePoint will apply a filter to the current view, showing only items that are tagged with a service offering type. In addition, users can use the Key Filters text box to type in the value of an offering, thereby applying the filter.

To configure metadata navigation, click the Configure Metadata Navigation link within the settings for the document library. Here, you can configure three items (see Figure 13-10):

- **Configure Navigation Hierarchies.** You can set navigation fields based on the following types: Content Type, choice, managed metadata. The properties of all Columns that satisfy one of those three types are enumerated here. You can choose any/all fields that you want users to navigate by using the tree view.

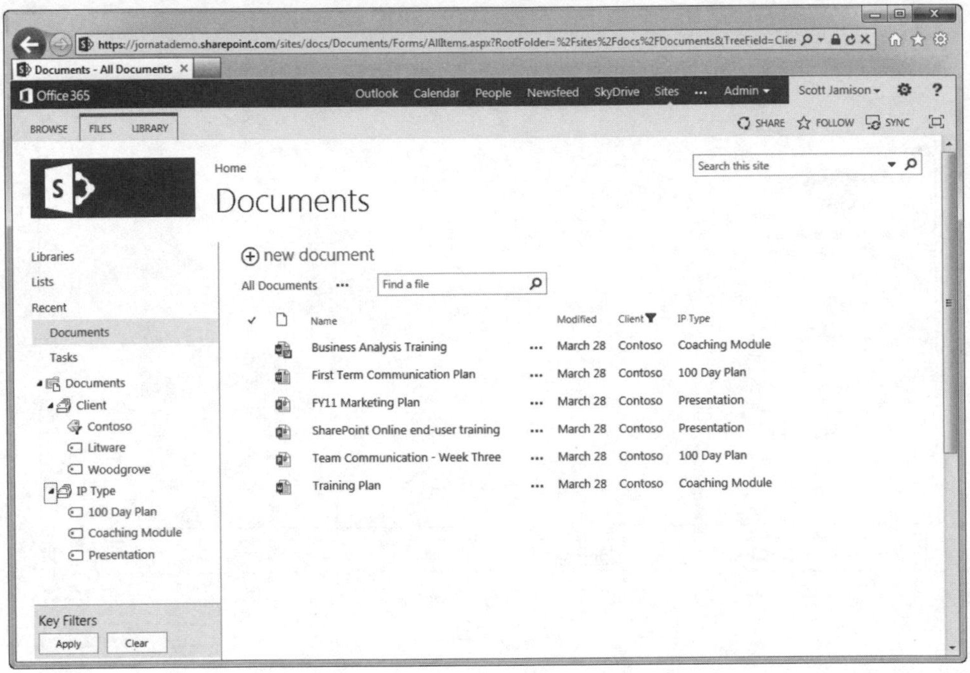

Figure 13-9 Metadata-based navigation provides a way for users to navigate lists and document libraries by using managed metadata values or folders

- **Configure Key Filters.** In addition to the tree view, you may want users to type in filter information for fast filtering. You can indicate which fields you want SharePoint to maintain an index on for filtering.
- **Configure automatic column indexing for this list:** Typically, you'll want SharePoint to manage Column indices on the list.

Location-Based Metadata

A very powerful feature that was introduced in SharePoint 2010 is the concept of default metadata values. The library administrator can set default Column values by location (see Figure 13-11); for example, all documents dropped into a specified library can have metadata values set automatically. This feature becomes even more powerful when combined with folders, since

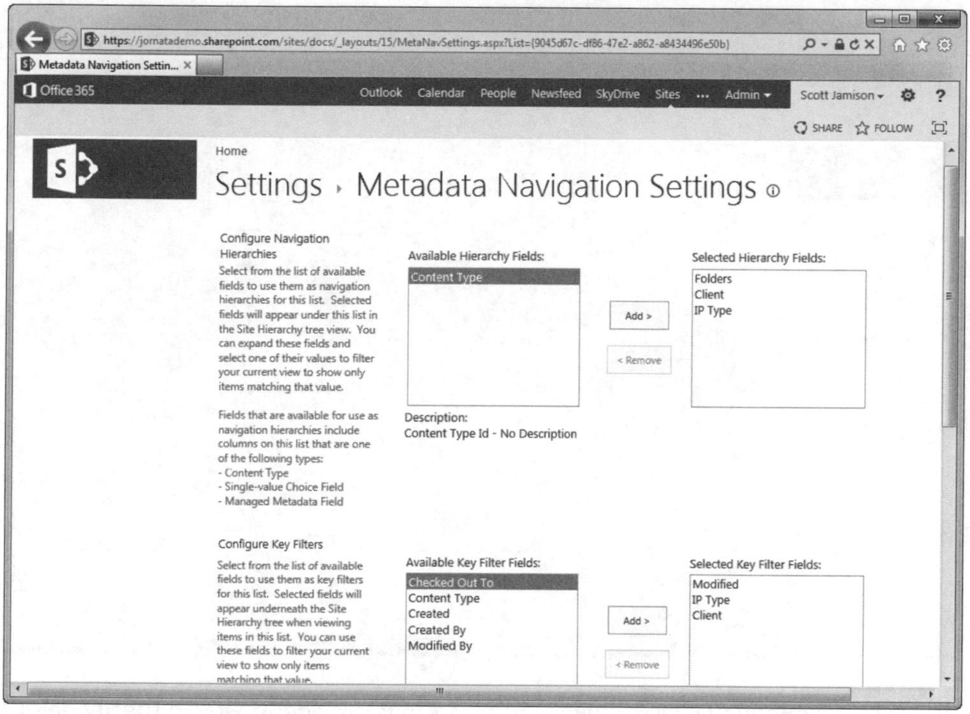

Figure 13-10 Metadata Navigation Settings enable you to configure document filtering based on metadata Columns, providing automatic filtering based on filters

content contributors can use SharePoint 2013's new drag-and-drop capability to move dozens of documents at once into SharePoint, select the proper folder, and apply correct metadata values on all documents automatically.

Document Sets

In many document management scenarios, users may produce several documents to accomplish one task or produce one deliverable. It can improve efficiency and consistency to manage the group of documents as one document set. Before you can create and manage SharePoint document sets, you must activate the site collection Document Set feature. Activating this feature creates a new Content Type that allows you to organize multiple documents into a collection of related documents that can be managed as one. In effect, document sets are folders where you can

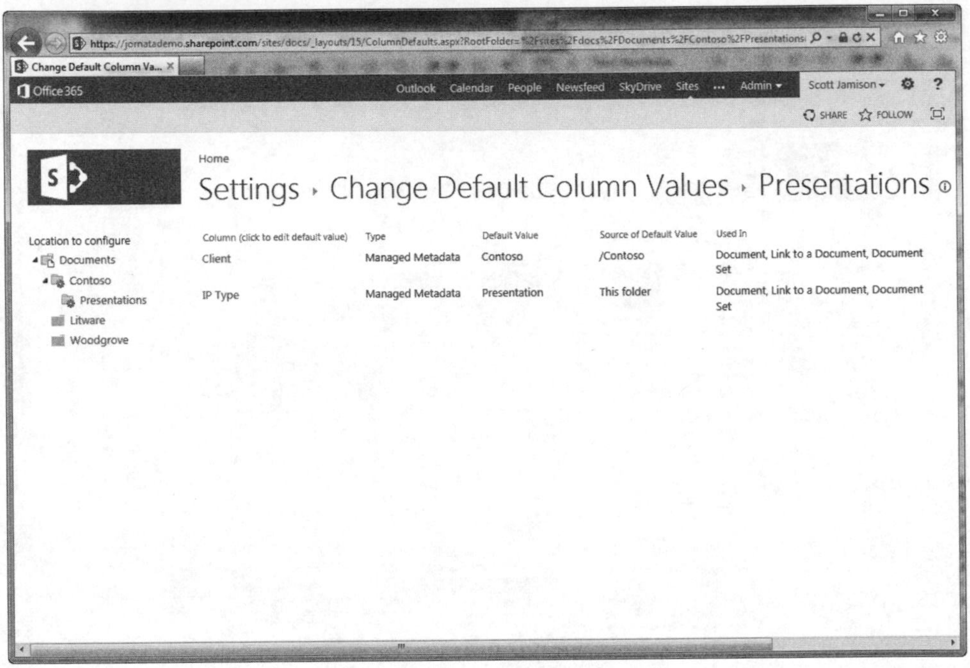

Figure 13-11 Configuring Column default value settings provides a way to specify default Column values; combined with folders, this feature enables contributors to simply choose a location and get metadata tagging for free

- Share metadata across documents
- Version the document set itself (instead of the individual documents)
- Initiate workflows for the whole document set
- Set permissions on the document set
- Download the documents within a document set to a .zip file
- Create a welcome page for the document set

The big advantage is that the entire collection of documents is effectively treated as one when used as part of a business process.

Document sets are implemented as a Content Type. To activate document sets, follow these steps:

1. Select Site Actions → Site Settings.
2. Under Site Collection Administration, click Manage Site Collection Features.

3. Click the Active button next the Document Sets feature (see Figure 13-12).
4. Return to the document library Advanced Settings page and enable management of Content Types.
5. Add the Document Set Content Type to the library by clicking "Add from existing site content types" (Figure 13-13) and selecting Document Set.

So when do you use document sets? Primarily when you want to treat a number of documents as a single item that has common metadata, permissions, and workflow. For example, you might be creating a proposal for a customer. While the proposal itself might be a single Word document,

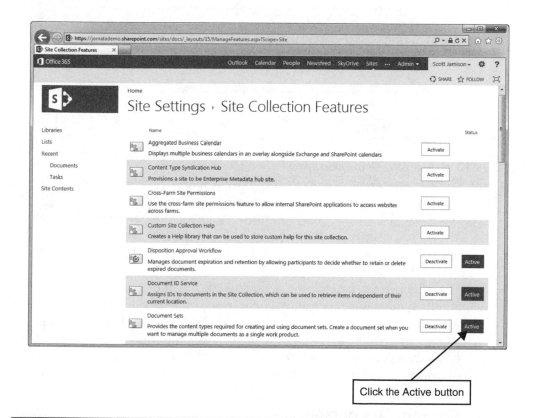

Figure 13-12 The Document Sets site feature and the Document ID Service feature are enabled at the site collection

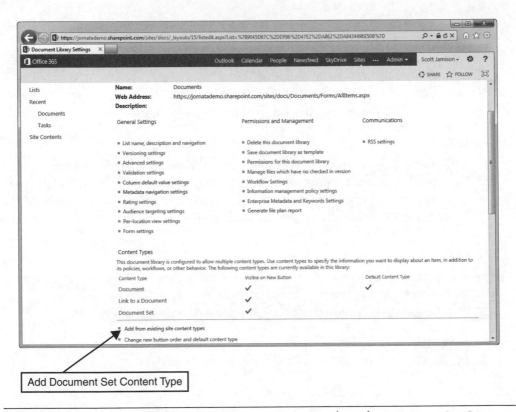

Add Document Set Content Type

Figure 13-13 Unless you use the Document Center site template, the Document Set Content Type must be added manually to the document library before you can create one

you'll also deliver a PowerPoint presentation, a video presentation, and an Excel spreadsheet for financial analysis. In this scenario, you'll probably want all of the items to share the same metadata (customer name, opportunity ID, and so on).

When users navigate to a document set, they will see information about the document set and can view and upload documents associated with the set. In addition, there is a special tab in the ribbon that appears when a user enters a document set. This ribbon button enables the user to create a version of the set, to start a workflow on the set, and to manage permissions on the set as a whole.

Content Organizer

The Content Organizer, introduced in SharePoint 2010, can automatically process content based on rules. This allows you to set up rules, such as specifying a drop-off library where users can centrally upload documents, having the system automatically create subfolders to partition items so that no folder has too many items, and sending documents to another location based on document attributes.

Document IDs

The Document ID service, also introduced in SharePoint 2010, enables you to assign unique IDs to documents within a site collection. Once this feature is activated, SharePoint assigns each document in the site collection its own unique identifier (permalink). This identifier can then be used to identify documents through either a direct link, page navigation, or a search. Users can then search for and retrieve documents based on ID independent of location.

Prior to SharePoint 2010, if a document moved within SharePoint, all references to it would break. With a document ID, that document now has a permanent path, independent of how many times it is moved. This provides a dependable method for retrieving the document and is a very powerful feature for those who point users directly to specific documents on their site. Since this feature is managed at the site collection level, there are additional settings that should be configured to ensure that document IDs are unique across all site collections. This is described in further detail later in this chapter.

To use this feature, activate it on the Site Settings page in the Site Collection Administration section. Then, click the Document ID settings page within Site Collection Administration.

There are two options within the Document ID settings page. The first setting is vitally important—it enables you to configure a prefix that will be applied to all documents within the site collection. Why is this setting so important? Provided you use unique prefixes across your site collections, it will ensure that your document IDs will be unique. The second option enables you to specify a search scope that is used for looking up documents using the ID field. An important note: Even though your document ID will be unique, if you move a document from one site collection to another, a new document ID will be created for it, since SharePoint considers it a copy.

As a best practice, make sure that each site collection has a unique document ID prefix properly configured. Don't just make something up; instead, use consistent prefixes according to your document management policies. Your governance committee should approve all document ID prefixes used in your enterprise; this will ensure that all document IDs assigned by SharePoint are globally unique. As a best practice, we recommend maintaining a master list to store the site collection names, the document ID prefix assigned to the site collection, the principal contact and backup contact for the site collection, and a description of the intent or focus of the site collection. Keep this with other governance plan documents for your environment.

Workflow

Workflow is a framework for defining rules and associated actions on a list entity (like a document). Workflow rules can be based on metadata (i.e., Create Date < 1/1/2014 or Status="Approved by Manager") and can trigger actions like document approval, removal, or movement. The workflow components of SharePoint 2010 proved popular for automating processes such as approvals and dispositions; SharePoint 2013 continues to add and enhance workflow capabilities by adding the new Workflow Manager role (for more information on workflows, refer to Chapter 17, "Planning Business Solutions").

The biggest advantages of workflow implementation are the consistency and structure it offers. Workflow rules are defined, and then SharePoint triggers the workflow actions when the specified criteria are met. From a document management perspective, workflow is interesting in that it enables content administrators to define rules for humans to interact with documents within SharePoint.

SharePoint 2013 contains a few out-of-the-box workflows that represent standard scenarios. One is an approval process. In this scenario, one or more approvers must confirm the validity of document content and acknowledge their acceptance through a formal process. The SharePoint workflow manages the process of notifying each approver of the requested action, captures the response, and notifies the next approver on the list of the request.

As stated earlier, workflow enables a framework for introducing a set of well-defined actions, with or without intervention, as they apply to documents stored in SharePoint libraries. In addition, actions can be defined so that appropriate activities can occur and be logged as documents are altered.

Document Information Panel

One of the toughest challenges in building a document repository is ensuring that each document is tagged with well-defined metadata so that it is easily discovered by an organization's members. Given the breadth of content that is often created in a corporate environment, this can be an overwhelming task (ask anyone who has tried to manage a document management system!). Content contributors are much more focused on the details within a document than on thinking about how best to tag it. Content discovery, after an item has been submitted, is an afterthought. Why is this bad? Search engines, even the best ones, cannot deliver optimal results if little is known about the content. In addition, it is hard to group similar content if the linking attribute is not consistently managed. This leaves many organizations in a stuck state. They have a SharePoint environment that contains the majority of business-critical documents but no easy way to find or associate key content.

Why is document tagging so difficult? Mainly it is because the tagging process happens too late in the document submission process. Just after a user uploads a document, he or she is asked for a bunch of metadata. Often, as a timesaver, little or no data is provided. Once a document is in the repository, it is very unlikely that it will ever be tagged again. The Document Information Panel (DIP), also available in previous versions of SharePoint and Office, is an interface within the Office 2013 products (such as Word or Excel or PowerPoint) that shows the metadata requirements for that document within the Office interface. A content contributor can update metadata as he or she is creating the document. Think about the power in that. SharePoint 2013 has moved the metadata entry process earlier in the document life cycle, where it should be, when the information is most readily available and makes more sense.

By providing an easier means of entering/updating document metadata (directly in the open document), the Document Information Panel can improve the probability that quality metadata will be entered for the document. This improved metadata has far-reaching impact as it offers a better user experience in terms of content discovery (i.e., search or filtering). In addition, it provides the data required to implement stronger audit policies around specific types of content.

Document Center

One of the final items to note regarding document management is the Document Center, which is a site template that enables you to centrally manage documents in your organization. Whereas most sites contain document libraries that are geared toward supporting that particular site only, the Document Center is for centrally managing documents.

What does the Document Center template provide? It's essentially a template with two key lists: a document library and a task list. The Document Center site template also configures the default settings in the document library to support strong content control. In contrast to generic site templates and libraries, default checkout is required before editing, major and minor versions are enabled, support for multiple Content Types is enabled, document sets are enabled, metadata navigation is enabled, and auditing is enabled to track content changes over time. The site template also provides a custom welcome page to facilitate easy upload and search (based on document IDs) (see Figure 13-14).

Figure 13-14 The Document Center template enables you to create a site specifically geared toward enterprise document management

Our recommendation is to use the Document Center site for documents that need centralized management. Use a Team Site template with document libraries to store documents that require active collaboration.

Records Management

Records management in SharePoint 2013 enables you to manage business documents that are necessary for regulatory compliance, business continuity, or historical interest. Records management is not new to SharePoint 2013, but it has been enhanced to enable retention policies on entire sites (in addition to retention policies on documents and other library items, which were available previously). In a nutshell, records management involves declaring the document(s) as a record and then applying records management policies and auditing to those records. Records management policies are an effective way to ensure that historical content is maintained by either marking the document in place or moving the document to a special repository with its own rules and security. Documents are effectively removed from the mainstream content so that they do not burden search engines and content navigation with excess clutter. If desired, a separate search page or navigational structure could be used for archived content.

Record Declaration

To start off, which do you use: in-place records declaration or the records archive? You'll likely use both and will need to decide which and when. There are certain issues you will need to consider:

- Records retention rules
- Which users can view records
- Ease of locating records (collaborative users versus the records manager)
- Maintaining each version as a record—do you need this?
- Records auditing—how often will you audit records?
- Site organization (and number of sites used)—what does your information architecture look like?
- E-discovery
- Security

If you plan to use a records archive, you will need a Records Manager role to ensure that records are well managed and that rules are followed. This person will likely set up a records archive using the Records Center template.

In-Place Records Management

You can also declare records in place. This requires you to do two things first: (1) activate the In Place Records Management site collection feature; (2) then enable manual declaration of records either at the site collection level or at the document library level (under "Record declaration settings"). You can also automatically declare items as records when they are added to specified libraries.

Note   Lists can also be configured to store records.

Once you enable manual declaration of records, users will see a new action in the ribbon that allows them to declare an item as a record (see Figure 13-15).

Records management involves "locking down" a version of a document to provide an immutable snapshot of that document at a point in time. This means that SharePoint 2013 can manage items as auditable sources of corporate content. With SharePoint 2007, this meant having to move the document to another location and/or tightening the security around it. With SharePoint 2013, documents can be treated as records either in a central location or in place. Thus, you have the choice of sending a document to a Records site, or marking the document as a record within the context of its original document library. In-place records management gives contributors more flexibility in managing documents and locking them down when each reaches a final state. Doing this will provide a proper audit trail and eliminate some current business processes associated with physically moving documents to new locations for archiving.

Because most users are not familiar with records management practices (and likely don't need that level of detail), the ability to implement consistent handling to ensure compliance/retention/disposition is a real value-add for many organizations. However, that does not obviate the need to make sure individuals who have overall responsibility for managing record content are actively engaged and well trained in defining

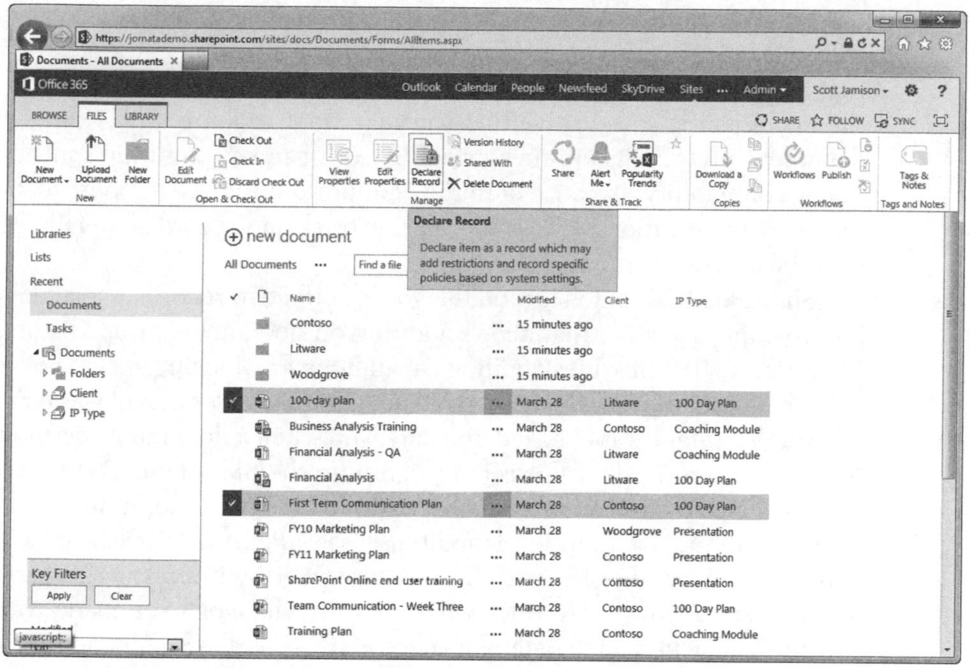

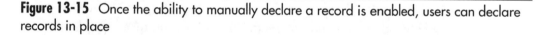

Figure 13-15 Once the ability to manually declare a record is enabled, users can declare records in place

and/or implementing policies and settings. You should make sure that anyone responsible for content management of any kind understands the expectations for how content is to be managed.

Auditing

For many organizations, especially those in industries that require a high level of regulatory compliance, storing documents in a repository is not enough. It is just as important to manage the activity around those documents. Activity management is all about auditing or recording the details around what happened to a particular document throughout its life cycle. Examples of audit information include who added particular sections and when, when a document was approved and by whom, what a document looked like on a certain date, and what the rules around document retention are.

Even more granular is the ability to record viewing statistics associated with a particular document. Let's say you have a new corporate policy that requires executive approval prior to publishing. The information in the document is so sensitive that you may want to know who viewed the document prior to its approved state. As you can see, auditing spills over into accountability. Because of this, it is important to have a robust records management solution in place to properly track and record all details associated with portal content.

SharePoint 2013 delivers on the goal of effective records management by providing a system that allows auditing on documents or any list item. SharePoint 2013 provides auditing capabilities for tracking specific events like when a document was opened or viewed, when a document was edited, when a document was checked out, and even when a document was moved to a new location. All of this is built right into the SharePoint 2013 system interface and is easily configured as part of a list library definition.

In addition to item-level auditing, SharePoint 2013 also provides auditing at a specific site level. This is an especially interesting feature as it allows site managers to track when security changes were made within the site and when metadata associated with a particular document was altered. Think about the impact of such a feature! Administrators can be assured that policies about site security and/or document definition can be effectively monitored and enforced. This is how the term *compliance* gets introduced in the SharePoint 2013 feature set.

Who can see details on audit data? Only administrators. Content contributors, whose activities are tracked, do not have access to audit reports. In addition, no one is allowed to edit or alter audit data. This lockdown ensures that audit trails are always complete and accurate. In addition, audit policies themselves can be audited so administrators can assess how well certain policies are being followed. This rules-based approach is yet another way SharePoint supports the effective management of sensitive information. Everything is monitored; policies are always tracked.

Information Management Policies

We've briefly talked about applying audit policies to specific documents or list items in SharePoint 2013. One of the obvious questions is how you ensure that these policies are in place, in all the right places. SharePoint provides the ability to set information management policies. These policies provide a structured way for administrators (or records managers) to define the proper audit policies and apply them consistently to all relevant locations. That way, no one has to worry about making sure that these policies extend into new sites or documents—they'll be applied automatically, ensuring that future content adheres to organizational rules.

As with most SharePoint 2013 functionality, information management policy management is built right into the interface. This allows administrators or records managers to define policies directly in the site settings of a particular document or site. In the Permissions and Policies section there is a link for "Information management policy settings." This is where policy is defined and applied.

Setting information management policies is intended to be simple and intuitive. No special skills are required to define policies. Administration is intended to be simple. For users, the experience is just as simple. When a policy is in place around a particular document, the user is made aware by a notification bar at the top of the document. All other functionality is normal.

There are several information management policy use cases, but let's look at a specific example associated with an expiration policy. Very much like metadata capture, document expiration is critical to the overall effectiveness of portal document delivery. Few documents should live forever (at least in the context of the corporate portal). Over time, a document becomes less relevant and therefore should be moved out of the mainstream. Without rules and policies in place, this becomes an overwhelming burden for document administrators. Who can be responsible for investigating all documents for usefulness?

SharePoint 2013 introduces the ability to have multistage expiration policies, which is a set of rules for executing activity on a particular document or group of documents. This is a two-step process.

The first step is to define *when* a document will encounter an expiration trigger. This is most easily done with logic against known metadata (another reason to properly tag content!). While most rules will be date driven (i.e., expire after 180 days), any metadata can be used to drive expiration.

The second step in the policy definition is to define *what happens* to the document when the criterion is met. This can take many forms; you can delete the document from the repository, or perhaps launch a SharePoint-based workflow that can move that document to an archive location. By setting expiration rules, administrators and records managers can ensure that the portal always contains relevant and timely data. See

Figure 13-16 for the compliance details on a particular item—this one has yet to have a retention policy defined.

As we have seen in this section, the document management and records management features in SharePoint 2013 enable you to create a repository to retain business documents that are necessary for regulatory

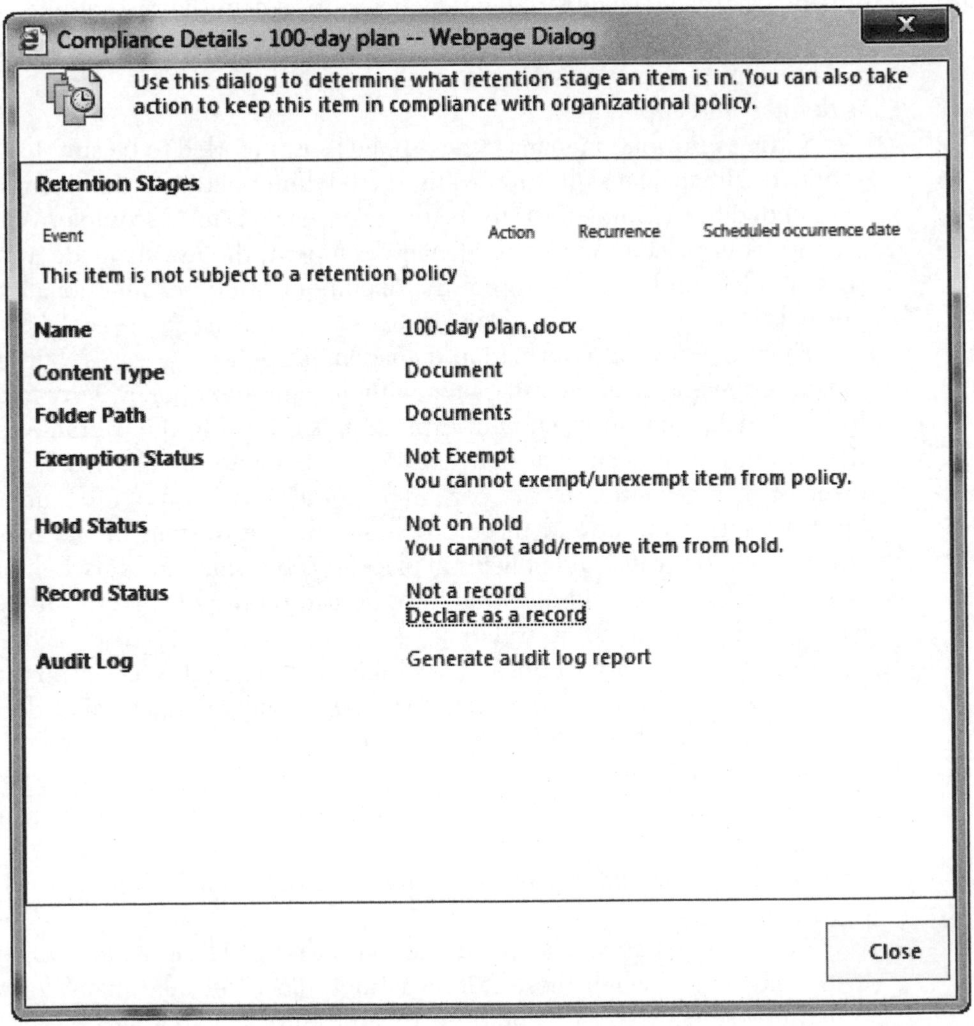

Figure 13-16 You can view the compliance details on any document, where you can see the document's scheduled retention policy, record and hold status, and audit information

compliance, business continuity, or historical interest. The ECM features of SharePoint 2013 enable you to set polices and auditing around documents. It's an effective way to ensure that historical content is maintained, not deleted, and does not burden search engines and content navigation.

Key Points

This chapter provided recommendations for using the enterprise content management (ECM) features of SharePoint 2013. In general, our recommendations are:

- Define Site Columns to capture metadata. Consider using folders for contributors, which enables you to define location-based default values for Columns. This provides a way for editors to provide metadata in bulk, or when using drag and drop.
- Use folders to apply security, define location-based default metadata, or partition large libraries. Train users to use Columns instead of folders to organize or display content.
- Set the default reader view(s) in a library to ignore folders. Then, provide a secondary view, called either Contributor or Folder View, for those users who want to navigate via a folder view.
- Define Content Types to standardize metadata across the organization, using Content Type syndication to keep document types consistent across site collections.
- Use a Team Site template with document libraries to store documents that will be actively collaborated on. Use the Document Center site template for documents that need to be managed in a centralized way.
- Make sure that each site collection has a unique document ID prefix configured. Your governance committee should approve all document ID prefixes used in your enterprise; this will ensure that all document IDs assigned by SharePoint are globally unique.
- If you have a records manager, use the Records Center site template to store and manage records. If you don't have a formal, centralized records manager, in-place record declaration will be easier for users to manage.

CHAPTER 14

MANAGING WEB CONTENT

SharePoint has continued to evolve into a premier Web content management (WCM) platform—more than ever with the 2013 release. SharePoint 2013 has added a significant number of features that enable an organization to host its Internet presence using the same set of technologies that many organizations—probably yours—already own.

WCM is one of the focus areas that is getting attention in SharePoint 2013 because it offers a rich functionality suite to manage, repurpose, deploy, and analyze content distributed to an Internet-based community. In addition, Microsoft has loosened its licensing model, no longer requiring a separate, costly server license to host Internet-facing sites on SharePoint. This can dramatically reduce the overall costs of using SharePoint for external publishing sites.

In this chapter, we will look at the WCM enhancements and how they can be used to build your publishing site.

Why SharePoint for Internet-Facing Web Sites?

Before we dive into some of the functionality associated with WCM, let's look at some of the key reasons why organizations use SharePoint for their publishing sites:

- **Ease of use.** Part of the appeal of SharePoint has always been its low threshold for entry. Users can be very quickly trained to use specific functionality and require very little training for uploading and managing content.
- **You already own it (business users).** Organizations that have already invested in SharePoint as part of an internal collaboration or communication initiative can leverage that very same software to manage Internet content with no additional training.

- **You already own it (IT).** Again, for organizations already familiar with SharePoint it is much easier to quantify IT support for a publishing site. IT knows how to manage and maintain a SharePoint environment because they already do that for internal use.
- **Leverage list data.** Web sites do not have to be a collection of static HTML content. SharePoint allows you to easily leverage list and library data for content presentation. This makes it easier to deploy and maintain dynamic content presentation without having to manage the underlying HTML.
- **Search.** SharePoint has a native search engine that will support the discovery experience associated with looking for keyword matches on your Web site. There is no need to purchase third-party search products to integrate into your WCM solution.
- **Content repurposing.** The life cycle of a document can transcend the boundary of the corporate firewall. What was once created through employee collaboration can ultimately provide high value to partners, clients, or customers. By leveraging SharePoint for intranet, extranet, and even Internet use, content can be shared naturally, via workflow, from one system to another.

And these are just a few reasons. Because of these and many others, SharePoint has gained tremendous momentum in the WCM space. SharePoint 2013 takes advantage of that momentum and raises the bar associated with what companies can do with their Web sites. It is now easier to leverage native capabilities in SharePoint to create a highly dynamic, rich, aesthetically pleasing corporate Web site.

What's New in SharePoint 2013?

Those who are familiar with WCM in SharePoint will be excited to learn that several features are improved in SharePoint 2013 and new features have been added. Let's take a look at some of these:

- **Content authoring.** There are many improvements to the content-authoring experience, starting with the content editor control. For example, a content editor can now copy content directly from Microsoft Word and have the document styles match the page styles. Small changes like this can make the difference in getting proper adoption for content-editing tools—and content is king when it comes to an Internet-facing site.

- **Multilingual sites.** While variations are nothing new with SharePoint 2013, one of the more significant improvements is the integrated translation feature. This feature can use the Machine Translation Service connecting to Microsoft Translator or can facilitate exporting/importing the content for third-party translation. This means that you can automatically translate your content into multiple languages.
- **Cross-site publishing.** Remote publishing in SharePoint 2010 required two separate farms. This was cumbersome at best and was an unacceptable expense to many. With cross-site publishing in SharePoint 2013, you can store and maintain your publishing content in the authoring site collection and then publish it to multiple destination publishing site collections—all within the same farm. This feature leverages built-in search functionality and the new Catalog Web Parts. With cross-site publishing you can
  - Share a list or a library as a publishing catalog
  - Display that catalog using search
  - Combine cross-site publishing with variations to provide multilingual sites

With the concept of catalogs and search Web Parts that can display core data in multiple areas, cross-site publishing is no longer restricted to a single site collection, or even a farm for that matter. Another great benefit of cross-site publishing is the ability to organize your source site independent from your destination site. This capability can benefit large sites with complex security requirements. For example, you will probably want to present content in your source site in a way that is logical for the content creators (e.g., based on your company's organization charts). However, you may choose to publish the content to one or more destination sites in a completely different hierarchy—one that is more end-user-friendly.

- **Catalogs.** Any list or library can be designated as a catalog. Why is that useful? Content from catalogs can then be displayed on other sites using smart search analytics and recommendations. For example, you may want to centrally define a catalog of products or articles and then leverage that catalog to display purchasing and/or reading recommendations on various pages throughout the site.

- **Web analytics.** The new analytics engine in SharePoint 2013, based on search, features greatly improved performance, along with new reports such as popularity trends, most popular items, and historic usage.
- **Search.** With the new Content Search Web Part, you can easily leverage search to display content from multiple site collections. Unlike the Content Query Web Part, which is restricted to aggregating content within a single site collection, the Content Search Web Part enables you to look across site collections—mainly since it queries the search index, rather than the content databases themselves.
- **Navigation.** Leveraging term sets, you can supplement the existing site navigation by using managed metadata. This allows you to take advantage of the term store features such as translations, ownership, and maintaining terms in a single, easy-to-update location. In SharePoint 2010, customers found themselves writing custom code to build a functional and stylish navigation menu that was created dynamically based upon site metadata. In 2013, this functionality is available out of the box by leveraging term sets.
- **Branding.** To the user, a branded site is just a single composition that simply looks good and works. To the developer (who owns the code) and designer (who owns the look and feel), a branded site is a set of artifacts that are often owned by two different groups. SharePoint 2013 provides for greater separation of the designer and developer roles by supporting a wider array of standard tools, allowing designers to focus on designing a site using the tools that they prefer (e.g., Dreamweaver). This design can then be imported as a package to be applied to a site, at which point the developer can add controls and other technical aspects to the page—rather than having to build the page from scratch or forcing the designer to use a specific tool.
- **Device targeting:** A major shortcoming in SharePoint 2010 was inadequate channel support for devices such as phones, tablets, and other mobile devices. The new device-targeting feature allows you to specify layouts that are specific to the device that the reader might be using. For example, an airline might have a full-featured page for laptops but display only flight status and check-in when a mobile device is detected. This provides the optimal experience for users so that on a small-screen device, the page isn't cluttered or too small to read. Layouts can be added or updated as new devices come on the market.

- **Friendly URLs.** URLs that were indecipherable by the user can now be converted to something much more readable. Using managed navigation and category pages, for example, you can produce a URL such as www.contoso.com/products/bicycle. Notice that there is no more mandate for "Pages" in the URL, as previous versions of SharePoint required.
- **Digital asset management.** Using photos and videos has been greatly improved, enabling the use of video thumbnails and image renditions, whereby different-size versions of the same image can be displayed in different situations automatically. For more detail on videos and renditions, see the next section, "Additional Features."

Additional Features

Beyond the highlights mentioned so far, there are a number of additional features worth exploring when it comes to content management in SharePoint 2013. These include

- Image renditions
- Video management
- Content Organizer
- Search engine optimization (SEO)
- Usage analytics

Let's dig a little into each of these items.

Image Renditions

Image renditions allow you to display different versions of the same image in different situations. For example, you may want the full-size version of the image displayed on an article page, and a thumbnail version of the image displayed in a highlight section on the home page.

When you upload an image to a library, SharePoint will create a variety of renditions based on rendition templates (see Figure 14-1). When you add the image to your page, you can then select which rendition to use from the ribbon control (see Figure 14-2). In addition to having multiple renditions, you can edit the rendition and define a cropped area to display instead of the full image.

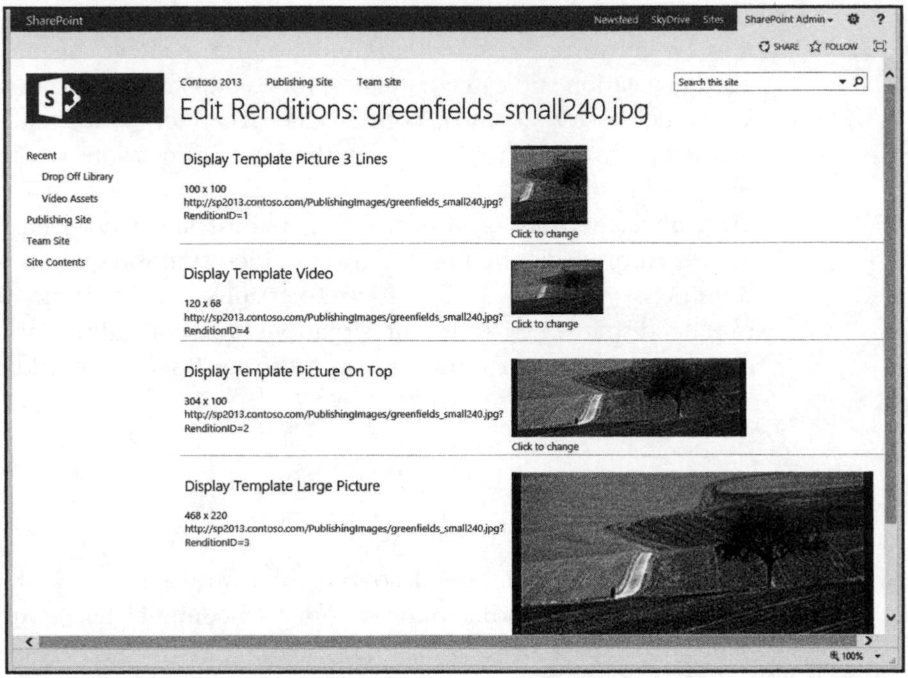

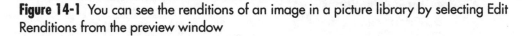

Figure 14-1 You can see the renditions of an image in a picture library by selecting Edit Renditions from the preview window

Video Management

Video management is one of many improvements included in the SharePoint 2013 asset library. The Video Content Type (see Figure 14-3) supports a thumbnail which can be taken from a video frame or from a separate image—even for cat videos. Similar to pictures, the Video Content Type also supports renditions. You can even link to external videos by saving embed code.

Content Organizer

The Content Organizer allows you to define rules-based logic to help determine where new content should be stored on your Web site. First, let's look at how to enable it. Under Site Settings, pick Content Organizer Rules. If you don't see it under Site Settings, the feature may not be activated; go to Site Features and activate it.

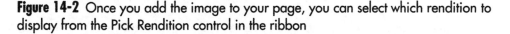

Figure 14-2 Once you add the image to your page, you can select which rendition to display from the Pick Rendition control in the ribbon

Rules can be based on any fields available to you on the specific page. These rules can help define where new content will be stored. Think of it as a wizard that understands your site topology. Figure 14-4 shows an example of a rules creation page.

This is a very nice way of controlling how new content is stored on your Web site. By setting up a few key rules, you can dictate the automatic placement of new content. This allows for consistency in how content is presented and maintained by enforcing an overall content topology.

Search Engine Optimization

Search engine optimization (SEO) helps users find information and is a key element in site adoption (or rejection). To access the SharePoint 2013 publishing site SEO configuration options, access the site home page and select "Edit SEO properties" from the Edit Properties ribbon. This opens

Figure 14-3 The asset library Video Content Type makes managing videos a lot easier by supporting thumbnails and renditions

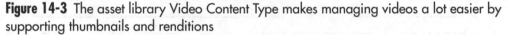

a page where you can add content that will improve the SEO of the site (see Figure 14-5). You can use the Meta Description and Keywords fields to add terms that will be picked up by search engines like Bing and Google, making your site easier to find on the Internet.

Usage Analytics

If you have a public-facing company Web site, or an internal corporate portal, knowing how your audience interacts with the content on your site is important to your ongoing improvements. SharePoint 2010 analytics were useful but had performance issues on large sites. With a new analytics platform, SharePoint 2013 has addressed these concerns while also adding many new features to better surface site usage details.

SharePoint Server 2013 includes the following default usage events:

- Views
- Recommendations displayed
- Recommendations clicked

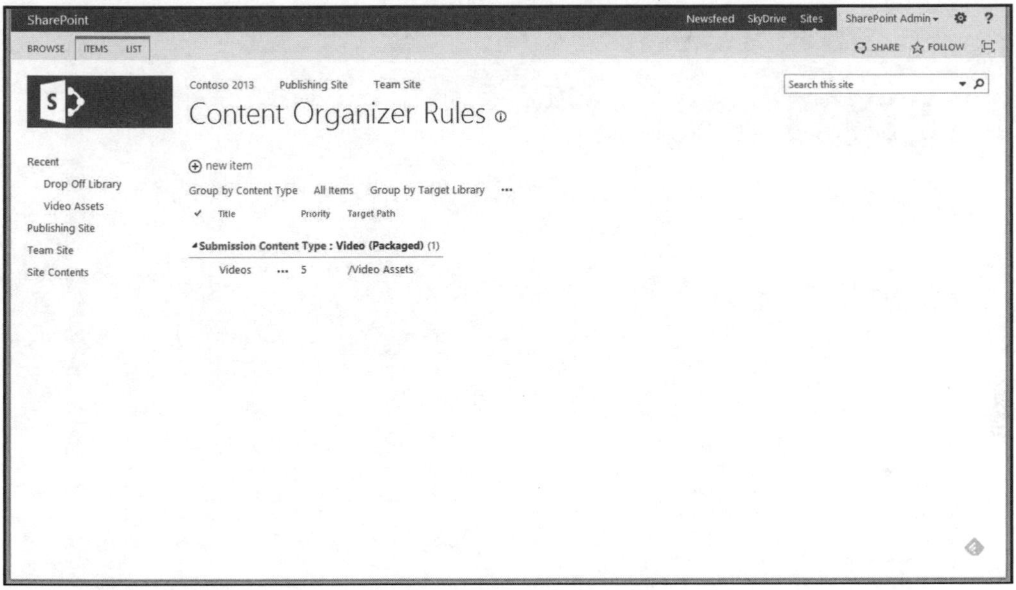

Figure 14-4 Users can create rules to determine where new content will be stored on the Web site

In addition to the default events, you can create your own custom events. An example of a custom event might be how often a page is viewed from an iPad.

Using these events, analytics performs the following analyses:

- Usage counts
- Recommendations
- Activity ranking (leverages search)

The analytics provide these reports:

- **Most Popular Items** displays ranking per usage event for all items in a library or list. An example of this is the most viewed document in a library.
- **Popularity Trends** produces an Excel report that shows the count (daily or monthly) per usage event for the item or site.

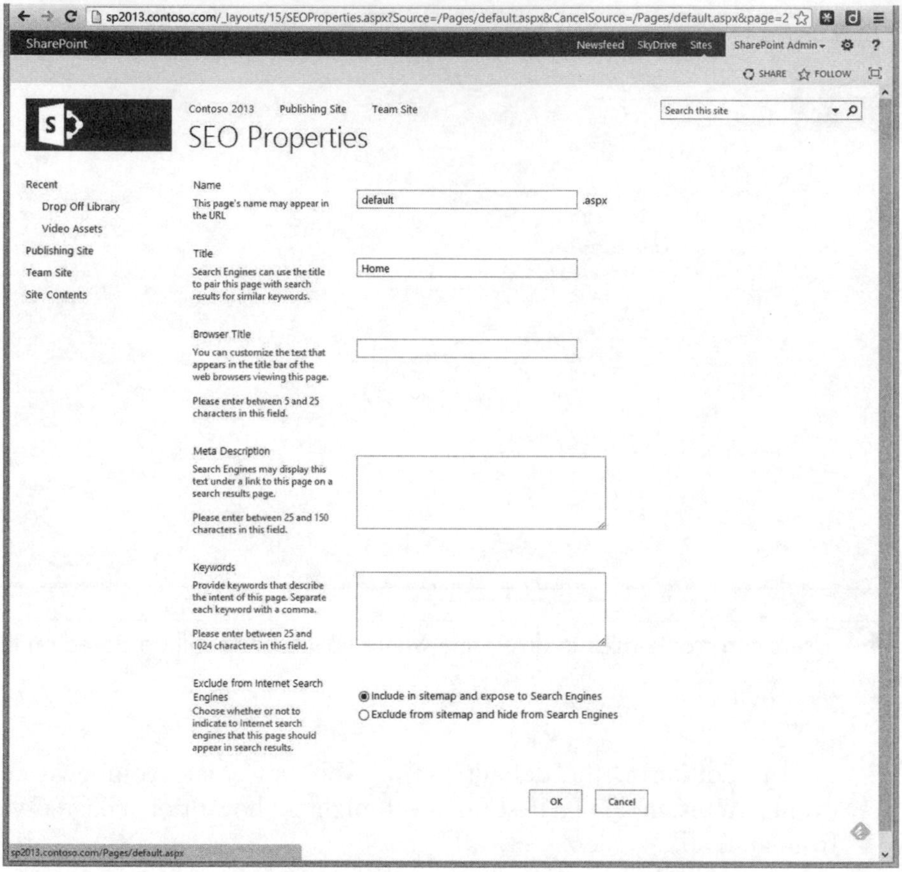

Figure 14-5 SharePoint 2013's new SEO features allow you to better describe and add properties to a page, which helps search engines find the page on the Internet

Web Content Management: The Basics

SharePoint 2013 offers the capability to manage Web content (pages, images, and HTML) in an easy way. This allows business users to author and publish Web content without having to involve IT or a Web master for each and every new page or update to a page. This enables your Internet site to take on any look and feel (unlike the default SharePoint UI that most people think of) and scale to the requirements of the world's most popular Web sites. For business users to change their page, it's as simple as clicking the Edit icon (the pencil icon at top right) in the toolbar or selecting Edit from the settings (gear) menu. They will then see their page change to "edit mode" (see Figure 14-6), where the familiar ribbon interface of Office will allow them to easily make content and formatting changes directly in the browser—eliminating the need for IT involvement. The one thing to remember is that your list of Web page editors should be well defined—and armed with guidance and policies that adhere to your overall governance strategy for Web content.

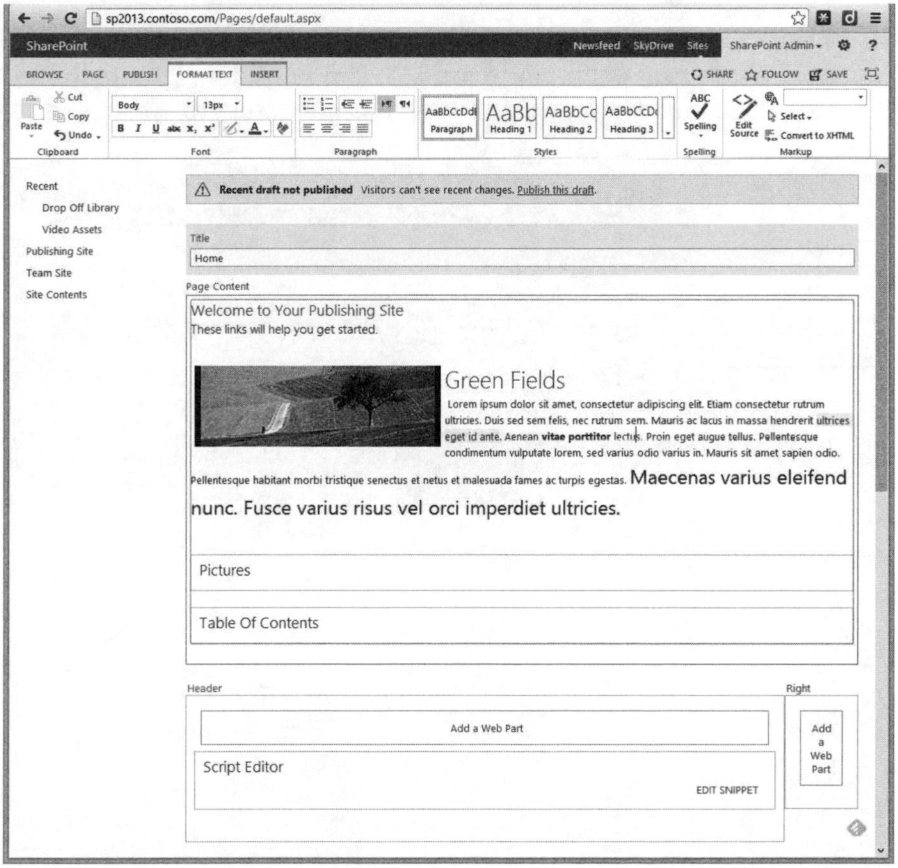

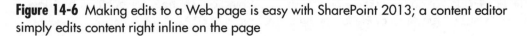

Figure 14-6 Making edits to a Web page is easy with SharePoint 2013; a content editor simply edits content right inline on the page

Finally, the page can be run through an approval process, ensuring that changes are reviewed before going live to the Internet. The ribbon provides options for publishing directly, publishing on a schedule, or putting the page through an approval process (see Figure 14-7).

There are entire books dedicated to creating, managing, and hosting Web-content-managed sites, so we won't try to recreate that information here in a few pages. Instead, we'll provide the basics of how SharePoint provides Web content management features and our recommendations on what to watch out for.

Publishing Sites

There are different kinds of site templates within SharePoint (collaboration, enterprise, publishing, custom). The Publishing Site templates provide additional features that enable business users to create and manage

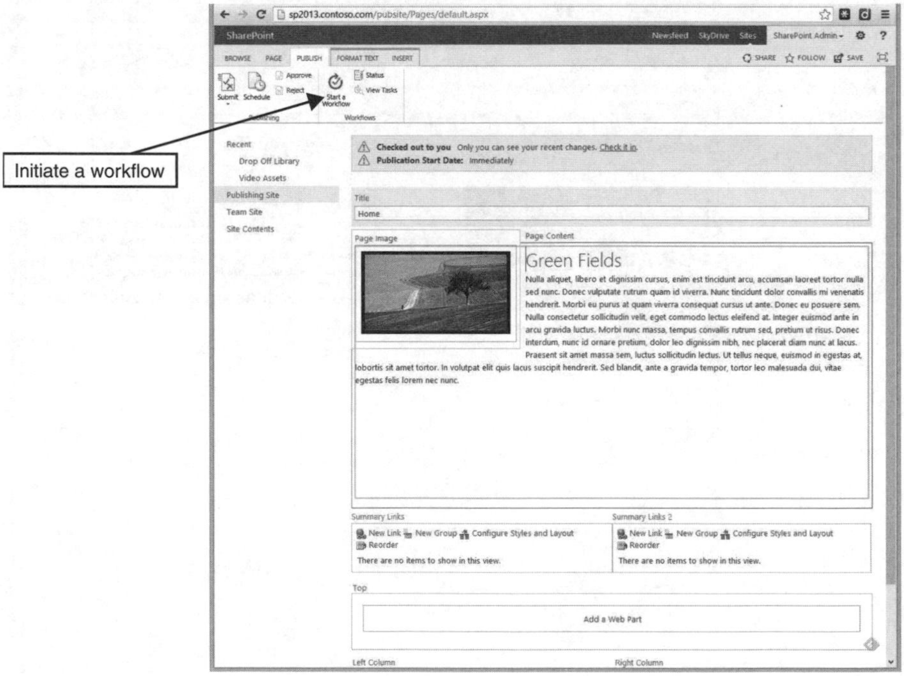

Figure 14-7 Initiating a workflow on a page or pushing out changes for publishing is done with the ribbon functions at the top of the page

Web content on a page (or create brand-new Web pages). For some people, this may sound a lot like a wiki site. Isn't a wiki site also an easy way to create new Web pages and update existing Web pages? Yes. The main difference is that wikis are geared toward sharing ideas within a community. Wikis provide Web pages that can be quickly edited to record information and then linked together through keywords, but they are far less powerful than the full-fledged Web-content-managed pages. For example, take a look at www.xbox.com. This is not a wiki—it is a highly stylized Web site with a number of controls to keep it branded properly. In publishing sites, contributors can work on draft versions of pages and publish them to make them visible to readers. Publishing sites also include document and image libraries for storing Web publishing assets such as site pages and images. You can find the Publishing Site with Workflow template within the Publishing tab of the new site wizard (see Figure 14-8).

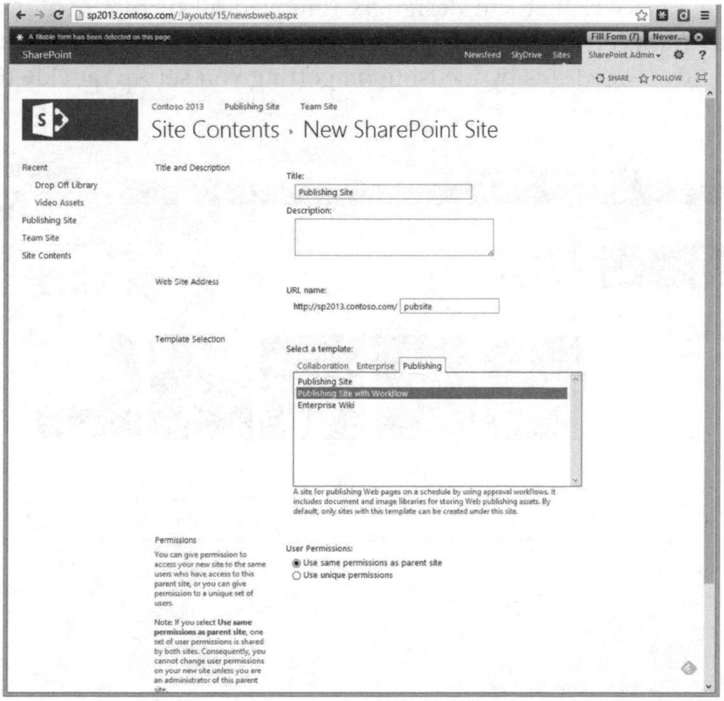

Figure 14-8 The Publishing Site template provides page layouts that contain field controls so that business users can add content without affecting the design of the page

The Web publishing features are provided by the SharePoint Publishing feature. This means that you can add publishing features to any SharePoint site. Try the following: Create a regular SharePoint team site. Next, click the gear icon and then select "Site settings" (see Figure 14-9). Under Site Administration, select Site Features. Enable the Publishing feature by clicking Activate next to SharePoint Server Publishing (see Figure 14-10). Go back to your site; it will look the same at first. But if you look more closely, you'll notice some key changes. For example, in the Site Actions menu, Design Manager has replaced "Change the look" (see Figure 14-11), and you will see additional apps on the Site Contents page.

Although the Publishing feature can be used with any SharePoint site, you'll probably plan to use it more for consumer-based sites. Previous versions of SharePoint provided *starter templates*, such as the Internet Presence template, and the previous Publishing Site template, which contained stub-out images and content as well as sub-sites for search, news, and other items. These templates were also branded out of the box. The reality is that site designers removed all of that content and design and replaced it with company branding and content. Microsoft has now acknowledged this by focusing on getting you set up quickly to apply your

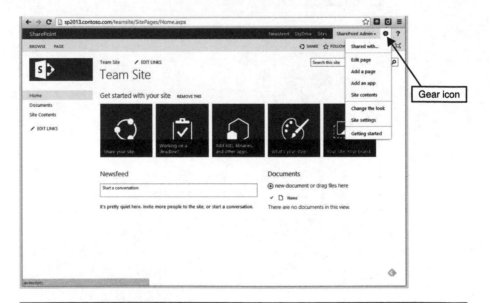

Figure 14-9 Site settings are available by clicking on the Site Actions menu (gear icon)

Figure 14-10 The Publishing Site feature can be activated in Site Settings

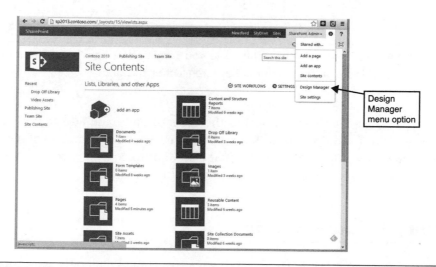

Figure 14-11 After enabling the Publishing feature within a site, users with appropriate permissions will see publishing options such as Design Manager as well as more apps

own brand and implement content. Instead of the typical SharePoint starter content home page, the first publishing site you will create starts with a task-based page that will walk you step by step through the process of creating your branded site (see Figure 14-12).

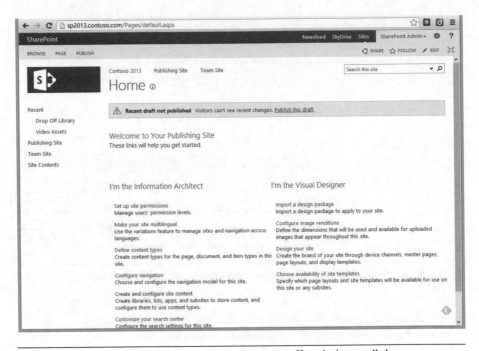

Figure 14-12 The first publishing site you create offers links to all the areas you need to focus on as an information architect or designer

Once you have completed the tasks to build and add content to your site, you should remove the task list that is composed of two Web Parts that are easily deleted. You might also want to consider creating your own "starter" site if you plan to work on multiple publishing projects.

Branding a SharePoint Site

So far we've taken you through some functional elements associated with content on your site. However, there is still a big part of WCM related to defining and managing the user experience (UX). In fact, some would argue that the user experience is the true measure of the overall success of an Internet-facing Web site.

What is UX? A user's experience on a Web site can be segmented into four categories: branding, usability, functionality, and content. One segment is no more important than the others; they all need to be optimized for users to embrace and appreciate the overall experience of interacting with a Web site. To this point we've touched upon how SharePoint 2013 offers certain functional elements to make it easier for visitors to navigate and discover information, where the focus has been on making it easy to update and present important content on the Web site. Let's extend our discussion into a key UX segment: branding.

Does Figure 14-13 look like a typical SharePoint site? This is a standard SharePoint publishing site to which we have applied custom branding. By using SharePoint 2013 and its adherence to standard branding techniques, it's easier than ever to make great-looking SharePoint sites.

Figure 14-13 A SharePoint site does not have to look bland. Applying a slick design greatly enhances the user experience

Branding is an essential part of any Web site. It defines the aesthetic appeal and visual presentation of your Web pages. At the highest level, branding provides visitors with an engaging experience (which increases the likelihood that they will buy your product or at least return for another visit). To create a strong impact, remember that branding is about consistency: consistency among the Web pages (in terms of color palette, content organization, layout, and navigation) and consistency with the brand identity (as it relates to an organization's other public materials like print collateral). In addition, graphics, collateral, and multimedia are all part of branding and are used to add value to the overall experience.

With regard to SharePoint 2013, you have to consider the following elements to help you define and build your brand:

- Master pages
- Page layouts
- Web Parts
- Themes
- Design Manager

Master Pages

Master pages define the look and feel and standard behavior that affect all of the Web pages in a site. For those familiar with SharePoint 2007 or 2010, master pages function similarly in SharePoint 2013—but the way you create them has changed somewhat. The concept is that a master page defines a template for how content will be presented, and that template is applied to all associated pages so you don't have to keep building pages from scratch. In addition, the use of a template makes the propagation of changes to all pages quick and seamless.

When you create a new publishing site, you have two master pages to choose from: Seattle and Oslo. There does not appear to be much difference between the two other than page layout (Seattle displays a Quick Launch menu on the left; Oslo does not).

If you browse to the Master Page Gallery, you will also see a master page called "v4.master"—this master page supports upgrading from SharePoint 2010 sites.

To change the master page associated with your site, go to Site Actions → Site Settings, then select "master pages." You can change the master page by altering the selection shown on the master page administration screen, as seen in Figure 14-14.

If you are planning to create a custom master page, you can use the new Design Manager to either start with a "minimal" master page, or you can create a new master page from existing HTML.

The core feature of Design Manager is that it converts your HTML design into a SharePoint master page. To render successfully, a SharePoint master page must contain many ASP.NET elements and elements that are specific to SharePoint. When you convert an HTML file to a master page, Design Manager creates a .master file that contains all of these required elements, so you don't have to know about them (at least not right away). During conversion, some HTML markup, such as comments, gets added to your original HTML file.

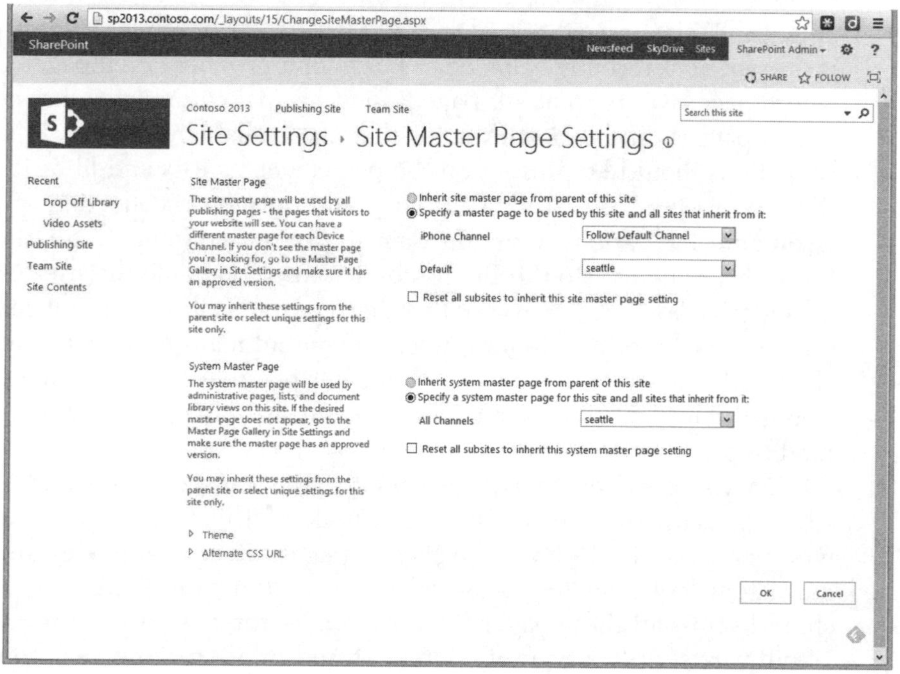

Figure 14-14 You can alter the selected master page for your site by changing the option on the master page screen

After the conversion, your HTML file and the SharePoint master page are associated, so that when you edit and save the HTML file in your mapped drive, the master page is updated automatically. In Design Manager, the HTML master page has a property named Associated File that determines whether changes to the HTML file are synced to the .master file.

As we mentioned, Design Manager also provides an option to begin your design by using a minimal master page. In this scenario, you don't have to begin with an HTML design; instead, you can create an HTML master page that contains the minimum page elements necessary to render the master page correctly in SharePoint, and then build out your design by editing the HTML master page.

Page Layouts

Master pages are an essential component of a good Web site as they establish a consistent look and feel. However, content presentation across an entire Web site might need to be different. For example, a home page is presented differently from a news page or a product detail page. That's where page layouts come in. Page layouts are page templates that define how a page should look, the fields that are available, and exactly which collections should be present on the page (such as lists and libraries). In the construction of a Web site, you would develop a collection of page layouts for the various ways you want to present content. In SharePoint Web sites, you activate the Publishing features to enable the use of publishing page layouts. The use of these page layouts allows content submitters to work directly in their browser for content management and submit changes for approval when done. While it is possible to create a new page layout through the browser UI, you should use SharePoint Designer to modify it.

Do you need custom page layouts? For most custom publishing sites, the answer is probably yes. Think of the master page as the wrapper around all of your Web site pages. This wrapper enforces a consistent look and feel as it relates to content or graphics that are shared across all these pages (i.e., header, footer, navigation, etc.). Page layouts are simply a type of content stored in SharePoint that controls how content is presented and is unique to the page, or at least the type of page (see Figure 14-15). As mentioned, you might have one page layout for your home page, another that is used on your various

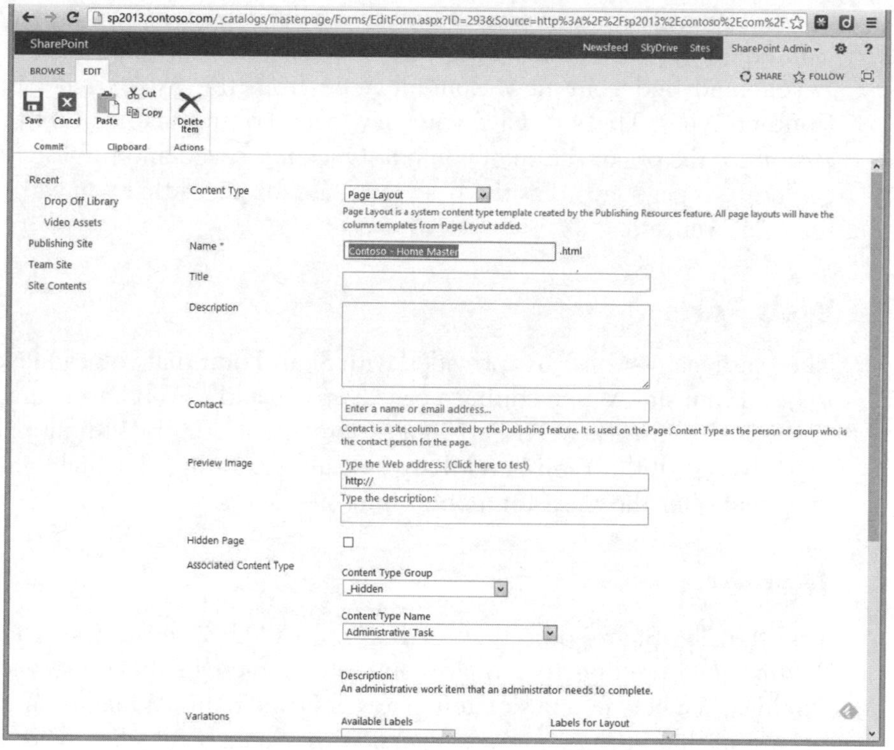

Figure 14-15 Content Types are stored in the Master Page Gallery. The properties allow you to associate a master page with a Content Type

product pages (which may show different content but should show it in a similar way to other product pages), another that is used when only simple HTML is needed, and another when you are pulling data from SharePoint lists.

Note For more information on the SharePoint 2013 page model, visit http://msdn.microsoft.com/en-us/library/jj191506.aspx.

After you create a new Content Type, you can create a new page layout from it. Before you do this, make sure your Content Type has any additional custom Columns that you might need for your content presentation. Now, in SharePoint Designer 2013, open the Web site for which you want to create the page layout. From the menu, select New → SharePoint Content. From the dialog box, click SharePoint Publishing. Click Page Layout and find your new Content Type from the list of Page Layout Content Types. That's it. Give your new page layout a name and title and customize the organization of content. Once it is saved and published, you can use this page layout as the base template for pages that you will create for your Web site.

Web Parts

There are many Web Parts provided with SharePoint that you can leverage to build your site. When editing a page, you can add a Web Part in any Web Part zone or insert a Web Part in a page content editor. Without exhaustively listing all the Web Parts that you can use, Table 14-1 highlights the ones that offer the most for a publishing site.

Themes

Traditionally, SharePoint themes have provided a quick way to apply *lightweight* branding to a SharePoint site—much in the same way you would switch between design templates in PowerPoint. While themes have been available in many previous versions of SharePoint, they were rarely used, mainly because the options were limited (i.e., "all or nothing") and they included only the most basic of formatting—primarily CSS styling for colors and fonts.

With SharePoint 2013, theming has been completely redesigned to make the experience more powerful and a lot easier. The user interface to manage and apply the themes has a fresh and simple look. To see this interface, perform the following steps:

1. Open Design Manager. The Welcome page displays.
2. On the Welcome page, click "Pick a pre-installed look." The "Change the look" page will appear (see Figure 14-16).

After selecting your theme, you will be able to further refine it by selecting such properties as color, layout, and fonts (see Figure 14-17).

The "try it out" link gives you the ability to preview your theme applied to your site before you commit to it (see Figure 14-18).

Table 14-1 SharePoint 2013 Web Parts Most Commonly Used in Internet Publishing Sites

Web Part	Category	Description
Content Query	Content Rollup	Displays a dynamic view of content from your site
Content Search	Content Rollup	Allows you to show items that are results of a search query you specify
Summary Links	Content Rollup	Allows authors to create links that can be grouped and styled
Content Editor	Media and Content	Allows authors to enter rich text content
Media	Media and Content	Used to embed media clips (video and audio) in a Web page
Picture Library Slideshow	Media and Content	Used to display a slideshow of images and photos from a picture library
Pictures	Search-Drive Content	Shows any items that are derived from the Picture or Image Content Type
Popular Items	Search-Drive Content	Shows items that have been recently viewed by many users
Videos	Search-Drive Content	Shows any items that are derived from the Video Content Type, sorted by number of views

Design Manager

While the individual components of branding have changed little in SharePoint 2013 (master pages, page layouts, and themes), the most significant change from previous versions is how to implement these elements to brand your site. As we've mentioned previously, SharePoint 2013 offers a new feature called Design Manager as part of a publishing site. Design Manager (see Figure 14-19) allows you to create a custom branded design using the Web design tools that your design team is used to (Dreamweaver, for example).

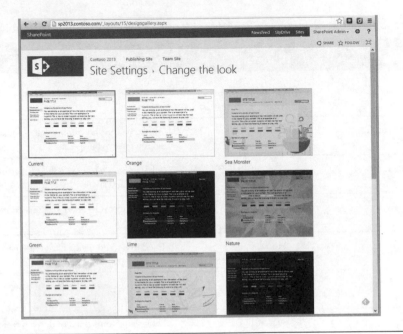

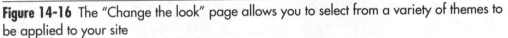

Figure 14-16 The "Change the look" page allows you to select from a variety of themes to be applied to your site

With Design Manager, you can

- Manage device channels
- Upload design files
- Edit master pages
- Edit display templates
- Edit page layouts
- Publish and apply a design
- Create a design package

Managing Device Channels

With your users relying more and more on mobile devices, it is critical that you provide an acceptable experience for users who may access your site from a tablet or phone or an alternate browser. This was very challenging (if not impossible) in earlier versions of SharePoint. SharePoint 2013 addresses this using Device Manager and device channels (see Figure 14-20).

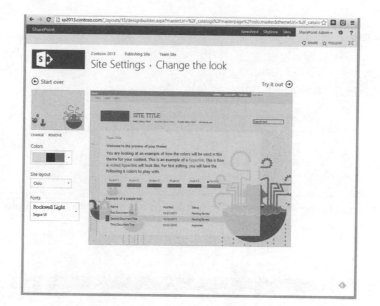

Figure 14-17 Once you select your theme, you can modify it by selecting a different color scheme, site layout, and fonts

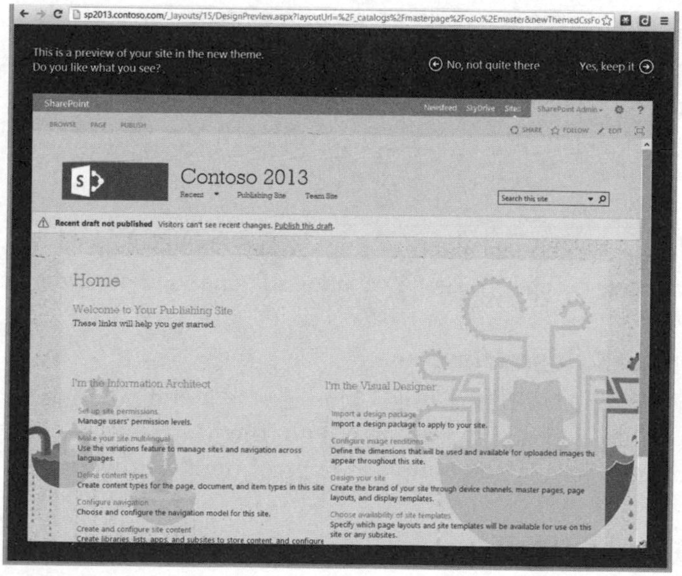

Figure 14-18 Previewing your theme lets you take a quick look to see what it may look like when applied to your site

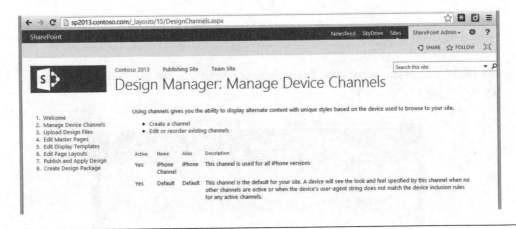

Figure 14-19 The Design Manager in SharePoint 2013 makes it easy to implement a custom design as part of your brand

Figure 14-20 The device channel manager ships with a default channel. You can add several more channels to support iPhone, Windows Phone, and other devices

Upload Design Files

This function of the Design Manager is a simple page to explain where your uploaded design files should go (the Master Page Gallery). It is a little odd that there is not an upload control right on this page.

Edit Master Pages

This page displays the master pages. It allows you to upload HTML pages and have them converted to SharePoint master pages. You can also create a minimal master page directly from here.

Edit Display Templates

Search results and other search-related Web Parts rely on display templates to control the appearance and behavior of search results. This page displays all the site control templates. All of these control templates are stored in the Display Templates folder of the Master Page Gallery.

Edit Page Layouts

This page displays existing page layouts and also allows you to create a new page layout.

Publish and Apply Design

Once you have all the design elements in place, you can apply them to your site from this page. Clicking the link to assign master pages brings up the Site Master Page Settings page (see Figure 14-21), where you select the master page for each device.

Create Design Package

With your new design in place, you may want to save it and apply it to a different site. Design Manager allows you to save your design as a complete exportable package. This will create a SharePoint solution file (.wsp) that can be imported and applied in another site. This solution file contains all the master pages, page layouts, and other elements that make up the design. To import a design package, navigate to the Design Manager Welcome page and click the link to import a design package.

The Content Editor Experience

One of the themes you will hear a lot about with SharePoint 2013 is the notion of a richer user experience. Let's take a minute to explain what that means. Fundamentally, when we talk about ease of use with SharePoint, it is centered on allowing users to gain the most functionality with the least amount of intrusion (defined as required training or tools). SharePoint 2013 handles this by offering improvements in two key areas. The first, as discussed previously, is the ability to make many, if not all, page edits right on the page (i.e., fewer clicks). This allows users to easily see the impact of the changes without having to go to a different page or tool to do so.

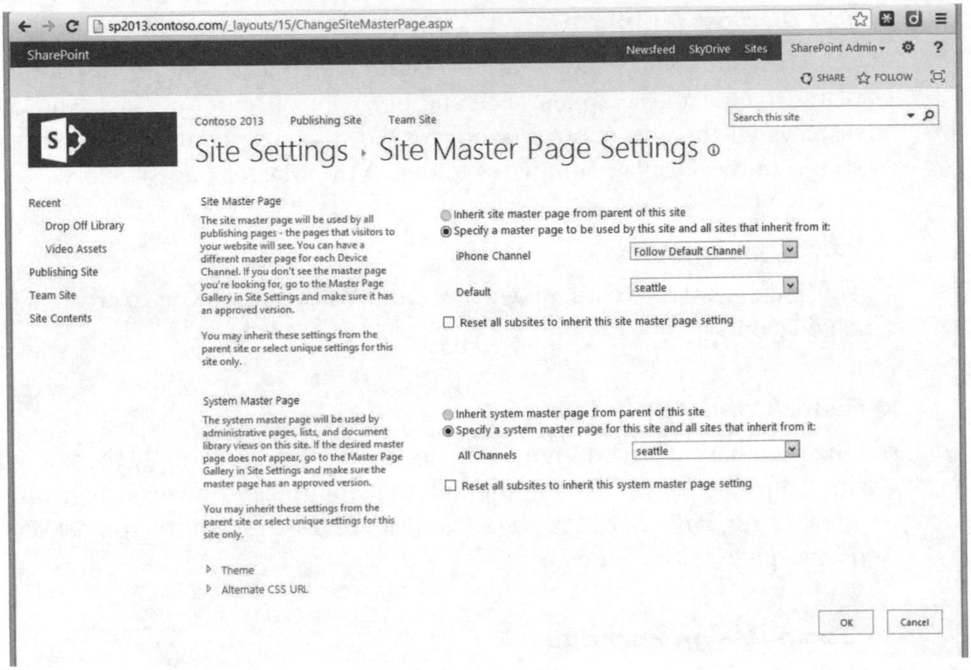

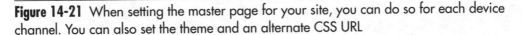

Figure 14-21 When setting the master page for your site, you can do so for each device channel. You can also set the theme and an alternate CSS URL

More important, for SharePoint users who don't use Internet Explorer, this experience also holds for Safari, Firefox, and Chrome. Users with the appropriate permissions can get to this mode in one click and begin to make changes immediately.

Another important improvement in the user experience is the ability to better manage rich content. The Content Editor Web Part (CEWP) is still a very powerful native Web Part based solely on its simplicity. Just type in the box and format the content accordingly—no Web development or HTML skills required! However, in some ways the CEWP is not needed with WCM. With SharePoint 2013, you can add content practically anywhere on the page. You are now entering data in field controls, not the CEWP text box, and have more freedom to decide where and how HTML is presented.

While the field control worked well in SharePoint 2010 also, it has been much improved for SharePoint 2013. A bit of a downfall of previous versions was the lack of support for pasting in content from editors such as Microsoft Word. Previously, the result of pasting in content was very

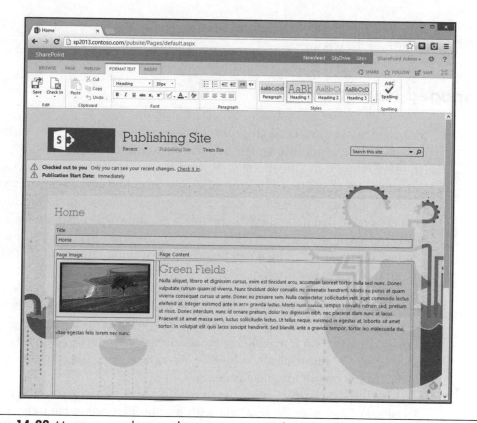

Figure 14-22 Users can make text changes on a page by using the improved field controls

unpredictable and often simply would not work at all. Now, when you paste in content, the styles associated with the layout will be applied to the pasted text. This makes bulk editing a lot easier, as often when you are loading a new site you will be loading the content from other Web sites or Word documents. You also have the options to control how you paste from the paste icon. You can choose to Paste as is, Paste Clean, or Paste Plaintext. A feature as simple as this is very welcome to a Web site content manager. Figure 14-22 shows the new field control in action, whereby a content editor can edit right in place using a WYSIWYG interface.

What does this have to do with WCM? Simple. It allows more freedom to manage the content on the Web site, and it allows more users to be empowered to make changes and to easily deploy those changes right to the Web. This offers the potential to change the way companies manage their Internet-facing content. Intranet site was altered with the enablement of the employee community, There is a potential with SharePoint

2013 to change the way Internet-facing content is managed and, more important, by whom.

Managed Navigation

Managed navigation in SharePoint 2013 enables web designers to build navigation for a publishing site by using a managed metadata taxonomy (the term store). In SharePoint 2010, you had to either base navigation on the structure of a site, or use a custom method like a site map provider. By using managed navigation, you can design site navigation around business concepts, maintained by the people who know that business the best. Managed navigation also enables you to create friendly URLs (no more "Pages" in the URL), which can help Search Engine Optimization (SEO) and simply make more sense.

To use managed navigation, you simply enable it under Navigation Settings on the site collection. (Managed navigation is enabled by default for Publishing site collections and Enterprise Wiki site collections.) When managed navigation is enabled, two additional settings are also enabled: new pages are automatically added to navigation, and friendly URLs are automatically created for new pages.

Managed navigation works by enabling you to map your terms to global and local navigation, along with an automatically generated page. You can define the page that is generated by setting attributes on the term in the navigation term set itself. You can specify values for a friendly URL, a target page (the page to show when the actual URL is visited), and a catalog item page (which allows you to specify a page that is loaded when a visitor views an item from the product catalog that is tagged with the term). Figure 14-23 shows an example of a term set that is used for managed navigation mapped to a sample page layout.

While managed navigation is great for dynamically controlling your navigation taxonomy, the key downside is that your navigation will only work within a single site collection. In addition, the lack of publishing and approval workflows means that changes take effect immediately. For example, there is no version control on terms. If you make a change to a term, you can't later revert the change back to an earlier version of the term. In addition, there is no publishing workflow on terms. As soon as you make a change to a term, the new term will appear in navigation (unless you hide the term(s) from navigation until the content is published and indexed by search).

Our recommendation is to leverage the managed navigation feature if you want to have consistent navigation within a site collection (for example,

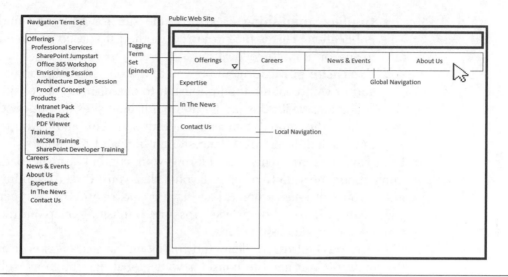

Figure 14-23 Managed navigation enables you to use a term set for your global and local navigation, providing a more dynamic and easier-to-maintain technique for managing your navigation taxonomy

in an intranet or Internet site), mainly since it allows you to de-couple the actual structure of your site from the navigation itself—an extremely useful capability. And although you'll be able to change your navigation easily, don't be tempted to change it without planning. You must carefully plan your global navigation taxonomy since you don't want your primary global navigation to change often—it will just confuse users.

Managed navigation is great for dynamically keeping your detailed (local) navigation up-to-date, maintaining your navigation separately from your site structure, and for creating sites that show catalogs of information, since you can combine friendly URLs, automatically generated product pages, and search keywords for an easy-to-use interface for users. Just beware of the limitations.

Planning for Web Content Management

Before you jump into building your new site, step back for a minute and think through all the factors that you need to consider for your site:

- **Plan for publishing.** When considering how you want to publish your content, you need to consider if you want to do it in place or use a push model.

- **In-place publishing** uses the same site for authoring and publication. This is the preferred method if you do not need to author in multiple locations.
- **Cross-site publishing** allows you to use one site collection to author your content, then publish it to one or more target site collections. With this model, the publishing sites do not need to have the same design as the author site. This allows you to provide a different experience for authors and consumers.

- **Plan for content.** When considering your content, you need to think about the variety of page layouts that you need. At a minimum, you will need a home page layout and one or more inner page layouts. If you chose to use cross-site publishing, map out the content source and destinations.

- **Plan for navigation.** A clean and functional navigation is critical for your site. You need to consider your global navigation as well as page navigation (or quick links). With SharePoint 2013, you can leverage the Managed Metadata Service and term stores to build your navigation. Plan your term sets to use for global and faceted navigation.

- **Plan for devices.** With more and more users accessing sites from phones and tablets, you need to factor these devices into your site. Plan for page layouts for the various devices that you intend to support.

- **Plan for branding.** Branding is an important consideration for any published site. Consider whether you are going to use standard master page deployment or the new Design Manager.

- **Plan for multiple languages.** If you intend to provide content in multiple translations, you need to plan for implementing variations and how you are going to support the translations. Even if you do not initially plan to deploy more than one language, if it is a possibility in the future, you should implement variations now so the ability is in place.

- **Plan for search.** Search is critical for any Web site, and with SharePoint 2013 you have no excuse to not provide a great search experience.

- **Plan for content approval.** With any publishing site, it's often easy to leave the approval process to the last minute. The earlier you can think about and plan for this, the better, so you are not scrambling at the end to implement your process. To plan for approval, you need to consider the flow process. Will the default publishing approval be sufficient? Who will be involved?

Putting It All Together: A WCM Strategy

OK, let's say you have read the previous pages, are an existing SharePoint user (internal only), and are excited about the potential of using SharePoint 2013 to refresh your Internet presence. Where do you begin? Let's start with some key questions about the current site:

- How much of your current Web content is static HTML?
- Do you post documents on your Web site?
- Who manages and approves content on your Web site?
- What is the process for submitting new content to your Web site?
- Do you track user activity on your Web site?
- What is the competitive advantage of having a new Web site?
- Who "owns" the Web site?
- How much external content is repurposed from internal content?

Do you know the answers to all of these questions? If not, the first step is to assemble a team of representative internal resources who, collectively, can answer them. Once you have these answers, you are ready for design sessions. The goal of these sessions is to lay out an overall information architecture for your Web content, defining what goes where, who will manage it, how content is deployed, and how you will monitor user activity. Think about some of the new features highlighted earlier in this chapter. All may not be right for you, but because your organization has already invested in SharePoint, you will recognize obvious gains by leveraging an existing technology and empowering another group of users and consumers. Here are additional questions to ponder once you have more details on your SharePoint Web site:

- How will your users use search to find content?
- Should you "push" content from the intranet to sections of the Web site?
- How important is the site branding?
- Will the site be in multiple languages?

- Will there still be a Web master or will ownership be distributed?
- What is the long-term vision for the Web site?

Think about how your employees have changed the way the business processes work inside your organization as SharePoint has been widely used. Extend that now to include changes in how your customers or prospects learn about who you are and what you do based on the content that you present. Dynamic organizations have dynamic Web sites. It's time to stop apologizing for your old static Web site and realize that it is an asset that can be leveraged for competitive business gains.

Key Points

This chapter provided some suggestions for using the WCM features of SharePoint 2013. In general, there are many features to take advantage of for your site. Some of our recommendations are:

- Leverage the Design Manager to separate your design from your content.
- Plan your content distribution, and leverage cross-site publishing to reuse content in multiple sites.
- Use Content Organizer rules to automate the placement of new content.
- Optimize your site design and content for multiple devices using device channels.
- Enable more users to participate in the management of Web-based content.
- Optimize your content by analyzing the usage reports and set up key alerts for monitoring activities.

CHAPTER 15

PLANNING FOR SOCIAL COMPUTING

On Thursday, October 4, 2012, the CEO of Facebook, Mark Zuckerberg, updated his status to announce that "there are more than one billion people using Facebook actively every month."[1] If Facebook were a country, it would be the third-largest in the world. A research study published by comScore in late 2011 found that "nearly 1 in every 5 minutes spent online is now spent on social networking sites."[2] Clearly, social computing technologies are deeply integrated into popular culture. But while consumers are leveraging social networking solutions such as Facebook, Twitter, and LinkedIn, enterprise social computing has been slower to take off. Many organizations are just beginning to try to determine the business value of these tools.

SharePoint 2013 includes a vast new collection of social computing capabilities, and with the acquisition of Yammer in July 2012, it is clear that the direction for SharePoint and for Microsoft in general is getting more social. However, just as social technologies have changed the way many people live, social technologies have the potential to transform how people work. That transformation often comes with a significant amount of change and disruption to organizational hierarchies, processes, and cultures. While it is technically possible to just "turn on" the social features of SharePoint and see what happens, smart organizations carefully consider both the technical features and the organizational change impact before they leap into the new world of social computing in SharePoint 2013.

---

1. Mark Zuckerberg, Facebook update, October 4, 2012. Retrieved from https://www.facebook.com/ajax/sharer/?s=22&appid=25554907596&p%5B0%5D=4&p%5B1%5D=10100518568346671
2. comScore, Inc., "It's a Social World: Top 10 Need-to-Knows About Social Networking and Where It's Headed," comScore.com, December 21, 2011. www.comscore.com/Press_Events/Presentations_Whitepapers/2011/it_is_a_social_world_top_10_need-to-knows_about_social_networking, accessed October 6, 2012

What's New in SharePoint 2013?

While SharePoint has had social capabilities in previous releases, earlier versions lacked some of the core features that consumers have come to expect in social tools, such as the ability to use @mentions, likes, and #hashtags in activity posts. Social features have had a complete overhaul in SharePoint 2013, and as Yammer becomes more integrated, these features will continue to evolve.

The following list highlights the primary new social features in SharePoint 2013:

- **My Site evolution, including rich microblogging capabilities.** In earlier versions of SharePoint, users had a personal site that functioned as the hub for interacting with others in the organization. For SharePoint 2013, the My Site branding has been deemphasized and the functionality has evolved to better support discovery of social information, task management, and sharing documents. The set of features formerly known as My Site comprises four key functional areas, as shown in Table 15-1.

Table 15-1 New Personal Features in SharePoint 2013

Feature	Summary of Capabilities
Newsfeed	The newsfeed in SharePoint 2013 is a "microblog" where users can post short messages. Think of the newsfeed as "Twitter for the enterprise." It's like a blog because one person posts and others can reply—but it's not for long messages because you are limited to 512 characters. The newsfeed provides the ability to "follow" people, tags, sites, and individual documents. Every SharePoint 2013 user can have a personal newsfeed where the content that is posted is shared with the entire organization. Teams can also have a site feed in their team site, which is a type of newsfeed secured just to the people who have access to that site. When you make a post in the site feed of a team site, the post will show up only on the personal newsfeed of someone who has access to and is following the team site. When you make a post to the general organizational newsfeed, it can be seen by anyone in the organization. In order to post to a site feed, you need Contribute permissions for that site. Site feed and newsfeed posts can appear in search results, but site feed contents are security trimmed so that they will never appear in search results for someone who doesn't have access to the site.

Feature	Summary of Capabilities
	Until the release of SharePoint 2013, organizations interested in providing microblogging and activity post capabilities internally had to leverage products such as Jive, Yammer, Chatter, NewsGator, and Neudesic Pulse. One of the big challenges for organizations that also use SharePoint for collaboration has been the requirement to purchase and integrate these separate products in order to create a consistent user experience. Even with integration, in previous SharePoint releases, the user experience could feel disjointed since users may have needed to log in to different systems to see their aggregated activity feed aligned with their core document, workflow, and task management collaboration activities. With SharePoint 2013, microblogging and activity feed content are directly incorporated in an individual's personal site, and as Yammer becomes even more integrated into SharePoint, you will have more options for best-in-class microblogging and community collaboration in a completely connected user experience.
	Every fully licensed SharePoint 2013 user can have a personal newsfeed where the content that is posted is shared with the entire organization. (Guest users do not have access to a newsfeed.)
	Though Yammer is not technically fully integrated into SharePoint as of this writing, organizations have the option of replacing the SharePoint 2013 Newsfeed with Yammer as their microblogging platform, and Microsoft has announced (and is continuing to evolve) a detailed plan for Yammer integration with SharePoint.* In this chapter, unless specifically called out, we will use the term *newsfeed* to refer to the concept of microblogging, whether you are leveraging the SharePoint 2013 Newsfeed or Yammer.
SkyDrive Pro	SkyDrive Pro replaces the default shared documents and personal documents libraries that were part of earlier My Sites. The functionality is similar to other SharePoint document libraries but is also accessible via a constant link in the main SharePoint navigation bar. The SkyDrive Pro desktop client (formerly SharePoint Workspace) enables you to sync your documents and work offline by integrating directly into Windows Explorer.
	SkyDrive Pro is personal storage for each SharePoint user in your organization. In Office 365/SharePoint Online, each user gets 7GB of space that is not counted against the overall pooled SharePoint storage quota that is allocated to the organization. In an individual SkyDrive Pro library, a user can synchronize up to 20,000 items and no single file can be greater than 250MB in size. Microsoft is working to increase these storage limits in future updates of SharePoint Online. In SharePoint on-premises, you can determine what the default storage space is for each SkyDrive Pro user.
	Your users may be familiar with SkyDrive, the consumer service with nearly the same name, which provides consumers with 7GB of free cloud storage and is similar to other public file-sharing services such as Dropbox. The consumer version of SkyDrive has nothing to do with SharePoint and doesn't support any of the advanced functionality that is available only with SkyDrive Pro, such as document versioning and alerts. SkyDrive Pro allows your users to work with business documents offline. SkyDrive "consumer" is for personal, non-business content.

(continues)

Table 15-1 New Personal Features in SharePoint 2013 *(continued)*

Feature	Summary of Capabilities
"About me"	"About me" is where users update their profiles and list areas of interest and topics that others may ask questions about. The search function uses this information to identify subject matter experts based on keywords.
Tasks	My Tasks is the area where users can centrally view and manage items assigned to them across SharePoint, Exchange, and Project Server. Users can also mark a newsfeed post or reply for follow-up so that it will show up in their My Tasks list.

*In March 2013, Microsoft announced updates to the integration roadmap for Yammer initially outlined at the SharePoint Conference in November 2012. Not all of the details were announced by the time this book went to print, but the March blog post can be found at http://blogs.office.com/b/sharepoint/archive/2013/03/19/yammer-and-sharepoint-enterprise-social-roadmap-update.aspx. Refer to the end of this chapter for a brief discussion of what to expect in the Yammer integration roadmap.

- **Conversation concepts.** In SharePoint 2010, users were able to post a status update in their activity feed, but the activity feed capability in SharePoint 2010 was not interactive. In SharePoint 2013, users have a rich interactive capability in both the new newsfeed and the enhanced discussion forums. Table 15-2 lists key SharePoint 2013 conversation concepts.
- **Support for communities.** Communities are groups of people who collaborate around common goals. SharePoint's support for communities at the time of this writing is better thought of as an "embarrassment of riches" rather than a "one size fits all" approach. Both Yammer and the new Community Site template provide an opportunity to encourage people in your organization to share both tacit and explicit knowledge in an engaging, feature-rich environment. A community might choose to leverage one or perhaps both enabling technologies, and until the integration between Yammer and SharePoint is as extensive as the native SharePoint capabilities including the new Community Site template, you will need to consider your specific use cases and desired outcomes in order to make the best decision about which tool to use to support the communities of interest or practice in your organization. Microsoft has been clear about recommending

Table 15-2 New Conversation Concepts in SharePoint 2013

Concept	Description
Post	A post is an initial message created by a user in the newsfeed or in a discussion list. A post can also be system-generated. A newsfeed post that shows you that someone has updated a document you are following is an example of a system-generated post.
Reply	A reply is a response to a post. A reply can be made by the person who created the post (for example, to provide clarification) or by someone else.
Follow	Following is an action taken by a user that indicates interest in a specific document, person, site, or tag. When you follow a document, activities related to that document are reported in your newsfeed.
Mention	When you create a post or a reply, you can refer to other users by mentioning them. To mention someone in a post, you place an @ symbol in front of the person's name. As you are typing, the user profile service in SharePoint 2013 returns a list of names that match what you have entered. When people are mentioned in a post or reply, they receive a system-generated activity in their newsfeed and an e-mail that alerts them to the mention. Users also have a mentions view on their newsfeed where they can see all posts in which they have been mentioned.
Hashtag	When you post or reply, you can associate the item with a topic by using a hashtag. To assign a hashtag, you place the number # symbol in front of the term that you want to include in the hashtag. The managed metadata service returns a list of terms that match your entry based on hashtags entered by other users. When a post contains hashtags, the newsfeed displays an activity related to that hashtag, and users who follow that hashtag see the activity in their newsfeed. Using hashtags helps focus attention on a specific topic and can be used to filter posts and replies in search. Hashtags must be entered as one word and are not stored in the same term set as enterprise keywords, which can include multiple words. For example, if you wanted to assign a hashtag for Business Development, you could enter #BusinessDevelopment. Entering #Business Development would count only "Business" as the associated hashtag.
Like	When someone makes a post or replies to a post, other people can "like" the post or reply. Likes provide a method to collect support for a post or indicate agreement. In your personal SharePoint 2013 newsfeed, you can use the likes view to look at the newsfeed activities that you have previously liked. Likes can also be used to indicate support in discussion forums. Within a community or team site with a community-enabled discussion board, members can improve their reputation by building up likes from others.
Activity	An activity is either a post or a reply or a system-generated message.

(continues)

Table 15-2 New Conversation Concepts in SharePoint 2013 *(continued)*

Concept	Description
Conversation	A conversation consists of a single post and all of its associated replies. The terms *thread* and *conversation thread* are alternative terms for conversation. Note that you can have a conversation using two different SharePoint 2013 features: a newsfeed or a discussion board. Refer to Table 15-5 for a detailed comparison of conversation options.
Notification	A notification is a system-generated e-mail that notifies you about an activity occurring on a thread to which you have contributed, notifies you that someone has started to follow you, or notifies you that someone has mentioned you. You can edit the newsfeed settings in your profile to determine which activities you are notified about. Determining notification settings, all of which are enabled by default, is a personal preference. Turning on notifications is a really helpful way to ensure that you don't miss a reply to an important question or post you have made. (An example of which activities generate notifications is provided later in this chapter.)

that organizations leveraging Office 365/SharePoint Online take advantage of Yammer for microblogging, but the integration that would be required for Yammer to support all of the needs of a community of practice, including support for document collaboration and a fully integrated search experience, are not yet implemented—at least not if you are reading this book in 2013 or perhaps 2014. Support for communities and the integration story for Yammer is evolving much too quickly to be adequately covered in a book. If you are responsible for implementing technology to support communities, you need to pay attention to ongoing announcements from Microsoft about integration updates so that you can make the best decision for your organization and for the specific communities that you plan to support.

In this chapter, we will focus on the features that are currently available directly as part of SharePoint 2013. However, our discussion and recommendations for ensuring that communities have moderators to nurture and monitor their health are important whether or not your community leverages Yammer alone, Yammer plus a community site, or any other enabling technology.

The new Community Site template in SharePoint 2013 is a new type of site that provides a forum experience for community members and visitors that allows them to share expertise and seek help from others who have knowledge in a specific topic area. It is similar to the Team Site template because it has a wiki editing experience for the home page, but unlike the team site, the community site does not have a document library, site notebook, or site feed included by default. What makes the community site even more different is that it has some built-in features to encourage and reward participation in collaborative activities and is fundamentally based around the new, enhanced discussion list. The new discussion list with community features includes the ability to feature questions, mark a reply as the best answer, and provide incentives and rewards for participation by awarding "badges" for different levels of participation or expertise as part of SharePoint 2013's support for the emerging industry hot topic: "gamification." Table 15-3 provides an overview of the new features and concepts in community sites.

Table 15-3 Community Site Features and Concepts in SharePoint 2013

Concept	Description
Category	A category is a term that allows you to group similar discussions in a discussion list. For example, in a community site for products, there might be a separate category for each product that a company manufactures.
Discussions and threads	Categories contain discussions, which in turn contain threads. Discussions often focus on a question or a specific area of interest on which you want feedback from others. Members of a community contribute to discussions by replying to the original post, which creates a thread within the discussion. The term *member* in this context means people who have actually contributed to or explicitly joined the community site. Discussions can be just that—discussions—but an individual discussion post can also be marked as a question. When this happens, the question remains visible in the unanswered questions view until either the original "poster" or the moderator marks one (and only one) answer as the best reply.
Membership	Users who visit a community site can "join" and become a member of the community. The owner of a community site has different options for allowing users to become members, including allowing all users to automatically be members of the site or requiring that users request access to become a member and get approved by a moderator.

(continues)

Table 15-3 Community Site Features and Concepts in SharePoint 2013 *(continued)*

Concept	Description
Moderator	A moderator is a community member who has permission to access the special tools to manage, or moderate, the community conversations.
	Moderating involves reviewing and addressing posts that are flagged as inappropriate, setting rules for discussions, specifying interesting content as featured discussions to promote them, and also recognizing key subject matter experts. Having a moderator is especially important for community sites because good moderation helps ensure successful outcomes for the community. Later in this chapter, we talk more about the important role of the moderator and some of the characteristics to look for in selecting people to serve as moderators of a community.
Reputation	Each member of a community site earns a reputation within the community. Out of the box, users earn reputation based only on specific activities (creating or replying to a post) and feedback from other members (when the member's posts are liked frequently or rated as a best reply).
	Reputation functionality is specific to an individual site—it does not span sites. This is by design because a member might be considered more knowledgeable in one community than in another community. Moderators and site owners can define and adjust reputation settings for the community as a whole and can, if necessary, award a "gifted badge" to a user in their community site.
Gifted badges	Moderators and site owners can give a user a gifted badge to designate the user as a special contributor to the community. Gifted badges replace earned reputation. For example, you might give a gifted badge to highlight users who are experts in a specific topic area.
Best reply	In a discussion, one reply can be designated as the best reply. Only the original poster (the person who poses the question) or moderators can designate best replies. When an answer to a question is marked as the best reply, the question is removed from the unanswered questions view. SharePoint 2013 does not support identifying more than one reply as "best."

- **Improved support for "social on the go."** SharePoint 2013 introduces new support for mobile devices. In addition to improved mobile browser support, Microsoft has also built native applications for Windows Phone and iOS devices. These mobile applications allow you to view and interact with your newsfeed (post new messages, reply to and like existing messages), see posts where you have been mentioned, and view others' profiles. These mobile applications are discussed in more detail in Chapter 19, "Planning for Mobility."

Getting Started: Planning and Governing Your Social Strategy

The absolute worst way to get started with the social features of SharePoint is to jump right in because it's trendy, cool, or "the millennials expect it." Leveraging social features might help attract new talent to the organization, but the features still need appropriate context and organizational support to deliver value. Even more important, it's not the social features themselves that help organizations get business results, *it's what the tools let users do* to solve real business problems that drives business value. If you are not already leveraging this type of technology in your organization, you need to evaluate the social features in SharePoint 2013 the same way you would evaluate any other new capability or emerging technology. To determine if you should be using these features, you need to have a business problem to solve. This probably bears repeating: You need to have a *real* business problem to solve for which social computing technologies can be an effective solution. Otherwise, you will have a very limited chance of driving the organizational change that is necessary to ensure success. First, define your desired outcome, and then determine how the SharePoint social features address this challenge.

If you haven't done so already, it's probably time to read (or reread) Chapter 2, "Planning Your Solution Strategy." In that chapter, we talk about clearly identifying the outcomes you are trying to achieve with your SharePoint deployment. As you think about how and when to deploy SharePoint 2013 *social* features, remember what you read in that earlier chapter and consider the following key strategic steps:

- Clearly identify the business problem.
- Identify use cases.
- Be prepared to respond to barriers.
- Define your governance plan.
- Define a "do-able" pilot project.
- Prepare a launch and communications plan.

Clearly Identify the Business Problem

It's important to clearly associate a business outcome objective with any collaboration technology, but especially for social. Consider some of the typical business problems that social technologies can help address:

- **Providing improved access to internal experts.** In many organizations, people complain that it just takes too much time to figure out "who knows about" a particular topic. Expertise is often needed quickly, and even the most connected people in the organization may not know whom to contact for every possible topic. User profiles and expertise search can quickly connect people who need help with people who have the knowledge to help them—a frequent issue in large, global organizations where people often complain, "I know someone must have already addressed this issue someplace in the organization; I just have no clue how to find them."

- **Building relationship capital.** It often takes several months if not years for new employees to develop the social networks necessary for them to be effective and productive. Relationship capital—who knows whom—is an underdeveloped asset in many organizations. Often, people have trouble solving problems because the right people in the organization don't connect. Features in SharePoint such as the organization chart browser help employees understand formal relationships in the organization, and social tags, likes, ratings, activity posts, and blogs help people understand more informal knowledge relationships so that they can quickly figure out how to get to the tacit expertise distributed across the enterprise.

- **Improving the connection between people and the content and processes they need to get their jobs done.** Authoritative metadata improves search results significantly, but not all organizations have a good plan for assigning metadata to content. User-assigned tags help add context to content even when there is authoritative metadata available. Ratings can also help identify useful content, *as long as there is a clear understanding of what ratings mean in each context*.

- **Identifying new opportunities for mentorship and knowledge sharing.** In large, geographically dispersed organizations, it is difficult to match up existing experts with emerging experts. User profiles, blogs, newsfeed posts, and discussion lists on community sites help people identify opportunities for mentoring relationships on their own.

- **Allowing users to add content to information repositories.** When users add keyword tags to content (via the Tags and Notes feature in the document ribbon), they help make the information more useful to themselves, but if they allow the tag to be exposed publicly, they may also make the information more relevant to others and improve the relevance of search results for the entire organization. Social tagging is a very personal activity—users generally do it so that they can find or group information in a way that is meaningful to them. However, the added benefit of social tags is that they may also help others find information, either because they improve search results or because users may discover what someone else is thinking about or working on through the activity feeds that show what that person is tagging.

- **Moving conversations out of the limited range of e-mail and hallways and into online spaces where more people can benefit.** A lot of tacit knowledge transfer happens in the private space of e-mail and hallway conversations. Blogs, shared notebooks, and wikis help make some of these conversations more public, addressing the "holy grail" challenge of knowledge management: sharing knowledge that is not yet available in formal repositories. In addition, posts in the newsfeed and posts to discussions in community sites provide a real-time way of connecting people in the organization and disseminating tacit knowledge. In addition, having these conversation options available internally may provide employees with an outlet for collaborating and airing grievances without resorting to public social networks or even public blogs. Providing an internal outlet with moderation may be a way to improve morale and employee engagement.

- **Making it easier to recruit and retain new, Internet-savvy employees.** We said earlier that deploying SharePoint social features shouldn't be done just because younger employees expect to see them. Simply having the functionality available doesn't guarantee that it will be used effectively. That said, the availability (and active use) of social technologies can help your organization attract and retain the next generation of employees who are familiar with and expect to use this type of technology at work.

Note that in this context, we're primarily talking about internally facing business scenarios. However, if you invite external business partners into your SharePoint 2013 environment, you can extend the benefits of these same scenarios to your partners, suppliers, and even customers. Organizations that use SharePoint 2013 Online have the capability to invite external users to participate in SharePoint sites at no additional cost as part of a "guest access" license. This capability provides a cost-effective opportunity to interact with the "extended enterprise." However, external users in SharePoint Online do not have access to the same social features that fully licensed users do. Table 15-4 provides a comparison of the features available to each type of SharePoint 2013 user.

Table 15-4 SharePoint 2013 Online User Experience Differences

Functionality	Fully Licensed User	External Guest Share-Point Online User
Top navigation	Newsfeed (activity feed), SkyDrive Pro (personal online document storage), and sites (communities) available in the top navigation bar.	No links in the global navigation bar. No newsfeed, SkyDrive Pro, or page where all sites are listed.
Newsfeed	Full features, including the ability to add hashtags and mentions. E-mail and indication in the mentions view.	No newsfeed, but can get an e-mail when they are mentioned in a post.
User profile	Rich options for describing interests, skills, and expertise in the user profile, including the ability to upload a picture and identify topics with which the user can help others.	No options to describe personal interests or abilities.
Search for people	Yes, can view other user profiles.	No, cannot view other user profiles.
Follow	Ability to follow people, hashtags, documents, and sites.	No ability to follow people or content.
Contribute documents or post to discussions	Ability to be invited to a community or team site and contribute to a discussion and upload/edit documents for sites where the user has been assigned Contribute permissions.	Ability to be invited to a community or team site and contribute to a discussion and upload/edit documents for sites where the user has been assigned Contribute permissions.

Identify Use Cases

One of your key goals for social computing inside the organization is to make it "real" for executives and other key stakeholders. This essentially means being able to describe the scenarios or stories where using the SharePoint social features can add value to the organization's objectives. Turning these stories into hard dollar values may be difficult, but it will be much easier if you can tie them to key business activities people do every day. (But don't forget the investment that will be required for the training, communications, organizational change, and support efforts required to get people to use them.)

Professional services companies use user profiles to identify internal expertise to quickly assemble the best-qualified team for a client engagement. Large global companies with distributed IT staff members use blogs to share "how I did it" stories and software code across the enterprise so that people don't reinvent the wheel. Organizations all over the world, in the public and private sector, use wikis to collaboratively create software documentation and Wikipedia-type term definitions that are shared and updated by a broad community of users.

You will need to identify use cases that apply in your own organization. Start with your list of business objectives and derive use cases from this list and from the stakeholder objectives you collected at the start of your SharePoint project.

In January 2011, Geoffrey Moore, author of *Crossing the Chasm* and the managing director of TCG Advisors, produced a white paper for AIIM (The Global Community for Information Professionals) entitled "Systems of Engagement and the Future of Enterprise IT."[3] In it, Moore talked about identifying "critical moments of engagement" in your business and focusing on how you can leverage social capabilities in these already complex organizational activities. For example, in a services business, a critical moment of engagement might be engaging with a new client during the sales process. Reaching beyond the customer relationship management system to engage in a dialog with colleagues who have expertise in the industry, customer, or sales process via social tools provides an opportunity for knowledge transfer that can drive meaningful business results. Similarly, in a product development scenario, social technologies can be extremely valuable to an engineer struggling with a problem.

---

3. Available from www.aiim.org/Research-and-Publications/Research/AIIM-White-Papers/Systems-of-Engagement

The social features of SharePoint 2013 include several that most organizations will be able to leverage in one or more strategic use cases. These features include

- Enabling online conversations
- Supporting online communities
- Providing the ability to work with personal SharePoint content across devices and offline

Enabling Online Conversations

The organization-wide newsfeed and enhanced discussion lists offered in community sites create a potentially disruptive alternative to the most common collaboration technology in use today in virtually every organization: e-mail. If your organization chooses to enable and promote the use of the social features of SharePoint 2013, you will need to consider if and how you want these features to change the way people collaborate currently. You will need to answer the fundamental strategic question: Do social features replace or complement the existing tools we have for electronic collaboration such as e-mail and instant messaging?

The newsfeed offers a serendipitous information discovery experience. It offers the opportunity to see, like, or reply to any public discussion occurring throughout the organization. You can sort and filter this public stream of information based on hashtags that are relevant and of interest to you.

Whether you are building a new house or a new social intranet, a key principle for design and build is using the right tool for the right job. The newest version of SharePoint gives your organization new tools beyond e-mail and instant messaging to use for having conversations. There is no universal answer to the question of how each organization will decide whether new social tools will replace or complement existing methods for having conversations. Moreover, even if your organization decides to adopt one approach over another, there is no guarantee that all users will immediately understand which method is the right tool for each type of conversation. It may take time before the right approach emerges for your organization.

One way to think about which tool is right for which type of conversation is to think about two dimensions: privacy and length of relevance. Figure 15-1 places the following ways to have online conversations in a privacy and relevance matrix:

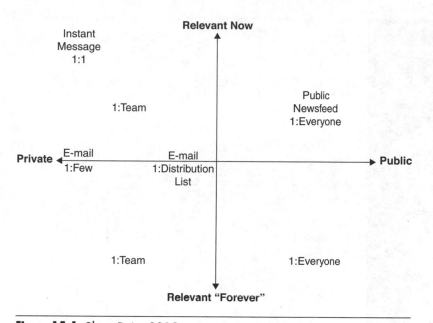

Figure 15-1 SharePoint 2013 conversation matrix

- Instant message (most private)
- E-mail
- Team discussion
- Site newsfeed
- Public discussion
- Public newsfeed (most public)

Table 15-5 compares and contrasts the different conversation options along even more dimensions. This table describes the spectrum of online interaction methods and suggests use cases and specific features that might cause you to promote one method over another in your organization. Note that instant messaging is not really part of SharePoint 2013, but it is an online conversation option that may be available to your users. Note also that this table is not meant to imply that any of these methods replaces the need for telephone or face-to-face conversations. There are clearly situations for which having any type of online conversation is not as effective as face-to-face or phone. We'll leave that discussion for another book and focus on the options you can promote within the context of SharePoint 2013 and related technologies.

Table 15-5 Conversation Options in SharePoint 2013

Functionality	Instant Message	E-mail	Team Discussion (Community Features)	Private Site Feed	Public Discussion (Community Site)	Public Newsfeed
Best for	Urgent chat with one person or small group	Private conversation	Topic-focused Q&A and conversation with a team where content preservation is important	Short, time-sensitive conversations within a team	Topic-focused Q&A where content preservation is important	Short, time-sensitive conversations—hallway chatter
Maximum length	For Lync, the maximum is 800 characters for the initial message and 8,000 in subsequent messages	None, but long messages are more easily consumed as documents	None, but long messages are more easily consumed as documents	512 characters per post, maximum of 100 replies/post	None, but long messages are more easily consumed as documents	512 characters per post, maximum of 100 replies/post
Acknowledge agreement with likes	No	No	Yes	Yes	Yes	Yes

Privately target a specific person	Yes, can send privately	Yes, can send privately	No, can @mention a person but everyone can see the post	No, can @mention a person but everyone on the team can see the post	No, can @mention a person but everyone can see the post	No, can @mention a person but everyone can see the post
Ability to encourage/reward participation	No	No	Yes, community features encourage and reward members for participation	No	Yes, community features encourage and reward members for participation	No
Ease of content "findability"	Difficult, unless instant messages are saved to conversation history within e-mail	Difficult, unless you have saved the e-mail messages personally	Easy, because content is categorized	Possible, but only via search because the conversation space is not optimized for reuse	Easy, because content is categorized	Possible, but only via search because the conversation space is not optimized for reuse

(continues)

Table 15-5 Conversation Options in SharePoint 2013 *(continued)*

Functionality	Instant Message	E-mail	Team Discussion (Community Features)	Private Site Feed	Public Discussion (Community Site)	Public Newsfeed
Visibility of historical content	Depends on organizational policy	Only for people in the distribution list	Anyone added to the site as a visitor; content is permanent, list contains a history of any posts and replies before a user has even joined	Only for team members (or users with Read access to the site) and only as long as newsfeed content is preserved	Anyone added to the site as a visitor; content is permanent, list contains a history of any posts and replies before a user has even joined	All users, but only as long as newsfeed content is preserved
Interact using free mobile apps for SharePoint	N/A	N/A	No*	Yes (Windows and iOS)	No	Yes (Windows and iOS)

Moderation	No	No	Yes, built-in capabilities, but someone has to be assigned the Moderator role	No	Yes, built-in capabilities, but someone has to be assigned the Moderator role	No

*Third-party applications, typically fee-based, allow you to work with any type of content on SharePoint sites offline on mobile devices, such as SharePlus or Colligo Briefcase for iOS, and this includes the discussion lists. In addition, assuming that your organization allows you to connect to your SharePoint environment from a mobile device, you can also view and work with SharePoint content on a Windows Phone.

Over time, we will likely see these technologies being used in different ways as users "settle in" with the new capabilities and organizations define specific scenarios in which one type of conversation space is preferred over another, and as Yammer becomes more integrated into SharePoint. While e-mail may continue to be used for direct communication among small groups of people, the expectation is that community sites with discussion features (or Yammer communities when they are fully integrated into SharePoint) will evolve into places where groups of people get together to discuss and share common interests, lessons learned, and best practices. Ideally, an increased use of communities should help to decrease the reliance on e-mail and help unclutter overloaded inboxes.

Supporting Online Communities

Community sites provide an engaging way to support practice- or topic-focused business communities. Built-in "gamification" features in SharePoint encourage users to participate in activities such as moderation and marking "best" replies, earning them badges and increasing their reputation scores within the site. While it may be tempting to run off and build hundreds of individual topic-specific community sites, this is not a recommended approach. Communities thrive when the community site (or Yammer community) is configured to enable a real business community or an important organizational topic, not when the site is enabled just to see if users will come.

Moderation is an important critical success factor for online communities. Moderators help facilitate an environment where members share and exchange ideas, questions, and concerns and contribute resources that benefit the community. The Community Site template includes a new security role that provides the moderator with permissions that help the moderator build an environment of safety and trust, encourage and promote conversations and people, inspire members to act, and curate success stories that demonstrate the value of the community to the members and sponsoring executives.

One way that that the new Community Site template helps the moderator focus the attention of members and encourage conversation is by providing the ability to create "sub-areas" in which to have focused conversations called categories. Categories are predefined metadata tags for a specific conversation. One of the most engaging features of SharePoint 2013 is that when you create categories in your community discussion, they are automatically featured in a tile with which you can associate a relevant image. These featured categories can quickly direct users to a particular conversation topic (see Figure 15-2). (Note that the community site featured in this example has been configured to include both custom categories and a document library.) There is no absolute limit to the number of categories, but in general, no more than about a dozen mutually exclusive topics are recommended so that users can quickly post and find content relevant to the topics of interest for their community.

Providing the Ability to Work with Personal SharePoint Content across Devices and Offline

SkyDrive Pro provides an opportunity to ensure that users save key files to a location where they will be automatically backed up, can be discovered, and can be accessed from other computers and devices as well as offline. This has many benefits, including enabling users to work across multiple machines without losing information. It also is helpful if you want to share information with others in a way other than e-mailing file attachments and trying to manage versions. SkyDrive Pro can also be used as a replacement for personal drives and the use of non-IT-approved consumer sites such as Dropbox.

Most organizations do not want people using SkyDrive Pro as a document dumping ground. It is important to consider both quotas and retention policies for content stored in SkyDrive Pro. You will also want to provide guidance to ensure that users understand when content should be stored in their SkyDrive Pro space and when content should be posted to a team site or another more appropriate location.

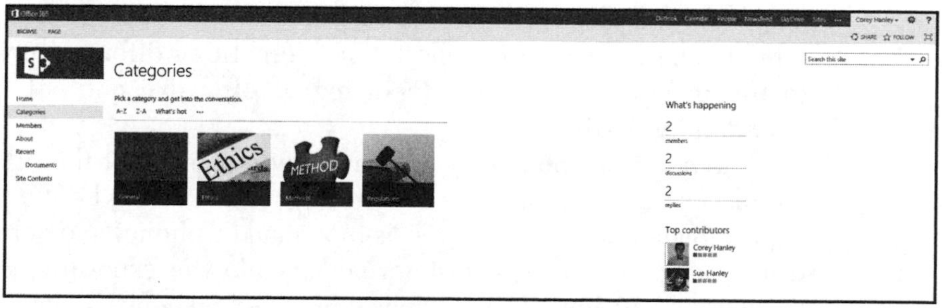

Figure 15-2 Community site categories

Be Prepared to Respond to Barriers

Even with well-described, relevant, and meaningful use cases, you may still see some resistance to deploying social features. You may find the ideas in the following sections helpful as you think about your social computing strategy.

Understanding the Risk of Exposing Inaccurate Information

The barrier: *If we allow any user to contribute content (to a discussion board or a wiki or a blog), we risk exposing inaccurate information.*

This objection is one of the barriers often expressed in organizations where executives are concerned about allowing employees to have blogs. It may also be a concern in an environment where content is collaboratively edited in a wiki. The concern is often not that users will intentionally post inaccurate information, but that they might be misinformed and unintentionally post information that is not correct.

Blogs, discussions, newsfeeds, and wikis tend to be "self-policing," especially if multiple users have the ability to comment on a post or edit a wiki. If everyone in the organization has commenting privileges and can reply to or comment on incorrect entries, the risk of incorrect information being exposed is temporary—only until someone catches and corrects the error. (You can also require approval before posts or comments are visible to all users using the approval settings in lists, but this is recommended only if you have resources available to review submitted posts on a timely basis.) Moreover, unlike on the Internet, on an internal site, inappropriate or incorrect content can always easily be removed by the site administrator. Within the new SharePoint 2013 community sites, any user with Moderator privileges can remove an inappropriate discussion post. You can also optionally enable the capability to allow any user to report a problematic or offensive post directly to the moderator via the "Reporting of offensive content" option in Community Settings.

The question you may want to ask is whether or not the risk of exposing inaccurate information is any greater than it would be if a user asked a question in another way (such as by e-mail or phone) and got an answer from someone who was misinformed. While the exposure risk may be small if only two people are involved in an e-mail conversation, the potential damage is probably greater in the one-to-one conversation because there is no opportunity to catch the error unless the person asking the question seeks a "second opinion." Blogs, newsfeeds, and wikis are actually more transparent than e-mail. In other words, social technologies make it easier to catch problems, not harder.

A possible strategy to gradually decrease barriers might be to start by limiting users who can have blogs to subject matter experts and similarly restricting Edit privileges on wiki sites until the organization is more comfortable with the technology and explicit positive results can be demonstrated.

Understanding the Risk of Accidental or Inappropriate Disclosure

The barrier: *If we allow people to post anything they want in their profiles or on their blogs, they may talk about inappropriate topics or about other people or about information that can't or shouldn't be universally shared.*

This barrier may be a legitimate concern in some organizations, especially those where "ethical walls" apply. In general, most organizations already have a policy regarding the appropriate use of corporate IT resources, and this policy typically already covers the type of content referenced in this objection. If it doesn't, it is time to update the policy, not necessarily ban the activity.

As a general rule, most people will do the right thing when it comes to sharing online. One of the reasons that you may see a "flame war" on the public Internet is that people are often anonymous on the Internet and can hide behind pseudonyms. This is not the case inside the organization where a general best practice is to ensure that all users "own" their comments and content. It would defeat the purpose of connecting people to other people inside the organization if anonymous contributions were the norm. Even if contributions are allowed to be anonymous in some circumstances, it is almost always possible that at least the system administrator will be able to see who is posting what content. With a documented policy and usernames associated with content, this barrier becomes much less of a real risk.

Understanding the Risk of Losing Stature

The barrier: *I don't want to share what I know in a blog because then someone might take my idea and use it without giving me any credit.*

We've heard this as a barrier in organizations with a culture that rewards and values innovation and individual contribution over collaboration and teamwork. The barrier is often expressed about collaboration solutions in general, not just social technologies.

One of the important things about knowledge is that it is an asset that you don't lose when you give it away—if I share my knowledge to help you out, I still have the knowledge to share again and reuse for myself and with others. People are naturally "wired" to be helpful, but sometimes organizational norms and reward structures create artificial barriers that limit the success of solutions that promote collaboration and sharing. It is actually harder to not assign credit to others or at least identify the source of an idea when it comes from a dated blog post or shared document or activity post since the evidence for an idea or concept is relatively easy to find.

To mitigate this barrier to successfully deploying social technologies, it may be necessary to look at how people in your organization are rewarded—how they are measured for both regular and incentive compensation. It may also be necessary to reinforce that the organization wants people to feel safe to share ideas, within the guidance provided by your social media policy. Some of the barriers to collaborative technologies are not risks associated with the technology itself but the fact that there are organizational barriers that discourage the desired behaviors.

Understanding the Risk of E-Discovery

The barrier: *If we allow people to create blogs, post notes and comments, and narrate their work in a status update, we might create additional discoverable content that would have to be turned over as part of a lawsuit.*

This is probably a valid risk but no more so than any other type of content in the organization, especially e-mail. Remember that unlike e-mail, social content is *always exposed*. In other words, there are many opportunities to correct inappropriate content or remove it simply because it is "social," not private. While there may be additional legitimate risks if community content is exposed in your public-facing Web site or extranet environment, internally this content is likely to be far less problematic than e-mail or instant messaging. Most organizations have every employee sign an "appropriate use of internal technology resources" contract when they join the organization. Some have employees re-sign this agreement annually. The bottom line is that most people know how to behave online. If they don't, the content is both easily identified and removed.

Understanding the Risk of Distraction

The barrier: *Status updates and notes will be used for trivial purposes and provide a distraction from the main event—work.*

There are plenty of opportunities for people to become distracted at work. In general, people understand what is appropriate at work. If they don't, there are already performance measures in place to ensure that employees get their work done on time. In addition, by adjusting their preferences, users can control the information they share and see. The best mitigation strategy for this objection is a success story—an example of a situation where a connection made via social technologies benefited a project team or an individual or the organization as a whole. If you're responsible for the deployment of the social features of SharePoint 2013, your project plan should certainly include a plan to capture and evaluate metrics. Be sure to include success stories as a qualitative metric for your initiative.

Note   For a more comprehensive discussion of how you can demonstrate value from the social features of SharePoint 2013, refer to Chapter 8, "Developing a Value Measurement Strategy."

Define Your Governance Plan

Ideally, you thought about your governance plan when you were reading Chapter 4, "Planning for Business Governance." If you have not yet thought about how you want to approach governance for the social features in SharePoint 2013, it's time to do it now. The most important general governance policy when it comes to social features is to not allow users to post anonymous content. To get value from social features, people need to know who is posting content. "Owning" your social content helps ensure that everyone plays by the rules and makes it very easy to ensure that governance policies are followed.

Configuring the User Profile

The user profile contains attributes about each user such as name, e-mail address, organizational hierarchy, skills, and phone numbers. Some of this information can be automatically populated from a system of record such as Active Directory or a human resources information system. SharePoint

2013 has several standard user attributes that are provided out of the box, and these can be customized and extended to meet the needs of your organization. You have most of the same capability to change the user profile attributes in SharePoint Online as you do when you install SharePoint 2013 on-premises.

The user profile is where individuals can specify their privacy settings for what fields are shown to everyone within the organization or are just available for personal reference. This is also where preferences are set for what activities people want their followers to see about themselves in their newsfeed and what events they want to be notified about via e-mail.

The first item for which your users will need some "social" guidance is their profile. Figure 15-3 shows an example of the Basic Information section of the SharePoint 2013 user profile. One challenge organizations often face when introducing SharePoint is getting people to create their initial profiles. It's very frustrating to search for people in organizations where some users have a well-defined profile and others have virtually no content. Consider hosting a profile-building "jam session" to encourage users to create their initial profiles. One organization created a rap video to get employees to update their profiles and showed the video at an all-hands meeting. In the back of the conference room, they set up several "kiosks" (tables with laptops) where users could update their profiles during breaks and after the meeting ended. Another organization hosted a very successful "profile week" where the department that completed the highest percentage of profiles was given the opportunity to select a charity

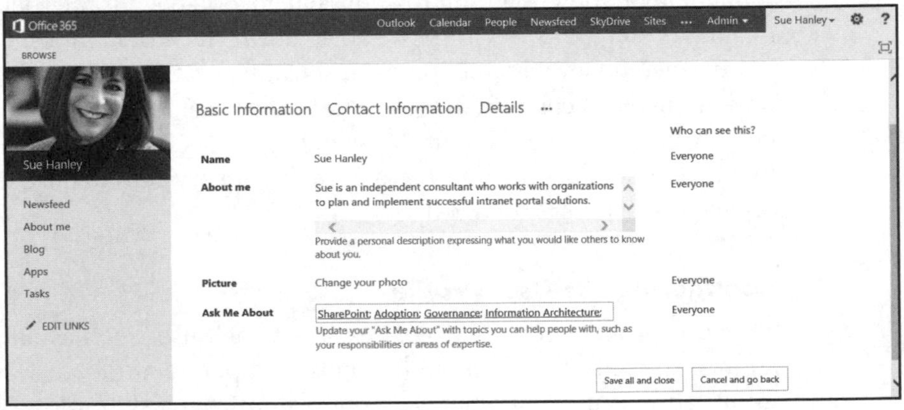

Figure 15-3 SharePoint 2013 user profile

to which the organization donated $1,000. The campaign was part of a "do good for us and do good for others" message that was very well received and resulted in the majority of the staff creating a meaningful user profile.

Your governance plan should have a suggested format for the "About me" description and provide examples of well-written descriptions. Users will want to know what you expect them to write in their "About me" statement, and they will be especially interested in understanding how much personal versus work information is appropriate. An HR executive recommended a 90/10 rule for content in the "About me" area. She suggested that in her organization, she would expect 90% of the "About me" content to be work-related and about 10% personal.

Consider whether or not you want users to be able to upload a picture of their choice and whether or not you need to provide guidance for the types of pictures that are acceptable. If you plan to automatically populate pictures from another source (for example, badge pictures), check with your legal and human resources departments to find out any requirements to allow users to opt out of sharing a picture. And consider local laws about sharing and storing any personal information, including pictures, as you plan for the attributes you will capture in the user profile.

The Ask Me About field is particularly important to address in your governance plan. For example, at what degree of knowledge is it appropriate for users to say that you can ask them about a topic? How well do you have to know something before you should declare this expertise to your colleagues? Do you want users to declare that you can ask them about any topic in which they are interested or only those in which they have some degree of expertise? The answers to these questions will likely vary based on the nature and even size of your organization, but you will want to provide some guidance to users about what is or is not appropriate based on the outcomes you are trying to achieve. Topics that users identify in their Ask Me About profiles are weighted higher in search results, so it is important to clearly identify what type of information should be included in this part of the profile. If expertise location is among your business objectives, you might want to think about the following guidelines for users:

- Add a topic to your Ask Me About profile if you have advanced knowledge of that discipline, even if you are not necessarily using that knowledge in your current role. This should mean that you have used the discipline extensively and can assist others in applying it to complex problems or that you are a true expert—you are experienced in all aspects of the discipline and are able to develop creative solutions to complex problems and can educate others.

■ Also add a topic to your Ask Me About profile if you know the discipline is new or new to the organization, even if all you can do is answer basic questions and direct inquiries to people with more expertise.

Figure 15-4 shows the fields in the Details area of the profile.

You will certainly want to provide guidance about adding information to the "Past projects" field if you are going to use it. This property is very difficult to keep up-to-date if users are expected to maintain it manually. As a general rule, it is better to hide or remove a field rather than allow it to go stale, so if you plan to use this profile attribute, be sure that you have an organizational process that ensures that it will be maintained over time.

Decide whether or not you want to include Skills and Interests (refer to Figure 15-4) in the profile. Most organizations find a lot of value in

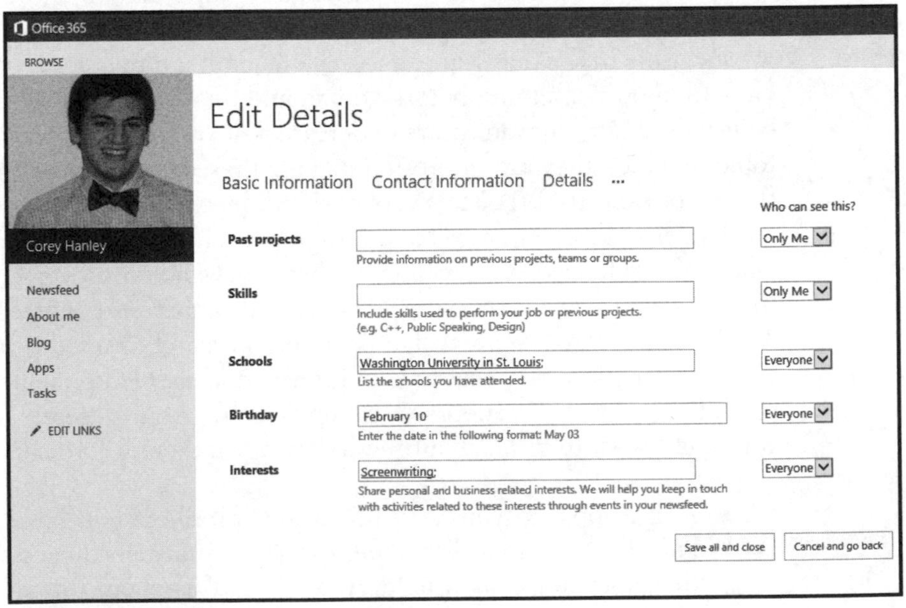

Figure 15-4 SharePoint 2013 profile details

encouraging users to include personal interests (within reason, of course) and relevant skills that they have that might not be used in their current assignment, such as language skills or experience with specific technologies that the organization may not be using at this time. Some organizations find that the field for Skills is too informal and unstructured to be of much value. In this case, it is helpful to replace the Skills list with a more structured list of suggested skills so that users select meaningful values. In one organization, a user entered "Jack of All Trades, Master of None" in his skills list. Not only is this entry not helpful, but because a comma was used as a separator, this user actually was identified as having two separate skills—Jack of All Trades and Master of None—so the joke didn't even work. At a minimum, you need to provide guidance regarding what types of skills are relevant if you choose to use this field. Skills and Interest values are "sourced" from the enterprise keywords list. An easy way to ensure consistency in this list is to "prime" the enterprise keywords list before you launch.

Many organizations worry about privacy issues when it comes to exposing birthdays, even if you are exposing only month and day. Be sure to check with your HR or legal departments, but in our experience, people really like to know this information about their colleagues. Many HR departments allow the information to be shared as long as providing it is "opt in," but in some countries, even an "opt in" field is not acceptable. As with all personal fields in a user profile, you have the option of removing them, but if you choose to use them, be sure to define your governance policies for their use and maintenance. Refer to Chapter 4, "Planning for Business Governance," for additional issues to consider regarding governance of profile information.

In SharePoint 2010, users had the ability to restrict who could see some of their personal information to just their colleagues or manager. This capability is not available in SharePoint 2013. There are only two visibility options for attributes in the profile: Only Me and Everyone. You can change whether a user can set the visibility for an attribute at the organization level for many attributes, but individual users get only two choices.

The last section of the profile allows users to set their preferences for how they want to be notified about the events associated with their newsfeed. These attributes allow users to control the amount of information they receive to prevent information overload and ensure that they are focused on the social information that they find most helpful. Figure 15-5 shows the available Newsfeed Settings in the user profile.

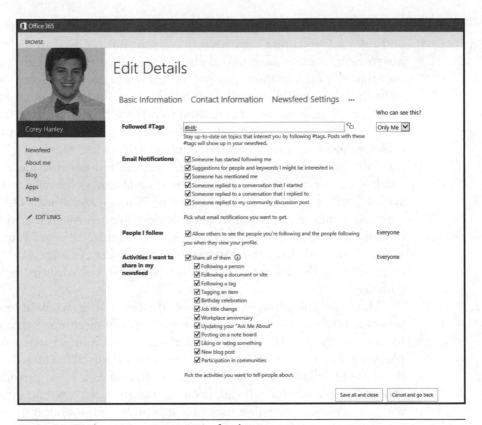

Figure 15-5 SharePoint 2013 Newsfeed Settings

Managing Newsfeed Posts

Many users will not need guidance regarding what type of content is appropriate for an enterprise newsfeed post—but that doesn't mean you shouldn't have a social media policy that reminds users of what is and isn't appropriate. If your organization does not already have a social media policy in place, the Online Database of Social Media Policies, available at http://socialmediagovernance.com/policies.php, is an excellent reference that includes many examples of social media policies to leverage as a starting point.

Users may need guidance regarding when it is appropriate to use a newsfeed to have a conversation rather than e-mail or a discussion list. Use the concepts in Table 15-5 to help promote the use of and guidance for newsfeeds.

Managing Blogs and Wikis

Many of the barriers to social computing described earlier are expressed in the context of blogs and wikis. The objections rarely play out with any negative consequences, but they are very real to the executives who express them. Your governance plan should explicitly address policies and content for blogs and wikis, including how content will be maintained and removed.

Wikipedia provides an excellent resource for governance policies for enterprise wikis that are known as the "Five Pillars of Wikipedia." These rules define how conflicts will be resolved and prescribe a code of conduct for all contributors.[4] Consider assigning a moderator for each wiki site. The moderator is an individual who agrees to be accountable for providing oversight to the wiki site, with a role similar to the role of a moderator for a community site. The moderator periodically checks to see that content pages are complete, that the site's organization still makes sense, and that content is appropriate.

Understanding Likes and Ratings

Likes and ratings are two alternative ways that users can acknowledge a newsfeed post, a discussion entry, or a document or list item in an app where this feature has been enabled. Both approaches provide a way to indicate agreement and collect support.

Likes provide a way to indicate agreement or affinity with an item. (As with consumer social sites like Facebook, there is no corresponding "dislike" to indicate disagreement.) Ratings allow users to evaluate an item on a five-point scale. Ratings are more controversial and probably deserve more thorough attention in your governance plan because users need to understand what you are asking them to rate—for example, do ratings apply to the quality of the writing or the usefulness of the content or something else entirely? If you are going to leverage ratings in a list or library, the best practice is to provide context or direction so that users understand what you are asking them to rate.

Deciding whether to use star or like ratings will largely be based on your organizational culture and style. We expect that most organizations will choose to use the like rating method since it is more consistent with other areas for providing social feedback within SharePoint (such as in newsfeeds and discussion posts), and it is not as specific and granular as

---

4. http://en.wikipedia.org/wiki/Wikipedia:Five_pillars

trying to determine whether to rate something as two or three stars. For some organizations or departments within an organization, having a more precise star rating system may be desirable. This is why SharePoint offers the choice and flexibility to make this selection at the list level.

Understanding Social Tags

Social tags allow users to add their own personal metadata to content, which supplements the authoritative metadata assigned by content owners. Users can click the Tags and Notes icon to associate their own personal terms to a document. Note that the social tags added by individual users are stored in the system-wide keywords term store as managed metadata. The hashtags associated with discussion or newsfeed posts are stored in the separate hashtags term store. The tag might describe what the content contains or what it does or just add the user's personal term for the topic covered by the content. Because these keyword tags are intended to be personal, you don't want your governance plan to be overly directive about what users should do. In SharePoint 2013, social tags are not used in search refinement, ranking, or recall by default, but you could create custom search experiences that leverage social keyword tags. If your organization chooses to do this, you may want to provide some additional guidance about keyword tagging for users.

Managing Discussions

The simple discussion list from earlier versions of SharePoint has an entirely new life in SharePoint 2013; it forms the foundation of the concept behind a community site. If you have existing team sites, you can activate community features to get the enhanced discussion list in them.

One of the challenges with the previous versions of the discussion list in SharePoint was that the user experience for discussion lists did not facilitate engaging users. The new community features for discussion lists and the Community Site template add moderation and gamification capabilities to conversations that can encourage participation, which can, in turn, help ensure that discussions provide value to the organization. There are two types of features that you will need to evaluate as part of your social strategy and governance plan:

- **Moderation.** Community sites and team sites with community features activated include a new security role for a moderator. Among other things, an important role of the moderator is to pay attention to the conversations inside the community site to ensure that great content and great contributors are recognized and to keep conversations going by monitoring the list of unanswered questions. Assigning a moderator to a discussion forum has always been our recommended best practice—and with SharePoint 2013, Microsoft has provided features to help a forum moderator be more effective. Moderators manage the community conversations by setting rules, reviewing and addressing inappropriate posts, marking interesting content as featured discussions, and marking an answer as a best reply. Moderators can also assign gifted badges to specific members to visually indicate that the member is recognized as a specific kind of contributor in the community, such as an expert or a moderator. Each community contains information about member and content reputation, which members earn when they actively post in discussions, and when their content is liked, replied to, or marked as a best answer.

While it is likely that the time involved in moderation will diminish once a community gets going and becomes more vibrant, active, and self-managed, the role is a critical one nonetheless. You will need to consider who will fill this role for each community and how much time and how many people are needed to focus on critical community forums. The best community moderators are users who are already interested and active members of the community. Emerging experts in a subject area make particularly good moderators because they already have an incentive to learn more about what is going on in their emerging area of expertise. In the best communities, moderation is far more than an administrative role. Since it can take time to be a good moderator, you might want to consider sharing or rotating moderator responsibilities so the burden is not too great on any one person.

- **Gamification.** As described in Chapter 7, "Planning Your Adoption Strategy," gamification is the use of game thinking and game mechanics in a non-game context. Three basic elements of games are incorporated in the SharePoint 2013 community features: points, badges, and leaderboards. SharePoint 2013 includes the ability to assign and collect reputation points within a community based on how a user participates. Points can be accumulated so that a user can earn a particular level status or "badge" within the community. Moderators can also "gift" badges to specific members to visually indicate that the member is recognized as a specific kind of contributor in the community, such as a subject matter expert or a moderator. Members of a community earn points when they actively post in discussions and when their content is liked, replied to, or marked as a best answer. While this can be fun and engaging in some communities, it may be completely inappropriate in others. Moreover, if people are actively participating in conversations because they really enjoy helping others, rewarding them with points might actually backfire because the visible recognition might make the activity that people love seem more like work—which will defeat the purpose. Be sure that the gamification features in SharePoint 2013 community sites are appropriate for your community—and that you have a plan for evaluating how these features can be used as part of your overall adoption strategy. At the time of publication, SharePoint 2013 includes only a limited amount of functionality to support gamification. If you determine that more capabilities are required, you can develop them using custom code or consider integrating a third-party product such as Badgeville (www.badgeville.com).

Another consideration for social governance is determining how aggressive to be about regulating social content. Community features in SharePoint 2013 include the option to enable the capability to report abuse to the moderator. Other social features of SharePoint 2013, including the newsfeed, do not have this capability. Should you be concerned? Probably not. Unlike the Internet, people communicating within an enterprise social environment generally understand the rules of engagement. Just as your users probably know better than to send a nasty e-mail or post certain types of documents and photos, they also know better than to post inappropriate comments. However, as stated earlier, that doesn't mean that you shouldn't have a social media policy. Within SharePoint, every element of content, including social activities, has an associated user ID and timestamp logged. But, as the saying goes, "you can say anything you want on your last day at the organization."

While there are legitimate business needs for restricting and monitoring content, especially in highly regulated industries, you should look for a balance between being too restrictive and being too flexible. If your business outcome goal is to encourage information sharing, you probably don't want to have every post and comment go through a formal review process. Instead, you may want to consider leveraging SharePoint's search, retention policy, and eDiscovery capabilities to have a regular process for identifying and handling inappropriate content. You should also be sure to update your existing acceptable use and HR policies to reflect the new capabilities—just as organizations did when e-mail, the Internet, and instant messaging were first introduced.

Many organizations seek to reward contributors to encourage a change in behavior. There are many reasons for this. First, there is great benefit in getting conversations out in the open and sharing information more broadly than individual e-mail threads. This creates an opportunity for information to be discovered and leveraged by others. Second, it is helpful for an organization to get the real-time pulse from their employees about what is on their minds and what the key concerns and questions are—this is a key benefit of the public newsfeed. Third, organizations often prefer encouraging the use of internal enterprise social tools for information sharing and debate because internally, the discussions can be audited and secured. Without a safe, internal forum, your users may leverage public consumer social tools like Twitter or Facebook for what should be a private internal conversation. As stated earlier, avoiding insecure public tools can be an important benefit of leveraging the social computing capabilities available within SharePoint 2013 and Yammer.

Define a "Do-able" Pilot Project

A small deployment pilot for an audience predisposed to adopt new technologies is a good way to create a successful outcome for SharePoint social features. Your goal is to find a community that is going to create an initial critical mass of information with a well-connected and vocal leader. As you deploy more broadly, users will see and benefit from this initial content and ideally be inspired to contribute themselves, especially if your vocal leader uses every opportunity to talk about the benefits. Building support from the ground up allows you to attract rather than mandate participation. Look for a community that may already be using social technologies as a good candidate for your pilot. For additional recommendations for successfully launching and encouraging adoption for social computing features, refer to Chapter 7, "Planning Your Adoption Strategy."

Prepare a Launch and Communications Plan

Use the feedback from your pilot to help plan an organization-wide launch plan. Be sure to capture user stories focused on how the social features helped them do their jobs more effectively. Use these stories in your communications activities to help spread the value proposition across the enterprise. Consider how you might want to use incentives to drive initial participation. Refer to Chapter 7 for specific examples of effective communications strategies.

The most successful technology solutions are designed so that employees can use them easily without the need for special training. However, you can't assume that everyone in the organization is familiar with social technologies and how to use them effectively, even if the technology itself is very intuitive. Your launch plan will need to ensure that users understand the value proposition for the technologies as well as how to use them to be more effective.

Consider that the successful adoption of most of the SharePoint social features requires the organization to change—and for individual users to change the way they work. Therefore, it's especially important to be patient. You may be able to launch your pilot in a very short period of time, but the organizational and cultural changes required to sustain a social computing initiative take time, sometimes as long as several years, and you may need to wait a while before their use becomes pervasive. At the same time, remember that you don't need 100% participation to achieve value with social technologies. Often, getting the right set of users solving meaningful business problems is far more valuable (and encouraging) than setting a target for 100% participation.

In addition, for social programs to succeed, people need to feel that it is OK to use the technology to speak openly (within appropriate human resources policies, of course!) without fear of retribution or censorship. If your organization is not comfortable with this concept, you may want to defer or limit the scope of your social strategy.

Using Social Features to Engage Others and Get Work Done

In earlier releases of SharePoint, the center of "social gravity" was the My Site. In SharePoint 2013, the concept of a My Site has evolved and the term is actually no longer being used—though there really is no good single replacement term for the "set of features and functions previously known as the My Site." If you still want to use the term *My Site*, that's OK—we won't tell anyone. What makes SharePoint 2013 really different is that there is really no one single place that is the center of social gravity anymore. In fact, there are multiple places where users can engage to get work done. This section approaches the social features of SharePoint 2013 from the perspective of the individual and describes how individual users can leverage each core element.

Personal SharePoint 2013 Sites

Your personal space in SharePoint 2013 is much more than a site where you share documents—it is where you go to see what is important to you. Your newsfeed (see Figure 15-6) shows you what is new for the people, sites, documents, and tags that you are following. You can interact with this activity feed—for example, by replying to newsfeed updates or liking activities done by others. As stated earlier, the newsfeed examples in this edition of the book show the internal SharePoint 2013 Newsfeed. Depending on if, how, and when your organization chooses to integrate Yammer for newsfeed-type conversations, the newsfeed in your SharePoint deployment may look different. One thing to note is that while Yammer can be integrated with SharePoint on-premises and/or SharePoint Online, Yammer is exclusively a cloud-based storage solution, so that should be considered as part of your deployment strategy.

When others visit your personal site (Figure 15-7), they can view content that you have shared with them such as documents or blog posts

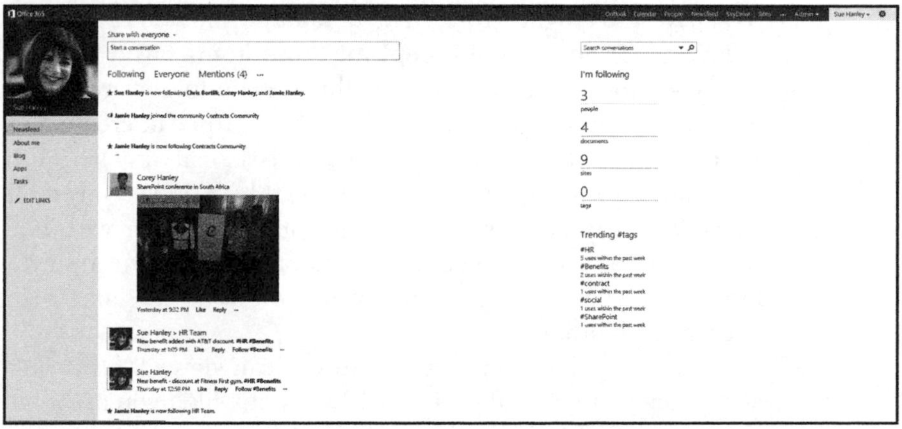

Figure 15-6 SharePoint 2013 Newsfeed

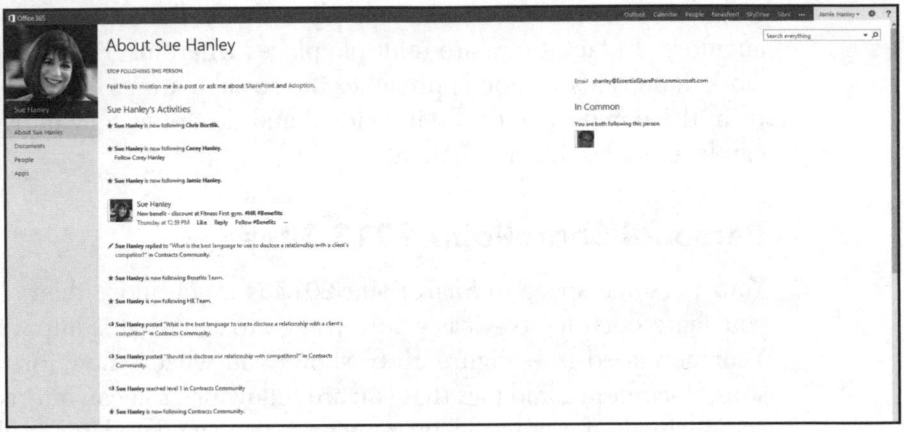

Figure 15-7 Viewing another person's personal site

and see the people who are following you as well as those whom you are following. They can also view your recent activities such as newsfeed posts or replies you have made, new sites or documents that you are following, and community site posts to which you have replied.

In SharePoint 2013, your personal site still includes a repository in which you can publish your personal documents. However, in this release, there are no longer separate "personal" and "shared" document libraries. By default, your personal site has a single document library called SkyDrive Pro (Figure 15-8). The default permission setting for this library is Private for all content except for those items saved in the Shared with Everyone folder. Permissions for this special folder are set to View Only for everyone in the organization by default. You can create and share folders or documents with others from your personal SkyDrive Pro by inviting them and specifying whether they should have View Only or Edit permissions. This approach is more consistent and familiar with how consumer file-sharing services function. It allows you to have a single document library that you can access across your various devices and selectively share content with others.

Your personal site is also where you can view all tasks assigned to you across the various SharePoint 2013 sites of which you are a member, your Exchange 2013 tasks, and your Project Server 2013 tasks. This capability solves a problem that existed in earlier versions of SharePoint where tasks (e.g., workflow assignments to review or approve items) were scattered

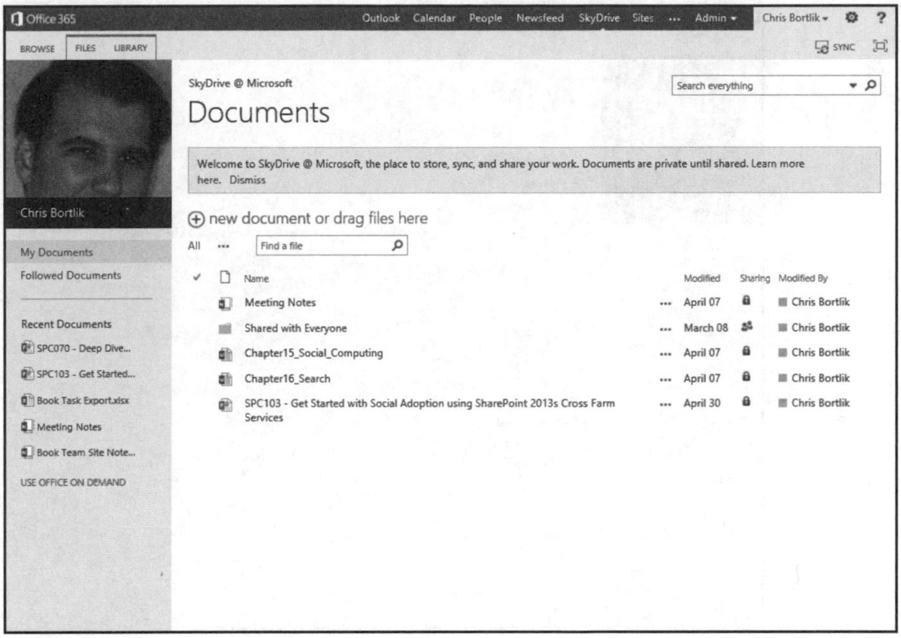

Figure 15-8 SkyDrive Pro

across multiple individual sites. With SharePoint 2013, you now have a central view and a single place to review and update tasks assigned to you (Figure 15-9). From your main newsfeed, you can mark conversation posts or replies for follow-up and have those items show as tasks in the consolidated task view on your personal site. This feature makes the social features more actionable and improves SharePoint's ability to support getting work done.

Newsfeed

Consider the following tips to get the most out of working with your newsfeed:

- **@Mention others in your post to focus their attention.** To direct a post to someone, type the @ symbol and a list of related names appears. When you select the person to mention, he or she is notified of your post via e-mail and will also see it in the mentions view on his or her personal newsfeed.

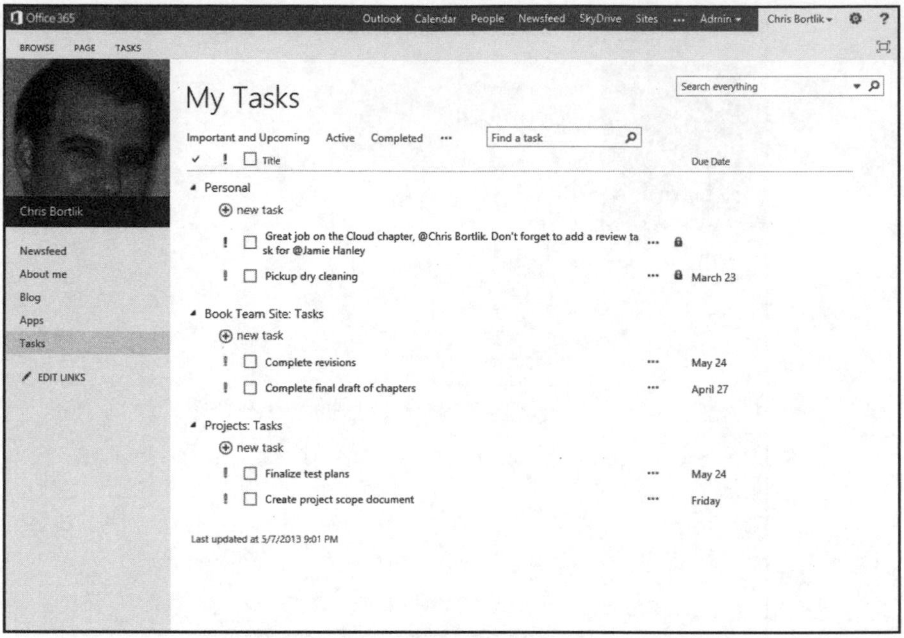

Figure 15-9 SharePoint 2013 personal task list

- **Add #hashtags to posts with one or more topics.** The use of hashtags allows you to categorize your post based on the topics it is about. When you type # within a post, existing hashtags are displayed. You also have the option to create a new hashtag. One of the main values of adding hashtags to your posts and replies is that it enables your post to show up in the newsfeed of other people who are following the tag but may not be following you. This is very helpful when you are asking questions and interested in discovering relevant subject matter experts. As a best practice, don't add more than three hashtags to a single post.
- **Share your post with specific teams.** By default, your newsfeed posts are visible to everyone in the organization. If you want to have the post be shown only to specific teams, you may want to change the "share with" option above the post to direct the post to a specific team site you're following or post directly to the site feed within a team site. In these cases, the post will honor the security permissions set for the team site and be shown only to those authorized. You may also want to consider posting to a community site discussion

instead of your newsfeed if the topic is one that you think will have long-term value to the community (refer to Table 15-5 for suggested use cases where this might be appropriate).

■ **Attach an image to your newsfeed post.** This image is automatically uploaded into the microfeed list within your personal site, which is where your newsfeed is stored and managed.

■ **Add hyperlinks.** When you post a link, you have the option of changing the display text rather than showing the full URL in your post to make it easier for people to read. One benefit of this is that it helps you to stay within the 512-character limit per newsfeed post while also improving readability for others. Note that you cannot attach a document to a newsfeed post, but you can insert a link to the document.

■ **Post a link to a video.** If you post a link to a video that is stored in SharePoint or YouTube, a video player is displayed and the video can be played directly from the post.

■ **Share a link to a document written in one of the Microsoft Office applications.** When links to Office documents are included and the Office Web Apps server is available, you have the option to preview Word, Excel, and PowerPoint documents directly within the post.

■ **Indicate agreement or affinity with someone else's post.** When you like a post or reply created by someone else, other people who follow you will see this activity in their newsfeed.

■ **View a list of all of the items that you liked as a special view within your newsfeed.** This view is accessed via the ". . ." menu of more options.

■ **View additional actions you can take on your newsfeed with the ". . ." menu.** The ". . ." menu on individual posts enables you to perform actions such as marking a post or reply for follow-up. This action creates a task for you on your personal site. The ". . ." menu is also one of the ways that you can select to follow a hashtag that is included in a post. Doing this will make items tagged with this hashtag show up within your newsfeed.

■ **Use the Newsfeed Settings in your profile to set which activities you want to be notified about via e-mail.** For example, when someone mentions you in a post, starts to follow you, or replies to a conversation in which you are participating, you can elect to receive an e-mail notification. You can also use these settings to manage what activities you want others to be able to see.

There are two main locations to interact with the SharePoint newsfeed. This chapter has focused primarily on the public newsfeed integrated within the personal site. Newsfeeds can also be included within team sites. SharePoint allows you to interact with both private (team site) site feed and public (Everyone) newsfeeds from within your personal site. Figures 15-10 and 15-11 show an example of a newsfeed post that was initiated from a personal site and published within a private Book Team site.

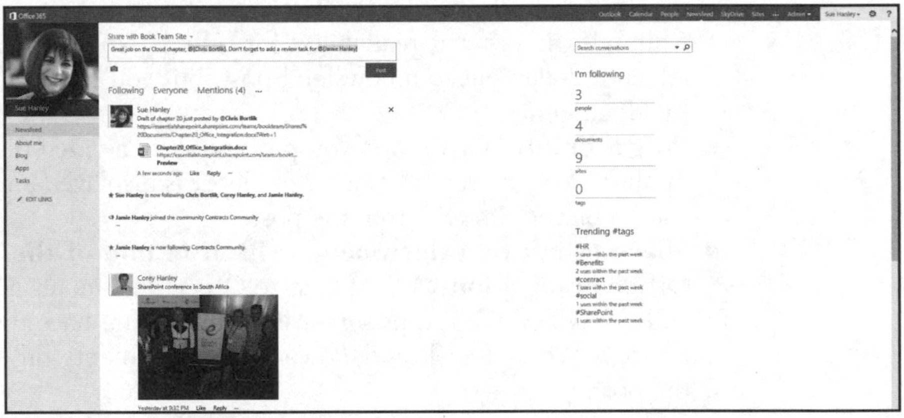

Figure 15-10 Posting to the Book Team site from a personal site

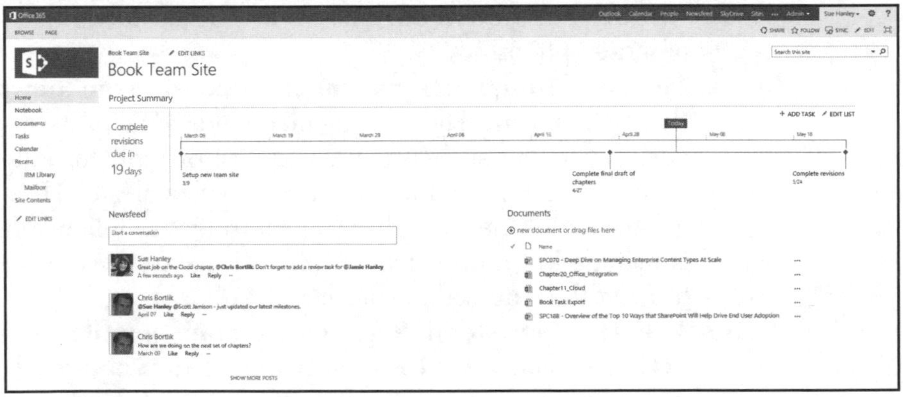

Figure 15-11 Newsfeed within the Book Team site

The same features and concepts apply when using newsfeeds within a team site as with the public newsfeed, including being able to mention people and use tags in your posts. One major difference is that newsfeed posts targeted at team sites are security trimmed to be visible only to members of the team site. SharePoint includes newsfeed posts for team sites you are following in the main newsfeed view within your personal site so you can follow all of the activities of interest to you in a single location.

Ratings

One of the benefits of social computing is getting richer feedback from others and allowing people to have conversations around a particular document or topic. SharePoint 2010 introduced the concepts of ratings and social tagging. Both of these areas continue to be important considerations in SharePoint 2013. When you socially tag or rate items, these events are shown to others who follow you in their newsfeeds. By interacting with content in your intranet or team sites, you can enhance the value of that content for both you and others.

Ratings can be enabled on a variety of SharePoint list and library types, including documents, blogs, and wikis. By default, ratings are disabled on most list types. For lists and libraries, ratings can be based on either stars (0–5 stars) or likes (Figure 15-12). This is an improvement over SharePoint 2010, where there was a disconnect between rating and using the "I Like It" tag.

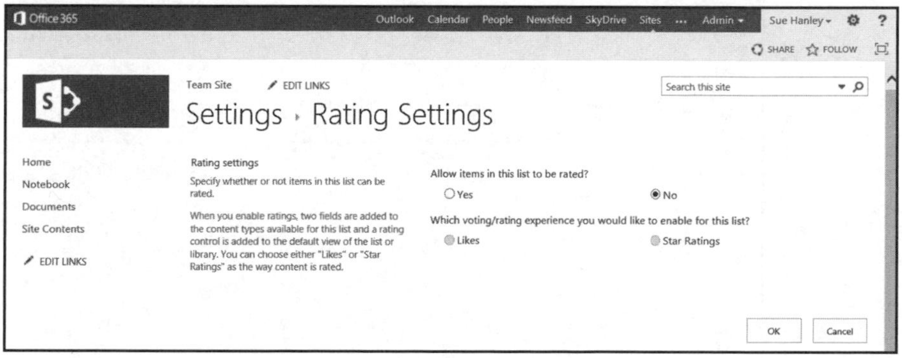

Figure 15-12 Enabling ratings on a document library

When star ratings are enabled (Figure 15-13), SharePoint shows you the average of the ratings and the total number of people who have rated the item. The total number is important because it helps to determine how relevant the average rating is. For example, if 50 ratings for an item have an average rating of 4.5 stars, it is considered more relevant than if only one person rated an item with 5 stars. Content can also be sorted and filtered based on its ratings.

When like ratings are enabled, SharePoint shows you the total number of likes (Figure 15-14) for each item.

Social Tagging

Social keyword tagging was introduced in SharePoint 2010 and works similarly in 2013. To add a keyword tag to a document or list item, you click the row for the item and then click the Tags and Notes option in the ribbon (Figure 15-15). When the dialog box appears (Figure 15-16), you can start typing the name for the tag you want to apply. If the tag already exists as an enterprise keyword, you can select it. If not, you have the option of

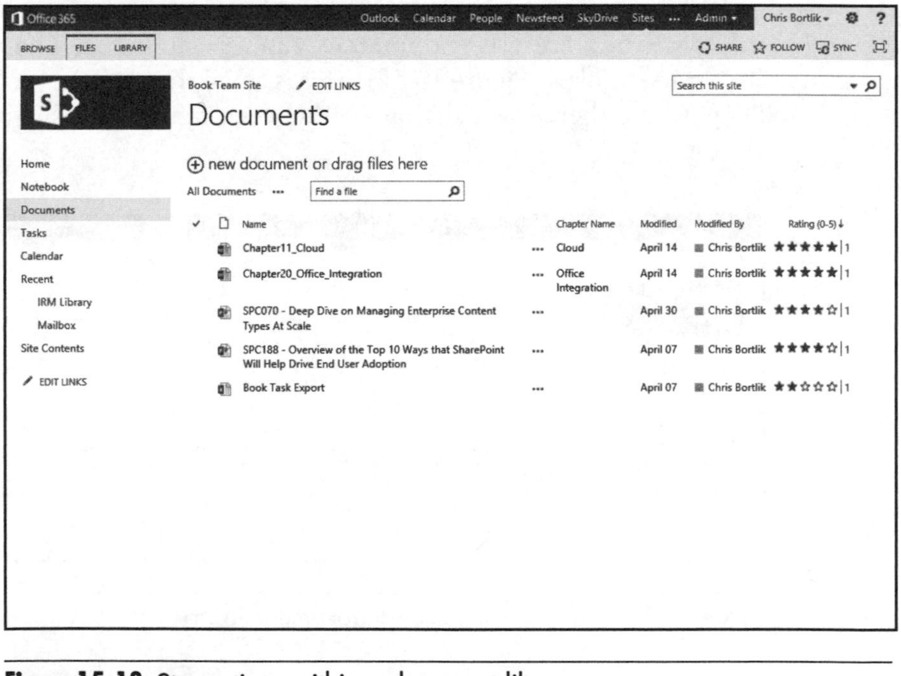

Figure 15-13 Star ratings within a document library

creating a new social keyword tag. Unlike hashtags, social keyword tags can include multiple words or a short phrase. You can use multiple tags by separating them with a semicolon. You can also specify whether the

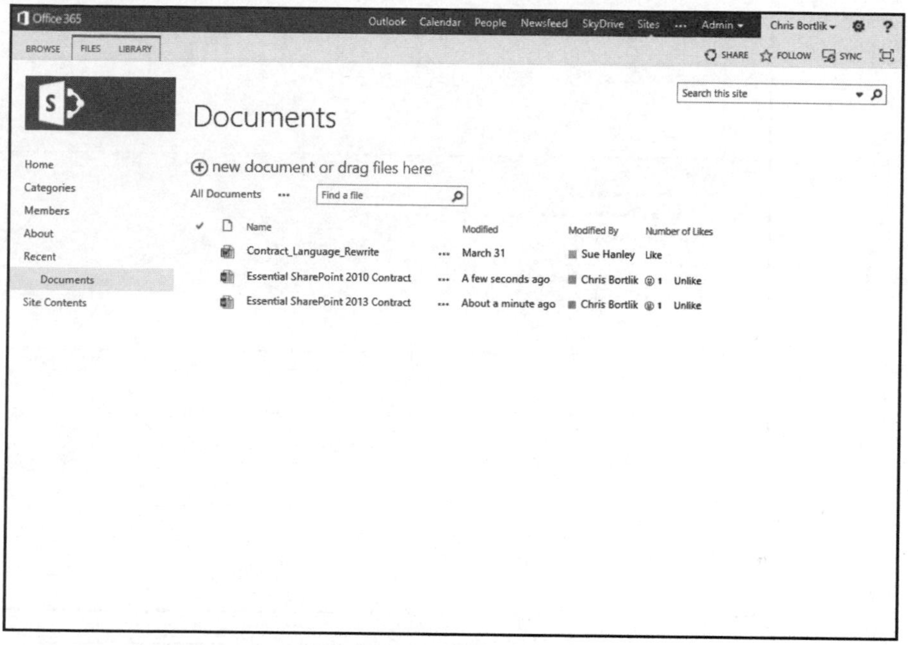

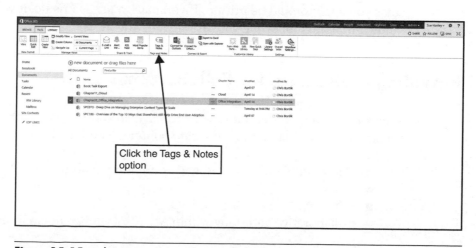

Figure 15-14 Like ratings within a document library

Figure 15-15 Selecting an item to socially tag

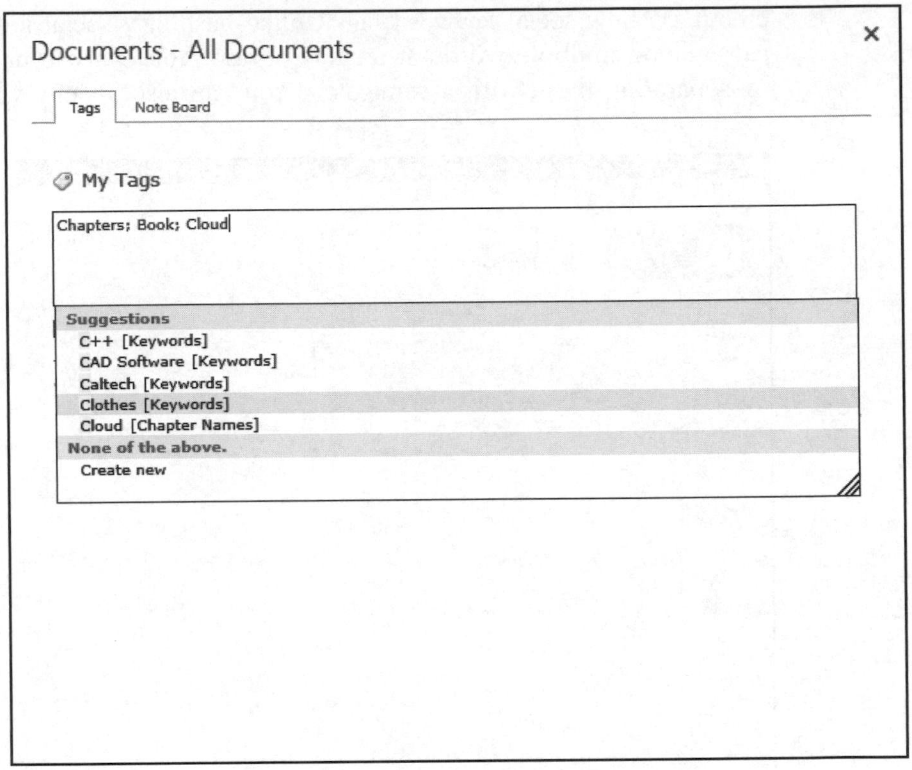

Figure 15-16 Applying a social tag to an item

tags you apply should be private. If you mark a tag as Private, it will not be shown to others following you or following the tag.

Providing a Structure for Collaborating

SharePoint supports multiple ways to have structured, collaborative conversations and collaborating to create content. These include

- Community portals, sites, and community features
- Blogs
- Wikis
- Collaborative authoring within Microsoft Office documents

Community Portals, Sites, and Community Features

Community sites, discussed earlier, are one of the main areas of social investment for SharePoint 2013. Community sites are a major step forward from the SharePoint discussion lists that existed in prior releases.

A new Community Portal site template is available in SharePoint 2013 (Figure 15-17) that aggregates all SharePoint sites in your environment that have been created using the Community Site template. The community portal provides an easy way to discover and join communities. While it is possible to enable community features in other SharePoint sites, such as a team site, only sites created from the Community Site template are displayed in the community portal.

Community Sites

By default, community sites are public, so anyone can join a community, but site owners can change the access permissions to either make the community private or require that join requests be approved before someone can become a member. When you join a community, it automatically shows up in your sites list as a site that you are following. As a member of the community, there are many activities that you can perform. The most typical activities are posting and answering questions. Figure 15-18 shows the default view when you first enter a community of which you are not a member. The discussions with the most recent activity are shown higher in

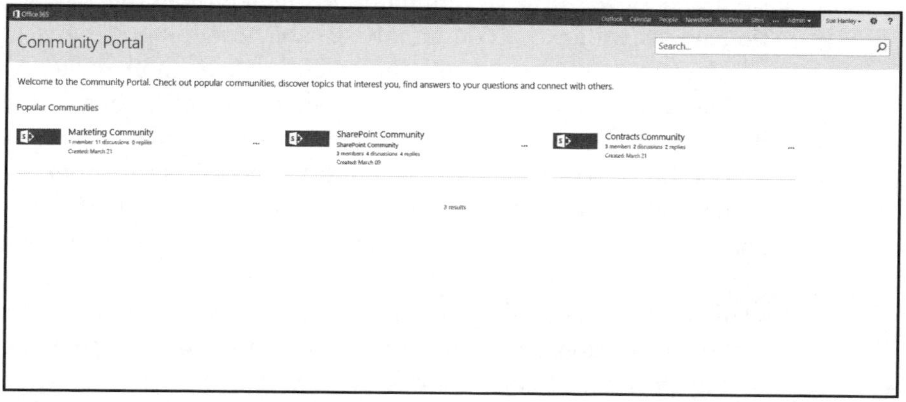

Figure 15-17 Community Portal

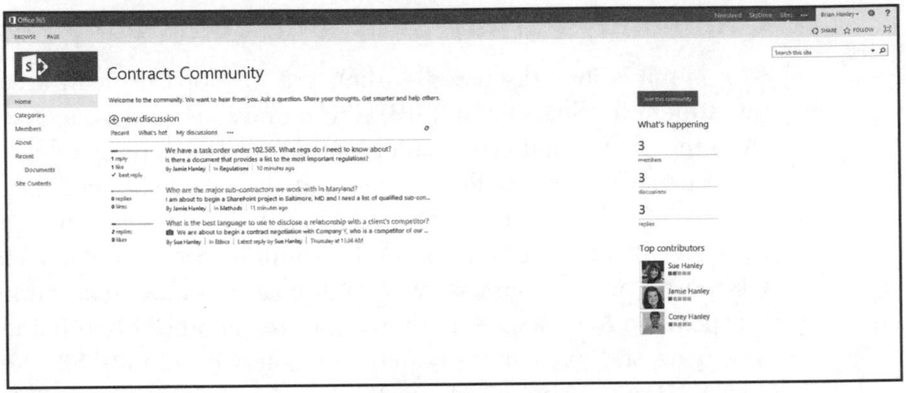

Figure 15-18 Community recent discussion view

the list. You can also select prebuilt views to sort and filter the list to show only unanswered questions or to see just questions that you have posted.

When community sites are established as unique site collections, the owner or moderator has the option of enabling "auto-approval" for permission requests. When this feature is enabled, prospective members can join the community by clicking the "Join this community" button shown in Figure 15-18. When users click the join button, SharePoint automatically moves them from the Visitor to the Members security group for the site collection, surfaces their name and activity status within the community on the members view for the community, and enables them to start earning reputation points within the community. Enabling auto-approval is not available when you create a community site as a sub-site of another site. An advantage of implementing communities as separate site collections is that a site collection is the most scalable model for long-term growth, but other than the auto-approval feature, there are no differences in user experience between community sites implemented as site collections and those implemented as sub-sites. As a best practice, always configure community sites with unique permissions, and do not share the sites with users until you have completed configuration so that they do not appear in the community portal before you are ready to expose the site to new users. In addition, if you are not using an independent site collection for your community site, consider adding the Everyone security group to the Members SharePoint Group for your site so that your entire organization will be able to contribute content and join the community without having to submit an access request (though you can both not enable auto-approval and require users to request access if that better meets the specific needs of your community).

When you start a new discussion (Figure 15-19), you have the option to identify your post as a question. This indicates that you are seeking answers. When members start posting replies to discussion questions, others within the community can reply and like replies posted by others. The person who asked the original question or the moderator of the community site can identify one response as the best reply, and that response will be shown at the top of the discussion (Figure 15-20) as well as in search results.

Community members can see how active others are within the community from the members list (Figure 15-21).

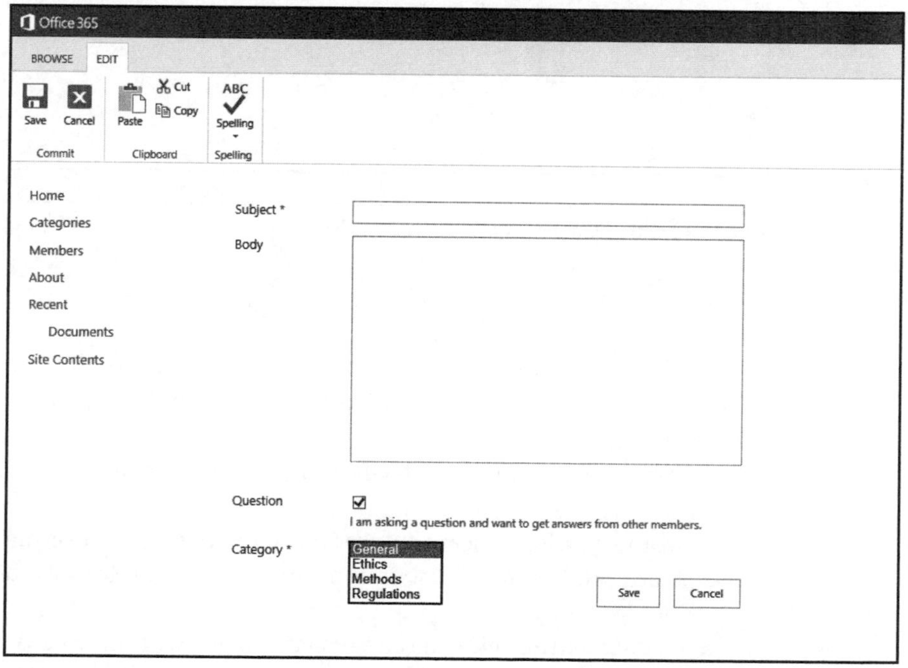

Figure 15-19 Posting a new question in a community

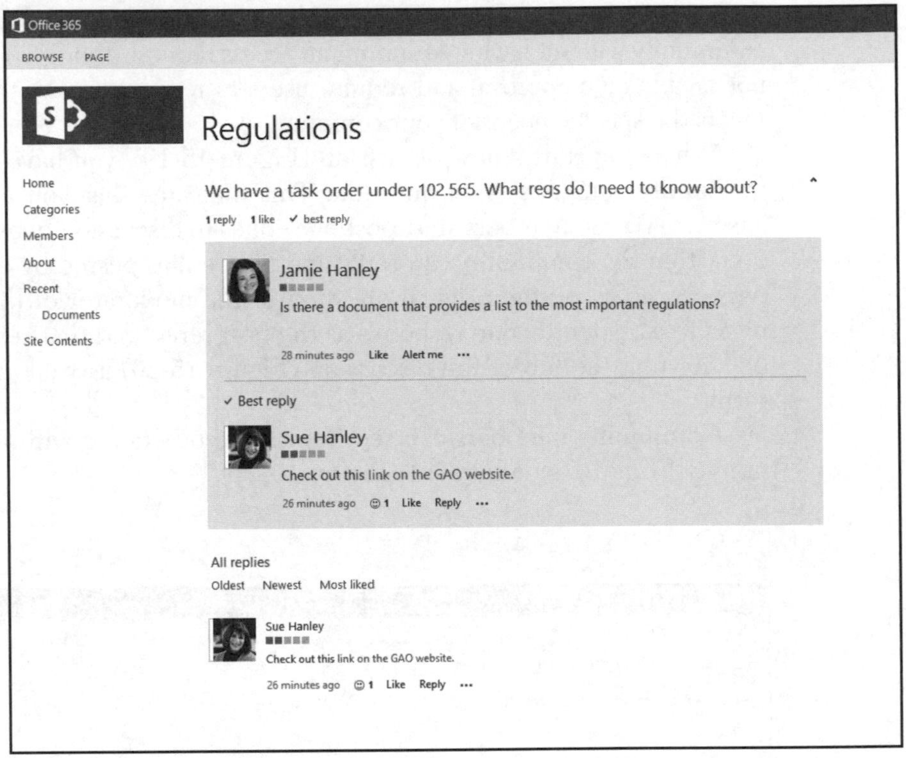

Figure 15-20 Question with a best reply

Community moderators can see additional details and perform additional actions using the links in Community Tools as shown in Figure 15-22.

The links in Community Tools allow moderators to

- **Manage discussions** where they can delete a post or mark a post as featured. Featured discussions are listed at the top of each category view.
- **Create categories** and associate images with new categories.
- **Create badges** in addition to the two default badges: Expert and Professional. Badges created on the Badges screen can be "gifted" to

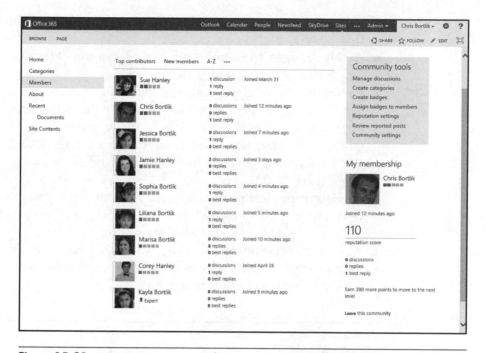

Figure 15-21 Top community contributors

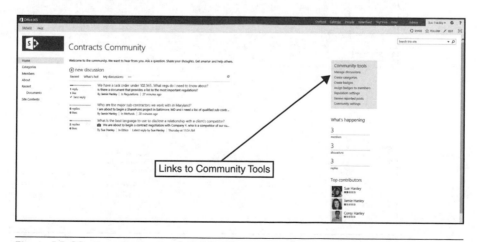

Figure 15-22 Community Tools Web Part

members, essentially overriding the need to earn reputation points to achieve levels.

- **Assign badges to members** based on criteria determined by the moderator or the community as a whole.
- Determine **reputation settings**, including whether or not items can be rated using stars or likes, whether the achievement points system will be enabled and how many points each activity is worth, how many points are required for each level, and whether the achievement level should be displayed as an image or text (see Figure 15-23).
- **Review reported posts** where they can examine posts that members have tagged using the "Report to moderator" link available in the ". . ." menu for an individual post or reply.
- Manage the **community settings** where they can enter the date the community (not the site) was established and enable auto-approval and/or reporting of offensive content.

Rating settings

Specify whether or not items in this list can be rated.

When you enable ratings, two fields are added to the content types available for this list and a rating control is added to the default view of the list or library. You can choose either "Likes" or "Star Ratings" as the way content is rated.

Allow items in this list to be rated?
◉ Yes   ○ No

Which voting/rating experience you would like to enable for this list?
◉ Likes   ○ Star Ratings

Member achievements point system

Within the community you can allow members to collect points based on their participations.

☑ Enable member achievements point system

Specify the point values for the following activities

Creating a new post	10
Replying to a post	10
Member's post or reply gets liked or receives a rating of 4 or 5 stars	10
Member's reply gets marked as 'Best Reply'	100

Achievement level points

As members accumulate points, they can reach specific levels as milestones of achievement. Specify the number of points required for members to reach each achievement level.

Specify achievement levels

Level 1	More than	0
Level 2	More than	100
Level 3	More than	500
Level 4	More than	2500
Level 5	More than	10000

Achievement level representation

Specify whether achievement levels are represented as a series of boxes or as a textual title. You can customize the title for each level.

◉ Display achievement level as image ■■■■■
○ Display achievement level as text

Specify a title for each level

Level 1	Level 1
Level 2	Level 2
Level 3	Level 3
Level 4	Level 4
Level 5	Level 5

Figure 15-23 Community reputation administration

What Does "Member" Mean in the Context of a Community Site?

Microsoft has built in some special permissions for community sites and, unfortunately, changed the meaning of the term *member* in the context of sites built using the Community Site template. Actually, the term *member* in the context of a community site is probably closer to the generally accepted English definition of this term. The use of the term *member* in the context of all other types of SharePoint team sites is extremely confusing because it is used to refer to a permission group, not the group of people who are actually members of the team. In the context of a community site, there are actually two completely different types of "members":

- **Community Members, the SharePoint security group:** Just as for other team sites in SharePoint, when you create a new community site with unique permissions, SharePoint 2013 automatically creates default security groups [Site Name] Owners, [Site Name] Members, [Site Name] Visitors, and the new [Site Name] Moderators. These default groups have Full Control, Contribute, Read, and Moderator permissions, respectively. This is actually different from "regular" team sites, where [Site Name] Members have Edit permissions by default. The primary difference between Contribute and Edit is the ability to create lists and libraries.
- **Members of the community site (who will be listed in the members view):** In the context of the community site, "member" also means someone who has explicitly joined the community using the join button. Until users explicitly join a community, they are not listed in the members view of the community, even if they might otherwise be in the Members security group. So, in the context of the community site, there are *community members* and people who are in the security group called *Members.* You must be in the Members security group in order to post to the discussion list, but you won't be listed in the members view of the community until you have explicitly joined the community (or made a contribution). Yes, it's confusing, but perhaps this explanation makes it less so.

Blogs

SharePoint 2013 continues to support blogging, and there have been minor updates to the blogging features in this release. Typically, a blog site is created as a sub-site within an individual's personal site or as a sub-site of a team site. Blogs are a great way for a person or team to share thoughts and best practices with others within the organization—especially when it is a more involved topic that does not lend itself to a quick update via a newsfeed or a discussion post—but it is not as structured as creating a formal document. For example, the executive team may choose to maintain a blog to share thoughts and solicit feedback from others (Figure 15-24).

Blog posts can be authored either directly in your Web browser or by using a blogging application such as Microsoft Word. Rich text, tables, pictures, and videos can be included or embedded within the blog post. You also have the ability to link to other pages and upload a file that gets related to the blog post. Categories can be created to group related blog posts together.

Figure 15-24 Executive blog

People reading the blog post have the ability to rate (stars or likes) and comment on the blog post as well (Figure 15-25). When you post or rate a blog post, people following you see the activity in their newsfeed. Unfortunately, blog posts and comments do not currently support the ability to direct posts with @mentions or assign hashtags.

Wikis

SharePoint 2013 offers in-browser wiki page editing, which takes advantage of many of the new SharePoint enterprise content management and Web content management enhancements in this release. Wikis are great for working together with others to manage pages. The SharePoint Team Site template uses the SharePoint wiki platform for editing pages in the browser. You can also create a dedicated enterprise wiki site for creating documentation or a shared acronym list. Some of the key features of SharePoint wikis include the following:

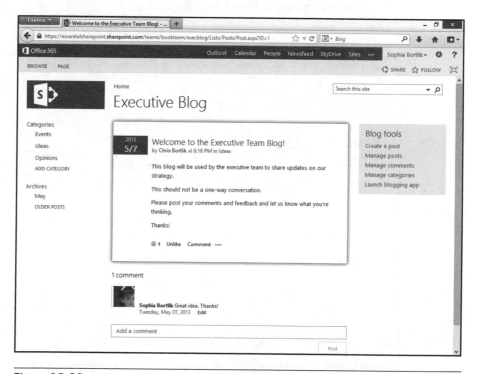

Figure 15-25 Commenting on and liking a blog post

- Wikis offer the ability to insert various objects, including tables, images, links, documents, and videos, and embed code to show content from other sites inline, such as a video from YouTube (Figure 15-26).
- Wiki pages can be categorized. Categories can be created and managed using the SharePoint Managed Metadata Service to drive consistency across wiki pages (Figure 15-27).
- Wiki pages can be rated (stars or likes); the rating activities are displayed in the newsfeed.
- Wiki pages leverage a publishing workflow and can be versioned. You can compare changes between versions of the page as well.
- Wiki pages can be created or linked to from within existing wiki pages by typing [[. When you enter [[(two "open" brackets), SharePoint will show a list of existing pages available within the library. You can select an existing page to link to or type a new page name and then type]] (two "close" brackets) to let SharePoint know that the name of the page is complete.

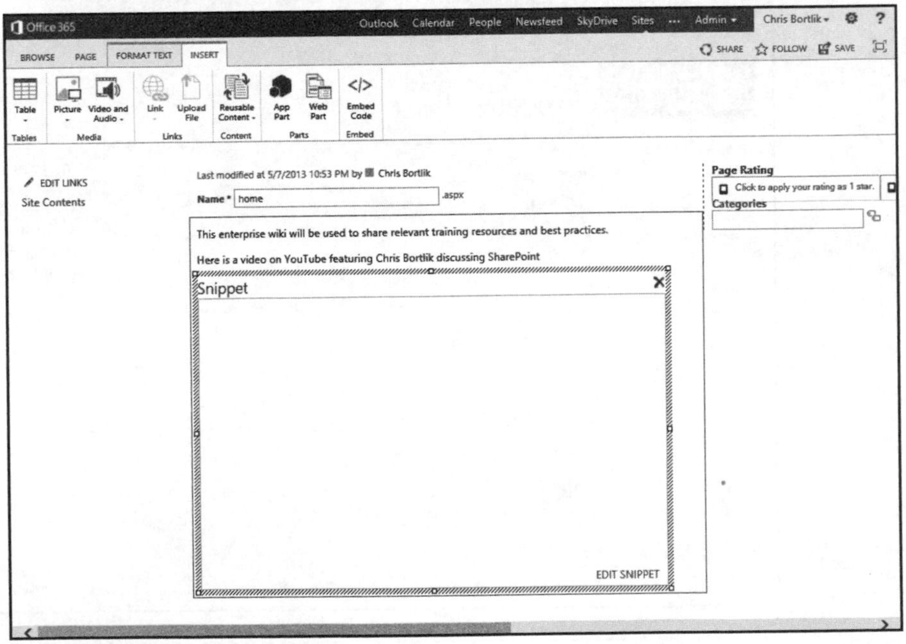

Figure 15-26 Editing a wiki post

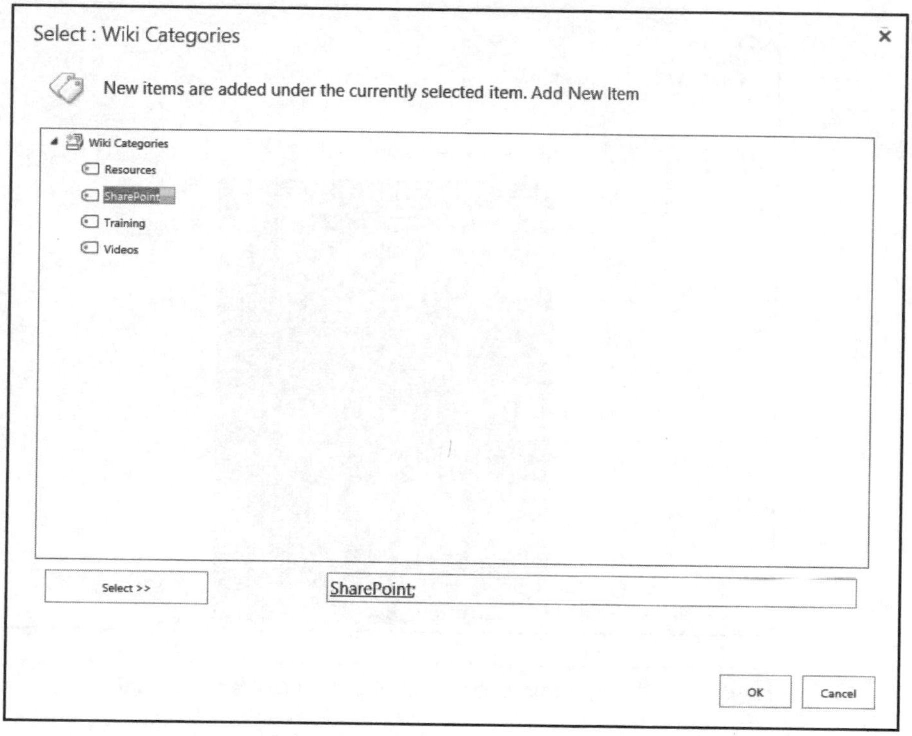

Figure 15-27 Wiki categories

Collaborative Authoring within Microsoft Office Documents

The Microsoft Office rich clients and Web applications have added additional support for collaborative authoring—cases where multiple people are simultaneously editing the same file. In some organizations, the use of Microsoft Office OneNote for shared note taking and brainstorming has started to replace other forms of social collaboration, including wikis. Figure 15-28 shows an example of team members using OneNote in a Web browser to work together at the same time to add meeting notes. By default, team sites in SharePoint 2013 include a team notebook for sharing meeting notes via OneNote.

Various Microsoft Office clients and their browser-based Web Application Companions (WACs) support the ability for people to work together on editing the same document at the same time. Table 15-6

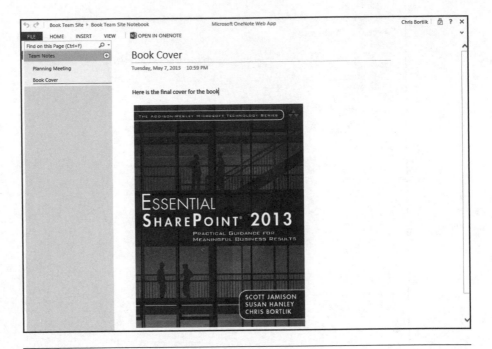

Figure 15-28 OneNote shared notebook in a Web browser

Table 15-6 Collaborative Authoring Supported in Office 2013

Application	Rich Desktop Client	Web Application Companion
Excel		√
OneNote	√	√
PowerPoint	√	√
Word	√	√

provides a summary of the applications that support collaborative authoring via the rich desktop client or the WAC.

Note Chapter 20, "Integrating Office Applications" discusses these capabilities in more detail.

Understanding the Architecture for SharePoint Social

In SharePoint 2013, personal sites must be enabled for users to participate in newsfeed activities and to have the ability to follow sites, documents, and people. When a personal site is created, it also (by default) provides the ability to store documents and other types of content such as custom lists, calendars, and tasks.

Most of the social information in SharePoint 2013 is stored within site collections and their related content databases. For example, newsfeed posts for individual users are stored within the personal site, and newsfeed posts for team sites are stored within the team site. This is a significant change from SharePoint 2010 where most social information was stored within a single shared social database. SharePoint 2013 also leverages in-memory "velocity cache" to allow social information to quickly be displayed in various individual and team newsfeeds. These result in some specific considerations for architecting an on-premises SharePoint 2013 environment:

- Storage of social information now needs to be factored into determining whether or not to allow personal sites for individual users. If users do not have personal sites, many of the new SharePoint 2013 social features (for example, the newsfeed) are not available since they require the personal site to store social data.
- SkyDrive Pro is part of the user's personal site and needs to be factored into the quota assigned to the user. In SharePoint Online, each user is automatically assigned a 7GB storage quota for SkyDrive Pro content. Within SharePoint Server on-premises, you can specify smaller or larger quotas within the constraints of the regular SharePoint guidance and recommendations for the maximum size of site collections and content databases.
- Social information related to team sites, such as private site feeds within a team site, are stored within the sites themselves. The storage and management of this information need to be considered when setting site-based retention policies and site collection quotas.
- The reliance on the in-memory velocity cache service may require additional memory to be allocated to SharePoint 2013 servers within your farm.

- Many of the new social features rely on SharePoint search to function. For example, the recommendations SharePoint displays to each user of people, documents, sites, and tags to follow are all driven via search. SharePoint search also includes a conversations search result scope to display information across SharePoint newsfeeds and community sites.

Note   For more information about these capabilities, please see Chapter 16, "Planning Enterprise Search."

Preparing for Yammer Integration

As discussed earlier in this chapter, Microsoft acquired Yammer in July 2012, and Yammer is now a member of the SharePoint product team within Microsoft. At the time of this writing, Yammer and SharePoint 2013 have significant overlap in the area of social computing—especially the newsfeed capabilities. Microsoft has stated publicly at the SharePoint Conference, and via numerous blog posts and press stories, that the majority of its social investments going forward will be in Yammer.

Even before Microsoft acquired Yammer, Yammer offered Web Parts for integration with SharePoint 2007 and 2010. Yammer also offered federated search with these versions of SharePoint to help expose Yammer information within SharePoint search results.

Yammer also has the ability to be embedded into other applications including CRM solutions such as Salesforce.com and Microsoft's own Dynamics CRM product which now leverages Yammer for its social features.

In March 2013, Microsoft took the first step toward integrating Yammer into SharePoint: it began to include Yammer Enterprise licensing with customer purchases of SharePoint Online. This is important since Yammer will be powering more of SharePoint's social features going forward.

Microsoft plans to extend the Yammer integration with SharePoint 2013 over time. At the time this book went to print, SharePoint customers have the option to replace the SharePoint newsfeed with the Yammer newsfeed within both personal sites and team sites.

Microsoft plans to offer quarterly updates to Yammer and SharePoint Online, which means that customers using Office 365 will have access to tighter Yammer integration, and likely newer capabilities, before SharePoint on-premises customers will.

Microsoft has also disclosed plans to have Yammer leverage the Microsoft Office 365 identity management platform (technically known as Windows Azure Active Directory) in the fall of 2013, which will lay the foundation for offering single sign-on across Yammer and Office 365 and enable tighter integration of the two services in the future.

As we look forward to 2014 and beyond, there are numerous possible opportunities for SharePoint and Yammer to come closer together. Some areas to keep an eye on are seeing how Yammer may be able to store documents directly inside of SharePoint and be more tightly integrated with other SharePoint features such as following documents, sites, and people. Longer term, it is also likely that Microsoft will want to integrate Yammer with SharePoint's search and eDiscovery capabilities.

Microsoft's roadmap for Yammer integration is obviously an important input into your immediate social computing strategy. However, it doesn't necessarily mean you have to wait for Microsoft to provide integration for you. It definitely means that you need to be aware of the latest integration plans from Microsoft and be sure you understand when specific features will be available. However, you need to make decisions about what to do based on your own organizational use cases and desired outcomes. Start with the most important outcomes for your business scenarios and then determine whether Microsoft's integration roadmap aligns with your needs and if you can wait for deeper integration, or whether your business needs require an accelerated timeline and you want to invest in doing the integration yourself. There is no one best decision for all organizations. Some will choose to wait to implement Yammer until Microsoft has completed more of the integration, and others will make the leap now because they prefer the experience in Yammer. And still others, who for business reasons do not want any enterprise data in the cloud, will stick with the SharePoint newsfeed and community support available in the on-premises version and, if necessary, look to third-party tools like NewsGator which provide features similar to Yammer in an integrated, on-premises SharePoint 2013 environment.

Key Points

Social computing capabilities may provide meaningful efficiency gains and cost savings in your organization, but almost all organizations will see less tangible but equally important benefits, including

- Increased collaboration by providing a greater voice to everyone in the organization
- Competitive advantage by breaking down some of the traditional barriers across the enterprise such as language, time zone, and geographic dispersion
- Increased flexibility to respond quickly to business needs by empowering business users with capabilities that previously required support from IT staff
- Elimination of redundancy by allowing teams throughout the organization to share ideas and knowledge across organizational silos

Leveraging the social capabilities in SharePoint 2013 in your organization will not automatically result in these or other benefits. As we discussed throughout this chapter, social computing needs a plan, and you need to think about how each social feature in SharePoint 2013 addresses key issues for your organization. Keep in mind:

- Introducing social computing into an organization is more than just introducing new technology. You need to assess the potential impact on your organizational culture and how this technology will change how people work with each other. As with any new technology, to be successful with social computing, you need to have a business problem to solve. Be sure that your SharePoint strategy includes business problems that can be solved with social computing features. Reread Chapter 2, "Planning Your Solution Strategy," as well as the first section of this chapter for business ideas you can leverage.
- Social computing features can be fun, and they also provide a compelling way to encourage collaboration and sharing. Don't be afraid to take "baby steps" as you deploy social computing functionality in your organization. Identify early adopter people and projects, and take the time to collect user stories that build both the business case and the value proposition for these features.

- Don't allow perceived risks to stop you from trying the rich social features of SharePoint 2013. Provide basic ground rules, plan carefully, and remember that it's really hard to find any good examples of horror stories of social computing disasters inside the enterprise. Unlike the public Internet, if inappropriate or inaccurate content gets posted, you can easily take it down. Moreover, if you are careful about ensuring that your users have the appropriate information literacy skill to distinguish between authoritative and opinion content, your actual risk will be minimized.

- It is important to think about training and adoption for these new social features. SharePoint 2013 introduces many different social features, and you will want to assess which capabilities to enable and provide guidance on how and when they should be used.

- SharePoint's architecture has changed to support the new social computing features and needs to be factored into your capacity planning and quota setting. The personal site (formerly known as My Site) in particular needs to be assessed to make sure adequate quotas are allocated to support the SkyDrive Pro and newsfeed storage requirements.

- Don't try to look for hard-and-fast ROI on your social computing investment, but look for progress toward your overall business goals, which might include a reduction in e-mail traffic or an improved business process.

- Above all, be patient. Organizational change takes time. Plan a persistent communications plan and tolerate a few mistakes—it may not be easy to get adoption of every feature, so you may have to try a few different approaches before you find the best approach for your organization and each business scenario.

CHAPTER 16

PLANNING ENTERPRISE SEARCH

Enterprise search in SharePoint 2013 has significant changes from previous versions. In this release, Microsoft has unified its prior SharePoint, FAST, Exchange, and Search Server search platforms into a single engine. This search engine is also now available via SharePoint Online as part of Office 365.

In this chapter, we will explore

- What's new in SharePoint 2013
- Planning for search
- Understanding search from a user perspective
- SharePoint 2013 search administration
- Search-driven applications

What's New in SharePoint 2013?

SharePoint 2013 introduces major changes to search that are based on the key concepts and features available in SharePoint 2010 standard search and FAST search for SharePoint, plus new capabilities.

Microsoft acquired FAST Search & Transfer in April 2008. In SharePoint 2010, Microsoft introduced a new version of FAST search built specifically for SharePoint. This version of FAST leveraged the same user interface and Web Parts within SharePoint 2010 but still had separate search services and required separate application servers under the covers. All that has changed in SharePoint 2013; there is now a single search platform.

This new search engine powers all versions of SharePoint 2013: Foundation, Standard, and Enterprise as well as SharePoint Online via

Office 365. Depending on the version of SharePoint 2013 you implement, you will see different features and Web Parts available. Microsoft has published a detailed matrix of search features available across the different types of SharePoint 2013 licenses at: http://technet.microsoft.com/en-us/library/jj819291.aspx.

Search has a much more prominent role in SharePoint 2013. Search is used to aggregate, analyze, and recommend sites, people, and documents that SharePoint will suggest for you to follow as well as social tags that are trending within your organization (see Chapter 15, "Planning for Social Computing," for more discussion on these concepts). There are many search-driven Web Parts, such as the new Content by Search Web Part, which can be configured to display content across multiple site collections.

With the release of SharePoint and Exchange 2013, Microsoft has moved toward using the same enterprise search platform to power both of these products. One area that this benefits is the new eDiscovery features that allow you to find and take legal action on content that may come from SharePoint, Exchange, Lync, or file shares. For example, placing a team site or mailbox on hold will benefit from the search integration. You can find more information on eDiscovery and Site Mailboxes in Chapter 13, "Managing Enterprise Content."

Another major change is the integration of the Office Web Apps server into search results. Now, if an Office document (Word, Excel, or PowerPoint) is included in the search results, you see a live preview of the document and can jump to specific sections in Word documents or slides within PowerPoint presentations. Office Web Apps are discussed in more depth in Chapter 20, "Integrating Office Applications."

Planning for Search

Many organizations have stated that enterprise search remains a top priority for their business. Unfortunately, many organizations think that just implementing an enterprise search tool will solve all of their information discovery challenges. At a minimum, organizations should plan to allocate part of a resource to *regularly review* search reports and to help improve search relevancy by promoting or demoting certain sites and documents. The responsibility for managing search should be considered carefully to ensure that search results are optimized across site collections, represent organizational priorities, and are linguistically sensitive. In some organizations, search may be centrally managed; others may elect to delegate the responsibility for managing search to SharePoint business owners.

In the following sections, we'll discuss important considerations when planning for search such as:

- Why does search matter?
- What are some common enterprise search terms and concepts?
- How does content management affect search?
- Why is configuring and managing SharePoint 2013 search important?
- What content should you expose via SharePoint search and how?

Why Does Search Matter?

One of the biggest challenges in most organizations is finding the answers to frequently asked questions. Sometimes what people are searching for is a document or a Web page. Other times it is a video. Many times people are trying to identify a subject matter expert.

In many organizations, trying to find the answer to a query across a variety of sources is challenging. People often need to know what systems exist, and then they need to execute a search in each system. Some solutions just identify results based on metadata attributes such as the document title or author but not necessarily the contents of the document itself.

Finding people is often even more challenging—especially in large global organizations. What if your organization has multiple divisions or subject matter experts (such as engineers or human resource professionals) working in a decentralized manner? Most times people have to rely on talking to the people they know within the organization or performing Internet searches to find experts outside of the organization.

SharePoint search seeks to address these challenges and others by bringing together the ability to search across structured (e.g., line-of-business) data and unstructured (e.g., Word documents) data sources from a single place. The content may be stored inside of SharePoint, or it could exist elsewhere such as on file shares, in other document repositories, or in LOB systems, such as your human resources or sales applications.

What Are Some Common Enterprise Search Terms and Concepts?

A number of different terms and concepts are commonly used in enterprise search. It is helpful to understand the following when planning for search:

- **Indexing**, which is sometimes referred to as crawling, is the technical term for when the search engine processes various types of content and catalogs the key attributes (e.g., Document Name, Author, Modified Date) and contents of files.
- **Querying** is the action of the search engine looking at the index to see if there are any documents or other items that meet the search criteria specified by the user.
- **Search results** are what the search engine returns after a query is passed to it. For example, if the query was "Boston," the search engine would display all items that contain the word *Boston* in their metadata or their contents.
- **Federation** is the action when one search engine passes a query on to another search engine to provide search results without having to index the same content source. For example, Wikipedia contains content that you may want to display in your search results. Chances are that you do not want your SharePoint environment to index all of the Wikipedia content. In this case, you would enable search federation between your SharePoint environment and Wikipedia. When a user performs a search in your SharePoint environment, SharePoint can pass the query on to Wikipedia's search engine and then display the results that Wikipedia returns.
- **Search Center** is typically a central site where individuals can go to perform a search across various sites and systems within an organization. SharePoint contains an Enterprise Search Center site template that includes prebuilt pages for handling user search queries and displaying search results. Like other SharePoint site and page templates, the Enterprise Search Center can be customized to meet the needs of your organization.
- **Search refiners** enable a user to visually filter search results. The search refiners are typically shown on the left side of the search results page. SharePoint automatically displays refiners for common metadata attributes such as the type of result (e.g., Word document, PowerPoint

presentation), the name of the author of the item, and when the item was last modified. Users can click on a refiner to display search results for only specific criteria, such as only PowerPoint presentations that have been modified within the past week.

- **Result sources** are used by SharePoint to define different actions to perform against different types of content. For example, SharePoint enables you to handle search results differently for document content and social conversations. You can also define new result sources to specify how to handle searching content from other sources such as Microsoft's Exchange e-mail platform or content sources with which you are federating. Result sources also incorporate what were formerly known as "search scopes" in prior releases of SharePoint. Out-of-the-box search scope examples include having different views of the search results page to show only "People" or social "Conversations" results.

- **Result blocks** contain a set of related results. For example, results that are PowerPoint documents automatically appear in a result block when the word *presentation* is part of a search query. You can also define your own custom result blocks.

- **Promoted results**, which were formerly known as best bets, allow you to specify that certain items should always be shown at the top of the search results for specific keywords entered by the user. For example, if a user searches for the word *sales*, you can have the sales team site show up at the top of the list of search results. Promoted results can be targeted to specific groups of users (known as segments) and can be set to be used only during a specific time frame within a date range.

- **Crawled properties** are metadata that is extracted from items during content indexing. Metadata can be structured content (such as the name of the author of a Word document) or unstructured content (such as the language in which the content is written).

- **Managed properties** have metadata that is either automatically created by SharePoint or created by a search administrator. Crawled properties are mapped to managed properties so that they can be included in the search index. Managed properties can also be used as search refiners and can be used to sort search results.

- **Entity extraction** is the process of SharePoint search parsing content during the crawl process and dynamically building search refiners. One example of this is the built-in "Company name extraction" process where SharePoint can create a refiner based on a list of company names. This enables the search engine to create a company refiner automatically, which allows users to filter search results based on the company names contained within the content that has been crawled—even though the content may not have been explicitly tagged that way.

There are many additional terms and concepts to consider. Microsoft has published documentation to assist with planning and understanding enterprise search. These resources can be found at http://technet .microsoft.com/en-us/library/cc263400.aspx.

How Does Content Management Affect Search?

While SharePoint's enterprise search engine can perform advanced content processing, such as performing entity extraction to automatically generate search refiners, search results are much more accurate when content is tagged with explicit metadata. There is a tight relationship between effective information classification and taxonomy and search results. For example, SharePoint Content Types and managed metadata can be leveraged to properly classify content within SharePoint, which can then be used by search for displaying and filtering content. By using Content Types, you can classify items as being related to a sales proposal. Search can then be leveraged to find all sales proposals stored across your organization. You can also use managed metadata to apply consistent attributes to content within SharePoint. Perhaps there is an attribute within your organization that tracks the industry of the customer for which a proposal was created. You can then index these attributes and display them as search refiners to be able to filter search results to show sales proposals only for customers that are in the financial services industry.

Why Is Configuring and Managing SharePoint 2013 Search Important?

In SharePoint 2013, the role of search is much more prominent than in previous versions. Search is no longer just a box you type in when you're looking for something. Search is now leveraged directly by other areas of SharePoint to drive Web content display via page templates and suggest social recommendations for people, sites, tags, and documents that you may want to follow. Search also drives the new usage analytics capabilities in SharePoint as well as the new eDiscovery capabilities.

Many organizations and individuals make the incorrect assumption that enterprise search performs magic and is a totally automated task. They believe that consumer search tools such as Google and Bing operate automatically without human interaction. These are false assumptions. The reality is that human intervention is required to optimize SharePoint search. One example is promoting sites and documents to make sure that the most important content is being shown as a promoted result at the top of the page. For example, when someone searches for "benefits" during the last quarter of a calendar year (October through December), your organization may want to link to a site or page with information on benefits open enrollment. Individuals can also define search synonyms so that when a person searches on a particular term or acronym it can be mapped to display other similar search results. A search administrator can also help to demote documents or sites to push less authoritative content sources to be displayed lower in search results.

Note   SharePoint 2013 does not fix content problems such as incorrect document titles. If you're not getting very good search results in SharePoint 2007 or SharePoint 2010, an upgrade to SharePoint 2013 won't fix your problem. In fact, it could make the problem worse. Take the time during the upgrade to educate users on the importance of the Title property, which is used for displaying search results. Search results that look incorrect could simply be reflecting bad data. Remember: garbage in, garbage out.

What Content Should You Expose Via SharePoint Search and How?

When developing your enterprise search strategy, there are a number of key questions to consider, including the following:

- What content needs to be indexed via the SharePoint search engine?
- Where does that content reside today?
- Do you need to crawl content over a wide area network (WAN)?
- Are there any time zone considerations? Crawling can impact the source system that you're crawling—you might be scheduling crawls off-hours where the search server is located, but it could be the middle of the workday for content owners.

- Does the content being indexed have adequate security controls in place, or do people practice "security by obscurity" and basically "hide" content by burying files many folders deep? If so, search may now "expose" that "hidden" content, which was never really secured in the first place.
- Do you have other search tools already in place that currently index the content?
- Do you want to have a single search engine crawl the content so you can have a single source of relevancy for ranking and displaying the results?
- Do you have to federate with other search engines internally or externally (e.g., Google, Bing) to also display results for content SharePoint does not crawl? If so, do these other search engines support the OpenSearch federation standard?
- Should you feature and promote certain content for certain roles?
- What content sources should be indexed as opposed to federated?
- What file types do you need to index (e.g., Word, .pdf, CAD, videos, etc.)? Do you need any additional iFilters to crawl the contents of these files (if SharePoint does not already include them), or is indexing the metadata alone sufficient?
- What languages do you need to support? Is there any LOB system data (e.g., CRM, ERP) that you want to display via search? If so, are there existing BCS connections already in place, or do you need to create new ones for search purposes?
- Will you need to implement a hybrid search architecture to display search results across both SharePoint Online and SharePoint Server?
- What are the roles and responsibilities for search administration?
- What training is required for managing search?
- Will SharePoint 2013 search be the first service implemented on the new platform to perform a "search first" migration where existing content is crawled and displayed in place and gradually migrated or archived?

These are just some of the key questions that we suggest you consider as part of developing your enterprise search strategy. The remainder of this chapter will help you to understand what SharePoint 2013 offers from a user and administrative perspective to guide you in answering these questions and developing new questions of your own.

Understanding Search from a User Perspective

The user search experience has evolved from what was available in SharePoint 2010. There are two primary ways to search: using a Search Center landing page (see Figure 16-1) or directly within a SharePoint site page (see Figure 16-2).

Users can access standard result sources (functionality that replaces search scopes in prior versions) from a SharePoint site page. Result sources include the following:

- **This Site** is the default search, which includes content stored in the current site and its child sites.
- **Everything** includes content ranked across a variety of sources such as SharePoint sites, people, file shares, or other document management solutions.

Figure 16-1 SharePoint 2013 Enterprise Search Center

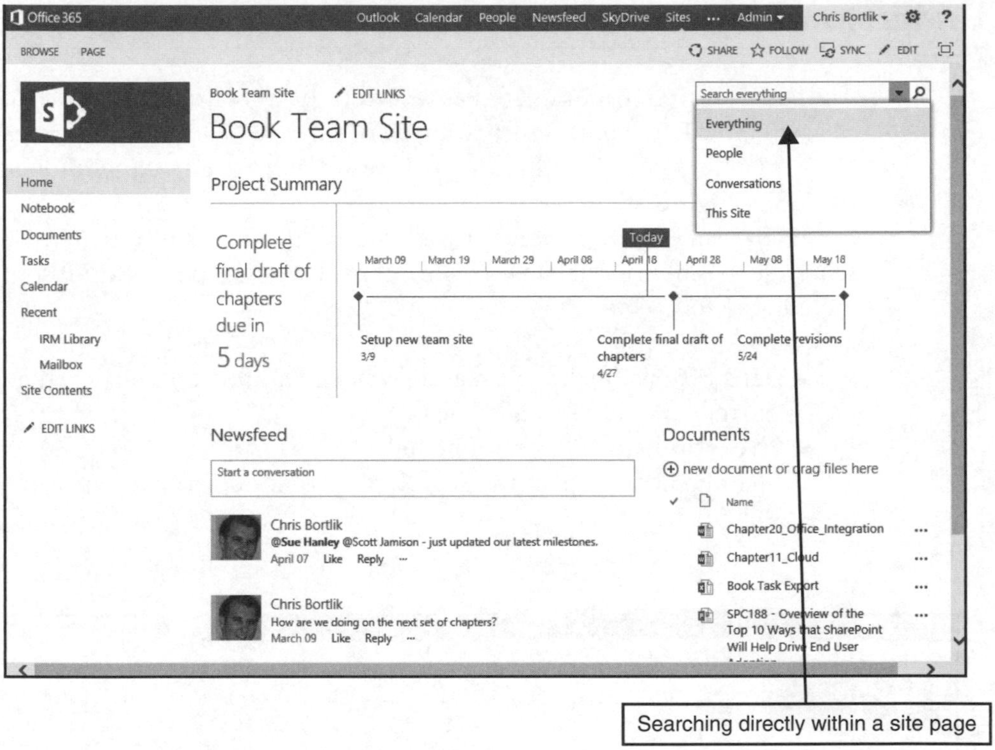

Figure 16-2 SharePoint 2013 site search

- **People** focuses just on information from other people's profiles within SharePoint and provides the option to review results by relevance (how likely it is that the person has skills or interests that match your search) or social distance (looking at the people you follow and those that they follow).

- **Conversations** includes results across the public newsfeed, team newsfeeds, and community site discussions based on your permission level. More information on these capabilities can be found in Chapter 15, "Planning for Social Computing."

SharePoint 2013 search remembers your prior search history and can recommend recently used search terms. It can also suggest search terms (also referred to as queries) based on similar phrases that are trending in popularity across your environment.

SharePoint search result pages provide search refiners to help you filter your results. The refiners vary based on the result source. For example, the Everything result source provides options to refine by the result type (e.g., Word document, .pdf, Web page, etc.), the author of the document, and the date the content was last modified. The Author refiner enables you to also enter a specific name to find results just from a particular person. You can also create your own custom search refiners, such as the Chapter Name refiner shown in Figure 16-3.

Figure 16.4 shows a sample search result from within a team site. One major change that users coming from FAST search for SharePoint will notice is that by default the search refiners do not show the count for the number of items that are of that type, such as that there are 250 Word documents. While the counts are not shown by default, you should know that SharePoint search does do deep refinement as part of the content-crawling process and does sort some of the result types, such as the author,

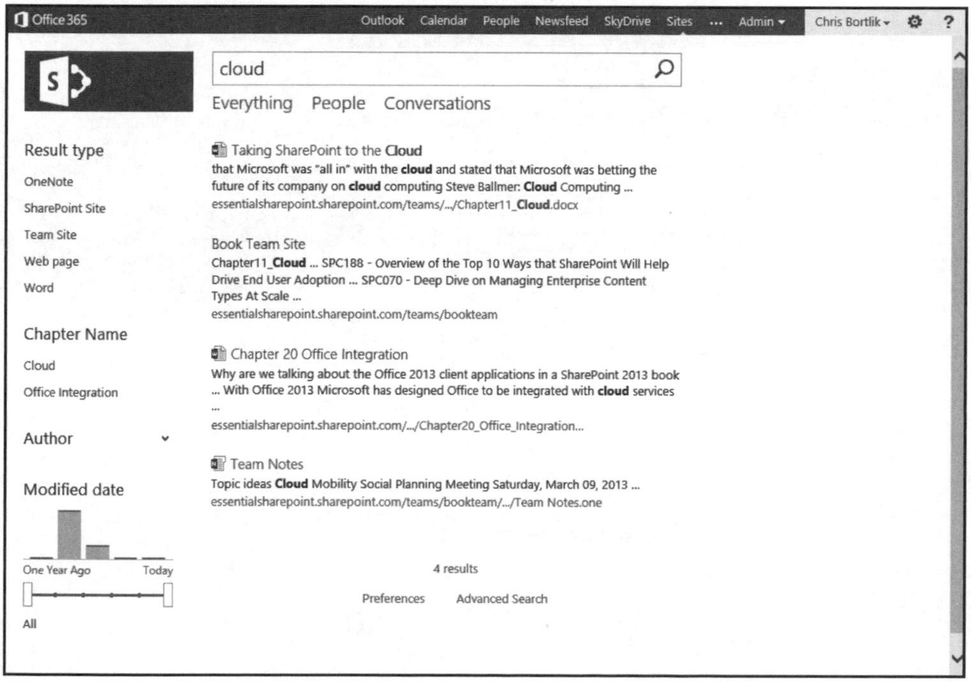

Figure 16-3 SharePoint 2013 search refiners

in descending order so that refiners with the most items will be displayed at the top. The counts can also be displayed in the search results, if desired.

There are many changes within the search results as well. As Figure 16-4 shows, when SharePoint 2013 is used with the Office Web Apps server, search results for Word, PowerPoint, and Excel documents include a full live preview of the document that you can scroll through. Word and PowerPoint results provide you with links to jump directly into the document at specific sections or slides.

Even without the Office Web Apps, search results now provide much richer context. Document results give you the direct ability to follow the document from the search results and see important metadata such as who authored the document, when it was last modified, and how many times the document has been viewed.

Conversations search results look across SharePoint community sites and newsfeeds. Community results show how active a given community is, including the number of members, discussions, and replies. You can

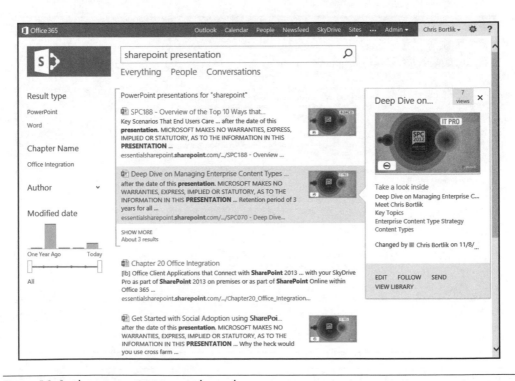

Figure 16-4 SharePoint 2013 search results

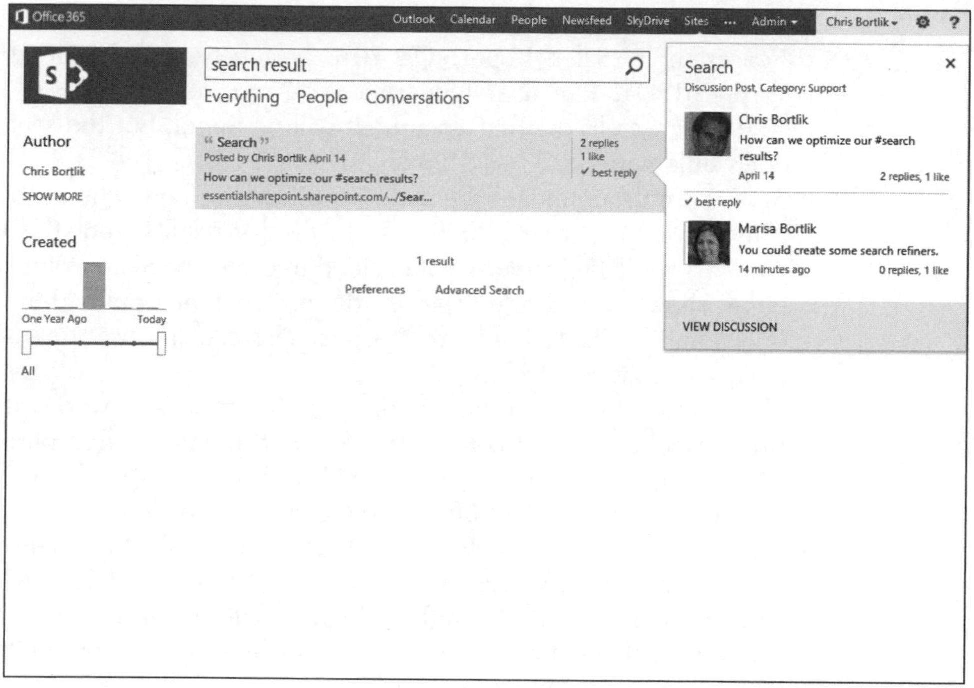

Figure 16-5 SharePoint 2013 Conversations search

quickly go to specific discussions within a community (see Figure 16-5) or visit the community site.

Search Tips and Syntax

When performing searches, there are a number of options available to help you target search results. Many people will use the built-in search refiners to narrow down the search results to include only specific file types or dates or locations or authors. However, more advanced querying options are available. Some examples of search tips and advanced query options are listed below. Additional tips are summarized in the Appendix.

- Put search phrases in quotes to indicate that you're searching for an exact phrase, for example, "business intelligence."
- When naming content, use whole words and use underscores to separate those words. This is due to word breaking, which splits

the file name into real words that are used as search keywords. For example, Sales_Report_Q4_2013 is a better file name than slsrpt-2013Q4. If a user types in "sales" or "report" or "Q4" or "2013" in search, the first document will be found, but the second one would not.

- Make sure users update the Title property for document content. This property is what search uses to display results—not the file name. If the Title property is not filled in correctly, SharePoint will either show the bad title or arbitrarily use content from within the document for displaying search results. This can confuse users and make them think search is bad.

- Place an asterisk at the end of the search phrase as a wildcard to bring back results that contain the first part of your search phrase. For example, searching on "shar*" will return search results containing words such as *SharePoint*, *sharing*, and *shared*.

- Use search operators such as AND, OR, and NOT. For example, you can perform a search such as ("SharePoint" OR "SPS") AND (title:"search" OR title:"workflow"), which will return search results for items that contain *SharePoint* or *SPS* where the title of the item includes the words *search* or *workflow*.

SharePoint 2013 also provides an Advanced Search screen that lets any user perform a complex query without having to understand SharePoint search syntax. Figure 16-6 shows one example to find all documents in English created by any author whose name is "Bortlik"; where the document was last modified on or after September 1, 2012; and where the word *SharePoint* or *search* is contained within the body of the document or any of its metadata. The Advanced Search page also includes a link to a help resource with additional search tips.

Additional Search Options

Two additional capabilities are available to users to help them make search work the way they want it:

- **Search alerts** allow you to have a search query run automatically on your behalf and send you the results via e-mail. For example, you could receive an e-mail daily when new items are available for keywords of interest to you. Note that search alerts must be enabled in Central Administration as part of the Search service application for this capability to work.

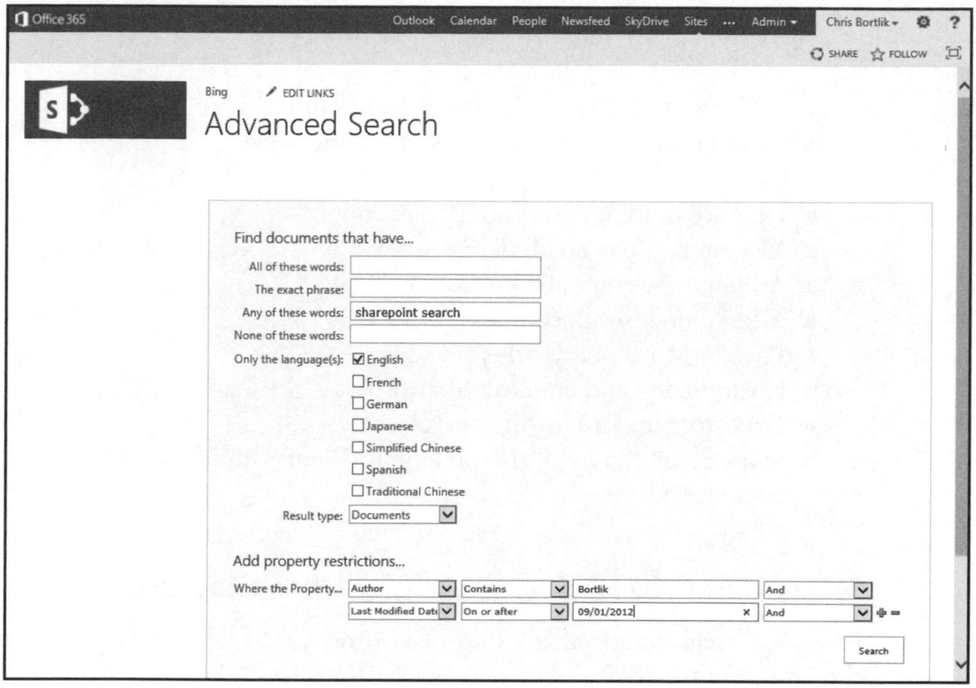

Figure 16-6 SharePoint 2013 Advanced Search page

- **Search preferences** allow users to specify whether they want SharePoint search to suggest search phrases to them and whether the search engine should use their personal search history to suggest previously used search phrases. Users can also specify their default search language (e.g., search results for content in English or Spanish), whether to use the Office Web Apps or Office desktop clients to open search results that are clicked on, and to manage their existing search alerts. Users can access their search preferences at the bottom of the search results page.

SharePoint 2013 Search Administration

The SharePoint 2013 search architecture is different from how search was performed in previous SharePoint and/or FAST versions. This section describes the logical architecture, physical architecture, and options for managing SharePoint 2013 search crawling and results display and includes the following topics:

- SharePoint 2013 search logical architecture
- SharePoint 2013 search physical architecture
- Capacity planning considerations
- Upgrading to SharePoint 2013 search
- Managing SharePoint 2013 search
- Adding new content sources
- Adding new result sources
- Working with query rules
- Customizing and creating SharePoint 2013 search refiners
- Exporting and importing search settings
- SharePoint Server 2013 and SharePoint Online search capability comparison

SharePoint 2013 Search Logical Architecture

From a logical perspective, content is processed by SharePoint 2013 as shown in Figure 16-7.

- **Content source** is the system that SharePoint is crawling. The content source could be SharePoint itself, a file share, a Web site, or some other system.
- **SharePoint crawler** uses a connector to get content and metadata from a content source.
- **Content processing** occurs for each item, such as a document or Web page, that comes from the crawler. The appropriate iFilter is

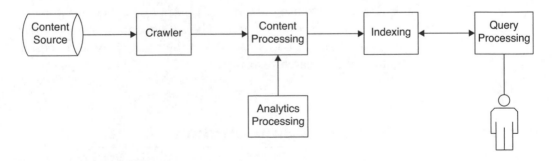

Figure 16-7 SharePoint 2013 logical architecture

used to analyze the full text of the item, such as a .pdf file. Additional steps are performed to process metadata and extract entities to refine by, such as the built-in Companies refiner.

- **Analytics** processing information is processed to see how often an item is viewed and linked to by other items.
- The **indexing component** uses the output of content processing to create index files. The indexer is also used to provide search results to the query-processing component when a user makes a search request.
- The **query-processing** component performs a number of key tasks after accepting the search request. These include applying query rules, performing linguistics tasks (e.g., stemming, word breaking, spell checking, etc.), and processing result sets before displaying the results to the user.
- The **search administration component** (not shown in Figure 16-7) handles the system processes for search and manages the other search components.

SharePoint 2013 Search Physical Architecture

From a technical implementation perspective, outside of SharePoint Online, you have the option of scaling the various search roles across multiple servers (physical or virtual). Figure 16-8 shows the view in central administration that helps you review which servers in your SharePoint farm are handling the various search roles. In this example, we are running all roles on a single test server. In the real world you would have multiple servers handling different roles for both redundancy and scalability.

Figure 16.8 also shows the various search databases that are created by the default search configuration wizard. The primary function of each of these databases is as follows:[1]

- **Administration database** stores settings for the Search Service application, such as the topology, crawl rules, query rules, and the mappings between crawled and managed properties.
- **Analytics reporting database** stores the results of usage analysis, such as the number of times an item has been viewed. It also stores

---

1. "Overview of Search in SharePoint 2013." http://technet.microsoft.com/en-us/library/jj219738(v=office.15).aspx

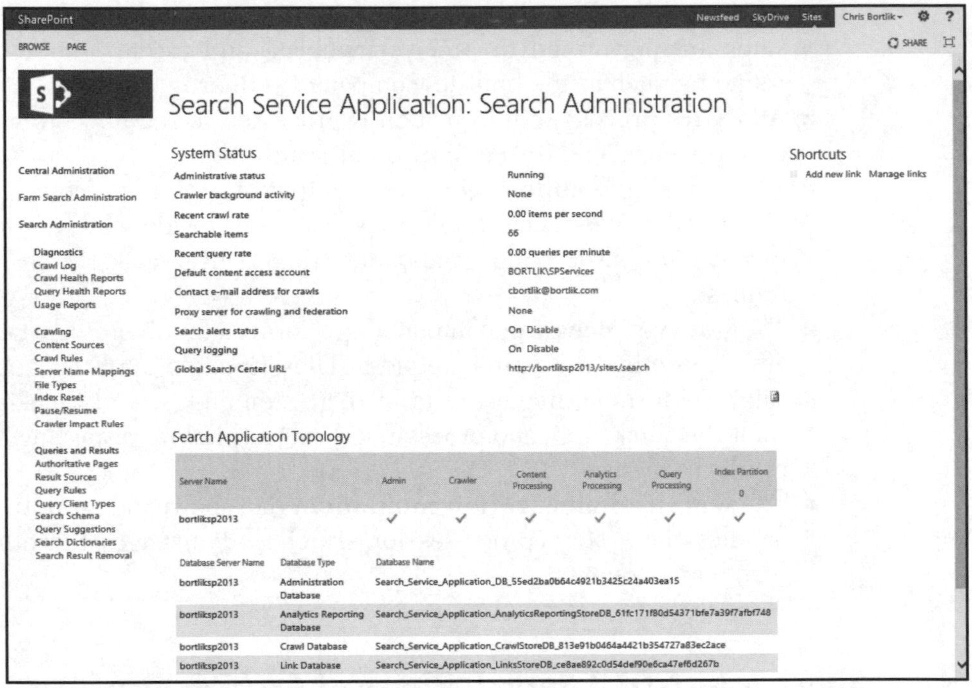

Figure 16-8 SharePoint 2013 search application topology

statistics from the different analyses. These statistics are used to create usage reports.

- **Crawl database** stores tracking information and details about crawled items such as documents and URLs. It also stores information such as the last crawl time, the last crawl ID, and the type of update (add, update, delete) during the last crawl.

- **Link database** stores unprocessed information that is extracted by the content-processing component and information about search clicks. The analytics-processing component analyzes this information.

Note   Additional information and details on the SharePoint 2013 search architecture can be found on the Microsoft TechNet site at http://technet .microsoft.com/en-us/library/jj219738(v=office.15).aspx.

Capacity Planning Considerations

When planning for search as part of SharePoint Server 2013, there are many factors to consider. Microsoft has published guidance and reference architectures to help you calculate the number of search servers (physical or virtual) you may need as well as what the hardware specifications are, including the amount of memory, storage, and processor power required. This information is published at http://technet.microsoft.com/en-us/library/jj219628(v=office.15).

Some of the key inputs that you will need to identify in your capacity planning include the following:

- How many items do you plan to crawl?
- How large are the items being crawled (e.g., average file size)?
- How much metadata will be indexed?
- How many content sources do you plan to index?
- How often will you index the content sources (full, incremental, or continuous crawl) and how frequently does the source content change?
- What do you expect to be the average number of queries per second that you need to support?
- What are your disaster recovery and high-availability requirements for search?

Upgrading to SharePoint 2013 Search

When upgrading to SharePoint 2013 search from SharePoint 2010, there are a few key scenarios and options to consider:

- If upgrading from SharePoint 2010 standard search to SharePoint 2013, you have the option to perform a database-attach and upgrade in SharePoint 2013. You will be able to upgrade the SharePoint 2010 Search Service application administration database, which includes existing content sources, crawl rules, and federated locations. Please see Chapter 10, "Planning Your Upgrade," for more details on upgrading to SharePoint 2013.
- If you are using FAST search for SharePoint 2010 or any other prior version of FAST, you will need to do a manual migration to SharePoint 2013 search, although Microsoft may be making some

migration tools and resources available at a later date. You will need to inventory any existing content sources and processing changes that you have made and implement them in SharePoint 2013.

- Since SharePoint 2013 introduces so many new search changes, you may choose to recreate your content sources and processing rules manually in SharePoint 2013.

Managing SharePoint 2013 Search

Many of the core search administration capabilities are managed in SharePoint central administration (SharePoint Server) or tenant administration (SharePoint Online). There is no longer a separate search administration server as there was with FAST search for SharePoint 2010.

When defining new content sources to crawl in SharePoint Server, one decision that needs to be made is how often the content needs to be indexed. You can also define a schedule for full and incremental crawls. A new capability added for SharePoint Server content is the option to perform a continuous crawl, which enables SharePoint content to be available in the index in near real time, which is important for many of the new search-driven features such as using the Content by Search Web Part to aggregate Web content.

Most organizations establish a single enterprise Search Center where corporate-wide result sources and query rules are defined. In some organizations, however, it is desirable to have departmental search centers that have unique rules and displays available for certain functional areas such as research or legal. If you create different strategies based on the search source, consider how you will communicate this difference to your users.

Adding New Content Sources

When working with SharePoint Server 2013, you can add new content sources to be crawled and indexed by SharePoint search. By default, SharePoint 2013 crawls local SharePoint content (sites, lists, people information, documents, pages, etc.) on the SharePoint farm of which the search server(s) is a member. Typically, organizations set up SharePoint to perform a full crawl once per week (such as Saturday evenings when there typically is lower system load from users) and to have incremental crawls performed throughout the day at scheduled intervals (for example, once every hour).

SharePoint 2013 introduces the concept of continuous crawls to enable specified SharePoint content to be made searchable without going through the full indexing process. This is very important for search-driven Web sites that have dynamic content. You can select to implement either continuous crawling or incremental crawls. We expect that most organizations will choose to use continuous crawls—especially for farms with frequent content updates.

In addition to crawling SharePoint content stored in your SharePoint environment, you can also crawl and index content from other locations. SharePoint 2013 supports the following content source locations out of the box:

- Web sites
- File shares
- Exchange public folders
- Line-of-business data via Business Connectivity Services within SharePoint that support content retrieval from external data sources such as a customer relationship management (CRM) or enterprise resource planning (ERP) system.

SharePoint supports the ability to connect to additional content sources if the appropriate custom repository connector is installed and configured. For example, Microsoft offers custom connectors for Lotus Notes and Documentum. You can also purchase connectors from other organizations or build your own.

Adding New Result Sources

A result source is simply a collection of settings that defines what the user will get back when issuing a search query. A result source is defined mainly by three parameters: a source URL (from where do I get results?), a protocol (local SharePoint? OpenSearch?), and a query transform, which allows the user to narrow the results to a subset (just .pdf files? just a particular Content Type?). In prior versions of SharePoint, this concept was referred to as search scopes.

SharePoint 2013 provides 16 preconfigured SharePoint result sources including conversations (social newsfeeds and community sites), documents, people, and video results. More likely than not, you'll be able to stick with this collection of out-of-the-box result sources. However, if you have a specific scenario that you want to customize, SharePoint provides the capability to create custom result sources if needed.

SharePoint 2013 supports working with the following result source protocols:

- **Local SharePoint** content within the current farm
- **Remote SharePoint** content coming from another SharePoint farm or SharePoint Online
- **OpenSearch 1.0/1.1** federation with other search engines such as Bing or Google
- **Exchange** server content such as public folders

The remote SharePoint result source is key in a few scenarios. One of the primary use cases is in hybrid environments that include both SharePoint Server on-premises and SharePoint Online, for example, where the organization's intranet is based on SharePoint on-premises but team and personal sites are provided via SharePoint Online. In this scenario, you will want to enable people to see search results across both environments. Another example may be cases where customers have multiple SharePoint geographically distributed farms and these farms may not be using a single search service. One important aspect to be aware of is that when different result sources are being leveraged, such as when using a remote SharePoint farm as a source, there is no ability to have a single relevancy ranking applied. This means that the local SharePoint results will be indexed and ranked separately from the remote SharePoint farm's results. If it is important that the relevancy of your search results be factored into how they are displayed, you may want to consider crawling all of the content via a single search engine (if possible) or trying to leverage result blocks (discussed later in this chapter) to highlight and promote certain result sources to have a higher priority over others.

Result sources also allow you to define and apply custom handling and display templates to different results coming from different locations or different types of content within a given source. This is useful since you might want to display product catalog searches differently from people searches.

A final decision in search administration is which result sources should be defined at the farm (SharePoint Server) or tenant (SharePoint Online) level so they can be reused across multiple site collections. Result sources can also be defined at the site collection or site level, which enables greater flexibility, such as for different business units, departments, or team needs.

Working with Query Rules

SharePoint 2013 has somewhat deemphasized the concept of identifying content as a "best bet"—which is now referred to as promoted results. For example, whenever someone searches on a particular keyword (such as SharePoint), a specific result is always shown at the top of the page (see Figure 16-9). Setting promoted results does not change an authorized user's ability to access content; it simply changes the item's position in the search result listing.

Promoted results can be defined as query rules based on specific content sources, such as SharePoint search results. Promoted results can be set to be shown only during specific time periods, for example, only showing benefits open enrollment links between September 1 and December 31 for a given year. Promoted results can also be shown to

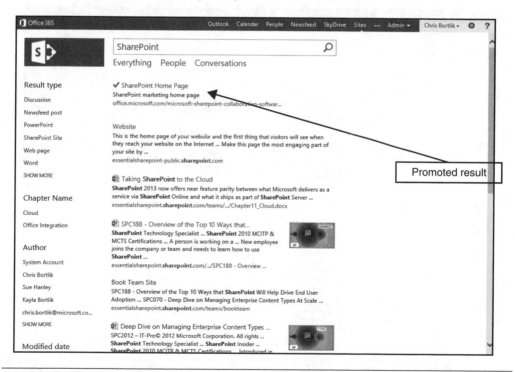

Figure 16-9 SharePoint 2013 search with promoted result

specific user segments, which allows you to target recommended results at different groups of individuals such as people in sales or research roles.

Query rules also allow you to define result blocks. Result blocks are a powerful tool you can configure to inspect the query results and then take additional actions before displaying the results to the user. For example, if a user searches for a product name, you can display not only documents that match that search criterion but also related product inventory data from an ERP system (such as SAP or PeopleSoft) as part of the search results. SharePoint 2013 ships with many standard result blocks. Figure 16-10 shows an example where the keyword presentation is detected in the search query. Because a result block has been defined for this keyword, SharePoint groups all PowerPoint presentations and displays them at the top of the page.

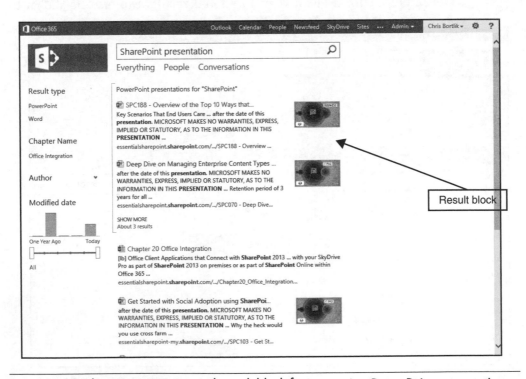

Figure 16-10 SharePoint 2013 search result block for promoting PowerPoint presentations

Customizing and Creating SharePoint 2013 Search Refiners

SharePoint 2013 search enables you to manage and create search refiners that display as part of the search results. There are a few areas to consider:

- **Managing the search schema** allows you to modify managed properties and map crawled properties to managed properties. Crawled properties are automatically extracted from crawled content. You can use managed properties to refine search results and present the content of the properties in search results. For example, you can specify which properties included in the search crawl should be displayed to the user as part of the "About me" search refiner that is shown in people search results.

- **Adding and displaying new search refiners** may not be obvious to most SharePoint search administrators. Since this is such an important and often overlooked capability, we strongly encourage readers to review this article from Microsoft that describes how to create custom search refiners: http://office.microsoft.com/en-us/ office365-sharepoint-online-enterprise-help/manage-the-search- schema-in-sharepoint-online-HA103628856.aspx. Once created, these custom search refiners can be added to your search results page by customizing the built-in Refinement Web Part and using the Choose Refiners feature to select the refiners you want to display.

- New in SharePoint 2013 are **search dictionaries** that are defined and managed via the term store, also known as the Managed Metadata Service (managed metadata is discussed further in Chapter 13, "Managing Enterprise Content"). Search dictionaries allow you to specify the list of values that SharePoint search should include or exclude when it is building the list of a search refinement. For example, in a company name extraction process, search can identify words such as *Microsoft, Jornata,* or *General Electric* as names of companies and then let you create a refiner to filter search results to show only items that contain those company names. You can also manage the list of phrases to be included or excluded as "did you mean" search phrases when users search for similar phrases. For example, search could suggest the word *SharePoint* if someone entered the search term "SharePint." Out of the box,

SharePoint search will also automatically handle suggesting "did you mean" search phrases for commonly used words that may be misspelled in user searches.

■ Using PowerShell scripts, you can also create your own custom **entity extractors** that can then be mapped to managed properties within search. For example, search could dynamically identify and build search refiners based on a list of your organization's product names.

Exporting and Importing Search Settings

SharePoint 2013 search enables you to export and import search settings. This is important when you want to reuse search query rules across SharePoint tenants or site collections. Exporting search settings includes all customized query rules, result sources, result types, ranking models, and site search settings that your organization has customized but not any that shipped with SharePoint.

Comparing SharePoint Server 2013 to SharePoint Online Search

Table 16-1 provides a summary of the key search administration features and indicates what is available within SharePoint Server 2013 compared to SharePoint Online. As noted earlier in this chapter, Microsoft has published a complete licensing matrix that shows what license level is needed to use specific features. A few of the major functional differences between SharePoint Server and SharePoint Online are that the following options are currently available only with SharePoint Server (please see Chapter 11, "Taking SharePoint to the Cloud," for a more thorough comparison):

■ The new **Content by Search Web Part** is key to many search-driven intranet site experiences. This Web Part enables aggregation of content across site collections by using the content available in the search index, rather than querying the content databases themselves. Note: This Web Part is part of the Enterprise CAL and as of this writing is not available in Office 365.

Table 16-1 Comparison of Search Administration Options

Capability	SharePoint Server	SharePoint Online	Setting Level
View crawl log	Yes	Yes	Farm or tenant
Crawl health reports	Yes	No—managed by Microsoft as part of the Office 365 service	Farm
Query health reports	Yes	No—managed by Microsoft as part of the Office 365 service	Farm
Usage reports	Number of Queries Top Queries by Day Top Queries by Month Abandoned Queries by Day Abandoned Queries by Month No Result Queries by Day No Result Queries by Month Query Rule Usage by Day Query Rule Usage by Month	Same as Share-Point Server	Farm or tenant
Content sources to index	SharePoint Sites (with continuous crawl option and ability to change full/incremental crawl schedule) Web sites File shares Exchange public folders LOB data Custom repository via custom connector (e.g., Documentum)	SharePoint Online only but can add additional result sources (see below)	Farm
Crawl rules	Yes	No	Farm
Server name mappings	Yes	No	Farm

(continues)

Table 16-1 Comparison of Search Administration Options *(continued)*

Capability	SharePoint Server	SharePoint Online	Setting Level
File types	58 included (e.g., .docx, .pdf) and can add additional iFilters	58 included as part of SharePoint Online service	Farm
Index reset	Yes	No	Farm
Crawler impact rules	Yes	No	Farm
Authoritative pages	Yes	Yes	Farm or tenant
Result sources	16 included; additional sources can be added: Local SharePoint Remote SharePoint OpenSearch 1.0/1.1 Exchange	Same as SharePoint Server	Farm, tenant, site collection, or site
Query rules	Yes	Yes	Farm, tenant, site collection, or site
Query client types	Yes and can add additional client types and change throttling priority	Same as SharePoint Server	Farm or tenant
Search schema	Yes and can add additional managed properties and edit crawled property mappings	Yes and can add additional managed properties and edit crawled property mappings	Farm, tenant, site collection, or site
Query suggestions	Yes and can specify phrases to always or never suggest	Yes and can specify phrases to always or never suggest	Farm or tenant
Search dictionaries	Yes via Managed Metadata Service	Yes via Managed Metadata Service	Farm or tenant
Search result removal	Yes	Yes	Farm or tenant

Capability	SharePoint Server	SharePoint Online	Setting Level
Specify default Search Center URL	Yes	Yes	Farm or tenant
Import/ export search configuration	Yes	Yes	Tenant or site collection
Result types	Yes	Yes	Site collection or site
Search navigation settings	Yes	Yes	Site collection or site
Searchable Column exclusions	Yes	Yes	Site
Exclude site from search	Yes	Yes	Site
Mark site for reindex	Yes	Yes	Site

- **Advanced content processing** allows you to manipulate some of the internal search relevancy algorithms and weightings via PowerShell scripts.
- **Custom entity extraction** is a capability to define your own metadata attributes for SharePoint 2013 search to dynamically determine during the crawl process and display as search refiners. In SharePoint Online you cannot define your own list of custom entities to derive from the crawled content; however, you can modify the built-in list of companies to include or exclude from the companies refiner.

Search-Driven Applications

One of the emerging trends is to use search as an interface to navigate content. Public-facing Web sites such as bestbuy.com, financialtimes.com, and treasury.gov have made search part of their core user experience. Rather than relying on a relatively static information architecture and site hierarchy, many sites are now leveraging search to drive a more dynamic and personalized experience.

SharePoint 2013 has implemented a number of new capabilities designed to make it easier for companies to implement search-driven Web sites.

Video Search Results

Out of the box, SharePoint 2013 provides a custom search results page showing videos that are tagged to match the keywords you're searching for. Note that this feature does not index the audio and video—SharePoint bases the search on the metadata and file type.

SharePoint 2013 also provides a new way of viewing and interacting with video search results. This includes the ability to see a thumbnail preview for the video, the ability to play the video in the context of the search results using either a built-in HTML5 or Silverlight viewer, and the ability to perform actions such as following the video or sending a link to others.

New Search-Driven Content Web Parts

SharePoint Server 2013 introduces a number of new search-driven Web Parts. These Web Parts enable dynamic aggregation and viewing of content via crawled search results and are highly configurable without requiring developer assistance. There are 11 Web Parts in SharePoint 2013 in the new Search-Driven Content Web Part category. These include Web Parts to dynamically display popular and recommended items.

For example, you may want to leverage a Search-Driven Web Part to dynamically display a summary of article pages. Inserting the Articles Web Part on a page offers you the option to configure various items for how you want the search results to be displayed and how many items to show.

Changing the query displays a query builder wizard that enables you to perform multiple tasks, including selecting from various search refiners.

For example, you can filter the search results to show only the content based on the Article Page template.

Key Points

There are significant changes to enterprise search in SharePoint 2013. Some of the main topics covered in this chapter are:

- SharePoint 2013 introduces a brand-new enterprise search engine which is based on the "best" concepts and features that were available in SharePoint 2010 and FAST while adding new capabilities.
- There is now a single integrated enterprise search engine that exists across all versions of SharePoint 2013 (Foundation, Standard, Enterprise, Online), and this engine now also powers Exchange 2013 search.
- Effectively implementing enterprise search requires up-front planning and review of your search requirements. Some items to plan for include identifying what content sources (e.g., SharePoint, file shares, Documentum, etc.) need to be included, what type of content is being indexed (e.g., Office documents, Web pages, Adobe .pdfs, etc.), understanding how often the content is updated and needs to be made available in search results, and determining what sort of query and result processing you want to perform against search to promote certain search results.
- Search is now key to many other areas within SharePoint 2013. Many of the new Web content management features leverage search to dynamically aggregate and display content as well as to recommend content. The new social features leverage search to recommend sites, documents, and people for you to follow. Search is also used to drive the new usage analytics components within SharePoint.

CHAPTER 17

PLANNING BUSINESS SOLUTIONS

In Chapter 5, "Planning for Operational Governance," we discussed the importance of governing the customizations made to your SharePoint environment that support business solutions built with SharePoint. In this chapter, we discuss three key concepts that enable you to create and manage those business solutions by customizing SharePoint, along with the changes to these functions that have been introduced in SharePoint 2013:

- **Composite Applications**, which are a way to assemble business-critical solutions via premade components
- **Business Connectivity Services**, which enable you to connect SharePoint to external data sources
- **Workflows**, which provide the basis for automating business processes within the organization

Companies far and wide struggle to connect their users with the business data stored in various locations such as databases and file shares across the organization in a simple, easy-to-use manner, and to use that data in business processes, making sure employees are performing the right tasks in the right order. As these companies become more successful at getting the data into an electronic format, IT departments are under pressure to meet the demands of the data consumer to build complex applications to manage that information. In most cases, custom development has been required to build those applications—which increases time, effort, cost, and project risks.

SharePoint Composite Applications were introduced to address this issue. By using the suite of client applications (SharePoint Designer, InfoPath, Excel, Access, and Visio), and leveraging the flexible nature of SharePoint Web Part pages, IT departments can enable a self-service environment for the business—significantly reducing the need for IT to be involved in data-driven solutions while still maintaining control over the systems and the data itself. Another way to connect users with business data is to leverage the SharePoint platform to enable business process automation, specifically through workflows and tasks. Solutions in this category can provide functionality to capture data and move it through a defined business process. These business processes, whether connected to external databases or not, are another must-have solution set in the business user's arsenal. Assigning and managing user tasks in SharePoint is a way to keep business processes running smoothly, especially when associated with a project or process.

What's New in SharePoint 2013?

Before we dive into the details, here's a summary of what is new in SharePoint 2013 with respect to Composite Applications, business connectivity, and workflows:

- **Business Connectivity Services (BCS).** BCS has been enhanced in SharePoint 2013 to connect to OData sources (an industry-standard way of accessing data) and receive events from external systems. In addition, External Content Types can now be scoped at the application level. Finally, support for Representational State Transfer (REST) and the client object model has been enhanced. These features provide the ability to create sophisticated, modern applications without significant coding. We'll review the core pieces of BCS and how to plan for it in the first half of this chapter.
- **Access Services.** Access Services still provides a way to put an Access database into SharePoint, giving you the ability to manage, secure, and control databases that would otherwise have existed on someone's hard drive away from the control of IT. This feature was available in SharePoint 2010. However, in SharePoint Server 2013, an Access Services database is actually a SQL Server database, rather than a list as it was in SharePoint 2010. When you create an Access Services app, SharePoint talks to a SQL Server 2012 instance and creates tables within SQL Server for the tables in the Access database, giving you a SQL Server database that you can use directly, or

with the front end in SharePoint. We don't cover Access Services in this book; for more information, check out http://technet.microsoft .com/en-us/library/ee748634.aspx.

- **Napa.** The new Napa Office 365 Development Tools, which are Web-based and used with an Office 365 tenant, can be used to build apps for Office or SharePoint without the need for Visual Studio. Instead, you use an Office 365 developer site and a supported browser. That said, Napa apps will still require coding, which is outside the scope of this book (for more information, check out http://msdn.microsoft.com/en-us/library/jj220038 .aspx). We'll stick to the browser and SharePoint Designer in this chapter.

- **Work management.** The Work Management Service application provides functionality to aggregate tasks to a central location, where users can view and track their to-dos and tasks. In addition, tasks can be cached to a user's personal site, aggregated from Exchange, Project Server, and SharePoint. The Work Management Service is usually exposed as part of each user's My Site/newsfeed experience. If you use tasks with Project Server, SharePoint sites, or Outlook/Exchange to-dos, this feature alone can help social adoption within your organization by consolidating task management. For more information on work management, visit http://social.technet.microsoft.com/wiki/contents/articles/12525 .sharepoint-2013-work-management-service-application.aspx.

- **Workflow Manager.** Workflow in SharePoint 2013 introduces a number of enterprise features such as fully declarative authoring, REST and Service Bus messaging, elastic scalability, and managed service reliability. SharePoint Server 2013 can use either the old SharePoint 2010 engine or a new workflow service built on the Windows Workflow Foundation using .NET Framework 4.5. The new service, called Workflow Manager, is designed to play a major role in the enterprise by organizing central processes. We'll discuss workflows in the second half of this chapter.

Note that we didn't mention enhancements to InfoPath Forms Services. This is because Forms Services in SharePoint 2013 is essentially the same as in SharePoint 2010. We cover InfoPath and Forms Services very briefly at the end of the chapter.

What Is a Composite Application?

SharePoint 2013 provides users with a suite of applications and functionality to allow them to take more control over how they represent their data. With the help of Visio Services, Excel and Access Services, and SharePoint Designer, it is possible for these users to build no-code collaborative solutions through browser-based customizations.

Note With SharePoint composites you can
- Rapidly create no-code collaborative solutions
- Unlock the value of enterprise data
- Maintain control over user solutions

Prior to SharePoint, those client applications could be used to create solutions that were trapped on a single machine. With SharePoint in the mix, Visio 2013, Excel 2013, and Access 2013 allow the user to work on local data and then publish it to SharePoint, leveraging enterprise-class services such as scalability, a Web-based interface, and IT control for things such as backups and permissioning. Even with this level of functionality, accessing external data has always been a challenge. Microsoft recognized this and filled this gap in SharePoint 2010 with Business Connectivity Services.

Using Business Connectivity Services

Business Connectivity Services is a component of SharePoint 2013 and Office 2013 that provides a way to create business solutions for scenarios that require integration of external data sources. With BCS, you can use SharePoint 2013 sites (and Office 2013 clients) as an interface into data that doesn't live in SharePoint 2013 itself (see Figure 17-1).

Back in SharePoint 2007, the Business Data Catalog (BDC) was introduced as a way to bring enterprise data from SQL Server, Oracle, and other sources directly into SharePoint in a real-time manner. This was the first step in bridging the gap between SharePoint data and external enterprise data. While it was an important step, it proved to be difficult to work with and limited in functionality. In SharePoint Server

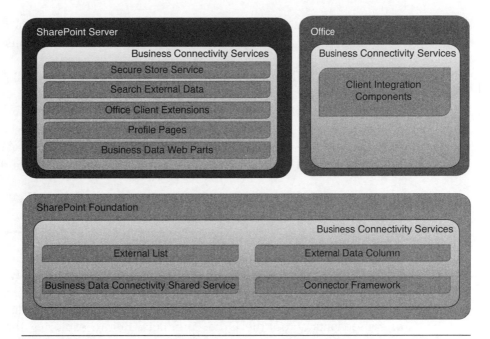

Figure 17-1 Business connectivity services provides the ability to connect SharePoint to other databases, such as Oracle, a line-of-business database, or a SQL database running on Azure

2010, Microsoft took a giant leap forward by introducing BCS. With BCS in SharePoint 2010, users could read and write data as easily as they interacted with a standard SharePoint list. In addition, business solution designers could use SharePoint Designer to create and manage external connections. The Business Data Web Parts helped expose the external data for building Composite Applications. SharePoint 2013 continues the evolution of BCS, providing enhanced access to data sources using OData (the Open Data Protocol) for developers.

In short, BCS provides the ability to

- Expose enterprise data from external sources such as databases and Web services through the user interface in SharePoint 2013 and Office 2013
- Map Office-type objects and capabilities such as appointments, tasks, and contacts to external data

- Enable a two-way synchronization between the external data and SharePoint, allowing the data to be updated as well as consumed in SharePoint
- Provide offline accessibility to the external data using clients such as Outlook

While the BCS platform gives power users great functionality and flexibility to create data-centric applications, IT departments need not fret, as SharePoint still allows IT to control who gets to create what and where.

Understanding BCS Components

BCS provides many tools for connecting to and managing how users interact with external data. While SharePoint Server 2013 Enterprise license holders get more goodies, SharePoint Foundation 2013 is certainly not left completely out in the cold. Figure 17-2 shows the distribution of components across the Office products. Before exploring the various

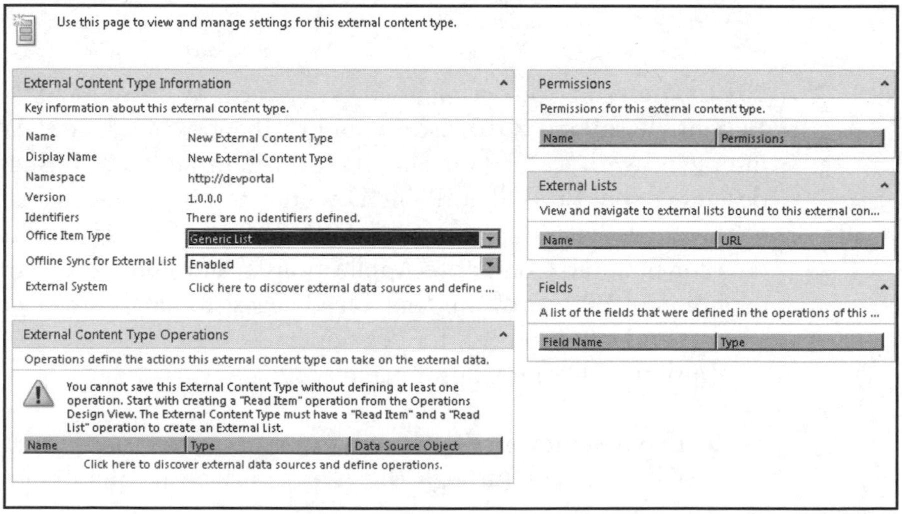

Figure 17-2 Business Connectivity Services provides a number of components depending on the version of SharePoint 2013

components, however, it is important to understand the fundamental building block of BCS—the External Content Type.

External Content Types

External data is represented through an object called an External Content Type. With an External Content Type you get to define the following for the data connection:

- External data source (What is SharePoint connecting to?)
- Office item type (What is the data mapped to as far as Office is concerned?)
- Operations (What can the user do? Create? Read? Update? Delete? Query?)
- Fields (What data Columns do we have access to?)
- Permissions (Who has access to do what?)

Once you have defined your External Content Type, you can use it directly from within SharePoint lists. In doing so, all the data from the external source will now be available in what appears to be a standard SharePoint list. Using an External Data Column, several of the external data Columns can be added to other lists.

As you can see, there are many pieces to the BCS puzzle. Table 17-1 summarizes the components and capabilities for each of the SharePoint deployment options.

Types of BCS Solutions

Given the list of components described in Table 17-1, it is easy to see that you have many options when it comes to building solutions. Whatever solution you choose to build will fall into one of the following categories:

- SharePoint Web-based solution
- Simple solution in Outlook 2013
- Declarative solution in Outlook 2013
- Code-based solution using the BCS API

Table 17-1 Comparison of Capabilities of BCS in Various Flavors of SharePoint

Function	Description	SharePoint Foundation 2013 and SharePoint Server Standard	SharePoint Server 2013 Enterprise	SharePoint Online
Access on-premises data	Connect directly to on-premises data sources	√	√	
Access cloud data	Connect directly to cloud data sources	√	√	√
External list	Special list type that interacts directly with an external data source	√	√	√
External Data Column	Special data type that allows you to add external data to any list	√	√	√
Secure store service	Handles credential mapping, allowing single sign-on functionality		√	√
External data search	Exposes the external data to SharePoint search for indexing		√	√
Rich client extensions	Allows Office clients to connect directly to the external data through SharePoint		√	√
External Data Web Parts	Several Web Parts allowing you to build Composite Applications from your external data		√	√
Profile pages	Exposes the external data in a single page for a single item		√	√

The SharePoint Web-based solution is the type that will be created most frequently, and this is the one we will cover in the rest of this section.

BCS Web Parts

BCS provides several Web Parts that you can use to build a Composite Application. Out of the box, you get the Web Parts listed in Table 17-2.

Note The Business Data Web Parts are part of the Enterprise license; to access them you must activate the Enterprise Site Collection Features through Site Settings.

The BCS Web Parts (see Figure 17-3) provide options for creating Composite Applications for integrating SharePoint pages with your enterprise data. Let's say that you want users to be able to review invoice information from your accounting system right within a SharePoint site. A SharePoint site could use the Business Data List Web Part to show a list of active invoices, for example. When a user clicks on an invoice, the Business Data Item Web Part displays detail for the invoice, such as an invoice due date and a total amount. Finally, the Business Data Related List Web Part could show detailed line items if the user elected to drill down.

Table 17-2 Out-of-the-Box BCS Web Parts

Web Part	Description
Business Data Actions	Displays a list of actions from an External Content Type
Business Data Item	Displays a single item from an External Content Type
Business Data Item Builder	Uses the query string to create a business data item and provides the value to other Web Parts
Business Data List	Displays a list of items from the External Content Type
Business Data Related List	Displays a list of items related to one or more parent items from an External Content Type
Business Data Connectivity Filter	Uses values from the External Content Type to use to filter the contents of Web Parts

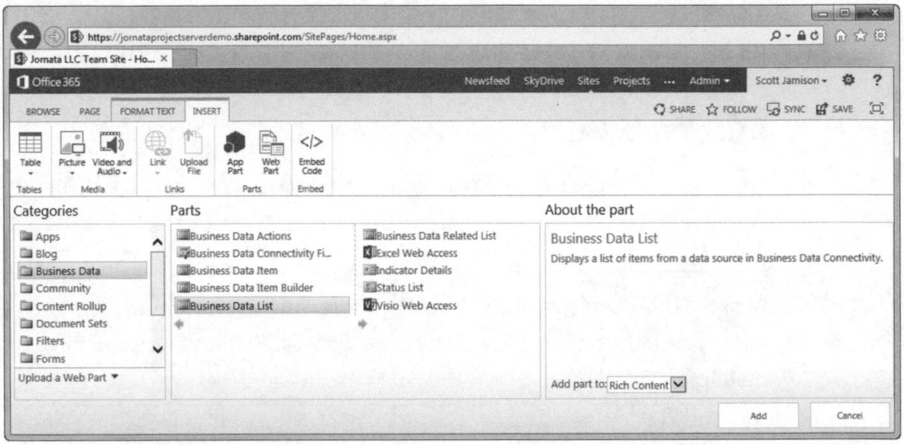

Figure 17-3 The BCS Web Parts can be found in the Business Data category after you enable Enterprise features

Planning for BCS Solutions

Since business solutions are typically built for the specific need that they will serve, BCS solutions are harder to plan for than most other SharePoint features. Until you build a solution, you probably don't know exactly how they will be used. Therefore, this book won't go into the detailed walk-through needed to build effective solutions using BCS—that's a topic for an entire other book. Instead, we'll focus on how to plan for BCS solutions if your organization will be using them.

What's the first step of building a BCS-based solution? Planning. Before you design a Business Connectivity Services solution strategy, seek to understand the business needs that are driving the solution and the environment in which the solution must operate. As with any solution in SharePoint, involve your stakeholders to make sure that they understand how external data will be used and the responsibilities of the user, designer, developer(s), and the owner of the external data itself—now and over time.

Let's walk through the list of design factors that you'll establish when you set out to build a solution that relies on BCS—and the "gotchas" that come with each:

- Location of the data
- Access protocols

- Security and permissions
- Presentation layer

Location of the Data

Your external data could be located in many possible places. In most cases, it's probably in a database on your corporate network. If so, you can only use an on-premises SharePoint environment. If your data is in the cloud, you can use either an on-premises SharePoint environment or SharePoint Online. What's the implication here? SharePoint Online cannot be used to access data in your corporate environment. So if you've deployed SharePoint Online and want to use BCS, you'll need to ensure that your data is accessible in the cloud—most typically through SQL Azure. SQL Azure provides a way for you to use SharePoint Online and still access corporate data—so consider this in your overall cloud strategy.

No matter where the data resides, you'll need to work with the person or group who has daily administrative responsibility for the external data source. You'll want to make sure you're ready to answer questions about your use of the data and its potential impact on the performance of its primary solution. For example, if you're looking to connect SharePoint to an Oracle ERP system, the Oracle administrator might not take kindly to you wanting to connect SharePoint to it. This is why you'll likely need a planning team—aligned with your governance strategy—to help get buy-in on your overall design.

Access Protocols

Now that you've solved what you are connecting to, the next question is "How do I connect SharePoint to it?" BCS can connect to external data through OData, SQL Server, SQL Azure, WCF endpoints, and .NET assemblies. This topic is important for two reasons: (1) the protocol in question could impact internal firewall ports, so work with your network team to make sure you can talk to the data source; and (2) the choice of protocol will impact your choice of development tools. Table 17-3 provides a list of which tool should be used with which protocol.

Security and Permissions

The next item you'll need to consider is security—both of the external data (or the system that owns the external data) and of your solution and its

Table 17-3 BCS Tools and Corresponding Data Access Protocols

Data Access Protocol	Development Tool
OData	Visual Studio 2012
SQL Server	SharePoint Designer 2013
SQL Azure	SharePoint Designer 2013*
WCF endpoints	SharePoint Designer 2013
.NET assemblies	Visual Studio 2012

*SQL Azure requires that you design against a local SQL Server, then modify the connection manually to work with your SQL Azure instance.

capabilities. Business Connectivity Services supports three authentication models for connecting to data:

- Credentials-based authentication models, where a username and password are sent to the external system
- Claims-based authentication, where the external system accepts credentials from a third-party authentication service that it trusts
- Custom authentication, where you develop a custom solution (mainly since the external solution doesn't support credentials or claims)

You'll also need to identify which users will have permission to use various parts of your solution. You should plan for things like who will administer the solution, because the administrator will need permission to connect your model to the external data source; who will design the solution, because that person will need access to the admin screens and the BDC model itself; and who will use the solution, because users will need a way to query and update the data via BCS Web Parts and the sites and pages in which they live. This is another topic to discuss when you meet with the owner of the external system or database.

Presentation Layer

The final item you'll need to consider is the user interaction method—will it be external lists, BCS Web Parts, SharePoint search, or Office 2013 clients? Will users need access to external data as a substitute for the external system's regular user interface? If so, that's probably a good candidate for BCS Web Parts. Do users need to find information from an external system based on keyword searches? That's a good candidate for crawling the external system and enabling external data search and search profiles. What about adding metadata to documents? In addition to standard text fields and Managed Metadata Columns, external data connections can also be used as a data type in a document library or list. In short, make sure you think through the way that external data will show up in SharePoint, mainly since most enterprise databases contain a large number of rows. If you simply create an external connection with a "Select * from DatabaseTable" approach, you might be disappointed by performance—along with all of your users. Be sure to understand where the connections will be used, how much information will be pulled back from the external data source, and whether enabling updates is really necessary. Just because a solution is easy to pull together via BCS, it doesn't mean you can ignore basic application design principles.

In short, Business Connectivity Services can provide a powerful mechanism to connect SharePoint to external data sources. Be sure to plan using the recommendations listed here. Once you get your data sources planned, you can move into another key business solution area: business processes and workflow.

Understanding Business Processes

Organizations large and small typically need to capture documents and/or data—and then act upon that set of information through a defined process. In this section, we'll cover two key SharePoint functions—workflow and electronic forms—that help to meet this business need.

Workflow

SharePoint workflow features enhance the document library and list functionality inherent in SharePoint. Workflow features are useful when you want to orchestrate document authoring, review, approval, and publishing processes—or to simply capture information and then put it through a repeatable set of steps.

Many business processes are somewhat ad hoc and loosely defined. A challenge of network-drive-based and e-mail-attachment-based collaboration (admit it—this is still the way most folks collaborate) is the proper routing of content to "the right people at the right time." Typically, coworkers are either blind to activity on shared drives or inundated with e-mail discussions about content that they are not actively monitoring. Automated workflows ease this burden by offering a structured means of transporting content, typically documents or forms, to the appropriate reviewers for comments, approval, or publishing. In some ways, think of workflow as a manageable business rules engine that allows administrators to predefine the routing of information across its life cycle. As an example, consider a standard employee expense reimbursement form. Typically, a manager or supervisor must review or approve the submitted claim before it is processed. Let's say that the approvals happen over ad hoc e-mail. This causes two challenges: (1) the coordination among employee, reviewer, and finance representative is sometimes clunky and error-prone, and (2) there is no auditing maintained around the form activity (e.g.: Who approved the submission? When? Why haven't I received my check?). Workflow solves both problems by allowing for the routing and auditing of content in a standardized way, along with on-demand status information.

You can also use workflow in business scenarios—for example, invoice approval, purchase order routing, and other scenarios. The workflow engine manages the execution of activities by enabling business users to extend SharePoint by providing rules, conditions, and activities. SharePoint can also do simple approval scenarios, supporting both parallel and serial processes.

If you're already familiar with SharePoint workflow, SharePoint 2013 changes workflow by providing two engine options: stay with the SharePoint 2010 engine, or use the new 2013 Workflow Manager. The SharePoint 2010 workflow platform has been carried forward to SharePoint Server 2013, so workflows that were built using SharePoint Server 2010 will continue to work in SharePoint Server 2013. As in SharePoint Server 2010, the workflow engine is installed automatically with the product. If you simply install SharePoint Server 2013 and do nothing else, you will have a nearly identical experience with building workflows as you did in SharePoint Server 2010.

SharePoint 2013 workflows, on the other hand, are powered by Windows Workflow Foundation 4 (WF), which was substantially redesigned from previous versions. If you want to use the new SharePoint 2013 workflow tools, you need to download and install the new Workflow

Manager service and configure it to communicate with your SharePoint Server 2013 farm. The Workflow Manager is separate from SharePoint. Microsoft did this to allow for enterprise scenarios where SharePoint can be the conduit and user experience for a business process that can scale separately from SharePoint itself—even into the cloud if necessary.

From a SharePoint perspective, workflow allows for the management of content movement (through a review or approval cycle), auditing of all activity associated with the content, and task list integration that allows users to see the items that are pending their review or approval. This is all done in an interface that most employees interact with regularly. Notifications from workflow processes can be e-mailed so users do not have to monitor task lists. In addition, exceptions can be defined, so if unexpected delays in processing occur, someone is notified.

One of the biggest challenges in implementing a successful workflow strategy is not so much becoming an expert in the custom workflow creation process as understanding how to define a clear and accurate business process. Before associating a workflow with a SharePoint list or document, ask:

- How do you define the life cycle of the associated business process? (Who should approve it first? How many people should we ask for feedback? If this document should go to someone's manager, does the system have that data?)
- What is the current process? What are the benefits of automating this process?
- How do you deal with exceptions (i.e., if someone is away or sick)?
- How important is it that we log all activity associated with this list item or document? Do we need to look back historically at previous content for insight into the approval process?

Whether it is a simple serial, single-person approval process or a complex workflow associated with many conditional layers and approvers, designing the business rules *first* will ensure that the right technology decisions are made later. As you'll see in the coming sections, SharePoint offers some native workflow processes as well as integration with SharePoint Designer custom workflows (and even Visio, .NET-based, or third-party -created complex solutions). In every case, it is important to effectively manage the processes and expectations surrounding business-critical content movement.

Understanding Workflow Terminology

SharePoint 2013 includes the capability to use workflows within a list or document library as well as at the site level (i.e., not associated with a list item). While both SharePoint Foundation and SharePoint Server offer the same fundamental platform (Windows Workflow Foundation), the difference comes down to what default workflows are offered (see Table 17-4). Beyond the default workflows, custom workflows can be developed using SharePoint Designer 2013 or Visual Studio 2012. Since this book focuses on creating solutions without custom code, we'll focus on the SharePoint Designer solutions only, which we will cover later in the chapter. For now, let's focus on the

Table 17-4 SharePoint 2013 Standard Workflow Templates

Name	Description	Use for . . .	Available in Share-Point Foundation 2013?	Available in Feature Named . . .
Approval— SharePoint 2010	Routes a document (or list item) to one or more users for approval via a Web-based form.	Generic approval processes in document libraries and publishing sites.		Workflows
Collect Feed-back— SharePoint 2010	Routes a document (or list item) to one or more users for feedback. Reviewers can provide feedback, which is then compiled and sent to the person who initiated the workflow once the workflow has completed.	Aggregating feedback on a document.		Workflows

Name	Description	Use for . . .	Available in Share-Point Foundation 2013?	Available in Feature Named . . .
Collect Signatures—SharePoint 2010	Routes an Office document to one or more users to collect approval via digital signatures. Note: This workflow must be manually started from within Office 2007 or 2013.	Digital-signature-based approval processes for Office documents.		Workflows
Disposition Approval	Manages document expiration and retention by allowing participants to decide whether to retain or delete expired documents.	Records management (retaining or deleting expired documents and/or list items).		Disposition Approval workflow
Three-State	Manages business processes and complex workflows. Lets you choose what happens re: choice fields in a list and its initial, middle, and final states.	Tracking items in a list—things like issues, tasks, etc. Useful for adding to a task list as "stage 2" of an approval workflow to track the actual task.	√	Three-State workflow
Publishing Approval	Routes a page for approval. Approvers can approve or reject the page, reassign the approval task, or request changes to the page.	Approving Web pages as opposed to documents.		Publishing Approval workflow

fundamentals of workflow in SharePoint, including the differences among workflow templates, workflow associations, and workflow instances.

Templates, Associations, and Instances

There are three ways to describe a workflow. A workflow *template* is the initial description of what should happen (steps, conditions, activities, etc.). When you bind a template to a list or library, that linkage is called an *association*. When you add an item to a workflow-enabled list, the workflow that starts up and processes that item is called a workflow *instance*.

Let's say you have a workflow template called Approval. You could associate the workflow template to three separate lists (list A, list B, and list C). Within each list, there are ten items, each in one of the various stages of workflow processing. In this scenario, there is a total of

- One workflow template
- Three associations (one template x three lists)
- Thirty workflow instances (three associations x ten items each)

Using the Standard Workflows

To get you started, SharePoint provides several out-of-the-box standard workflows that can be applied to your lists and libraries. While SharePoint Foundation 2013 users get only one such workflow (the Three-State workflow), SharePoint Server 2013 users have several to choose from. The advantage of using these workflows is that users can simply apply them directly without waiting for custom workflows to be built and deployed. The standard workflows are designed to be generic enough that they can be applied to many review and approval processes. Table 17-4 lists some of the more popular standard workflows.

Associating a Workflow with a List

By default, workflows are not associated with any of the list templates provided, but using them is very simple. To see the workflows that are available for a list, look at a document library. To associate a workflow, simply open the document library and select the Library tab in the ribbon. In the settings section on the right, you will notice an icon menu for Workflow Settings (see Figure 17-4).

From here, you can select to Add a Workflow to your library. This will open the Add a Workflow page shown in Figure 17-5.

On the Add a Workflow page, you will find several options:

- Select a workflow template
- Enter a unique name for this workflow
- Select a task list
- History list
- Start options

The template list displays all the workflows available for your library. For example, you could use the Approval workflow for your Annual Newsletter Review. The task list is used to store tasks that are assigned during the workflow (in this case reviewer tasks). The history list is used by the workflow to store messages such as status, errors, and general feedback. Table 17-5 shows the start-up options on workflows.

Once you have all options configured, the Properties page for the workflow lets you define the default list of approvers among other values such as approval order, notification message, and task due dates. When you choose to let users initiate the workflow manually, these settings can

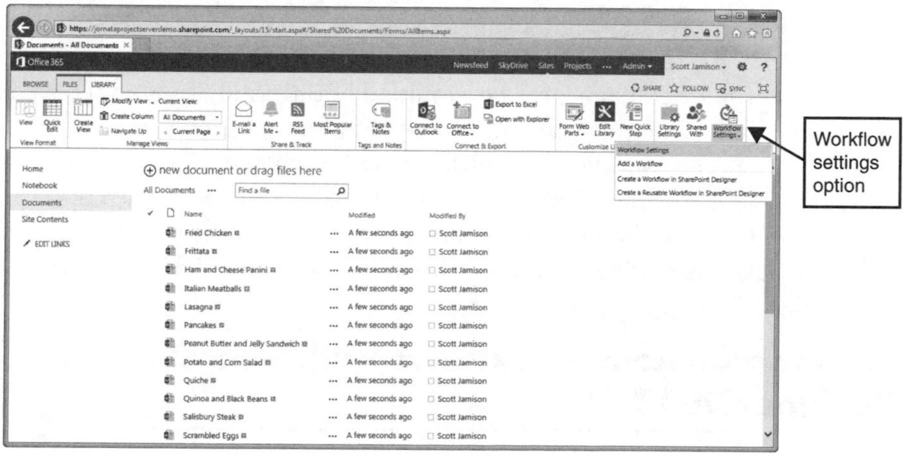

Figure 17-4 The workflow menu under Workflow Settings on the list ribbon allows you to add a workflow to your list

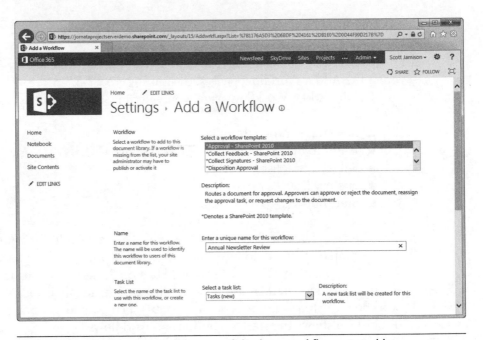

Figure 17-5 The first page of the out-of-the-box workflow wizard lets you configure its name, associated template, and start-up parameters

be overridden by the user who initiates the workflow. If you elect to start the workflow automatically, the default settings will always be used when the workflow begins.

If you select a different workflow, the options presented in the properties page may be completely different. Indeed, certain workflows may not require default properties at all.

The workflow templates that SharePoint Server 2013 provides have plenty of functionality that will suit the majority of simple approval workflows. However, the user is not limited to these workflows alone. The next section discusses using SharePoint Designer to take workflows to the next level.

Creating Custom Workflows with SharePoint Designer 2013

If you find that the workflows SharePoint provides do not quite fit your process, Microsoft SharePoint Designer 2013 provides the ability to modify them or even design your own from scratch. This gives business

Table 17-5 Workflow Start-up Options

Name	Description	Use for . . .	Notes
Allow this workflow to be manually started.	A user can manually initiate this workflow for an item.	Letting users selectively run workflows on items.	The default settings on workflows can be overridden by the user initiating the workflow.
Start this workflow to approve publishing a major version of an item.	This workflow starts when a user marks (publishes) a document as a major version.	Making sure published items get approvals. Uses the content approval feature, which keeps items in draft state until approved.	Out-of-the-box workflows only. Available only for libraries with major versioning enabled.
Start this workflow when a new item is created.	Automatically initiates the workflow when a new item is added or created.	Ensuring that workflows always run for newly added items (approvals, etc.).	
Start this workflow when an item is changed.	Automatically initiates the workflow when an existing item is modified.	Ensuring that a workflow runs for modified items (approvals, etc.).	

analysts or power users the ability to create their own workflows without requiring IT involvement and/or developer time. It also enables developers to create workflows quickly without having to write custom code. Using a predefined list of activities, users can create a workflow to route their documents for approval, move their documents, modify properties, and so on.

Note SharePoint Designer is an essential tool for managing SharePoint content by both IT personnel and power users. SharePoint 2013 features controls and settings for IT administrators to have more granular control over who can use SharePoint Designer, the actions they can perform, and on which sites.

SharePoint Designer connects directly to a SharePoint site and allows the user to manage content in a rich user interface. The workflow tools within Designer allow the user to develop a workflow specifically for a list, or a generic workflow that can be used by many lists.

Introducing SharePoint Designer (for Workflow Development)

SharePoint Designer 2013 is a free download that can connect to SharePoint 2013 on-premises and SharePoint Online. Figure 17-6 shows SharePoint Designer 2013 opened at its home page for a site. From the home page you can get a quick overview of the site, including general information, permissions, sub-sites, and other settings.

In the navigation pane on the left, you will see a list of all available objects such as lists and libraries, workflows, site pages, and so on. As you can see, you can browse the majority of objects within SharePoint related to design. With our focus being on workflow, let's open that tab to see what there is.

Figure 17-7 shows the Workflows tab selected. You will notice that the options on the ribbon are related to the various ways to construct a new workflow. The main pane lists the available workflows; because we have not created any custom workflows yet, this list displays only the reusable workflow templates provided with SharePoint Server 2013—in this case, we see the Approval workflow for all of the language packs we have installed. The ribbon keeps us focused on the task at hand by making only our workflow options available.

Clicking any of the workflows listed will open an information page for that workflow template (see Figure 17-8). This gives a quick overview of information about the workflow, start options, and even the forms associated with the workflow. This is very useful for troubleshooting.

Workflow Types

There are three types of workflows that you can create with Designer: list workflows, reusable workflows, and site workflows. The differences are explained in Table 17-6.

Let's say you want to build a custom workflow that is targeted at SharePoint 2013 and doesn't need to be backward compatible with SharePoint 2010. In addition, you want the workflow to be available for any list or document library. To create the workflow, simply click on Reusable Workflow in the ribbon, which presents you with the Create Reusable

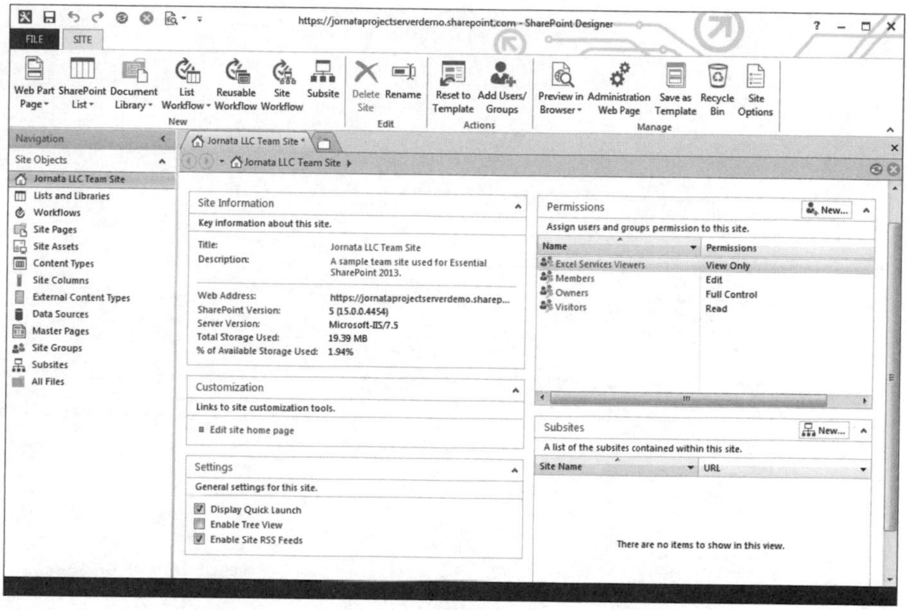

Figure 17-6 The SharePoint designer 2013 home page displays general site information as well as sub-sites and permissions for the site

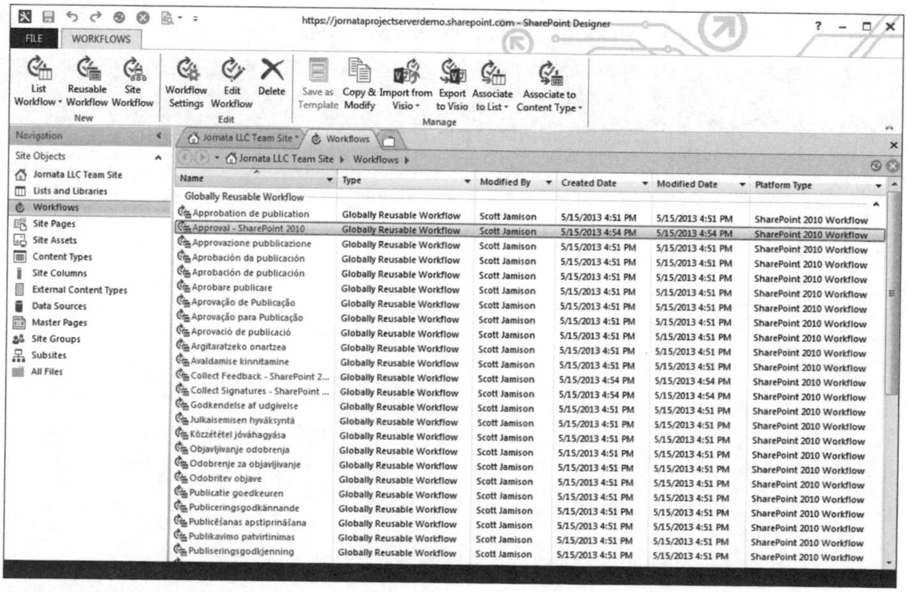

Figure 17-7 The Workflows tab displays the available workflow templates and provides all workflow options in the ribbon

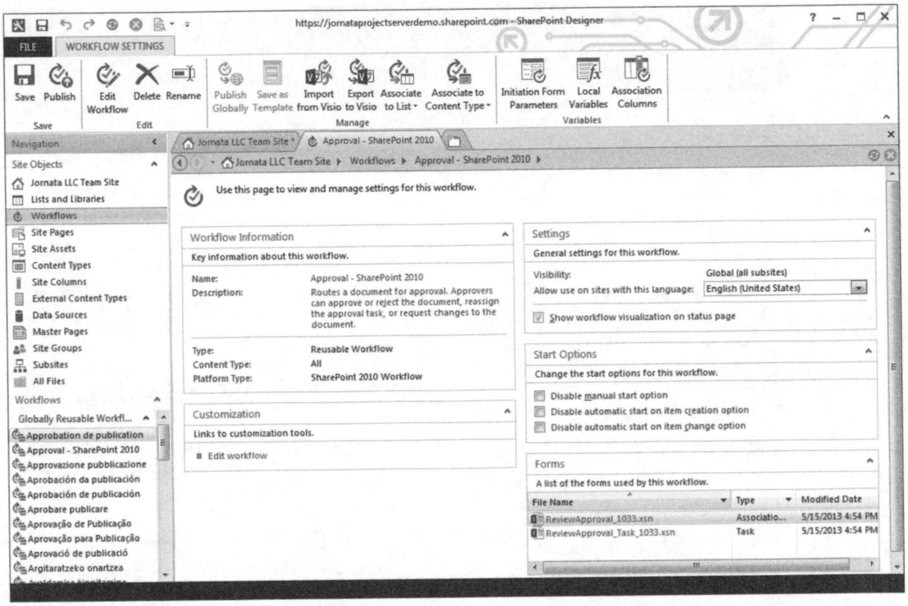

Figure 17-8 The Workflow Information page displays an overview of the workflow, including the forms that it uses

Table 17-6 SharePoint Designer 2013 Workflow Types

Workflow Type	Description
List workflow	Associated directly with a list. Cannot be reused on a different list. Is content sensitive, so can work directly with list values.
Reusable workflow	Not associated with any list. Can be associated with any list once created. Is not content sensitive.
Site workflow	Associated with the site and not a list. Can be used for workflows that are not associated with list data. Manually run from the Site Actions menu.

Workflow dialog box (see Figure 17-9). Note that you can give the workflow template a name and a description and indicate which version of SharePoint you're targeting.

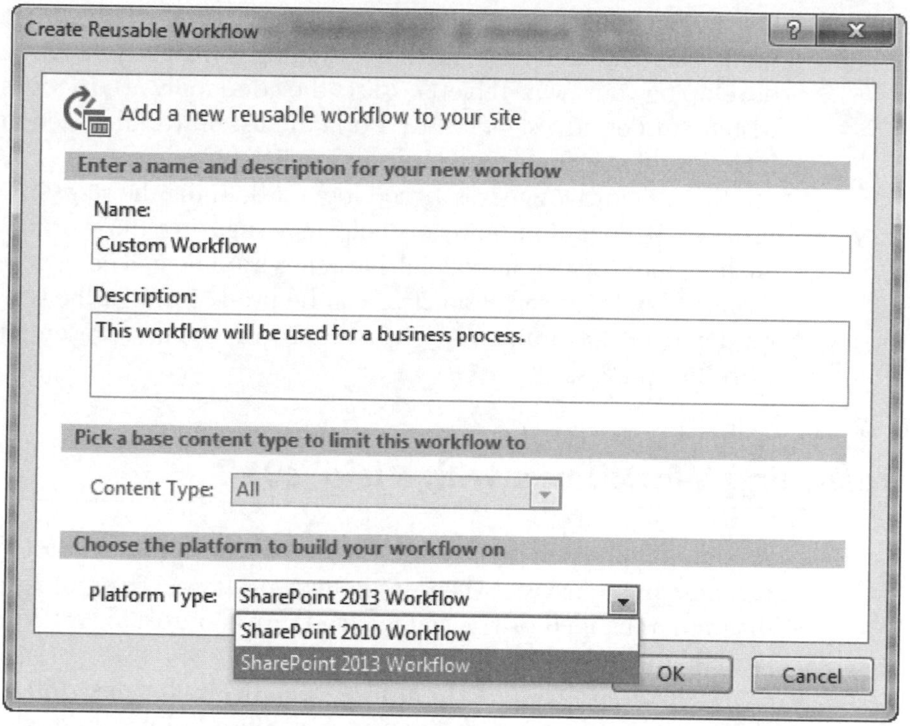

Figure 17-9 The Create Reusable Workflow provides a way to use SharePoint Designer to create a custom sequential workflow by using workflow actions

Workflow Association Options

When you create a reusable workflow, it cannot be used until it has been associated with a list or Content Type. When you open the workflow in Designer, you will have both association options in the ribbon in the Manage section. When you click Associate to List, you will see the available lists to associate with. Similarly, when you click Associate to Content Type, you will see available Content Types. The benefit of associating a workflow to a Content Type is that it will work for all items using that Content Type in any list.

Workflow Actions

As your workflow is moving through its steps, you'll need to define things that happen—in other words, what *actions* will occur. SharePoint Designer ships with a set of actions specifically for SharePoint interaction—things like doing calculations, sending e-mails, and updating properties on an item. This list can be extended by installing third-party actions or even by developing your own. Table 17-7 lists the commonly used actions provided with SharePoint Designer 2013. For a full list of workflow actions, refer to http://msdn.microsoft.com/en-us/library/jj164026.aspx.

SharePoint Designer is a good tool for defining the steps in a workflow process. It does not, however, help in visualizing the workflow process itself as the steps in SharePoint Designer are linear. The next section will discuss how Microsoft Visio 2013 can be used to design the workflow and render it in the browser to give the user a visual representation of the workflow process.

Designing Workflows with Visio 2013

A common practice in organizations is for a business analyst to work with business users in Visio when designing workflows. The end result, a Visio diagram, is handed to a developer, who turns it into a SharePoint Designer workflow or Visual Studio workflow.

Visio 2013 provides a template specifically for designing workflows that can be imported directly into a SharePoint Designer workflow. Selecting the SharePoint workflow template in Visio 2013 Pro opens

Table 17-7 SharePoint Designer Actions for Workflows

Action	Description	Available in Visio
Core		
Add time to date	Adds a time period to a date variable.	√
Do calculation	Does a basic calculation such as addition and outputs to a variable.	√
Log to history list	Writes an entry to the workflow history.	√
Pause for duration	Pauses the workflow for a defined period.	√

Action	Description	Available in Visio
Pause until date	Pauses the workflow until a defined date.	√
Send an e-mail	Defines e-mail recipients, subject, and body.	√
Set time portion of Date/Time field	Sets a time value and outputs to a variable.	√
Set workflow status	Sets the status of the current workflow.	√
Set workflow variable	Uses a workflow variable to store values.	√
Stop workflow	Terminates the workflow.	√
Document Set Actions		
Capture a version of the document set	Can specify a document set with major or minor versions.	
Send document set to repository	Copies or moves a set to a defined content organizer.	√
Set content approval status for the document set	Set the status with comments.	√
Start document set approval process	Kicks off an approval process for the set for a list of users.	√
List Actions		
Check in item	Checks in an item and provides comments.	√
Check out item	Checks out an item.	√
Copy list item	Copies an item from one list to another.	√
Create list item	Creates an item and outputs it to a variable.	√
Declare record	Declares the current item as a record.	

(continues)

Table 17-7 SharePoint Designer Actions for Workflows *(continued)*

Action	Description	Available in Visio
Delete item	Deletes a defined item in a list.	√
Discard checkout item	If an item is checked out, it will be discarded.	√
Set content approval status	Sets the status to Approved, Rejected, or Pending.	√
Set field in current item	Updates a field value.	√
Undeclare record	If an item is a record, it will be reverted.	
Update list item	Commits any changes made to an item.	√
Wait for field change in current item	Pauses the workflow until a field value condition is met.	√
Relational Actions		
Look up manager of a user	Gets the manager from Active Directory.	√
Task Actions		
Assign a form to a group	Defines a form with simple fields and assigns it to a list of users.	√
Assign a to-do item	Creates a task for a user and adds it to the workflow task list.	√
Collect data from a user	Builds a custom form and outputs values to a variable.	√
Start approval process	Kicks off an approval workflow.	√
Start custom task process	Kicks off a task workflow.	√
Start feedback process	Kicks off a feedback workflow.	√

Action	Description	Available in Visio
Utility Actions		
Extract substring from end of string	Manipulates a string value.	
Extract substring from index of string	Manipulates a string value.	
Extract substring from start of string	Manipulates a string value.	
Extract substring of string from index with length	Manipulates a string value.	
Find interval between dates	Manipulates a string value.	

up shape stencils specifically for SharePoint workflows. Each of these shapes relates to the actions and conditions that are available in SharePoint Designer. As in any Visio diagram, these shapes can be dragged onto the canvas to build a full workflow solution. Each shape reflects a default action, so dragging it onto the canvas has the same effect as adding the action to the SharePoint Designer canvas. It is not possible to define the properties on the shapes, however. For example, adding the "Log to history list" action does not allow you to define the message you are logging to history. These properties need to be set *after* the workflow has been imported into SharePoint Designer. Even though the properties cannot be set by the workflow designer from within Visio, you can add details to each step specifying what any values should be. This additional description can be added directly on the design canvas and will be ignored by SharePoint Designer on import.

Once the workflow is imported into SharePoint Designer and deployed to SharePoint, Visio Services can be used to display a Web-based view of the workflow process. Visio Services is part of the SharePoint Enterprise CAL.

Creating Electronic Forms

When you create a new item, SharePoint displays a form that enables you to enter data into the associated list. Sometimes, however, the default SharePoint forms are not sufficient for capturing data in a complete way, since you may need to look up information from other sources, make one choice field be dependent on another, and so on. In addition, users may be used to filling out paper-based forms, so you might want to make a form that behaves like the paper form. For example, you may want to enable job applicants to fill out a fairly complex application form.

So do you really need electronic forms? In most cases, organizations are using SharePoint lists, Word documents, or Excel worksheets. But a real forms package gives you rich design, validation, prepopulation of information, multiple roles, digital signatures, and rich security. Take a look at this list of common issues and see if any of them sound familiar:

- In your existing forms-submission process, do you have challenges around incomplete, inaccurate, or lost information? Do you face challenges around locating that information? Does it take too long for information to get to its final destination(s)? Electronic forms can drive business processes so that these issues are minimized or eliminated, validating the data by checking it as the user is supplying it.
- Are your users overwhelmed with the number of business processes or sources of information that exist within your company? Electronic information capture helps streamline the complex processes sitting behind forms.
- Are people filling out paper forms that need to be rekeyed? Electronic forms capture data at the source.

If you are experiencing any of these issues, you're probably a good candidate for capturing information via electronic forms. InfoPath 2013 is Microsoft's offering for electronic forms creation and use. In the next section, we'll describe the process of using an InfoPath-based electronic form with SharePoint. We'll focus not on the technical details of InfoPath, but rather the key integration points with SharePoint.

Introducing InfoPath 2013

InfoPath 2013 is a client application that lets you visually design forms using layout tables and controls for gathering data such as text boxes, choice fields, and buttons. In addition to quickly formatting a form, InfoPath allows you to connect the form to various data sources such as a database or a SharePoint list. InfoPath is divided into two key tools: InfoPath Designer 2013, which enables a developer or designer to create a new form, and InfoPath Filler 2013, which enables a user to make use of a form to enter data.

InfoPath Forms Services

SharePoint 2013 allows you to create forms libraries that capture form data, enabling users to publish their information directly to SharePoint via InfoPath. In this scenario, all users need to have the InfoPath Filler 2013 client installed on their computers to work with the forms.

SharePoint Server 2013 Enterprise provides InfoPath Forms Services, which can render a published form template as a Web page. This eliminates the need for the user to have the InfoPath client installed. The experience in the browser is exactly the same—allowing the user to pick dates using a date picker, for example, and even adding additional rows for fields with unlimited line items.

Note While InfoPath Forms Services can convert many form elements from the client to the browser, it may have difficulty with certain controls depending on how complicated your form is. For this reason, InfoPath provides a Design Checker to check compatibility.

InfoPath 2013 gives the business user tremendous power for creating forms quickly and relatively easily. Even developers can take advantage of the advanced features such as data connections to really bring the forms to life. With the addition of InfoPath Forms Services, the need for another deployed client can be eliminated, which is always welcome by IT departments.

Key Points

In this chapter, we reviewed the various business services that SharePoint 2013 provides for creating business solutions, including connectivity to external databases and workflows for business processes. The following list is a review of the key points:

- Composite Applications are a way to assemble business-critical solutions via premade components by using SharePoint and Office.
- Business Connectivity Services is a component in SharePoint 2013 and Office 2013 that provides a way to create business solutions for scenarios that require integration of external data sources.
- External Content Types allow you to easily connect to external data from sources such as SQL, Oracle, or Web services.
- OData is a new protocol that is supported for BCS connections and used by developers via Visual Studio 2012.
- External lists in SharePoint can display content directly from an external source using an External Content Type.
- External content can be updated directly from an external list as if you were updating a standard SharePoint list item.
- BCS provides several Web Parts for creating Composite Applications.
- SharePoint 2013 introduces a new workflow engine powered by Windows Workflow Foundation 4.
- SharePoint 2013 provides several out-of-the-box workflows, including
    - Approval
    - Collect Feedback
    - Collect Signatures
    - Disposition Approval
    - Three-State
    - Publishing Approval
- SharePoint Designer 2013 allows you to modify out-of-the-box global workflows as well as design unique ones.
- Visio 2013 allows you to design SharePoint workflows that can be imported directly into SharePoint Designer 2013.

- With SharePoint Server 2013 Enterprise, Visio Graphical Services allows you to render your Visio workflow in the browser.
- With InfoPath 2013, you can publish form templates to document libraries as well as submit the form data to a SharePoint list.
- With SharePoint Server 2013 Enterprise, you can publish an InfoPath form and have it rendered as a Web form.
- Advanced workflows can be created by using Visual Studio 2012 (which is beyond the scope of this book).

CHAPTER 18

PLANNING FOR BUSINESS INTELLIGENCE

Business intelligence (BI) is the art and science of transforming data and information into knowledge and wisdom. BI requires both attention to detail and big-picture thinking. And SharePoint 2013 can make it all possible through a nicely improved toolset—definitely the most comprehensive and well-performing set of tools on the Microsoft platform to date.

Before we get deeper into what SharePoint itself has to offer, let's take a closer look at BI in general. Ask any CxO what his or her number-one need is for enabling solid business decisions, and the answer will most likely come down to one word: information. These people need the right information, in just the right amount, at just the right time. Understanding what has happened in the past, and what is happening right now, can help in the process of determining what an executive should do next. This, of course, assumes two key elements about the available data: quality and timeliness. Organizations today need to have real-time, visual cues that tell them how they are performing, both operationally and strategically. If reports are generated too far after the fact, or without proper cross-correlation, it may be too late to change course if there is a problem. If your organization can't react fast, your competition probably can, and that's a problem.

This transformation of data into actionable information is at the heart of business intelligence. And while quality and timeliness are essential to building a BI solution, it is also very important to decide how best to present the information gathered. Do you use a report? A chart? A scorecard? A dashboard? Telling a story through data is a big part of success with BI. SharePoint 2013 helps in this way by providing users with several options to analyze information and help facilitate decision making.

First, let's discuss what SharePoint 2013 is not. It is not a data warehouse for storing large amounts of corporate data. Nor is it a data-cleansing tool that will automatically correct bad or incomplete data. SQL Server's Analysis Services and Data Transformation Services are in charge of those items. Instead, think of SharePoint as both the facilitator and the presentation tier for business intelligence data. SharePoint is becoming *the* presentation hub for all Microsoft Business Intelligence solutions, from Excel to SQL Server Reporting Services to PerformancePoint. For users, SharePoint is the common destination to find the business information they need to make decisions. In short, SharePoint is there to help present key data to users to help them make the right decisions faster and more easily.

This chapter provides an overview of key business intelligence capabilities that are provided by SharePoint 2013, including report delivery, dashboards, scorecards, key performance indicators, and server- and client-side Excel calculations and charting. Full coverage is well beyond the scope of this book, so we'll stick to providing advice on the best way to think about BI in the context of SharePoint. The key topics covered in the chapter are

- What's new in SharePoint 2013?
- Planning for business intelligence
- Which presentation tool is right for you?
- Excel Services
- Excel BI and PowerPivot
- PerformancePoint Services
- Visio Services

What's New in SharePoint 2013?

The BI enhancements in SharePoint 2013 are quite compelling. At first glance, it might appear that Microsoft hasn't changed much in the feature set since SharePoint 2010, but that's not the case. Microsoft has significantly polished the overall quality and usability of the toolset. The overall goal of the core Microsoft BI tools hasn't changed much, but the execution has improved significantly. The full set of tools includes Excel 2013 (the client application), Excel Services in SharePoint 2013, PerformancePoint Services in SharePoint Server 2013, Visio Services in SharePoint 2013, and Microsoft SQL Server 2012. The following BI feature changes are of particular note:

- Excel Client BI provides additional capabilities to analyze and visually explore data of any size, including data sets with millions of rows.
- Excel Services enables users to view and interact with Excel workbooks that have been published to SharePoint sites with a number of improved features and better analysis support.
- PerformancePoint Services enables users to create much better interactive dashboards for key performance indicators (KPIs) and data visualizations in the form of scorecards, reports, and filters, including a new BI Center template and support for iPad.

Planning for Business Intelligence

Business intelligence is very personal. Independent of the challenges of getting corporate data collected, completed, and cleansed, the "right" delivery method is highly subjective. One user may be satisfied with a static report that simply delivers information; another user wants the ability to drill down into specific sections of a report to interact with more detail; still another may want to spend no more than three seconds looking at a picture to determine whether action is required.

Given all of that, how do you get started? The first step is to recognize that delivery around BI has evolved. It used to be that you needed to know all user requirements and know exactly what users wanted to see. That's changed. Now, business intelligence is much more about putting tools in the hands of the users and letting them have control over what they see. This is sometimes called "BI for the masses." In the next few sections, we highlight various options for BI delivery in SharePoint, including report storage and delivery, charts, dashboards, scorecards, and KPIs. In a later section, we discuss the options and how to select the delivery choice that is most appropriate for your organization.

Reports

It is pretty safe to say that every person in an organization, independent of roles or responsibilities, interacts with some type of report. In the "old days," reports were delivered in paper form, perhaps through interoffice mail. With technology advances, this has changed so that most report delivery occurs through e-mail attachments or interactively via a real-time online system.

At the highest level, there are two types of reports: static and dynamic. A static report is a presentation of information in a locked-down view, meaning the reader can see the information only in the format that is shown and is exposed only to the level of detail provided on that report. The report itself may have been generated from any enterprise database, or perhaps an accounting system. For example, your bank statement might be delivered as a .pdf file. A dynamic report, on the other hand, is more flexible. It allows the user to manipulate the presentation of data and/or access detail that may not be presented in the default view. Think of a sales performance report available in a spreadsheet. Perhaps the presentation is revenue per region, but the user is allowed to drill into an individual office's detail. Or, the user may be able to request additional information by clicking a check box. Again, this report may have been generated from any number of external systems, but since there's a "live" link to the data (which is not likely real-time itself but more likely an aggregation of many transactions over time), the report is more flexible.

From a SharePoint perspective, the type of report or the data source is irrelevant. Again, think of SharePoint as the delivery tool. While SharePoint is not typically a data repository for report information, it *is* a document repository. And reports are documents. This means that you can deliver corporate reports by storing them in SharePoint. You may get the reports into SharePoint manually or provide access to a reporting source like SQL Server Reporting Services (SSRS) or through custom development. The value of placing reports in SharePoint versus e-mailing them directly to users or placing them on a network drive is significant. A SharePoint document (report) library

- Can be secured, at either the library or the item (report) level. This allows you to easily apply permissions so the reports are seen by only the appropriate resources.
- Is crawled by SharePoint's search engine so reports can be returned in search results.
- Has version control; as reports are updated, the new version overlays the old and there is no confusion about which is the most current version.

- Can meet compliance requirements through defined document management workflows to control approval, publication, and disposition.
- Is familiar to users in an existing SharePoint environment, so it is easier to train users on how to access new reports.
- Has alerts; specific users can be notified of new or updated reports automatically without having to spam every employee.

In addition, SharePoint has tight integration with SSRS so that reports generated in SSRS can be shown in the context of a SharePoint site and can provide users with a single access point for reports and supplemental structured and unstructured data.

Charts

Reports typically contain mostly text—characters and numbers formatted in a certain way for presentation. Another way to show data is in a graph (see Figure 18-1). A pie chart or bar graph can "tell a story" with fewer words and numbers than a traditional report. The value of a chart is that it leverages a visual indicator to quickly highlight specific data elements (i.e., sales are way down this year because the current-year bar is much smaller than last year's). Business users have long been familiar with charts through their use of Microsoft Excel. Excel provides an easy way to transform data into a picture.

From a SharePoint perspective, there are three main ways to present charts as part of a business intelligence solution. The first and simplest is to store the spreadsheet that contains the chart(s) in a document library (similar to the Reports section). This requires very little effort but forces the user to click the correct file and launch Excel on the desktop. A second choice is to use a charting tool, such as the SharePoint 2010 Chart Web Part, that offers SharePoint integration where the charts themselves are actually Web Parts that have been configured to point to a specific data source and present results in a specific way. The benefit here is that the user interface is much richer, and access to the visual indicators is faster. The challenge is that this requires an additional purchase and at least some training in the third-party solution. The final choice is to use Excel Services, which is part of SharePoint and discussed in more detail later in this chapter. Excel Services requires that the organization have the

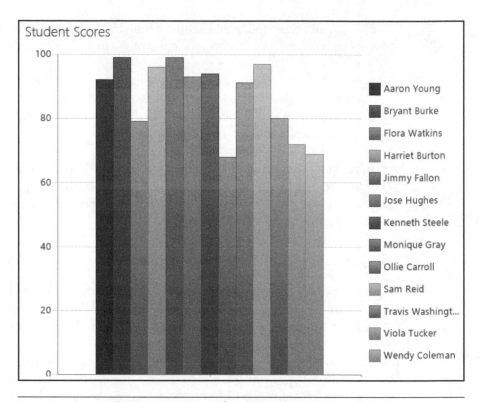

Figure 18-1 Most business users are familiar with Excel-based charts, which can describe data in a visual way

Enterprise version of SharePoint Server 2013. It allows users to publish a chart or collection of charts directly from Excel and have them rendered directly into a SharePoint Web page. This offers the rich and instant presentation without the overhead of an additional software solution.

Dashboards

A dashboard contains a collection of BI elements such as reports, filters, and scorecards, typically in real time. Dashboards are used to show how an organization (or, more often, a part of an organization) is performing against real-time, tactical goals as of this moment. Most often, the metrics that are displayed in a dashboard reflect data that is constantly changing (How many support calls do we have in queue? How many units have we manufactured today?). Dashboards are most often watched by members of the organization who are responsible for specific day-to-day goals.

The information used in a dashboard is usually "raw" data, but in an effective dashboard it is displayed in such a way that there is instant recognition of performance against a target. So, for instance, if there are fewer than five support calls in queue, we can show the number 5 in green; if there are six to 20, we can show the number in yellow; and if there are more than 20, we can show the number in red. This commonly understood color scheme provides instant feedback to supervisors or staff members on how they are doing at any moment in time. Additional cues such as shapes or symbols can be used to clarify indicators for users who are color-blind or who have visual limitations. At a glance, someone can look at a dashboard to spot the trouble areas and investigate further or take action. The use of gauges or progress bars or charts can also provide visual cues about the information that changes regularly. In our example, we can see at a glance that Northwind Traders is falling short of revenue targets (see Figure 18-2).

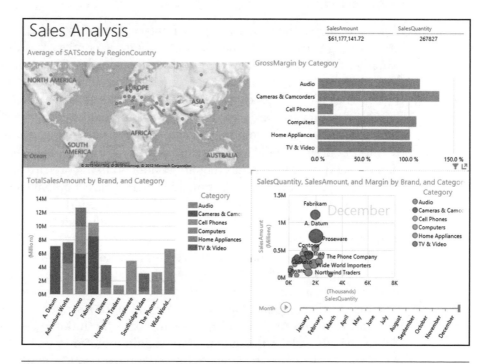

Figure 18-2 PerformancePoint Services in SharePoint 2013, which is vastly improved over SharePoint 2010, provides a way to build sophisticated dashboards without programming effort

The most critical action to perform before setting up a dashboard is to identify which metrics are going to help drive the organization's performance. Too often, information like the current weather or the company's stock ticker is dropped onto a dashboard because dashboards are easy to create. However, unless you are in the snowplow business, a weather dashboard is not likely to provide a metric that drives performance.

Dashboards are not "one size fits all." Different people in the organization need to see different information to understand performance. Sometimes this just means a different level of granularity (how many support calls for software product X versus software product Y versus for all software products), but it can also mean different metrics for different parts of the organization. Because of this, you need to carefully plan so that you are sure that you are providing the right information to the right people at the right time in your dashboards.

Scorecards

Many people use the terms *dashboard* and *scorecard* interchangeably, but there is a significant difference between them. Whereas a dashboard is a container for a related group of report views and other indicators that are organized together, a scorecard is a specific type of report that displays a collection of KPIs together with performance targets for each KPI.

Often, scorecards are used to show how an organization is performing against *strategic* goals, rather than day-to-day tactical goals. In addition, the metrics are generally from a snapshot in time ("this fiscal year") rather than in real time. The metrics that are contained in a scorecard also can be viewed from an overall organizational level (How are we doing against our revenue goals for the year?) or cascaded down to the individual level (How much have I sold this year?). Scorecards are usually watched most closely at the top level of an organization.

The most important step in creating a scorecard is to do careful analysis. An organization's strategy is almost always difficult to articulate outside the boardroom. Scorecards are a way to make strategy real to everyone in the organization. If your organization's strategy is to be the best and best-known service provider in a specific industry, you need to identify which metrics the organization should monitor to understand how it is doing against that strategy. Scorecards have been around for a long time, and many organizations think that they have a handle on theirs if they are watching financial metrics. However, it is just as important to watch metrics that show how the organization is performing from a customer perspective, from a business process perspective, and from a learning and growth perspective. The reasons for this are many. Revenue might be going through the roof, but if the staff is leaving in droves, there's a problem. If profits are way up but no one can understand when they should report a critical defect, there is a problem that might impact future profits.

The visual representation of scorecards is similar to that of dashboards but is usually simpler. The red/yellow/green approach is the most common, given that users are interested in how they are performing against a fixed set of metrics in a specific time period. The visuals won't change in real time but will change on a periodic basis, whatever period makes sense for the overall organization. Usually these periods are monthly or quarterly since they coincide with financial reporting periods, and monthly/quarterly reporting is well ingrained in the corporate psyche.

Let's assume that you have done all of the up-front analysis for your dashboards and scorecards (no small feat, but too large a set of topics to cover here). Once you have SharePoint up and running, enabling collaboration and teamwork across the enterprise, it's time to consider using the platform as a basis for business intelligence. SharePoint provides a rich set of new tools to facilitate building up your dashboards and scorecards.

Key Performance Indicators

A key performance indicator is one element of a scorecard (see Figure 18.3). Organizations use KPIs to monitor business activity and performance. Simply stated, KPIs are metrics (data values) that are compared against a benchmark and scored. KPI indicators (also known as status indicators) are intended to spur action. If the sales KPI is red, it indicates that an issue has arisen and that action is required. Status indicator lists are one way to implement a simple dashboard or scorecard. A scorecard is more formal and has more rollup and drill-down capabilities that allow for views into supporting metrics. Status indicator lists in SharePoint are meant to be simpler. They are linear and represent the presentation of a group of items that share a common data point (that is, they all relate to the organization).

Traditionally, corporate executives have used KPIs to "take the pulse" of business performance. Examples include sales pipeline, revenue, and products sold (all for a specific point in time). Increasingly, however, all levels of an organization are being exposed to KPI lists as a way to present performance data. Think of project teams being exposed

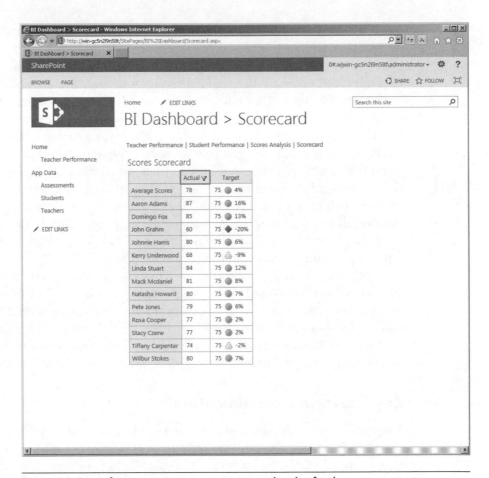

Figure 18-3 PerformancePoint services provides the facility to create KPIs, enabling easy-to-use scorecards

to project performance (utilization or budget versus actual) in a master list. The power of a KPI list is that it presents, in a very simple interface, information about collected data measured against predefined goals. One of the key challenges of any sort of dashboard or scorecard is that it seeks to aggregate a wide variety of data—data that may come from multiple systems. Worse yet, the necessary data may not exist in any systems, or it may be very complex to calculate or locate. Presenting the red/yellow/green on a scale is often the easy part. Defining and locating the actual data is the hard part.

In SharePoint Server 2013, KPIs are typically created within PerformancePoint Services. Like scorecards, a traditional KPI list typically has three main color codings (although it is possible to use a number of graphical icons, including smiley and sad faces):

- **Green:** positive results against a measurement
- **Yellow:** borderline results
- **Red:** poor results

Which Presentation Tool Is Right for You?

Reports, charts, dashboards, or scorecards—which is best for your users? Remember, business intelligence is highly subjective, so you may need to use some or all in an overall deployment. Table 18-1 may help in your decision-making process.

Excel and Excel Services

We have seen two main trends in business intelligence adoption within organizations: (1) the vast majority of companies have implemented or are implementing a strategy for BI, and (2) the most popular tool for delivering BI data continues to be Microsoft Excel. Excel offers users (typically business analysts or knowledge workers who work closely with specific business data) a familiar environment for manipulating corporate data. For years, many software companies have tried to recreate this experience in a Web-based environment with the goal of better leveraging workbook-based results in a broader medium. Most solutions failed because they could not effectively mimic the simplicity that Excel offers users.

Excel Services, a BI component of the SharePoint 2013 Enterprise Edition, addresses that need by validating what business users have known all along—that Excel is a great tool for ad hoc manipulation of business data. Excel Services takes the concept to a new level by allowing data owners not only to acquire and manipulate business data but, ultimately, to publish it to a Web-based environment that is highly secure. One of the

Table 18-1 Selecting the Right BI Delivery Tool

Requirement	Delivery Tool
Presentation of existing static reports generated from another system or compliance library/archive of static, file-based reports	Report: document library
Presentation of dynamic reports that allow drill-down	Report: SSRS reports shown with Web Parts on SharePoint site
Charts generated and managed by business users that need to be shared with an organization's members (where SharePoint 2013 Enterprise is not being used)	Chart: spreadsheets in a document library
Charts generated and managed by business users that need to be shared with an organization's members (where SharePoint 2013 Enterprise is being used)	Chart: Excel Services
Charts that need to be ultra-rich with customizable capabilities and can be managed by IT development resources	Chart: third-party charting tool with SharePoint integration
Executive presentation on the health of the business with key metrics measured against previous reporting periods	Scorecard (using PerformancePoint capabilities)
Business manager's daily summary of key metrics, including the overall health of their organization, details of recent closed deals, top prospects this week, and top-performing sales team members	Dashboard (using PerformancePoint capabilities)
Business process diagram that shows stages and analytics associated with performance in each stage	Chart (using Visio Services)
Reports, dashboards, and charts from very large data sets	Excel BI and SQL Server 2012 SP1 (see the Excel Services section)

biggest strengths of Excel Services is that it not only allows users to publish Excel-based content (entire workbooks, individual worksheets, or even a single chart), but it also offers the ability to publish only what the data owner wants to be seen. For example, a business analyst may use specific formulas and business logic to take raw data and deliver a set of charts to make predictions or show trends. The analyst would like to share these results with a broader audience but cannot e-mail the workbook without the risk of compromising the formulas and proprietary logic. Excel Services offers a solution by allowing the business analyst to create the chart using native Excel capabilities in an Excel workbook and then to publish only the content (the specific chart or perhaps the single worksheet) from the spreadsheet that the analyst wants to share to a SharePoint portal, all without exposing the detailed data and formulas (see Figure 18-4).

Excel Services in SharePoint 2013 continues to be a major component of the business intelligence integration into SharePoint technologies. It truly offers business users the best of both worlds; users can continue to build and analyze using a tool that is very familiar and are empowered to publish results without having to work through an IT department to build custom Web pages or dashboards.

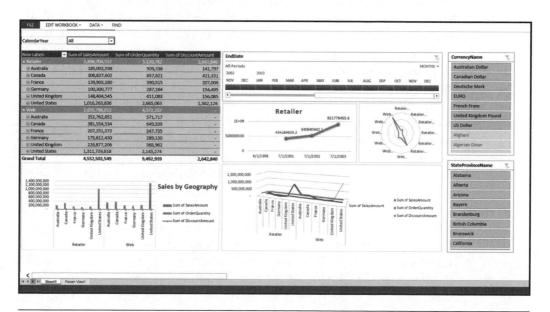

Figure 18-4 Excel Services can render interactive dashboards that are based on Excel; this provides a way for business users to create their own reports and publish them via a Web page

Getting Started with Excel Services

One of the first things to look at is the three core components of Excel Services:

- **Excel Calculation Engine**. This is the main engine responsible for managing the data and calculations associated with workbooks.
- **Excel Web Access**. This is the Web Part within SharePoint that allows the rendering of Excel-based content in a browser-based environment. It can be associated with dashboards and can be connected to other Web Parts.
- **Excel Web Services**. These are APIs that developers can use to build custom solutions that leverage Excel workbooks.

How Does Excel Services Work?

Let's take a look at how to publish Excel-based content to SharePoint. One of the first things you need to do is tell Excel Services where to look for the Excel workbooks you want to render as HTML on your portal. When you define a trusted source file location, you can specify a path to a specific SharePoint-based site or file system file (UNC path) or an HTTP location that is Internet-based.

Note that when you work with SharePoint-based sites, you can enable Excel Services workbook acquisition in all underlying child sites as well. The advantage of doing so is that it allows administrators to apply more granular security on sub-sites when maintaining navigation among Excel charts. There are several options associated with setting a trusted connection, including limits on a workbook's size and number of calculations.

A trusted file location acts as a master address book that indicates the portal sections or file system locations that are enabled for Excel Services consumption. One of the important things to note is that this capability is an administrative task. It is assumed that the definition of trusted locations will be managed by a SharePoint administrator and *not* the business users, mainly since Excel Services is not intended to give business users full control or management of SharePoint security or administration, but to focus on the content itself.

Let's assume a sample Excel file contains a worksheet dedicated to salesperson bonus calculations. In this scenario, a manager is using Excel to manage employee compensation based on performance. He or she is using a formula based on some personal definitions to calculate bonus amounts and show the data in a simple pie chart. The goal is to share the data with the team but not share the formulas associated with the results. How does Excel Services enable this outcome?

- **Business process.** Without Excel Services, the manager would be forced to take manual steps to separate the pie chart from the calculations. This would have included things like hiding a calculation worksheet, copying the chart to another workbook, or generating a .pdf file with the chart. All of these require manual steps every time the data changes. Obviously, it is an inefficient process. Excel Services, on the other hand, allows for publishing and protection within the same environment.
- **Presentation.** Let's say that the table associated with salesperson data has graphical indicators for performance. This is done using Excel's conditional formatting, which looks like a KPI list. Conditional formatting in Excel is another way of publishing performance data.
- **Security.** The goal of the publishing portion of the process is not just to display the pie chart, but also to protect the formulas and business logic. Excel Services allows a user to publish an entire workbook, a single worksheet, or any chart. This is a very powerful tool. Consumers of the content cannot edit the data; the transmission is unidirectional. They can, however, do many things with the end results. This includes sorting and filtering, recalculation, and PivotTable capabilities.
- **Ease of maintenance.** Manual manipulation of Excel files is manageable but not very scalable. Yes, it is possible to manipulate the workbook or segment charts through a manual process. This process, however, requires the same effort every time data needs to be republished. One of the biggest advantages of the Excel Services model is that it allows for a continuous "dialog" between producer and consumers through the connection it provides to the data.

In this example, the business user was able to create the data presentation, secure the business logic, and publish the results to the intended audience—all with no code or direct IT involvement other than initial administration settings. That is the true power and value of Excel Services. It empowers business users to leverage the tools they have (and know) to effectively and securely publish results, all in an effective and efficient manner.

Excel Services can be a great accelerator of BI activity for a business that has invested in a SharePoint environment. As mentioned earlier in this chapter, however, it is not a substitute for coordinated activities between business and technical resources. In a standard corporate setting, business users will continue to "own" and manage the data in an Excel environment. They should be supported by an IT staff that helps them easily connect to back-end corporate data as well as provides them with the necessary SharePoint support to securely store Excel files. While the advertisement around Excel Services states a "no code" deployment, it does not include a "no IT" process. It is important to leverage the value of this new and exciting tool within a framework of coordinated business and technology activities.

What's New in Excel Services with SharePoint 2013?

If you're familiar with Excel Services from SharePoint 2010, you'll be pleasantly surprised to know that while Excel Services operates basically as before in SharePoint 2013, there are a number of improvements and additions that make it an appealing BI tool—both on the server side with Excel Services, and on the client side with Excel.

Let's review each of the aforementioned features in more detail. Table 18-2 describes the features you get for Excel and Excel Services when combined with SQL Server 2012 SP1.

Excel BI (Client Features)

In SharePoint 2013, Excel BI offers certain new features to support business intelligence applications. These include the following:

- **In-Memory BI Engine (IMBI).** The in-memory multidimensional data analysis engine allows for almost instant analysis of millions of rows and is a fully integrated feature in the Excel 2013 client.
- **Power View add-in for Excel.** Power View enables users to visualize and interact with modeled data by using highly interactive visualizations, animations, and smart querying. Users can present and share insights with others through rich storyboard presentation capabilities.
- **Decoupled PivotChart and PivotTable reports.** Users can now create PivotChart reports without having to include a PivotTable report on the same page.

Table 18-2 Key SharePoint and SQL Server Features and Components

	Specific Features You Get	Components You'll Need
SharePoint only	Native Excel Services	Excel Services Service Application
SharePoint with Analysis Services in SharePoint mode	Interactive PowerPivot workbooks in the browser	Install Analysis Services in SharePoint mode Register Analysis Services Server in Excel Services
SharePoint with Reporting Services in SharePoint mode	Power View	Install Reporting Services in SharePoint mode Install Reporting Services add-in for SharePoint
All PowerPivot features	Access to workbooks as a data source from outside the farm Schedule data refresh PowerPivot Gallery Management dashboard	Deploy PowerPivot for SharePoint 2013 add-in

Excel Services (Server Features)

Excel Services offers new features to support business intelligence applications. These include:

- **Data exploration improvements.** People can more easily explore data and conduct analysis in Excel Services reports that use SQL Server Analysis Services data or PowerPivot data models. For example, users can point to a value in a PivotChart or PivotTable report and see suggested ways to view additional information. Users can also use commands such as Drill Down to conduct analysis. Users can also apply the Drill Down command by using a single mouse click.
- **Field list and field well support.** Excel Services enables people to easily view and change which items are displayed in rows, columns, values, and filters in PivotChart reports and PivotTable reports that have been published to Excel Services.

- **Calculated measures and members.** Excel Services supports calculated measures and calculated members that are created in Excel.
- **Enhanced timeline controls.** Excel Services supports timeline controls that render and behave as they do in the Excel client.
- **Application BI servers.** Administrators can specify SQL Server Analysis Services servers to support more advanced analytic capabilities in Excel Services.
- **Business Intelligence Center update.** The Business Intelligence Center site template has been streamlined. It not only has a new look, but it is also easier to use.

PerformancePoint Services

Those who tried using PerformancePoint Services in SharePoint 2010 might have been a bit disappointed by some of the bugs in the product— we were.

PerformancePoint Services in SharePoint 2013 is vastly improved. In short, PerformancePoint Services is a performance management tool that an organization can leverage to monitor and analyze its business. In an earlier section, we talked about building dashboards and scorecards for graphical presentations of key decision-making data. In SharePoint Enterprise, the definition, construction, and management of dashboards and scorecards are done with PerformancePoint Services. The high-value proposition here is that because PerformancePoint Services provides a rich and easy-to-use way to construct dashboards, scorecards, and KPIs, and SharePoint offers a natural presentation tier for this data, the bar has been raised on the business intelligence capabilities that can be originated within SharePoint. Remember, we talked earlier about using SharePoint to store reports or present information gathered in other places, like Excel. With PerformancePoint Services, we're actually talking about a front-to-back business intelligence solution that offers a full range of tools for gathering, analyzing, and presenting corporate metrics—all for any data source.

How Does PerformancePoint Services Work?

PerformancePoint Services stores its data in SharePoint document libraries and lists. Because of this, it can naturally take advantage of the features that exist natively with SharePoint, the most compelling being security integration. Very much like Excel Services, PerformancePoint Services is a service within SharePoint 2013 that is integrated with the SharePoint software; when you have the Enterprise version of SharePoint 2013 enabled in your environment, you have full access to the capabilities of PerformancePoint without having to install or configure anything new, aside from a client tool that helps create and display key reports and dashboards.

Why Use PerformancePoint Services?

PerformancePoint Services is specifically targeted as a performance management solution. Performance management allows business users to monitor and analyze their businesses by presenting key data and metrics that can facilitate change (from business process to product development to staffing).

With PerformancePoint Services:

- An organization can use a single platform for "pushing" key business metrics to all employees. The "outreach" component of the PerformancePoint Services tool (and thus SharePoint) is very important in that a company can get data in the hands of decision makers of all levels more quickly and efficiently.
- Individual business users can take advantage of metrics presented via PerformancePoint Services as one component of their collective business activities, meaning that it can be integrated with native collaborative tools in SharePoint to offer context and execution outside the data that is shown.
- IT can provide the business with a single tool for showcasing data that has been aggregated through a master repository such as a data warehouse. By using a tool like SharePoint, which is already highly leveraged for collaboration and communication, IT has fewer systems to support and less effort associated with monitoring and training users in diverse business applications.

PerformancePoint Services provides all of the functionality needed for performance management, including scorecards, dashboards, management reporting, and analytics. Reporting is also integrated with PerformancePoint Services to provide planning, budgeting, and forecasting output. As mentioned before, all of this is done within the context of an existing SharePoint environment, offering business users a single interface for collaboration and analysis. The main advantage of PerformancePoint Services is that users can see more robust scorecards and dashboards and then click a metric to drill down to sub-dashboards or even the raw data.

Visio Services

What does Visio have to do with business intelligence? Well, if you recall an earlier definition that stated business intelligence is mostly about "telling a story" with few words, then showing information in Visio diagrams is just as impactful. Business users have used Microsoft Visio for some time to represent corporate data. One of the challenges, however, has been that not all content consumers had Visio on their desktops, so distribution of Visio charts was sometimes a challenge. Visio Services operates very much the same way as Excel Services or PerformancePoint Services in that it acts as a service in the context of a SharePoint environment and provides a view of the information in a browser-friendly format.

Why Use Visio Services?

There are three main benefits to using Visio Services:

- A business user can share a presentation of data created in Microsoft Visio in the browser without requiring the content consumer to have Visio installed on his or her desktop.
- Once a diagram from Visio has been deployed, information can be refreshed so that changes made in Visio can automatically be refreshed in the browser presentation. This is great for workflow visualization, for example.
- Much like Excel Services and PerformancePoint Services, Visio diagrams can be shown in the context of an already familiar SharePoint environment.

Visio Services supports diagrams connected to one or more of the following data sources:

- SQL Server
- SharePoint lists
- Excel workbooks that are stored in SharePoint
- Any ODBC data source that you can normally connect to

Visio Services is an effective tool that offers business users an easy way to share diagrams. Because it operates as a service within SharePoint, Visio Services has a very low overhead for IT in terms of management and support. It is important to remember that Visio Services does require both the Enterprise version of SharePoint 2013 for presentation and Microsoft Visio 2013 on the desktop of users who will create diagrams that will be published to SharePoint.

Putting It All Together

At this point, you should have an appreciation for how dashboards and scorecards (and perhaps even Visio diagrams) can be used within SharePoint through Excel Services, PerformancePoint Services, and Visio Services. But what are the benefits of these technologies?

The business benefits of using Excel Services are many. When an analyst can take a key set of charts based on Excel spreadsheets into the portal for wider consumption, he or she is able to inform the organization in ways that are not always possible when a spreadsheet is distributed by e-mail. Having a single place where a spreadsheet is stored and can be viewed by the people who are allowed to see it ensures that everyone is getting the same message. Is the spreadsheet that you e-mailed to me on Tuesday the right one, or is it the one that Bob said he got from you on Wednesday? What changed? Do I need to compare the two? If it's in only one place, there is only one answer. In addition, Excel Services allows an analyst to control and protect the published information. The user is not simply uploading a spreadsheet into a document library; a subset of the data is shared in a controlled and secure manner.

PerformancePoint Services can provide an additional visual layer on top of large amounts of information. Are we trending up or down? Are we more productive or less? Again, with a single glance, you can tell. If you see a problem, you can click on the indicator and see what's driving the trend, and most important, you can then do something about it in an informed way. It's all about what the numbers *mean*, not what the numbers *are*. There's a reason that visual representations are more helpful than long lists of numbers. With a single glance, you can tell whether things are good, not so good, or bad.

Visio Services offers the ability to present business intelligence data in a diagram format. Think of the presentation of a business process (or workflow) now integrated with back-end data that shows performance at each phase in the process. That is a very compelling presentation that is not easily done with a chart or scorecard or dashboard. That's where Visio adds another layer of value.

As you start to think about how all this hangs together and how you might deploy business intelligence solutions in your organization using SharePoint, keep a few things in mind:

- **Understand your strategy.** Many times dashboards and scorecards can enforce exactly the opposite behavior from what is intended. Think about a scorecard that tracks the number of new accounts. What is going to happen to your existing accounts? Will they get neglected inadvertently? Isolating your metrics without respect for the overall picture can potentially have an adverse impact somewhere else. Make sure it is all strategic and will influence the right behavior.

- **Keep it simple.** Giving people hundreds of metrics to watch regularly will hide the important messages. Decide which metrics (or more likely a combination of metrics) indicate good performance and use those. Build up a high-level dashboard or scorecard for general consumption, listen to what people find helpful or not, and go from there. Don't try to build the be-all and end-all solution from Day 1.

- **Expect things to change.** When the novelty wears off, dashboards can get dull. They need to evolve both to keep people's focus but also to reflect any changes in the organization's underlying strategy or business processes. Having agility in your dashboard and scorecard development capabilities will translate into agility against your competition and in the marketplace.

- **Make sure the data is accurate.** A dashboard or scorecard is useless (and dangerous) if it's wrong. Ensure that data delivery is complete and accurate. Remember, this presentation is driving business decisions.

- **Target an audience.** A dashboard tells a story. That story is specific to certain data elements and is presented to convey a certain message. Keep the messaging focused and target a specific set of users. If dashboard viewers want more metrics, maybe a new dashboard is required.

- **Business intelligence, especially in SharePoint, is not about "one size fits all."** Know your users and target the right presentation of corporate data with the one that tells the story in the easiest and most useful way. For example, if you want to stress the number of new clients acquired in a given quarter, your charts and graphs should emphasize growth—so use a bar graph, not a pie chart. Take advantage of the robustness and integration that SharePoint offers to map the solutions one-to-few (versus one-for-all). Provide a generic data source and teach people how to make their own reports—doing so will empower business users without overburdening IT.

Key Points

Bringing business intelligence to your knowledge workers is a key feature of SharePoint. Features such as SSRS report delivery, Excel Services, Excel BI, and PerformancePoint Services provide fantastic ways to harness and distribute analytics information. When using SharePoint for business intelligence, remember these key points:

- BI is the art and science of transforming data and information into knowledge and wisdom; it requires both attention to detail and big-picture thinking.
- Dashboards are used to present a summary of information, typically in real time, on how certain measures are performing against tactical goals—typically with a collection of charts, KPIs, and report snippets.
- Scorecards are typically used to show how an organization is performing against strategic goals by using KPIs.
- KPIs are a simple way to map business metrics to existing data values to provide a green/yellow/red presentation of performance.
- Excel Services empowers business users to publish Excel-based content in an environment that offers visibility without compromising security.
- PowerPivot is a component within Excel BI that enables the ability to work with millions of rows of data in a fast, efficient manner.
- PerformancePoint Services allows you to create more advanced business intelligence presentations and to create and manage metrics for scorecards, dashboards, and KPIs, all with drill-down capabilities.
- Visio Services allows users to publish Visio diagrams to a browser and to connect those diagrams to corporate data, thus providing a different type of business intelligence solution.

CHAPTER 19

PLANNING FOR MOBILITY

Many organizations list mobility as a key requirement for collaboration solutions such as SharePoint. Organizations are increasingly supporting remote and flexible work styles, including bring-your-own-device (BYOD) policies. The explosion in the use of tablets, smartphones, and other mobile devices makes mobility an important consideration when planning for SharePoint 2013.

SharePoint 2013 has improved support for mobile devices, including Windows, iOS, and Android platforms. In this chapter, we will cover the following topics:

- What's new in SharePoint 2013?
- Planning for mobile
- Mobile usage scenarios
- The SharePoint phone and tablet experience
- SharePoint Newsfeed mobile applications
- SkyDrive Pro mobile applications
- Office Mobile and Web Apps
- Third-party mobile applications

What's New in SharePoint 2013?

SharePoint 2013 has improved support for mobile devices. The default SharePoint mobile pages have been slightly improved for smartphone access to SharePoint sites. On a tablet, such as an Apple iPad or Microsoft Surface, SharePoint has a touch mode that enables you to hide all navigational elements such as the ribbon commands, links, and menu bars. This mode is helpful when your primary goal is to read and consume content within SharePoint.

Chapter 14, "Managing Web Content," discusses the new device channel SharePoint capability. Channels allow your organization to optimize the SharePoint user experience for specific mobile device platforms. This will most often be used for public-facing Web sites on the Internet and intranets.

SharePoint 2013 has new mobile applications to support the new social and SkyDrive Pro features described earlier in this book. The SharePoint Newsfeed mobile application enables you to view and respond to items in your social newsfeed and post new items, including photos, directly from your mobile device. The SkyDrive Pro client enables you to view and edit documents stored within your personal document library within SharePoint 2013.

Windows Phone 8 includes updated versions of the Office Mobile Applications which can be used for viewing and editing Microsoft Office files (Word, Excel, PowerPoint, OneNote) opened from SharePoint.

The Office Web Apps have improved support for mobile device viewing and editing Office documents stored within SharePoint. These applications are useful in many scenarios—especially when working on a device such as an iPhone, iPad, or Android that does not have native Word, Excel, or PowerPoint applications.

Note In March 2013, Microsoft provided an update of its SharePoint mobile applications. This blog post provides information on the current and future state of SharePoint mobile applications at the time of the writing of this book: http://blogs.office.com/b/sharepoint/archive/2013/03/06/out-and-about-new-sharepoint-mobile-offerings.aspx. We will discuss these new mobile applications and features further within this chapter.

Planning for Mobile

A key first step in planning for mobility is to understand your business requirements and typical use case scenarios. Some questions to consider include the following:

- Does your organization have a large population of mobile device users?

- What are the typical activities and functions that people need to perform while they are mobile?
- What devices will people be using—a PC, a laptop, a tablet, and/or a smartphone?
- Will your organization allow people to access corporate content from a personal device?
- Will people outside of your organization (e.g., customers, partners) be accessing SharePoint via a mobile device?
- How will mobile access to SharePoint be provided? Your implementation and architecture will be different if you are running SharePoint on-premises or SharePoint Online.
- Will people have reliable network connectivity or will they require offline access?
- Do you need to update your existing security, governance, and information classification policies to support these new mobile scenarios?
- How will mobile devices be supported? Will user support be available outside normal business hours?

Mobile User Personas

When planning for mobile, it is helpful to think about the various user personas that will need mobile access to SharePoint. Many scenarios are common across organizations:

- Sales personnel often require access to their customer and supplier information while on the go. This typically includes documents and meeting notes.
- Field workers, such as those who perform inspections or servicing at a customer site, may need access to company procedures, forms, and knowledge bases.
- Customer service interaction may require that staff be able to access and input data without the barrier of a tethered PC or laptop.
- People who work from home will often have access to SharePoint from their organization-issued devices. Many organizations are being asked to extend this same access to personal devices and computers that may not be managed by the organization today.
- Customers and partners may be accessing your public Web site or an extranet based on SharePoint.

- People who are active using SharePoint's social features will want to be able to review their newsfeeds, post a question, reply to others, or post a photo while on the go. Mobile access to consumer social networking tools such as Facebook, LinkedIn, and Twitter has set the standard for enterprise social networking solutions. People expect that they will be able to access their social resources from their phones and tablets, and if they cannot, they often will not adopt enterprise social networking solutions and instead will continue to use e-mail and consumer tools to meet their collaboration needs.

Mobile Device Management

Many organizations have existing mobile strategies and device management policies. Some organizations restrict access to content to corporate-issued devices, such as a company laptop. Other organizations allow a BYOD policy where users can use their device of choice.

Often organizations are leveraging some form of mobile device management (MDM) technology to validate that the devices connecting to their corporate resources have adequate security controls in place, such as device encryption and password policies, to ensure that the organization is protected in the event the device is lost or stolen. These MDM tools often support the ability to locate a mobile device and perform a remote wipe of the device's contents when necessary.

Good Technology and Microsoft's Windows Intune are two examples of MDM solutions that are available to help manage mobile devices across a variety of platforms, including Windows, iOS, and Android. Microsoft Exchange ActiveSync is often used by organizations as well for some forms of mobile device and policy management.

Mobile Architectural Considerations

Once your organization has decided to support mobile device access to SharePoint, you will need to consider how people will access your SharePoint environment. Some organizations will allow access to SharePoint only from an organization-issued device when the device is connected to the organization's network, whether that be physically in the office or over a VPN or DirectAccess (DA)-type technology that supports remote access.

Other organizations have evolved beyond supporting access only while connected to the organization's network. Some organizations have allowed connections to their internal SharePoint environment from external devices. Some organizations have created a SharePoint extranet to support mobile access and extended this environment to support collaboration scenarios with external customers and partners. Organizations are now also evaluating hosted solutions, such as Microsoft's SharePoint Online (which is discussed in detail in Chapter 11, "Taking SharePoint to the Cloud"), to provide access to SharePoint outside of the organization.

As part of identifying your technology requirements for mobile, you should also review what content will be accessible via mobile devices and determine if you will require data loss prevention (DLP) solutions to protect information leaving the company. One example is leveraging IRM technologies to protect sensitive files or document libraries that may be accessed from mobile devices. IRM technologies allow you to restrict viewing, sending, and/or editing of content opened from SharePoint and include the ability to set an expiration time for when rights are revoked. Consider a scenario where a salesperson has access to a PowerPoint presentation that contains confidential information on future product roadmaps. IRM can be leveraged to ensure that the salesperson cannot edit the document; to prevent others from viewing the file if it is sent to them via e-mail; and to have permissions on the document automatically expire on a specific date, which will require the user to go back to SharePoint to obtain the most current version of the presentation.

You may also want to revisit your information classification policies to consider what content should be accessible via mobile devices. You may choose to allow mobile access only to certain SharePoint environments or sites. For example, you may choose to have different security policies for content that is considered HBI such as SharePoint sites that contain organization trade secrets or customer confidential information such as Social Security or credit card numbers.

Another key aspect to consider is how people will authenticate with SharePoint from their mobile devices. One option is to leverage multifactor authentication technologies to add an extra layer of security when accessing content on mobile devices. This technology is helpful as an additional security check above and beyond the user's network account and password. Common examples of multifactor authentication tools include RSA's SecurID and Microsoft's PhoneFactor, which require users to enter a second secure code (in addition to their SharePoint username and password) to gain access to content.

Depending on how your SharePoint environment has been architected, additional networking and security server infrastructure may be needed to enable people to access your SharePoint environment outside of your organization. To help on-premises customers set up SharePoint 2013 for mobile connectivity, Microsoft has published documentation and reference architectures on its TechNet site at http://zoom.it/E1BL#full.

SharePoint Online (as part of Microsoft's Office 365 online service) is designed for secure external access and does not require any additional configuration or infrastructure to be accessed from mobile devices.

Mobile Usage Scenarios

There are a variety of mobile use case scenarios that we typically see. Some of these are:

- Anywhere, anytime access to SharePoint content. The content may be documents that you are working with, Web pages, wikis, blogs, or various types of list data. Often when working with this form of content on a mobile device the goal is content viewing as opposed to content creation.
- Electronic forms are often used on mobile devices by individuals who spend most of their day on the road. For example, they may be used as an inspection checklist for a field engineer working for an insurance company, or to sign up a customer for a new banking account while in a supermarket.
- Workflow and task management scenarios are often used in conjunction with documents and forms. Often we ask people to review and approve items, and they may receive the workflow task while on the road.
- Social computing is exploding from a consumer perspective. People are checking in on Foursquare, posting photos on Facebook, connecting with business colleagues on LinkedIn, and sharing news and information via Twitter. Many organizations are seeking to leverage similar tools securely within their organization to encourage information sharing, knowledge transfer, and connecting people across the organization. SharePoint 2013 now offers many new social tools that people will be looking to access when they are on the road,

waiting for a meeting to begin, or sitting in the airport getting ready to board a flight.

- As more documents, forms, and discussions are posted within SharePoint, people are looking for the ability to search this information while on the go regardless of the device.
- Business intelligence, such as executive scorecards and dashboards, are great candidates for mobile applications since they are typically more about content viewing and consumption.
- Sites and content will be accessed by people outside of your organization. Thus, you will need to determine which content needs to be optimized for mobile devices. For example, an airline may want to have special mobile pages for key functions that its customers will want to access from their mobile devices such as checking in for a flight or reviewing their flight status.

The SharePoint Phone and Tablet Experience

The native SharePoint pages have been enhanced with SharePoint 2013. SharePoint's automatic mobile browser redirection feature is able to detect the capabilities of the mobile device and then render the appropriate page. For mobile devices that support HTML5, a new contemporary page view will be rendered (see Figure 19-1). This page view has been optimized for modern mobile devices. If the device does not support HTML5, SharePoint will fall back to rendering mobile pages with a classic view, which is similar to what existed in SharePoint 2010. Users also have the choice of rendering SharePoint pages in full site views, which provides a similar experience as if the user were accessing SharePoint from a personal computer. Note that for most mobile devices the full site view will often result in extensive horizontal and vertical scrolling since the screens on mobile devices are not as large as traditional desktop or laptop monitors.

SharePoint 2013 has been optimized for tablet devices that support touch, such as Apple iPad and Microsoft Surface. SharePoint has a new touch mode which removes the SharePoint ribbon and other navigational elements and allows the user to focus on viewing and interacting with SharePoint content (see Figure 19-2).

For organizations that want to have greater control over how SharePoint 2013 renders Web pages on mobile devices, a new "channel" feature

Figure 19-1 SharePoint team site mobile view

has been created. Typical use cases for the channel functionality are for organizations that are using SharePoint's Web content management (WCM) capabilities for their intranet or public-facing Internet sites. The channel feature allows SharePoint 2013 site designers to implement different page templates for different device types. For example, your organization may have different page designs for users accessing SharePoint on an iPhone and on a PC. The key benefit of channels is that they allow content owners to manage one version of the content within SharePoint and enable

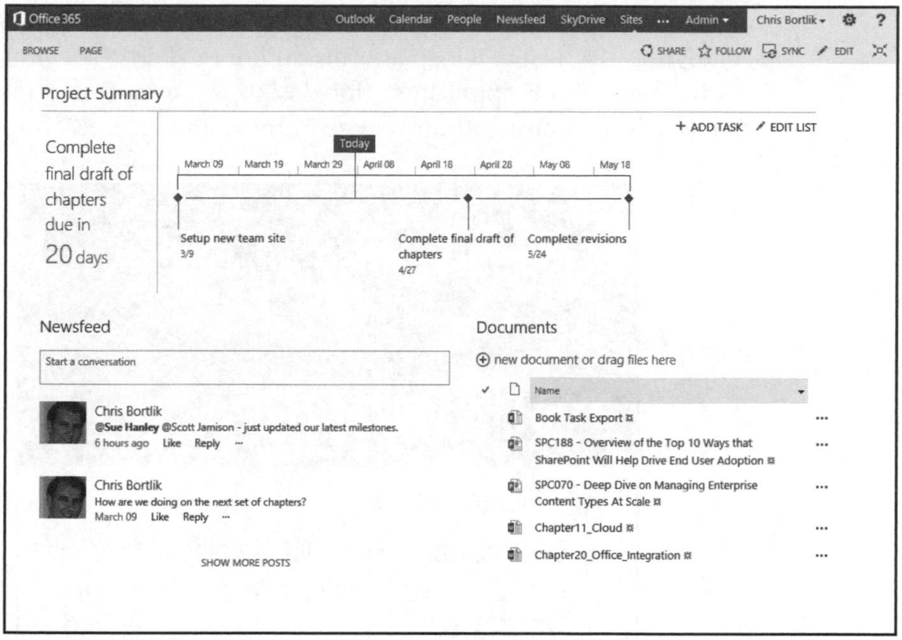

Figure 19-2 SharePoint team site in touch mode

SharePoint to detect the device (such as an iPhone or PC) viewing the page and then render the appropriate page template specified by the site designer. As mentioned earlier, while channels are a powerful tool in the toolbox of a SharePoint site designer, you should carefully consider what SharePoint sites and pages require this level of design and customization based on the key use cases of your site. Channels are discussed in more detail in Chapter 14, "Managing Web Content."

SharePoint Newsfeed Mobile Applications

Organizations rolling out SharePoint 2013's new social capabilities will want to consider supporting the new SharePoint Newsfeed mobile application. The SharePoint Newsfeed application enables people to keep up-to-date on their organizational newsfeed and to post new messages, including photos that they may want to take with their mobile device.

The SharePoint Newsfeed application is available on Windows Phone (see Figure 19-3) and iOS platforms (iPhone, iPad) (see Figure 19-4). A native Windows 8 application (for desktops, laptops, and tablets) is in development and targeted for release in the summer of 2013.

Figure 19-3 SharePoint Newsfeed application on a Windows Phone

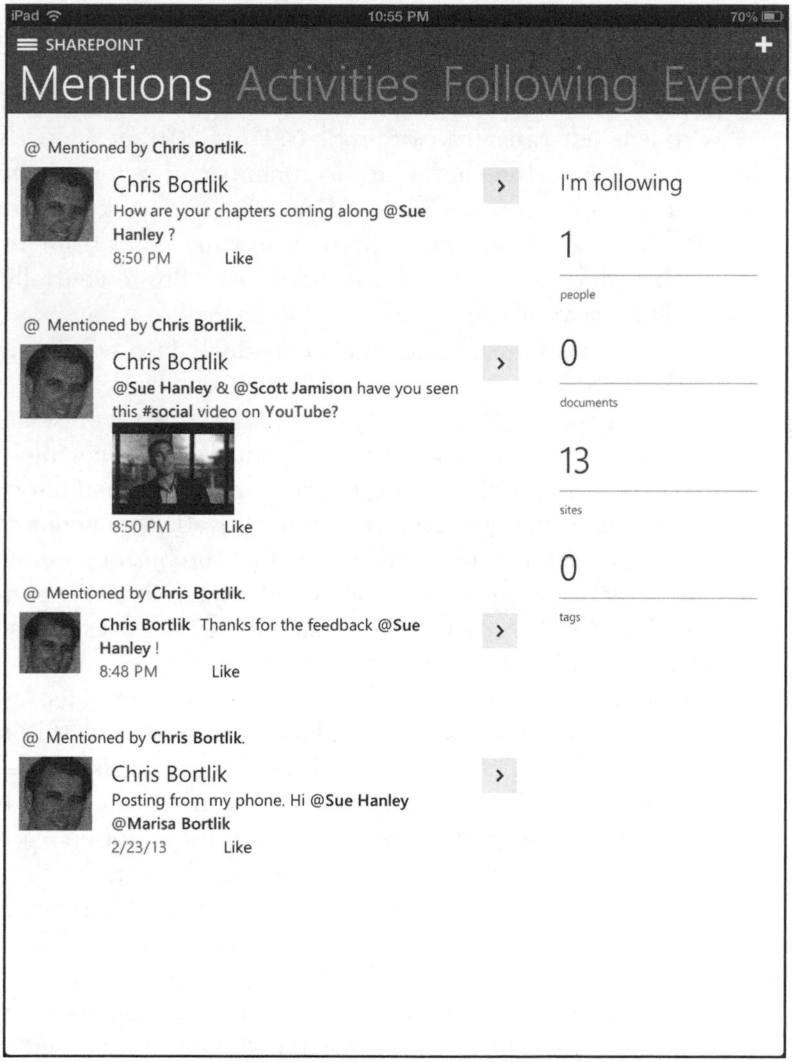

Figure 19-4 SharePoint Newsfeed application on an iPad

Note   The SharePoint Newsfeed can also be accessed from other platforms and devices via Web browsers that include Internet Explorer, Firefox, Chrome, and Safari. Please see Chapter 15, "Planning for Social Computing," for more information on the SharePoint Newsfeed.

SkyDrive Pro Mobile Applications

As described in Chapter 20, "Integrating Office Applications," SkyDrive Pro is a new capability within SharePoint 2013 designed to enable secure anywhere, anytime access to documents and notebooks from any device. For example, you can store a OneNote notebook on your SkyDrive Pro and have access to your important meeting notes from any PC, tablet, or mobile device. You can also use SkyDrive Pro to centrally store, manage, and access your key documents. SkyDrive Pro is intended to solve a variety of business challenges that individuals face when they want to work on content across various devices (such as a work laptop, home tablet, or mobile phone) and are today e-mailing files to themselves or using USB thumb drives. In some cases, individuals are using file-sharing services such as Box, Dropbox, Google Drive, or other consumer-oriented applications that, if not approved by the organization, may not offer the level of IT management, audit, and control that the business requires.

In addition to the desktop-based SkyDrive Pro experience described in Chapter 20, Microsoft is scheduled to release new SkyDrive Pro mobile applications in the summer of 2013. These applications will support Windows 8 and Windows RT devices (such as the Microsoft Surface RT tablet) and iOS platforms (iPad and iPhone) to facilitate working with documents stored on a personal SkyDrive Pro document library within SharePoint. Windows Phones have direct integration with SkyDrive Pro as part of the Microsoft Office Mobile Applications, which are discussed in the next section of this chapter.

In addition to these mobile applications, SkyDrive Pro can also be accessed from a variety of platforms and devices via Web browsers that include Internet Explorer, Firefox, Chrome, and Safari. This assists with creating, viewing, and editing content stored on your SkyDrive Pro site within SharePoint. The SkyDrive Pro desktop client described in Chapter 20 supports full offline scenarios on Windows 7 and Windows 8 devices.

Office Mobile and Web Apps

Microsoft's Windows Phone includes Office applications for Word, Excel, PowerPoint, and OneNote. These applications can be used to view and edit documents stored on SharePoint sites and have integration with SkyDrive Pro (see Figure 19-5). The Office mobile client also allows you to see your recent document history across your devices (see Figure 19-6). This is very helpful for quickly finding the documents that you have been working on and then being able to view and edit them directly on the phone.

Figure 19-5 SkyDrive Pro is integrated with the Windows Phone Office application

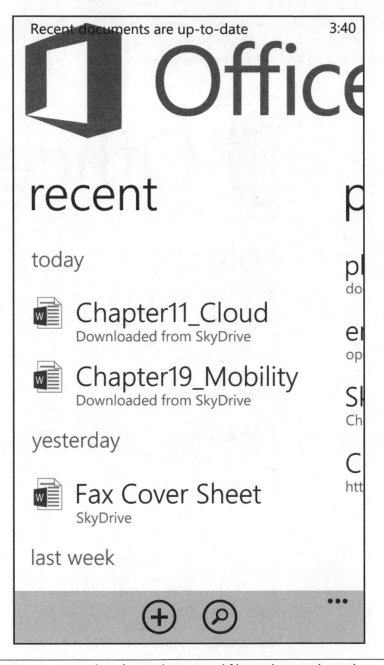

Figure 19-6 Viewing a list of recently accessed files in the Windows Phone Office application

This includes the ability to view and edit a PowerPoint presentation (see Figure 19-7) or to add comments to Word documents.

Microsoft's Outlook client for Windows Phone supports the ability to view and edit SharePoint and Project tasks that have been synchronized with Microsoft Exchange. This is helpful for having mobile access to the key tasks that you need to perform.

Microsoft also offers a Lync client for Windows Phone which helps with viewing others' presence status (free, busy, do not disturb, etc.) and joining meetings while on the go without having to dial in to the meeting and put in your meeting and leader codes; this is very useful if you need to join a meeting while at the airport, for example.

Microsoft currently offers Lync and OneNote applications on iOS and Android devices. These applications work similarly to the way they do on the Windows Phone platform and are regularly updated.

Microsoft also offers mobile versions of the Office Web Apps for Word, Excel, PowerPoint (see Figure 19-8), and OneNote. These mobile clients support both viewing and lightweight editing of Office documents stored in SharePoint and work across various PC, tablet, and mobile device platforms.

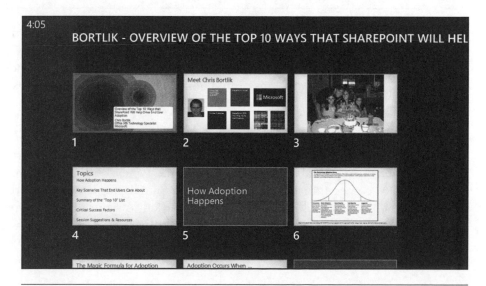

Figure 19-7 Viewing slides in the PowerPoint mobile application

Figure 19-8 Viewing a PowerPoint presentation via the mobile Web application

Third-Party Mobile Applications

In addition to Microsoft mobile applications, a number of third parties have built mobile applications that support SharePoint. Mobile Entree provides mobile applications that extend SharePoint in a variety of use cases including business intelligence. Formotus has solutions targeted at delivering forms from SharePoint to a variety of mobile device platforms.

Our recommendation is to start by evaluating the native mobile applications, tools, and experiences delivered by Microsoft. If your organization finds that the capabilities are limited, the typical evaluation of build versus buy comes into play. In these cases, purchasing specialized third-party solutions may offer a faster time to market for your organization and save money in the long run since these third parties are continually updating their mobile applications to support common business requirements.

Key Points

When planning for supporting mobile use cases with SharePoint 2013, there are a number of areas to consider. These include the following:

- SharePoint 2013 has added improved support for mobile devices, including native browser features and a new device channel feature that enables optimization of SharePoint Web pages based on the capabilities available on the mobile device.
- Microsoft has released new mobile clients for the SharePoint Newsfeed and SkyDrive Pro capabilities. These clients support the new SharePoint social and personal document storage features.
- Microsoft has updated the Office Mobile and Web Apps with the 2013 release.
- Many third parties offer mobile applications for SharePoint— beyond what Microsoft provides.
- When planning for offering SharePoint mobile capabilities, you should evaluate the different use cases and scenarios that apply to your organization. You also need to think about the governance, security, support, and architectural areas that may be impacted. For example, will your organization support only corporate-issued mobile devices or also end-user-supplied tablets and phones?
- When planning support for multiple devices and browsers, you should consider the need to test any applications that you build or purchase for use on top of SharePoint 2013. Microsoft does extensive testing of SharePoint 2013 to ensure that it is compatible across these platforms—you will want to do the same for your customizations.
- As you map your business and technical requirements, make sure you keep the user in mind. Often organizations place significant security and technical burdens on users, making it challenging for them to access the content they need from their mobile devices. This often results in poor user adoption of the solution and ultimately drives users to collaborate using alternative consumer solutions or e-mail, for which the barriers to entry are lower.

CHAPTER 20

INTEGRATING OFFICE APPLICATIONS

Why are we talking about the Office 2013 client applications in a SharePoint 2013 book? The answer is simple: to maximize the value of your investment in the SharePoint platform, you will want to evaluate and take advantage of the integration and capabilities that are "lit up" through the Office client.

There is business value here: if you make it easy for users to work with SharePoint from within the context of the Office applications with which they already spend most of their time (e.g., Outlook, Word, Excel, PowerPoint), you will give them the incentive to use SharePoint over other tools such as file shares and e-mail. It's a virtuous cycle: as more properly tagged content is added to SharePoint, the more relevant search results will be; this then drives people to use your SharePoint environment and begin to access the social features, business intelligence, forms, and other tools.

The Office 2007 system added many features that worked "best" with a combination of Office 2007 client versions and SharePoint, for example, offline information and easy access to advanced SharePoint document management features such as workflow, metadata, and version control. Office 2010 extended integration with SharePoint via the Backstage and new Web-based versions of Word, Excel, PowerPoint, and OneNote.

With the 2013 release, Microsoft has further advanced the role of the Office client in the SharePoint experience by enhancing integration with SharePoint in a number of areas, including the new SkyDrive Pro capabilities for personal file storage. The following topics are covered in this chapter:

- What's new in Office 2013
- Office client applications that connect with SharePoint 2013
- SkyDrive Pro—taking SharePoint content offline

- Document and data caching
- Backstage
- Other clients: Office Web Apps and Office Mobile Applications

What's New in Office 2013?

Microsoft designed Office 2013 to be integrated with cloud services. From a consumer perspective, Office suggests SkyDrive as the preferred file storage location. From an enterprise perspective, Office integrates with SkyDrive Pro as part of SharePoint 2013 on-premises or as part of SharePoint Online within Office 365. Similar to SharePoint, Microsoft's Office strategy is moving away from major releases every three years to a much more frequent set of regular quarterly updates. Microsoft will be regularly releasing updates to Office via Office 365.

- **Office 2013 Professional Plus** requires Windows 7 or Windows 8 on a personal computer. Prior versions of Windows, including Windows XP, are no longer supported with Office 2013.
- **Office Home & Student 2013 RT**, released for the new Windows RT operating system, is installed with the device. For example, when you purchase a Surface RT tablet device from Microsoft, Office 2013 is included, with Word, Excel, PowerPoint, and OneNote.

There are also new Windows 8 applications available for Lync and OneNote which can be downloaded for free from the Windows Store. These applications are optimized for a touchscreen. Updates are coming soon for Office on the Mac.

Also updated in 2013 are the Web and mobile application companions for Word, Excel, PowerPoint, and OneNote that provide lightweight viewing and editing capabilities and are integrated with SharePoint. These applications are comparable to Outlook Web Access and Outlook mobile application access to an Exchange mailbox. The Office Web Apps have a new architecture in 2013: they can no longer be installed in a SharePoint farm. Office Web Apps, on-premises, must be installed on a separate set of servers that can now be shared with multiple SharePoint farms and other server applications that integrate with the Office Web Apps, such as Exchange 2013. The Office Web Apps are also available for free consumer use via SkyDrive and for enterprises via Office 365 subscriptions, including integration with SharePoint and Exchange Online.

Similar to SharePoint 2013, Office 2013 introduces a new apps model and marketplace. Previous Office applications and extensions, such as add-ins and macros, are still supported. The new Office apps model allows applications to be built using Web technologies such as HTML5, CSS3, and JavaScript. This model enables Office applications to run in both the Office clients and the Office Web Apps. The Office Marketplace provides a new way to publish and acquire applications for Office. Microsoft manages a public marketplace where third parties can make Office applications and document templates available for download (Figure 20-1). Organizations can also have a private Office application catalog for only their internal applications or to centrally manage third-party applications and licenses.

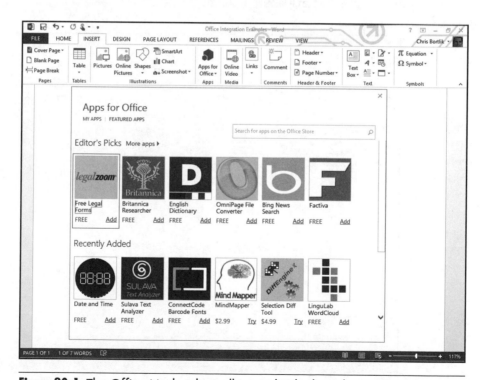

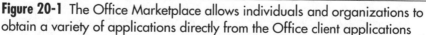
Figure 20-1 The Office Marketplace allows individuals and organizations to obtain a variety of applications directly from the Office client applications

The new Office has a special mode that is optimized for use with touch devices. In this mode (Figure 20-2), the icons are larger to make them easier to access with a finger, and the Office user interface is adjusted to place frequently used functions (e.g., the Delete button in Outlook) near the edges of the screen to enable people to easily work with content with their thumbs. Applications such as Word also have a new reading mode that is optimized for content consumption on a tablet device.

Office 365 adds new capabilities to Office that are available only with Microsoft's managed cloud offering. The new Office subscription service (named Office 365 ProPlus) enables organizations to license Office on a per-user basis. Users can install and use Office on up to five PC or Mac devices. Office 365 ProPlus enables software to be streamed to these devices where Microsoft can manage the updates. Organizations can elect to manage and distribute updates on their own, if so desired.

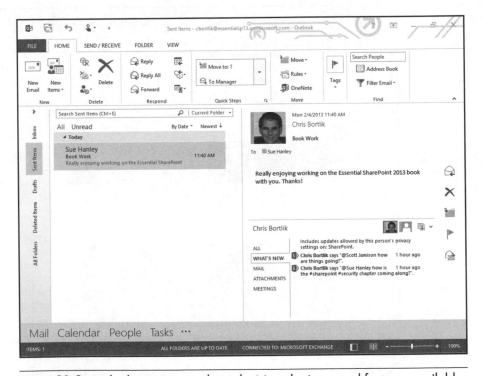

Figure 20-2 Outlook 2013 in touch mode. Note the icons and features available on the left and right sides of the screen which are designed for use on a tablet

Office 365 ProPlus supports the ability to perform side-by-side installations where Office 2013 can coexist on a PC with older versions of Office, such as Office 2007 or 2010. The benefit of this is helping organizations to roll out the new Office while enabling users to use prior versions of Office which may be required for legacy applications and add-ins. Office side-by-side installs also help with training and communication plans to phase in the introduction of the new Office clients within organizations.

Office on Demand (Figure 20-3) is also available via Office 365. This capability allows individuals to temporarily install an Office application (e.g., Word, Excel, or PowerPoint) on another device. This feature is available when a user is viewing his or her SkyDrive Pro site within SharePoint Online. For example, say you were visiting a family member's house on vacation and you needed to make an important update to an Office document that you have shared with others on your SkyDrive Pro. You could use the Office Web Apps to view and edit the document through the browser. But what if you needed to use an advanced capability in Word that is not supported in the browser, and the PC you are using does not have Office

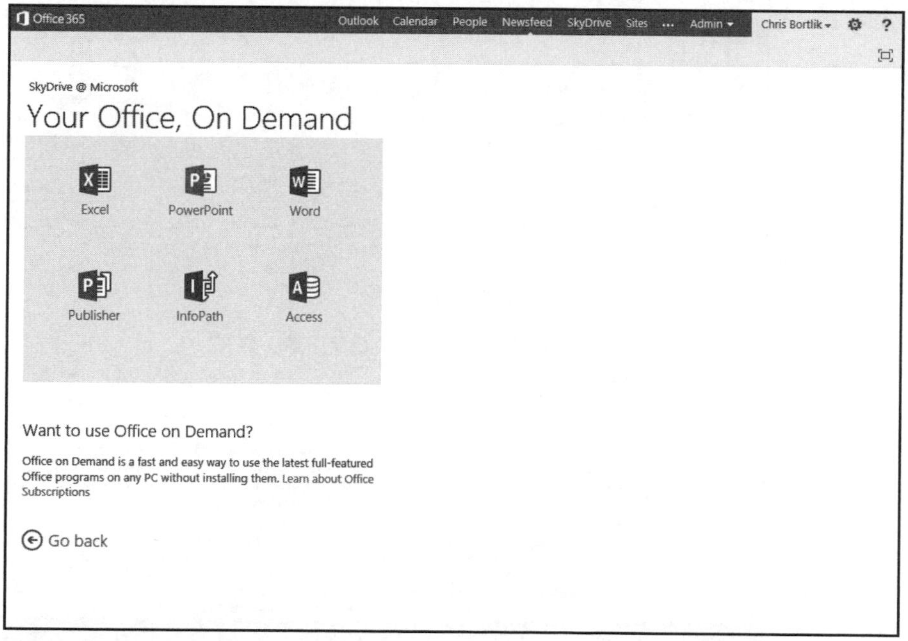

Figure 20-3 Office on Demand enables temporary use of Office client applications on other PCs

installed? In this case, Office on Demand allows you to temporarily stream and install Word on the PC (Windows 7 or Windows 8 only) that you are currently using. You can then perform the tasks needed, and when you exit Word, the program and your document are no longer available on the PC.

When Office is connected to SkyDrive or Office 365, it also enables Office to "roam" with you. This means that Office can remember the documents you most recently viewed or edited, regardless of the PC, tablet, or mobile device you last used. Office can also remember your exact location within a document when you closed the Office client so you can pick up right where you left off (Figure 20-4).

Office 2013 also improves the way that people collaborate on documents. Collaborative authoring, first introduced in the Office 2010 client and Web Apps, has been enhanced in Word, Excel, PowerPoint, and OneNote—including the ability for people to simultaneously edit Word or PowerPoint documents via the Web browser. For example, multiple people can edit the same presentation file at the same time so team members can

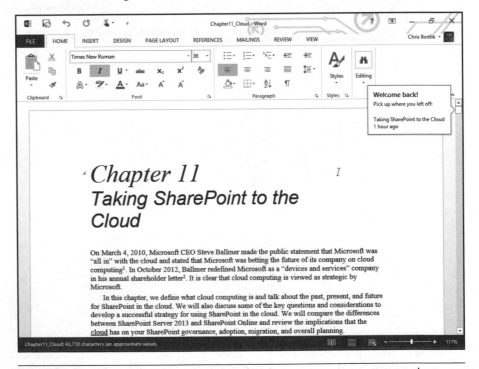

Figure 20-4 Office 2013 can remember the documents you were recently working with and where you left off

make their edits to different slides without the need to work serially and go through a series of document handoffs. Office has added threaded commenting within documents so people can have a "conversation" via comments (Figure 20-5) and reply to each other—similar to working within a discussion list but scoped to a specific document. Sharing (Figure 20-6) has also been integrated directly into the Office clients to make it easier for people to grant others View or Edit permissions to individual files and automatically send e-mail messages to invite others to access the document.

From an administrative perspective, Office 2013 introduces new capabilities. The new Office telemetry dashboard helps to monitor usage of Office documents and add-ins. This analytical information can help organizations to identify the Office documents and add-ins that are used most frequently and by which individuals and teams. This information is very helpful when planning for testing, upgrades, training, and migration and for being proactive in detecting and addressing support issues. The built-in Office 2013 telemetry capabilities replace the various stand-alone

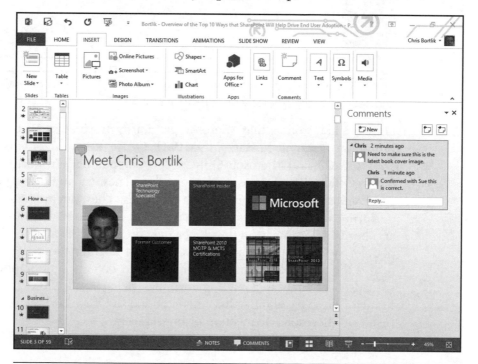

Figure 20-5 Office 2013 offers the ability to have threaded comments within a document

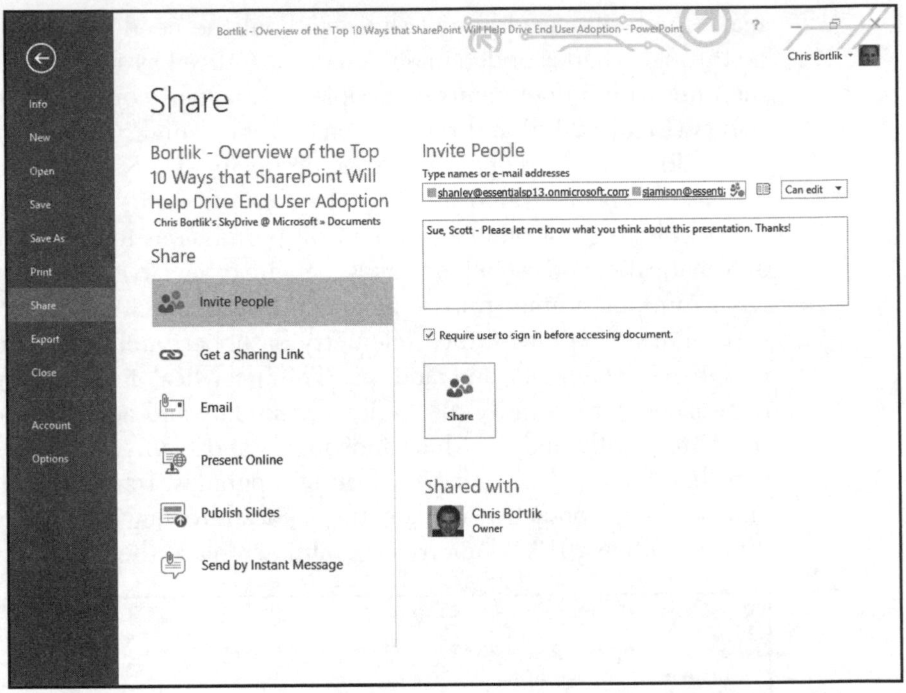

Figure 20-6 Office 2013 makes it easier to share SharePoint content with others and specify if they can view or edit the file

utilities and resources that Microsoft previously provided, such as the Office Migration Planning Manager (OMPM), Office Environment Assessment Tool (OEAT), and Microsoft Office Code Compatibility Inspector.[1]

In Office 2013, Microsoft also introduced new capabilities to help manage Excel spreadsheets and Access databases. These include the ability to perform comparisons to see what has changed from one version of a file to another (similar to what a developer may do with application code or how people have compared differences in Word documents in the past) and to use the new Excel "Inquire" capability to detect potential issues with spreadsheets such as analyzing formulas being used within workbooks. Many of these capabilities have been added to Office and SharePoint as a result of Microsoft's acquisition of Prodiance.[2]

---

1. Microsoft Office 2010 migration-planning resources. http://technet.microsoft.com/en-us/library/ee460876(v=office.14).aspx

2. Microsoft Prodiance acquisition pathways Web site. www.microsoft.com/pathways/prodiance

One of the biggest changes that will affect SharePoint is the upgrade and repositioning of SharePoint Workspace (formerly Groove), which has been morphed into the SkyDrive Pro client. SkyDrive Pro provides offline file and folder synchronization from SharePoint to your local file storage. Once installed, SkyDrive Pro creates a folder directly within Windows Explorer without requiring you to open a separate application to view, add, or edit files. Unfortunately, not all of the capabilities that existed within SharePoint Workspace are available in SkyDrive Pro. We will discuss these differences in depth later in this chapter.

OneNote has also been improved in 2013. OneNote is an application for capturing information from various formats (text, audio, images, etc.) and integrating them on one canvas. OneNote has rich integration with SharePoint, so multiple people can concurrently collaborate on a page within a shared OneNote notebook and have their changes automatically synchronized and tracked so people can see who changed what section and when. In some ways OneNote is like a wiki editor on steroids and can be used for various tasks such as meeting notes, brainstorming, policies, procedures, and training materials.

Business Connectivity Services (BCS) has also been improved in SharePoint 2013 as the successor to the Business Data Catalog (BDC) that was introduced in SharePoint 2007. BCS enables you to establish a read/write connection with a back-end database such as a CRM (e.g., Salesforce, Siebel, or Dynamics) or ERP system (e.g., PeopleSoft or SAP) using tools such as SharePoint Designer or Visual Studio. Once created and published to SharePoint, the BCS connection can be reused by SharePoint lists and the Office 2013 clients (e.g., Outlook and Word) to view and edit data that is stored in the back-end system. More detailed information on BCS is provided in Chapter 17, "Planning Business Solutions."

Note While the Office 2013 clients add tighter integration with the latest SharePoint 2013 server product, it is not required that you upgrade your clients and servers at the same time. Microsoft will be publishing a "Business Productivity at Its Best" white paper that describes the integrated client and server capabilities and differences across versions of SharePoint and Office in more detail. Unfortunately, this document was not publicly available at the time this book was written. Microsoft's TechNet Web site (www.technet.com) will have the document when it is available.

Office Client Applications That Connect with SharePoint 2013

The user interface in SharePoint 2013 has been improved, and many people work directly in their Web browser. But what if you're going to be offline or you prefer to do your SharePoint work right in the context of the document that you are working on? Maybe you're somewhere with very low bandwidth and you're working with large files. Good news: Office 2013 has a few different options to help you out.

SharePoint 2013 has increased the integration with various Office 2013 clients. The SharePoint ribbon browser interface directly links you with the following Office and Windows clients, offering you the choice and flexibility to work with SharePoint in the context of the client tool that best supports the task you are performing:

- **Access.** Enables you to work with SharePoint list data offline in a read/write fashion. Also great for mashing up SharePoint data with other data sources (databases, spreadsheets, etc.) and creating queries and polished reports. This fits in well with the overall SharePoint Composite Application strategy and provides you with another alternative for migrating local Access databases to a shared and managed platform, including the updated Access Services SharePoint capabilities. Access Services enables you to publish an Access database and have the data, forms, macros, and queries be usable via a Web browser.
- **Excel.** Continued support for browser-based Excel Services. Updated Office Web Apps companion for browser-based viewing, editing, and coauthoring of spreadsheets. Continued integration of Excel with SharePoint for saving documents, adding metadata, checking in/checking out, and workflow. Great for taking a list offline and performing advanced analysis using capabilities such as charts, graphs, slicers, and PivotTables. New business intelligence capabilities including PowerPivot and PowerView for creating advanced reports and publishing them to SharePoint via Excel Services. Excel also has a new "Inquire" capability that helps with inspecting Excel files to look for issues and irregularities such as cells within a table that may be missing formulas—which is key since many organizations rely on Excel for financial analysis and modeling. Inquire helps

to flag cells to inspect closely to make sure there are no irregularities within your spreadsheets.

- **InfoPath.** Tool for making advanced forms which can then be reused across SharePoint (via InfoPath Forms Services) and other Office applications (Word, Access, Outlook). InfoPath supports the creation of InfoPath Forms Services Web Part controls so you can mash up InfoPath controls on the same as page as other SharePoint data and Web Parts.

- **Lync.** Application for providing instant messaging and presence (free, busy, in a meeting, etc.). Lync can also be used for audio, video, and desktop sharing. Integration with SharePoint and other Office applications to see when someone is online and to then engage with that person directly—for example, when coauthoring a Word document.

- **Office Upload Center.** Performs per-document-level caching and central access to see all SharePoint files you have viewed recently and which items are pending check-in, regardless of which SharePoint site the content originally came from. Synchronizes changes only between the client and server applications across the Office suite.

- **OneNote.** Advanced wiki capabilities for collaborating, brainstorming, and sharing information. Updated Office Web Apps companion for browser-based viewing and editing of information, including coauthoring support in both the browser and rich desktop client for concurrent editing.

- **Outlook.** Primarily used for personal information management (PIM) and a personalized view of SharePoint team information. Examples include read/write access to SharePoint calendars, tasks, contacts, and discussion boards—even while offline. Outlook includes an updated Outlook Social Connector (OSC) which displays news and activity feeds for your contacts from SharePoint 2013 as well as other social systems (e.g., LinkedIn, Facebook) in a centralized view to help improve your collaboration experience. Outlook 2013 also integrates with the new Site Mailbox capability that has been added to SharePoint and Exchange 2013.

- **PowerPoint.** Continued integration of PowerPoint with SharePoint for saving documents, adding metadata, checking in/checking out, and workflow as well as slide libraries. Updated Office Web Apps companion for browser-based viewing and editing of presentations. Client supports coauthoring so multiple people can edit the same presentation concurrently. Web companion now supports coauthoring as well. Updated features to add videos and photos directly from SharePoint and the Internet and to edit these digital assets (e.g., change display, trim, resize).

- **Project.** Supports exporting SharePoint task lists into Project for more sophisticated reporting on project tasks, milestones, dependencies, resources, and so on.

- **SharePoint Designer.** A free desktop application provided by Microsoft for advanced SharePoint site customization, including creating and managing reusable workflows and BCS. One major change in SharePoint Designer 2013 is the removal of the design view while working with page design. This topic, and alternative approaches, is discussed further in Chapter 14, "Managing Web Content."

- **SkyDrive Pro.** Replaces SharePoint Workspace. Used for taking SharePoint document libraries offline—either at the site or per library level. Synchronizes changes only to efficiently use network bandwidth.

- **Visio.** With Visio you can create workflows graphically through new integration with SharePoint Designer 2013. You can also create browser-based Visio diagrams (using Visio Services as part of SharePoint) and export SharePoint task lists to a graphical Visio diagram.

- **Windows Explorer.** SharePoint continues to integrate with Windows Explorer for both uploading and copying documents between SharePoint and another file storage location such as your local PC storage or a network file share. Integrate with SkyDrive Pro to have direct offline access to SharePoint files without opening another desktop application.

- **Word.** Continued integration of Word with SharePoint for saving documents, adding metadata, checking in/checking out, and workflow. Updated Office Web Apps companion for browser-based viewing and editing of documents. Both client and Web application now support coauthoring so multiple people can edit the same document concurrently.

SkyDrive Pro—Taking SharePoint Documents Offline

The SkyDrive Pro (SDP) desktop client is the replacement for SharePoint Workspace (SPW). SPW was the evolution of the product that was formerly known as Groove, which Microsoft purchased in 2005.

The SDP client is currently installed as part of Office 2013 Professional. There is also a free standalone download of SkyDrive Pro available from Microsoft. Microsoft has also released SkyDrive Pro applications for iOS and Windows RT. We will focus in the remainder of this chapter on the SDP client that ships with Office 2013 for Windows 7 or Windows 8. SDP has the following primary capabilities:

- **Sync.** SDP enables you to synchronize a SharePoint document library offline. The document library could be from your personal site, or it could be a document library from a team or project site.
- **Windows Explorer integration.** SDP integrates directly into Windows Explorer and appears as any other folder within the file system. Files and folders can be created, copied, or moved into the local SDP folder and synchronized with SharePoint automatically.
- **Conflict resolution.** SDP manages conflicts (cases where more than one person updates the same file at the same time) at the item level. This means that if two people edit the same document in a shared library at the same time, SDP will identify the conflict and allow the user to select which version of the file to keep. This also allows multiple people to edit the same file concurrently without the need to have people serially check the document in and out of SharePoint.
- **Binary differentials.** When SDP syncs data, it syncs only changes since the last sync. For example, if you have an 8MB PowerPoint file synced locally in SDP and someone makes a change to one slide, SDP will sync only the parts of that single slide that changed. This is great in general and especially when you're on a slower network, wireless, or mobile connection.
- **Desktop search.** SDP enables you to use desktop search to locally search for and find content that has been taken offline within the tool.

Using SkyDrive Pro

The SkyDrive Pro client application can be used in two primary ways. The typical use case is to synchronize files and folders from your personal SkyDrive Pro (documents that are stored as part of your SharePoint 2013 personal site) to your local computer. You can also synchronize document libraries from SharePoint sites. Since the user experience is similar when you are synchronizing documents from personal sites or team sites, we will focus in this section on setting up your personal site to sync.

To access your SkyDrive Pro library (Figure 20-7) click the SkyDrive link at the top of any page within SharePoint 2013. The first time you click the Sync icon on a PC that has Office 2013 installed, the SkyDrive Pro configuration wizard will prompt you for a local storage location to synchronize your files and folders (Figure 20-8).

After the SkyDrive Pro wizard completes the initial setup, clicking the "Show my files" option takes you to the location that you specified to synchronize your files to (Figure 20-9). You can now create, copy, delete, and rename files and folders locally within your SkyDrive Pro folder (Figure 20-10). These files are visible within Windows Explorer, and any changes that you make locally, or on the SharePoint server, are automatically kept in sync. By default, each SkyDrive Pro document library within SharePoint 2013 has a Shared with Everyone folder; content stored in this folder is visible to anyone within your organization. File and folder permissions and sharing within

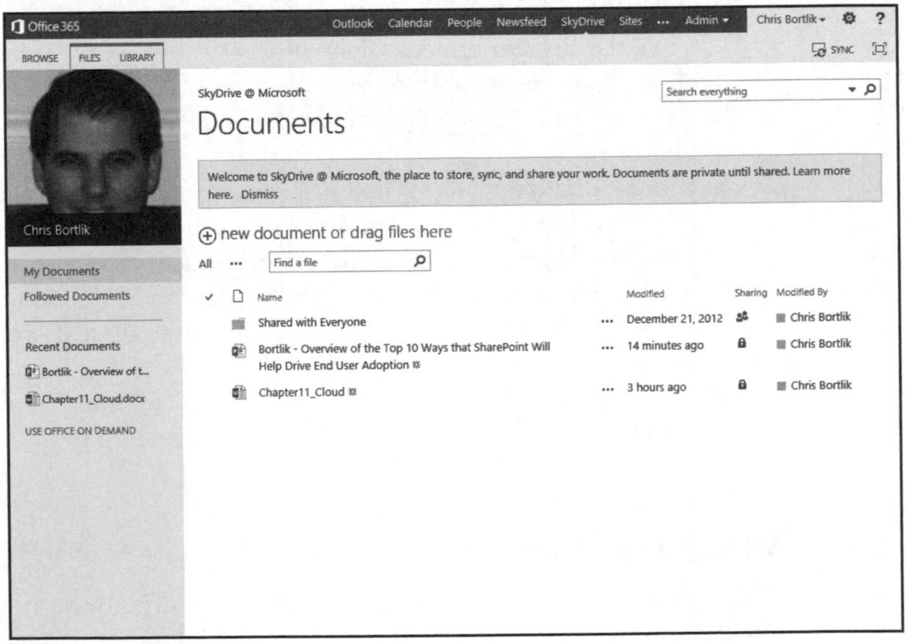

Figure 20-7 A typical SkyDrive Pro library for an individual using SharePoint 2013

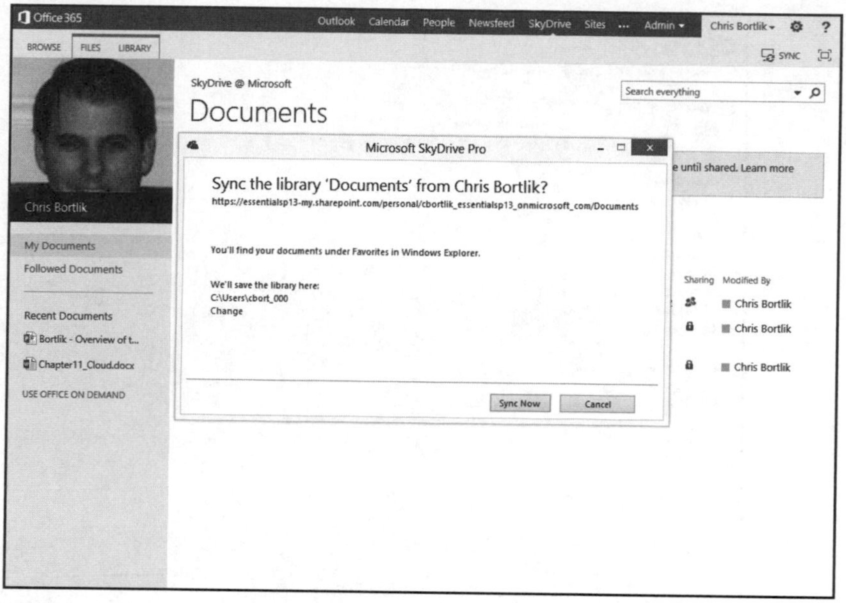

Figure 20-8 Initial SkyDrive Pro setup

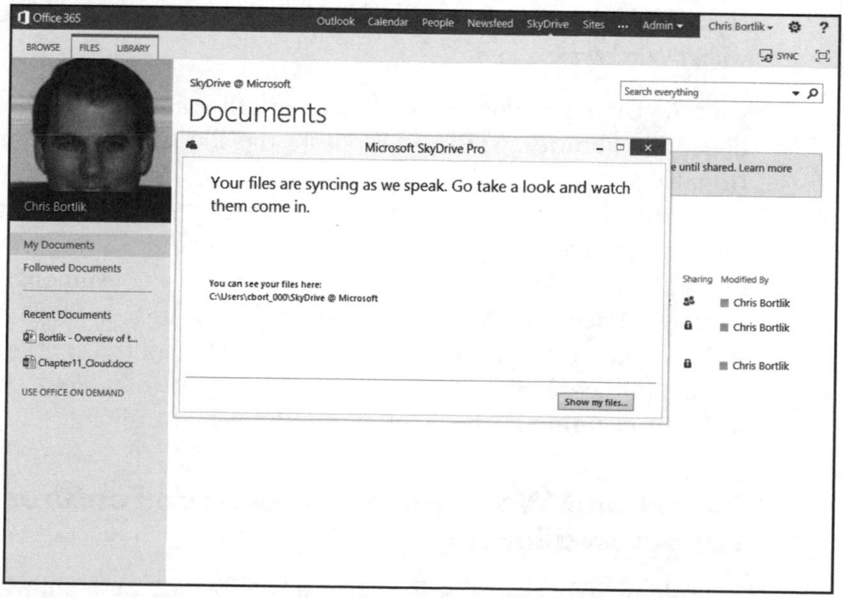

Figure 20-9 SkyDrive Pro initial setup completion screen

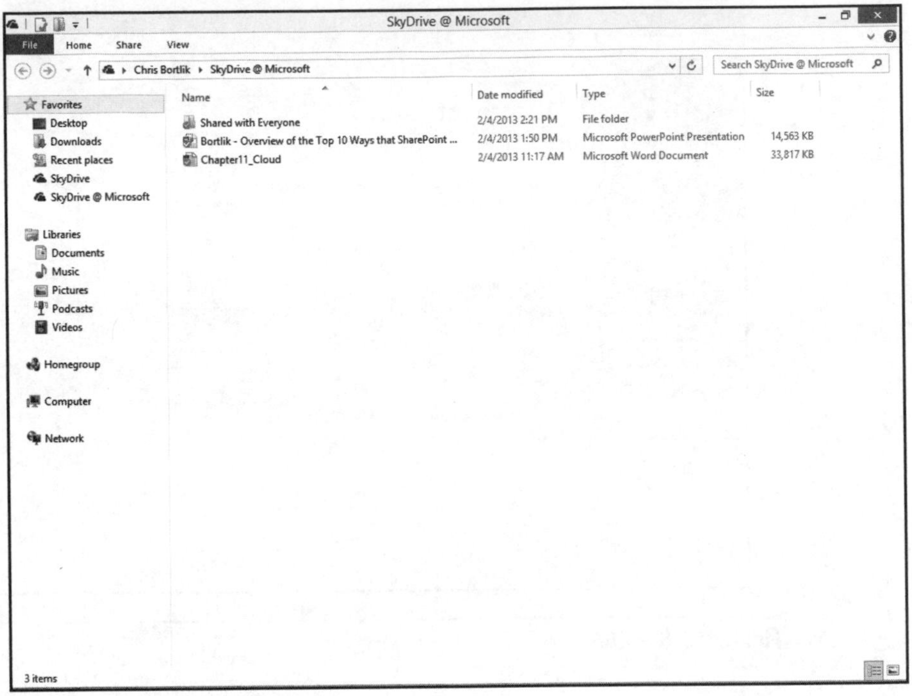

Figure 20-10 Your SkyDrive Pro folder and files are made available directly within Windows Explorer

your SkyDrive Pro document library work the same as for other SharePoint document libraries. SDP will replicate the file synchronization experience from SPW.

Note that in Figure 20-10 there are two Favorites folders with the name SkyDrive in them. The first folder named SkyDrive is the local integration and synchronization with Microsoft's consumer SkyDrive file-sharing service. The SkyDrive @ Microsoft location is SkyDrive Pro since in this example, SkyDrive Pro is hosted at Microsoft as part of SharePoint Online (Office 365). This is something that you will want to consider during your planning for user communications and training.

SharePoint Workspace and Groove Features No Longer Available

SharePoint Workspace (SPW) had a number of capabilities that are not available in SkyDrive Pro. These include

- **Extended offline capabilities.** SPW allowed you to take non-document SharePoint library data offline. For example, you could use SPW to synchronize an offline copy of a custom SharePoint list that you may have been using to track customer support information.
- **Version management.** SPW allowed you to directly check documents in or out of SharePoint without having to access SharePoint in a Web browser.
- **Metadata attributes.** SPW showed SharePoint metadata for files in the offline list view.
- **Business Connectivity Services (BCS).** BCS integration via SharePoint lists allowed you to use SPW to work with external data lists offline. Examples of this included working with CRM, ERP, or custom LOB systems.
- **InfoPath forms integration.** SPW used InfoPath for its forms and allowed you to work offline with a set of SharePoint forms.
- **Classic Groove workspaces.** These were used for non-SharePoint-based collaboration and information exchange both within the organization and externally with customers and partners. These Groove workspaces worked via either a peer-to-peer synchronization or via Groove relay, audit, and management servers.

Migrating from SharePoint Workspace to SkyDrive Pro

There is no direct migration path from SharePoint Workspace to SkyDrive Pro. In most cases, customers were using SPW for synchronizing files offline from SharePoint. SDP should work fine for organizations in most cases and may offer an improved user experience since the SPW client is gone and SDP integrates directly with Windows Explorer and functions similarly to the consumer SkyDrive client. Note that SDP can also work with SharePoint 2010 document libraries. Unfortunately, Microsoft does not provide an upgrade path to move existing document library synchronization relationships from SPW to SDP: individuals will need to manually re-sync libraries with SDP, or organizations can create scripts to automate this process on behalf of their users.

If your organization was relying on SPW for offline usage of SharePoint lists and forms, you will want to review the capabilities built into other

Office client applications such as Excel, Access, and Outlook. These Office clients provide much of what SPW did for working with SharePoint lists and have additional capabilities, such as reporting, that SPW did not include.

Organizations that will feel the largest impact are those that were relying on Groove workspaces for peer-to-peer synchronization without the use of SharePoint. In these cases, your best temporary option may be to keep SPW installed side by side with SDP using the Office 365 ProPlus capabilities or other client virtualization technologies, such as Microsoft's Application Virtualization (App-V) software, which will allow you to run multiple versions of the same product side by side. One important technical consideration is that both SPW and SDP run as the "groove.exe" process under the covers.

Documents and Data Caching

Office 2013 offers several different ways to handle document and data caching. Choosing the tool that is right for you will depend on what you need to do.

Documents

When working with documents, your primary tools are

- SkyDrive Pro
- Office Upload Center
- Outlook 2013
- Windows Explorer

SkyDrive Pro

SkyDrive Pro is the tool to use for SharePoint sites that you frequently use and/or where you want to make sure that you always have the latest copy of documents synchronized and available—even when you are not connected to the corporate network. Personal and team collaboration sites are two examples of sites that are well suited to use SDP to keep content up-to-date.

Office Upload Center

What if you only occasionally browse SharePoint sites and have trouble remembering the sites where you've checked out files and those where you have pending check-ins? Or maybe you're in a remote location and have a low-bandwidth connection? Good news: Office 2013 includes an application named the Office Upload Center. When opening the Office Upload Center, you can see the documents you have most recently opened from SharePoint, manage your locally cached copies, and review and check in documents (see Figure 20-11).

You can also customize how the Office Upload Center works, how you are notified of changes that are pending or failed to upload, and the amount of disk space allocated to the file cache (see Figure 20-12).

Using the Office Upload Center is the default option in Office 2013 for caching Office files on your PC. It is not required. If you want to change Office to instead use a "local server drafts folder" on your computer and have this work as it did in Office 2007, you can change that option under the Offline Editing Options for the Document

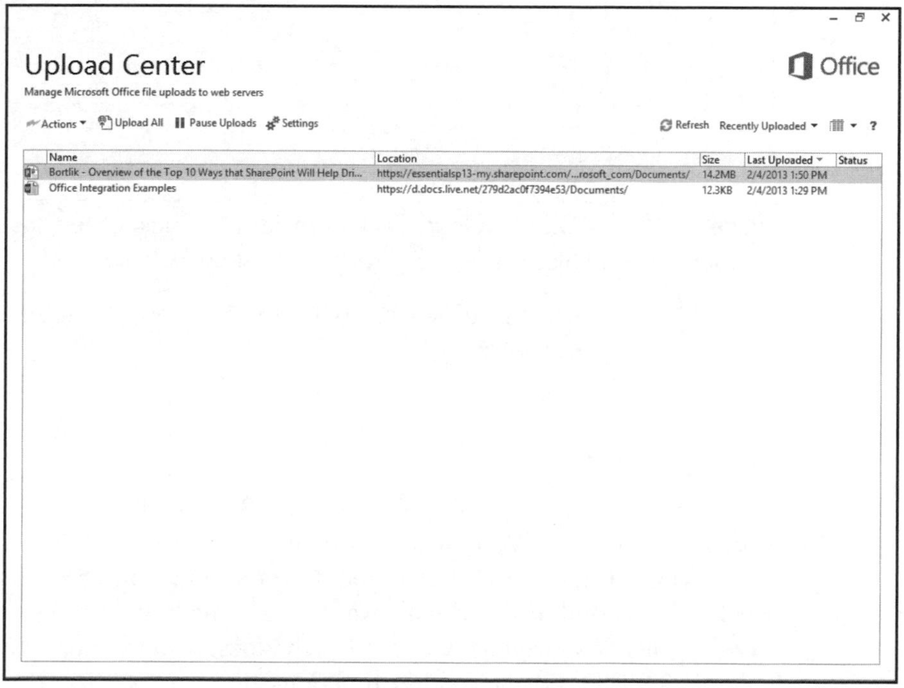

Figure 20-11 The Office Upload Center is a central location for caching all SharePoint files and providing a consolidated view of all files checked out and pending upload back to SharePoint. The Office Upload Center is also used with Microsoft's consumer SkyDrive service

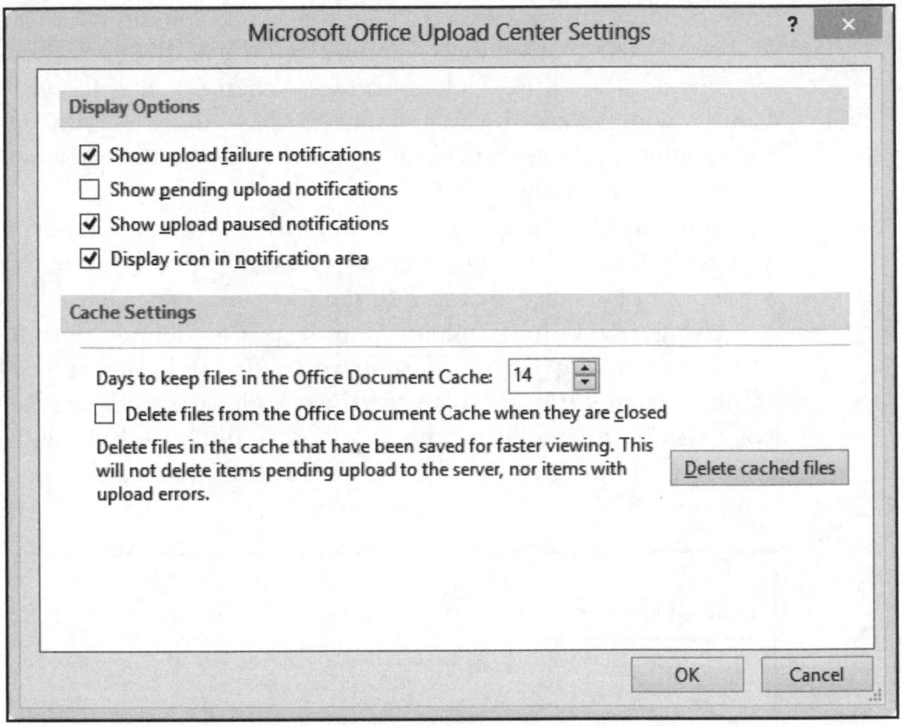

Figure 20-12 The Office Upload Center provides a variety of settings, including how long cached files are kept and whether to show notifications

Management Server Files setting within the Save options in any Office client product (Figure 20-13).

Outlook 2013

Like Office 2007 and 2010, Outlook 2013 supports the ability to take documents offline. We typically discourage the use of this feature for a few reasons. First, Outlook document synchronization with SharePoint is read-only. Second, do you really want your e-mail client to be synchronizing documents as well as what it already does around your e-mails, tasks, calendars, RSS feeds, and other functions?

There is one important exception to this recommendation: Office, Exchange, and SharePoint 2013 have introduced a new Site Mailbox capability (Figure 20-14), which enables you to have a unified view of messages

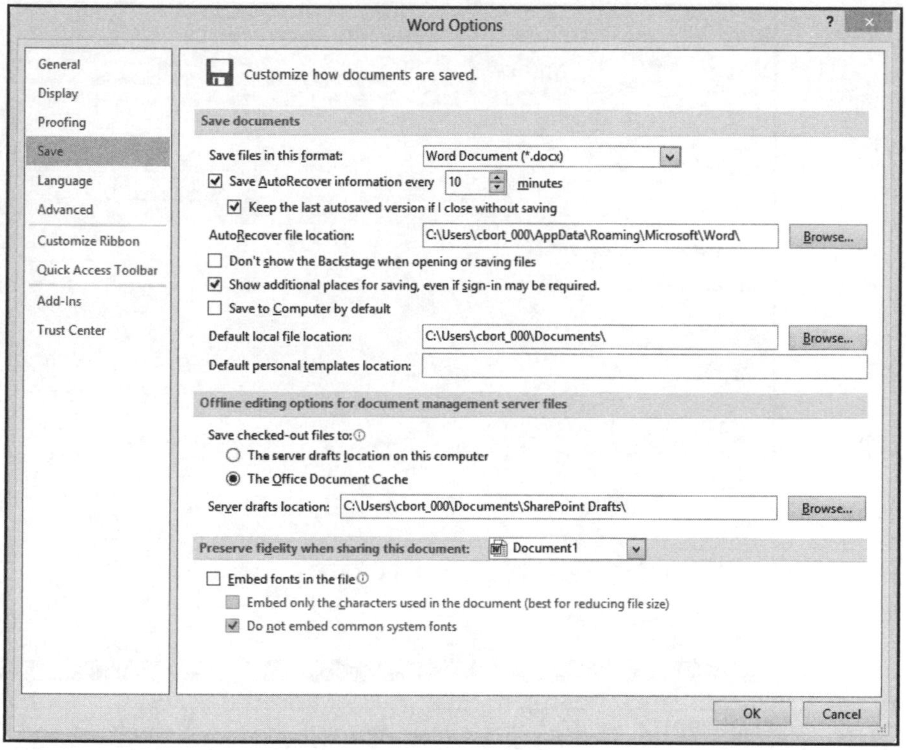

Figure 20-13 Setting Office 2013 to use Office Document Cache or a local server drafts location

from Exchange and documents from SharePoint, and to drag and drop files into SharePoint from within Outlook.

Note Chapter 13, "Managing Enterprise Content," discusses the new Site Mailbox feature in more depth.

Windows Explorer

Use Windows Explorer to quickly move files between SharePoint and other file systems (e.g., a network file share or your local PC storage) if you are not concerned about applying new SharePoint metadata (inbound transfer) or preserving existing SharePoint metadata (outbound transfer).

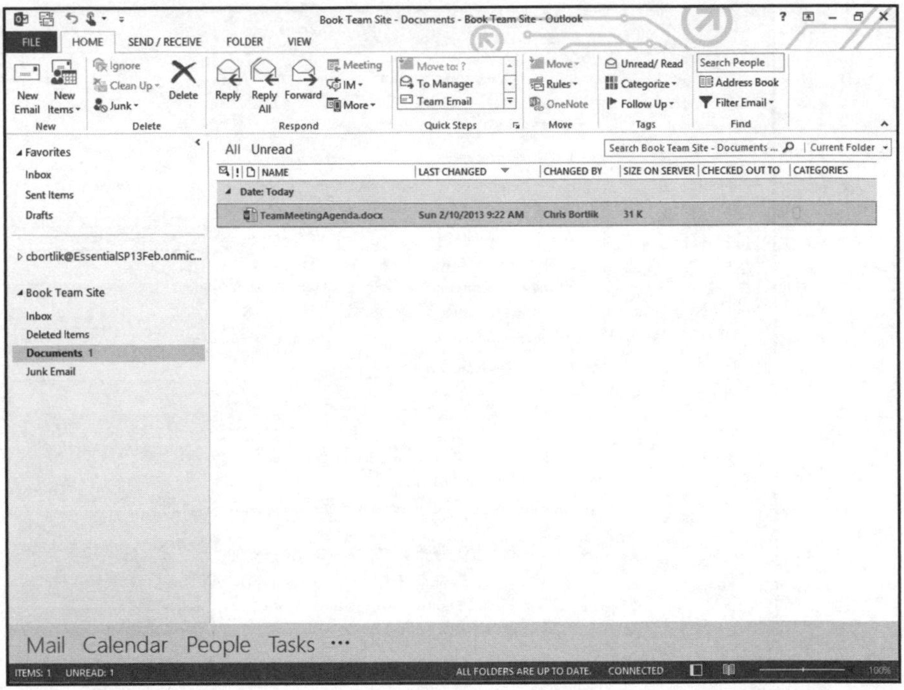

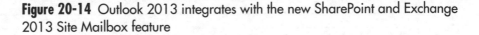

Figure 20-14 Outlook 2013 integrates with the new SharePoint and Exchange 2013 Site Mailbox feature

If you use Windows Explorer to perform an initial upload of files, you can use the SharePoint interface or edit using the Quick Edit view to apply metadata. If, however, you use this function to re-upload documents, you may overwrite your metadata. Documents you download from SharePoint will retain both file property and SharePoint metadata—but only if you download them back from SharePoint after your initial upload and replace them in the source location.

SkyDrive Pro and the Office Upload Center offer richer capabilities than Windows Explorer for working with SharePoint files offline. In addition, for Office-based documents, the Backstage feature (described in greater detail later in this chapter) provides extensive capabilities for working with SharePoint while authoring the documents; this makes it easier for people to perform tasks such as managing document metadata tags, viewing other authors, and interacting with workflows.

Other Considerations: Synchronization of Office Document Changes and Branch Cache

Office 2010 and SharePoint 2010 made significant improvements behind the scenes in terms of how document changes are managed and synchronized between the server and your offline copy. For these scenarios, only the changes are synchronized between your PC and the server when updates are made. For example, consider a scenario where you have a copy of a 5MB Word document on your PC that has been opened from SharePoint. When someone adds a new table and saves the changes to SharePoint, the next time you open the file from the server, only what has changed will be sent to your PC. This is a major improvement that both enhances user performance and minimizes network traffic and impact.

Windows Server 2008 R2 and Windows 7 added a new capability known as Windows Branch Cache. Branch Cache helps geographically distributed offices access SharePoint documents over a WAN efficiently. If this is enabled in your environment, SharePoint can take advantage of it. With Branch Cache, the first time a person in a remote office accesses a file from the remote SharePoint server, a cached copy of that file is stored on a server located in the remote (branch) office. Subsequent requests for that document within the office are fulfilled from the local branch copy of the file, saving what is often a slower network call over the WAN. Branch Cache and SharePoint work together to manage changes and to make sure that security continues to be enforced so that only people authorized in SharePoint can access the right version of the document.

SharePoint and Office 2013, as well as Windows Server 2012 and Windows 8, build upon this foundation and continue to support Branch Cache.

Data Caching

Office 2013 offers a number of choices for working with SharePoint data offline. These choices include

- Outlook
- Access
- Excel

Outlook

Outlook remains the primary option for easily taking a SharePoint calendar offline (Figure 20-15). One benefit of doing this in Outlook is that you can then compare, overlay, and update both your personal and shared calendars in the same client tool. In Outlook you can also view and edit contacts from SharePoint. Tasks can be synchronized from SharePoint to Outlook—including the new unified My Tasks view from your SharePoint 2013 personal site, which provides a single rolled-up view of all tasks assigned to you across Exchange, SharePoint, and Project (Figures 20-16, 20-17). The Outlook Social Connector allows you to surface SharePoint social updates directly within Outlook (Figure 20-18).

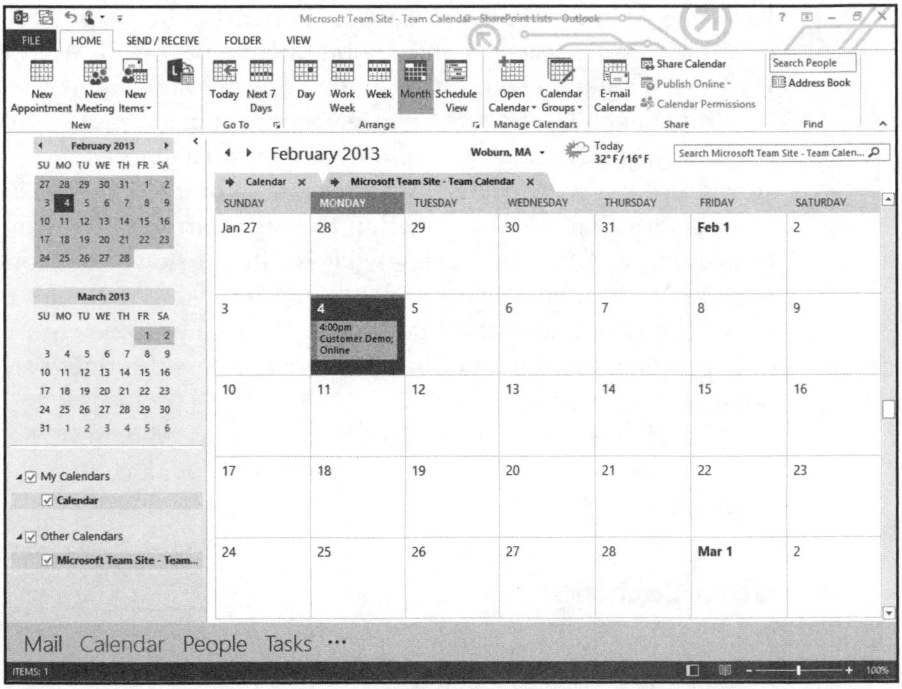

Figure 20-15 Outlook continues to be the best tool for taking a calendar offline from SharePoint and having read/write access. To take a calendar offline, select the Connect to Outlook option from the Calendar tab in the Calendar Tools section within the SharePoint ribbon

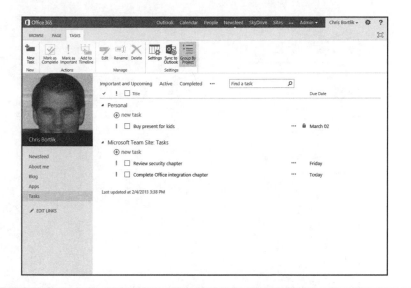

Figure 20-16 SharePoint 2013 can aggregate all tasks assigned to individuals across team sites, project sites, and personal tasks within Exchange

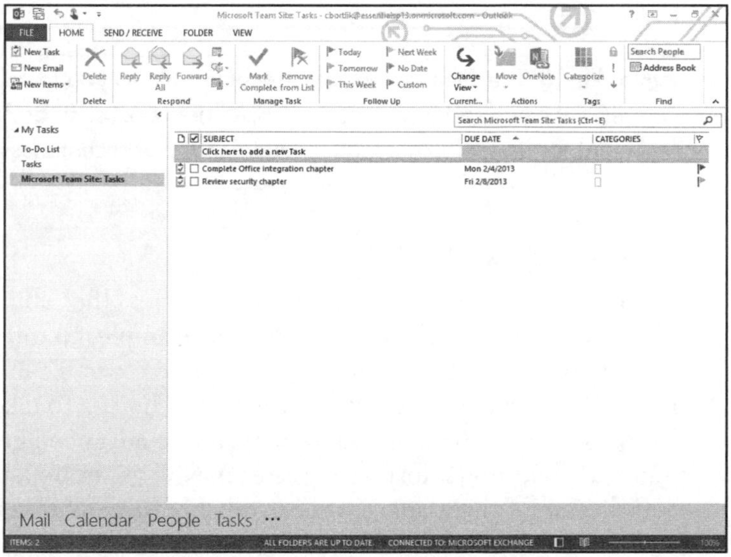

Figure 20-17 Outlook 2013 can synchronize tasks from SharePoint where they can be viewed and edited. Tasks are grouped by the site of which they are a part. Updates made in Outlook and SharePoint are synchronized automatically.

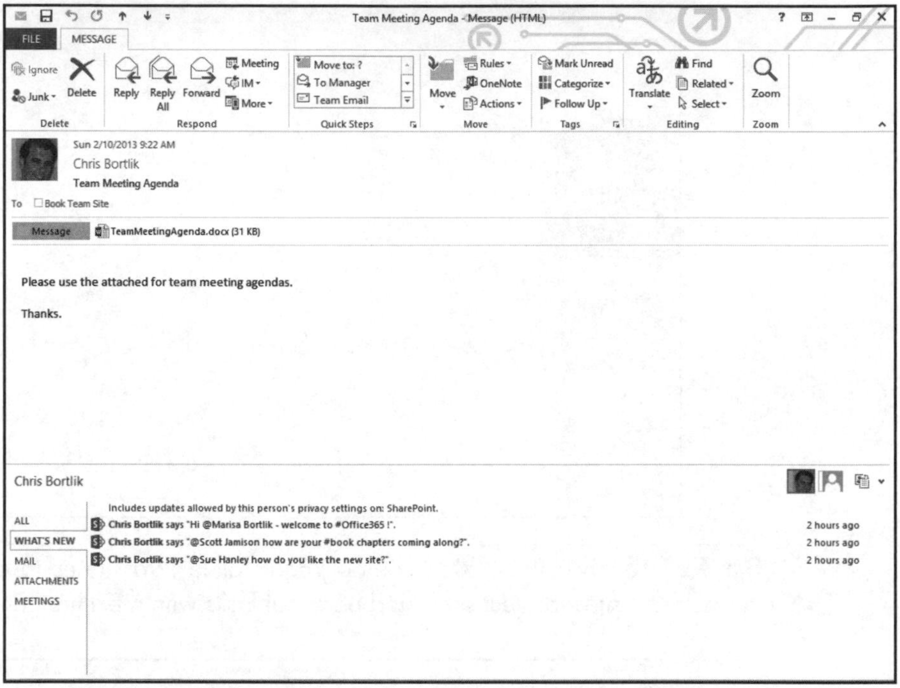

Figure 20-18 The Outlook Social Connector allows you to connect to your SharePoint newsfeed (and external social networks such as Facebook and LinkedIn) to see social messages in the context of recent messages

Access and Excel

Both Access and Excel continue to offer the ability to work with SharePoint offline (Figure 20-19). For example, to quickly integrate and join SharePoint data with other data sources so you can run complex queries and reports, Access is likely your best choice. To take your SharePoint list data into a rich client where you can do advanced graphing and charting, add conditional formatting, and maybe generate a pivot table to slice and dice all of that data, Excel is probably the tool to use.

Recommendations

Office and SharePoint 2013 offer a few different choices for working with documents and data. In summary:

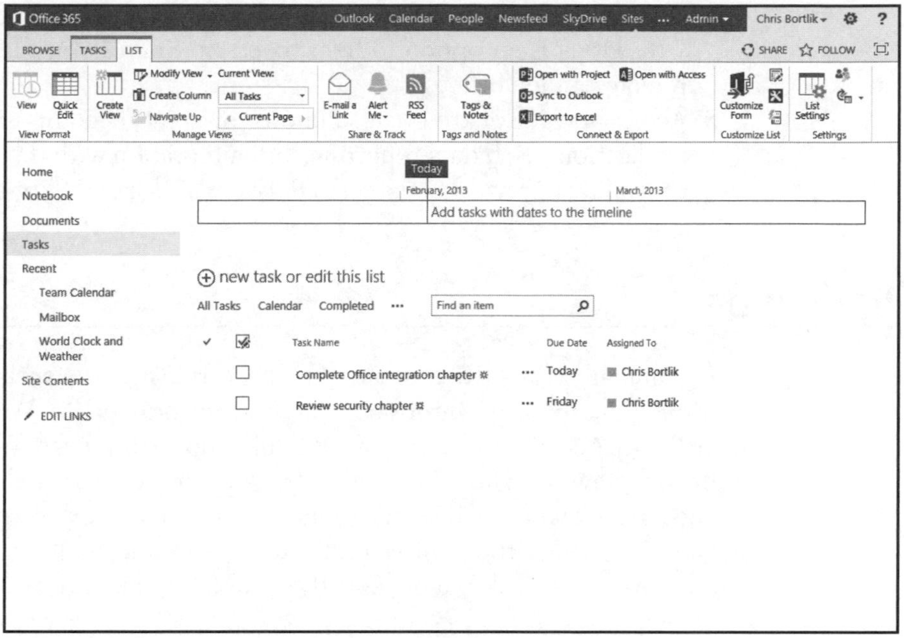

Figure 20-19 The ability to take list data offline in Excel, Access, and other Office clients can be located in the Connect and Export section of the List Tools command group within the SharePoint ribbon

- SkyDrive Pro should be used for sites that you use often, such as collaborative team sites or your personal site, or those sites where you need to have offline access to your SharePoint documents.
- Use the Office Upload Center as a one-stop shop for information and usage for all of the SharePoint files that you have viewed and checked out—regardless of which site the files originated from. This is especially useful for those sites that you access infrequently.
- Outlook should be used only for working with SharePoint team data that intersects with your personal information. Calendars are one example. Tasks, contacts, and discussion boards are other examples. In general, using Outlook to synchronize document libraries is discouraged with the exception of the new Site Mailbox capability.
- Windows Explorer should be used as a last resort for copying files offline if you find that working through SkyDrive Pro, the Office Upload Center, or the browser is not appropriate for your specific document management scenario.

- Branch Cache in Windows Server 2008 R2 (or later) and Windows 7 (or later) is an option to help speed up SharePoint file access for remote branch offices.
- Access and Excel are great solutions for creating composite mashup applications, rich data reporting, and integration with the server-side capabilities provided by Access Services and Excel Services.

Backstage

Users familiar with Office since the 2007 release are accustomed to the ribbon fluent user interface that was introduced in Word, Excel, PowerPoint, Access, and parts of Outlook (those that used Word as the editor and viewer). The ribbon was designed to address usability issues that occurred over the past 25 years as more features were added to the menus in the Office suite. Past attempts at addressing these issues included toolbars, task panes, and the character that everyone loved to hate: Clippy.

The ribbon was Microsoft's attempt to press the reset button on the Office user interface and implement a design that addresses how we work and collaborate today. Office 2007 was designed to make features more accessible and discoverable by users of the products. The ribbon was so successful that in 2010 it was extended to other Office system applications, including SharePoint, the rest of Outlook, OneNote, InfoPath, Visio, and Project.

The Office 2007 ribbon addressed the usability issues for operations within a document such as text formatting, tables, charts, and Smart Art. In Office 2010, Microsoft sought to address things that happen outside of the document and had been a challenge to work with. For example, it was frustrating that only a limited context was provided for documents, including the inability to easily understand:

- What document library is this document from?
- What is the workflow status?
- Who are my coauthors and what is their status?
- What are my rights to perform updates and print this document?

To help answer these and many other common questions, in 2010 Microsoft introduced another Office UI innovation: the Backstage.

The Backstage replaces the old File menu and the Office "pearl" that was introduced in 2007 as the icon in the top left-hand corner of each Office product. The Backstage is launched when you click on the File menu tab in any Office client application (Figure 20-20).

In the Backstage area you find all of the things that you can do to the document as a whole. You can

- Assign Information Rights Management (IRM) to protect what people can do with the document
- Review the document for accessibility by those with disabilities
- Start or see the workflow status of the document (Figure 20-21)
- Publish the document to a SharePoint site
- Check the version history of the document

Like other parts of Office 2013, the Backstage is open and customizable. Using Visual Studio, your company and partners can create extensible

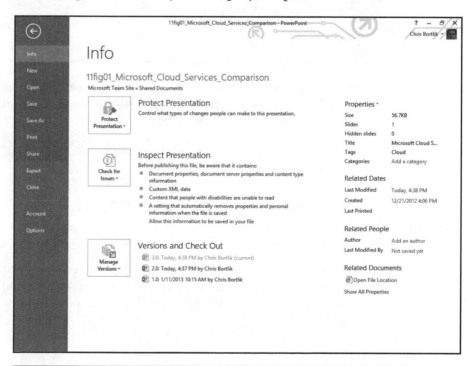

Figure 20-20 Use the Backstage view to review document information, properties, related authors, version history, metadata, and notes

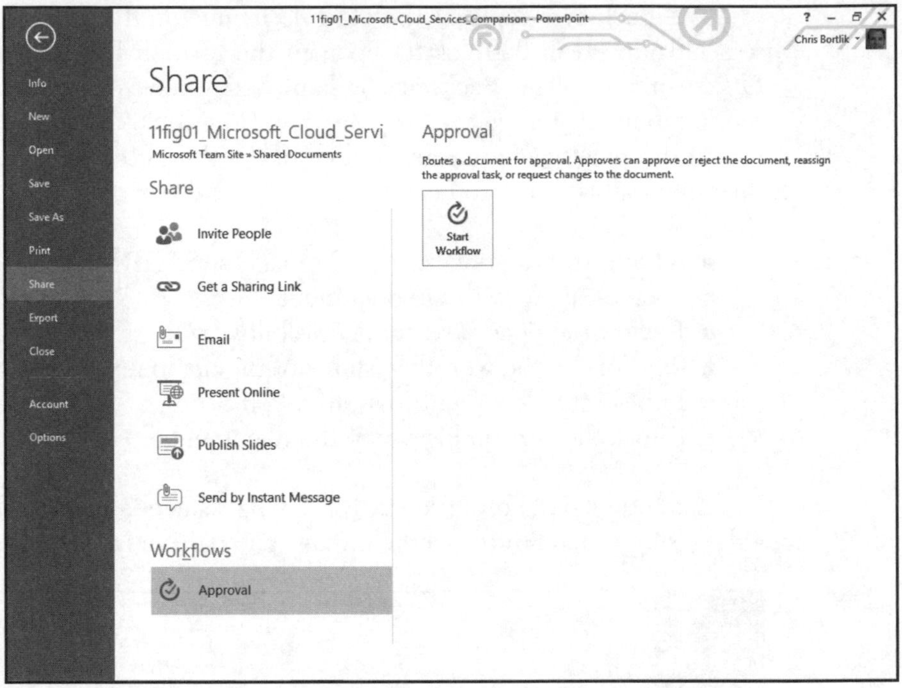

Figure 20-21 Sharing documents from the Backstage. From this section you can access SharePoint sites to save to and activate related SharePoint workflows

applications that plug information into the Backstage from other systems, databases, and processes.

Other Clients: Office Web Apps and Office Mobile Applications

One of the main themes across the Microsoft Office system since the 2010 release is the idea of choice and flexibility in how you work with SharePoint content. In 2013, the Office Web and mobile companion applications have been updated for

- Word
- Excel
- PowerPoint
- OneNote

The vision for these four applications is that you should be able to access them in the same way you can currently access your Exchange-based e-mail across three different devices: Outlook on the PC, Outlook Web Access in the browser, and Outlook mobile (or some other e-mail client) on your phone.

One of the fundamental design goals for Office 2013 is that documents should seamlessly travel from the PC to the browser to the phone and back without concern for loss of data or formatting. This is very important since you want to be confident that regardless of which application or device was used to make changes to a document, the integrity of the document is maintained. By leveraging the Office Open XML document file formats, SharePoint is the foundation and glue behind the scenes that makes this happen.

Describing each of these applications in depth is outside the scope of this book, but you should be aware of them and factor them into your solutions plans.

Office Web Apps

Office Web Apps is not intended to replace the Office products that you use on your desktop today, just as Outlook Web Access is not a replacement for the rich functionality that Outlook provides. Rather, Office Web Apps is intended to offer you the essential viewing and editing capabilities so you can work with documents stored in SharePoint wherever you are (Figure 20-22). For example, you can now perform lightweight editing in Word, modify slides in PowerPoint, and edit formulas and spreadsheet values in Excel. Office Web Apps, like SharePoint 2013, leverage open standards and work across different browsers: Internet Explorer, Safari, Chrome, and Firefox. In general, you will want to use these applications in cases such as when you're working on someone else's PC, using a kiosk at a conference, or working in a hotel lobby where the Office client application is unavailable.

Office Mobile Applications

The Office Mobile Applications for Word, Excel, PowerPoint, and OneNote enable you to read and edit documents on a Windows Phone device. There is also an updated SharePoint mobile client that allows you to take SharePoint content on your phone and participate in some key tasks such as social or approving a document as part of a workflow.

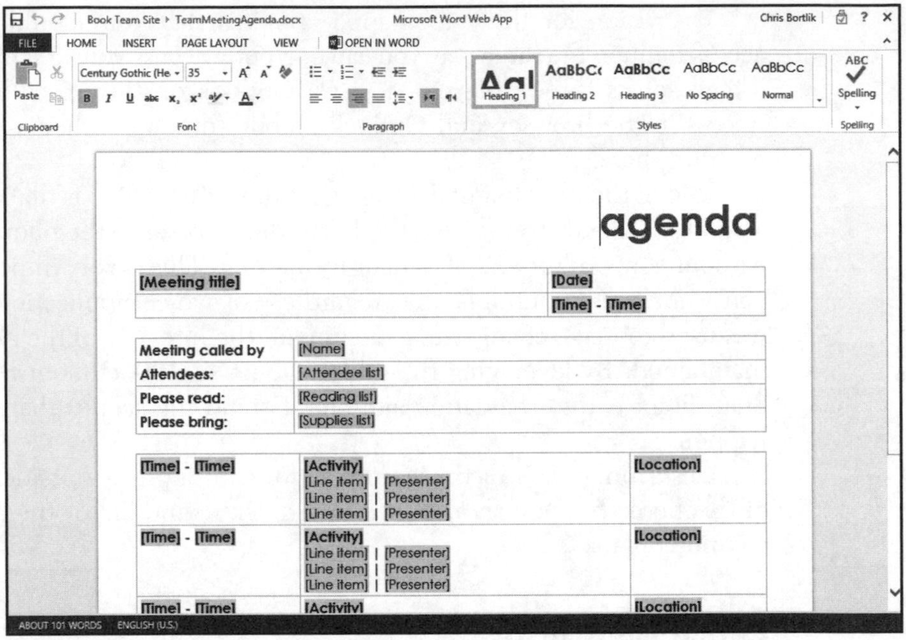

Figure 20-22 Editing a Word document in the Word Web application companion

What if you are not using a Windows Phone device and are using something like a BlackBerry, Android, or iPhone? Good news: SharePoint and the Office Web Apps also have micro-browser support for the most popular operating systems and browsers that run on other mobile device platforms.

Note More information on SharePoint and Office Mobile Applications is included in Chapter 19, "Planning for Mobility."

Key Points

In this chapter, we covered the key concepts about working with SharePoint using the Office 2013 client applications, and we touched on the updated Office Web and Mobile Applications for working with

SharePoint and Office when you don't have access to Office applications on the computer you are using. Some important things to remember include the following:

- SkyDrive Pro is the best way to take SharePoint documents offline and synchronize changes.
- The Office Upload Center manages the SharePoint documents that you access via the Office clients. It caches a local copy of the documents, synchronizes changes only when you access the server again, and provides a central place to review all files pending check-in regardless of which site you accessed the files from.
- Outlook remains the tool to use for viewing and integrating your personal calendar with shared calendars on SharePoint, as well as working with tasks, contacts, and discussion lists. Outlook 2013 also integrates with the new Site Mailbox feature that was added to SharePoint and Exchange 2013.
- Access and Excel continue to provide rich advanced support for charting, graphing, filtering, and reporting on data. Improvements have been made around Excel Services, including support for the new PowerView capabilities. Access Services has been updated with SharePoint 2013 as an option for publishing Access data and forms for centralized browser-based access.
- The Backstage within the Office 2013 client applications can be launched from the File button. This is where you can clearly view the context of your document as part of SharePoint libraries, workflows, and authoring permissions and apply metadata and tagging.
- The updated Office Web Apps for Word, Excel, PowerPoint, and OneNote are integrated with SharePoint and provide Read and Edit access to documents using the Internet Explorer, Firefox, Chrome, or Safari Web browsers. With the 2013 release, the on-premises Office Web Apps servers must be installed on separate servers from SharePoint 2013. Office 365 offers the Office Web Apps as an online service for customers using SharePoint Online.
- Microsoft now offers Office as a service via Office 365. Organizations can subscribe to Office 365 ProPlus on a per-user basis. Capabilities such as Office on Demand, roaming settings, and Office "remembering" recent documents you have worked with work only when

Office 2013 is connected to a Microsoft cloud service such as SkyDrive for consumers or Office 365 for organizations.

- Office Mobile Applications for SharePoint, Word, Excel, PowerPoint, and OneNote provide access to your content on the go while using Windows mobile devices. Micro-browsers are also supported on many other non-Windows mobile device platforms such as BlackBerry, Android, and iPhone.

CONTENT YOU CAN REUSE

Most of the focus of *Essential SharePoint 2013* is on thinking strategically about planning and deploying SharePoint solutions for your organization. This section (available as a download from www.jornata.com/essentialsharepoint) is designed to provide content that you can use as part of your governance and training plans as well as some of the trickier "how to" information for new capabilities in SharePoint 2013 that users and site owners should know.

For the most part, we have included the topics that our clients have found particularly confusing or challenging, and we just couldn't find a place to share these tips, lessons, and best practices in other chapters of the book. Our goal in creating this appendix is to provide something that you can literally copy and paste into your training, governance, or how-to guides, so that you can benefit from the lessons we have learned the hard way!

In this appendix, you will find the following:

- Content for your governance and training plans
  - Tips for writing great content for SharePoint sites
  - Naming conventions that improve "findability"
  - Tips for writing better search queries
  - Glossary of social terminology for SharePoint 2013 (including an explanation of the difference between getting an alert in the newsfeed and setting up a notification alert)
- New or different user tasks in SharePoint 2013
  - Creating and displaying views in lists and libraries
  - Managing copies of documents (Send To and Manage Copies)
  - Following documents, sites, people, and topics
  - Tips for creating posts in the newsfeed

- New or different site owner tasks in SharePoint 2013
  - Sharing sites and documents with people outside your organization
  - Adding an app to a site
  - Using Promoted Links

Content for Your Governance and Training Plans

This section includes content that you can include as part of your governance documentation (either on a wiki site or as part of a short guidance document) and training material.

Tips for Writing Great Content for SharePoint Sites

Content management is a critical element of your governance plan. But before you manage the content, you had better decide that it is worth managing! Writing content for the Web is different from writing content that will be consumed as a document. The tips in Table A-1 will help your content authors create great content for Web pages in SharePoint.

Table A-1 Best Practices for Great Content for SharePoint Sites

Topic	Recommendation
Remember your audience.	When creating content for your page, be sure to consider the user. When structuring your content, group ideas that are relevant to a specific audience.
	Web content editors should write copy with a specific person in mind—and think about that person as they write their content.
	Site users are in search of information and tools for specific tasks. Before creating any type of content, think about these questions:
	• What would the user want or expect to find?
	• Are there common requests for information from your department or team? If so, make sure that this content is easy to find on your page or site.
	• Is there an obvious path to and from content that users would look for?
	• Are the headlines and copy written in an engaging, concise, and relevant manner?

Topic	Recommendation
Think about the delivery context.	Make sure that your page template designer has considered the different types of devices on which your content might appear. Sometimes this means writing short, medium, and longer versions of your copy. For example, your page template could include a content placeholder for headline text that would be the primary display for smartphones and a placeholder for a one- to two-sentence abstract that could be combined with the headline for delivery on a tablet, and a longer placeholder for the complete article that might be linked to from one of the shorter versions.
Limit the message.	Online attention spans are short. Limit your message to three key ideas within a content "block."
	In calendar and announcement entries, keep the content short. If you need to reference more information, write a document, upload it to the appropriate document library, and add a link to your calendar or announcement entry.
Keep the content fresh.	Encourage return visits to your Web site by giving users something new to learn.
	Keep your site current with value-added information.
	Check and update your page regularly and review all document content according to the governance plan, deleting or updating content that is no longer relevant.
Spelling and grammar count.	Check your content for spelling and grammatical errors every time new information is added or changed.
Start with the main topic.	Think like a journalist when you write text for a content block. Start with the main point, follow with supporting information, and end with a link to more detail on a subsequent Web page or attached document if needed.
	Users who are scanning your site will quickly see what is on the site and then be able to click through for more information.
Write concisely.	People read differently when looking at a computer screen. Make the content easy to scan, using short bullet points whenever possible.
	Do not WRITE IN ALL CAPITAL LETTERS.
	Do not use an <u>underline</u> to emphasize a point. On Web sites, an underline implies that the content is a hyperlink.
	Use **bold** if you need to emphasize a point, but don't use it too much.
	Italics do not display well in a browser. They should be used sparingly, for example, to refer to proper names or to emphasize text.
Watch the fonts in rich text fields.	Don't go overboard using all the features, colors, and capabilities of rich text fields. Refer to your corporate style guide for specific font and color requirements.
	Be very mindful about using multiple colors, fonts, and highlights in text content.
	If possible, choose fonts designed for on-screen reading.

(continues)

Table A-1 Best Practices for Great Content for SharePoint Sites *(continued)*

Topic	Recommendation
Use numerals— don't write out numbers.	The best practice for the Web is to write numbers with digits, not letters (23, not twenty-three). For the most part, use numerals even when the number is the first word in a sentence or bullet point.
Write effective hyperlinks.	Write links as you would write a heading—use eight words or less. On any one page, every link should be unique, independent, and separate. As a best practice, have just one link to a particular piece of content (usually the first mention or section where it is most meaningful) on each page so that you don't confuse your users. "Lead with the need"—if you have a guide for how to install a widget, write the link: "Installation instructions." Don't write: "How to install this widget." Otherwise, you will have a lot of links beginning with "How to."
	Use the following guidelines to create hyperlinks: • OK: Click here for the latest application form. • Better: Download the latest application form. • Best: Latest Application Form
Always add a "user-friendly" description to SharePoint hyperlink Columns.	Write a user-friendly description for all hyperlink Site Columns (in lists and libraries). Enter the URL in the URL field and a "friendly" name for the description as shown in Figure A-1.

Naming Conventions That Improve Findability

There are two types of naming conventions that will help improve the "findability" experience for users. The first type are conventions geared toward site owners, users with Full Control privileges. The second are naming conventions for content contributors.

What's Up with %20?

All SharePoint users immediately notice something funny in the URLs for sites and documents: if the site or document name has any spaces in it, the spaces are replaced with "%20" in URL references. The "dreaded %20" makes it very difficult to read URLs for SharePoint content.

SharePoint itself isn't responsible for inserting the %20 characters in your URLs. This is what happens when your references are "URL encoded."

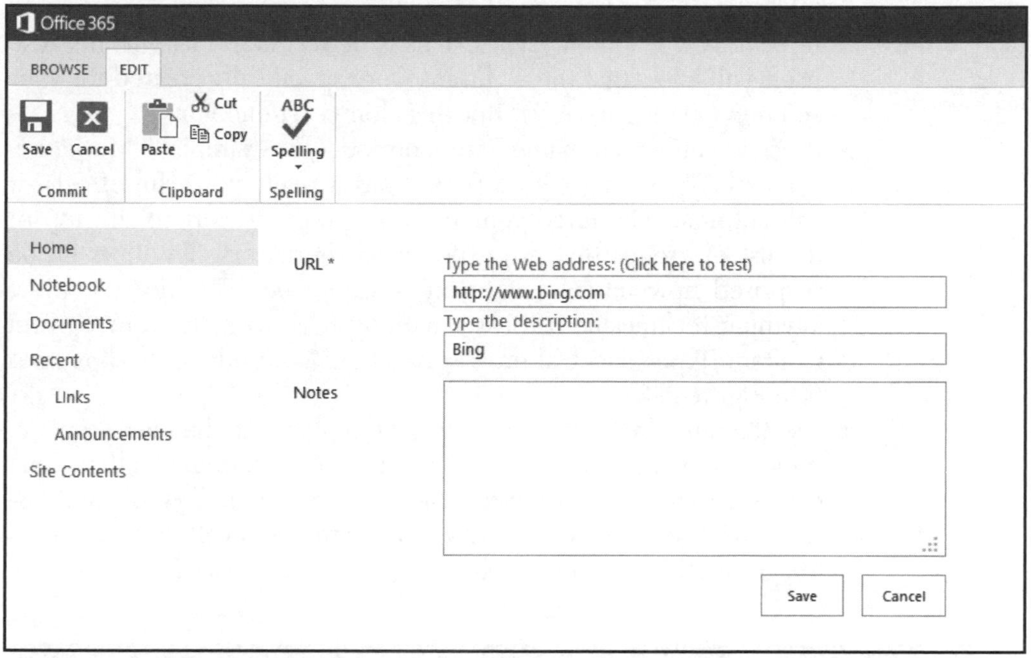

Figure A-1 Enter a "friendly" description for all hyperlink Columns

A single character space in a name translates to %20 (three characters). Since your URL cannot be longer than 255 characters and the %20s are not very readable, it's a good idea to eliminate as many spaces as possible—without compromising usability. As with most user experience items, you need to balance readability with usability. For the most part, the one tip to remember is to create most assets that power users can create (such as sites, lists, libraries, and views) using "CamelCase" names—in other words, smushing words together with no spaces but using capital letters to distinguish the words, for example, "ProposalTemplate" rather than "Proposal Template." For file names, the tip is to use either a hyphen (-) or an underscore (_) to separate words.

Naming Conventions for Site Owners

- Create meaningful names for the groups that you will use for your custom Columns, Content Types, and custom templates—use a name that is associated with the most common way that the objects will be used. For Site Column or Content Type group names, it's

OK to use spaces between the words. So, an acceptable name would be *Marketing* Content Types. This is better than "custom" because users will know that the Columns were specifically created for your solution (see Figure A-2). But this alone isn't enough.

- Precede your group name with a period—for example, ".Marketing Content Types." That little period has a really powerful effect—it will automatically force your custom groups to sort to the top of the list of groups that are exposed to your users. Try it; you'll be surprised how much easier your life will be. This doesn't affect anything technically; it's just a naming trick to make your custom Content Types and Columns sort "above" the out-of-the-box ones (see Figure A-3).

- Use the same trick with custom page templates. In the ideal scenario, remove templates that you don't want your users to use so they don't even see them. If that's not feasible, put a period in front of your custom template names so that they will sort to the top of lists when users are given selection options when they create new pages.

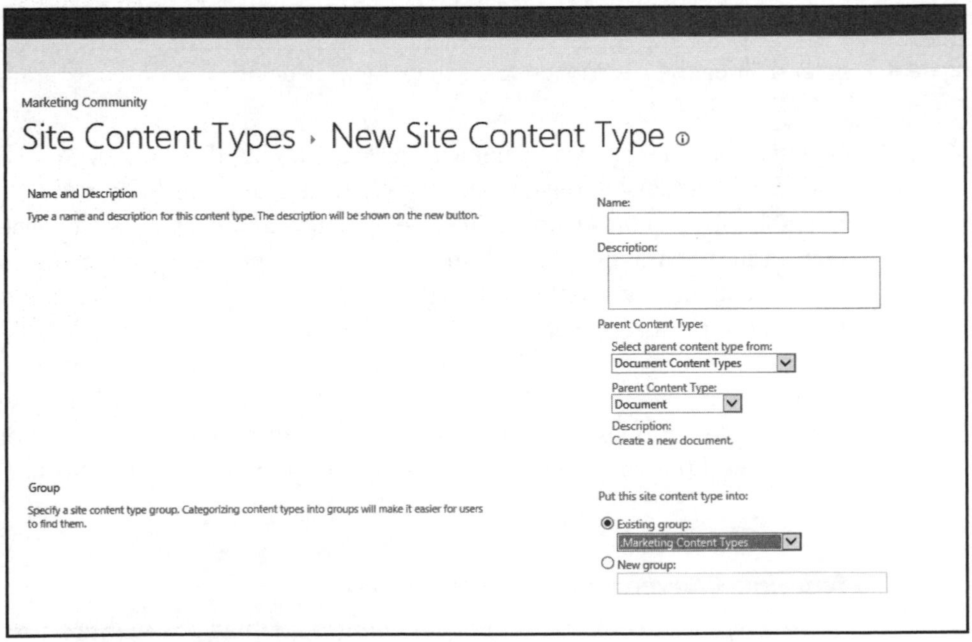

Figure A-2 Create a meaningful group name for your custom Content Types and Columns

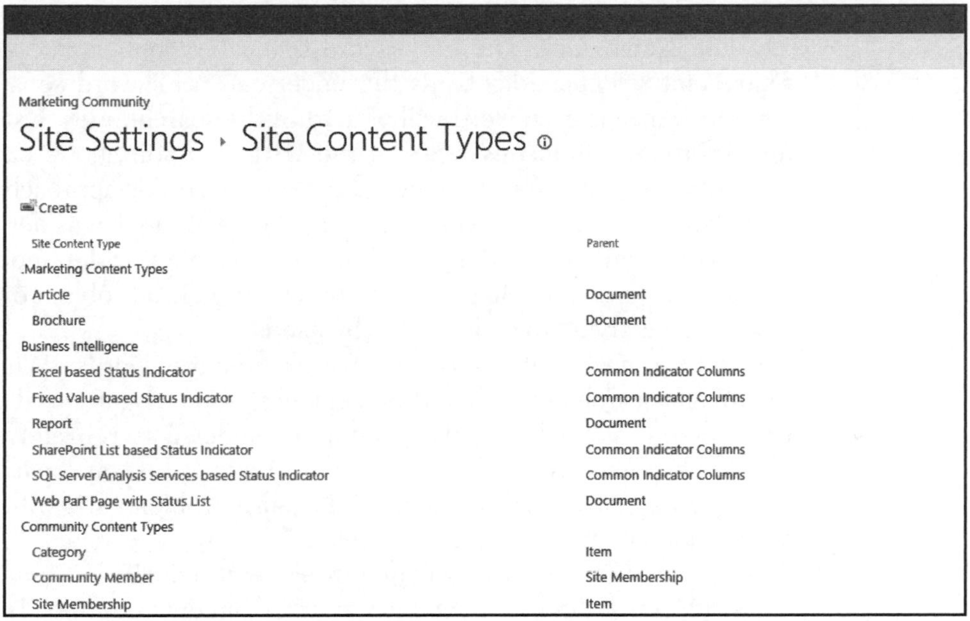

Marketing Community

Site Settings ⟩ Site Content Types ⓘ

📖 Create

Site Content Type	Parent
.Marketing Content Types	
Article	Document
Brochure	Document
Business Intelligence	
Excel based Status Indicator	Common Indicator Columns
Fixed Value based Status Indicator	Common Indicator Columns
Report	Document
SharePoint List based Status Indicator	Common Indicator Columns
SQL Server Analysis Services based Status Indicator	Common Indicator Columns
Web Part Page with Status List	Document
Community Content Types	
Category	Item
Community Member	Site Membership
Site Membership	Item

Figure A-3 Naming groups with a preceding period (.) automatically sorts your custom groups at the top of Content Type and Column lists

- Create all site, list, library, and view names using CamelCase, and then after the list, library, or view is created, go back into the settings and rename the Title (or view name) to include spaces in the names. This will eliminate %20 in the URL and still support a friendly user experience. (It's like having your cake and eating it, too!)

Naming Conventions for Users with Document Contribution Permissions

- SharePoint won't allow many special characters in file names, so make sure you document these characters for your users. Refer to http://support.microsoft.com/kb/905231 for a complete list of the characters that cannot be used in site, folder, server, and file names in SharePoint.
- When creating file names for documents, use an underscore (_) in place of a space between words if file names have more than

one word. Capitalize each word of the file name, for example, My_File_Name.docx. The underscore is the best option because SharePoint search understands the underscore as a word separator, which means each word will be part of the search index. Using an underscore eliminates %20s in the URL and still allows each word of the file name to be indexed for search, so this approach is definitely recommended over using spaces. One of the downsides of this recommendation is that it is difficult to distinguish the underscore from a space in a hyperlink, but this is usually a problem only if someone is trying to copy a URL by hand.

- Try not to use hyphens or dashes to separate words. While SharePoint search (and other search engines) also recognizes a dash or hyphen (-) as a valid word separator, the underscore is preferred because hyphens are used as break points to wrap text on separate lines. URLs that contain hyphens often cause problems when they are included as links in e-mail messages.

- To give your documents a user-friendly name, use the Title Column to create an additional name for your documents. In the Title Column, spaces, special characters, and punctuation marks are fine. It's a good idea to always have a non-blank Title because the Title is displayed by default in search results and in Content Query Web Parts. You can also create a default "reader" view that displays the file icon and the Title to create a better user interface for folks who do not manage the file content.

- If you absolutely have to have folders in your document libraries, you need to consider balancing readability of folder names with the goal of eliminating %20s in URLs. If you are more concerned about URL length and your folder names have more than one word, use underscores (_) to separate words in the folder names, for example, Folder_Name. If you can live with eliminating the biggest %20 offenders (site, list, library, and view names), use spaces to separate words in folder names because the underscore is not as readable in views that show folder names as a simple space between words.

Tips for Writing Better Search Queries

We have all heard the quote "Give a man a fish; you have fed him for today. Teach a man to fish and you have fed him for a lifetime." This quote can be rewritten in the context of search (and modern usage): "Give a person a document; you have answered today's question. Teach a person how to search and you have answered all the questions for a lifetime."

The following list of very simple search tips can help your users find content not only in SharePoint, but also on the public Internet. Some of these tips are provided by SharePoint as a hyperlink if no results are returned in a search query. You might want to consider adding a Web Part to your search results page with a permanent link to tips for searching that are relevant to your content or site.

- **Use search "groups" or verticals to narrow the scope of your search.** On a Search Center site, use the preconfigured search "verticals" to narrow the scope of your search to just specific types of content. These verticals can be customized for your organization. For an example, see Figure A-4.
- **Click query suggestions that appear as you type search queries.** As you type a search in the search box, SharePoint search provides suggestions. These suggestions are based on past queries and include the items that you have searched for and clicked before.
- **Review the "did you mean" suggestions after you submit a search query.** SharePoint search provides suggestions if the terms in your search query are similar to other queries that have been submitted frequently. This will help if you make a mistake as you type in the query box.
- **Use logical operators to narrow or expand your search.** You can use the operators AND, OR, and NOT to expand or narrow your search query. Be sure to type the operator in all capital letters. For example, let's say you are looking for your organization's social media policy but you don't know if it is called a policy or a manual

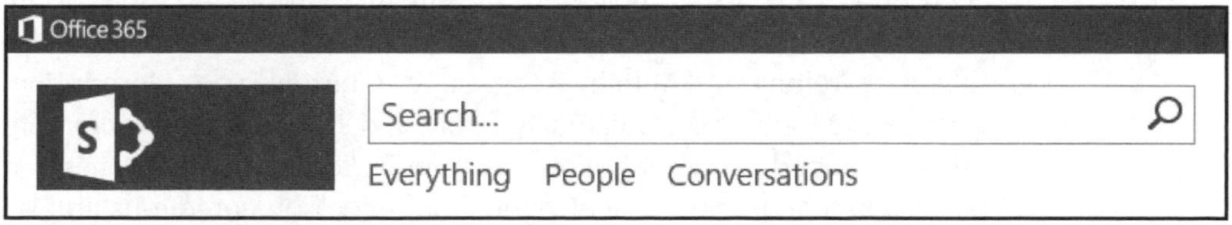

Figure A-4 Use search verticals to narrow the scope of your search

or a handbook. You could write your query as "social media" AND (handbook OR policy OR manual). Notice the parentheses, which are used just as in algebra. (Note that you probably wouldn't need to write a query that is this complicated to search for your social media policy, but you *could*!)

- **Capitalize operators in search.** Normally, search does not care about capitalization. However, you *must* capitalize the words AND and OR if you want search to recognize the words as operators.

- **To make sure you find words with any term listed, be sure to separate terms with the OR operator.** If you just string words together, SharePoint search assumes you are using the AND function. To make sure you find any term, separate terms with OR. For example, to find cats or dogs, type "cats OR dogs" as your query.

- **Use quotes to ensure that words must be found together, as in "social media."** If you were to type the two words without the quotes, search will interpret the query as (social AND media), which means that both words have to appear in results but not necessarily together as a single phrase. When you use quotes, be sure you know that the exact phrase in quotes is in the content you are looking for because search assumes that all of the words in quotes must appear in the content in order for it to be returned.

- **Use an asterisk as a wildcard (*) to find words that begin with a character string.** For example, you can search for "Micro*" to find all documents that contain *Microsoft* or *microchip* or *microscope*.

- **Use [Property Name]:[value] to find content in managed properties.** For example, to find all the documents written by Maureen Smith, you could use the query Author:Maur* or Author: "Maureen Smith." Note that the results would be slightly different in the first query because that query (with the wildcard) would find documents written by anyone named Maureen or anyone named Mauro (or any name beginning with Maur). Note that this syntax works only for managed properties, which may be different in each organization. Some of the default managed properties that you may find particularly helpful for searching are Author, AssignedTo, ContentType, Description, Filename, ModifiedBy, CreatedBy, Skills, and Title. There is a complete list of managed properties, along with an indicator of which ones can be used in search queries, at http://technet.microsoft.com/en-us/library/jj219630.aspx, though the list is not particularly end-user-friendly.

Glossary of Social Terminology for SharePoint 2013

Don't assume that all of your users are familiar with the "social" features of SharePoint 2013. Following is a brief glossary that will help users become familiar with the basics of social in SharePoint.

- **Post.** A post is an initial message created by a user in a newsfeed (or in Yammer) or discussion board or generated by the system in a newsfeed. An example of a system-generated message is a post that shows you that someone updated a document you are following.
- **Reply.** A reply is a response to a post. A reply can be made by the person who created the post (typically, just to clarify the initial post) or by someone else.
- **Activity.** An activity is either a post or a reply or a system-generated message. Examples of activities include
  - Microblog activities such as posts, replies, likes, mentions, and tagging
  - Following activities (people, documents, sites, and tags)
  - User profile activities (birthdays, job title changes, anniversaries, updates to Ask Me About, creating a blog post, or posting on a community site)
  - Document activities when a document is edited or shared
- **Conversation.** A conversation consists of a single post and all of its associated replies. The terms *thread* and *conversation thread* are alternative terms for conversation. Note that you can have a conversation using several different SharePoint 2013 features: the newsfeed, Yammer, or a discussion board.
- **Likes.** When someone makes a post or replies to a post, other people can "like" the post or reply. Likes provide a method to collect support for a post or indicate agreement. In your personal newsfeed, you can use the likes view to look at the newsfeed activities that you have previously liked. In a community site or in a discussion board where community features have been enabled, likes are also available for posts and replies. Within a community or team, members can improve their reputation by building up likes from others. You can also enable ratings on any list or library in a SharePoint site and choose one of two ways to allow users to rate an item—either likes or star ratings. The likes and star ratings for documents appear in the newsfeed for content you are following.

- **Mentions.** When you create a post or reply, you can refer to other users by mentioning them. To mention someone in a post, place an @ symbol in front of the person's name. As you are typing, the user profile service returns a list of names that match what you have entered. When users are mentioned, they receive an activity in their newsfeed that alerts them to the mention.

- **Tags.** When you post or reply, you can associate a post with a topic by using a hashtag or just tag. To assign a tag, you place the number symbol (#) in front of the term that you want to include in the tag. The Managed Metadata Service returns a list of terms that match what you have entered. When a post contains tags, the newsfeed displays an activity related to that tag, and any users who follow that tag see the activity in their newsfeed. Using tags helps focus attention on a specific topic and can be used to filter posts and replies in search. Hashtags must be one word; to tag a post with the term "business development, use #BusinessDevelopment.

- **Discussion list versus newsfeed** (which may be implemented via Yammer or the SharePoint 2013 Newsfeed). Both discussion lists and the newsfeed can be used to ask questions of colleagues. The newsfeed is like an internal Twitter site, where you can post timely questions that are not necessarily intended to become part of the overall corporate knowledge base. A discussion board, on the other hand, is often used to create more permanent answers to questions and can be used to build up your corporate knowledge base, especially with the ability to flag an answer as the "best reply" or to "feature" a particular conversation to call attention to it. The lines between the newsfeed and the discussion board are actually pretty blurry right now and are likely to get even blurrier as Yammer becomes more tightly integrated into SharePoint.

- **Newsfeed versus alert.** Both the newsfeed and alerts are used to automatically give you information about activities or content that you care about in SharePoint. As a general rule, newsfeed activities stay in SharePoint, but you can choose to receive some of them in e-mail as well. Your preferences for the newsfeed are set in your profile, on the Newsfeed Settings page (see Figure A-5). Your newsfeed history is available in SharePoint for as long as your organization chooses to keep posts.

  Alerts are sent from SharePoint to either your e-mail or your mobile device as an SMS message, but you cannot find your "alert history" in SharePoint. If you delete your SMS message or e-mail

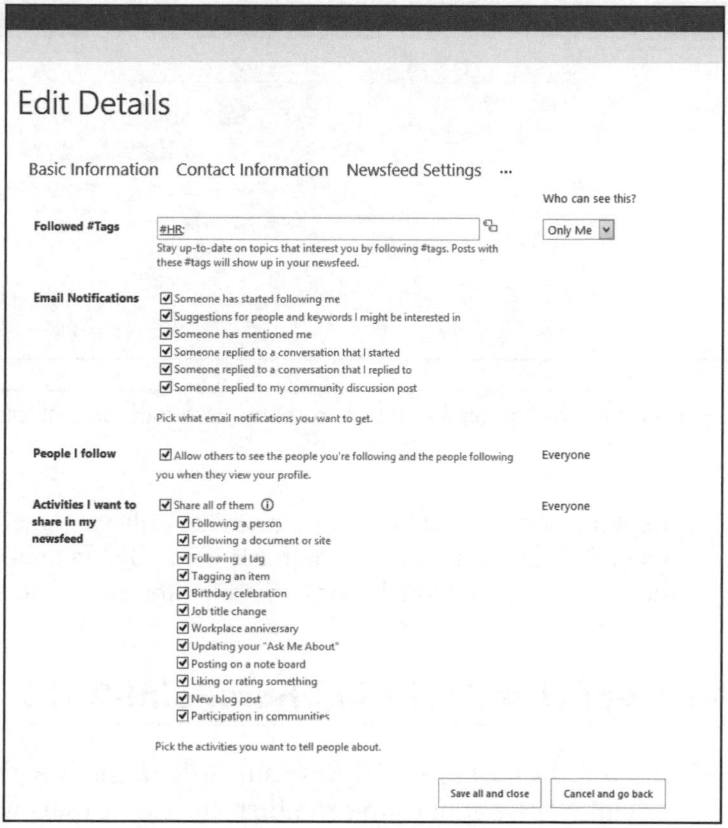

Figure A-5 Set your newsfeed preferences in the Newsfeed Settings area of your profile

alert, the information is no longer available. To set up an alert, you must go to the page or document or list or library that you want to be alerted about and select Alert Me from the ribbon, as shown in Figure A-6.

When you set up an alert, you have the option of indicating what you want to be alerted about and how often you want alerts to be sent to you. The options for alerts are shown in Figure A-7. Alerts are helpful when you are working collaboratively on a document and you want to know immediately that someone has made an edit to the document. You can also find out about updates via the newsfeed if you are following a document, so whether you use an alert or the newsfeed will depend on your personal preference. Alerts are

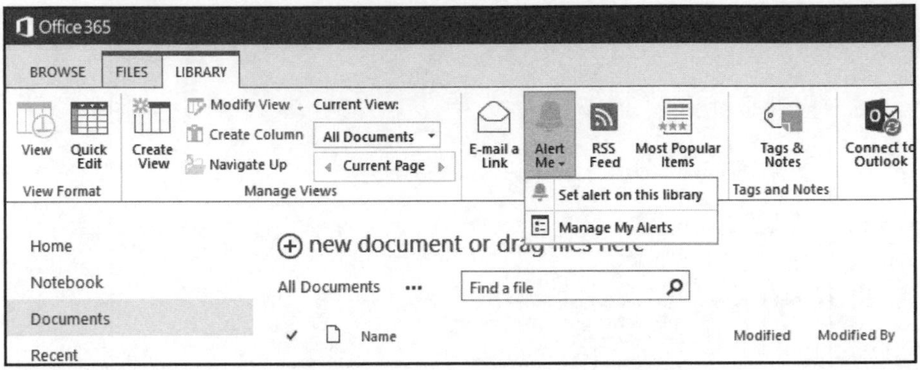

Figure A-6 Use the Alert Me button on the ribbon to set up an e-mail or SMS alert

helpful when you want to monitor activity only via e-mail or SMS or when the item you want to monitor is not available to be tracked via the newsfeed, such as a list or individual items in a list.

New or Different User Tasks in SharePoint 2013

Many of the tasks for users work very similarly to the way they worked in SharePoint 2010, but of course the first thing your users will notice is that the way to access the menu function formerly known as Site Actions is now back in the upper-right corner of the page where it used to be in SharePoint 2007—and looks like a gear icon. Clicking the gear icon and clicking the Site Actions button perform the same function—but from a different side of the page. In this section, we describe some additional actions and activities that are different enough that you should consider providing some tips or instructions as part of your training material.

Creating and Displaying Views in Lists and Libraries

Creating views in lists and libraries in SharePoint 2013 is essentially the same as in SharePoint 2010, but there are some new (and helpful) features. The default view for lists and libraries shows all items in the list (up to 30 per page). Creating alternative views helps users quickly examine the contents of a list or library from different perspectives. For example, you can

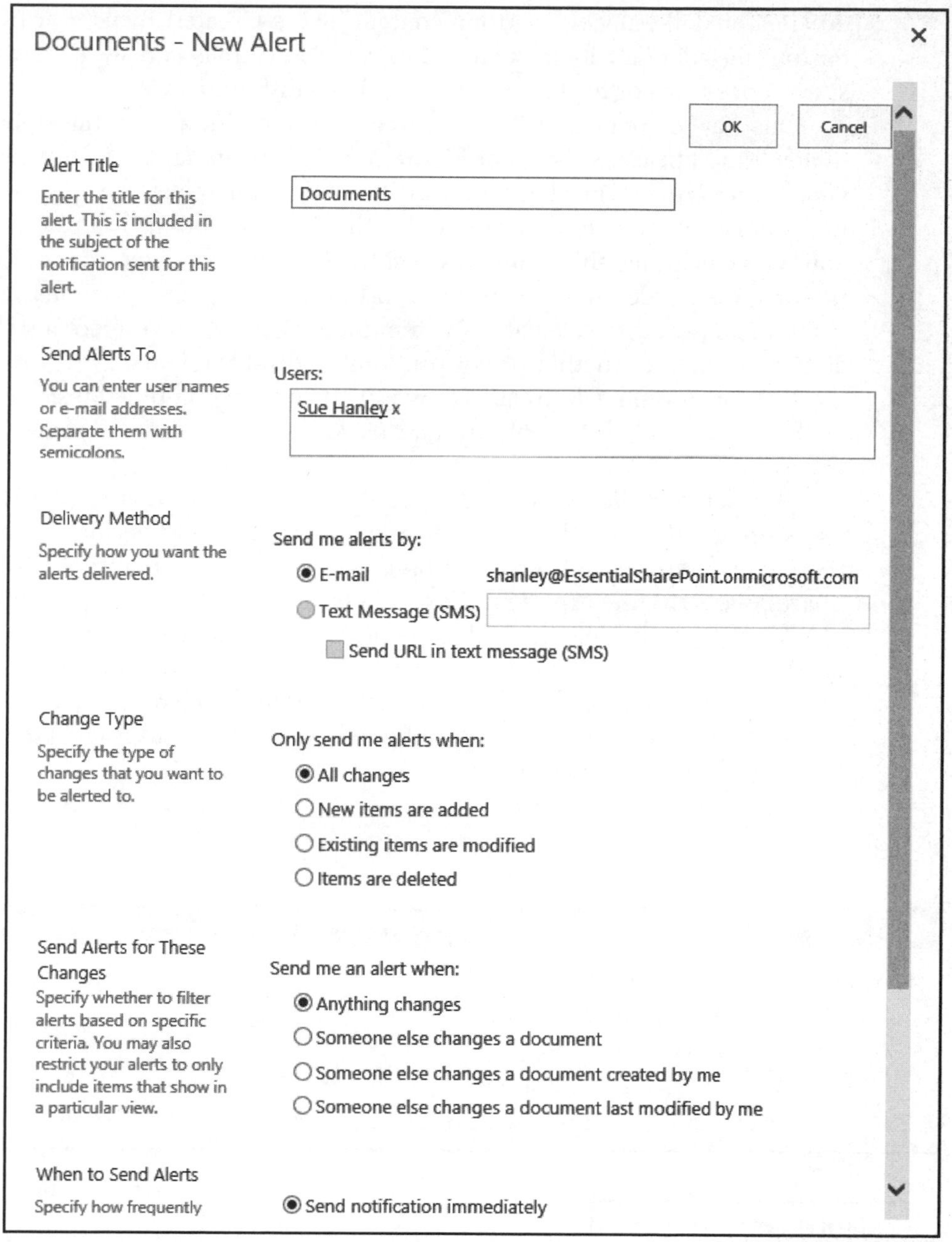

Documents - New Alert   ×

OK   Cancel

Alert Title

Enter the title for this alert. This is included in the subject of the notification sent for this alert.

Documents

Send Alerts To

You can enter user names or e-mail addresses. Separate them with semicolons.

Users:

Sue Hanley x

Delivery Method

Specify how you want the alerts delivered.

Send me alerts by:

⦿ E-mail   shanley@EssentialSharePoint.onmicrosoft.com

◯ Text Message (SMS)

☐ Send URL in text message (SMS)

Change Type

Specify the type of changes that you want to be alerted to.

Only send me alerts when:

⦿ All changes

◯ New items are added

◯ Existing items are modified

◯ Items are deleted

Send Alerts for These Changes

Specify whether to filter alerts based on specific criteria. You may also restrict your alerts to only include items that show in a particular view.

Send me an alert when:

⦿ Anything changes

◯ Someone else changes a document

◯ Someone else changes a document created by me

◯ Someone else changes a document last modified by me

When to Send Alerts

Specify how frequently

⦿ Send notification immediately

Figure A-7 Alerts provide several options about what you want to be notified about and how often you want to receive notifications

create a predefined view to group content by the Created By user or by a custom metadata attribute such as Project. You can also create a view to show more items or to show the items using a different style.

One way to create a new view is to click Create View from the ribbon in any list or library as shown in Figure A-8. This is similar to the way new views were created in SharePoint 2010. When you select the option to create a new view, you are presented with all of the options to customize your view, including the ability to select the Columns that you want to display and their order, how you want to sort or filter or group the items, and whether you want to calculate any item totals. You can also select a style, an item limit, and whether or not you want to display folders.

You can also quickly create a new view by clicking on the ellipsis (. . .) at the top of your list or library and clicking Create View as shown in Figure A-9.

One of the challenges with alternative views in SharePoint 2010 is that users often didn't see that alternate views were available because to see them, you had to click the view drop-down, as shown in Figure A-10. In SharePoint 2013, the experience for users is improved because up to three views are shown by default for document libraries as shown in Figure A-9. The order of the views shows the view selected as the default view first; the remaining views are listed in alphabetical order by view name. If there are more than three views, users are forced to click the ellipsis (. . .) to see a listing of the additional views.

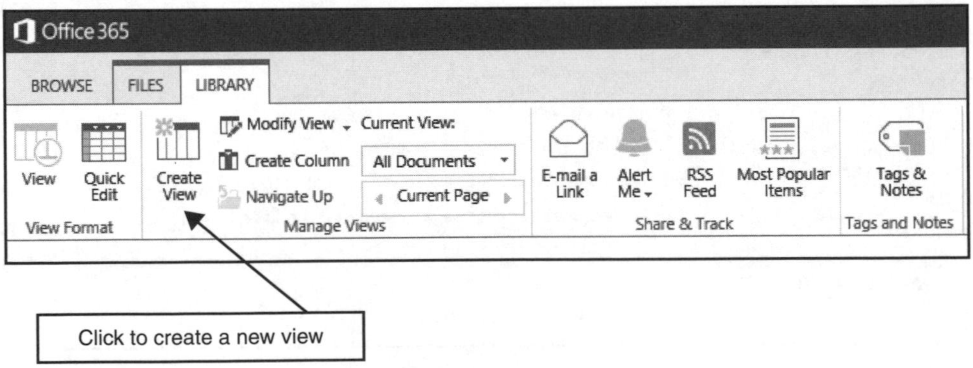

Click to create a new view

Figure A-8 Create a new view from the library or list ribbon

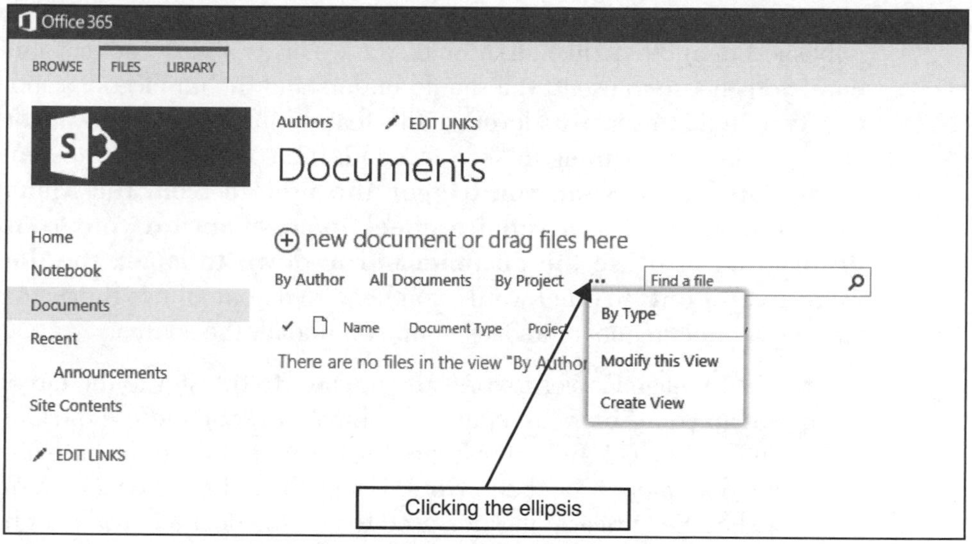

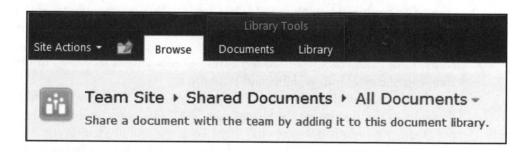

Figure A-9 Create a new view from the list of views

Figure A-10 Alternate views were hard to find in SharePoint 2010 unless you clicked the drop-down arrow next to the name of the default view

Managing Copies of Documents (Send To and Manage Copies)

The Send To command is a handy feature that allows you to copy a file to a different library and then manage the different copies of a source file after they are created. It is primarily helpful in publishing environments. In other words, the Send To command allows you to keep in sync documents that are created in one place (such as a private team site) and published in another (like an intranet site). This is a very cool capability, but if you choose to use it, you should understand the implications and be very certain that users who leverage this feature understand how it works. One very important thing to keep in mind: the copies of your document are **updated only when you trigger the update from the Manage Copies page or if you require check-in/checkout on your source library and also use the document drop-down to check the document in and out.** In other words, you need to do one of two things to get your target documents to update when you update the source:

- Use Manage Copies to force the updates to transfer to the targets.
- Set up your library to require check-in/checkout *and* use the Check Out and Check In buttons from the document drop-down to check the document in and out. Note: Using check-in and checkout from within the Office application used to edit the document will not trigger the update prompt.

Editing the source does not automatically update the target copies unless you trigger the update action using one of the two methods described. For this reason, you will want to make sure that when you choose to enable this feature, all users have sufficient training to understand exactly how it works. While this functionality can provide very useful file controls, to prevent errors in content publication, it is essential that contributors and site owners who use these tools have a thorough understanding of the system benefits and limitations.

In SharePoint 2010, the Send To command was available as a drop-down from the document. In SharePoint 2013, this command is available only from the ribbon. To access the Send To command in SharePoint 2013, select the document you want to work with, click Files in the ribbon, and locate the Send To command as shown in Figure A-11.

When a file is copied in this way, the copy maintains a relationship with its source file, and you can choose to update this copy with any changes that are made to the source file (upon check-in, as stated earlier). In addition, if the document Columns in the target library are the same as those in the source library, those Columns or fields are also updated when the copy is updated. (The Content Types in the source and target libraries do not have to match, but if they do, all of the metadata will be available in the target.) When you use the Send To command, you can choose to be prompted to update any existing copies whenever the source document is checked in as shown in Figure A-12 (although at the time of this writing, we have not been able to get this feature to work as described).

Figure A-11 The Send To command in SharePoint 2013 is available only in the ribbon

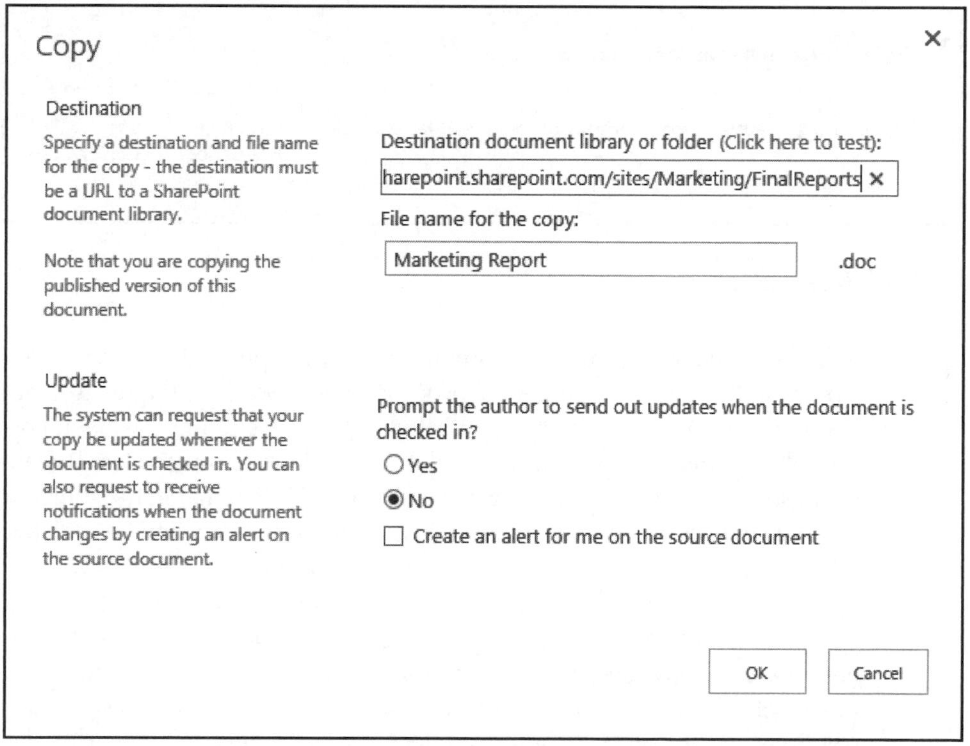

Copy   ✕

Destination

Specify a destination and file name for the copy - the destination must be a URL to a SharePoint document library.

Note that you are copying the published version of this document.

Destination document library or folder (Click here to test):

harepoint.sharepoint.com/sites/Marketing/FinalReports ✕

File name for the copy:

Marketing Report   .doc

Update

The system can request that your copy be updated whenever the document is checked in. You can also request to receive notifications when the document changes by creating an alert on the source document.

Prompt the author to send out updates when the document is checked in?

◯ Yes
◉ No

☐ Create an alert for me on the source document

OK   Cancel

Figure A-12 Send To command options

The Send To command makes it easier to maintain files across libraries and sites because when files are copied by using the Send To command, the server tracks the relationship between the source file and all of its copies. You can view and manage all copies of a document centrally from the Manage Copies page as shown in Figure A-13, which is available on the ribbon just below the Send To button (see Figure A-11). You will need to access this page

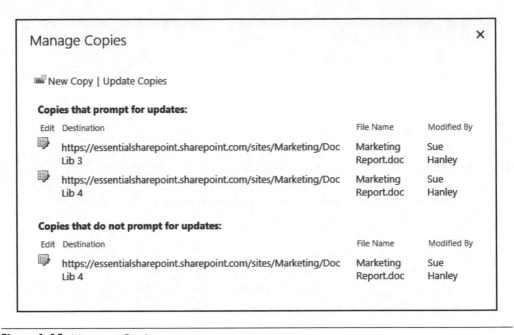

Figure A-13 Manage Copies page

to actually update the target documents when you update the source. Manage Copies in the source document shows you which locations the document has been copied to, but the only way to find out if a document has been copied is to click Manage Copies, which might be a little confusing unless the entire purpose of your library is to manage source files. Notice that in the source, you can indicate whether you want all or just some of the copies to be updated. If you choose to update a target document, the target gets completely overridden—so if there have been changes in the target, they will be lost.

Notice that the Manage Copies page has an option that allows you to create a new copy directly from the page. However, this option will not work unless check-in/checkout is required on the source. If you have checkout required on the source, when you check the document in after editing, you get a prompt in the check-in options that asks if you want to update the copies. If you say yes, the target copy will update—but only if you check the document in and out from the document context ellipsis (. . .) as shown in Figure A-14. When you check a document in from the document context, you will see the prompt to automatically update copies as shown in Figure A-15.

If you have Edit privileges in the target library and you edit a document that is connected to a source, you will not know this unless you first

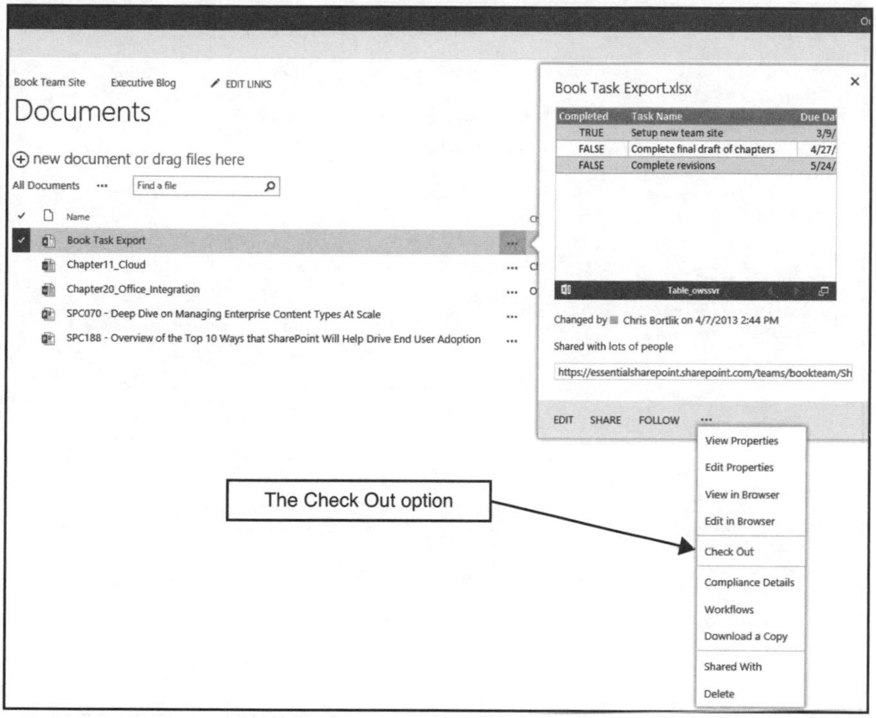

Figure A-14 You must use the document context to check out and check in a document to automatically trigger updates to target copies

either view or edit the document's properties. So, if you choose to take advantage of this capability, you should consider very strictly limiting Edit privileges in the target library. Figure A-16 shows the properties view in the target library.

In summary, the Send To command is a very powerful option, but using it is not trivial, so you will want to leverage this capability only in scenarios where you have a trained user group that updates content on a regular basis so that they follow the process that results in the desired and expected outcomes.

Following Documents, Sites, People, and Topics

SharePoint 2013 provides the ability to keep track of documents, sites, people, and topics of interest with the "follow" feature that users may be familiar with in consumer social media.

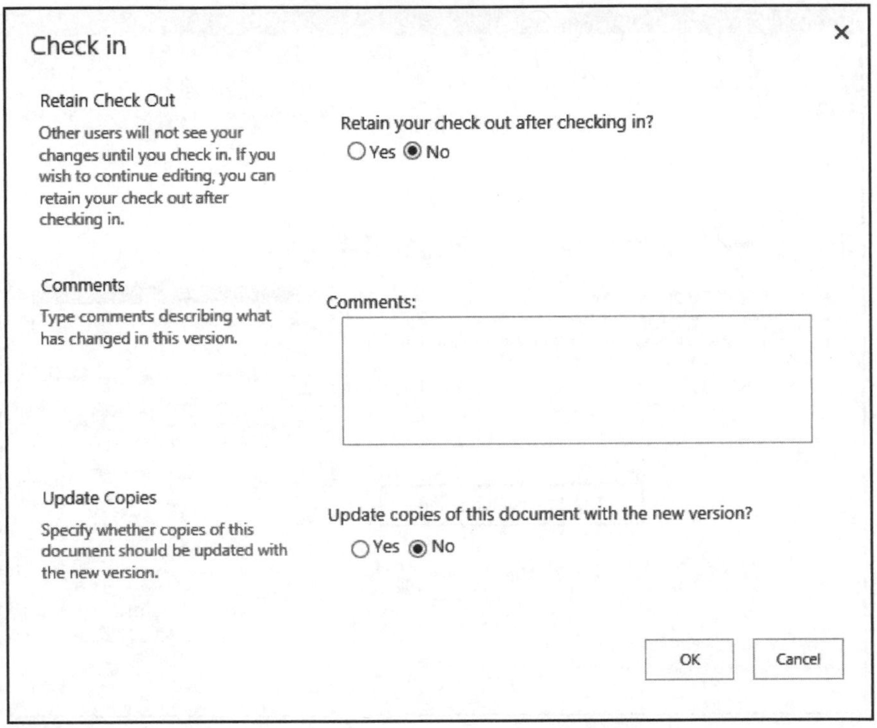

Figure A-15 The prompt to update copies is displayed only when you check a document in from the document context

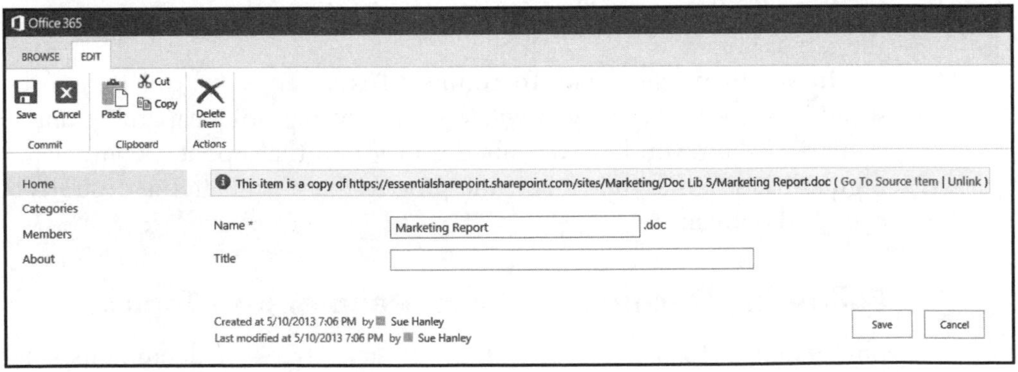

Figure A-16 Document properties of a Send To document in the target library

Following Documents

Following documents and SharePoint sites makes it easy for you to keep on top of the information you care about in SharePoint. When you follow content, there is no need to search for files to check their update status because you automatically receive notifications in your newsfeed whenever updates occur.

To follow a document, click the ellipsis (. . .) next to the document file name and then click Follow in the callout window. The document or file is added to the list of documents that you follow so that you can easily find it again. Updates to the document are automatically flagged in your newsfeed so that you can see what is happening to the document. Note that you do not get an e-mail when a document you follow is updated; you will only be notified in your newsfeed. If you want to get an e-mail message when a document is updated, you will need to set up an alert, which is done by selecting the document and then clicking Alert Me in the ribbon.

To find documents that you are following, click Newsfeed in the Suite Bar and open your list of followed documents as shown in Figure A-17. To stop following a document, click "Stop following" under the name of the document you no longer wish to follow in the list of documents you are following.

Following Sites

To follow a site, click Follow in the upper-right corner of the site home page (and all other pages), as shown in Figure A-18. If you are already following a site, SharePoint will display a pop-up that says, "You're already following this site." You can see all of your followed sites by clicking the Sites tab of the Suite Bar. From the Sites page, you can stop following any site in which you are no longer interested.

Following People

When you follow people, you see the conversations they start in your newsfeed. You can also get updates when people start to follow a document, site, tag, or person if they have chosen to display these actions in their newsfeed settings. In addition, you will see a notification when they upload content to sites to which you have access and when they create new sites.

Following people is a social activity; following people allows you to discover information based on what your colleagues are interested in or

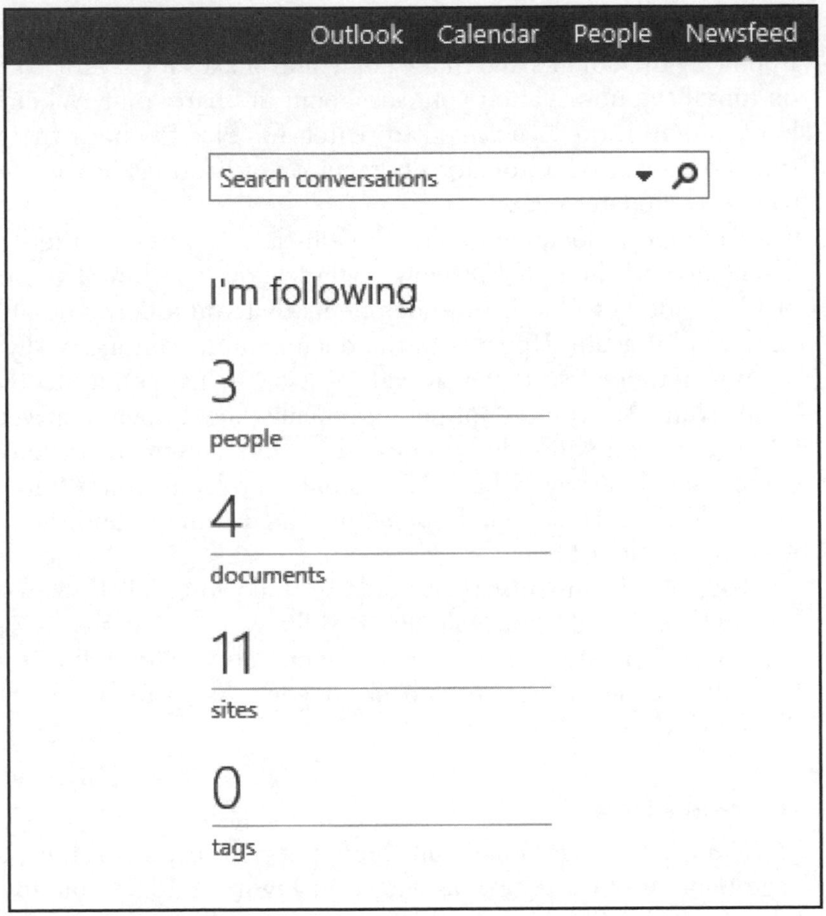

Figure A-17 Click the number above "documents" in the "I'm following" list to see a list of the documents you are following

what they are doing. It is one of many ways to help transfer the elusive tacit knowledge of an organization.

When someone follows you, you will get a notification in your newsfeed and in your e-mail as well, if you have not disabled the default setting that sends you an e-mail automatically when someone follows you. You cannot say no when someone chooses to follow you (and vice versa). You can, however, control which of the actions you take will appear in your newsfeed (and in the newsfeeds of others) in your newsfeed settings.

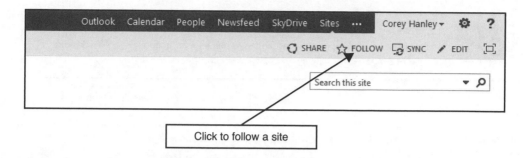

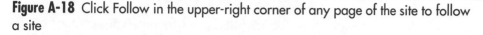

Figure A-18 Click Follow in the upper-right corner of any page of the site to follow a site

There are several ways in which you can sign up to follow a person:

- To start following someone who posts to a newsfeed, click the "Follow [name]" link that appears under the post. You will see this link only for people you are not currently following.
- To follow someone who is mentioned in a newsfeed post or someone whose name is listed as liking a post, click the person's name and go to his or her profile page. On this page, click "Follow this Person."

To stop following people, go to the list of people you are following on your newsfeed page and click the ellipsis (. . .) to open their callout. From the callout, click "Stop Following." You can also stop following a person from his or her profile page.

Following Topics

To get information in your newsfeed about a topic that interests you, you can follow a tag for that topic. Tags are terms preceded by a hash symbol (#) in your newsfeed. When you start following a tag, you'll get newsfeed notifications whenever someone uses that tag in newsfeed conversations or discussion board posts as long as the person mentioning the term uses the hashtag symbol, for example, #HR. When you're no longer interested in news about the tag, you can stop following it.

When you see a tag in a newsfeed post that you want to follow, click the Follow tag below the post. If you don't see that option, click the ellipsis (. . .) and then select the tag from the drop-down list as shown in Figure A-19.

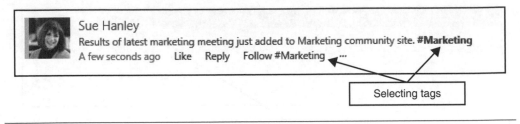

Figure A-19 Follow a #tag from the newsfeed by clicking follow #[term]

To post a new tag that you or others can follow, type a #[tag] (such as #Legal or #Marketing) in your post window, click Post, and then click Follow #[tag] below the post.

To see how a tag is being used in conversations and documents associated with that tag, click a tag that interests you in a post in your newsfeed. An "About #[tag]" page appears with a list of all the content items that are associated with that tag. You can follow the tag from this page if you are not doing so already.

To stop following a tag, find the tag in the list of followed tags (refer to Figure A-17) and then delete it.

Tips for Creating Posts in the Newsfeed

Posting to the newsfeed allows you to both ask questions and share important information with your colleagues. The newsfeed is not intended to be a place where you post what you had for lunch or what you are planning to do this weekend. Think of the newsfeed in SharePoint as a way of narrating your work—sharing important project milestones, letting your colleagues know when you are struggling with an issue, or congratulating someone on an important achievement. Whether you are using the SharePoint 2013 newsfeed or the Yammer newsfeed, you can enrich your newsfeed posts with two special features: #tags and @mentions.

Mentioning people in a newsfeed post is a way of directing a post to specific people to get their attention (because when you @mention people, the post shows up in their newsfeed and possibly e-mail) and also a way of helping people make connections.

To mention someone in a post, type an @ character and start typing the name of the person you want to mention. As you type, SharePoint assumes that you're most likely to mention people you're currently following and lists them first. SharePoint then lists all the other people in your organization whose name matches what you have just started to type.

Adding a #tag (also called a hashtag) to a post is a way of helping group and organize posts by attaching a keyword to the post. Tags need to be one word (no spaces are allowed), so if the tag you want is a short phrase, you can combine the words in "CamelCase," such as #BusinessDevelopment.

To add a tag to a post, type the # symbol and start typing a word. Previously entered tags will then appear for you to select. It's always better to choose an existing tag if you can. (If your organization has a collection of topics that you typically talk about, for example, engineering disciplines in an engineering firm, the site administrator can predefine hashtags in the Managed Metadata Service.) As a best practice, try to limit the number of hashtags in a post to no more than three.

There are several other ways you can add interest and value to your newsfeed posts:

- Add a hyperlink by cutting and pasting the URL of the link in the post box. When you do this, you are prompted to display a "friendly" name for the URL in the "Display as" box as shown in Figure A-20. You can use this same approach to create a link to a SharePoint document.
- Add a picture to a post by clicking the camera icon below the post box.
- Add a video to a post using the same method as adding a hyperlink. When you post the entry, the video appears as a thumbnail, ready to be played.

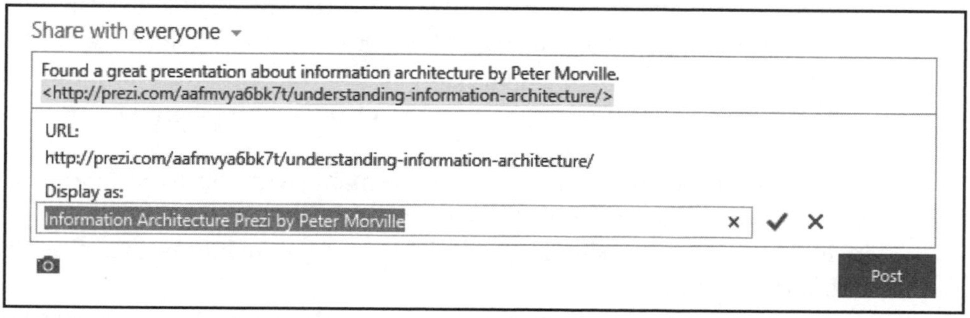

Share with everyone ▾

Found a great presentation about information architecture by Peter Morville.
<http://prezi.com/aafmvya6bk7t/understanding-information-architecture/>

URL:
http://prezi.com/aafmvya6bk7t/understanding-information-architecture/

Display as:
Information Architecture Prezi by Peter Morville   × ✓ ✕

Post

Figure A-20 SharePoint prompts you to enter a friendly "display as" name for hyperlinks in posts

New or Different Site Owner Tasks in SharePoint 2013

Managing security has always been an important task for site owners. Determining when and what to share is a very important role for them. In previous versions of SharePoint, securing content was easier than sharing content, and as a result, users often complained of getting way too many "access denied" messages. SharePoint 2013 makes it much easier for site owners to share entire sites and individual documents with both internal and, in the case of SharePoint 2013 Online, external users. This can provide a significant benefit in making it easier to break down information silos, but with this new great power comes an even greater responsibility to pay attention to the entire sharing process.

Sharing Sites and Documents with People Outside Your Organization

If you are using Office 365 or SharePoint Online, you can share content with people who are outside your organization. This is very helpful in scenarios where you want to collaborate on a document with a partner, supplier, or customer. In order for this feature to work, external sharing must be enabled for your environment and also for your site collection by the site administrator.

Sharing a Site

If you are the site owner (or you have Full Control permissions) in a SharePoint Online site and this feature has been enabled, you can share an entire site with an external user. To share your entire site, click the Share button in the upper-right corner of the page and enter the e-mail address of the user with whom you want to share the site. Note that users who do not have Full Control permissions will not be able to share an entire site with an external user.

The external user will receive an e-mail invitation to join your site. The e-mail will come from the Microsoft Online Services Team and will include a link to your site. Figure A-21 shows the invitation to a site called Marketing Community.

When the external user clicks the link in the e-mail message, he or she is invited to sign in to your site with either an existing Office 365 ID or a free Microsoft account as shown in Figure A-22.

When you give external users access to an entire site, you are giving them access to the site and any sub-sites that share permissions with that site. For this reason, you need to be very careful when you provide access

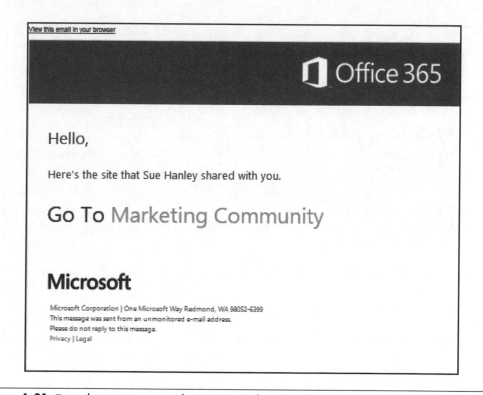

Figure A-21 E-mail invitation to a SharePoint Online site

to external users. As a best practice, you can set up a site that you use specifically for external sharing and make sure that it has unique permissions from all of your other sites. Each organization will need to determine the scenarios in which external sharing is appropriate, and policies and guidelines for sharing should be documented as part of the governance plan.

Sharing a Document

You must have Full Control permissions to share a document with an external user in a SharePoint Online environment. There are two ways you can share a document with external users:

- You can require them to sign in to your site to view the document. This is recommended if you are going to allow the external user to edit the document.
- You can send them a guest link, which they can use to view or edit the document without signing in. This is recommended only if you are going to restrict the external user to Read access only and not

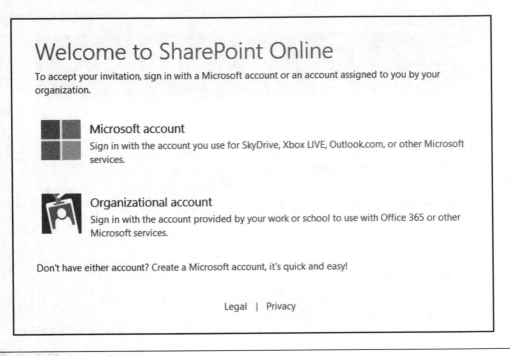

Welcome to SharePoint Online

To accept your invitation, sign in with a Microsoft account or an account assigned to you by your organization.

Microsoft account
Sign in with the account you use for SkyDrive, Xbox LIVE, Outlook.com, or other Microsoft services.

Organizational account
Sign in with the account provided by your work or school to use with Office 365 or other Microsoft services.

Don't have either account? Create a Microsoft account, it's quick and easy!

Legal | Privacy

Figure A-22 External user sign-in screen

allow editing. When you allow external users to have Edit access to a document without requiring sign-in, you will not be able to tell who made which change to your document because all anonymous users are identified as Guest Contributor.

To share a document externally, go to the document you want to share and click the ellipsis (. . .) to open the menu, and then click Share in the properties dialog box. Type the e-mail addresses of the external users with whom you want to share the document. In the drop-down, select the permission level you would like to grant and type a message letting the people you are inviting know what you would like them to do. As stated previously, if you want someone to be able to edit your document, it's a good idea to select the "Require sign-in" check box as shown in Figure A-23.

Review What Has Been Shared

You can use the Share command to quickly see the list of people with whom a document or site has been shared. To see who has access to a site,

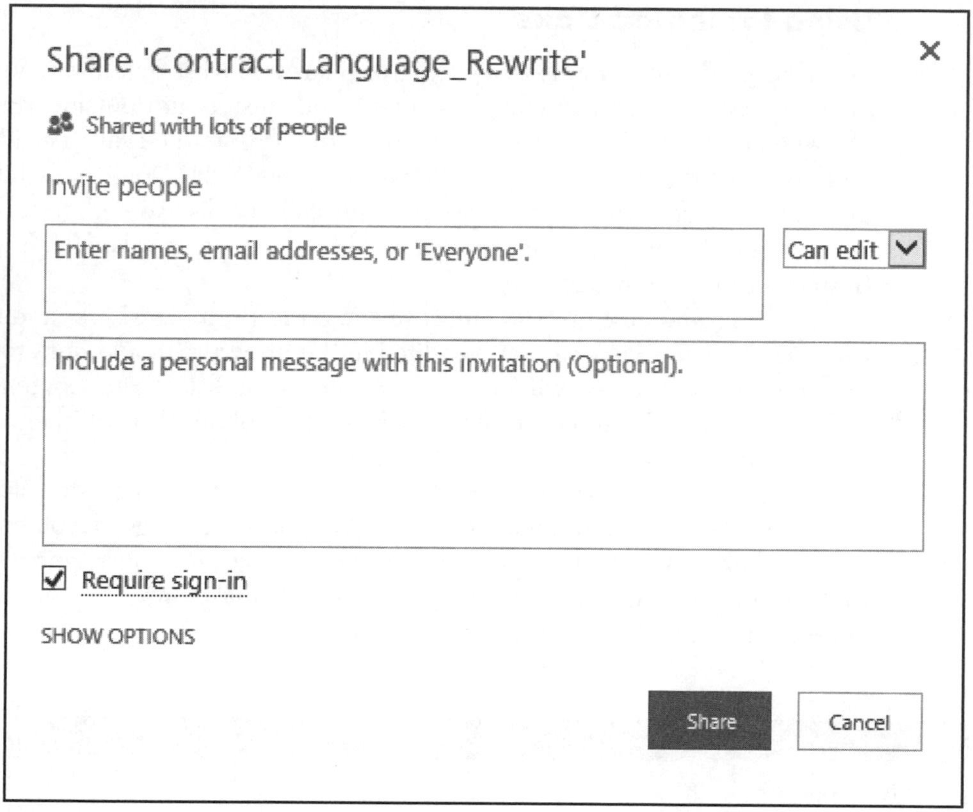

Figure A-23 Require sign-in if you plan to allow external users to edit your document

click Share at the top right of the page and then click the "Shared with" link to view a list of people who have access to the site. To see who has access to a document or folder, select the item in the document library and then click "Shared with" on the Files tab in the ribbon.

Adding an App to a Site

In SharePoint 2013, the lists and libraries with which you are familiar from SharePoint 2010 are now called "apps."

To add an app to a site, click the gear icon in the upper-right corner of the page and then the "Add an app" link in the drop-down. You will then be presented with all of the available apps for your site, including any apps in the SharePoint store that your organization has enabled.

Using Promoted Links

The Promoted Links app is a new type of SharePoint list that allows you to use images in tiles to highlight content both inside and outside your SharePoint site. When a user hovers over the Promoted Link tile, the description of the link pops up as shown in Figure A-24. Note that while the app is called Promoted Links, you can call the list something else on your site. In this example, the Promoted Links app is called Helpful Resources on the HR team site.

To use Promoted Links, you must first add the Promoted Links app to your site. The tiles view cannot be edited in the browser. To add links to a Promoted Links list, you will need to navigate to the list in Site Contents and select the All Promoted Links view from the ribbon. You will then be able to add a new link as shown in Figure A-25.

Think about the images or icons you want to use to create interest in your Promoted Links. You will need the URL for each image as you create each link item. As a best practice, store the images for your Promoted Links in the Site Assets library for your site and make sure they are no more than about 100KB for best performance.

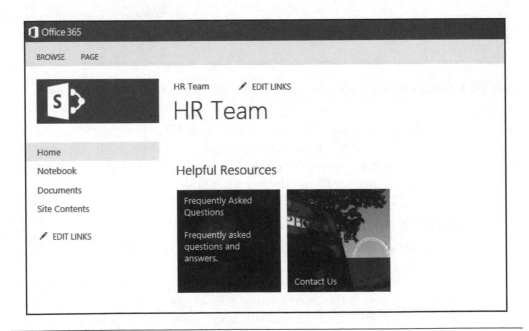

Figure A-24 Promoted Links allow you to create visually appealing links to your content

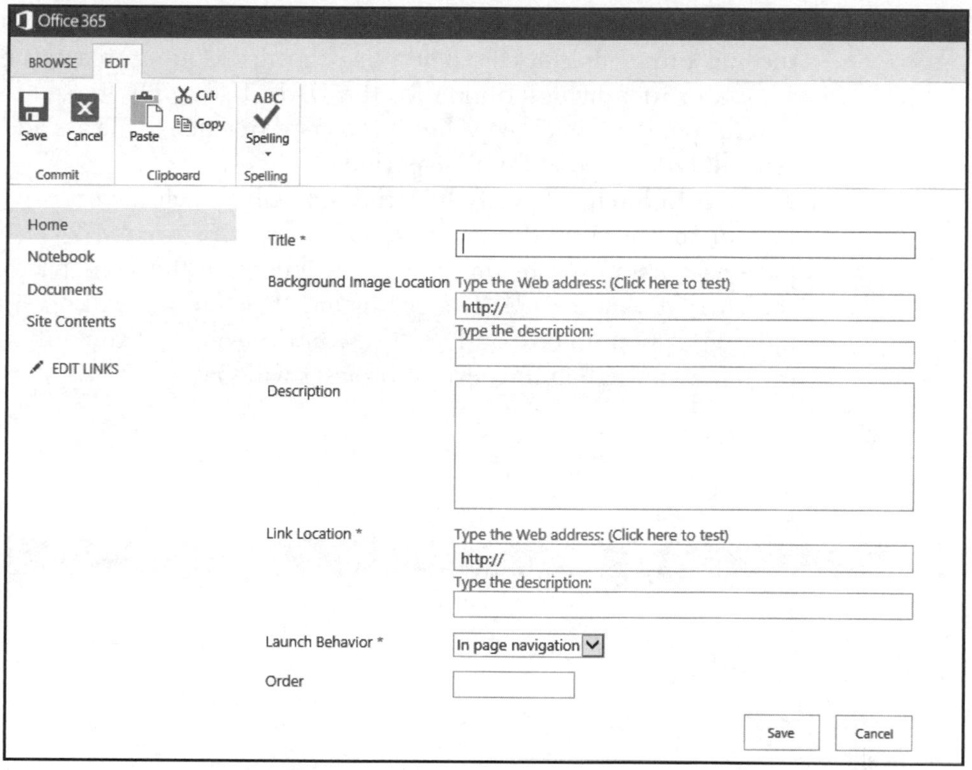

Figure A-25 New Promoted Link form

Enter the following information about each Promoted Link:

- **Title.** This is the text that users will see at the bottom of each image in the tiles view of the Promoted Links list. In Figure A-24, the Title of the first link is Frequently Asked Questions and the second is Contact Us. Keep your Titles short; use just a few words.
- **Background image location.** Enter the hyperlink to the image for the link in this field. Be sure to add a user-friendly description for the link. If you do not specify an image, the default image is a blue square.
- **Description.** Enter the "hover message" that users will see as they mouse over the link in the tiles view. The description can be a short sentence that tells your users what they will find if they click the link.

- **Link location.** Enter the target URL for the link. You must enter the full http:// link in this field. Use the description area to create a user-friendly description for the URL. Users will not see this description in the tiles view, but it is a good practice to always add a "friendly" description for all hyperlinks.
- **Launch behavior.** Specify how the link will launch for users who click on it. There are three options as shown in Figure A-26: (1) "In page navigation" means that the link will open in the same page as the current window, (2) "Dialog" means that the link will open in a dialog or pop-up box, and (3) "New tab" means that the link will open in a new tab in the current browser window.

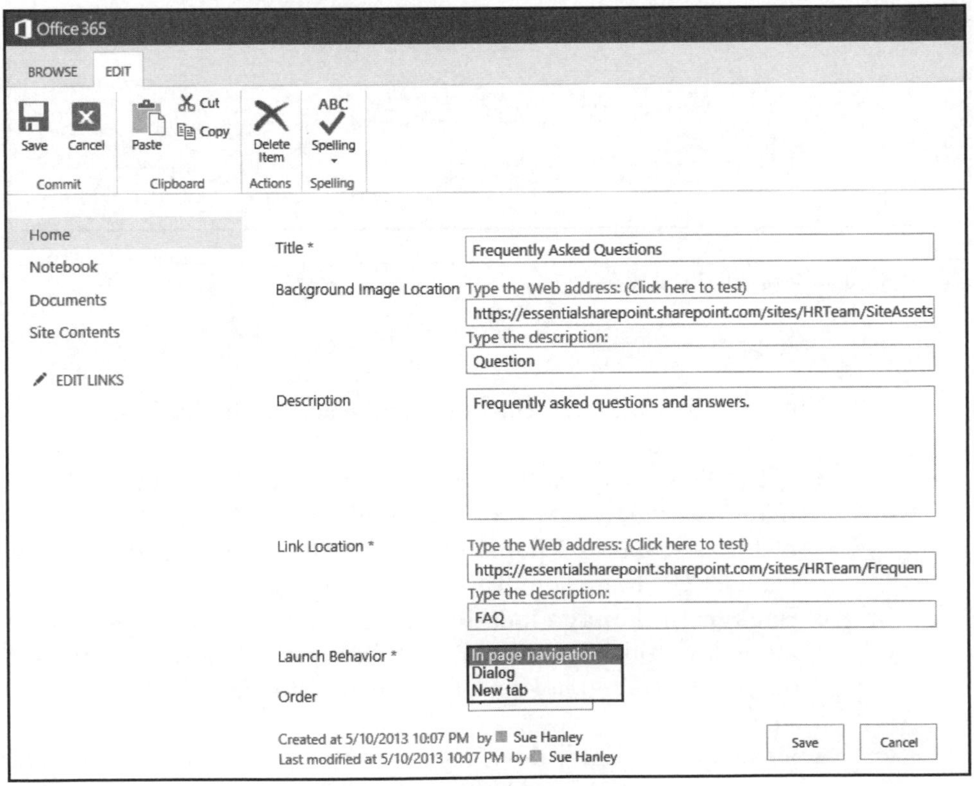

Figure A-26 Launch behavior options in Promoted Links

- **Order.** Specify an order in which you want your links to be displayed with 1 being first. If you leave the order blank, the links will be displayed in reverse order of when they were created, with the newest link listed first.

Be sure to test your Promoted Links to make sure that the launch behavior mode you have selected will work for each of your links. Note that Promoted Links in the Web Part tiles view does not wrap. If you have more tiles than can be displayed in your browser width, you will see a Previous/ Next button in your Web Part. As a best practice, limit the number of Promoted Links to those that will be visible in most browsers. If you need or want to add more links, be sure to adjust the order of appearance so that the most important links will not be hidden behind the Next button.

Index

FREE
Online Edition

Safari
Books Online

Your purchase of **Essential SharePoint® 2013** includes access to a free online edition for 45 days through the **Safari Books Online** subscription service. Nearly every Addison-Wesley Professional book is available online through **Safari Books Online**, along with thousands of books and videos from publishers such as Cisco Press, Exam Cram, IBM Press, O'Reilly Media, Prentice Hall, Que, Sams, and VMware Press.

Safari Books Online is a digital library providing searchable, on-demand access to thousands of technology, digital media, and professional development books and videos from leading publishers. With one monthly or yearly subscription price, you get unlimited access to learning tools and information on topics including mobile app and software development, tips and tricks on using your favorite gadgets, networking, project management, graphic design, and much more.

Addison Wesley   AdobePress   ALPHA   Cisco Press   FT Press   IBM Press.   Microsoft Press   New Riders   O'REILLY

Peachpit Press   PRENTICE HALL   Que   Redbooks   SAMS   SAS Publishing   vmware PRESS   WILEY   wrox